Essays in Ancient Philosophy

The University of Minnesota Press
gratefully acknowledges publication assistance
provided for this book by Princeton University.

Essays in Ancient Philosophy

Michael Frede

University of Minnesota Press   *Minneapolis*

Published by the University of Minnesota Press, 2037 University Avenue Southeast, Minneapolis, MN 55414. Published simultaneously in Canada by Fitzhenry & Whiteside Limited,
Markham. Printed in the United States of America.

Library of Congress Cataloging-in-Publication Data

Frede, Michael.
  Essays in ancient philosophy.

  Bibliography: p.
  Includes index.
  1. Philosophy, Ancient.   I. Title.
B171.F69 1987   180   86-6974
ISBN 0-8166-1274-9
ISBN 0-8166-1275-7 (pbk.)

See p. vi for further copyright information.

Contents

Preface

This volume contains seventeen papers which I have written over the course of the last twelve years, and an introduction, written for this volume, in which, with some hesitation, I try to explain how I conceive of my study of ancient philosophy. Most of the papers have been published before, but some of them were published in volumes which are not readily accessible, and three of them had appeared only in German. Hence, I am grateful to the University of Minnesota Press for this opportunity to present these papers in a form which makes them more easily available, and to Princeton University which, by a grant, made this publication possible. But, in particular, I would like to thank the editorial staff of University of Minnesota Press, who went through the manuscript with extraordinary care and tact, and Wolfgang Mann, who did an excellent piece of work in translating the rather stubborn German of Chapters 2, 4, and 10. I am also indebted to the various publishing houses which allowed me to reprint papers in this collection. Finally, I am glad to have this opportunity to express my gratitude to Pearl Cavanaugh, Ann Getson, and Bunny Romano, whose patience I have tried too often in the course of the years.

Introduction: The Study of Ancient Philosophy

Ancient philosophy can be studied in many ways.[1] The thoughts of ancient philosophers are of great interest not just as philosophical thoughts. Many of them, in one way or another, are also of great historical importance. They help to explain a great many historical facts, not just in the history of philosophy, but in many other histories, e.g., the history of theology, the history of political theory, even the history of literature. Or they are reflections of some historical development we may be interested in; again, this may be a development in the history of philosophy or in some other history, even one that at first may seem to have very little to do with philosophy, e.g., the rise of literacy. In historical accounts of ancient life there are few aspects of that life which do not involve some reference to the fact that some philosopher had a certain view and many aspects of that life into which philosophy enters quite substantially, e.g., Roman law. Equally, there is hardly a facet of ancient life that does not find its reflection in ancient philosophy, and there are many aspects of that life which seem to have a substantial influence on the thought of philosophers. Thus there are many approaches to the thought of ancient philosophers, all of which contribute to a better understanding of it. One can pursue each of the many histories in which ancient philosophy, either as a whole or in part, plays a role and try to determine what this role is in a manner appropriate for the history in question. One reason why the study of ancient philosophy is so attractive and so lively is that it allows for so many interests and approaches. Clearly it would be a mistake to think that there is only one way to study ancient philosophy.

It would be as great a mistake to think that one could fruitfully study the subject in any way one cared to. The different approaches have to be carefully distinguished and kept distinct. Different approaches are appropriate for different interests, and the results one obtains are relative to this interest and to the approach chosen. Thus one might well imagine that one could explain the thought of a political philosopher on the distribution of goods in terms of the history of that philosopher's society and social status in it, if this is the kind of history one is interested in and if one chooses this approach to the thought of the philosopher in question. But it would be a mistake to think that the explanation one found was the only possible explanation. For the philosopher may have had very good reasons for his views on the distribution of goods, reasons that we find so convincing that we feel the need to explain why not everybody in his society adopted them. Moreover, we may have no reason to doubt that it was for these reasons that he adopted the view in question. Thus, depending on the way we approach his thought, we account for his thought in two quite different ways. This does not mean there is anything wrong with either of these explanations or that we have to declare one of them illegitimate. All this does show is that the fact that someone had a philosophical view is an extraordinarily complex fact, and that, if we want to capture some of its complexity, we have to allow for a wide variety of approaches to it and resist the temptation to declare one of these approaches the only legitimate one.

In principle one can look at a philosophical view that someone has held in two different ways. One can look at it primarily as a philosophical view that someone might entertain; one may wonder whether or not it is true, for what kinds of reasons one might want to take this view, what its implications are, and entirely disregard, as irrelevant to one's purposes, the fact that it is a view that has actually been taken by a certain person under certain circumstances. To consider a view in this way is to consider it philosophically. But one can also look at this view primarily as one that was actually held, be interested in the fact that it was the view of a certain person under certain circumstances, and try to understand it as such. Now, presumably, one is not interested in understanding the fact that someone had a certain philosophical view quite independently of who had the view and what the view was. We are interested in understanding the fact that someone had a certain philosophical view only if we think this fact has some significance, is in some way revealing. The fact that someone held a certain philosophical view has some significance, is somehow revealing, if the view intrinsically is of philosophical interest or if it has considerable historical influence, either in the history of philosophy or in some other history; or it might be revealing in a number of other ways, e.g., because it shows how considerations or events that form part of some other history influence the thought of philosophers, or how the influence of certain events and changes was so pervasive that it was reflected even in the thought of philosophers. I will call facts about the past that have this significance, that are revealing, historical facts. One might, of course, call all facts about the past historical facts. But it seems important to emphasize that history in the sense in which the historian is concerned with it is not the whole of the past, but some abstractions from it into which only some facts about the past enter, namely those we find interesting or important or those that we have to refer to account for those facts that we deem interesting or important. To do justice to this it seems preferable to restrict the notion of a historical fact to those facts about the past that enter into a history. To understand the historical fact that someone took a certain philosophical view is to be able to explain it in the way in which one explains historical facts.

Now if the historical fact is the fact that a certain agent performed a certain action, we try to explain it in the way in which we normally try to explain why someone did something. We first ask ourselves whether the agent had good reason to do what he did, and if we see that he did, we think we have understood his action. By "good reason" I mean here and throughout what we ourselves would regard as good reason. It is, of course, quite true, that the agent in question may have a different view of what constitutes a good reason and may act on what he considers to be good reasons. But in this case his behavior would not be readily and immediately intelligible to us, precisely because we would first have to realize that he acted on a different conception of what constitutes a good reason, and then we would have to understand why he had this different conception. In the end we have no alternative but to understand what others did or thought in terms of our notion of what constitutes a good reason, though in trying to understand others we may come to realize that it is our notion of what counts as a good reason that needs to be changed and that stands in the way of understanding them. But we may also come to the conclusion that the person, even given his own conception, did not have a good reason to do what he did. And in this case, we have to try to find a more complicated explanation that will explain why the agent did what he did, though he had no good reason for it. Now, what is true of action seems also to be true of taking a philosophical view. If we think that a philosopher had a good reason to adopt a certain view, we think we understand why he held this view. It may take us some time to find out that he had a good reason. It may be that the reason we do not readily understand the thought of a philosopher is that at first we fail to see that he in fact did have a good reason to adopt his view; it may take us some time to change our own views and possibly even our notion of what constitutes a good reason before we can realize that he had a good reason for holding his views. One reason we study the thought of great philosophers with such care would seem to be precisely this, that we trust that in many cases they had good reason to say what they did, although, because of limitations in our understanding, we do not readily understand it. These limitations are one of the things we hope to remove by studying the great philosophers of the past. We may, of course, in some cases come to the conclusion that the philosopher, after all, had no good reason to adopt the view in question.

It is, perhaps, worth pointing out that it often is not easy to come to this conclusion. For to claim that someone did not have a good reason to think what he did is to claim that it is not owing to our lack of understanding that we find it difficult to understand why the person held this view—a claim not easily made in the case of philosophers whose peer power of intellect and depth of insight generally far exceeds our own. Still, we may feel sufficiently confident that the philosopher had no good reason to think what he did. In this case, we think we have to look for a more complex explanation of why he took the view, in spite of the fact that he had no good reason to do so. If this is correct, it is apparent that a full historical understanding of the fact that somebody held a certain view will always involve a philosophical understanding of the view itself. For how is one to judge whether someone had a good reason to hold a view, unless one has a philosophical understanding of that view by virtue of which one knows what it is to have a good reason for holding it? Even if the philosopher did not have good reason for holding the view, the explanation of why he held it will have to make some reference to the fact that it was not for a good reason that he adopted it. It is an explanation of why the philosopher held the view, in spite of the fact that he had no good reason for doing so. For instance, merely to cite the bad reason he had will not satisfactorily explain the fact that he held the belief, though it was, in fact, for this reason that he held it. We would still not understand why he held the belief for this reason, unless something were added that made us understand why he held the belief, though his reasons for doing so were bad.

But even in the case where we have come to the conclusion that the philosopher held his view for no good reason, there are two quite different kinds of explanation that might account for the fact that he held it. In one kind of case we can explain why the philosopher held the view he did by providing him with a set of assumptions and a line of reasoning such that we can understand how someone who made these assumptions and argued in this way could think that the inadequate reasons he offered for adopting his view did constitute a good reason to do so. We would not share these assumptions or we would find fault with the argument, or both, but we might be able to understand how even one of us might make these assumptions or use an argument of this kind. We might, e.g., decide that the author had fallen victim to a simple fallacy, the kind of fallacy we can see ourselves committing, and this might explain why he thought what in fact are bad reasons to constitute a good reason to adopt the view. Hence we have an explanation for why he adopted the view, though he had no good reason for doing so.

In another kind of case, though, no explanation of this kind may be available. However hard we try, there is no set of assumptions and no line of philosophical argument that we could easily see ourselves adopting and that would explain why the philosopher thought his bad reasons good reasons. It is in these cases that we think we have to appeal to some historical context from which we can explain why the philosopher held the view. Thus, we might discover that all of the philosopher's contemporaries made certain assumptions, which, although none of us would make them, readily explain why the philosopher in question took his reasons to be good reasons to adopt his view.

Now all the explanations we have considered so far are explanations of a historical fact, and in that sense one might call all these explanations historical explanations. But these explanations are of two radically different kinds in that only the last kind of explanation tries to explain the historical fact from its historical context. It may be useful, then, to make a distinction between these two kinds of explanation by reserving the term "historical explanation" for the kind of explanation that must appeal to a particular historical context to explain the fact that someone held a certain philosophical view.

How, then, do we explain historically the historical fact that someone held a certain philosophical view, if he had no good for reason for doing so, and if we cannot find some line of reasoning and certain assumptions that we can easily imagine ourselves using? We consider the historical context of the thought to see whether there is some history that will help explain why someone, given his historical situation, would come to hold this view.

But at this point it is, perhaps, worthwhile to note the fact that it does not follow from the fact that someone held a philosophical view which has to be explained historically that it has to be explained in terms of the history of philosophy, by the historian of philosophy. Perhaps we can avoid some confusion if we distinguish between ancient philosophy, or quite generally the philosophy of the past, on the one hand, and the study of this philosophy, on the other. There is an object, ancient philosophy, and this object allows for a certain kind of study. Often one uses the expression "the history of ancient philosophy" to refer to the object as a whole, but to avoid confusion we may prefer to reserve the term "history of philosophy" for a certain kind of study of this object and for the aspect of the object that is studied this way, namely the kind of study that tries to do philosophical justice to ancient philosophy.

The reason I think it is useful to make this distinction is this: it is not the task of the historian of philosophy to explain whatever philosophical view someone may have had, even if it is a historical fact, i.e., a fact of some significance, that a certain person held this view. Nor is it the task of the historian of philosophy to find some explanation or other for such a historical fact. It is, rather, his task to find a certain kind of explanation for the view in question, namely the kind of explanation that is appropriate for the history of philosophy, rather than, say, the history of morals. Thus it may be a historical fact of great significance that a certain politician held certain philosophical views, and this fact may admit only of a historical explanation. But this may be a fact of no significance for the history of philosophy. The thought may not be remarkable as a philosophical thought, it may shed no light on the thought of earlier philosophers, and it may be of no help in understanding the thought of later philosophers. It may even be that it is an important historical fact that a philosopher held certain philosophical views, but this in itself does not guarantee him a place in the history of philosophy, since the only reason his views were so important may have been that he was the friend of an important politican whose politics were very much influenced by his philosophical views.

It is easy to see that some philosophical thoughts do not enter the history of philosophy because they lack historical significance. It is also easy enough to see that some philosophical thoughts do not enter the history of philosophy because they are of no significance for this history. It is not so easy to say positively that a philosophical thought is to be considered a part of the history of philosophy. Ultimately this will depend on the conception one has of the history of philosophy. But it does seem safe to say that we want those philosophical thoughts to be part of the history of philosophy that had a considerable philosophical influence on later philosophical thought. A thought may have philosophical influence on later thought in any number of ways: it may make the philosophical problem at issue appear different, it may suggest other views one could take on this problem, it may open up new ways to argue for a given view, it may reveal the limitations of a line of argument that had been accepted thus far. If a good deal of later philosophical thought can be seen to depend on some earlier philosophical thought in this way, the earlier thought no doubt forms part of the history of philosophy. And the more the thoughts that are influenced by earlier thought in turn are philosophically influential, the clearer it will be that the original thought should be part of a history of philosophy.

Now, to say that a philosophical thought has been philosophically influential is to say that there are philosophical thoughts that somehow depend on it, that in some way have to be explained in terms of it. But a thought may depend on an earlier thought in several ways. The simplest case would seem to be one in which a later philosopher adopts a view for a good reason, but the view and the reason are sufficiently complex so that one assumes that his taking this view for this reason was facilitated, or even made possible, by the fact that an earlier philosopher had taken this view for this reason. More complex cases are those in which a later philosopher adopts a view for reasons that do not constitute good reasons because he has convinced himself that some earlier philosopher who adopted the view for these reasons had good reasons to adopt it, or, more generally cases in which a later philosopher adopts a view for reasons that do not constitute good reasons because he has been persuaded by the thought of some earlier philosopher that what he regards as reasons to adopt the view are good reasons. Almost all philosophical thought depends on earlier thought in this way. What this reflects is simply the fact that we always do philosophy against the background of the philosophical views and the philosophical reasoning of at least our immediate predecessors, that we cannot, at least to begin with, see the problems except in terms of the views and the reasons of our predecessors, and that however much we free ourselves from their views and reasons, there will always be some dependence on them. And, in general, even in the case of highly original philosophers, this dependence seems to be overwhelming. If early modern philosophy seems or even at times pretends to stand on its own feet, it can do so only as long as we know very little about the history of Hellenistic and late Medieval philosophy. So what the history of philosophy in the narrower sense seems to be made up of are those philosophical thoughts which are influential in this way.

Nor is it the task of the historian of philosophy to find some explanation or other for the philosophical thoughts that enter the history of philosophy. The historian of philosophy will, rather, go on the assumption that philosophical views are usually set forth for philosophical reasons. He recognizes that sometimes philosophical views are put forth by philosophers who are quite aware that they do not have a good reason to hold them, but the historian of philosophy, nevertheless, and often rightly, thinks that it would be worthwhile to consider these views. More may be gained by this than by considering uninteresting or boring views for which excellent reasons have been offered. But the paradigm is that of a philosopher who adopts a view because he thinks he has a good reason to do so. The historian of philosophy will try to identify the reasons for which he adopts the view and will see whether they constitute a good reason for doing so. Failing this, he will see whether he can reconstruct some line of reasoning that would make it intelligble why the philosopher thought his reasons constituted good reasons and hence adopted the view, a philosophical line of reasoning that even one of us might still avail himself of. Only if this also fails will the historian of philosophy resort to a historical explanation in terms of the history of philosophy. But he will still insist that it is because the philosopher had reasons for holding a certain view and that there must be some philosophical considerations that will explain why the philosopher in question took these reasons to be adequate reasons, except that now these philosophical considerations are dated; only someone in the historical situation of the philosopher in question could avail himself of such considerations. They are the kinds of considerations we would expect someone who is dependent on the thoughts of those predecessors to take seriously. We ourselves can imagine that if we were in those circumstances there would be nothing remarkable, noteworthy, surprising, or astonishing, if we examined these considerations and concluded that the reasons we had for the view in question constituted good reasons to adopt it. It is at this point in particular that the historian of philosophy will have to display all his historical learning and his philosophical ingenuity. For he will have (i) to try to reconstruct some philosophical line of reasoning that would explain why the author in question thought his reasons for holding the belief adequate, and (ii) to make a case for saying that it was, indeed, because of such a line of reasoning that the author thought his reasons adequate. To do the first often requires much philosophical resoucefulness; to do the second requires a firm grasp on what kind of reasoning, which kinds of philosophical considerations were available at the time.

Nevertheless, however successful we may be in reconstructing a line of reasoning that we can imagine ourselves espousing in this historical context, and that we have reason to think the philosopher adopted, or at least might have adopted, it will still be a flawed line of reasoning. It must rely on assumptions that not only are unwarranted, but that one can plausibly make only in such a historical context. Or it will rely on a mode of reasoning that is inconclusive, and that could be found acceptable only in such a historical context. And we must be able to identify these flaws or mistakes. For we do want to say that the author came to hold his view because he made these mistakes and that it was because of these mistakes, understandable as they may be, that he thought that his reasons for holding his view were adequate.

Often, though, not even this kind of explanation is available to us. For, however hard we try, we are not able to find a set of philosophical considerations we ourselves might have used in this historical situation on purely philosophical grounds. Even given the thought of the relevant predecessors, we cannot see ourselves making these assumptions or finding these arguments acceptable. In purely philosophical terms and in terms of the history of philosophy in the narrow sense, there is something remarkable, noteworthy, surprising, astonishing about the flaws and the mistakes that led the philosopher to take his reasons to be good reasons for his view. It is at this point that we have to look for a historical explanation outside the history of philosophy, an explanation in terms of some other historical context, some other history. Thus we might conclude that the only way to understand why the philosopher came to avail himself of a certain line of reasoning is by assuming that he found it difficult to avail himself of certain lines of reasoning that would have been preferable on philosophical grounds because of his religious convictions, the religious convictions of the time, and because of the way in which such convictions were encouraged and conflicting views were discouraged.

One may note, first, that in actual practice it is quite difficult to determine in a particular case how far one should go in trying to provide a philosopher with a line of reasoning that is intelligble at least in the light of the history of philosophy, and when one should just give up and look at an explanation in terms of some other history. Naturally enough, historians of philosophy try to take the philosophers of the past seriously as philosophers and hence go as far as they possibly can to explain their thought in terms of purely philosophical considerations.

Secondly, we may assume that the selectivity with which the historian of philosophy deals with the philosophy of the past results in much philosophical thought that stands in need of a historical explanation in terms of some history other than the history of philosophy being dropped from consideration. Philosophers who adopt philosophical views for reasons that could not make much philosophical sense even to their contemporaries tend to have little philosophical influence and hence to disappear from the history of philosophy. It seems that the philosophers who play a crucial role in the history of philosophy are in general those whose thought we can explain without having to refer to some other history. But however narrowly we conceive of the history of philosophy, it will still be the case that some of the thought it deals with will have to be understood in terms of some other history.

So though the historian of philosophy usually explains those philosophical views of the past that enter into the history of philosophy in terms of philosophical considerations, it is obvious for the reasons given above that this will often not suffice to understand the fact that a philosopher took a certain view, because it will not suffice to explain the mistakes he made. And unless these mistakes are trivial because they are the kinds of mistakes any of us occasionally make, they need an explanation in terms of some other history. We might, e.g., think that the fact that a philosopher availed himself of a certain line of reasoning could be understood only in terms of something in the history of his life that suggested this line of reasoning to him, which made it tempting for him to think of a particular matter in a certain way, which made it difficult for him to think of it otherwise. We might come to the conclusion that the fact that a philosopher availed himself of a certain line of reasoning had to be understood in terms of the history of the social structure of his society, which made it very difficult for him to think of certain matters other than as he did. We may suspect that the reason he was inclined toward a certain line of philosophical reasoning has something to do with the history of religion and that this will also explain why it was rather difficult to adopt certain lines of philosophical reasoning, though on purely philosophical grounds they may have seemed preferable even then. Neither last nor least, it might occur to one that the pursuit of philosophy is also a social institution, with its history in terms of which we can explain that students have views resembling the views of their teachers, and that at times it would have been quite difficult to have views different from the views of one's teachers or one's school. There are any number of ways in which some history other than the history of philosophy may interfere with the thought of a philosopher in such a way that it no longer is intelligible just on philosophical grounds, not even on the philosophical grounds available at that point in the history of philosophy.

Now, though I think that one should conceive of the history of philosophy in this way, I also think that thinking of it in this way involves an enormous abstraction and idealization. One goes on the assumption that, in general, philosophers adopted certain views because they had certain philosophical reasons for doing so. But, in fact, it seems that philosophical views grow on one in a highly complex manner, of which our philosophical reasons and our philosophical considerations form only a part. We have seen that even in the case in which a philosopher has a good reason for adopting the view he does and no doubt holds it for this reason, we may, nevertheless, think that he depends for his view on some earlier philosopher from whom he has learned to see the matter correctly and without whom, we might think, he would never come to hold the right view for the right reasons; and this, in turn, is perfectly compatible with the further assumption that our philosopher, given his nonphilosophical, e.g., moral, concerns, could under these historical circumstances, e.g., these social conditions, hardly fail to avail himself of this line of reasoning and adopt the view in question. We will never understand the origins of Greek philosophy by looking only at the philosophical considerations that led Thales, Anaximander, and Anaximenes to their philosophical views, unless we understand enough about the history of Greek society to understand why at this point this society needed something like philosophy, and how this influenced the thoughts of the first philosophers. That philosophers hold their views for philosophical reasons is perfectly compatible with the assumption that there are many other histories influencing their thought. This is most apparent when their thought gets derailed in such a way that we can no longer understand it in terms of purely philosophical considerations. But the same kinds of influences that reveal themselves in this case are also operative even when the philosopher adopts a view for purely philosophical reasons.

In fact, one may become quite impressed by how firmly embedded the thought of philosophers is in the life of their societies and even in their own lives. I have been struck for a long time by how autobiographical, as it were, the thought of philosophers is. It does not take much reflection to see that it is not surprising that the topics philosophers concentrate on, the general approach they take to their topics, the way they argue, the way they set forth their views, and often even the questions they consider are very much a reflection of their life and their personality. And it is no less surprising that the thought of philosophers should closely reflect the life, the history, and the character of the societies they live in. One cannot understand why friendship plays such an important role in ancient moral philosophy that Aristotle devotes two books of his *Ethics* to it unless one understands the enormous role friendship played as a social institution in classical Greece. One cannot understand why Plato and Aristotle subordinate ethics to politics unless one recognizes that the relation between the individual and the political community was very different in classical Greece from what it is now and, correspondingly, that it was conceived of rather differently. It is difficult to understand on purely philosophical grounds why almost the whole philosophy of late antiquity should be some form of Platonism; obviously, there is a connection between the dominance of Platonism and the new religions that conquered the Roman Empire. But it would be a mistake to be so impressed by this thought to think that the reasons philosophers offer for their views, or the philosophical considerations the historian of philosophy attributes to them, are mere rationalizations of views that they, in fact, held for other reasons. To think this is to underrate the intellectual power, ingenuity, resourceful-ness, and honesty of certain philosophers who would have been ready to trans-form, modify, or, if necessary, give up any of their views, to arrive at a set of beliefs for which they could have produced satisfactory reasons, even though they might have started out by trying to justify a view they were inclined toward on other grounds. And it is in terms of these reasons that we have to try to under-stand their views, unless we want to think that there is something misguided about the whole enterprise of philosophy that allows us to discount the philosophers' claim to hold philosophical views for philosophical reasons. More-over, we have to keep in mind that even if we came to believe that the philosophical reasons given frequently are mere rationalizations, they nonethe-less are reasons that have to be considered as such, and that they might turn out to be perfectly good reasons, in spite of the fact that they may have been es-poused for other reasons. What is more, the way they influence this history of philosophy is not as rationalizations, but as reasons, as good or bad, plausible or implausible reasons. It is because of this that the history of philosophy tries to explain the views of philosophers, as far as this is possible, on purely philo-sophical grounds.

But even if we think of the history of philosophy in this way, we may, for the reasons given, also want to insist that the thought of philosophers is tied to various histories, several of which may help to explain why a certain philoso-pher held a certain philosophical view, even if it was for philosophical reasons, or even good philosophical reasons, that he held it. What is more, these histories often help to shape philosophical thought, namely when its precise form and content is no longer determined by purely philosophical considerations. More-over, we have to keep in mind that philosophical thought itself helps to shape many other histories.

Thus, if we regard ancient philosophy an an object, this object, either as a whole or in part, enters into many histories. It is because of this that it can be pursued in many different ways, all of which have something to contribute to a fuller understanding of this object. To consider the philosophical thoughts of ancient philosophers only as such, will provide one with a very partial under-standing of ancient philosophy. The history of philosophy goes further than this. But it, too, does not provide us with more than an abstract, general understand-ing of ancient philosophy. To understand it, as much as possible, in its concrete, complex detail, one has also to look at all the other histories to which it is tied by an intricate web of causal connections which run both ways.

Hence, if I were asked whether my interest in ancient philosophy was primar-ily an interest in philosophy or an interest in the history of philosophy, I would say neither, since I am primarily interested in ancient philosophy itself, as it turns up in the various histories into which it enters, and in the way it actually enters these various histories.

It is because I conceive of my interest in ancient philosophy in this way that I have taken an interest in the whole history of ancient philosophy. For if, as I believe, a good deal of ancient philosophical thought cannot be understood in terms of reasons we might avail ourselves of, and if even what can be understood in this way is more fully understood if we also understand it in terms of the history of ancient philosophy, then an understanding of the history of ancient philosophy is crucial. But one does not arrive at a full understanding of a history by looking at just a few parts of it, especially if these parts are not selected with a view to what is important in terms of this history, but, rather, in terms, e.g., of our current philosophical interests and tastes. One cannot hope to understand the history of ancient philosophy by looking at just its beginnings, for obviously how the history is to be constructed depends crucially on how it continues and how it ends. This is just another way of saying that we can understand a philosophical view only in terms of the history of philosophy, that is, only if we see how it fits into this history as a whole, that is, if we understand not just what leads up to it, but also how it leads up to what follows. If we try to understand Aristotle's *Ethics,* we are not only greatly helped by seeing it against the background of Plato's moral philosophy, but also by considering what became of it as it was passed down in the Peripatetic school and by considering how Stoics, Epicureans, and Skeptics reacted to it and transformed it.

Hence, a large part of my work has been devoted to Hellenistic philosophy, in particular to the Stoics and the Skeptics, because until fairly recently we had very little understanding of this part of ancient philosophy. One reason for this was that Hellenistic philosophers were regarded as second- or third-rate philosophers, of little or no philosophical interest. As we come to have a better understanding of them, we increasingly realize three things: (i) Hellenistic philosophers are extremely interesting philosophically, once we do the tedious work of the historian to restore and reconstruct their actual views, instead of just believing what philosophers have been telling us about them since the beginning of modern times; (ii) We will understand early modern philosophy from Descartes to Kant much better once we fully realize how enormous the debt of early modern philosophy to Hellenistic philosophy is; (iii) Pre-Hellenistic ancient philosophy begins to appear in a different and better perspective. Hence, it is not surprising that the last ten years have seen an enormous increase in the interest in Hellenistic philosophy.

I very much hope, though, that one will soon be able to say the same about the philosophy of late antiquity. The objection is that it is philosophically boring, if not repellent. Again, the judgment is not based on careful study of the evidence, but on what has been commonly said about the philosophy of late antiquity. It seems clear to me (i) that Plotinus is extremely interesting philosophically, (ii) that we will never be able to understand medieval philosophy in its various traditions (the traditions of Byzantine philosophy, Islamic philosophy, and the Latin West) unless we understand the philosophy of late antiquity, and (iii) that the philosophy of late antiquity sheds a great deal of light on the history of Hellenistic philosophy and classical philosophy. One can learn much more from Plotinus about Aristotle than from most modern accounts of the Stagirite. Thus, I am confident that the near future will bring us a renaissance of studies of late ancient philosophy.

Because it seemed to me that one has a chance to understand the fact that someone took a certain view only if one fully understands that view, I chose to study the ancient history of one subject-matter, namely logic. Since we now seem to have a particularly clear understanding of the subject-matter, it is relatively easy for us to attain an unusually high level of understanding of views of logic held in the past. And, indeed, the enormous advances logic has made in the course of the last century have had the effect that we now have vastly better accounts of ancient logic. But this case also shows that a mere understanding of the subject-matter is not sufficient. To explain the reasons for which views were held, we also have to know which lines of reasoning were available and which not. Modern accounts of ancient logic almost invariably suffer from anachronism, and often grossly so.

Moreover, it seemed to me a good thing to take particular views or complexes of views and to follow them through history, to see how they were interpreted and reinterpreted, what was made of them in which context. A treatise like Aristotle's *Categories* offers a unique opportunity to do this, since it is one of the two or three philosophical texts that have been studied continuously throughout the history of philosophy, there are commentaries on it from all periods, it has had an enormous influence on the history of philosophy, and its contents were diffused at all levels of learning through compendia. Hence, a good deal of my work has centered on this treatise, in particular its metaphysics with its doctrine of substance.

Given that I am interested in the way in which ancient philosophy fits into the life of antiquity in general, I have not only tried to come to some understanding of ancient philosophy in terms of the history of ancient philosophy as a whole, but I have also taken an interest in some of the other histories in which parts of ancient philosophy play an important role. In particular I have been interested in the connections between philosophy and other branches of learning, e.g., grammar, medicine, and rhetoric.

Grammar seemed to me to be a particularly interesting case for the following reason. In school I had great difficulty understanding traditional grammar, whether Greek, Latin, or German. Later I learned from modern linguists that traditional grammar is utterly confused. Part of the reason for this confusion, though, seems to me not to have been properly understood. Traditional grammar was heavily influenced first by Stoic philosophy and later by Peripatetic philosophy. But, of course, the quite substantial philosophical assumptions that explain many of the features of traditional grammar were no longer accepted, under-stood, or even acknowledged when the subject had gained a life of its own and was pursued by scholars who knew little more of Stoic philosophy than its name. Hence, crucial features of the theory were no longer understood by those who were supposed to teach, revise, and expand the theory. In this one can see how far and in what disguise philosophical ideas can travel and what damage they can do if they go unrecognized.

Ancient medicine is of particular interest because here we have a case where there is a close connection on different levels which goes in both directions. There is not just a close connection between philosophical theory and medical theory, owing to the fact that both philosophers and doctors are interested in physiology and even pathology. There is also a connection between philosophi-cal views concerning the nature of human knowledge, the sciences and arts, and the way doctors conceive of their art. In fact, doctors develop quite elaborate philosophical theories concerning their expertise and expert knowledge in general, which in turn influence philosophers. Moreover, one might at least think that these philosophical views that are of great concern for ancient doctors might significantly affect their medical practice. One can observe that they did, but it is more interesting to notice how principles, based on philosophical con-siderations, which one might imagine would lead to wide divergences in practice in the end are supplemented by further principles, so that differences in medical practice between adherents of different schools were greatly reduced, if not abolished.

The case of medicine is also of interest in this context because ancient doctors had their own tradition of philosophical thought, they, as it were, insisted on their own philosophy which is rich enough to have its own history, closely inter-woven with the history of philosophy of the philosophers, but not part of it, rather parallel to it. To make things more complicated, some ancient doctors, like Asclepiades of Bithyma, Menodotus, Sextus Empiricus, and Galen, were also philosophers of sufficient stature to secure themselves a place in the history of philosophy. But it is the history of philosophy within medicine, as it were, which has been my particular concern. For, naturally enough, historians of phi-losophy have not taken much interest in it, and historians of medicine, equally naturally, have been reluctant to deal with philosophical matters.

So I have tried to study ancient philosophy in these various ways in the hope of getting as complex an understanding as possible of its complex reality. It seems to me that all these are perfectly good ways to study ancient philosophy, to shed light on the subject. Sometimes, though, philosophers talk as if there were only one way to study ancient philosophy and the philosophy of the past in general. And sometimes they talk as if it were not really worthwhile to study ancient philosophy and the philosophy of the past in general, obviously assuming that there is this one way to study the philosophy of the past, but that not much profit is to be gained by studying it this way. I am sure that no one really means this, but some comments on the matter may at least clarify my view.

To start with, it is merely an institutional fact that ancient philosophy is mainly studied in philosophy departments by philosophers. There is no separate profession of students of ancient philosophy. And this is all for the better, since to understand ancient philosophical thought one first of all has to understand it philosophically. It does cause a noticeable problem, though, for classicists, ancient historians, Roman lawyers, historians of medicine, historians of science, historians of theology, and a great many others, who may get the feeling that they are supposed to approach the subject in the way philosophers tend to approach it, when they, in fact, have their own legitimate approaches to it. For philosophers naturally want to study ancient philosophy in such a way as to understand it philosophically and to benefit philosophically from this understanding. It goes without saying, or rather apparently it does not, that this is not everyone else's ultimate aim in studying ancient philosophical thought. The one great history of ancient philosophy was written by a theologian, E. Zeller, whose primary interests in writing this history were in theology and the history of theology. But the philosophers are encouraged in their attitude toward the study of the philosophy of the past by a historical accident, namely the accident that ancient philosophy and the philosophy of the past in general came to be a subject of research and teaching by philosophers for a certain reason. It seems that the philosophy of the past came to be studied and taught by philosophers at the end of the eighteenth and in the course of the nineteenth century to complement or supplement the systematic study of philosophy. It seems that it was thought that the great philosophers could serve as models of what it is to do philosophy, that they had raised certain questions in an exemplary way and that they had formulated classical answers to them, from the study of which one could greatly benefit, even if one disagreed with their views, because they were exemplary even in their mistakes.

This attitude toward the great philosophers of the past had, of course, a long tradition. The tradition of studying great philosophers as philosophical classics goes back to antiquity. At the end of the second and in the first century B.C. certain figures in the history of philosophy, primarily Plato and Aristotle, were singled out as classical philosophers, just as one singled out classical historians, classical orators, classical dramatists, authors who were supposed to serve as a model for, and in a way to define, a genre. Within another two centuries the study of philosophy was reduced to the study of these classical philosophers. Philosophy was taught by commenting on the texts of these historical authors. Much historical and philological learning went into their study: reliable editions for these authors had to be prepared, authentic writings had to be distinguished from inauthentic ones, numerous historical allusions in the text had to be clarified. To understand what Plato and Aristotle say, one often has to know that they are addressing certain long-forgotten philosophical views. In short, men like Alexander of Aphrodisias and Porphyry were men of vast historical learning, but there is no reason to suppose they had an interest in the history of philosophy as such. They just learned what it took to determine Plato's and Aristotle's thought and to understand it philosophically. For their purposes it was an accident that Plato and Aristotle were figures of the past, historical figures.

Obviously, this way of teaching and studying philosophy by studying classical texts was no longer acceptable in modern times. It had been a strain already in antiquity, and in the Middle Ages literary forms were developed that allowed one to formally comment on a text when, in fact, one was systematically expounding one's own views, e.g., the questiones commentary. Once one started to study and to teach philosophy by setting forth systematically one's own views or by teaching from a contemporary textbook, another problem arose. The views of earlier philosophers may have been outdated, but one could not fail to realize that there was a noticeable difference between Descartes, Leibniz, Locke, Hume, and oneself or the author of the textbook one used. There is something strange in the notion that Baumgarten, Reimar, Cruse, Knutzen should take the place of these earlier philosophers, and there is something incongruous in the idea that Kant should teach philosophy by commenting on these authors. In any case, it is easy enough to see why it could be thought that the systematic study of philosophy should be supplemented by a study of the great philosophers of the past as philosophical models, to be understood and appreciated as philosophers. And this kind of study came to be called the study of the history of philosophy, since it was after all a study of the philosophy of the past and since it could involve some, or even a great deal of, historical learning, as we saw above in the cases of Alexander and of Porphyry. Hence, it is only natural that philosophers to the present day should think of the study of the history of philosophy in this way and decide that it should be abandoned if it no longer benefited us philosophically. After all, it was introduced for this purpose, and if it no longer serves it, it has lost its rationale.

But, clearly, there is an equivocation here. The study of the history of philosophy as a subject as I described it, i.e., as a systematic historical discipline is quite a different enterprise from the study of the philosophy of the past as it has been practiced by philosophers from the nineteenth century onward and continues to be practiced by them to the present day, though both come under the title of "history of philosophy." The historian of philosophy wants to understand the history of philosophy, and he wants to explain philosophical views of the past in terms of this history. He is not, at least as such, concerned to fully appreciate how past philosophers have managed to think or fail to think the way we think or the way one ought to think.

This switch in approach to past thought and the resulting equivocation may have been obscured for a long time by a certain conception of the history of philosophy in the historian's sense of history. If one conceives of the history of philosophy as essentially a process in which certain questions that define the philosophical enterprise are seen and understood ever more clearly and in which the answers to these questions become more and more apparent, if it is perhaps even assumed that there is some mechanism or force that guarantees this kind of progress and in terms of which the history of philosophy, therefore, has to be understood, the two appraoches to the philosophical past might easily seem to coincide. For now the philosophical classics will serve to show a certain understanding of the philosophical problems, but also the limitations of this past understanding and the necessity to overcome these limitations by the progress later thinkers have made. This seems to be the spirit in which the first detailed histories of philosophy were written at the end of the eighteenth century. But, surely, it was a mistake to think that the proper way to understand and to explain Aristotle's thought was to see it as a crucial step forward in the direction of Kantianism, or some other philosophical view. The nineteenth century abounded in views that explained why philosophy, along with the culture of which it is a part, was set on a steady path of progress, in which the steps could be understood, almost teleologically, in terms of the position they led up to. But if the history of philosophy is as much a history of failure where success was possible, as of achievement where failure was possible or almost guaranteed, what reason do we have to think that there is something that guarantees philosophical progress such that we have to understand the history of philosophy in terms of it?

Thus, it seems to me that there is no reason to suppose that the study of the great philosophers of the past as models of philosophical thought and the study of the history of philosophy in the historian's sense will somehow amount to the same thing. And, hence, I think that the question whether the study of the great philosophers of the past as philosophical models is philosophically profitable is quite different from the question whether the study of the history of philosophy is philosophically profitable. In both cases I find it difficult to believe that the answer should not be positive. It is difficult not to see, even without any historical learning, that Kant is a much better philosopher than the famous Kruse, not to mention any of our contemporaries, and that much is to be learned from the complexity of his thought. It is equally difficult to see how one would not benefit philosophically when, in doing the history of philosophy, one tries to find as good a philosophical reason as possible to take the most diverse, if not perverse, philosophical views. What better way could there be to expand one's repertoire of philosophical lines of reasoning than to find one for almost any conceivable philosophical position? What better way is there to learn to see things in fundamentally different ways and to appreciate the merits and the defects of the different positions one could take?

In all this it should not be forgotten, either, that the philosophical views of contemporary philosophers are as much a part of the history of philosophy in the wider sense as the philosophical views of the past. If, then, by chance, we should be interested not just in some contemporary philosophical view, but also in the question why a certain philosopher holds it, we will try to get the kind of answer we are looking for when we do the history of philosophy, or, more generally, study the philosophical thought of the past. One would expect that the answer one gets is the kind of answer one gets throughout the history of philosophy, an answer that will show how much the view depends on earlier views, at least as likely as not there is no good reason to hold the view, but there are considerations that allow one to understand why the philosopher does think that he has a good reason to hold the belief. One thing, though, that will almost never happen is that we come to think that the philosophical considerations we attribute to the author are dated, are the kinds of considerations we would no longer avail ourselves of, and, hence, have to be explained in terms of the history of philosophy. This must be part of the reason why some philosophers seem to think that contemporary philosophy does not depend on its history. For one can, indeed, understand contemporary philosophical thought, at least in general, without reference to the history of philosophy, because the kinds of philosophical considerations contemporary philosophers avail themselves of are the kinds of considerations in terms of which we can understand any philosophical view, whether present or past, without having to have recourse to the history of philosophy. But, of course, it does not follow from the fact that one can explain someone's having a philosophical view without recourse to the history of philosophy that it does not depend on the history of philosophy. In fact, it might depend so heavily on it that in the future one will no longer be able to understand it except in terms of the history of philosophy. This is just obscured from us by the fact that we have little idea which contemporary considerations in the future will appear dated.

Now if one does not take the view that the history of philosophy by its very nature is a history of increasingly rational and philosophically satisfactory answers to a set of pernennial problems, but, rather, a history of achievements and failures, where the failures often had more influence than the achievements, and if one believes that philosophical thought does heavily depend on the history of philosophy, there might be something to be learned philosophically from the history of philosophy as described above. If we were able to get a good enough grasp on the actual history of philosophy, we should be able to see ever more clearly how our own philosophical thought depends on the philosophical failures of the past. As long as the history of philosophy is seen primarily as a series of achievements that did not go far enough and, hence, naturally invited further achievements that would take the matter a step further, it seems that not much is to be learned philosophically from the realization that one's thought is indebted to one's predecessors. But it is exactly because the historian of philosophy tries to take the philosophers of the past seriously as philosophers that he might come to the conclusion that the history of philosophy at crucial junctures has gone in the wrong direction.

If this were a fact, it would be difficult for us to see. For we would have to make such judgments in terms of what we think of as good reasons or at least as considerations in the light of which someone might take something to be good reasons. Given that these are matters conditioned by the history of philosophy, they are likely to be conditioned by the very failures we want to diagnose in their terms. Obviously, this will be a difficult task. For to the extent that our notions and assumption of what is rational and reasonable are conditioned by the history of philosophy, they will make that history appear rational and reasonable, a history of achievements rather than of failures.

Fortunately, the historian of philosophy has more to rely on than contemporary philosophical views. His work, ideally, would have taught him new views that one could take, new reasons for or against old views; he may have discovered there was good reason for views which at first seemed unreasonable. All this work may have substantially changed his notions and his assumptions of what constitutes good reason and of what at least is reasonable. Hence, the historian of philosophy might very well be in a position to diagnose a development in the history of philosophy as an aberration, when, from the point of view of contemporary philosophy, this development seems entirely reasonable. The difficulty, of course, is that the historian of philosophy should be able to persuade philosophers that this is so on purely philosophical grounds.

But if one studies the philosophy of the past not just as a historian of philosophy, but in all its aspects, one has further resouces to fall back on. It may be that at some of the junctures in the history of philosophy where the historian of philosophy believes he has to diagnose a failure, the failure may be the result of thoughts which themselves are to be explained in good part in terms of some other history. One may even be able to show that this other history interfered with the "natural" development of philosophical thought at this point, however philosophically reasonable this development may now seem to us.

Once one asked questions such as "What is philosophy?" A way to answer this question is to look at the thought of the past, to study ancient philosophy, e.g., in the way I propose to do, not just by studying ancient philosophers as paradigms, nor by just trying to fit them into the history of philosophy, but by looking at all the histories in which they occur, to see by their example, as concretely as possible, what it actually means and amounts to when one does philosophy. One thing one can learn from this is that to be a philosopher in antiquity was something rather different from what it is today. There is no doubt that the *Lives and Views of the Philosophers* of a Diogenes Laertius are bad history of philosophy, but perhaps they do capture an aspect of ancient philosophy that the scholarly history of philosophy, given its aims, passes over, but that, nonetheless, is real and of interest.

Plato

1

Observations on Perception in Plato's Later Dialogues

Ast, in his *Lexicon Plantonicum,* gives the following as the general meaning of the verb "aisthanesthai" in Plato: "to sense, to perceive by a sense, and hence generally to perceive by the senses." This not only seems to me to be wrong, it also seems to be seriously misleading if one wants to arrive at an understanding of what Plato has to say about perception. For it suggests that in general when Plato uses the verb "aisthanesthai," he is relying on a common notion of sense-perception, a notion which Plato just tries to clarify. This suggestion seems natural enough. Surely, one will say, the Greeks even before Plato must have had a notion of sense-perception, and "aisthanesthai" must have been the verb they commonly used when they wanted to talk about sense-perception. And yet it seems to me that one fails to understand what Plato is trying to do, in particular in the *Theaetetus,* unless one understands that it is only Plato who introduces a clear notion of sense-perception, because he needs it for certain philosophical purposes. What he has to say about perception has to be understood against the background of the ordinary use of the verb "aisthanesthai" and against the background of the philosophical intentions with which Plato narrows down this common use so that it does come to have the meaning "to perceive by the senses."

Though "aisthanesthai" presumably is formed from a root which signifies "hearing," its ordinary use is quite general. It can be used in any case in which one perceives something by the senses and even more generally in any case in which one becomes aware of something, notices something, realizes or even comes to understand something, however this may come about. There will, of course, be a tendency to use the word in cases in which it is particularly clear that somebody is becoming aware of something or noticing something, as opposed to just venturing a guess, making a conjecture, learning of something by hearsay. These will be cases of seeing, but then also cases of sense-perception quite generally. But the use of the verb is not restricted to these cases. It is used whenever someone becomes aware of something. And up to Plato's time, and often far beyond it, there is no clear recognition that there are two radically different ways in which we become aware of something, one by way of sense-perception and the other in some other way, e.g., by a grasp of the mind. Thus, there is no reason to suppose that the verb "aisthanesthai," strictly speaking, refers only to sense-perception, but is also used metaphorically in other cases. It, rather, seems that all cases of becoming aware of something are understood and construed along the lines of the paradigm of seeing, exactly because one does not see a radical difference between the way the mind grasps something and the way the eyes see something. Both are supposed to involve some contact with the object by virtue of which, through a mechanism unknown to us, we become aware of it.

But in addition to this very general use of the verb "aisthanesthai," we find in Plato a second, narrower use of the term, e.g., in the *Phaedo* and in the *Republic*. In this use the term is restricted to cases of awareness that somehow involve the body and that constitute an awareness of something corporeal. But even now it would be rash to assume that the verb means "sense-perception." For in these cases it is used almost interchangeably with "dokein" and "dox-azein," "to seem" and "to believe." The realm of belief, as opposed to the realm of knowledge, is the bodily world with which we are in bodily contact as a result of which this world appears to us in a certain way, as a result of which we have certain beliefs about it. There is no "doxa," no belief about the ideas, because ideas are not the kinds of things with which one could have the kind of contact that gives rise to a belief or a perception. But, just as it would be a mistake to infer from this that "doxa" means "sense-perception," so there also is no need to assume that "aisthesis" means "sense-perception," though standard cases of "aisthesis" will be cases of sense-perception.

It is also in the later dialogues that we clearly have an even narrower use of "aisthanesthai," in which it, indeed, does mean "to perceive by the senses." And it is this third sense of "aisthesis" whose introduction I want to discuss.

Unfortunately, our main evidence for this very narrow notion of "aisthesis" is contained in a passage of the *Theaetetus*, 184–187, whose interpretation has become highly controversial, since it involves basic claims about Plato's philosophy and his philosophical development.

In this passage Plato tries to show not only that perception is not identical with knowledge, but that no case of perception as such is a case of knowledge. The argument assumes that if we perceive something, a bodily sense-organ is affected, and that through this change in the sense-organ a change is brought about in the mind (186 Cff.; 186 D). What the argument, as I want to interpret it, mainly turns on is that if we have a clear and precise notion of perception, we see that perception is a purely passive affection of the mind and that for that very reason it cannot constitute knowledge, since knowledge minimally involves true belief and since any belief involves an activity of the mind.

If this is correct, then it would seem that Plato's point in introducing this very narrow notion of perception is to untangle the conflation of perception, appearance, belief, and knowledge with which the main discussion of the dialogue begins in 151 D ff. There perception is first identified with knowledge in Theaetetus' first definition of knowledge as perception, and perception gets quickly identified with appearance (152 C 11), which then throughout this section of the dialogue is treated as if it were the same as belief (cf., e.g., 158 A 1 with 158 A 2 and 185 B 2). But, obviously, it is useful to distinguish between these cognitive states: to perceive is not the same as to believe (though in the middle dialogues we had not paid much attention to the distinction); neither is the same as to be appeared to, and to know is yet a fourth thing. But it is not only useful to make these distinctions, as Plato tries to make them in the *Theaetetus* and the *Sophist* (264 A-B). It is necessary to make these distinctions if we want to combat a certain philosophical view that we first encounter in Protagoras, but that, in one version or another, will later be espoused by some rhetoricians, Skeptics, and the so-called Empiricists, namely the view that the beliefs which we have are just a matter of how things appear to us, how they strike us, of what impression, given the contact we have with them, they leave on us. Plato and the philosophical tradition that depends on him, on the other hand, think that we should not rest content with how things strike us, that we have to go beyond that to find out how they really are, quite independently of how they appear to us. The opponents, like Protagoras, question or deny the possibility that we ever get beyond appearance, seeming, belief. And, hence, they doubt or deny that there is any point in reserving the term "knowledge" for something that goes beyond belief. It is in this context that I want to see the argument of the *Theaetetus,* and in particular the section from 184 to 187. Plato thinks that our beliefs and our knowledge about the physical world involve a passive affection of the mind, but he also thinks that they go much beyond this passive affection. And he wants to reserve the term "aisthanesthai," or "to perceive," for this passive element in our beliefs, which he was willing to grant the opponents. It is in this way that the term came to have the meaning of sense-perception.

With this as a background let us turn to the details of the argument. The conclusion that perception and knowledge are two different things is drawn in 186 E 9–10 on the basis of the argument in the preceding lines, 186 E 4ff. It is assumed that to know is to grasp the truth and that to grasp the truth is to grasp being. But in perception we do not grasp being, hence we do not grasp truth. Therefore, to perceive is not to know. This argument has two crucial assumptions: (i) to grasp the truth is to grasp being, and (ii) to perceive is not to grasp being. It is difficult to understand and to evaluate these assumptions, since we do not know what is meant by "to grasp being." There is no argument for the first assumption that can shed light on the meaning of the phrase. But the second premise is supposed to have been established by the argument that extends to 186 C 6. Hence, we can look at this argument to see whether it gives us a clue to what is meant by "to grasp being."

Now, if we look at the argument, it seems that the reason given for the assumption that in perception we do not grasp being is that the mind considers questions concerning the being of something by itself, rather than by means of one of the senses. This would suggest that the mind grasps or gets hold of being in the relevant sense when it manages to settle the question concerning the being of something which it has been considering by itself. This seems to be confirmed by the final comments on the argument in 187 A 1ff. There Plato says that we have learned from the argument at least that we have to look for knowledge not in perception, but in what the mind does when it considers questions concerning being by itself (187 A 5–6), when it forms beliefs (187 A 7–8). It is because we are supposed to draw this moral from the argument that the dialogue proceeds to discuss the suggestion that knowledge is true belief (187 B 4–6). It is in belief that we grasp truth, if the belief is true, though, as the further argument will show, this is not yet a sufficient condition for knowledge, since knowledge requires that this truth be grasped in a particular way.

But if it is in true belief that we grasp truth, it is also in true belief that we grasp being. This suggests that by "grasping being" Plato here means no more than that the mind in forming a true belief manages to settle the question of the being of something correctly. And it is easy to see how Plato could think this, given his views on being. For he assumes that any belief, explicitly or implicitly, is of the form "A if F," and he thinks that in assuming that A is F one attributes being both to A and to F-ness. To assume that Socrates is just is, on this view, to attribute being to Socrates and to justice. Hence, any true belief will presuppose that one has correctly settled questions concerning the being of something.

One may, of course, think that by "grasping being" Plato here means something much stronger than settling the question whether being should be attributed to something in this way. One may think that Plato wants to distinguish two kinds of grasps or intutions, a perceptual grasp or intuition and an intellectual grasp or intuition. Thus, one may think that Plato, having distinguished two kinds of features, perceptual features and nonperceptual or intelligible features, wants to claim that knowledge involves the intellectual grasp of intelligible features and hence that perception will never give us knowledge. But even if this should be Plato's view, this is not the way he argues in this passage. Instead of distinguishing two kinds of features and correspondingly two kinds of grasps or intutions, he distinguishes two kinds of features and correspondingly two kinds of questions the mind considers and tries to settle (cf. 185 E 6ff.). If F-ness is a perceptual feature, then, when the mind considers the question whether something is F, it draws on the testimony of the senses (cf. 185 B 10–12). If F-ness is a nonperceptual feature like being, then the mind considers the question whether something is F by itself. What little Plato has to say about how the mind goes about doing this makes no reference to some intellectual grasp. Plato is referring to comparisons and to reasonings the mind goes through to come to a judgment (186 A 10ff.; 186 B 8ff.; 186 C 2ff.), the kinds of things the mind does when it tries to decide a matter. And the fact that Plato is 187 A 5ff. characterizes what the mind does when it considers questons by itself as "doxazein," i.e., as coming to form a belief, certainly should warn us against assuming that some special power of the mind to grasp intelligible entities is appealed to here. All that seems to be appealed to is what the mind has to be able to do to form beliefs. And this is a great deal, though Plato here does not care to spell it out in any detail. To be able to form the belief that A is F, the mind has to have arrived at some idea of what it is to be for A and what it is to be for F-ness, or what it is to be for an F and it has to find out whether A is such as to be an F. What Plato here wants to emphasize is the mere fact that the perception is a purely passive affection (cf. 186 C 2 and 186 D 2), whereas the simplest belief even if it concerns a perceptual feature, requires and presupposes a great deal of mental activity. And he infers from this that since all this activity is needed to arrive at truth, perception itself does not give us truth and, hence, cannot be knowledge.

Now one may want to interpret the argument of 184–187 differently and argue thus: Plato distinguishes two kinds of questions, those the mind settles by itself and those the mind settles by relying on a sense. Since there are questions the mind has to settle by itself, and since, presumably, the answer to these questions can be known, we here have an argument which shows that knowledge is not to be identified with perception. But we do not have an argument, nor does Plato intend to argue, that perception never gives us knowledge. After all, there are questions for whose solution the mind relies on a sense. The answer to these questions seems to be provided by perception. It seems to me that this interpretation is wrong. Plato is quite careful never to say that some questions are settled by perception or by a sense. All questions are settled by the mind, though for some it does rely on perception. Thus, I take it that Plato wants to argue that even the question whether A is red is not settled by perception. We may be passively affected by the color red, but to form the belief that something is red presupposes and takes a great deal of activity on the part of the mind. Hence, we perceive the color red, but we do not, strictly speaking, perceive that A is red. Hence, knowledge, since it always involves belief, never is just a matter of perception.

The only textual evidence that seems to stand in the way of this interpretation is the following. In 186 B 11-C 5 we are told that whereas animals and we as children perceive many things right from birth, there are other things that it takes us a long time, much trouble, and some education to grasp. Surely, one will say, to see that something is red does not take much trouble and a lot of education. It is something any infant can do. But, it may be worth remembering that even the Stoics later will deny that children, properly speaking, perceive that something is red. For perception in this wider sense presupposes a state of the development of reason that allows us to articulate a visual impression in terms of concepts and that allows us to accept such an impression as true. Thus, even the simple judgment that something is red presupposes some notion of what it is to be and some notion of what it is to be red. And this we do not have right from birth. Nor is it given to us by perception, but only by reflection on what we perceive. What we perceive, strictly speaking, are just the proper objects of the different senses, e.g., colors in the case of sight (184 E 7ff.). Thus, strictly speaking, we do not even perceive the object of which we come to believe that it is red. And if this is so, it is even more difficult to see how we could be said to perceive that something is red, given this very narrow notion of perception.

Now, Plato, in restricting perception to a passive affection of the mind and in emphasizing the activity of the mind in forming beliefs, thinks of beliefs as something we deliberately arrive at after a good deal of consideration and ratiocination. As Plato puts it later in the dialogue (189 E-190 A), belief is the result of a silent discussion one leads with oneself. In the *Sophist* (263 Eff.) and in the *Philebus* (38 C-E), we get a similar view of belief. Thus, belief is conceived of as something that is actively espoused on the basis of some conscious, deliberate activity. This, no doubt, is an idealization of how we come to have beliefs. For many beliefs we just find ourselves with, and in their case there is no reason to suppose that we ever went through a process of deliberation as a result of which we espoused the belief. The Protagorean view, on the other hand, and the other views alluded to in the beginning, which are like it, assume that beliefs normally are something we just find ourselves with, which have grown on us, which we have just come by by being struck by things in a certain way. And they try to assimilate all beliefs to what they take to be the normal case. Hence, they emphasize the passive element in belief-formation. Thus, one can see why Plato should be interested in emphasizing how small the passive element in belief-formation is. To do so, he restricts the general notion of perception to sense-perception in such a narrow sense and, moreover, to such a narrow notion of sense-perception that we cannot even any longer be said to perceive that something is red. It is this philosophical motivation that underlies Plato's introduction of a narrow use of "aisthanesthai" in the sense of "sense-perception," a sense which the word did not have ordinarily and which it did not have in Plato's earlier writings.

Aristotle

2

The Title, Unity, and Authenticity of the Aristotelian *Categories*

I. Introduction

The *Categories*, ascribed to Aristotle, has played a unique role in our tradition. It is the only philosophical treatise that has been the object of scholarly and philosophical attention continuously since the first century B.C., when people first began writing commentaries on classical philosophical texts. From early late antiquity until the early modern period, one would begin the study of Aristotle and the study of philosophy quite generally with the *Categories* and Porphyry's *Isagoge*. For several centuries, these two treaties, and the *De Interpretatione*, formed the core of the philosophical corpus which was still being seriously studied. Thus, it is hardly surprising that our received view of Aristotle—whether we are aware of this in all its details or not—was colored substantially by the *Categories*.

Already in late antiquity, however, doubts were raised about its authenticity,[1] though we know of no ancient scholar who, on the basis of such doubts, declared the treatise to be spurious. On the contrary, Ammonius claims that everyone agreed that it was authentic.[2] The writers of the Middle Ages and the scholastics of the early modern period seem to have had no doubt about the authenticity of the treatise;[3] presumably, they were relying mainly on the authority of Boethius.[4] It is tempting to suppose that this acceptance of the treatise by the scholastics is precisely what led Renaissance scholars like Luis Vives[5] and Francesco Patrizi[6] to raise doubts about this very foundation of both scholasticism and traditional logic, though they did not attempt to provide any detailed arguments for their conclusion. It remained for the nineteenth and twentieth centuries to examine the *Categories* critically with the aid of the new philology. And soon enough, there was an impressive roster of those staunchly maintaining that the treatise was not genuine.[7] Even H. Bonitz considered it to be of doubtful authenticity.[8] During the present century, opinion has again shifted in favor of the view that it is a genuine work of Aristotle's, though, to be sure, the doubts have not been entirely silenced. I.M. Bochenski, writing in 1947, thought the treatise of doubtful authenticity;[9] and in 1949, S. Mansion tried to argue against its authenticity.[10] Doubts especially about the second part, the so-called *Postpraedicamenta,* have never really ceased.[11]

Given the enormous influence this treatise has had on our view of Aristotle and on our interpretation of his writings, it seems extremely important to me to try, as far as possible, to lay these doubts to rest. Yet, I hope this investigation will also be of interest to those already firmly convinced that the *Categories* is a genuine work of Aristotle's; for it raises questions that interpreters of the treatise, in general, do not address and whose answers might well alter the standard view of this text.

The question of authenticity, however, turns out to be crucially linked to the question of unity. Given that it seems highly questionable whether the *Postpraedicamenta* were originally part of the treatise or were appended by a later editor,[12] it might seem as if the question regarding the authenticity of the treatise needs to be asked as two questions, viz., questions regarding the authenticity of the first and second part individually. Many authors have indeed taken this for granted and have thus assumed that the first part was authentic, the second either probably or certainly not.[13] Since, however, interest traditionally has focused almost exclusively on the first part of this treatise, we also find the tendency to regard the question of authenticity as primarily the question of the authenticity of the first part and so to leave the question of unity and the problem of the authenticity of the second part to more or less take care of themselves. Buhle already exhibits this tendency characteristic of many modern interpreters.[14] After having called attention to the apparent lack of connection between the *Postpraedicamenta* and the *Praedicamenta* and after briefly remarking (without providing any specifics) that some things in the *Postpraedicamenta* do not mesh well with other aspects of Aristotle's thought, he writes: "sed fac esse postpraedicamenta spuria, non idem tamen de Categoriis statuendum est." It is obvious—as long as the authenticity of the first part is secure, it does not much matter to Buhle whether or not one considers the second part genuine. Such an approach, however, is methodologically highly suspect because the questions of unity and of authenticity cannot be separated without both prejudging the issue of unity and presupposing a certain interpretation of the *Categories,* especially since the lack of unity itself has been taken as providing strong *prima facie* grounds for judging the treatise to be spurious.[15] Therefore, in what follows, I will pay particular attention to the question of unity. The dangerous tendency to consider this treatise almost exclusively with reference to the first part and thus to jeopardize the status of the second part is, of course, reinforced considerably by the title. Hence, I will also discuss the title in connection with the question of unity.

II. The Unity of the Treatise I

There can be little doubt that the treatise, in the form in which we have it, is not by Aristotle. Like many other of Aristotle's writings, it shows signs of the activity of a later editor. Cook Wilson, in the *Göttinger Gelehrte Anzeigen,* already showed that for linguistic as well as doctrinal reasons lines 11b 10–15 cannot be by Aristotle.[16] Minio-Pauluello has shown that, for the same reasons, the following lines, 11^b 15–16, also are not by Aristotle.[17] This view seems to have prevailed,[18] though it should be pointed out that Colli, despite all his doubts, felt he could not adopt it.[19]

We can even ask if the doubts ought not to be extended to the preceding lines as well. The "hyper" which, especially by being iterated, seemed objectionable in 11b 10–16 already occurs in 11^a 20.[20] In 11^a 37–38, we find the strange claim that if something is both a *quale* as well as a *relativum* nothing prevents us from assigning it to both genera. The claim is strange in three respects. First, there is no other place in the corpus where the possibility is considered that the highest genera are not mutually exclusive. In fact, even the author of our treatise is willing to introduce a new definition of relatives to exclude the possibility that substances should fall under the definition of relatives (cf. 8^a 13ff.). Even if, in light of 11^a 35–36, we—to my mind, incorrectly—construe the term *quale* in 11^a 37 as referring not to a quality but to something having a quality, we still have a problem: though this solves our immediate difficulty, that one and the same thing should be both a quality and a relative, we are faced with a new difficulty; now it seems as if the genus of quality is the class of things having a certain quality not, as we might have thought, the class of qualities. Second, however we construe this sentence, it contributes nothing toward solving the difficulty raised in 11^a 20–22. Third, in this treatise, we find "genos" used in the sense of highest genus only here and in the interpolated part, at 11b 15. Finally, it should be noted that the discussion of the genera of doing and of being-affected is highly schematic, mechanical, and incomplete; someone who actually had something to say on the matter ought not, under ordinary circumstances, write lines like these.

Of course, all that is relevant for our argument here is that lines 11^b 10–16 are not by Aristotle; for these lines establish the formal unity of the treatise. The *Categories* clearly falls into two parts, Chapters 1–9, on the one hand, and Chapters 10–15, on the other. As far as content is concerned, the two parts seem quite unrelated; nothing in the first part prepares us for the second part, and the second part neither builds on the content of the first part nor does it formally refer back to it; instead, it begins abruptly with an entirely new subject—the kinds of opposites—a subject entirely unmotivated by what came in the first part. In particular, the second part of the treatise is not at all concerned with categories. It would be impossible to read the two parts (whether we think of the first part as ending at 11^a 19, or 11^a 36, or 11^b 8) as a single text without being troubled by the lack of transition; for (i) the discussion of genera at the end of the first part is obviously incomplete, and (ii), the shift to an entirely new subject in the second part is abrupt and unmotivated. Thus, it seems likely that the interpolated lines are by an editor who simply could not avoid tampering with the text, if he intended to publish the two parts as a single text.[21]

However, given the disparity between the two parts, we need to ask ourselves what could have motivated the editor or, perhaps, even the editors, to join the two parts into a single text. In connection with this, it is important that neither of the two parts, on its own, could stand as a complete and self-contained text.

This is especially noticeable in the case of the second part. Chapters 10 and 11 form a unit in both language and content; they treat of opposites. But then, without any transition and without any connecting particle, we have a discussion of priority and simultaneity. Chapter 14 provides a short treatment of the kinds of motion, which seems out of place in both language and content. The final chapter, again beginning without any connecting particle, gives an enumeration of eight senses of 'having'. We get an idea of how great the difficulties surrounding the inner unity of just the second part are by seeing that the tradition never succeeded in providing an even somewhat plausible account of its unity. It is instructive to see how many interpreters sought to escape the problem by simply ignoring the textual situation. Al-Farabi, for example, simply does not discuss the final two chapters; Ps.-Archytas, in *Peri antikeimenon,* restricts himself to the chapter on opposites; the *Paraphrasis Themistiana* recapitulates the contents of c. 15 at the end of the discussion of the ten genera, as if it were a chapter on the category of 'having'.

However, it would be a mistake to follow Brandis[22] in concluding that the second part consists only of three or four unrelated fragments that were simply appended to the main text, i.e., to the first part, by an editor. For the second part does indeed have a certain unity of both language and content (leaving aside the chapter on motion). As for language, compare, for example c. 12, 14^b 7–8 esti men dē schedon allotriotatos tōn tropōn houtos with c. 15, 15^b 28–29 eoike de allotriotatos ho nun rhetheis tropos tou echein einai. In both sentences we find "tropos" used in a sense which, while relatively rare in the rest of the corpus, is characteristic for this text; in both, a use of "allotrios" that is rare in the rest of the corpus; and the combination of the two words, which seems to appear nowhere else in Aristotle; in both cases we have the superlative, and eoike in the second sentence corresponds to "schedon" in the first. All the pieces of the second part, except that on motion, have in common that they discuss the tropoi in which something is the case (12^b 3; 12^b 11; 13^a 16; 13^b 1; 14^b 8; 14^b 9; 14^b 11; 14^b 22; 15^b 17; 15^b 29; 15^b 31); and even the bit on motion discusses the kinds of motion. Thus, it very much looks as if the pieces of the second part belong to a single bit of text, even if not to one intended as a continuous discussion, much less one that could stand on its own. We seem to have an unfinished fragment; and if we knew more about its original context we could, presumably, also see its unity of content.

However, it is also by no means the case that at least the first part forms a self-contained unit. We often hear that the first part is an independent text, namely the actual treatise on categories, to which an editor has added the problematic second part. Against this, it must be pointed out—what has already been noticed for quite some time[23]—that the first part too is a fragment which never could have been published as a separate essay in its present form. E. Zeller[24] already saw this when he suggested that the editor had removed the rest of the treatise on categories to replace it by 11^b 8–14. Of course, not only is it difficult to see what could have motivated an editor to mutilate a text in this way in order to be able to append the *Postpraedicamenta,* but this hypothesis also does not begin to account for the full extent of the first part's fragmentariness. The problem is not just that it ends abruptly in the middle of the discussion of genera. The treatment of the genera of doing and being-affected is grossly incomplete;[25] it provides no general characterization of these genera, no discussion of their species, no mention of their propria, all of which we would expect from the schema (admittedly, only incompletely followed in c. 7) of the other chapters. The fact that the third chapter is not tied to its context in either language or content also seems objectionable, as does the fact that c. 4 begins without a connection particle. In fact, it has always seemed troubling that the connection between the first three chapters, the so-called *Antepraedicamenta,* and the following chapters is by no means made sufficiently clear. It is also not sufficiently clear what the actual subject of the treatise is supposed to be. This certainly is something we would expect of a finished and complete treatise, and the *Categories'* lack of explicitness on this point has given rise to the never-ending debate about whether the treatise is primarily about expressions or parts of expressions or about the corresponding entities and their genera. Even though Chapters 5 through 9 clearly are about genera of objects, we can easily imagine that the author, having discussed true genera, was going to turn to the corresponding expressions and to the propositions formed from them which had been the subject of the first part of the treatise. Moreover, the chapter on relatives is lacking a specification of their propria. In short, the first part as well seems to be an unfinished fragment. This suggests that the editor was dealing with a single, fragmentary, perhaps never completed text, or with two related fragments which for some reason he sought to combine into a single text.

Against the assumption that the pieces were all originally part of a single work, it has been argued, since Andronicus, [26] that the second part has nothing to do with the subject of the treatise, namely, the theory of categories. Supposing that it was clear that this, in fact, was the subject of the treatise, people have traditionally countered this objection by trying to construct a connection between the theory of categories and the second part of our treatise. Porphyry's attempts along these lines already seemed hopelessly inadequate to Simplicius.[27] Porphyry himself may not have been convinced that it was a single treatise; his commentary, at any rate, breaks off at Chapter 9, and all the frequent references to his commentary by Simplicius are concerned with the first part. Simplicius himself[28] follows Iamblichus' attempt at a reconstruction, which is hardly any less contrived. On this line, the treatment of the various genera presupposed the notion of contrary opposites which, however, could not have been discussed in Chapters 5–9, since such a discussion would have interrupted the main line of thought. In the chapter on relatives, Aristotle holds that though correlatives form pairs of opposites, these are not contrary opposites; thus, it was necessary to distinguish between the various kinds of opposites. Furthermore, since Aristotle discussed priority, posteriority, and simultaneity in the first part of the treatise, these notions, too, needed to be clarified. Since the genera of doing and of being affected subsume notions, these needed to be discussed as well. Finally, the word 'having' has many senses; Aristotle thus needed to clarify in which sense we should talk of a genus of having. The artificiality of this explanation is hardly worth remarking on; if anything is worthy of note here, it is how convinced of the unity of this text Simplicius must have been to fall back on such an explanation even in desperation.

Now, the difficulties confronting Andronicus and the tradition that follows him arise only because they assume that this text is a treatise on the categories. This assumption, however, was never justified in the tradition which has come down to us, and it is difficult to see how it could be justified. If we leave aside the title for the moment (I will return to it later), we find that very little tells in favor of this assumption, just enough to see how anyone could ever have made it, but by no means enough to justify it. The second part of the treatise, indeed, seems to rule out this assumption. It may be objected that this argument just involves a *petitio principii;* it is just the reverse of the argument that the second part could not originally have been part of the treatise, since it does not deal with the categories. Even if we disregard the second part, there is still very little that tells in favor of the assumption that the subject here is categories. It is hardly worth mentioning that the treatise nowhere says that it is about categories; indeed, the very word 'category' appears only once (10^b 19–20) in this text, near the end, and there in a very subordinate role. Nor do we find some synonym used in its place. Categories simply are not explicitly discussed in the treatise, except once, in passing, in the passage mentioned. Finally, it is not as if the contents of the treatise are about categories in the Aristotelian sense. When I speak of categories in the Aristotelian sense, I am assuming that we need to distinguish between categories (that is, kinds of predication in a special, technical sense which we find in *Top.* I 9), genera of being, and categories of 'being' (i.e., kinds of predication of "being"). In terms of this distinction, the first part of the treatise, at least in the form in which we have it, deals with the genera of being and not with the categories. There is, of course, a close connection between *Cat.* 4 and *Top.* I 9, and we can well imagine that the author of the first part, after having treated the various genera, either would have proceeded or even did proceed to consider the corresponding categories. The fact of the matter is that in the text as we have it categories in the Aristotelian sense are only alluded to at the beginning of the first chapter. And so it is telling that the ancient commentators, when explaining the title 'Categories', do not refer to some special technical use of the term in Aristotle but simply, in an *ad hoc* manner, come up with a more or less suitable meaning. Porphyry, for example, thinks that categories in the sense of expressions that are predicated of things are what are being discussed here.[29] Most commentators, however, including Simplicius, maintain that terms or genera, like substance, quality, quantity, etc., are being considered, which, because of their complete generalilty, cannot be subjects but only predicates.[30] Aristotle himself does not, however, speak of categories in either of these senses. Even if we disregard this point and, like Simplicius, proceed to identify the highest genera with the categories, we will notice that the genera or genera of being are also not explicitly discussed as such in our text, with the exception of the two occurrences, in the passages of doubtful authenticity, which I mentioned above (11^a 38; 11^b 15). This would be strange at best if these genera were the subject matter of the treatise.

The text itself, then, does not give one grounds for assuming that the subject matter is the theory of categories. We need, rather, to ask what could have led to this assumption in the first place, not to mention how it could ever have come to be taken for granted. The title, once it became established, naturally furthered this assumption. Yet, if we look at the history of the title, we will see that the title probably did not originally lead to the assumption, but, rather, the assumption led to the title.

III. The Title

Whether the title "Categories" is Aristotle's original title, as Th. Waitz[31] and others have thought, is of crucial importance for my argument. Some later commentators[32] do, indeed, claim that Aristotle himself referred to the treatise with this title. No such passage in Aristotle, however, has come down to us, and we must doubt whether there ever was any: if antiquity had known of texts in which Aristotle himself refers to the *Categories* as the Kategoriai, it would be impossible to explain why it was a debated question what the correct title was, since the time of Andronicus, at the latest.[33] And discussion of what the correct title was always seems to have focused on which title was appropriate, given the contents and function of the treatise. No one seems to have argued that this or that title was Aristotle's original title. Clearly, already in antiquity, there was no reason to suppose that Aristotle himself called the treatise the *Categories*. Otherwise, we could also hardly account for the larger number of different attested titles. Besides Kategoriai we find Deka Kategoriai[34] or Kategoriai deka,[35] Peri tōn deka genōn,[36] Peri tōn deka genōn tou ontos,[37] Peri tōn genōn tou ontos,[38] and Pro tōn topōn resp. Pro tōn topikon.[39] These titles clearly fall into three groups, corresponding to three interpretations of what the treatise is about. The title that took the genera of being as the subject matter of the treatise seems to have fallen by the wayside, presumably because it was linked to a view on which the *Categories* was primarily about objects and not about expressions. The scholars known to us all decided on one of the following: Kategoriai or Pro tōn topōn or Pro tōn topikōn, resp. It has been suggested,[40] that "Categories" is the original or correct title which came to seem too restrictive once the *Postpraedicamenta* had been appended to the *Praedicamenta* and thus was sometimes replaced by Pro tōn topōn. This view is hardly justified by the facts. We have seen that "Categories" can scarcely be Aristotle's title; there is also reason to suppose that Pro tōn topōn is the earlier title or at least a title that was widely used early on, and that Kategoriai was widely used only later.

Andronicus is not only the first person we know to have preferred the title "Categories," he is also the first person whose use of this title is even attested; though it is certain that Andronicus, in fact, took the title over from others, there is no reason to suppose that it originated much before Andronicus' time. All the catalogs of Aristotelian writings list this title; yet the catalog of Ptolemy already has the *Organon* in its familiar place and thus is from a period after Andronicus, and in the two surviving Greek catalogs the title is interpolated, as we can see from its position in them.[41] This title seems to gain the upper hand near the end of the second century A.D., under the influence at first of Alexander and then of Porphyry. These two authors use it, and we find it in all surviving commentators. It is presumably not a mistake to assume that the title succeeds to just the extent that the *Organon*, in its present form, comes to be accepted. For the title Pro tōn topikōn corresponds to the sequence, *Categories*, *Topics*; the present order of the books of the *Organon*, however, rests on the view that the *Categories* treats of categorematic terms that are the building-blocks for propositions, which the *De Interpretations* deals with, and these, in turn, are the material for arguments, which are discussed in the *Analytics*, but also in the *Topics* and *Sophistici Elenchi*. From this point of view, it seemed incomprehensible why defenders of the other title should have thought that the *Categories* is only about the elements of dialectical propositions, that the terms treated in the *Categories* were not the terms for propositions and arguments of all sorts, but only for the dialectical ones treated in the *Topics*.[42] Though Simplicius[43] says the order suggested by the title Pro tōn topōn is "absurd," we should not forget that his own view of the *Organon*, of the order of its books and thus of the functions of the individual books, is one that arose only after Andronicus, and it is not justified by the *Categories* itself.

Given how badly the title Pro tōn topōn fits with the general view of the *Categories* in later antiquity, it is surprising just how well attested the title is. Andronicus again is the first person of those known to us by name who knew this title.[44] It is, however, also mentioned by Porphyry,[45] Andronicus,[46] Simplicius,[47] Boethius,[48] Olympiodoros,[49] Elias,[50] the anonymous scholiast in Urbinas 35[51] and the writer of ms. Vat. Gr. 1021.[52] Even in the second century A.D., there were two scholars who preferred this title; Adrastus,[53] who seems to have researched this question,[54] and Herminus,[55] who gained a reputation precisely as an interpreter of the *Categories*.[56] Olympiodorus even claims that the majority of scholars preferred this title.[57] This claim seems surprising at first, because in Olympiodorus' time presumably no one still opted for this title; all authors known to us since Alexander and Porphyry did not choose this title. And Simplicius[58] apparently contradicts Olympiodorus when he says that most people choose the title "Categories" for this treatise. Perhaps the difficulty can be solved if we assume that Olympiodorus' remark derives from a source that dates from a time when the prevailing title still was Pro tōn topōn and that the title "Catgorics" only slowly came to gain the upper hand. There is at least one indication that Pro tōn topōn was the title common in Hellenistic times and thus that Adrastus and Herminus were not trying to push for an unusual title with somewhat paltry arguments, but that they were, rather, defending the traditional title against Andronicus and his growing following. Both of the two surviving Greek catalogs list the title Ta pro tōn topōn a. The identification of the work with this title has been the subject of controversy;[59] since there is no longer any doubt, though, that Pro tōn topōn is a Hellenistic title that was known to Andronicus, nothing should stand in the way of identifying the title in the catalog with the title of our treatise.[60] That suggests that Pro tōn topōn or Ta pro tōn topōn, resp., was the prevailing Hellenistic title of this work.[61]

In connection with this, we should at least note that the catalog of Theophrastus' writings also has an entry Ta pro tōn topōn.[62] O. Regenbogen thought[63] that, perhaps, there was a single treatise whose authorship—by Aristotle or Theophrastus—was the question. If our identification of the Aristotelian treatise is correct, Regenbogen's hypothesis can hardly be correct, since antiquity did distinguish a treatise on the categories by Theophrastus from the treatise attributed to Aristotle. Regenbogen[64] also thought that the Theophrastus title obviously referred to the first part of Theophrastus' *Topics*.[65] This is not obvious. It seems reasonable, rather, to suppose this title refers to Theophrastus' *Categories*.

What follows for what has been said of our treatise? It seems we must suppose that the first editor of the treatise came upon an obviously fragmentary bit or bits of text, without any title. Furthermore, it seems that the treatise received the title Ta pro tōn topōn early on, perhaps, even in the first edition. One possibility we need to consider is that the treatise was given this title because of its obvious similarity to Theophrastus' treatise of the same name. The other possibility is that this title was arrived at only as a result of considering the contents. Clearly, defenders of this title relied on the close connection between our treatise and the *Topics*. The fact that *Cat.* 4 has its closest parallel in *Top.* I 9 must have been especially conspicuous. In fact, on reading *Top.* I 8 and 9, one could easily come to think that, as a preparation for the *Topics*, one really needs a discussion of predicables (which Porphyry then provided) and a treatment of the categories. Chapters 4–9 of our text, without a doubt, were closest to this among the surviving writings of Aristotle. Some of the remaining material may well have also seemed useful for the *Topics* – for example, the distinction between homonyms, synonyms, and paronyms, or the doctrine of opposites,[66] but also the chapters on priority and simultaneity. It certainly was not completely misguided to regard our treatise as an introduction to the *Topics*. In connection with this, one might bear in mind that I. Bekker still saw fit, in 1843, to publish a separate edition of the *Categories* and the *Topics*.

That this does not provide a truly convincing solution to the problem of what actually is the subject matter of this treatise and whether is it a unified work is obvious. It is, for example, difficult to see how the notions of motion and of having are especially relevant to dialectic; in the *Topics*, at any rate, they play no role. Thus, it is not surprising that this title proved to be unstable.

This defect, though, does not seem to be what ultimately led to the demise of this title. For the assumption that the subject matter is the theory of categories, however generously construed, necessarily leads to the same difficulties. The chapters on motion and having seem unmotivated on this assumption as well. The consideration that led to the new title seems, rather, to have been that a theory of the predicables and a theory of the categories were required not just for dialectic but for the whole of logic; thus, the particular connection to the *Topics* would seem much too narrow.[67] There was no treatise on the predicables, but our treatise, if the matter were not considered too strictly, seemed at least to fulfill the function of providing a theory of categories. Thus the title. The attempts, beginning in the first century B.C., to create a corpus of Aristotle's logical writings, namely, the *Organon*, which was also to serve as a compendium of Peripatetic logic, served to make this the stable title. It is difficult to imagine an arrangement of the books of the *Organon*, which makes systematic sense, that has the *Topics* immediately following the *Categories*. The view that logic is the theory of terms, propositions, and arguments became established together with the familiar order of the books of the *Organon*. Thus, the necessity arose of interpreting the *Categories* in such a way that it would fit the *Organon* so conceived and would harmonize with the conception of logic underlying it.

That this failed to do justice to the treatise, taken only by itself, did not escape the notice of even those who defended this new way of looking at it. Thus, it is not surprising that Andronicus sought to evade at least some of the difficulties by supposing that the second part did not originally belong to the treatise.

However this may be, it should be clear from what has been said that "Categories" is not Aristotle's title, but, rather, a product of the later history of the *Organon* and the later conception of Peripatetic logic. It should also be clear that the view of the *Categories* which prevailed together with the ordering of the books of the *Organon* gives strong support to the case against the second part and prejudices its relation to the first part. On this view, it was hardly avoidable that one came to see the second part as a more or less intrusive appendix that did not really belong there.

IV. The Unity of the Treatise II

This leads us back to the question whether or not the two parts of the treatise originally were parts of a single treatise. As should be clear by now, it will not do to rely on the fact that the second part is not concerned with the theory of categories to show that it did not originally belong to the treatise. One also cannot say that there is no connection in content between the two parts and that, thus, they could not have been parts of a single work. For although it is true that there is no obvious connection between the two parts, this is of little weight if we consider the fragmentary nature of the treatise. The perhaps substantial missing text would have allowed us to see much more clearly what the connections were. Nor can we conclude on the basis of its language that the second part does not belong. Criticism of the unity of the treatise rests, it seems to me, on weak foundations.

The attempts, however, to prove its unity are not much better. In recent times, there have been few defenders of its unity, and these generally limit themselves to pointing out that the treatise survives as a single treatise. The last attempt to provide a detailed proof of its unity was undertaken by R. Witten[68] in 1903, with so little success that it is pointless here to consider his work more closely. What, besides the fact that it is transmitted as a single treatise, can be said in favor of its unity?

It seems to me that precisely this lack of obvious internal coherence is an indication of its unity. Though it has been claimed again and again that the second part was appended by a later editor, it is telling that no one since Ch. A. Brandis[69] has attempted to explain just how we are to imagine this having taken place. To put the point very simply: it is difficult to see what would induce an editor to publish two texts that are entirely unrelated as a single treatise. There just is no reasonable motive. The first part is easily long enough to fill a whole book-roll. There is no conception of the treatise that would be benefited by the addition of the second part. On the contrary, the second part causes difficulties for every view of the treatise we encounter in antiquity, difficulties which cannot be overlooked and which can barely be overcome. The use to which one can put the second part, on the other hand, is very limited, as we can see from ancient and modern commentaries. At the time of the first edition, it could hardly have been a matter of saving a stray piece of Aristotle's writing from oblivion by incorporating it into our text. What could have motivated the editor to edit this work as a single text except that his source provided grounds for thinking he was dealing with pieces of a single text? The original source, the archetype, must at least have looked like a single text.[70] The fact that both versions of the treatise contained the second part perhaps also tells in favor of this. Moreover, Andronicus, Adrastus, Alexander, and Porphyry were not able to find any concrete reason for thinking the second part had ever not belonged to the treatise, and this despite their extensive researches.

The fact that the 'archetype' must have seemed as if the treatise were a single treatise is at least an indication in favor of its unity, but hardly conclusive evidence. Fortunately, we do not need to rely on this indication. It was pointed out long ago[71] that the language of the two parts is quite similar, though this was not spelled out in detail. In fact, the linguistic similarities between the two parts are so extensive that it is difficult to account for them except by supposing that we do here have two pieces of a single text. The agreement between 10ᵃ 25–26 and 15ᵇ 30–32 is especially conspicuous: isōs men oun kai allos an tis phaneiē tropos poiotētos, all' hoi ge malista legomenoi schedon toioutoi eisin. / isōs d' an kai alloi tines phaneiēsan tou echein tropoi, hoi de eiōthotes legesthai schedon hapantes katērithmēntai.

Worthy of note, among other things, is the use of tropos in connection with legesthai, which we otherwise find chiefly in the *Topics* but not as in this case with tropos as subject.

The expressions kata mēdemian symplokēn legesthai, kata symplokēn legesthai and aneu symplokēs legesthai occur only in the two parts of the *Categories* (1ᵃ 16–18; 1ᵇ 25; 2ᵇ 8; 13ᵇ 10–13). This is especially striking in view of the fact that the notion of symplokē is closely tied to the contents of the first part and that it can hardly be a coincidence that in the second part we also find kata mēdemian symploken and aneu symplokēs. With the exception of one or two passages in the *Topics* (cf. 127ᵇ 1–4), there seems to be no clear case of "en" used in the sense so prominent in the second and fifth chapters of the *Categories;* this very same use also occurs in the *Postpraedicamenta* (14ᵃ 16–18).

The second part of the *Categories* follows the first in its characterization of relatives as being that which they are of something ē hopōsoun allōs pros auto (6ᵃ 37; 6ᵇ 7; 7ᵃ 13; 10ᵃ 28; 10ᵇ 1; 11ᵇ 25); this characterization of relatives does not seem to occur elsewhere in the corpus.

Both parts use epidosin lambanein (10ᵇ 28; 13ᵃ 25; 13ᵃ 27; 13ᵃ 28; 13ᵃ 29) which, according to Bonitz's *Index* otherwise occurs only in the *Topics* (146ª 8; 183ᵇ 21); both parts have apokathistēmi (9ᵇ 25; 9ᵇ 28; 13ª 30). The only other occurrence, in a genuine part of the corpus, is, according to Bonitz, at *Met.* Δ 8 (1014ª 3).

In addition, there are a number of expressions which, though they occur elsewhere in the corpus, are striking here because of their frequency, e.g., apodidonai and tropos.

We should also note the agreement between 4ᵇ 8–10 and 14ᵇ 21–22. "tō gar to pragma einai ē einai, toutō kai ho logos alēthēs ē pseudes einai legetai," "tō gar einai to pragma ē mē alēthēs ho logos ē pseudēs legetai."

I am certain that closer examination would reveal still more linguistic agreements; but it seems to me that those features of language listed above already can hardly be accounted for except by assuming the two parts are pieces of a single text. This view, of course, would be more plausible if we could succeed in showing how the two parts could be parts of a single treatise as far as their content is concerned. If we compare the chapters of the treatise, we notice that, with the exception of the first four chapters, they have two things in common. First, with the exception of the chapter on motion, they all treat notions that are also treated in *Met.* Δ; both texts have a chapter on the word 'have'; this is especially worthy of note, precisely because this chapter of the *Categories* is one that causes major difficulties for finding a unified interpretation of the treatise. Second, the chapters of *Met.* Δ, as well as Chapters 1–15 of the *Categories*, treat of pollachōs legomena. The Chapter 5 begins ousia de estin hē kyriōtata te kai prōtōs kai malista legomenē and goes on to distinguish between primary and secondary substances. In Chapter 6 (5ª 38–39), we find: kyriōs de posa tauta mona legetai ta eirēmena, ta de alla panta kata symbebēkos. Chapter 7 distinguishes between pros ti in the sense of pros ti pōs echein and pros ti in a narrower sense. Chapter 8 opens: esti de hē poiotes tōn pleonachōs legomenōn.

Chapter 9 is an exception, but, given the fragmentary condition of this chapter, that is of little significance. Chapters 10 and 11 are introduced by the sentence: legetai de heteron heterō antikeisthai tetrachōs. Chapter 12 begins with the sentence: proteron heteron heterou legetai tetrachōs. Chapter 13 opens with the remark: hama de legetai haplōs men kai kyriōtata, hōn hē genesis en tō autō chronō.

Chapter 14 distinguishes between at least six kinds of motion, and Chapter 15 begins: to echein kata pleionas tropous legetai.

Brandis[72] already conjectured that the second part consisted of fragmentary sketches for a study of philosophically important synonyms. Perhaps this conjecture can be extended to cover the whole treatise. For as we can see from Chapters 2–4, it differs from *Met.* Δ mainly in trying to give some sort of account of the systematic relation of the various things treated; how the author would have tried to show the systematic relation among the things treated in Chapters 10–15 we can no longer determine, especially since we do not know whether the surviving chapters were to have been supplemented by a large number of other chapters. The first chapter, on homonyms, synonyms, and paronyms, could then be regarded as a general introduction to a treatise of this sort.

For my argument here, of course, it does not matter whether one accepts this view of the treatise or not. What is important is that one sees that the two parts may very well form a unit even in content, though we may no longer be able to see just what it was, given the fragmentary state of the treatise.

V. The Authenticity of the Treatise

It can hardly be proven with certainty that the treatise is a genuine work of Aristotle's. There is no passage in which Aristotle himself clearly and unambiguously refers to our treatise. On the other hand, given the fragmentary and incomplete state of the work, we can say with some confidence that it is not a forgery. What a forgery would look like, we can see from Ps.-Archytas, who simply sets out to eliminate all cruxes that cause us so much difficulty with the *Categories*. Ps.-Archytas does not even attempt to establish the inner unity of the two parts; he just writes two treatises corresponding to the two parts; the difficulties surrounding the unity of the second part he evades by simply not discussing the content of the final chapter.

Judging from the language, content, and condition of the treatise, it can only be a work of Aristotle or of one of his students. We know that students of Aristotle wrote treatises on categories. Philoponus[73] tells us that Eudemus, Phanias, and Theophrastus all eagerly imitated their teacher and wrote a *Categories, De Interpretatione*, and *Analytics*. David[74] reports that Theophrastus wrote a *Categories* in imitation of his teacher. The truth of these reports has, of course, been questioned.[75]. People have appealed to the fact that Philoponus' claim can only be sufficiently substantiated in the case of Theophrastus' *Analytics*. But that is hardly the case. First of all, there is good reason to suppose that Theophrastus' Peri kataphaseōs kai apophaseōs is the counterpart of Aristotle's *De Interpretatione*. Furthermore, we have other evidence of Eudemus' *Categories*.[76] In addition, it should be remarked that while all sorts of, especially logical, works were attributed to Theophrastus and Eudemus[77] in late antiquity, the mention of Phanias[78] should lead us to conclude that this testimony is based on fact. Moreover, there is sufficient reason for believing that Eudemus, too, wrote *Analytics*.[79] Also, we need to keep in mind that there is a whole series of passages where it is claimed that students of Aristotle wrote *Categories*.[80] Finally, there are a considerable number of references to Theophrastus' *Categories*.[81] Olympidorus even claims that Alexander of Aphrodisias wrote a commentary on Theophrastus' *Categories*.[82] We may be inclined to doubt Olympiodorus here; for it is difficult to explain why we know nothing more about the contents of this text if Alexander still had it and even commented on it, especially given the great interest in the categories. We should not, however, forget that Alexander seems to have known Eudemus' Peri lexeōs,[83] and that Galen wrote a commentary on this text[84] but that in the period after Alexander, people knew virtually nothing about this treatise, even though it must have been of interest if for no other reason than its closeness to the *De Interpretatione*. Olympiodorus also reports[85] that Theophrastus wrote a *hypomnema* to his own *Categories,* which was, however, frequently mistaken for a commentary on Aristotle's *Categories.* The remark, in Al-Nadīm's Aristotle chapter in the *Fihrist,*[86] that Theophrastus belongs to the ranks of writers of commentaries on Aristotle's *Categories,* and the further remark, in the Theophrastus chapter of the *Fihrist,*[87] that this commentary is falsely attributed to Theophrastus, seem to be connected with this point. Finally, we have to remember that the title ta pro tōn topōn appears in the list of Theophrastus' writings, and that it may well refer to his *Categories.* It simply is not the case, then, that there are no parallels for the claims of Philoponus and David that students of Aristotle, especially Theophrastus, wrote treatises on categories. On the contrary, it seems as if the passages mentioned provide sufficient evidence for the existence of these writings.[88]

Our treatise cannot be the work of Theophrastus, if it is true that Alexander of Aphrodisias wrote commentaries not only on Aristotle's *Categories* but also on Theophrastus'. It also cannot be the work of one of the younger students of Aristotle—as Jaeger had supposed[89]—since given the views we find there, it must be an early work most nearly comparable to the *Topics.* If the treatise, however, is neither by Theophrastus nor by some later Peripatetic, it must be that Aristotle himself is the author. Otherwise, it would also be difficult to explain why this treatise was preserved, despite its obviously fragmentary and incomplete condition.

The decisive fact, it seems to me, is the one Husik[90] above all called attention to: in language and content the treatise is so close to the *Topics* that, in my opinion, one cannot avoid ascribing both texts to the same author, except if there were very weighty reasons against this.

There do not, however, seem to me to be such reasons. Every objection that has been raised against the treatise in the course of history has been satisfactorily met, except one: the theory of substance in the *Categories* is quite un-Aristotelian compared to the one in the *Metaphysics.* This contradiction was already found objectionable in antiquity.[91] Felix Accoramboni,[92] writing in the sixteenth century, seems also to have found this objectionable. At the beginning of this century, the objection was revived again by Dupréel,[93] and it has found its classical formulation in the papers by S. Mansion referred to at the beginning (n. 10).

The conflict can be described as follows. According to the *Categories,* our ontology contains both substances and non-substances; but not all substances are substances in the same sense—we need to distinguish between objects, the primary substances, on the one hand, and their species and genera, or secondary substances, on the other. For the concept of substance that applies to primary substances only applies to secondary substances with some deletion: it is not true, in the case of secondary substances, that they have no subjects; and, hence, it is also not true that they are the ultimate subjects for all other elements of the ontology. They have the primary substances as their subjects, so it is only true that they underlie everything else.

Nonetheless, it is also true of secondary substances that they underlie all nonsubstantial items. To put the point another way: if A is an arbitrary nonsubstance, individual or universal, there not only is a primary substance, B, which is A's subject, but also a secondary substance, C, which is also A's subject; the existence of A presupposes the existence of both a primary substance like B and a secondary substance like C. In this sense, secondary substances, too, are substances.

We have grown so accustomed to talking of genera and species that we do not ascribe as much significance to this way of speaking in the *Categories* as we should. When Aristotle speaks of species and genera as substances in the *Categories,* he is relying on a view in which species and genera are also objects that lose none of their reality by being ontologically dependent on the primary substances. We can see from the *Metaphysics* that Aristotle was clear about how weighty an assumption this was. For in the central books of the *Metaphysics,* there are no longer any genera or species; the secondary substances of the *Categories* have not just disappeared in name; genera and universals quite generally, so Aristotle argues (cf. *Met.* z 13), cannot be substances; since, however, species and genera are not qualities either, in the Aristotelian sense, they disappear completely from the ontology. Moreover, although he retains the primary substances of the *Categories,* namely objects, these must now yield their status as primary substances to their substantial forms which now come to be called primary substances. The substantiality of concrete particulars is thus now only secondary. The idea of the *Categories* that substances are that which underlies everything else is retained, as we see from z1 and z3. However, the answer to the question what is it that underlies everything else has changed: now it is the substantial form. Aristotle also adds two new conditions for substancehood quite generally, conditions which, in the *Categories,* applied only to primary substances. They must be tode ti, and they must exist independently, i.e., not depend for their existence on any other entities.

The two theories of substance are thus radically different; that of the *Categories* is realistic, that of the *Metaphysics* nominalistic. Yet, as E. Dupréel and S. Mansion saw clearly, this does not yet mean that one of the treatises must be spurious. We can come to that conclusion only if we can also show that a historical development from one position to the other is inconceivable. In our case it not only seems as if such a development did take place—quite independently of whether we see the *Categories* as authentic or not—but also as if this development fits in well with an overall development.

That Aristotle changed his mind about the matter at issue we already know, since the ontology of the *Topics* hardly differs from that of the *Categories*. The *Topics* do not, to be sure, explicitly talk of primary and secondary substances; but in the *Topics,* too, Aristotle considers both individual objects as well as their genera and species as substances (cf. 103^b 27ff.). Nevertheless, Aristotle refuses, in the *Topics* or, to be more precise, in the *Sophistici Elenchi* (178^b 38ff.) to consider genera and species as tode ti, i.e., he does not ascribe the same ontological status to them as to individual substances. The *Topics* says nothing about substantial forms, much less that substantial forms are prior to the objects whose forms they are. We need in any case, then, to assume that Aristotle's theory of substance changed fundamentally from the *Topics* to the *Metaphysics*.

Yet it also seems as if this change of view fits in very well with an overall development that I want, in concluding, to sketch briefly. The species and genera of the *Categories,* whose existence Aristotle dismisses later in the *Metaphysics,* do not differ substantially from the genera and species that occupy such a conspicuous place in Plato's later dialogues—initially in the *Phaedrus,* but especially in the *Sophist,* the *Politicus,* and the *Philebus.* In both cases, the genera consist of species and, ultimately, individuals, into which they can be divided. That, at any rate, is the way Plato talks in the *Philebus,* when he speaks of that which is one, but also many and even indefinitely many, because it can be divided into its species and the individuals which fall under them (*Phil.* 16^c 9-e2). Though this would require a lengthy argument, it seems to me that what Plato has to say about being in the *Sophist* can best be understood on the assumption that this genus itself consists of everything it comprises. We seem to find the same conception in the second part of the *Parmenides,* where, e.g., the various numbers are considered as parts of number (144^a 7-9).

If this is so, the genera of the later dialogues can hardly be the forms we know from the middle dialogues. For those are characterized precisely by the fact that they exist separately from the particulars participating in them. Plato repeatedly calls attention to this assumption in the later dialogues; he does so especially clearly at the point of the *Parmenides* at which he begins criticizing the theory of ideas (130 b2, b3, b4, c1, d1; cf. 129 d8, 131 b1, b5) and at the point, in the *Sophist,* where he speaks of the friends of the forms as if he wants to distance himself from them (248^a 7-9) and, finally, in the *Philebus,* where he speaks of the difficulties (clearly referring back to the first part of the *Parmenides*) which arise from assuming self-existent forms which particulars, however, are to participate in (15b 1 ff.). Genera in the sense in which we find them in the *Philebus* precisely are not subject to these difficulties. It seems to me that Plato in the later dialogues, beginning with the second half of the *Parmenides,* wants to substitute a theory of genera and theory of principles that constitute these genera for the earlier theory of forms.

There is, of course, one major difference between the genera of the later dialogues and those of the *Categories*. While we may assume that Plato regards the genera as ontologically prior to their species and individuals, Aristotle reverses this relation exactly: individuals are prior to species, species to genera. With this move in favor of the particular at the expense of the general, he takes a large step in the direction of the theory of the *Metaphysics,* which, in B, still asks, which is prior, the general or the particular. Additional steps, of course, were necessary to reach the doctrine of the *Metaphysics,* especially, the introduction of the form-matter analysis and, then, the reconsideration, in light of it, of the question what is ultimately to count as the subject or substrate of all that is.

Thus, it is by no means the case that the incompatibility of the two theories of substance forces us to reject the *Categories* as spurious. On the contrary, it seems as if the theory of the *Categories* ought, rather, to be seen as a stage in a long development that proceeds from the forms of Plato's middle dialogues to the substantial forms of Aristotle's *Metaphysics.*

Thus, we have met the objection against the authenticity of the *Categories* that has survived the longest; and so we can, indeed, follow the tradition and attribute the treatise to Aristotle. However, we have also seen that we have reason not to follow the tradition blindly in its understanding of the treatise. Unlike the tradition, which sought to gloss over the differences between the *Categories* and the *Metaphysics,* we ought to take care not to project the universals of the *Categories* into the ontology of the *Metaphysics.*

3

Categories in Aristotle

There is a theory called the theory of categories which in a more or less developed form, with minor or major modifications, made its appearance first in a large number of Aristotelian writings and then, under the influence of these writings, came to be a standard part of traditional logic, a place it maintained with more or less success into the early part of this century, when it met the same fate as certain other parts of traditional logic.

There are many questions one may ask about this theory. Presumably not the most interesting question, but certainly one for which one would want to have an answer if one took an interest in the theory at all, is the following: What are categories? It turns out that this is a rather large and difficult question. And hence I want to restrict myself to the narrower and more modest question, What are categories in Aristotle?, hoping that a clarification of this question ultimately will help to clarify the more general questions. But even this narrower question turns out to be so complicated and controversial that I will be content if I can shed some light on the simple questions: What does the word "category" mean in Aristotle? What does Aristotle have in mind when he talks about "categories"?

Presumably it is generally agreed that Aristotle's doctrine of categories involves the assumption that there is some scheme of classification such that all there is, all entities, can be divided into a limited number of ultimate classes. But there is no agreement as to the basis and nature of this classification, nor is there an agreement as to how the categories themselves are related to those classes of entities. There is a general tendency among commentators to talk as if the categories were just these classes, but there is also the view that, though for each category there is a corresponding ultimate class of entities, the categories themselves are not to be identified with these classes. And there are various ways in which it could be true that the categories only correspond to, but are not identical with, these classes of entities. It might, e.g., be the case that the categories are not classes of entities but, rather, classes of expressions of a certain kind, expressions which we—following tradition—may call "categorematic." On this interpretation these categorematic expressions signify the various entities we classify under such headings as "substance," "quality," or "quantity." And in this case we have to ask whether the entities are classified according to a classification of the categorematic expressions by which they are signified or whether, the other way around, the expressions are classified according to the classification of the entities they signify. Or it might be thought that the categories are classes of only some categorematic expressions, namely, those which can occur as predicate-expressions. Or it might be the case that the categories themselves are not classes at all, neither of entities nor of expressions, but, rather, headings or labels or predicates which collect, or apply to, either entities or expressions, i.e., the category itself, strictly speaking would be a term like "substance" or "substance word." Or it might be the case that categories are neither classes nor terms but concepts. All these views have had their ardent supporters.

Given this rather bewildering choice of answers to our question it is too tempting to turn for enlightenment to an obviously very early writing of Aristotle's which by its very title *Categories* seems to promise an answer to our question. This is, in fact, how the treatise traditionally has been read, and the traditional views concerning Aristotle's categories to a good extent are based on taking the treatise in this way. Moreover, these views on the categories to a good extent are based on a certain view of the position of the treatise in the so-called *Organon,* the collection of Aristotle's logical writings. The order of this collection clearly suggests the view that in logic we first deal with terms, then with propositions, and finally with arguments, a view still current in modern times. And the ordering of the treatises in the collection thus suggests that the first treatise, the *Categories,* in providing us with a doctrine of categories provides us with a theory of terms. Hence a traditional tendency to regard the categories as classes of terms or expressions rather than as classes of entities.

But for the following reasons it seems to me that the unfortunate state of our question is largely due to the fact that scholars have been turning to the treatise *Categories* for an answer. I will leave aside the fact that the present order of the writings of the *Organon* was only established in the second century A.D., that there is no good reason to think that Aristotle himself had meant these writings to be read in this order, that it is even far from clear whether Aristotle himself would have classified the *Categories* as a logical treatise, and that hence the position of the treatise in the *Organon* and the view of logic which goes with it should not have had any influence on what we take categories in Aristotle to be. More important, it seems to me, is that it is far from clear whether the treatise *Categories* in whole or even in part was meant to be a treatise on categories. We cannot rely for this on the title *Categories*. For this is just one of a good number of titles the work had in antiquity and possibly not even the most common one. There is no good reason to think that the title is Aristotle's own. As to the content, it may have seemed obvious that the treatise is a treatise on categories. But if it did seem obvious, this—apart from the title—was due to the fact that the second part of the treatise, the so-called *Postpraedicamenta,* was not taken seriously. Hence, one focused on the first part, and this part, of course, would seem to constitute a treatise on categories, if one made the additional assumption that the genera of entities distinguished in this part are just the categories or that the categories amount to a classification of expressions depending on the classification of entities given in this part of the treatise. It is revealing that ancient supporters of the title *Categories* claimed that the *Postpraedicamenta* were material alien to the purpose of the treatise, added by somebody who wanted to turn the treatise into an introduction to the *Topics* and who gave it a corresponding title, namely, *Introduction to the Topics,* becoming thus responsible for the other title of the treatise common in antiquity[1] and for another ordering of the treatises in the collection.

But we cannot take it for granted that the categories are the classes of beings distinguished in the first part of the treatise or the corresponding classes of expressions. Nor do we have the right to disregard the *Postpraedicamenta.* For the case against them has not been made successfully, and there are strong philological and linguistic reasons in their favor. The presence of the *Postpraedicamenta* and the further fact that there is a clear gap in the text between the first part of the treatise and the *Postpraedicamenta,* which may be quite extensive, do make it almost impossible to say with any confidence what the treatise originally was meant to be about. We are certainly not in a position to say that the book as a whole was meant to be a treatise on categories. But there is also no reason to think that the text as we have it, or even that at least a part of it, namely, the first part, was meant to deal with categories. The treatise as we have it does not say anything to the effect that it is going to deal with categories. In fact, it does not even use the word "category" except in two lines (10^b 19; 10^b 21) toward the very end of the first part. And here the word is used in such an incidental way that nothing of interest can be inferred. Nor does the treatise use any other word for "category." It twice uses the term "genus" in a relevant way, but one of these occurrences is in a passage which is clearly spurious (11^b 15) and the other occurs in a stretch of the text which I take to be suspect, both on linguistic and doctrinal grounds (11^a 38). But even if these two passages were authentic they would be of no use for our purpose. For "genus" in these passages in used to refer to the classes of entities which one has to assume anyway on any account of what the categories are. Hence to assume that the genera referred to are the categories is just to beg the question at issue. And for reasons of this sort it seems to me that there is no non-question-begging way in which we can expect the treatise *Categories* to provide us with an answer to our question.

For a good number of reasons the text to turn to seems, rather, to be Aristotle's *Topics.* In date, language, and doctrine the *Topics* seem to be very near the

Categories. In particular, the two are the only treatises in the corpus which give us the full traditional list of ten classes of entities. The *Topics* explicitly talk of the categories in a nonincidental fashion, they give us a clue to the technical sense of the word "category" and how it came to be used this way, and they give us at least some indication of what the distinction of categories was introduced for. The idea to approach the doctrine of categories through the *Topics* rather than through the treatise called *Categories* is by no means new. It was chosen, e.g., by Kapp in 1920. But it seems to me that it has not yet been exploited sufficiently.

The crucial text for us in the *Topics* is Chapter 9 of the first book. But before we turn to this chapter a few words need to be said about the preceding chapter. In this chapter Aristotle distinguishes what later came to be called the predicables: genus, definition, proprium, and accident. For our purposes it is important to notice that these kinds of predicate are distinguished according to the predicative relationship in which they stand with reference to a given subject. For something to be the genus of something the genus-term has to be true of that thing in a certain way. To characterize these predicative relationships Aristotle uses the Greek verb "kategorein" and a compound of it. In ordinary Greek this verb means "to accuse," but it is clear that Aristotle here is using it in the unprecedented sense of "to predicate" or, one should say, in the sense of "to predicate truly." For clearly what makes something a genus of something is not that somebody happens to predicate a genus-term of that thing but that the term is true of the thing in the appropriate way.

With this in mind let us then turn to the first sentence of Chapter 9. Unfortunately, no two translators seem to agree on the translation of this sentence, and, as far as I can see, none of the translations is satisfactory. Hence let us proceed very cautiously. Leaving the crucial phrase untranslated, the sentence seems to run as follows: "Next we must determine the genera of the kategoriai in which one will find the four above mentioned." One immediately asks "the four above mentioned what?" It is clear from the grammar of the Greek sentence that "kategoriai" is to be understood again. Thus the full sentence runs as follows: "Next we must determine the genera of the kategoriai in which one will find the four above mentioned kategoriai." The next question obviously is how we are to translate "kategoria." It is clear from what was said about the preceding chapter that as a translation we need a noun which corresponds to the verb "to predicate." Given the word-formation of "kategoria" and its ordinary use in the sense of "accusation," we would expect this noun to be "predication." But translators and interpreters tend to prefer "predicate" as a rendering. Moreover, we have to take into account that abstract nouns like kategoria can be used in the sense of either "a particular kategoria" or "a kind of kategoria." When, e.g., Eurylochus tells his companions that all deaths are dreadful but that none is quite as dreadful as that of hunger, it is clearly that by "deaths" he means "kinds of death" (*Od.* 12, 341). Finally, it should be noticed that everybody agrees that the whole phrase "the genera of the katēgoriai" refers to Aristotle's categories in the technical sense which we try to determine. For the next sentence tells us that there are ten such genera and then lists them; what we get here clearly is the list of Aristotle's categories.

With this in mind let us first try to deal with the phrase "the four above mentioned katēgoriai." If it meant "the four above mentioned predicates," it would have to refer to the predicates genus, definition, proprium, and accident. But whatever view one has of Aristotle's categories, it seems clear enough that these predicates do not go into any of the categories. "Kinds of predication," on the other hand, might seem to fit. For given the standard views of Aristotle's categories, it will be true in some sense or other that predicates of the four kinds distinguished in Chapter 8 will go into one category or other. The translation "predication," on the other hand, will not work. For the preceding chapter did not mention four predications. What it did distinguish, though, were four kinds of predication, namely, four ways in which a predicate may be true of a subject such that, depending on the way the predicate is true of its subject, we have one or another kind of predicate. In fact, this distinction of four ways of being true of something was the main distinction of the preceding chapter, and hence the phrase "the four above mentioned katēgoriai" would most naturally be taken to pick up this distinction. There are, then, two translations of the phrase which deserve further consideration: (i) "the four above mentioned kinds of predicates" and (ii) "the four above mentioned kinds of predication."

Now, as to the open occurrence of the expression "katēgoria" in the phrase "the genera of the katēgoriai," it seems fairly clear that it should be translated either by "predicate" or by "predication." For the reference of the whole phrase "the genera of the katēgroiai" would seem to be either to kinds of predicates or to kinds of predications. Hence our problem of translation for the sentence as a whole seems to come down to the question whether we take the meaning of "katēgoria" to be "predicate" and hence also "kind of predicate," or "predication" and hence also "kind of predication."

I am inclined to think that the translation "predicate," at least in the Aristotelian sense of "predicate," would never have been suggested as a possibility if it had not been needed to make the text fit certain preconceptions as to what Aristotelian categories are. In any case, the following seems to me to strongly favor the translation "predication." The term "katēgoria" is used at least six times in the *Topics* outside our chapter (107^a 3; 109^b 5; 141^a 4; 152^a 38; 178^a 5; 181^b 27). In each case it can be taken to mean "predication," i.e., in no case do we have to take it in the sense of "predicate," but in at least three cases it definitely has to be taken in the sense of "predication" (109^b 5; 141^a 4; 181^b 27). Let us consider the two most questionable of the three remaining passages. In the first, 107^a 3ff., Aristotle considers the case of an argument whose validity turns on the question whether the predicate "good" is used univocally throughout the argument, e.g., in the premises "this food is good" and "this man is good." To check this, we are told, we should see whether "the genera of the kategoriai" are the same. The use of "good" in our examples fails to meet this test. For to say of food that it is good, according to Aristotle, is to say of food what it does: it produces pleasure, health, or whatever. But to say of a man or a soul that they are good is to say what they are like: they are courageous, wise, pious, and the like. This passage most naturally lends itself to the interpretation that it turns on the point that to say of something what it is like is to make one kind of predication and to say of something what it does is to make another kind of predication. In fact, in can hardly turn on the point that the genus of the predicate is different in the two premises. For Aristotle moves on to tell us that another test of univocity is to see whether the genus is the same (107^a 18). Hence "kategoria" here hardly can mean "predicate." For the first test would not be distinguishable from the second test.

Another questionable occurrence of the term is in 152^a 38ff. We are told that two things are not the same if they are not in the same genus of kategoria (en heni genei kategorias), but one signifies a quality, the other a quantity or a relation. Again it seems very difficult to assume that "kategoria" here might mean "predicate." For how should one in this case translate "genos kategorias?" And again it is clear from the following that the phrase cannot mean "the genus of the predicate." For Aristotle in this case, too, tells us that we should also check whether the genus is the same.

The interest of the passage lies in a curious way of talking which deserves closer attention. It says of items which can be predicated, i.e., of items like justice or the size of two feet, that they are in a genus of predication. We should have thought that genera or kinds of predication collect cases of predication. The language here suggests that there is also some sense in which kinds of predication collect kinds of predicates. But this is hardly mysterious. Assume that to say of something what it is like is one kind of predication and that to say of something of what quantity it is is another kind of predication. Now it would seem that qualities are exactly those items one refers to if one says of something what it is like and that quantities are exactly those things one introduces if one says of something of what quantity it is.

Given this, Aristotle's remarks here make perfect sense. Consider the question whether rationality and reasonability are the same. On this test, and given Aristotle's views, they clearly are not the same. For to say of something that it is rational is to say what it is essentially, whereas to say that it is reasonable is to say what it is like.

Thus the formation of the word, the ordinary use of "kategoria," and the use of this term in the *Topics* outside our chapter all strongly suggest that "kategoria" should be rendered by "predication." In this case we should translate the first sentence of A 9 in the following way: "Next we must determine the different genera or kinds of predication in which one will find the four kinds of predication mentioned above." And if this is the correct translation of the first sentence, the chapter allows us to draw the following conclusions concerning Aristotle's use of the word "kategoria" in the *Topics:*

(i) Aristotle uses the word in the sense of "predication";

(ii) Aristotle uses the word in the sense of "kind of predication";

(iii) A few lines into the chapter, in 103^b 25, Aristotle substitutes the phrase "the genera of the predications" by the simple phrase "the kategoriai" to refer to these same genera or kinds of predication, i.e., to the categories in the technical sense. Hence there is a third use of the term "kategoria" in this chapter, namely, exactly the technical use of "category" we are trying to determine. Given what has been said so far, the explanation of this use is fairly simple. "Kategoria" in its technical sense literally means "kind of predication," but in its technical use it is restricted to one of several distinctions of kinds of predication, namely, to the distinction of kinds referred to in the first sentence and listed in the second sentence of our chapter.

(iv) Unfortunately, there is yet another use of the term "kategoria" in our chapter, the one we find in 103^b 29. To understand this use we have to keep in mind that the kinds of predication define classes or kinds of predicates, namely, the classes of those predicates which occur in a statement of a given kind of predication. The category of quality, e.g., defines the class of predicates called qualities, the category of quantity the class of quantities. Aristotle here by extension ooomr to use "kategoria" also for the kinds of predicates thus defined. It may be suggested that it is this fourth use of the term which is the technical use for which we are looking. That this is not so will become clear later. It may be pointed out here, though, that this fourth use of "kategoria" would collapse with the technical use in question if we identified a quality or quantity with the properties of being thus qualified and the property of being thus quantified, if, e.g., we identified the quality health with the property of being healthy. For being healthy for Aristotle presumably is a kind of predication; something's being healthy certainly is.

If we accept these conclusions concerning the use of the term "kategoria," we will have to distinguish at least three kinds of things: (i) the categories in the technical sense of the word, (ii) classes of predicates defined by the kinds of predication in question, and (iii) the ultimate genera of what there is as they are distinguished, e.g., in the treatise *Categories*. For the ultimate genera of beings clearly are not kinds of predication. Nor can they be identified with the classes of predicates. It is not the case that these two distinctions fall apart because one is a distinction of kinds of nonlinguistic items, whereas the distinction of predicates is a distinction of expressions. For Aristotle tends to think of predicates as the nonlinguistic items introduced by predicate-expressions. The two classes, rather, seem to come apart insofar as the first class of predicates, i.e., the class of predicates defined by the first category, and the first class of entities, i.e., the class of substances, do not coincide. They differ in at least two respects: (i) the first class of predicates contains not only substance-predicates, but also qualities, quantities, and all other kinds of entities, all entities one could refer to in an answer to the question what something is essentially, whether that something be a substance, a quality, or a quantity. (ii) The first class of predicates will only contain predicates and not individuals, whereas the class of substances will contain individual substances, if anything.

The first of these differences is crucial in several respects. To show that there is this difference is to show a fortiori that the categories of the *Topics* cannot be identified with the ultimate genera of what there is. It also is to show that the categories are not to be identified with the classes of predicates defined by the kinds of predication. And, finally, it is to show that in a way there is no category of substance in the *Topics*. For if there were a category of substance, it would have to be the first category, i.e., the category of the what it is. But if we assume that the class of predicates collected by this category includes not just substances but entities of all other kinds, too, it will not be a category of substance in particular.

Hence, I will just consider this crucial difference between the classes of predicates and the ultimate classes of entities. Which position we take on this basically depends on how we interpret the phrase "what it is" in the list of categories in the second sentence of this chapter. And, hence, it might be appropriate to now move on to this second sentence. It runs as follows: "these [i.e., the kinds of predications] are ten in number: What it is, quantity, quality, relation, where, when, posture, having, doing, suffering."

It is generally assumed that the phrase "what it is" in this list must be just a variant on the term "substance." It is supposed that there is a special, technical use of the phrase "what it is" which restricts it to substances. It is easy to see why this would be assumed. It is taken for granted that there is a category of substance, and the only way to find a reference to it in our list of categories is to assume that the phrase "what it is" here has this special meaning. But if one did not already go on the assumption that the first category has to be the category of substance, one would naturally read the phrase as not being restricted in this way to substances. Given the context, I want to argue the only natural way to read the list is the second way. This will force us to include in the first class of predicates not just substances but qualities, quantities, and all other kinds of entities. The reasons why I take the phrase "what it is" not to be restricted to substances are the following: (i) as we know, e.g., from Plato's dialogues, the usual sense of the phrase in the context of philosophical or dialectical discussions, i.e., the kinds of discussions we are dealing with in the *Topics*, is not such that the phrase is restricted to substances. (ii) The phrase occurs eight times in our chapter, which is only twenty-two lines long, first in the list of categories, then in a repetition of the list of categories, and then another six times. But the other six times it is clearly used in its usual sense, not restricted to substance but neutral to the distinction of the various ultimate classes of entities. This strongly suggests that the phrase is used this way throughout the chapter. (iii) Taking it that way throughout the chapter makes excellent sense of the text. (iv) The phrase has been used in the *Topics* in preceding chapters and is going to be used throughout the treatise. But throughout it seems to be used in a sense which is neutral to the distinction of classes of entities. (v) The phrase is used neutrally even in places in which Aristotle clearly means to use his distinction of categories (cf. 144^a 17–18). Hence I conclude that nobody who just read the *Topics* could assume that the phrase "what it is" here in the list of categories is restricted in its use to substances.

If, then, the traditional view is to be defended, it would seem that the defense has to take the following form: it will have to be assumed (i) that the phrase "what it is" is used in two different ways in our chapter, in one way in the lists of categories and in a different way throughout the rest of the chapter, and (ii) that Aristotle presupposes that readers are aware of some fact or piece of Aristotelian doctrine which will enable them to see without a warning that the phrase is used ambiguously.

And, in fact, it would seem that readers at this point usually do rely on what they think they know from other writings of Aristotle's, e.g., the *Categories*, namely, the purported fact that the first category is the category of substance. To just assume, though, that this is what we know and can rely upon is to beg the question. What we would need is an argument to show that Aristotle quite generally takes the first category to be the category of substance. But I have already indicated why such an argument cannot rely on the treatise *Categories*, and I do not see how such an argument could rely on the *Topics*. To what extent it could be based on Aristotle's later writings remains to be seen.

At least since Alexander of Aphrodisias (*In met.* 473, 3ff.), commentators have relied on a genuine bit of Aristotelian doctrine which would seem to take care of the problem in a rather elegant way. Alexander pointed out that Aristotle himself in the *Metaphysics* (Z 4 1030^a 17ff.) tells us that the phrase "what it is" has different uses and that in its primary use the phrase applies only to substances. Unfortunately, this will hardly help, either. For at the time when he writes the *Topics* Aristotle does not yet seem to have developed the doctrine which will allow him in the *Metaphysics* to distinguish various uses of "what it is." And hence, when writing the *Topics*, he can hardly expect the reader to have a point in mind which he himself has not yet made. Moreover, it seems to be rather awkward to have to rely on an Aristotelian text whose main claim is that the phrase "what it is" does not have a uniform use across the various kinds of entities, given that Aristotle in our chapter, with the supposed exception of the list of categories, happily uses the phrase as if it did have a uniform use across the class of entities.

Sometimes commentators suggest a weaker explanation for the purported ambiguity of the phrase "what it is." They suggest that Aristotle assumes that we understand that the list of categories is a list not of the kinds of things we can say about anything whatsoever but of the kinds of things we can say about a given object or substance. And if this were true, it would, of course, be the case that the first class of predicates only collects substance-predicates. Now, it may be true that Aristotle should think, and that at times he does think, that of the various kinds of things one can say about things which he distinguishes here all but the first one apply only to substances anyway. The assumption could be that the only thing one can predicate of non-substantial items, given Aristotle's notion of predication, is what they are. If, then, Aristotle distinguishes ten kinds of things one can say about something, the suggestion runs, he presumably wants to distinguish the various kinds of things one can say about substances. Fortunately, we do not have to discuss the merits of this suggestion. It simply fails because it is clear from later passages in the *Topics* that Aristotle in the *Topics* thinks that the various categories do not just apply to substances. In 144^a 17–18, e.g., both the category of the what it is and the category of quality are applied to virtue. Since, then, (a) the text of the *Topics* in itself cannot justify the traditional reading of the phrase "what it is" and since (b) there does not seem to be a suitable piece of doctrine which the reader could be expected to import from the outside to get the traditional reading, we have no choice but to take the phrase to range over all classes of entities and not just substances.

But if we take the phrase "what it is" in this generous way, it is not just clear that the first category of the *Topics* is not a category of substance; it is also clear that the categories and the classes of predicates defined by them cannot be identified with the ultimate genera of what there is. Moreover, it is clear that the use of the term "categories" in 103^b 29 is not the technical use of the term. For it is now clear that, when Aristotle says in 103^b 27ff. that somebody who indicates the what it is either indicates substance or quality or quantity or one of the other categories, he is talking about predications in the one category of the what it is; i.e., in the sense of the list of categories in the second sentence only one category is involved whether somebody, in saying what something is, indicates substance or quality or quantity. Hence the use of "category" in this later sentence must be a different one. Finally, if we interpret the phrase "what is is" in the indicated way, we will also have to read the whole list of categories in a way that differs from the usual way. For if the category of the what it is not only collects substance-predicates but also qualities and quantities, the distinction of categories as given by the list can no longer be an exclusive distinction of kinds of entities like qualities and quantities. The only way to now preserve the mutual exclusiveness of the classification is to assume that the categories are distinguished according to whether a predicate is used to say of something what it is or of what quantity it is or of what quality it is, etc. And this, of course, fits well with the long observed fact that five or six of the category names are interrogative pronouns. It fits the fact that later in our chapter these category names repeatedly are used as indirect interrogative pronouns. And, finally, it seems to be confirmed by the later use of the categories in the *Topics*.

Given all this, it seems to me that the major threat to our interpretation of *Topics* A, 9 is this: everyone assumes that there is abundant evidence that for Aristotle in his later writings there is a category of substance which is the first category. Hence, there will be a tendency, hard to overcome, to read this later doctrine into the *Topics*, even if the *Topics* themselves do not naturally read this way and even if to read them this way is to beg the question at issue.

This tendency will be all the more difficult to overcome since there is one sentence in *Top*. A, 9 which seems to lend some support to it. Hence, I will first consider this sentence, then argue that the evidence for a category of substance is weaker than usually supposed, and finally argue that if there is a category of substance in later writings, this is due to a change in, or development of, doctrine.

In the sentence in question, 103^b 27–29, Aristotle says that someone who indicates the what it is of something either indicates substance of quality or quantity or some other category. Given the traditional view, it is very difficult not to see in this an open and obvious reference to the category of substance. But I have already argued that "category" in this sentence is not used in the technical sense of "category" in question. So it does not follow from the sentence that there is a category of substance in the required sense. But it does not even follow from the sentence that there is a category of substance in any sense of "category." Assume, e.g., that we had objects or substances and various kinds of features, namely, qualities, quantities, and whatever else there may be. Assume also that all the names we had were names either of objects or of features. In this case it would be true to say: "A name names an object or a quality or a quantity or another kind of feature." Now no one would take this sentence to mean that objects are among the kinds of features we find in the world. Everyone would understand that the word "another" in "another kind of feature" is restricted in scope to the kinds of features so far mentioned in the sentence. Similarly, the sentence in the *Topics* can only be construed as referring to a category of substance if we already assume that there is a category of substance. But the example shows that it does not have to be construed this way, and I have given independent reasons why it should not be construed this way.

The evidence that Aristotle accepts a category of substance is circumstantial. For Aristotle, as far as I can see, only once explicitly talks of a "category of substance," namely in *Phys*. 242^b 5. And in this one place in which this expression is actually used, it does not mean "category of substance." Given the enormous importance the category of substance is supposed to have in Aristotle, it should give one at least some pause that Aristotle himself never seems to talk of it in quite these terms. Nevertheless, there is circumstantial evidence for Aristotle's acceptance of a category of substance. This evidence in part is of the following kind. Consider the first lines of *Met.* θ: "That which is a being in the primary sense and which all the other categories of being have to be referred to, namely substance, has been dealt with. For all the other things (i.e., qualities, quantities, etc.) are called 'beings' in so far . . . " Here the phrase "all the other categories" only makes sense, or so it seems, if we assume that the other categories are contrasted with a category associated with substance. Hence, it would seem obvious that Aristotle here is referring to a category of substance.

A little consideration, though, shows that this is not obvious at all. For the phrase Aristotle uses here is not "the other categories" but "the other categories *of being*," and so what at best follows from this passage is that Aristotle accepts a category *of being* associated with substance. And from this it only follows that Aristotle accepts a category of substance if we assume that the categories *of being* are to be identified with the categories in the sense we are interested in. This, of course, is an assumption which is standardly made.[2] But for the following reason it is at least questionable, if not false. Aristotle's use of the term "category" seems to be such that if he talks of "categories" he is talking of the predication of predicates quite generally. If, on the other hand, he uses "category" with a dependent genitive, he often, if not always, is not talking about predication in general but about the predication of the predicates or terms specified in the expression in the genitive. Thus, when he talks about "katēgoria tou ontos," a "category of being," he can be understood, and presumably has to be understood, as talking about the predication of the term "being," about the, or a, use to which the term "being" is put.

If one has doubts about this, one should consider the following use of the term "category" in *Met.* Γ. In Chapter 2 of this book Aristotle points out that the term "one" has many uses, and that in a case like this, e.g., in the case of terms like "same," "other," or "contrary," one has to try to explain how the various uses of a term are related to a primary use of that term. He then goes on to say in 1004ᵃ 28: "Thus having distinguished in how many ways each term is used, we have, accordingly, to give an account how in each category a term is used with reference to its primary use." Now, "category" here obviously is not used in the technical sense of "category" in question. It, rather, seems that the categories Aristotle is talking about here are the categories of the one, the same, the different, and the like, i.e., the various kinds of cases in which we use the predicate "one," the predicate "different," or the predicate "same." And he is saying that with each of these predicates we should look for a primary use of this predicate in terms of which we can then explicate the other uses of this predicate. Keeping this in mind, it seems to be fairly clear that Aristotle in the opening remarks of

Met. θ just applies this general doctrine to the particular case of the predicate "being." Let me quote the relevant sentences of *Met.* θ again: "That which is a being in the primary sense and which all the other categories of being have to be referred to namely substance, has been dealt with. For all the other things [i.e., qualities, quantities, and the rest] are called 'beings' insofar as . . . " Applying the general point of *Met.* Γ, Aristotle here seems to be saying that the various uses of "being" in which things other than substances are said to be, or to be beings, have to be explained in terms of that primary use of the term "being" in which substances are said to be beings. Hence, it seems that when Aristotle is talking here of the other categories of being, he is not talking about the categories, but about the various uses of the particular predicate "being." And so it does follow from the passage that there is a category *of being* associated with substance, but it does not follow, at least not immediately, that there is a category of substance. For, as opposed to what is usually assumed, the categories of being cannot be identified with the categories themselves.

Now it will be argued that the reason why there is a category of being which corresponds to substance is that there is a category of substance underlying this category of being. One will point out, e.g., that the categories of being on the suggested interpretation are the various uses of "is" or "being" with reference to which Aristotle says in many places that there are as many of them as there are categories. And here by "categories" he clearly means categories in the technical sense in question. Hence it would seem that the fact that there is a category of being associated with substance rests on the fact that there is a category of substance.

This inference, however plausible, is not justified either. For one can arrive at the claim that there are as many uses of "is" as there are categories, including a particular use in which substances are said to be, without assuming a category of substance. To arrive at that claim it will do to assume the categories of the *Topics* as we have interpreted them. Hence, it does not even follow from the claim that there are as many uses of "is," including one for substances, as there are categories that there is a category of substance.

How, then, could the different uses of "is" be derived from the categories of the *Topics*, as we interpret them, i.e., without assuming a category of substance? A locus classicus for the claim that there are as many uses of " . . . is" as there are categories is *Met.* Δ 7, a most obscure chapter. Here Aristotle distinguishes per se being and being per accidens. I take it that per se being is the being of per se beings and that accidental being is the being of accidental beings; an accidental being seems to be something like a red thing or a just thing or a healthy man, as opposed to the color red, justice, health, or a man, all of which are per se beings. What makes them per se beings is that they are what they are, namely, the color red, justice, health, a man, not by being really something else which just happens to be that color or justice or whatever it is, but which also could be something else. The red thing, on the other hand, is an accidental being, because it is what it is, namely red, by really being something else which just happens to be red, but which might as well not be red. Given this distinction, Aristotle's claim is that there are as many uses of " . . . is" in which per se beings can be said to be, or to be beings or entities, as there are categories. What Aristotle seems to have in mind is this: there is no such thing as plain being such that there is something which all things which are share and which we attribute to them when we say of them that they are; rather, it is the case that it is one thing to say of a substance that it is, another to say of a quality that it is, and yet another thing to say of a quantity that it is. Depending on the ultimate genus of the subject, the use of " . . . is" or "being" is different. To say of a substance that it is, is to say that it is a substance of some kind or that it is of some substance of some kind; to say of a quality that it is, is to say that it is a quality of some kind. But why should this be so? Why should the use of "being" differ depending on the ultimate class of the being in question?

One might be tempted to assume that Aristotle relies on the thesis that quite generally a particular use of a predicate never extends beyond an ultimate class of entities, because the uses of predicates have to be defined with reference to a class of possible subjects and the maximal classes of subjects available are the ultimate classes of entities. Presumably there is enough evidence to show that this is what Aristotle thinks at times. But it does seem to be a very strong thesis, and hence it would be preferable if one did not have to rely on it for the claim in question.

If we go by the opening lines of *Met.* Z, e.g., it seems that Aristotle, when he talks about the different per se uses of " . . . is", has statements of the following kind in mind:

(i) Socrates is (i.e., a substance);
(ii) justice is (i.e., a quality of something);
(iii) the size of two feet is (i.e., a quantity of something).

Now these statements by themselves do not reflect differences in category, given our account of what categories are. If anything, the predicate, in each of these statements is in the category of the what it is. Hence, a consideration just of these statements will hardly help us to see why there should be as many uses of " . . . is" here as there are categories. But most of these statements do have counterparts which do reflect the differences in category. For their category does vary depending on the class of entities of the subject of the first kind of statement. This is most easily seen in the case of non-substantial items. For justice to be, i.e., for justice to be the quality of something, is for there to be something which is qualified by justice, i.e., for justice to be, or to exist, the following statement has to be true: (iiA) something is qualified by justice. Similarly, for the size of two feet to exist the following has to be true: (iiiA) something is quantified by the size of two feet. The predicate of (iiA) is in the category of quality, just as the subject of its counterpart (ii) was in the genus of quality. The same, *mutatis mutandis,* holds for (iiiA) and (iii) and for the corresponding pairs of statements involving the other kinds of entities. So, for non-substantial items it is easy to see how we always get a corresponding statement in the corresponding category. It is equally clear that there can be no such straightforward correspondence in the case of statements about substances. This just reflects the fact that substances are not the substances of something in the way qualities or quantities are the qualities or quantities of something. And this, in turn, just reflects the fact that substances have a special status in that they in some sense exist in their own right.

But how is all this supposed to help us to understand that there are as many per se uses of "is" as there are categories? Presumably, one can argue that for Aristotle to attribute, in one of the categories, something to something is to attribute some kind of being to it. Presumably it is also true, though this sounds strange to us, that this fact is supposed to be reflected by the use of the copulative "is." Presumably, we also can say that for Aristotle there are different forms or kinds of being which are reflected by different uses of "is." Being something essentially is one kind of being, being something accidentally is another kind of being which presupposes the first one. Moreover, there are different ways of being something accidentally; for being qualified in a certain way is one thing, being quantified quite another, and being in a certain relation to something yet another. But, if this is what we can assume for Aristotle, it also would seem that the kind of being which one attributes to something varies with the category of the statement. And, since the use of "is" is supposed to reflect the kind of being one attributes to something in such a statement, this would seem to give some content to the claim that there are as many uses of "is" as there are categories. But it still would not explain why there are as many per se uses of "is" as there are categories, and, in particular, it would not yet explain why there should be one per se use in which "is" is restricted to substances. For the statements with predicates in the various categories other than the first category involve the various accidental uses of "is" rather than per se uses, and, though statements in the first category involve a per se use of "is," this use is not restricted to substances since this category is not restricted to substances. It is at this point that our consideration of pairs of statements involving non-substantial kinds of entities becomes relevant. We saw that the per se being which we attribute to justice when we say that justice is, or that there is justice, is none other than the accidental being which we attribute to something when we say that it is just. It is one being which can be looked at in two ways: as attributed to objects it is accidental being and as attributed to the quality it is per se being. But if this is so, then there will be at least as many per se kinds of being as there are non-substantial categories. In addition there will be a per se kind of being which cannot be thus identified with some accidental kind of being. For the per se being of substances cannot be identified with the accidental being or any kind of being of anything else. Thus we arrive at as many kinds of per se being as there are categories, including one which is the per se being of substances. And hence we have as many per se uses of 'is," including one for substances, as there are categories, though we did not start out with a category of substance. What happened, rather, was that by applying our distinction of categories to the uses of "is" we were forced to introduce the notion of a substance.

Whatever the difficulties of this account may be, it would explain one fact about Aristotle's discussion of per se being in *Met.* Δ 7 which has exercised commentators considerably. And this is that Aristotle in his discussion of per se being considers as examples not only statements which involve a copulative use of "is" but statements which involve a clearly accidental use of "is." This strongly suggests that Aristotle for the claim that there are as many per se uses of "is" as there are categories is considering two sets of statements of the kind we have been considering: it suggests that in support of his claim about the use of "is" in one set of statements he has recourse to another set of statements which involve an accidental use of "is" and which differ in category in the sense of our explanation of what categories are. Thus it not only seems that, given the suggested notion of a category, we can given an explanation of Aristotle's claim but that we even can account for a detail of Aristotle's argument which otherwise would go unexplained. It does not seem to be the case, then, that we have to assume a category of substance to account for Aristotle's claim that there are as many uses of "is" as there are categories.

I have argued so far that the evidence that there is a category of substance is circumstantial and that a good deal of this evidence is inconclusive. I now want to argue that Aristotle in his later writings does restrict the first category to substances but that this is due to a development or change within his theory which does not affect the very notion of a category itself.

That Aristotle at some point comes to accept a category of substance is fairly clear from a passage like the following (*Met.* K 1068ᵃ 8ff.; *Phys.* 225ᵇ5 ff.): "Since the categories are mutually exhausted by substance, quality, place, etc. it is necessary that there be three kinds of motion, namely those with reference to quality, quantity, and place." So here we have a category of substance, and the subsequent remarks in the text make it clear that by "substance" Aristotle here does not mean "essence," as he often does, but substance in the sense in which Socrates is a substance. Hence, we have a category restricted to substances in the standard sense.

It seems to me that this acceptance of a category of substance is due to a development of doctrine which is reflected by a severe restriction on the use of the phrase "what it is" in this context. Consider, e.g., *Anal. Post.* 83ᵃ 21–23. Here Aristotle says that if one thing *A* is predicated of something *B*, *A* either is (part of) the what it is of B or signifies that B is of a certain quality or of a certain quantity, etc. There is no reason from the context to suppose that the what it is here is restricted to substance; in fact, the context strongly suggests that it is not (cf 84^a 14; 85^b 20). Thus we here seem to have the category of the what it is in its generous construal of the *Topics*. This, incidentally, makes it clear that the case presented here does not rest solely on the *Topics* and that the suggested interpretation of the *Topics* concerning the first category is not in conflict with all the rest of Aristotle's writing on the matter. In fact, the restricted use of the phrase "what it is" is much rarer than Bonitz's Index would make us believe and is largely, though not entirely, limited to the *Metaphysics*. Now, in contrast with this passage from the *Posterior Analytics,* consider the opening line of *Met.* Z 1028^a 10ff.: " 'being' is used in many ways, . . . for in one case it signifies what it is and a this, in another case a quality or a quantity or one of the other things thus predicated. . . . It is clear that of these it is the what it is which signifies the substance which is a being in the primary sense." In this passage the what it is obviously is restricted to substances, and, though the text does not explicitly mention categories under this name, parallel passages like 1026^a 36ff., where he does explicitly talk of categories, make it sufficiently clear that Aristotle here at the beginning of *Met.* Z is restricting the category of the what it is to substances. In *Met.* Z 4 1037^a 17ff., Aristotle is quite explicit about the restriction: "For the term 'what it is' in one way signifies substance and the this, in another each of the kinds of predicates, quantity, quality and whatever else there is of this kind. . . . And 'what it is' unqualifiedly applies to substance, whereas it only qualifiedly applies to the other kinds of things."

Why, then, is it that the what it is now is supposed to cover only substances, strictly speaking? To start with we have to take into account that for Aristotle a statement of the form "white is such-and-such a color" can be taken in two ways. It can be taken to tell us what the term "white" signifies or means (ti sēmainei). But it also can be taken to tell us what white is (ti esti). If taken this way, it is supposed to attribute being or existence to the color white and to specify the kind of being which is attributed to the color white, namely, the being of such-and-such a color. Secondly, the what it is of something is, or is part of, the essence of that thing or, to use Aristotelian language, the what it is to be for that thing. Hence to say of something what it is, is not just to attribute some kind of being to it; it is to specify the kind of being which is essential to it. Third, given Aristotle's developed view of what it is to be for the various kind of entities, it turns out that non-substantial items do not unqualifiedly have any essential being of their own to be specified by saying what they are. For, as we saw, the being of such-and-such a color is just the accidental being we attribute to something when we say that it is colored this way. In this non-substantial items differ from substances which unqualifiedly have an essential being of their own; their essential being is not just the accidental being of something else. Hence, it is only in a derived and qualified sense that we can speak of the what it is in the case of non-substantial items.

But why should this make us restrict the category of the what it is to substances? After all there still is an extended sense in which the what it is covers all kinds of entities, substances, and non-substances alike. Now it would seem that the truth of statements about non-substantial items rests entirely on truths about substances. In particular, the truth of statements of the being and the what it is of non-substantial items would seem to rest on the truth of statements about substances in the category of the what it is and on statements about substances in the category of the non-substantial item in question. The truths that there is white or that white is such and such a color, e.g., would seem to rest on the truth that some substances are of such and such a kind such that things of that kind are of some color or other, and on the truth about some substance of this kind that it is of such and such a color. Thus, statements concerning the what it is of non-substantial items are not really on a par with statements concerning the what it is of substances. The old category of the what it is collects disparate items insofar as statements of the what it is of non-substantial items presuppose statements of the what it is of substances, and, what is worse, they presuppose statements concerning substances in the other categories. To take account of this secondary and, in a way, parasitical nature of these statements, we restrict the category of the what it is to substances. This in any case is what Aristotle does.

Thus, we may conclude that the fact that Aristotle comes to accept a category of substance poses no threat to our interpretation of the *Topics*. For we can understand this development of Aristotle's doctrine as being due to the fact that Aristotle comes to think of statements of the form "white is such-and-such color" as having a more complex structure than it at first seemed and as being secondary to statements about substances in a rather radical way.

But there is nothing to force us to assume that Aristotle in the course of the development changed his notion of a category, unless one wants to say that the restriction of the distinction of categories to statements about substances amounts to a change in the notion of a category itself. But one should keep in mind in this connection that the distinction of categories was never meant to apply to any statement whatsoever. It hardly was meant to cover statements such as the following: "man is a species." "all species are constituted by a genus and a differentia," "the term 'being' has as many uses as there are categories." It, rather, seems that they were meant to apply to first order statements in which, as Aristotle sees it, an item in the ontology is predicated of an item in the ontology. If, then, Aristotle no longer thinks that a statement like "White is a color" is of this simple kind and, hence, no longer thinks that the distinction of categories applies to it, this in no way indicates a change in the notion of a category itself.

Having thus identified the notion of a category of Aristotle, let us, in conclusion, go back to our text in the *Topics* to look for at least some clarification of this notion. We are told in the first sentence of A, 9 that having distinguished the predicables we next have to distinguish the categories. Obviously our understanding of what the categories are supposed to be would be greatly increased if we had a better understanding of why Aristotle thinks that we have to make this distinction, of how he thinks it is to be made. Unfortunately, Aristotle in the *Topics* does not enter into a discussion of either of these questions. This may suggest that Aristotle relies on the fact that he has settled these questions elsewhere. But I do not think that has to be taken this way. It may very well be the case that Aristotle thinks that it is sufficiently obvious from the practice of the kind of dialectical discussion which is the subject matter of the *Topics* that we have to make that kind of distinction of predications. It would, e.g., seem to be clear to someone who had followed Platonic discussions that we had to distinguish carefully between saying of something what it is essentially and saying something else about it. And it would be clear from practice that one has to distinguish between a predicate which is true of something with reference to something else like " . . . is to the left" or " . . . is a father," and predicates which do not need that kind of complement. The actual use made of the categories in the *Topics* very much suggests that the crucial distinctions are picked up one by one and that it is long experience with arguments and the analysis of fallacies which will put one into the position to produce one list of such distinctions, filled up and completed by a general consideration of what kinds of things one can say about something, to arrive at a complete list of the various kinds of things one can say about something. For there does not seem to be any one problem whose solution requires the complete list of categories, nor is there any sign of a systematical derivation of the categories, e.g., in terms of a set of formal features. For if Aristotle in the *Topics* knew of such a derivation, we could count on his using it systematically to propose strategies for arguing for or against a statement on the basis of the formal features of the category involved. But one reason why he actually makes so surprisingly little use of the categories in the *Topics* seems to be exactly this, that he does not have a clear view of the logical properties which might serve to distinguish the categories from each other in a systematic fashion.

Nor does it seem that Aristotle arrives at his list of categories by grammatical considerations as has been proposed again recently by Benveniste. It is true that Aristotle thinks that certain grammatical forms tend to go with certain categories; the active form of verbs, e.g., naturally goes with the category of doing and the passive with the category of suffering. But he also is aware of the fact that grammatical form in this repsect can be quite misleading, and he thinks that a large number of fallacies are due to this.

It will, of course, be suggested that Aristotle arrives at his list of categories neither by logical nor by grammatical considerations, but by an ontological inquiry. It will be suggested that Aristotle first established a list of ultimate classes of what there is by an ontological inquiry into what there is and then just assumed corresponding categories. On this view Aristotle, e.g., first determined that there is an ultimate class of entities consisting of all qualities and then introduced a category of quality which is characterized by the fact that the item predicated belongs to the antecedently determined class of qualities. Now, though this matter would require quite a bit of detailed argument, it seems to me that things are exactly the other way round. When Aristotle in the treatise *Categories* tries to give a general characterization of qualities, he relies on the fact that we already know what it is to say of something what it is like. Qualities are just those items which we attribute to something when we say what it is like; quantities are just those items which we refer to if we say of something of what amount it is, and so forth.

On the other hand, it presumably is the case that for Aristotle the different kinds of entities like qualities and quantities differ from each other insofar as it is one kind of thing to be quantitifed in a certain way and quite a different matter to be qualified in a certain way. And, if we keep in mind that by "predication" Aristotle means here "true predication," it is clear that the distinction of categories just amounts to the distinction of these various ways of being and the corresponding various kinds of entities. And, hence, ontological considerations might well have an effect on the list of categories one draws up.

But if it does not just seem that Aristotle did not arrive at his list of categories exclusively by such ontological considerations, it would also seem that the notion of a category would lose much of its interest if the categories were simply arrived at by some ontological distinction of various ultimate classes of entities. For the real interest of the Aristotelian notion of a category seems to lie in the fact that we are supposed to have one set of notions, or, perhaps, two or three very closely related sets of notions, which do needed work in logic, in grammar, and in metaphysics. A serious study of Aristotle's categories would have to go in that direction. But such a study will not get off the ground unless certain rather simple facts have been straightened out. And I hope that the preceding remarks will be of some help for this preliminary enterprise.[3]

4

Individuals in Aristotle

By way of introduction, I offer a few remarks to give an overview of the subject of this paper. Aristotle assumes that, in addition to *objects,* there are *properties* of objects. This assumption is rather stronger than one might think, since it turns out that statements about properties are not just reducible to statements about objects; on the contrary, the truth of at least some statements about objects is to be explained by assuming that there are properties. For example, the truth of a statement like 'Socrates is ill' is to be explained by noting that there are not only objects, like Socrates, but that there are also such things as illness; illness is not to be construed as yet another object but as something standing in certain relations to objects, relations on the basis of which one can say of objects that they are ill. Besides this division of things into objects and properties, Aristotle, in the *Categories,* makes use of the distinction between *general* and *particular,* between individuals and universals. Although Aristotle does not, in this treatise, use any term like 'universal' (katholou), he does speak of 'individuals', and he contrasts these with their kinds. These two divisions, into objects and properties, on the one hand, and into particular and general, on the other, do not turn out to be the same. For Aristotle counts as general not only properties but also the kinds, into which objects fall, i.e., the genera, species, and differentiae of substances; and these are to be differentiated strictly from properties. When we say, 'Socrates is a man', we are not speaking of any property of Socrates'; rather, we are speaking of two substances, Socrates and the species man. When, however, we say, 'Socrates is ill', we *are* speaking of a property. The species is something general, yet, unlike illness, it is not a property. (Furthermore, for Aristotle, there is not, in addition to the species man, some property of being a man.) Both properties and kinds, then, turn out to be general. Moreover, Aristotle construes the distinction between general and particular in such a way that the notions of paticular and individual are not restricted to objects, but can also apply to properties. Thus, the two distinctions do not collapse into one, they cut across

49

each other, resulting in a four-fold division, into individual objects, individual properties, general properties, and general objects (cf. *Cat.* 2).

At this point, three difficulties arise. First of all, how is it possible to speak of individuals in the case of properties; second, how can there be a single notion of being an individual that can be applied to objects as well as properties; and third, what sorts of objects are these general objects, the genera and species, supposed to be? These difficulties, especially the first two, will be our concern in the first part of this paper, which deal with the *Categories.*

In the *Metaphysics,* Aristotle denies that there is anything general — at least, he denies that there are kinds, into which objects fall. Thus, he also abandons the notion of an individual which he had relied on in the *Categories,* since it presupposes that there are general things, that there are universals. Given that Aristotle does not identify properties with the general, denying that there is anything general does not result in the notion of an individual just collapsing into the notion of an object. Rather, the denial that there is anything general has this consequence: now the relation between objects and properties simply cannot be viewed as the relation between individual things and general concepts under which these fall. Because of this, Aristotle faces some odd results concerning what is actually particular, what is actually an individual object, what is to count as primary substance. These results will be our concern in the second part of this chapter.

I. Individuals in Aristotle's *Categories*

Looking at either Lewis and Short's *A Latin Dictionary* or Glare's new *Oxford Latin Dictionary* would lead one to conclude that, in ancient Latin, 'individuum' and 'individuus' were not used in the sense of 'individual'.[1] This conclusion, however, would be completely erroneous; for we find 'individuum' and 'individuus' used in precisely this sense rather frequently in later antiquity, especially in Marius Victorinus (*Adv. Ar.* I; 34, 20) and Boethius (*In de int. alt.* p. 334, 2 Meiser), but also in St. Augustine (*De trin.* VII, 6, 11), Martianus Capella (VI, 352), and Cassiodorus (*Inst.* II, 14; 123, 9), as well as in various grammarians, e.g., Priscian (*Inst.* II, 25; p. 58, 25).

The origin of this use of the word can be explained quite easily: it is simply the result of translating literally the Greek word "atomon," which can be used in just this sense of 'individual' or 'individual thing'. Aristotle, in the *Categories* (1^b 6; 3^a 34, 38, 39; 3^b 2, 7, 12), is the first to use the term in this way. However, for reasons of which I shall speak later, he seems to have given up this use of atomon in his later works. It is only with the increasing influence of the *Categories* in the 2nd and 3rd centuries A.D. that this term comes again to be used by Greek philosophers, albeit rather sparingly (cf. Plotinus VI, 3, 1, 15). Galen (*De Plat. et Hipp. dogm.* VIII, 2 p. 664, 6–7 (Müller), tell us that philosophers were in the habit of calling, e.g., Dion an individual substance. From the fact that Galen finds this worthy of comment and from the fact that he uses atmētos here, whereas the philosophers actually use atomos, we might infer that, in Galen's time, the philosophical use of this term was still rather rare (but, cf. Alexander *In Met.* 211, 30 and *passim*). At any rate, because of the influence of the *Categories* and Porphyry's introduction to the *Categories*—in which Porphyry speaks rather frequently of individuals (cf. 2, 18; 3, 3)—its use does come to be firmly established. This use, then, is simply taken over by the various Latin authors. The translations of the *Categories* and of the *Isagoge* by both Marius Victorinus and Boethius were, no doubt, of special importance in introducing and securing this use of the term in Latin.[2]

At any rate, it is especially these two, and authors depending on them, who use 'individuus' in the sense familiar to us. And the continued use of this term in this sense was assured by the prominent position in the curriculum of the schools the *Categories* and Porphyry's *Isagoge* came to occupy and continued to occupy till the very end of the Middle Ages.

If Aristotle, then, is the first writer to call individuals 'individuals', the question arises what is it he had in mind when he calls them 'indivisible'; for that is just what 'individuum', rather, "atomon" means. And given that "atomon" and "atomos" had already been used in two different philosophical contexts— atomists of all sorts had used the term for indivisible magnitudes, e.g., atoms, and Platonists had used it for *infimae species*—this question becomes all the more pressing.

Aristotle provides some indication of the answer when, in the first passage in which he speaks of individuals (*Cat.* 1^b 6–7), he offers "and that which is one in number" as a gloss on "individuals" (cf. also 3^b 12). As a matter of fact, Aristotle does, in various places, invoke the principle that that which is one is, as such, also indivisible; and so, we may assume that it is somehow with respect to their being one that individuals are said to be indivisible. However, being one is not a *proprium* of individuals: species and genera, i.e., the kinds into which objects fall, also have a kind of unity. One can, for example, count the species of a given genus. The kind of indivisibiliy characteristic of individuals must, then, be a special kind of unity. And it seems reasonable to suppose that the expression "in number," in the phrase "that which is one in number," serves precisely the function of pointing out the special kind of unity and so, too, the kind of indivisibiliy characteristic of individuals.

Now, Aristotle uses the expression "one in number" more frequently by way of contrast with "one in kind or species" and "one in genus." Two or more things are one in kind, if both belong to the same species. Thus, Plato and Socrates are one in kind, namely, man. Plato, Brunellus, and Fido, however, are only generically one, namely, animal. Since Brunellus is a donkey and Fido a dog, they do not belong to the same species and thus are one only in genus.

Now let us suppose that a genus is the set of objects that are generically one, and correspondingly, that a species is the set of objects that are specifically one. We could go on to say that the kind of unity that characterizes genera, i.e., that makes one genus *one* genus, is generic unity and, correspondingly, that the unity characteristic of species is specific unity.

If we go on to connect this division, of kinds of unity, with the notion that that which is one is, as such, also indivisible, we get the following result: something that has generic unity cannot be divided insofar as it has *this* unity. If we consider, for example, Socrates, Plato, Brunellus, and Fido only insofar as they are generically one and the same, namely, animal, we cannot distinguish them. They cannot be divided according to their genera. But, to the extent that Socrates, Plato, Brunellus, and Fido lack specific unity, we can distinguish them and divide them into their species, viz., into the sets of men, donkeys, and dogs, respectively. Now, if we go on to the set of men, Socrates and Plato, we cannot distinguish between them and cannot divide them as long as we consider them as a specific unity, i.e., as long as we consider Socrates and Plato insofar as they are one and the same, namely, man. Since, however, this set lacks numerical unity, we can indeed divide it, viz., according to number. And what we end up with, when we divide the set in this way according to number, are just the individuals.

In the *Categories,* then, Aristotle seems to be relying on a notion of division according to which genera and species, in a certain respect, *are* one and, hence, indivisible, but, in another respect, *are not* one and, hence, divisible; individuals, however, turn out to be completely indivisible on this schema of division. Indeed, this seems to me to be the explanation for the fact that Aristotle calls individuals 'indivisible' in the *Categories.* Yet, this explanation will be of little help in getting a grip on the notion of an individual as long as we do not have a clearer idea of what sort of division it is with respect to which the individuals are indivisible.

Some indication of what notions of division and part are at work here is provided by Aristotle at 3^b 16–18, where he explains that the species man and the genus animal are not individuals, because they have a plurality of subjects (hypokeimena); for there are many things of which one can truly say that they are a man or an animal. This explanation strongly suggests that an individual does not have any actual parts and is indivisible, because it has no subjects. In the relevant sense of 'part', then, x would be a part of y if, and only if, x is a subject of y. To distinguish between this sense of 'part' and the more familiar one, we can avail ourselves of the Scholastic terms 'integral' and 'subjective': a wall is an integral not a subjective part of a house, since we cannot say of it that it is a house; Socrates, though, is a subjective not an integral part of man, since we can say of him that he is a man. An individual, then, is something which has no subjective parts; indeed, it itself is a subjective part of an infima species into which the things having only generic or specific unity are themselves divided.

We shall have understood the relevant sense of 'division' and 'part', if we understand in what sense Aristotle is speaking of subjects here. According to the *Categories*, there are only two ways in which x can be the subject of y: either y is said of x as its subject, or y is in x as its subject. These two relations can be defined as follows:

(A) y is *said of* x as its subject if, and only if,
   (i) y is truly predicated of x; and
   (ii) the name of y occurs as a predicate-noun in the sentence in which y is predicated of x; and
   (iii) if, in that sentence, the definition of y can be substituted for the name salva veritate.

(B) y is *in* x as its subject if, and only if,
   (i) y is truly predicated of x; and
   (ii) y is not said of x as its subject.

These two definitions would require rather extensive elaboration. We would, for example, need to note that predication is a relation between entities not expressions, and we would need to explain what the name of an object is and what a definition is. I shall, however, restrict myself to providing an example to help clarify these definitions. Let us suppose Socrates is both healthy and white. Socrates, then, is the subject of health and of the color white, Now, health and the color will be in Socrates, as a subject, not said of him as a subject: for, when we predicate health of Socrates we do not use the name of health, viz., 'health', but the corresponding adjective; we do not say that Socrates is health but that he is healthy. As for the color, while we do use its name when we say that Socrates is white, we find that here the third condition is not satisifed; for we cannot replace 'white' by its definition and say that Socrates is such-and-such a color. If, on the other hand, we say that Socrates is a man, we do use the name of an object as a predicate-noun, viz., the name of the species man, and do not use a corresponding adjective. (If we were to say either that Socrates is manly or that he is humane, we would be saying something quite different and would be referring not to the species man but to the quality either of manliness or of humaneness.) In addition, we can replace the name 'man' by the definition of man; for we can say that Socrates is a rational animal. Thus, man is said of Socrates as its subject.

If we take this distinction as given, we can go on to ask in which way x must be a subject of y for x to be a subjective part of y. There are three possibilities:

   (i) x is a subjective part of y if, and only if, x is a subject of y, regardless of which way it is a subject of y, i.e., x is a subjective part of y if, and only if, y is truly predicated of x.

(ii) x is a subjective part of y if, and only if, x is a subject of y in this manner: y is *said of* x as its subject.

(iii) x is a subjective part of y if, and only if, x is a subject of y in this manner: y is *in* x as its subject.

The third possibility can be easily eliminated. Genera and species quite obviously have subjective parts, viz., individual substances, but they are not in anything as their subjects. The first possibility can be ruled out as well, for the following reason. As we can see from the second chapter of the *Categories,* Aristotle not only assumes that there are individual substances, but also that there are non-substantial individuals, individual qualities, and quantities. In addition, Aristotle assumes that an attribute, say, a quality, will belong to an individual substance as its subject in all and only those cases where this quality also belongs to the species and the genus of the individual substance. Aristotle can make this assumption, because (i) he takes a sentence of the form 'a man is running' to be a sentence about the species; and (ii) he believes a sentence of the form 'a man is running' is true only if a sentence of the form 'this man is running' is also true; and (iii) he believes that if a sentence of the form 'this man is running' is true, then sentences of the form 'a man is running' and 'an animal is running' also must be true. A result of these assumptions is that any attribute, whether it is individual or general, has at least two subjects, namely, an individual substance and a kind of substance. That, however, means that there could be no individuals in categories other than substance, if being an individual were only a matter of something having a plurality of subjects independently of which way these subjects are subjects. But since Aristotle wants to distinguish between individuals and their kinds also in the case of non-substances, and since this distinction can only be maintained if we distinguish between the two ways in which something can be the subject of something, only the second possibility remains.

We thus arrive at the following result: x is a subjective part of y if, and only if, y is said of x as its subject. Corresponding to this, we could define an individual in this way: x is an individual if (i) it is the subjective part of something, and (ii) it itself has no subjective parts. This definition seems to capture what Aristotle takes to be an individual in the *Categories.*

Two things strike me as worthy of note here. First, the negative character of this definition is surprising. Aristotle seems to proceed as if, quite independent of the distinction between individuals and non-individuals, it were clear what is to count as an entity, and the only problem was to make a cut within this given set of entities. And this cut is not made by using a positive condition for what is to count as an individual so that everything that fails to meet this condition is a genus or a species; rather, a condition is given for being a species or a genus—having subjective parts—and everything that fails to meet this condition counts as an individual. I shall return to this point briefly later.

Second, it is worth noting that this definition, together with the assumption that there are things besides substances, implies that not all individuals are substances. If, for example, there are properties or qualities, then, on this definition of individuals, there must also be individual qualities. For, suppose Q is a quality; either Q is itself an individual or it has subjective parts. If Q has subjective parts, these are either substances or non-substances. They cannot be substances, since substances are not qualities; at best, they have qualities. So, either Q is itself an individual or it has only subjective parts that are not substances. If Q has only subjective parts that are not substances, then it has parts that are individuals and not substances.

That this should be a consequence of a definition of individuals is by no means obvious, for we can easily imagine either a definition of individuals according to which only objects or substances are individuals or a definition which leaves the matter open. The definition implicit in the traditional definition of the universal is of this sort: according to *De int.* 7, the universal is that which is by its very nature predicable of a plurality of subjects. Since there is no requirement here that the subjects be of such a kind that the universal can be said of them as their subject, there can be properties without there being individual properties, since all the subjects of the properties could be substances.

The assumption that there should be, in addition to individual substance, individuals in other categories is difficult to get a grip on for a very simple reason. What makes the concept of an individual so readily available to us is the simple fact that the nouns for kinds, which objects fall under, can also be used in the plural, and that, when they are used in the plural, they apply not to kinds but to individuals: 'man' designates a kind, under which certain objects fall, and it forms the plural 'men'; when we speak of men, we are not speaking of kinds but of individuals. Moreover, we can use the plural with number-words. What we count in that case are again individuals not kinds. In counting, we have the problem of how to ensure that we count only those objects we mean to count, that we distinguish between the objects and not mistake two for one, and, finally, that we not count anything twice, having overlooked that we have already counted it. Thus, from the mere fact that we can count, we have access to a very rich notion of individuals when we are dealing with objects. By way of contrast, the definition of individuals arrived at above seems virtually contentless.

When we turn to non-substances, we do not quite know what to make of the notion of an individual. Let us, for example, consider qualities, to which I shall restrict myself in the following discussion. Terms for qualities, *nomina abstracta,* do not readily assume the plural. We do not speak of healths or courages, we form no plurals for 'warmth', 'anger', or 'paleness'. And even in those cases where there are plurals of terms for qualities, they do not seem to refer to individuals in the category of quality; rather, they seem to refer either to kinds of the quality, which, while they are qualities, are still general, or to examples of (having) the quality, which, while they may be individuals, are not qualities but only instances of (having) them. Thus, illnesses are kinds of illness, ways in which one can be ill; colors are general ways in which something can be colored. Beauties, on the other hand, are individual instances of beauty and, fortunately, not qualities but, say, persons like Helen or Alcibiades. Stupidities are instances of behavior that shows stupidity, not properties. Similarly, treacheries are not properties, but examples, instances of treachery or treacherousness; there are no treacherousnesses. These relatively simple facts about language seem to make it so difficult to understand what individual properties or qualities are supposed to be.

Given this state of affairs, there are at least two options. Either we can give up speaking of individual properties and turn, rather, to developing an adequate concept of individuals for objects, or we can insist that our difficulties with nonsubstantial individuals are just the result of, on the one hand, myopically focusing on the individuality of objects, and, on the other, giving excessive weight to these linguistic phenomena, which, as a matter of fact, are themselves subject to considerable variation. For if there had not suddenly been so terribly many abstract nouns in Greek, one could have continued with the attractive custom of referring to properties by neuter adjectives; in that case, all terms for properties would have had plurals. We could then, following Eudoxus, consider properties, in a manner analogous to homoiomerous things like gold, either as a single individual, scattered throughout the world, or we could say that the plural of the adjective actually refers to the scattered parts, and thus that it is these scattered parts which correspond to individual objects.

It would hardly be appropriate to ascribe the second position to Aristotle in the *Categories*. The explanation for Aristotle's position in the *Categories* seems, rather, to be that here he is taking a first step in making the distinction between objects and properties central for ontology. This distinction played virtually no role in Plato, and it was, in any case, completely overshadowed by the distinction between general and particular. It is the attempt to maintain this Platonic distinction between general and particular in addition to the new distinction between objects and properties that leads to our difficulties.

That Aristotle's schema of genera, species, and individuals amounts to Plato's distinction between particular and general is already suggested by the fact that, with one exception, the view in the *Categories* hardly differs from the Platonic theory of forms in the *Philebus*.[3] In the *Philebus*, Plato asks how forms can be both one and many. The answer is that they are at once one, many, and unlimitedly many; one, insofar as they are genus; many, insofar as the genus consists of many species; and unlimitedly many, insofar as unlimitedly many things are subsumed under the various species. Here we have not only the division into genera, species, and individuals, but also the notion that species and individuals are parts of the genus or form; the relation between genus and species, and between species and individual, seems to correspond exactly to the relation of being said of something as a subject; the individuals are again viewed negatively as what remains after one has divided the genus as far as it can be divided into species. The idea of things being one in genus seems to derive from the *Philebus* (12E), and in the *Philebus* (15A) forms are divided in just the way required here. The only difference is that Aristotle reverses the priority relation between forms and particulars. And this reversal seems to be a simple consequence of his giving precedence to the object/property distinction over the general/particular distinction.

Yet, if this is so, i.e., if Platonic forms include individuals as parts, and if the participation relation is precisely the converse of the relation of being said of something as a subject, there must also be non-substantial individuals, since there are forms not only of objects. Thus, we can give a historical explanation for Aristotle's countenancing non-substantial individuals—despite the obvious problems these seem to bring with them—by noting that he tries to maintain the Platonic distinction between general and particular, a distinction not restricted to objects.

Some philosophers, of course, do not shy away from the difficulties non-substantial individuals seem to involve; on the contrary, they seem positively enthusiastic about this notion.[4] They want to maintain not only that Socrates is an individual but that his wisdom also is, that is, the wisdom with respect to which we say of Socrates that he is wise. This wisdom, they maintain, is Socrates' and not Plato's. Similarly, that which makes Socrates healthy is not Plato's health but his own. Thus, it is claimed there are individuals also in the case of properties, namely, properties individuated by their bearers: the wisdom which is precisely Socrates' wisdom is an individual. And just such a view is ascribed also to Aristotle by almost all of his more recent interpreters. The only contemporary writer who has so far opposed this interpretation, Owen, can, thus, indeed speak of a dogma here, especially since the view was already accepted in later antiquity.[5] The reactions to Owen's criticisms of the received view show just how appropriate his choice of the word 'dogma' was.

Looked at from another aspect, of course, 'heresy' seems like a more appropriate term. Among the theses that Bishop Tempier condemned in his notorious decree of 1277 was that God cannot create any accident or attribute without its subject. Tempier seems here to be attacking a position like St. Thomas Aquinas' according to which properties are individuated by their bearers and, hence, cannot exist independently of them. What the ecclesiastical authorities were concerned with is the apparent incompatibility of this view of the individuation of properties with the doctrine of transsubstantiation. The doctrine of transsubstantiation seems to require that an object, say, the bread, have certain visible properties which, however, are not tied to the object, since they remain wholly unaffected by the change of the substance of the bread. But if, following trans-substantiation, the bread no longer remains, but its accidents do remain, then the identity of these accidents can hardly depend on their subject.

In the years following 1277, there are a large number of attempts to individuate properties independently of their bearers, of which some proved to be quite fruitful, e.g., the suggestion that properties be individuated according to their intensity.[6] Temperature or warmth is a universal; in any individual instance, however, warmth always appears with a particular intensity. And it is the degree of intensity—measured in Celsius, Fahrenheit, Reaumur, or whatever—which makes any given warmth the individual warmth it is. This suggestion presupposes a notion of intensive magnitude which Aristotle, presumably, did not have; however, the view that properties could be treated as intensive magnitudes was no doubt helpful in the mathematicization of physics. My concern here, of course, is only to show, on the basis of an episode in the history of philosophy, that the view, that if there are to be individual properties these must be individuated by their bearers, is by no means as natural and obvious as our recent Aristotle interpreters would have us believe.

I also do not intend to take up in all detail the reasons why it seems clear to me that a more careful reading of the relevant passages in the *Categories* not only does not require the standard interpretation but, in fact, precludes it. The received view, according to which properties are individuated by their bearers relies on an interpretation of 1^a 24–25. Here, Aristotle supposedly is giving a definition of the relation of 'x is in y as its subject'; and it is supposed that this can be rendered by something like this:

(C) x is in y as its subject if, and only if,
    (i) x is not a part of y, and
    (ii) x cannot exist independently of y.

According to this definition, a property can belong to an individual thing, say, Socrates, as its subject only if it could not exist independently of this individual thing. Yet, this implies that the properties which a particular thing has are peculiar to it and are not shared by any other thing; for if a property, e.g., a particular color, were shared by several objects, it would be difficult to see why this color should cease to exist as soon as one of the objects having it ceased to exist. Thus, this definition implies that we can attribute only such properties to individual things that are peculiar to them; and so, we end up with individual properties, properties peculiar to only one individual thing. Accordingly, then, individual things would have only individual properties as properties, while general properties, strictly speaking, would only have general things, like genera and species, as their subjects. But this cannot be Aristotle's view.

At 2^b 1–3, Aristotle says that one can only say that there is color in body if there is also color in a particular, individual body. A comparison with the immediately preceding sentence shows that he is speaking here of color in general and body in general, and that it is the universal color that is said to have the universal body as its subject only if there is also some individual body that color has as its subject. Color in general, then, is spoken of in a way as if it could and must have an individual object as its subject. Moreover, at 2^b 3ff., Aristotle says that all entities can be divided into two classes, individual objects or primary substances, on the one hand, and entities that are said of or are in these individual objects as their subjects, on the other. So, individual objects here are the subjects for everything else that there is; "everything else," however, includes general properties; hence, general properties, too, must have individual objects as their subjects. Finally, at 2^b 37ff., Aristotle explains why the genera and species of objects can also be called objects or substances. Just as the individual objects are the subjects underlying all properties, so too the species and genera underlie all properties as subjects. Since this is what makes substances, species and genera also deserve to be called substances. Again Aristotle speaks as if properties – regardless of whether they are universal or individual – have individual objects as their subjects; in addition, he also speaks here as if properties, both individual and universal, have universals as their subjects, namely, the species and genera of individual objects. After all, it is only this that justifies calling genera and species substances; they, just like the individual objects, underlie everything else. Nor can we charge Aristotle, either in this passage or in the preceding ones, with just expressing himself imprecisely. For his argument depends, in the one case, on the claim that all properties have individual objects as their subjects and, in the other case, on the claim that all properties, even the individual ones, have genera and species as their subjects.

We shall, therefore, have to find another interpretation of 1^a 24–25. These lines, it seems to me, do not provide a definition of the relation "x is in y as its subject"; rather, they provide a definition of the class of entities that are in something as their subject. What is characteristic of the members of this class is that, for each of them, we can specify at least one subject of which it is true that it could not exist without that subject. With one exception (which I shall come to later), this is not the case with entities that are only said of something as their subject and not also in something as their subject. While the species man would not exist, according to Aristotle, if there were no men, it is irrelevant to the existence of the species which men actually exist – as long as some do. There is no particular person, no one subject of the species man, to whom one could point and say that the species could not exist without this person as its subject. The same is true of the genus animal. The genus requires species and individuals as subjects to exist. None of these subjects, though, is so privileged that one could say of it, without it the genus could not exist.

In the lines following the definition, Aristotle tell us how matters stand with things that are in a subject. In 1^a 25–28, he explains how a particular knowledge of grammar and a particular white are the sorts of things that are in a subject (he does not even find it worth remarking that they are not said of a subject): " . . . and the particular white is in the body as its subject. For every color is in body (hapan gar chrōma en sōmati)." The last sentence is obviously meant to provide the explanation of *how* the body, mentioned in the preceding sentence, is the relevant subject with respect to which the particular white turns out to be something that occurs in a subject. Of course, it is not clear how we are to understand this explanation. At least initially, we might suppose that the explanatory sentence says that, for every color, we can specify some body that has this color; for if there were no body of this color, this color, too, would not exist. Applying this to the case at hand would lead us to suppose that for this particular white, too, some particular body can be specified which has just this color; this body, then, would be the relevant subject with respect to which we can say, of the particular white, that it is in a subject. Of course, the very language of the sentence seems to rule out such an interpretation. Both in this chapter and in the next, Aristotle—by using a special and rather unusual idiom—takes great pains to indicate when he is speaking of individuals: a particular, individual man is referred to by ho tis anthropos, a particular, individual white, by to ti leukon. Thus, if Aristotle had intended, in this passage dealing with the difference between universals and particulars, to say " . . . and the particular white is in a particular body as its subject," he would have written: kai to ti leukon en hypokeimenō men esti tō tini sōmati, hapan gar chrōma en tini sōmati.

Instead, the language Aristotle uses here is exactly like what he employs only a few lines later, at 1^b 1, where he is speaking of knowledge in general and soul in general, and what he employs at 2^b 1-3, where he is speaking of color in general and body in general. This strongly suggests that the body spoken of in 1^a 28 is not some particular, individual body but body in general, i.e., the genus body; it is thus parallel to 1^b 2, where he is referring to soul in general, not to some particular soul. But how are we now to understand the explanatory sentence? It must be saying that every color is in the genus body as its subject. Whatever, in any particular case, it may be that is colored, and whatever color it may be that it has, it must always be a body that has a color. Thus, if there were no genus body, there would also be no colors. Yet, the genus body is also the subject of every color, and this in accord with the rule previously mentioned: everything that is in an individual object as its subject also is in the genera and species as its subjects. How, though, does the fact that the genus body is the subject of every color explain the fact that the genus body is the relevant subject with respect to which one can say, of the particular white, that it is *in* a subject, that it is the kind of thing that occurs in a subject? The explanation is simple: things that are in a subject were defined (in 1^a 24-25) as those for which there is a subject without which they could not exist. For color in general, for any particular color and, hence, for a particular white, the relevant subject is body, that is, body in general or the genus body. If we assume — something we will need to assume in Aristotle for various reasons anyway — that, for every property, there is a species or genus outside which the property cannot occur because of how its range of possible objects has been defined, we shall be able to specify some universal without which the property cannot occur. Only living things are healthy or ill, only certain kinds of living things are male or female, only human beings are foolish.

It is important to note that 1^a 24–25 does not say that if something is in something else as its subject, it cannot exist independently of it. While it is natural and presumably also correct to assume that tou en hō estin in 1^a 25 refers back to en tini in 1^a 24, the reference of en tini is not fixed by the preceding words. As we have seen, everything that occurs in a subject must already have a plurality of subjects, at least some individual object and its species and genera. What is being claimed in 1^a 24–25 is not that for each of these subjects the property could not exist without it. What is being claimed, rather, is that if something is the kind of thing that occurs in a subject, then there is at least something, at least one subject, without which it cannot exist.

But is it even true that something which occurs in a subject differs from something which is said of a subject in this regard: for the former, we can specify at least one subject without which it cannot exist? As suggested earlier, with one exception, this is true; it is the case with genera and species; differentiae, however, at least differentiae on the schema of the *Categories*, form the exception. For, from the third chapter, we can see that Aristotle maintains that a differentia can occur only in a single genus and not in two independent genera. If 'rational' were the *differentia specifica* that constitutes the species man, 'rational' could not also, at least not in the sense relevant to the species man, appear in another genus; but this implies that we can specify a subject for the differentia without which it could not exist, viz., the species it constitutes. For the differentia is said of this species and, hence, has it as its subject.

Now it seems as if Aristotle wishes to rule out precisely this case by requiring, in 1^a 24–25, not only that there must be a subject, without which the thing in question could not exist, but also that this thing must not be a part of its subject. The differentia specifica, however, is a part of the species, since it constitutes it. This interpretation presupposes that Aristotle is thinking of 'conceptual' parts, when he is speaking of parts in 1^a 24–25. As we can see from Bonitz's *Index* (455^b 32ff.), Aristotle uses 'part' in this sense quite frequently. And it seems as if we must ascribe this use of 'part' to Aristotle here also, in 1^a 24–25. For there is a passage in the *Categories* where he explicitly refers back to 1^a 24–25; 3^a 29–32 (cf. elegeto, 3^a 32). There he is saying that the claim that parts of substances are substances is indeed compatible with the claim that what occurs in a subject is not a substance; for parts of substances are not *in* substances, in the sense of "being in a subject," just because they are their parts. If we were to suppose that Aristotle is thinking of physical parts of substances in 3^a 29–32, these lines would make little sense in the context either of what comes before or of what follows. For both the preceding as well as the following lines deal with genera, species, and differentiae. Thus, the continuity of the passage is preserved if we assume that, in 3^a 29–32, Aristotle is thinking of conceptual parts of substances. But if that is the case, then conceptual parts are also what he was thinking of in 1^a 24–25, as the line (3^a 32) referring back to the passage shows. At any rate, this part of 1^a 24–25 was so construed already in antiquity: cf. Plotinus, *Enn* VI 3, 5.8–9 and 25–27, and Simplicius, *In Cat.* 97, 14ff.

This interpretation of 1^a 24–25 has a further advantage. We no longer need to assume that the definition is circular because of the second occurrence of 'in' in the definiens. The 'in' in the definiens does not do any work, as we can see from the fact that we can also formulate our definition thus:

(D) x is in something as its subject, if there is a subject y such that
    (i) x is not a part of y, and
    (ii) x cannot exist independently of y

If we adopt this interpretation of 1^a 24–25, there is no longer any need, on the basis of the text, to assume that individual properties are peculiar to the individual whose properties they are. Furthermore, it is clear that individual properties also are not peculiar to the individuals whose properties they are; they are shared, at least, by the genera and species of the individuals. And nothing prevents individual properties from having a multitude of individual subjects. What is ruled out is that they should have a multitude of subjects which they are said of.

Moreover, the notion that individual properties are peculiar to their bearers seems itself an unsatisfactory one. It may be that people are struck by the thought that properties can occur in infinitely many variations so that, strictly speaking, it is never, say, the same illness that two different people have. And it may be that certain forms of empiricism rely on the idea that no schema of concept formation, however refined, can do justice to this infinite variability, rather, what is needed is experience and familiarity with individual cases. However, even if one wants to regard matters in this way, the result, at best, is that it is highly unlikely that the same property occur in two objects; but the standard interpretation requires not that it merely be highly unlikely but that it is impossible that individual properties ever occur in more than one object. Yet, the only way to ensure this is by assuming that properties are individuated by their bearers, that Socrates' health is the particular health it is, because it is Socrates' health and not anyone else's.

Such a view strikes me as wholly unsatisfactory. Its plausibility derives, it seems, merely from a special use of property-terms. Without question, it is my negligence, not someone else's, which caused the accident; no amount of philosophical argument will convince the police that negligence is something general and has nothing to do with me in particular. It is Plato's illness that causes his family concern, however much empathy they may feel toward others who have the same illness. The plausibility that the view in question derives from examples like these, however, evaporates as soon as one sees that the property-terms in these examples refer not to properties but to nominalizations of sentences in which the subject is the bearer of the property; and this creates the impression that the property-term, in these cases, is referring to some property uniquely possessed by the individual. It is the fact that I was negligent that explains why the accident occurred; it is the fact that Plato is ill in this way that causes his family concern. The assumption, then, that there are individual properties that are individuated by their bearers, is by no means as obvious or natural as its proponents would have us believe. Certainly it is not just a matter of common sense to suppose that there are such individual properties and to assume that they are what Aristotle has in mind when *he* speaks of individual properties. On the contrary, common sense, history, and the text itself seem to tell against this interpretation.

Summarizing this part of our investigation, we can say that, in the *Categories*, Aristotle wishes to maintain two distinctions, (i) that between objects and properties, which had been neglected by his predecessors and which he wishes to emphasize, and (ii) the Platonic distinction between general and particular. While it might have seemed natural to ground the notion of an individual in the notion of a thing or object, Aristotle grounds it in the notion of a particular. Thus, he ends up with non-substantial individuals and, indeed, his peculiarly weak notion of an individual; this strikes us as all the more strange, since we are inclined to ground our notion of an individual in that of an object. Individuals, in the *Categories*, are the parts into which a genus ultimately can be divided (where parts are to be contrued as subjective parts.) In this sense of 'part', the individuals themselves have no parts and are indivisible and thus are called 'individuals'.

II. Individual Substances in the *Metaphysics*

Aristotle seems to have given up using 'individual' in the sense discussed. We find the term employed systematically only in the *Categories*, the *Topics*, and in *Metaphysics*, B and I; it does not appear at all in the central books of the *Metaphysics*. We can, though, easily explain this. In the *Metaphysics*, Aristotle denies that there are genera or species, that is, he denies that universals really exist (cf. Z13). Yet, if there are no genera and species, individuals no longer can be taken to be the ultimate, indivisible parts of genera.

Though Aristotle denies the existence of universals, he does not assume that only individual objects really exist. He continues to maintain that properties exist. This has a strange consequence for the notion of an individual object which Aristotle arrives at in the *Metaphysics*. He continues to hold (cf., especially Z3) as he had in the *Categories,* that objects can be called substances because they underlie everything else that exists in such a way that everything else owes its existence to them. Illness, for example, exists only insofar as there are objects that are ill. However, while Aristotle had proceeded in the *Categories* as if the idea, that substances underlie everything else, were quite unproblematic, in the *Metaphysics,* he begins to draw out some implications of this notion for what is actually to count as an object or substance. As we can see from *Met.* Z3, he considers whether the substance that underlies everything else is the matter or the form; in the *Categories,* he had still spoken as if substances were the concrete particulars of ordinary experience: tables, horses, trees, and human beings. We must ask, why is it that Aristotle is no longer satisfied with the answer of the *Categories?*

He now sees that it cannot be the ordinary objects of experience that underlie the properties, if there are to be properties in addition to the objects; for the ordinary objects of experience are the objects together with their properties — an ordinary object has a certain size, weight, temperature, color, and other attributes of this kind. So, if we ask what is it that underlies all these properties and makes them the properties of a *single* object, we cannot answer: just the object. For the object, as ordinarily understood, already is the object together with all its qualities; what we, however, are looking for is that which underlies these qualities. Thus we can see why Aristotle now considers answers like "the form" or "the matter" when considering the question, what actually is the underlying substance.

An adequate answer to this question will need to satisfy at least these conditions: the substance must be the sort of thing that will allow us to understand why the object, whose substance it is, has the properties it has. Since an object can change its properties but still remain the same object, the substance should be the sort of thing that will enable us to see if the object, whose substance it is, is the same object despite any changes it may have undergone. Let us call the history of the changes an object has undergone, the history of the object; we shall want the substance of an object to be such that with reference to it we can explain how, despite all the changes, it is the history of *one* object. We also think an object might have had a history quite different from the one it actually had yet have been the same object; this, too, is to be explained in terms of substance. Furthermore, the substance must be an individual, since we are looking for the real individuals in the category of substance which are to explain the individuality of ordinary individual objects. Finally, there must be some sort of asymmetry between substances and properties, on the basis of which we can say of properties and everything else that exists that they depend on substances for their existence, but that substances do not, in any way, depend on properties for their existence. These are the requirements Aristotle lays down in the *Metaphysics*, when he says a substance must be a subject (hypokeimenon), "a this" (tode ti), and an independently existing entity (chōriston).

According to Aristotle, the *form* satisfies these requirements and thus is the substance. This, at least, is strongly suggested by those passages in *Met.* Z when Aristotle speaks of the form as substance and contrasts it with the derivative, composite substance (1037^a 29–30; 1037^a 25–26). At 1040^b 23–24, he seems to distinguish between two uses of 'substance', one picking out the form, the other the object having this form. At 1032^b 1–2, Aristotle says that, by form, he means primary substance, that is, what is substance first of all. In two passages (1037^a 28; 1037^ab 1), at least, he speaks as if the form were the primary substance. At 1037^a 5, he says that in the case of man, the soul, i.e., the form of man, is the primary substance. At 1037^b 3ff., he defines primary substance in such a way that forms satisfy the definition, but not composites of form and matter, much less ordinary objects. And at the very end of Book Z, Aristotle concludes that it is the *nature* of an object, that is, the form of a natural object, which is the substance. Aristotle, thus, does indeed seem to want to answer the question of *Met.* Z.1, 1028^b4 — what is substance? — by saying it is primarily the form.

How the form is going to satisfy all the conditions for substancehood laid down earlier is far from clear, though it is clear that Aristotle thinks it does satisfy these conditions. For example, it is clear that he thinks that the form is "a this" (*Met.* 1017^b 25; 1042^a 29; 1049^a 28–29; *De gen. et corr.* 318^b 32). Part of what Aristotle means when he says something is "a this" is just that it is an individual. That Aristotle really does think that the form of an object is an individual and not something general which all objects of the same kind share, we can see not only from the fact that he says the form is "a this" but also from the fact that he thinks the form's existence is temporally limited (cf. *Met.* 1039^b 24–26, 1070^a 22ff.). In at least one passage, Aristotle explicitly says that different things of the same kind each have their own form (*Met.* 1071^a 27–29; cf. 1071^a 21ff.; 1071^a 36-^{b}1). What we are interested in, for present purposes, however, is only to understand how Aristotle could think that an individual substance really is a form. In connection with this, it will be of some use to discuss, at least briefly, Aristotle's notion of a form.

Aristotle thinks objects have a function. We can readily understand what he means in the case of artifacts: they are constructed the way they are constructed to fulfill a certain task or to exhibit a certain kind of behavior. Fulfilling this task or exhibiting this behavior is their function; and if they do exhibit this behavior, we say they are functioning. Aristotle, like Plato before him, extends the notion of function to natural objects, especially to living things. If a living thing is functioning, it will behave in a certain, characteristic way; to behave in this way is its function.

In addition, Aristotle thinks that the capacity of an object to behave in this characteristic way depends on its organization, structure, and disposition, indeed, he thinks that it is just this disposition or organization that enables the object to behave the way it does. Now, for Aristotle, the form is this disposition or organization, while the matter is what is thus disposed or organized.

How could the form, so construed, satisfy the requirements laid down for being a substance? An important requirement was that the substance was to explain why, despite all the changes an object had undergone, it still is the same object. How the form could satisfy this requirement, we can see from the ancient example, expanded by Hobbes, of Theseus' ships, *Theoris,* which for centuries has been sent to Delos on an annual pilgrimage and whose return Socrates, in the *Phaedo,* must await before he may drink the poison.

Over the years, the ship is repaired, plank by plank, always, however, according to the original plan. Now, let us suppose there is a shipwright who keeps the old planks. After all the old planks have been replaced in *Theoris,* he puts them together again according to the original plan and thus has a second ship. It seems obvious to me that this ship, even though it is constructed from all the old planks and according to the original plan, is not the old ship, *Theoris,* but a new ship; the ship constructed from the new planks is, in fact, the old ship. No insurance company, presented with a policy written for *Theoris,,* would pay for damages suffered if the ship constructed from the old planks had been shipwrecked. Moreover, this would be so even if the planks had been changed all at once, not over many years; it would be even so if the ship constructed from the new planks were constructed according to a modified plan so that, perhaps, only the ship constructed from the old planks was constructed according to the original plan.

What makes for the identity of the repaired ship with the original ship is obviously a certain continuity. This is not the continuity of matter, or of properties, but the continuity of the organization of changing matter, an organization which enables the object to function as a ship, to exhibit the behavior of a ship. An object, then, exists as the object it is only as long as its capacity for functioning, i.e., for behaving in the way characteristic of it, has not been irretrievably lost.

This notion of the continuity of organization is even clearer if we consider living things rather than artifacts. It is presumably no accident that, in the *Metaphysics* Aristotle talks as if living things really are substances rather than artifacts. In the case of a living thing, its organization is such as to enable it to have a good chance of continuing to function for some time and so to stay in existence; such an organization will allow the living thing to change, for example, its place, to take in food or to evade an enemy, or adjust its temperature to the temperature of the environment.

The continuity of the organization, then, is part of the very notion of the organization characteristic of living things. In the case of living things, it is also clearer that this continuity of organization or capacity for functioning constitutes the identity of the thing over time. It is when a living thing has lost this capacity that we say it is no longer alive or no longer exists. All other changes in the thing — changes of matter or changes of properties — bear on the identity of the thing only to the extent that they influence its capacity for functioning. Since this capacity, in the case of living things, is the capacity for leading a certain kind of life, Aristotle calls this capacity, organization, or form, the "soul."

The substance is not only supposed to account for the identity of an individual object; it itself is supposed to be an individual. Against the view that the form or the organization of an object is an individual, it will be objected that, in the case of the two ships, for example, it would be much more natural to say that we have two individuals, say, *Theoris* and *Theoris II*, which have the *same* organization since they are built according to the same plan; this organization, then, is something general, since it can be realized in many objects. And there is no need to assume that in addition to this organization there also is an individual organization, peculiar to each ship. Likewise, then, with living things: we have many individuals, organized in the same way, but there is no reason to posit more than one, general form of organization common to them all. There might be any number of objects organized in the same way at the same time; and so, just as when several objects have, say, the same temperature, we feel no inclination to say that, in addition to this temperature, there are individual temperatures which each of them has (and these are completely alike), so too we should not feel inclined to suppose that, if several objects are of the same kind, in addition to one general form of being organized as this kind of thing, there are individual ways of being organized which each of them has. Looking at matters this way will lead one to the view that substantial forms, i.e., the forms of objects, are universals; that means that all living creatures of a certain kind, say, men, have one and the same soul.

Adopting this line presupposes, however, that the way in which an object has a form is relevantly similar to the way in which it has a temperature. One would need to assume that there is *one* object over some period of time that has a particular organization over this period of time just as it has a particular temperature over this period. This assumption, however, is false, if we want to hold — and this is what the example of *Theoris* suggested to us — that this *one* object, organized in a particular way over a period of time, in a certain sense, does not really exist, because, what is organized in this way, the matter, is continually changing or, at least, could be changing. We only have an individual object in virtue of the continuity of a particular organization; it is only the identity of this organization that makes the object the individual it is. Thus, if several objects have the same temperature or size, we are able to say that it is *one* size or temperature they have, because these objects are the objects they are quite independently of whether they have this particular size or temperature. But we cannot say there is only *one* form or organization which several objects of the same kind have, since these objects only are the objects they are because each has its own, individual organization.

If forms are individuals, the question arises, in what sense are they individuals. A condition that forms will need to satisfy, if they are to be individuals, is that forms of different objects of the same kind must be distinguishable and identifiable. That seems to involve certain problems. We certainly cannot individuate forms on the basis of the objects whose forms they are; for the objects themselves are to be individuated by the forms. Putting the matter differently, Socrates' soul is not Socrates' soul because it is the soul of Socrates, rather, Socrates is Socrates because of the soul he has. What, then, distinguishes Socrates' soul from Plato's soul?

This difficulty arises for the following reason. On the one hand, forms are supposed to be things like ways of being organized, dispositions, or capacities. Yet, it seems as if dispositions or capacities quite generally are individuated in such a way that any particular disposition or capacity is the sort of thing that can be had by several things. However detailed a specification of a capacity we come up with, it always seems to be such that more than one thing could have this capacity. One the other hand, the form is supposed to be an object, a substance, and, as such, not shared by several objects. Thus, in individuating a form, we shall need to go beyond a specification of a disposition or capacity, if we are to have an individual substance.

I am not at all certain that this difficulty results merely from our line of interpretation. It seems, rather, to arise whenever we consider the question, just what is it that makes an object precisely the object it is rather than another one of the same kind. My copy of a book, for example, is this copy and not the one borrowed from the library, because it is the one I purchased so many years ago in such and such a store, and because there is a continuous history linking the book purchased then with the one I now have. This history could be traced back to before the time of my purchase, say if all copies were numbered at the printing press, and mine were copy 100. Still, it is clear that this copy would have been the very same copy even if I had not purchased it then but the library had, and I was now borrowing it. If we do not want to posit anything which this copy has that makes it the copy it is and not another one, we shall need in some sense to go beyond the object to individuate it. One needs to point to some episode of its history or even pre-history, which, however, is not essential to its identity, since it still could have been the same copy even if its history had been quite different.

These considerations suggest that it is perhaps not problematic to go beyond the form in individuating it. Even if all the forms of a given kind were completely alike, we could distinguish between them on the basis of their histories. Now, of course, we are faced with a whole new set of difficulties. We need to ask in what sense can we speak of the history of a form. It is of no use that the history of the form is in a certain respect just the history of the object having this form, since we want to explain the identity of the object in terms of that of the form and not vice-versa. A detailed discussion of this difficulty would require, among other things, consideration of Aristotle's views in the *De Anima*. We would then see that the forms at least of ensouled things are not subject to change, at any rate, not in the sense in which Aristotle's natural philosophy approaches changeable objects, though they are principles of change and can have a very rich history, simply because the characteristic capacities of a living thing—which are what constitutes the soul, i.e., the form—can at various times be exercised or not exercised. If one sees something, it is not strictly speaking the soul which is undergoing some change but the living organism; nevertheless, the soul is a different soul, if one sees or has seen something.

For our present purposes, though, it should be sufficient to suppose that a form can have a history to the extent that it can be realized in different matter at different times. This seems clear enough in the case of living things; if it seems problematic in the case of artifacts or works of art, we can say that even in these cases the constitution of the matter is subject to at least minimal changes, induced, say, by wear.

We would thus be able to distinguish between various forms of the same kind on the basis of their histories, and between various forms of the same kind at a given moment, on the basis of the present stages of their histories—for example, we can say this form is realized in this matter, that one in that matter. This is possible only because, though Aristotelian matter can be identified only by means of the form of an object and hence be identified only with respect to a form, this form need not be the form of the matter at the time of its identificaiton; for example, the gold of this statue can be identified as the gold of this statue but also as the gold of that crown which was melted down. Thus, we can distinguish forms on the basis of matter without getting involved in the circle that this matter, in turn, can be distinguished only on the basis of the objects and hence the forms.

This interpretation on which individual substances are primarily substantial forms of objects leads to other difficulties as well. Yet not all of these difficulties tell against our interpretation. Aristotle himself seems to grapple with some of them. A problem, for example, is that Aristotle frequently talks as if knowledge, strictly speaking, were knowledge of the general or universal and as if knowing something were knowing its form or essence. But this seems to commit him to the view that the form of an object is something general, that the only thing that can be known, in the case of an object, is its form, because only it is universal, while the matter is what is peculiar to the object. However, *Met.* B 6, 1003ᵃ 13–14 and the relevant parallel passages show that Aristotle sees a problem here precisely because, on the one hand, he is inclined to think that the form, as the principle of substance, is individual, while, on the other, he does not want to say that there is no knowledge of that which strictly speaking is real, i.e., the form. This seems to explain why Aristotle, when he comes to *Met.* M 10, where he tries to solve this aporia, argues that knowledge is knowledge of the particular and only potentially also knowledge of the general.

This interpretation does not only lead to difficulties; it also helps shed some light on some old problems, e.g., the problem how Aristotle can claim (*Met.* E 1, 1026ᵃ 28–32) that theology also includes ontology, that *metaphysica specialis* and *metaphysica generalis* are the same discipline. Obviously, part of the explanation of this identification will involve explaining that a theory of substance will also be a theory of all being as such—however problematic that may be in all its details. But, then, the second part of the explanation will involve explaining why the theory of a certain kind of substances, namely, those studied by theology, will also be a theory of substance in general and thus also of being in general. This second part of the explanation—for which there is little direct textual support—could proceed from the fact that the predicate 'substance' does not have a single use either, just like the predicate 'being.' Though the use of 'substance' may seem relatively simple—especially compared to 'being'—closer analysis shows that here, too, there are several uses. That Aristotle thinks there are several uses of 'substance' seems evident from *Met.* Z. He arrives at a conception of substance on which primarily natural objects are substances (1041ᵇ 28–30), while artifacts count as substances as best in some extended sense of substance. In addition, *Met.* Z 3 and *Met.* A and H quite generally seem to allow for three different uses of substance even in the case of natural substances, uses that are systematically related: for the matter, the form, and the composite can be called "substance." However, of these uses, the one for forms is primary and the others are explained in terms of it.

In *Met.* Z there are various indications that we are dealing here with material substances, because these are known to us, but that our actual interest is in immaterial substances insofar as we want to know what substance is (cf. *Met.* 1029ᵇ 3–10, transposing with Jaeger; 1037ᵃ 10ff.; 1041ᵃ 7–9). If we consider that immaterial substances are pure forms and that they do not, for example, give rise to the problems about individuation discussed above, it seems reasonable to suppose that Aristotle could have thought that the idea of substance applies primarily to pure substantial forms, like God, then to substantial forms of natural objects, then to these objects and to their matter, insofar as it is potentially these objects, and only last to artifacts. Pursuing this line of thought will be the topic of another chapter.

5

Substance in
Aristotle's *Metaphysics*

Aristotle's ontology is very generous.[1] It contains objects like trees and lions.
But it also contains qualities, like colors, and quantities, like sizes, and all the
kinds of items Aristotle distinguishes according to his so-called categories. But,
of course, Aristotle does not assume that objects, qualities, quantities, and the
rest exist side by side, separately from each other. He thinks that qualities and
quantities exist only as the qualities and quantities of objects, that there are qualities and quantities only insofar as there are objects that are thus qualified or
quantified.

In taking this view Aristotle is making some rather substantial assumptions.
He assumes that the existence of properties[2] does not just amount to the existence of objects that have these properties, but, rather, that the existence of objects that have properties presupposes the existence both of objects and of
properties. Moreover, Aristotle makes a clear distinction between objects and
properties, and he regards this distinction as basic, i.e., he regards objects and
the different kinds of properties as basic ingredients of the world that cannot be
reduced to each other. His predecessors had had a tendency to blur the distinction, e.g., by treating qualities as somehow substantial and as thus constituting
objects, or by treating objects as insubstantial and as constituted, in some way
or another, by qualities. Furthermore, Aristotle assumes that, though both objects and properties are basic and irreducible to each other, there, nevertheless,
is an ontological dependence between them, that the existence of properties has
to be understood in terms of the existence of objects, rather than the other way
round. All these assumptions would need a good deal of discussion. In particular, it would be important to discuss the question whether it was not Aristotle
who first took the notion of an object sufficiently seriously and who, as a result
of this, was able to make the clear distinction between objects and properties,
which now seems so trivial to us that we have difficulty understanding how some
of the Presocratics and some of the Hippocratic doctors, but also even later many

Hellenistic philosophers and physicians, could try to reconstruct the world from properties like, e.g., warmth and cold, dryness and wetness. What the following remarks will be concerned with, though, are not these assumptions, but the way Aristotle tries to work them out in his theory. In particular, I shall try to show how Aristotle's notion of a substance underwent a considerable change when Aristotle, in the *Metaphysics,* tried to get clearer about the way in which properties ontologically depend on objects.

The first time, at least in the extant corpus, that Aristotle approaches this problem is in the *Categories.* There Aristotle distinguishes between objects and properties and explains how properties depend for their being on particular objects as their ultimate subjects. He calls objects "ousiai", i.e., by the term Plato had used to refer to the forms, because only they truly exist or because they exist in their own right and everything else that exists depends for its existence on them. In calling objects "ousiai," Aristotle claims for objects the central place in ontology that Plato had claimed for forms. Moreover, he can refer to them this way because he takes the view that objects exist in their own right and that all other things, i.e., the properties, depend for their being on these objects. Traditionally "ousia" has been rendered by "substance." The reason for this is that, on the view Aristotle puts forth in the *Categories,* properties depend for their being on objects in that objects are their ultimate subjects, they are what ultimately underlies everything else. Indeed, objects in the *Categories* are characterized by the very fact that they are the ultimate subjects which underlie everything, whereas there is nothing that underlies them as their subject. It is because of this characterization that the rendering "substance" seems appropriate.

The *Categories* are also very specific about the sense in which substances are the underlying subjects (hypokeimena). According to the *Categories,* something has something as its subject if it is predicated of it. It can be predicated of it as its subject in either of two ways: if it is in it, or inheres in it, as its subject, or if it is predicated of it as its subject in a narrow technical sense of "predication." The two ways roughly correspond to essential and accidental predication. Thus, something has something as its underlying subject if it is truly predicated of it. Now the argument of the *Categories* is that for any item in our ontology we can ask what its subject is. If it does not have a subject in either of the two ways, it itself is a particular object. If it does have a subject, either this subject is a particular object or it is not. If it is not, we can in turn ask of that subject what its subject is; and either this further subject is a particular object, or it is not. And so on, until ultimately we arrive at a subject that in turn has no further subject and thus is a particular object. So it is argued that any series of subjects, from whichever item in the ontology we start, ends with a particular object. It is in this sense that particular objects are the ultimate underlying subjects in the *Categories.*

The fact that particular objects invariably are the ultimate subjects seems to give them their status as ousiai in the following way. They must be assumed to exist in their own right, but everything else exists because it is involved in some truth about a particular object or because it is involved in some truth about something that is involved in some truth about a particular object, etc. It is in this way that properties depend on objects for their being.

When in the *Metaphysics* Aristotle tries to get clearer about the notion of substance, he starts his detailed discussion by first considering the suggestion he had followed in the *Categories,* namely, that substances are the ultimate subjects underlying everything else. But whereas in the *Categories* he had assumed that concrete particular objects play the role of ultimate subjects and hence of substances, Aristotle now clearly thinks that the assumption that substances are the ultimate subjects does not yet settle the question of what is going to count as a substance. For he now lists as candidates for substancehood that could play the role of ultimate subjects matter, form, and the composite of both (Z 3, 1029^a 2ff.).

The fact that Aristotle in *Met.* Z 3 is considering the suggestion he had followed in the *Categories,* namely, that substances are the ultimate subjects, is somewhat obscured by the fact that translations of the *Metaphysics* tend to render "hypokeimenon" by "substrate," rather than by "subject." But it should be clear from the characterization of the hypokeimenon in 1028^b 36ff. that Aristotle is talking here about subjects of predication, and it should be clear from 1029^a 8ff. that Aristotle is considering the notion of the *Categories* of substances as the ultimate subjects of predications.

Given that, we have to wonder why Aristotle now is considering matter, form, and the composite of both as possible ultimate subjects of predication. For none of these is identical with the particular objects of the *Categories*. This goes without saying for matter and form. But it also seems to be true for the composite of matter and form. It is true that traditionally the composite has been identified with the concrete, particular object. But the concrete, particular object, as we are familiar with it, actually is a composite not just of matter and form, but also of a large number of accidents; it is an object of a certain size, weight, color, and the like, i.e., a complex of entities. Hence, one should not assume without further argument that the composite of matter and form is to be identified without qualification with the concrete particular.

The reason why Aristotle now is considering matter, form, and the composite, rather than the concrete, particular object, as possible ultimate subjects of predication seems to be the following. Aristotle had assumed in the *Categories,* and still does assume in the *Metaphysics,* that a statement like "Socrates is healthy" introduces two entities, Socrates and health. But he now asks the question that he had not faced in the *Categories*: what is the subject of health, if health is an entity distinct from its subject, what in the bundle or cluster of entities that constitutes Socrates is the thing itself as opposed to the properties like health which it underlies? That this is what Aristotle has in mind is borne out by the way he argues in 1029^a 10ff. that matter is the most straightforward candidate for the title of the ultimate subject. For he argues that if we strip a particular object of all of its properties, nothing but matter will be left. So obviously he is looking for that element in a concrete particular object which underlies its properties, rather than for the concrete particular object itself.

Given this approach, it is easy to see why the composite of matter and form would be an ideal candidate for the title of the ultimate subject of all non-substantial entities. It is just that part in a bundle of entities which is a concrete object which is opposed to the non-substantial properties of the object, and since all non-substantial entities are predicated (or introduced by predicates) of objects, the composites will be the ultimate subjects of everything else in the ontology.

It is somewhat more difficult to see how matter could be the ultimate subject. 1029^a 20–23 suggests that all predicates can be construed as being directly predicates of some matter. But we have to keep in mind that the notion of a primary or ultimate subject (1029^a 1ff.) does not imply as such that the ultimate subjects are themselves directly the subjects of everything else. And, in fact, 1029^a 23–24 suggests that matter is the ultimate subject by being the subject of the substance in question which, in turn, is the subject of the non-substantial entities. All this raises considerable problems which I shall leave aside, though, since Aristotle himself here does not pursue the issue further because he thinks that matter for certain other reasons is not a good candidate for substancehood anyway.

Most puzzling, in any case, is his suggestion that there is a way in which substantial forms might be construed as the ultimate subjects and, hence, as the real things as opposed to mere properties of things. Bonitz thought that this suggestion was a mere slip on Aristotle's part, but it is clear from the introductory chapter of H (H 1042 1^a 28ff.) that it is Aristotle's considered view that in some way the form is the ultimate subject and hence substance. The view is puzzling in various ways. To start with, Aristotle does not tell us how statements are to be construed in such a way that it is forms that turn out to be the ultimate subjects.

Perhaps he thinks that statements about objects can be regarded as statements about forms insofar as they are either statements primarily about the form and only secondarily, derivatively, about the object, anyway, or insofar as they are statements about the form as it is embodied in matter. Thus, the truth that Socrates is an animal would be a truth about the form straightforwardly, whereas the truth that Socrates is healthy would be a truth about the form to the effect that the form constitutes a composite that is healthy.

But such a construal seems to be highly artificial, and, hence, we must assume either that Aristotle was driven to it because he had other reasons to think that forms are substances, but nevertheless wanted to retain the *Categories*' notion of a substance as an ultimate subject, or that there is a way of looking at the matter which makes it intuitively plausible to regard forms as the ultimate subjects. The following seems to me to be such a way of looking at things.

It is characteristic of ZHΘ that Aristotle tends to, or in fact does, restrict substances to natural objects (Z 7, 1032^a 19; Z 8, 1034^a 4; Z 17, 1041^b 28-30; H 3, 1043^b 21-22). It is not entirely clear whether this is supposed to restrict substances to animate things, but these certainly are paradigms of natural objects. So let us first consider them. In their case the form is the soul. Let us regard this soul as the organization of an object, or its disposition to behave or to lead the kind of life characteristic of that kind of object. The organization of the object is such as to have a good chance to survive changes in the environment, or such that the object has a good chance to keep functioning for some time and so to stay in existence. This will involve the thing's changing, e.g., its place to take in food or to evade an enemy, or its temperature in case of an inflammation. It also involves exchange of the matter so disposed.

So what has to stay the same as long as a particular animate object exists is just that organization or disposition to behave in a way characteristic of the kind. There always has also to be some matter that is thus organized, but it does not have to be the same matter. Similarly, there always have to be all sorts of properties, a certain temperature, weight, size, shape. In fact, the properties will ordinarily come within rather narrow ranges. For if we heat up an animate object, there will be a point at which it can no longer adjust to the change and the characteristic disposition will be destroyed. But though the object must always have a certain weight, size, temperature, and though it has to have these within certain narrow limits, there is no weight, size, temperature, etc. which it has to have all the time. If we, then, analyze an ordinary physical object into matter, form, and properties, the only item in the case of animate objects that has to stay the same as long as we can talk about the same thing is, on this account, the form. And this may give some plausibility to the assumption that it is really the form which is the thing we are talking about when we at different times say different things about an object.

As an example of an artifact let us consider Theseus' ship—let us call it *Theoris*—which is repaired again and again until all the original planks have been replaced by new ones. But a craftsman has kept the old planks. He now fits them together according to the original plan so that we have a second ship built according to the same specificiations as the other ship. Still, it is clear that it is the ship with the new planks which is the old ship, i.e., *Theoris I,* and that it is the ship with the old planks which is the new ship, i.e., *Theoris II,* though its planks and its plan are identical with the planks and the plan of the original ship, whereas the other ship has new planks.

Our theory will try to explain this in the following way: *Theoris I,* the ship with the new planks, is identical with the original ship because there was one disposition which was first the disposition of the original planks, then the disposition of a slightly different set of planks, and, finally, in a history that could be traced back step by step, the disposition of the set of new planks. The disposition of *Theoris II,* on the other hand, though it is a disposition of the original set of planks, and though the ship is built according to the same specifications, does not have that history and hence is not the disposition of the original ship.

It will be objected that, if the two ships are faithfully built according to the same specifications, they will have just one and the same disposition. There will be over a period of time some one thing, namely the *Theoris I,* which has that disposition and there will be, for an overlapping period of time, another thing, namely *Theoris II,* which has the very same disposition. But according to our theory, though it is true that as long as each ship is in existence there is always something which is thus disposed, namely the material, it is *not* necessary that that which is thus disposed be the same throughout the time of the ship's existence. Hence, the identity of what is thus disposed is not a sufficient condition for the identity of the ship; neither is it a necessary condition, as we can see from the case of the old ship with the new planks. And since we want to analyze the ship into a disposition and what is thus disposed, and since one of the two factors is to account for the identity of the ship, it has to be the disposition. And, hence, we have to distinguish the disposition of the two ships, though their specification may be exactly the same.

If we look at objects in this way, it is natural to look at the form as the centerpiece of the cluster of entities that constitute the concrete object. And so it is no longer counterintuitive to regard all truths about an object as ultimately truths about its form. They in some sense just reveal the particular way a form is realized.

But the claim that forms are the ultimate subjects is puzzling in yet another way. Traditionally it has been assumed that forms are universal. But it is of the very nature of ultimate subjects that they cannot be predicated and, hence, cannot be universal. Therefore, if substantial forms are the ultimate subjects, they must be particular. A moment's reflection, though, shows that this is a view that Aristotle is committed to anyway. For in Z 13 he argues at length that no universal can be a substance. But since he also wants forms to be substances, he has to deny that forms are universal. And, in fact, we do find him claiming that the form of a particular object is peculiar to that object, just as its matter is; Socrates' form, i.e., his soul, is different from Plato's form, i.e., Plato's soul (*Met.* Δ 1, 1071^a 24–29). We even find Aristotle claiming that the form is a particular this (a tode ti; 8, 1017^b 25; H I, 1042^a 29; Δ 7, 1049^a 28–29; *De gen. et corr.* 318^b 32). And, of course, he has to claim that a form is a particular this, if he wants forms to be substances, since he assumes that a substance has to be a particular this. It was for this reason that Aristotle rejected the claim of matter to be substance; matter is only potentially a particular this.

But though Aristotle clearly is committed to the view that forms are particular and no less clearly actually espouses the view that they are particular, we have to ask how he can assume that they are particular. For it would seem that all things of the same kind have the same form or are the same in form. But the answer to this is that things of the same kind have the same form only in the sense that for things of the same kind the specification of their form is exactly the same (1071^a 29). It is a basic nontrivial fact about the world that things come with forms that are exactly alike, and not just sufficiently similar to class them together in one kind. The reality of kinds amounts to no more than this: that the specification of the form of particular objects turns out to be exactly the same for a variety of objects. But for this to be true, there is no need for a universal form or a universal kind, either a species or a genus. And, in fact, the import of Z 13 seems to be that there are no substantial genera or species in the ontology of the *Metaphysics*. As universals they cannot be substances, and since they do not fall under any of the other categories either, they do not have any status in the ontology. Sometimes it seems to be thought that substantial genera and species could be regarded as qualities. But this cannot be Aristotle's view. For on Aristotle's view qualities are those things we refer to when we say what something is like. But even in the *Metaphysics* Aristotle takes the view that in referring to the species or the genus of something we say what it is, rather than what it is like.

Substantial forms, then, as ultimate subjects and as substances are particular. But we may still ask how they manage to be particular, given that their specification, down to the smallest detail, is exactly the same for all things of the same kind. To answer this question, though, we have to get clearer about what it is that is asked. If the question is how do we manage to distinguish particular forms at one time, the answer is simple: they differ from each other by being realized in different matter (cf. 1034^a 6–8; 1016^b 33) and by being the ultimate subjects of different properties. If the question is how do we reidentify a particular form at a later point in time, the answer is: it can be identified through time by its continuous history of being realized now in this and now in that matter, of now being the subject of these and then being the subject of those properties. But if it should be demanded that there be something about the form in and by itself which distinguishes it from other forms of the same kind, the answer is that there is no such distinguishing mark and that there is no need for one. It just is not the case that individuals are the individuals they are by virtue of some intrinsic essential distinguishing mark.

It turns out, then, that Aristotle in the search for what it is that is underlying the non-substantial properties of objects considers the form of an object as a serious candidate.

But it also seems to be the candidate he actually settles on. And so we have to see why he gives form preference over the two other candidates, matter and the composite. As we have already seen, Aristotle thinks that matter does not satisfy certain other conditions substances have to fulfill; it is, e.g., not actually, but only potentially a particular thing, and thus only potentially a substance. The composite, on the other hand, cannot be ruled out on the same grounds. And, in fact, Aristotle accepts its claim to be substance, but insists that it is substance only derivatively, that forms are the primary substances (1032^b 1ff.; cf. 1037^a 5; 1037^a 28; 1037^b 1).

It is easy to see why Aristotle thinks that forms are prior to composites (1029^a 5ff.; 1037^b 3): they are presupposed by the composites. But this in itself is not yet sufficient to think that they are prior as substances. The reason for this would seem to be that Aristotle thinks that substances are not as such composite. There are substances that are pure forms as, e.g., the unmoved mover. And it is clear from Z 3, 1029^b 3ff. and Z 11, 1037^a 10ff. (cf. also Z 17, 1041^a 7ff.) that Aristotle thinks that the discussion of composite substances in Z H is only preliminary to the discussion of separate substances. We start by considering composite substances because they are better known to us, we are familiar with them, and they are generally agreed to be substances. But what is better known by nature are the pure forms. Aristotle's remarks suggest that we shall have a full understanding of what substances are only if we understand the way in which pure forms are substances. This, in turn, suggests that he thinks that there is a primary use of "substance" in which "substance" applies to forms. Particularly clear cases of substance in this first use of "substance" are pure forms or separate substances. It is for this reason that composite substances are substances only secondarily.

It would seem, then, that there are two main reasons why the concrete, particular substances of the *Categories* in the *Metaphysics* get replaced by substantial forms as the primary substances: (i) Aristotle now is concerned with the question what is the real subject in itself as opposed to its properties; (ii) Aristotle now not only has developed his own theory of forms, but also has come to assume separate substantial forms which, on his view, are paradigms of substances, but which are not substances in the same way as the composites or the concrete particular objects are.

That substantial forms in the *Metaphysics* play the role of primary substances which in the *Categories* has been played by particular objects is obscured by a line of interpretation that one finds, e.g., in Ross (Aristotle, p. 166; 172) and S. Mansion (Melanges Merlan, p. 76). According to this interpretation, the question what is to count as a substance is already settled at the beginning of *Met.* Z; what, on this interpretation, Aristotle is concerned with is Z 3ff., rather, is the further question "what is the essence or substance of substances?", and "the substantial form" is supposed to be an answer to this further question. But this way of looking at what Aristotle says in the *Metaphysics* cannot be right. For in Z 3 Aristotle seems to set out to answer the very question raised in Z 1, "what is substance?". There is no suggestion that this question has already been an-

swered in favor of particular objects, and that we are now considering the further question "what is the substance of particular substances?" It, rather, seems
that Aristotle throughout Z is considering one and the same question "What do
we mean by 'substance' when we distinguish substances from items in other categories?", and he seems to be considering various candidiates for that one title.
If, then, Aristotle in the last chapter of Z (1041^b 30), where he makes a fresh
start at answering this question, again suggests that it is the nature or form of
a thing which is the substance we are looking for, we have to assume that this
is supposed to be his answer to the question of Z1: "What is substance?". When
in H 1 he again outlines the problem, he clearly puts the matter in such a way
that physical objects and the essences of objects, universals and ultimate subjects, were parallel candidates for the one title of substance (1042^a 3–15). Therefore, it should be clear that Aristotle now does mean to say that substantial
forms, rather than particular objects, are substances in the primary sense.

On the theory of *Metaphysics,* then, substantial forms rather than concrete
objects are the basic entities. Everything else that is depends on these substantial
forms for its being and for its explanation. Hence substantial forms, being basic
in this way, have a better claim to be called "ousiai" or "substances" than anything else does. Some of them are such that they are realized in objects with
properties. But this is not true of substantial forms as such. For there are immaterial forms. Properties, on the other hand, cannot exist without a form that
constitutes an object. Moreover, though certain kinds of forms do need properties for their realization, they do not need the particular properties they have.
The form of a human being needs a body of a weight within certain limits, but
it does need that particular weight. No form needs that particular weight to
be realized. But this particular weight depends for its existence on some form
as its subject. In fact, it looks as if Aristotle in the *Metaphysics* thought that the
properties, or accidental forms, of objects depended for their existence on the
very objects they are the accidental forms of, as if Socrates' color depended on
Socrates for its existence. However this may be, on the new theory it is forms
that exist in their own right, whereas properties merely constitute the way forms
of a certain kind are realized at some point of time in their existence.

Thus, a closer consideration of the way in which objects underlie the properties that depend on them for their being has led Aristotle in the *Metaphyics* to
a revision of his doctrine of substance.

6

The Unity of General and Special Metaphysics: Aristotle's Conception of Metaphysics

If one tries to get clearer about Aristotle's conception of metaphysics, one naturally turns to the treatise that by its very title promises to give us an account of Aristotle's metaphysics. Unfortunately, the title itself does not provide us with any clue. "Metaphysics" is not an Aristotelian term. It only gains some currency in late antiquity. Thus, the commentary on Isaiah attributed to St. Basil (164) speaks of those things, higher than the objects of the theory of nature, "which some call metaphysical." The earliest catalog of Aristotle's writings, the one preserved in Diogenes Laertius, does not yet contain the title "Metaphysics." Hence, it is clear that our title is the title later editors gave to the treatise. It is first attested in Nicolaus of Damascus' compendium of Aristotle's philosophy, i.e., in the first century B.C. But even these editors presumably did not mean to suggest any particular conception of the discipline by chosing this title. Probably, they were at a loss regarding a proper title for the treatise and just named it after its position in the corpus of Aristotelian writings, namely, as coming after the physical writings. It would also be a mistake to assume that the title indirectly expresses a certain conception of the discipline metaphysics by referring to its "natural" place in the order of Aristotelian writings. The place is anything but "natural." The order of the corpus follows the Academic, and then Stoic, division of philosophy into logic, physics, and ethics. And though there were subdivisions of this scheme in Hellenistic times, none made provision for a discipline metaphysics, whether called by that or another name. Not as if Hellenistic philosophers did not do any metaphyics, but they did not regard it as a separate discipline. Sometimes physics was divided into physics, more properly speaking, and theology. And since there is no natural place for the *Metaphysics* in Aristotle's corpus, a position after the physical writings must have seemed least disturbing, especially since Aristotle himself in the *Metaphysics* at times had identified the subject of the treatise as theology. Moreover, the treatise clearly belonged with the theoretical treatises, rather than with the *Organon* or the ethical writings, and hence had to come before or after the physical writings. But the basic order of the corpus is clearly didactic: we start with logic, proceed to a doctrine of the sensible world, on the basis of this move on to a doctrine of the intelligible reality underlying the sensible world, and, finally, in the spirit of Hellenistic philosophy, move to ethics as the ultimate end of all philosophical endeavor. In late antiquity it will become natural to identify the intelligible with the supra-sensible and to think of the move from the physical writings to the metaphysical treatises as the move from the doctrine of the sensible world to the doctrine of the supra-sensible world. And now the term "metaphysical" is easily understood to refer to the doctrine of supra-sensible entities, God, the ideas, the umoved movers, and or angels. But there is not sufficient reason to believe that this was what the Hellenistic editors of our text had in mind. If there is a question about why they chose the title "Ta meta ta physika," it is why did they not call the treatise "theology" or, at least, "first philosophy"? The answer to this must be that in Hellenistic philosophy one did not have much use for the notion of a first philosophy, and that the treatise did not fit the conception of theology one had, just as it does not fit our conception of theology. But that the matter is more complex we can see from the fact that Nicolaus of Damascus (p. 74 Dossaart-Lulofs) still identifies the subject of the *Metaphysics* as theology and calls it the "first science." Once we come to late antiquity, the situation has changed radically. Given the dominance of Platonism with its two-world view, its identification of the realm of forms with the Divine, and its doctrine of the ascent from the physical to the metaphysical, it became easy to see the *Metaphysics* as a theological treatise (cf. Asclepius in Met. p. 1, 18–2, 3). But this way of looking at things hardly fits into the first century B.C. Hence, we do not have sufficient reason to suppose that the title "Metaphysics" originally referred to anything more than the position of our treatise in the corpus.

To get a notion of Aristotle's conception of metaphysics, then, we cannot rely on the title, but have to turn to the treatise itself. Unfortunately, the treatise, too, does not owe its present form to Aristotle. There is good reason to believe that the treatise, as Aristotle left it, was composed only of books A, B, Γ, E, Z, H, θ, I, Λ, M, N, and that α, Δ, and K were added later. But even this underlying treatise turns out not to be of one piece. The evidence for this is abundant and well known. It will suffice here to recall that, e.g., the beginning of *Metaphysics* Z suggests a certain program in the course of which we shall deal with separate substances and the claim of ideas and mathematicals to be substances. But though we get these discussions in *Met. Λ* and *Met. M-N*, respectively, it is fairly clear that these books were not written in one piece with the beginning of *Met. Z*. They, rather, seem to be revised versions of treatises Aristotle incorporated to temporarily fulfill the need of a discussion of this sort. Once we realize this, it is also clear that to determine Aristotle's conception of metaphysics, we cannot look just at what we take to be the original treatise to see what kind of project he is carrying out. For the project never seems to have been completed. Thus, the only avenue that is left to us seems to be the following: we have to go by Aristotle's explicit remarks about the project he is engaged in, see to what extent this project actually is carried out, and extrapolate on what the finished project would have looked like.

Unfortunately, it turns out that Aristotle, on the face of it, does not even seem to have a clear conception of his project himself. Different parts of the *Ur-Metaphysik* seem to be written with different conceptions in mind. The most striking example of this is the following: the first lines of *Met.* Γ (1003ᵃ 21ff.) introduce the discipline as a science that considers being qua being quite generally and set it off from the particular sciences, which single out a particular part of being, particular kinds of beings, as their subject of study. And the rest of *Met.* Γ, in particular *Met.* Γ 2, tries to show how there could be such a universal, and yet unified, discipline. *Met.* E 1, on the other hand, introduces a discipline that is concerned with a particular subject matter, namely, with the kinds of beings that come first in the order of being. Hence, Aristotle calls the science "first philosophy" (1026ᵃ 24). And, assuming for the moment that there might be divine beings prior to natural objects, he also calls the discipline "theology" (1026ᵃ 19). Thus, we seem to have two radically different conceptions of the enterprise of the *Metaphysics*. According to one, we deal with what traditionally has been called "metaphysica generalis," a general study of being as such, of all there is insofar as it is, according to the other with metaphysica specialis, a study of a special kind of beings, supra-sensible beings.

Much modern scholarship has been devoted to the question how these two notions might be related. And yet agreement seems to be so far out of reach that, given the present state of the art, it might seem hopeless to make another attempt to arrive at a generally acceptable interpretation. If I, nevertheless, make the attempt, it is not because I think that I have a radically new answer, but because it seems to me that basically the correct answer was given by Patzig in his "Theologie und Ontologie in der 'Metaphysik' des Aristoteles" (an English version of which appeared in: J. Barnes, M. Schofield, R. Sorabji, eds.: "Articles in Aristotle," vol. III) in 1960, but this interpretation has not won the acceptance it deserves. This is in part owing to the fact that Patzig's view needs to be revised and elaborated in various respects.

Any interpretation has to start from the fact that it is clear from Aristotle's own remarks that Aristotle himself does not see a conflict between the two notions. Though E 1 introduces, in addition to physics and mathematics, a theoretical science of separate, unchanging substances as the object of our study, he, right from the beginning of the chapter, also talks as if he were still concerned with the universal discipline introduced in *Met.* Γ which studies being as such, and not just a particular kind of being (1025ᵇ 9–10). And toward the end of

Chapter 1, he faces the issue squarely by pointing out that there is a problem of whether first philosophy is universal or particular. But, obviously, for Aristotle this is not much of a problem. For, hardly having raised it, he settles it by the succinct remark: "it is universal in this way because it is first" (1026^a 30–31). This is all Aristotle cares to say about the matter.

How are we going to interpret this remark? We cannot follow Natorp who tried to deal with our problem in a manner fashionable in the late nineteenth century, namely, by excising from the text all references to the theological interpretation of the *Metaphysics* as later interpolations. This would not leave us with a coherent text for E 1. The remark at the end of Chapter 1 also excludes the possibility suggested by Jaeger (*Aristoteles* pp. 226ff.) that the two views reflect different stages in Aristotle's development. It also seems to rule out the attempt, suggested, e.g., by Merlan, to make the apparent conflict disappear by interpreting the phrase "being qua being" to refer to God's being, rather than to being in general. For the final remark of E 1 does assume that the study of being qua being as such is general or universal, and tries to explain how it could be so, given that it has a particular subject-matter. The problem raised in 1026^e 23 would not be a problem and would not need the answer it receives in the last sentence of the chapter, if the study of being qua being were not as such universal, but already in itself concerned with a particular kind of being. For we can hardly attribute to Aristotle the much later view that God is just being.

The explanation I want to offer for the final remark of E 1 is the following: (i) theology deals with beings of a certain kind, namely, separate substances. But in doing so, it also deals with a particular kind or way of being, a way of being peculiar to divine substances. (ii) It turns out that this way of being is the one in terms of which all other ways of being have to be explained, i.e., it turns out that a study of being as such resolves itself in three steps into a study of how all the different ways of being that characterize the different kinds of beings ultimately have to be explained in terms of the way of being that is characteristic of divine substances. (iii) Since theology studies this focal way or sense of being, it also provides the natural point to discuss how all other ways of being depend on this primary way of being, especially since this primacy would seem to reflect the very nature of divine substances. In developing this explanation, theology does carry out at least the substantial core of the program of general metaphysics and to that extent can be identified with general metaphysics. This is one way in which theology, because of the primacy of its objects, will be universal. For, in taking into account the primacy of the being of its objects, it will also deal with the ways of being that are dependent on it. (iv] But general metaphysics involves more than this kind of ontology. It also discusses certain universal principles, like the principle of non-contradiction, and certain notions of universal applicability like the notions of unity and identity. Again, this can be explained in terms of the primacy of theology. For though these principles and notions are universal, the first time they will be used in the hierarchy of sciences is in theology, and so it will fall to the theologian to introduce them in an appropriate manner. This will be all the more fitting, since ontology will, e.g., involve the distinction of various kinds of unity and identity; not only will some of these kinds be the ones needed by the theologian, but the theologian will be the one most competent to elucidate them. Thus, it turns out to be true in various ways that theology, because of its primacy, will be universal. (v) Admittedly, this will have the result that theology, or general metaphysics, has less internal unity than we might have expected. But Aristotle himself seems to envisage this result. Theology, or general metaphysics, will actually consist of a series of studies which have only generic unity. Only one of these studies will amount to theology in a narrow sense. But given the position of theology in the narrower sense in the hierarchy of theoretical sciences, which is, after all, owing to the nature of its subject-matter itself, it is embedded in a whole series of studies which, taken together, constitute general metaphysics.

Thus, let us try to understand how it is that theology is not concerned only with a particular kind of beings, but with a particular way of being, peculiar to its objects, and how it addresses itself to this way of being. By distinguishing a kind of beings and a way of being I mean to make a distinction of the following sort. Horses are a kind of beings, and camels are a different kind of beings, but neither horses nor camels have a distinctive way of being, peculiar to them; they both have the way of being of natural substances, as opposed to, e.g., numbers which have the way of magnitudes, or qualities which have a yet different way of being. The way magnitudes can be said to be is different from the way qualities or natural substances can be said to be. The claim, then, is that the way separate substances can be said to be is peculiar to separate substances. One reason why one has such difficulties with the identification of theology with general metaphysics is that one thinks of theology as just like other particular sciences, like astronomy or zoology, which deal with the nature of a particular kind of beings, but which could not be thought of as concerning themselves with the very way of being their objects have. For in the relevant sense, animals do not have a way of being peculiar to themselves; their way of being is the way of being of natural substances quite generally, and thus the zoologist presupposes, but does not concern himself with, a notion of a natural substance and what it is to be for such a substance. Similarly, the astronomer does not concern himself with the way of being the objects of astronomy have. They have the being of magnitudes, let us say, but it is not his concern to determine this way of being. For it is shared by the objects of many other disciplines. It would be a mistake, though, to think that it is true without qualification that particular disciplines are like that. It, rather, seems to be the case that we have to distinguish between the three particular theoretical sciences Aristotle distinguishes, namely, theology, physics, and mathematics, and the diverse particular sciences that constitute these three theoretical sciences by forming hierarchically ordered groups of disciplines. Once we make this distinction, it is clear that not just theology, but also physics and mathematics, i.e., all three of Aristotle's theoretical sciences, do concern themselves not just with a particular kind of beings, but also with a particular way of being peculiar to their objects. Though physics deals only with a particular part of reality, namely, natural substances, its objects do have a distinctive way of being, namely, the way of natural substances. And physics, as we can see from Aristotle's *Physics,* does address itself to this particular way of being by asking the question what it is to be a natural substance, i.e., by asking what it is to have a nature in the sense that distinguishes natural substances, whether there is such a thing as a nature, and what is involved in assuming natural substances to have such a nature. Even in the *Metaphysics* (Z 11, 1037^a 14–16) Aristotle tells us that in a way the, as we would say "metaphysical," inquiry into sensible substance is part of physics or second philosophy. And in E 1 he is quite explicit that were it not for the assumed fact that there are substances prior to natural substances, metaphysics would be part of physics and hence physics would be first philosophy (1026^a 27–29). Obviously, Aristotle is of a divided mind concerning the natural place of a theory of the way of being of natural substances. And this accounts for the strangely metaphysical character of Aristotle's treatise called "Physics." But there is no doubt that he does assume that the objects of physics do have a distinctive way of being, peculiar to them, and that the science of physics at least presupposes a theory of this way of being, if it does not itself involve it. For physics as an axiomatic science would have as one of its principles an assumption of what it is to be for a natural substance and of the existence of such things.

The situation in the case of mathematics is less clear. But, again, it seems that mathematical entities not only are a separate kind of entities, but also have their separate way of being, peculiar to them, namely, the being of magnitudes. Moreover, mathematics, as Aristotle conceives of it, does have a place at which the mathematician naturally would address himself to the peculiar kind of being mathematical entities have, or at which he would at least presuppose an answer to this question, namely, in general mathematics, a subdiscipline of mathematics Aristotle refers to in E 1 (1026^a 27). General mathematics deal with the nature and the properties of magnitudes in general, or as such, and thus at least presupposes a notion of what it is to be for a magnitude and that there are such entities with this kind of being. Thus, theology is unlike the particular sciences that fall under physics or mathematics, in that it is concerned with beings which have a way of being peculiar to them and in that it somehow has to address itself to this way of being by at least making an assumption about the nature of its objects and their existence, but it does not differ in this respect from physics or mathematics as a whole. This matter will need closer consideration at a later point. For the moment it suffices to recognize (i) that theology deals with beings that qua beings differ from all other beings and (ii) that theology somehow has to address itself to their peculiar way of being, if only to assume what it is to be for this kind of being and to assume that there are beings that have this peculiar way of being.

Now, this way of being, peculiar to divine substances, I want to suggest, is the focal way or sense of being in terms of which all other ways of being have to be explained. This explanation comes in three steps. The reasons why Aristotle thinks that all other ways of being presuppose, and have to be explained in terms of, the being of substances are well known and do not have to be rehearsed here. Aristotle thinks, e.g., that the being of qualities can be understood only in terms of the being of substances that are qualified in some way or other. But it would be a mistake to assume, as it often is, that Aristotle thinks that his task has been completed by showing how the various ways of being depend on the way of being of substances. For as soon as we start to pursue the question what is it to be for a substance, it turns out that this question has a single answer as little as the question of what it is to be for a being does. Even in the case of sensible, perishable substances, it has at least three answers, one for matter, one for substantial forms, and one for the composite of matter and form. What is more, these three ways of being a substance stand in a certain relation of priority and posteriority to each other. The being of a substance primarily belongs to the substantial form, only secondarily to the concrete physical substance in virtue of its having a substantial form, and in a third way to matter, insofar as it potentially is a composite substance. Thus, the focal way of being a substance, for sensible substances, turns out to be the being a substance of substantial forms. And since the ways of being of the entities in all the other categories depend on the way of being of sensible substances, the way of being of substantial forms turns out to be the focus for all non-substantial entities. Thus, in a second step, all ways of being are shown to be dependent on the way of being of substantial forms.

But there are not just sensible, perishable substances. Aristotle at times distinguishes as many as three different kinds of substances: sensible, perishable substances; the imperishable heavenly bodies; and immaterial, nonperceptible substances (cf. Λ 6, 1071^b 2ff.) And these are not just different kinds of substances in the sense in which horses and donkeys are different kinds of substances. They differ from each other qua substances. This is most easily seen if we just distinguish between sensible and nonsensible substances, as Aristotle himself sometimes does. The substantiality of sensible substances has to be explained in terms of the substantiality of their substantial forms, whereas nonsensible substances are just substantial forms. What is more, the substantial forms of sensible substances do not have the same way of being as the substantial forms that are separate substances. The substantial forms of sensible substances, in order to be at all, have to be realized in a composite substance that has various non-substantial characteristics, size, weight, shape, color, etc. Separate substances, on the other hand, exist without matter and without accidents. The unmoved mover, e.g., and quite generally divine substances, are such separate forms.

One may ask, though, what reason we have to believe that this difference in the way of being of substantial forms is relevant for Aristotle's account of what it is to be a substance and, hence, of what it is to be a being.

There are two passages in *Met.* Z which suggest that Aristotle himself thinks that the difference is relevant. In *Met.* Z 11 (1037^a 11ff.) he tells us "whether . . . we have to look for a different kind of substance (i.e., immaterial substance), like numbers or something of this sort, we will have to see later. For it is because of this that we try to get clear also about sensible substances. For in a way it is the task of physics and second philosophy to consider sensible substances." Aristotle here clearly assumes that separate substances and physical substances differ qua substances, and that in a way we in *Met.* Z only discuss physical substance to get clearer about separate substance. We find a similar thought in Z 3, 1029^b 3ff. There we are told that we will start with a consideration of sensible substances that are generally agreed to be substances. Thus, it is said, we shall proceed from what is better known to us to what is better known by nature, i.e., from what we are familiar with to what in the order of nature and hence scientific knowledge is prior such that ultimately what we are familiar with has to be explained in terms of it. Since both remarks are made in the context of a discussion of the question "what is substance?," these texts seem to suggest the following: (i) our discussion of the substantiality of sensible substances is preliminary to a discussion of the substantiality of nonsensible substances; (ii) nonsensible substances qua substances are prior to sensible substances; and thus (iii) we shall achieve a full understanding of the substantiality of sensible substances only when we have understood the substantiality of nonsensible substances.

Though Aristotle, unfortunately, does not explain this relation, one can still vaguely see what he must have in mind. Before we try to get clearer about this, though, it is important to distinguish two kinds of priority and dependence. It will be readily granted that, according to Aristotle, all other beings depend for their being on the being of separate substances, in particular the prime mover. And, hence, Patzig, e.g., originally thought that the relevant kind of dependence consisted in the fact that a complete account of the being of anything will have to make reference to the unmoved mover. But it seems that the kind of dependence we need for our account is not primarily this quasi-causal dependence, but a different kind of dependence. The kind of dependence we need for our account, rather, is of the following kind: sensible substances are dependent on separate substances qua substances, and this in the sense that their way of being a substance, and hence their way of being, has to be explained in terms of the way separate substances are substances.

But how could this be? Aristotle in *Met.* Λ not only assumes that the first unmoved mover is the primary being, but also that it is the primary intelligible object (1072^a 26ff.), thus giving rise to the medieval debate whether it is God or being that is the first object of the intellect, and hence the primary subject of metaphysics. Aristotle seems to assume not only that ultimately everything depends on God for its being, but also that ultimately nothing is intelligible unless it is understood in its dependence on God. And this in various ways. It is not just that everything depends on God as its first cause. There is also the notion, reflected in Aristotle in various ways, that lower forms of being somehow imitate higher forms of being. Animals procreate; this is their way of sharing in the eternal. The heaven eternally rotates to imitate, as well as it can, the unchanging nature of the unmoved mover. This suggests a scale of perfection in which the less perfect is to be understood in terms of the more perfect and ultimately the unmoved mover, as if everything was like him in the limited way it could be. But the central books of the *Metaphysics* seem to rely on a much more precise notion, though this never comes out explicitly.

To understand what it is to be a substance, and hence what it is to be a being, one has to understand, as *Met.* Z argues, what it is to be a substantial form or essence. For even if we consider a composite physical substance and look for what it is independently of its ever changing characteristics, look for what it is that remains the same throughout its life-span, while its matter is changing, it seems that it is the form that provides the object with its identity. But from the thought that it is substantial forms that are the substances, there are two lines of argument leading to the conclusion that it is separate forms that qua substances are prior to everything else.

The forms of sensible substances and separate substances are both substantial forms and they are both actualities, i.e., the reality of the object they are is constituted by their reality. But whereas separate substances turn out to be substantial forms and actualities without qualification, the substantial forms of sensible objects have to be understood as substantial forms and actualities of a certain limited kind. Thus, to understand them properly one first of all has to understand what it is to be a substantial form and an actuality without qualification, and then to understand the qualifications with which the substantial forms of sensible substances are substantial forms and actualities.

The forms of sensible substances involve potentiality in two ways, and hence are not pure actualities, though it is of the essence of a form to be an actuality. They need matter to be realized in, and thus are the forms of objects subject to change. But, what is more, when we turn to the paradigms of sensible substances, living beings, it turns out that their forms themselves essentially contain an element of potentiality. When Aristotle in *De anima* II, 1 defines the soul as the "first actuality" of a certain kind of body, this very language reflects the fact that the soul in a way is constituted by the various abilities to exercise the life-functions characteristic of the kind of living being in question, but that not all these life-functions are exercised all the time. What is more, some of the abilities that characterize the soul, like virtue or knowledge, are only acquired. Thus, the forms of sensible substances are not pure actualities; they in part are constituted by unrealized possibilities and in that sense are not fully real. The form that is the unmoved mover, on the other hand, is pure actuality. It neither needs matter to be realized nor does it involve any abilities that might or might not be realized or exercised. The unmoved mover is just eternally thinking the same thought. Thus, separate substances, in particular the unmoved mover, are pure actualities, and thus forms, and thus substances, and thus beings in a paradigmatic way in that they are perfectly real.

But, there is another line of argument which suggests that separate substances are paradigmatic as substances. Perhaps the most important characteristic of substances is that they exist in their own right, that they do not depend for their existence on something else, or, as Aristotle puts it, are separate. Now this requirement notoriously admits of various interpretations. But it seems that, on any plausible interpretation of it, it is only separate forms that satisfy this requirement straightforwardly. They do not in any sense need matter, or nonsubstantial characteristics, i.e., qualities, quantities, places, etc., or anything else to be realized. The forms of sensible substances are separate, too, but only qualifiedly so, namely, separate in account; the account of a form is self-contained in that it does not involve a reference to any other item in the ontology. Still, a material form needs some matter, and the composite substance needs nonessential properties, though these properties and their matter do not form part of the account of the form. The second most important condition of substances is that they should be particular or individual. This, again, is a requirement satisfied straightforwardly only by separate forms. The individuality of material forms, on the other hand, raises enormous problems, so much so that one may wonder *whether,* or even think that, as tradition indeed did, the forms of natural substances are universal. After all, the account of the form for all things of the same kind is exactly the same. Definition seems to be of the universal, and form or essence seems to be exactly what is given by a definition. To get particular forms at all we have to make up a complicated story about the way they are individuated by their history. Similarly, there is the notorious problem how the form of sensible substances, rather than the composite substances themselves or their matter, could come out as ultimate subjects of predication. Aristotle explicitly (Z 3, 1029^a 2–3) commits himself to the view that there is a way to construe the relation of being the subject of something in such a way that this comes out as true. But he also takes the view that the more natural way to construe the relation is such that it will be matter or the composite that comes out as ultimate subject. Thus, this requirement is met by the forms of sensible substances only by a somewhat artificial construction of the relation. Separate forms, on the other hand, are ultimate subjects of predication quite straightforwardly. Hence, separate forms satisfy all three requirements of substancehood mentioned in Z 3 straightforwardly, whereas the forms of sensible substances meet them only in some indirect or qualified way.

Moreover, Aristotle characterizes the difference between the objects of the three theoretical sciences by saying that the objects of theology are separate and unchanging, the objects of physics separate and changing, the objects of mathematics nonseparate and unchanging. Given this characterization of separate forms, it would seem that the forms of natural substances somehow are an inferior kind of forms in yet another way. For they are separate only qualifiedly, namely, in account; and they are unchanging, but only qualifiedly. For though they do not come into being or pass away, they, unlike separate forms, do not exist eternally, but go in and out of existence instantaneously. And though they do not suffer change, they really are different at different times, as one can see in the case of human souls.

Moreover, only in the case of separate substances are the form and the essence straightforwardly identical. For though Aristotle thinks that forms and essences quite generally are identical, he at times also talks as if the specification of the essence of a sensible substance in addition to a reference to the form had to include a reference to the matter. Thus, there is much reason to think that one will understand what it is to be a form, and thus what it is to be a substance, only if one has understood how separate forms are substances, and then understand how material forms, by a weakening of the conditions, count as forms and substances. And if this should be so, then the focal way of being a substance, and hence of being a being, is the way in which separate forms, or divine substances, are substances. Thus, general metaphysics would have as its core a study of the way of being of divine substances.

But why would it follow from this that theology would be the natural place to study the various ways of being, their systematical connections and thus being qua being? There are at least two other possibilities. There could be a universal discipline prior to theology, physics, and mathematics that studies the various ways of being and hence being qua being. And there is the other possibility that we leave it to the three sciences to study the ways of being peculiar to their objects.

To take the last possibility first, it deserves to be pointed out that it is a real possibility, one Aristotle himself seems to consider. For in the passage in Z 11 we looked at earlier, he does suggest that first philosophy is primarily concerned with the substantiality of nonsensible substances, whereas the substantiality of sensible substances in a way is the concern of physics. And since the way of being of nonsubstantial items like qualities and quantities depends on the way of being of natural substances, since only they have accidents, the natural philosopher would take care of all that, too.

But the shortcomings of this approach are obvious, too. Perhaps the most important difficulty with this approach would be that it would divide the account of being on three different subjects and thus would make it episodic, when in fact there is a continuous story to be told and when it is important for an understanding of the different parts of the story that they are just different parts of one account. It is for this reason that it would seem so much more attractive to give a continuous account of being as such, prior to the different accounts of the different kinds of beings, i.e., prior to theology, physics, and mathematics. And some remarks Aristotle makes might suggeest that this is the way he is inclined to deal with the problem. In E 1, 1025^b 10ff., e.g., he says that the different particular disciplines do not account for the essence and existence of their subject-matter, as if this was left to some prior discipline, i.e., general metaphysics. Since theology, physics, and mathematics are particular disciplines with a particular subject-matter, this might suggest that there is some discipline prior to all three of them which somehow accounts for their subject-matter. But the drawbacks of this approach are obvious, too. For there clearly is a sense in which it is the theologian who knows best about the way of being of divine substances, the physicist who knows best about the way of being of natural substances, and the mathematician who knows best about the way of being of magnitudes. If one insists that a full understanding of the way of being of magnitudes presupposes an understanding of the way of being of physical substances, and that this, in turn, presupposes an understanding of the way of being of separate substances, it will at least be true of the theologian that he knows best about the way of being of separate substances. For on the basis of what could somebody else know more about the way separate substances are? This could only be the case, if there were principles prior to separate substances in terms of which separate substances have to be understood, and these principles were the subject of some further discipline. But there are no principles prior to separate substances. Moreover, in the case of divine substances knowledge of them to a large extent, if not entirely, amounts to no more than a knowledge of their way of being. For assume that there is just one separate substance. In this case one might try to argue that whatever was true of it was true of it just in virtue of its being a separate substance, i.e., in virtue of its peculiar way of being. But even if there should be several separate substances, it still would be the case that much, if not most, of what is true of them would be true in virtue of their being separate substances. Thus, a study of the way of being of separate substances outside theology would, to a large extent, just reduplicate the study of the theologian. Moreover, as I suggested earlier, it would seem to be part of the essence of separate substances that all other ways of being depend on their way of being, just as it seems to be essential to natural substances that the way of being of accidents depend on their way of being.

It is for these reasons, I take it, that Aristotle decides, on the one hand, to give a continuous account of being as such, but, on the other, to do this within the framework of "theology" or "first philosophy."

But it has to be kept in mind that, though this kind of ontology forms the core of general metaphysics, there is more to general metaphysics than this. The metaphysician, according to Aristotle, does consider certain principles and notions of universal applicability, like the principle of noncontradiction and the notions of unity and identity and their various forms. Why would it be the task of the theologian to consider these matters? There are two possible explanations. The first is that since these matters have to be discussed somewhere, and since they are most naturally discussed in the context of ontology, it will be the task of the theologian to deal with them, since it is his task to do ontology. But there is another possible explanation which ties this fact to Aristotle's claim that first philosophy is universal, because it is first. Since it is first, and since these principles and notions are universal, first philosophy will be the first place where they are used. Hence, it will be the task of the theologian to introduce them.

Now, the only way in which theology could accommodate a general study of being as such as part of itself is by lacking the kind of unity we might expect of an Aristotelian science on the basis of what Aristotle says in the *Posterior Analytics*. But we have to keep in mind that, as we noticed earlier, physics and mathematics, too, are one science only in the sense that there is one subject-matter that is studied by a series of systematically connected disciplines. Moreover, Aristotle in Γ 1003^b 22 explicitly warns us that the study of being will be one science only generically, that it will be constituted by a series of studies that specifically deal with the various kinds of being. Thus, there is no reason why theology, too, should not be one only generically, why it should not actually consist of a series of studies. There is one disanalogy, though. Theology would not have one subject-matter in quite the straightforward way in which physics and mathematics have one subject-matter. It not only deals with the primary kind of beings, and thus the primary way of being, but also with being in general. Yet, there is also a sense in which these are not really two different subject matters. For to say of the primary way of being that it is primary, is to say that all other ways of being depend on it. And thus Aristotle can say that theology, being first, also is universal.

If this is correct, it also throws some light on the question whether Aristotelian metaphysics is a science. It has often been claimed that Aristotelian metaphysics is a dialectical enterprise, rather than a science in something like the sense of the *Posterior Analytics*. But it should be clear from what has been said that Aristotelian metaphysics, either as a whole, or at least in good part, is scientific. For otherwise, Aristotle could not in E 1 treat it as parallel to physics and mathematics. Moreover, it does seem that there is no reason why theology, at least in the narrower sense, should not be a science strictly speaking. But one can also see how, given the suggested conception of Aristotle's metaphysics, a much larger part of first philosophy could be considered as being strictly scientific. Both physics and mathematics, in addition to studies of the various kinds of natural substances and mathematical entities, involve a universal discipline that deals with natural substances, and magnitudes respectively, as such. In the case of mathematics this is obvious, since Aristotle explicitly refers to universal or general mathematics. But this is hardly less clear in the case of physics. For our treatise called "Physics" is the dialectical counterpart to such a science of natural substances quite generally. Thus, we may assume that theology, too, involves a discipline that we may call general or universal theology which will deal with separate substances as such, and, in doing so, with the way of being peculiar to separate substances. And there is no reason why general theology should not be strictly scientific, too. Immediately following general theology we shall have an exposition of the various other ways of being and how they depend on the way of being of separate substances. There is no reason why this exposition should not take a strictly scientific form with, e.g., definitions of qualities, quantities, relations, etc., and theorems concerning them. Having dealt with whatever needs to be dealt with in a study of being as such, we would move on to special theology which, again in a scientific way, would deal with the various particular kinds of separate substances, in case there should be more than one. Thus, it would seem that, if not the whole, then at least a very substantial part of metaphysics is scientific. But what reason is there to think that any part of metaphysics will not be scientific? The view that Aristotelian metaphysics is essentially a dialectical enterprise rests primarily on an interpretation of *Met.* Γ, and in particular the way Aristotle deals with the principle of noncontradiction. Aristotle says that principles like this are the concern of the metaphysician, but also says that they do not admit of proof in the strict sense, to then embark on a nonscientific discussion of the principle, which is regarded as an actual piece of doing metaphysics. This is the only evidence T. Irwin, e.g., refers to in order to arrive at the conclusion that first philosophy is not demonstrative, that the questions discussed by first philosophy are beyond demonstration (Aristotle's Discovery of Metaphysics, Rev. of Nov. 31, 1977, 78, p. 218). But this inference seem to me to be radically mistaken. For consider the following: another concern of the metaphysician must be God, his essence and existence, since God is a first principle. Moreover, Aristotle is committed to the view that strictly speaking there is no proof of the essence and existence of God. There will be a real definition of him as an axiom of special theology. And on the basis of this, there will be a deduction of theological theorems. Now imagine that we only had a text in which Aristotle says that the theologian is concerned with the existence of God, but that his existence does not admit of any proof in the strict sense, and then proceeded to give the kind of a posteriori proofs on the basis of the existence of motion which he in fact does give in the *Physics* and in the

Metaphysics. We could not possibly infer from this that Aristotle thinks that theology is not a science; here, we clearly could not argue that the proof constituted a piece of actual Aristotelain theology, but obviously was not, and could not by Aristotle be thought to be, demonstrative. For we would know that the assumption of God's existence was just a starting-point for scientific theology from which it would then deduce whatever there was to be deduced. Or consider the existence of nature. As we can see from the *Physics,* Aristotle thinks that it cannot be proved, strictly speaking, that nature exists. Nevertheless, he tries to establish it dialectically. But nobody is tempted to infer from this that Aristotle thinks that physics is not a science; nobody is inclined to argue that the discussion of the first book of the *Physics* is a piece of actual Aristotelian physics, and that, hence, Aristotelian physics is dialectical. But if these inferences would be misguided, it is equally misguided to infer from *Met.* Γ, or the *Metaphysics* in general, that Aristotelian metaphysics is not a real science. It is demonstrative, but, as with all other sciences, one arrives at its starting-points dialectically. And just as all other writings of Aristotle's do not pretend to present us with an actual piece of Aristotelian science, but, rather, show some of the work involved in arriving at the proper scientific axioms, so the *Metaphysics,* including *Met.* Γ, show us how we might arrive at the principles of the theory of being as such. In one important respect, though, metaphysics differs from all other sciences. Since it is the first in the hierarchy of sciences, it will also be the first to make use of the principles that all sciences will rely on, like, e.g., the principle of noncontradiction. And, hence, it will also be the task of the metaphysician to arrive at these universal principles and to provide them with whatever backing may be appropriate. Thus, the metaphysician, more than any other scientist, will be engaged in dialectical reasoning. But this goes no way to show that metaphysics is not a demonstrative science.

Thus, it seems to me that a proper understanding of Aristotle's conception of metaphysics, and in particular his remark that first philosophy is universal because it is first, will restore metaphysics to its proper place, that of the first of the demonstrative sciences.

Stoics

—

7

Stoic vs. Aristotelian Syllogistic

I. The Problem

At least since Lukasiewicz's paper "Zur Geschichte der Aussagenlogik" (*Erkenntnis*, 5, 1935, pp. 111ff.) historians of logic have usually contrasted Stoic and Aristotelian syllogistic as the ancient forms of propositional logic and term- or class-logic respectively.[1] One may have serious misgivings about the way this is usually interpreted and argued for. In fact, one could argue that, to contrast the two systems in this way, we would have to introduce many qualifications and explanations; indeed, so many qualifications that one may wonder whether it was not misleading to say that the relation between the two systems was that between propositional logic and term-logic.

There can be no doubt, in any case, that the Stoa and the Peripatus did not think that the difference between their logical systems was that between propositional logic and term-logic. For otherwise one would expect that Aristotelians to treat Stoic logic as a welcome and necessary complement to their doctrine of the categorical syllogism, and expect the Stoics in turn to regard Aristotelian syllogistic at least as a welcome supplement to their own hypothetical syllogistic. Yet the evidence we have suggests not only that both schools restricted their interest to their own logic but even that they rejected each other's syllogistic in some sense we shall have to specify. It is some aspects of this apparent rivalry between the two doctrines which I shall discuss in this chapter.

There would be little to discuss if we accepted Bochenski's explanation of this rivalry (*Ancient Formal Logic,* p. 81) Bochenski thinks that the ancient logicians somehow noticed the radical difference between propositional logic and term-logic and that "this difference was even felt as an opposition." Hardly more illuminating is Lejewski's account (in Edward's *Encyclopedia of Philosophy,* s.v. Logic, History of, p. 520): "As a result of interschool enmities and jealousies there was at first no cooperation in logical research between the Lyceum and the

Stoa. The Peripatetics limited their interest to the study of the categorical syllogism, whereas the Stoics did not look beyond those inference schemata which they could derive from the Chrysippian indemonstrables."[2]

More substance is given to the dispute by W. Kneale (*The Development of Logic*, p. 175); he thinks that the hostility was due to the fact "that the Stoics annoyed the Peripatetics by claiming priority for their own dialectic and pointing to Aristotle's unacknowledged use of its principles in such parts of his syllogistic as the theory of reduction." And Mueller, finally, agrees that the dispute was a dispute over priority though not for the reason suggested by W. Kneale (l.c., p. 173; 174; 181). But even if there was a dispute over the respective priority of the two systems—and we shall return to this question at the end (cf. p. 122)—this can hardly account for the behavior of the schools that we have to try to explain. For nobody refrains from doing predicate logic just because he wants to claim that propositional logic is prior. Nor does anybody who is interested in predicate logic get so annoyed by claims that propositional logic is prior to it that he loses any interest in propositional logic.

Now we know that the Stoics explicitly denied that Aristotelian syllogisms are syllogisms (Alexander *In an. pr.* 262, 28–29; 345, 15–16; 390, 16–18); and we also know that orthodox Peripatetics like Alexander claimed that Stoic hypothetical syllogisms were not really syllogisms at all (Alex. *In an. pr.* 265, 19–20; 390, 17; 256, 20–25); they even ascribed this doctrine to Aristotle himself (Alex. *In an. pr.* 42, 27–31). So if we can show that this was not just a mere quibble about words but reflected some serious disagreement we shall have an explanation of the fact that the Stoics and the Peripatetics did not regard their respective syllogistical systems as complementary but as competing on what was at least in part common ground.

I shall, then, first of all examine what reasons each side may have had for their disagreement about what is to count as a syllogism and why each party rejected the other's syllogistic; and here I shall first consider the Stoic point of view and then will take up the Peripatetic position. Only in the end shall I turn to the question whether or not the disagreement was affected by a dispute over the respective priority of the two systems.

II. What Is to Count as a Syllogism?

A. The Stoic Position

According to Diogenes Laertius (VII, 78) the Stoics defined as syllogisms those inferences which are either themselves indemonstrable or can be reduced by certain rules (the so-called themata) to indemonstrable inferences. The indemonstrables referred to in this definition are, at least in Chrysippean syllogistic, arguments of any of the five following forms (cf. D.L. VII, 80–81):

1. if p, then q; but p; therefore q
2. if p, then q; but not q; therefore not p
3. not both p and q; but p; therefore not q
4. p or q; but p; therefore not q
5. p or q; but not q; therefore p.

The themata referred to (again, at least in Chrysippean syllogistic) specify that an argument of a certain form is valid if another argument or other arguments of a certain form are valid. This first thema, e.g., presumably was a rule of the following kind (cf. Apuleius *De int.* 191, 7–10): if from a set of premises a certain conclusion follows, then the negation of any of these premises will follow from the negation of the original conclusion in conjunction with the other premises. So an argument of the form "p; but not q; therefore not: if p, then q" will be a syllogism because it can be reduced by means of this rule to a first indemonstrable inference.

Now, though the definition of the syllogism quoted above undoubtedly is the Stoic definition, it presupposes the complete system of Stoic syllogistic and tells us little about the notion of a syllogism in view of which the system was set up. But it is obviously this pretechnical notion of a syllogism which is relevant for our problem. For it could not have been a matter of dispute that, once the system was set up and the syllogism then technically defined on the basis of this system, Aristotelian syllogisms would not qualify as syllogisms: they neither belong to the class of indemonstrable inferences nor can they be reduced to such inferences by means of the Stoic themata. The basic dispute must have centered around a different question, namely whether or not the syllogistic system should be set up in such a way that it includes Aristotelian syllogisms; or whether, given a certain notion of a syllogism, we should or should not make the additional assumptions necessary for including Aristotelian syllogisms in the system.

We could get at this pretechnical Stoic notion of a syllogism if we could find out on what basis the Stoics divided valid arguments (D.L. VII, 78) into syllogistically valid arguments (syllogistikoi logoi) or syllogisms and merely valid arguments (perantikoi logoi). According to the Stoics, any argument is valid if the conjunction of its premises forms the antecedent and its conclusion forms the consequent of a true conditional (cf. Sextus Empiricus *P.H.* II, 113; 137; 138; 145; *A.M.* VIII, 304; 415; 417; cf. also D.L. VII, 77). Merely valid, then, are arguments which satisfy this general criterion of validity but do not satisfy certain further criteria which distinguish syllogisms from other valid arguments.

To find out what these further criteria are we could either look at what the Stoics actually are prepared to call syllogisms and see what they have in common as opposed to merely valid arguments; or we may look at merely valid arguments to see what they may be thought to lack. Fortunately, the evidence seems to be just good enough to claim that the Stoics distinguished two kinds of nonsyllogistical valid arguments and defined them with reference to what they lack in order to be syllogisms. For we hear of only two kinds of such arguments and they seem to be defined in such a way as to exhaust the class of nonsyllogistical valid arguments. These two kinds are the unmethodically conclusive (amethodōs perainontes) and the hyposyllogistical (hyposyllogistikoi) arguments.

Unmethodically conclusive are those arguments which satisfy the general criterion of validity of arguments but in which one or possibly more assumptions on which the inference is based have been taken for granted and not been made explicit (Galen, *Institutio logica*, 49, 8; Alex. *In an. pr.* 345, 13; 22, 5ff.; 24, 1ff.; 68, 29–31; 345, 22ff.; *In top.* 14, 22ff.; 15, 3ff.). Standard examples for unmethodically valid arguments are "a equals b; b equals c; therefore a equals c," "the first is bigger than the second; the second is bigger than the third; therefore the first is bigger than the third," or "Dio says it is day; but Dio tells the truth; therefore it is day." As Mueller (p. 180) has pointed out, this defect of taking something for granted, which should not be done if we want to proceed methodically, can always be removed just by adding a conditional with the conjunction of the given premises as antecedent and the conclusion as consequent. This will turn any valid argument (in fact any argument whatever) into a Stoic syllogism. But that certainly is not the only way and clearly not the most satisfactory way an unmethodically conclusive argument can be turned into a Stoic syllogism. A Stoic example of an argument which is unmethodically conclusive is: "if some god has told you that this man is going to be rich, then this man is going to be rich; but this god (i.e., Zeus) has told you that this man is going to be rich; therefore this man is going to be rich" (S.E. *A.M.* VIII, 308). Let us abbreviate this argument in the following way: "if p, then q; but p'; therefore q." In this case, the assumption that is taken for granted, and which would have to be made explicit, would most naturally be not the conditional "if, if p then q, and p', then q," but rather "if, if p, then q, then if p', then q," or simply "if p', then p."

Hyposyllogistical are those arguments one gets if one or more propositions in a syllogism are replaced by equivalent propositions but in such a way that the argument no longer is a syllogism (Alex. *In an. pr.* 84, 12–16; Galen *I.L.* 49, 6–7). Unfortunately, neither Galen nor Alexander gives us an example of such an argument in the passages referred to. But in *In an. pr.* 373, 29–35 Alexander criticizes the Stoics for maintaining that an argument of the form "q follows from p; but p; therefore q" is just valid but not a syllogism though (a) "q follows from p" and "if p, then q" are equivalent (isodynamousas lexeis, tauton sēmainontos) and (b) arguments of the form "if p, then q; but p; therefore q" are syllogisms. So we may assume that an argument of the form "q follows from p; but p; therefore q" will be a hyposyllogistical argument.

Now if we are actually given such liberty to turn unmethodically conclusive arguments into syllogisms, then all nonsyllogistical valid arguments will be either unmethodically conclusive or hyposyllogistical. This would also explain why the Stoics thought that any valid argument whatever is made up of elementary, indemonstrable syllogisms (D.L. VII, 79; D.L. actually says "every argument," but invalid arguments cannot be reduced to syllogisms). For, from what we have said, it seems that the Stoics thought that every valid argument will turn out to be a syllogism if only we supply the premises which have been taken for granted and formulate them properly; that is, it will turn out to be either an elementary syllogism or an argument which can be dissolved into or reduced to elementary syllogisms according to the themata.

If this is correct, we may assume that syllogisms according to the Stoics are characterized by the fact that they satisfy the following conditions:

(1) they are valid arguments;

(2) all the assumptions on which the inference is based have been made explicit as premises;

(3) all the assumptions and the conclusions have been put forward in a certain canonical form.

Having outlined the Stoic notion of a syllogism, we may turn to the question whether any of these requirements either by itself or in conjunction with some other assumption could have caused a disagreement about what is to count as a syllogism. Now, since the Peripatetics at least agreed that Stoic syllogisms are valid arguments, and since the Stoics did not want to deny that Aristotelian syllogisms are valid inferences (Alex. *In. an. pr.* 390, 16ff.), there could not have been a disagreement on the basis of the first requirement as such.

But some disagreement may have arisen about the question how something follows from something. We are inclined to think that " . . . follows from . . . " refers to a logical relation between propositions and that the fact that this relation holds between the conclusion and the premises of a given argument has to be explained in the case of formally valid arguments (if not generally) by reference to the logical form of the argument. But it is not as clear as it may seem that the Peripatetics and the Stoics shared this view. The Stoics talk of consequence and incompatibility as if they were relations between facts or states of affairs (cf. Plut. *De E ap. Del* 386F–387E; Cic. *De off.* I, 4, 11; *N.D.* II, 59, 147); and both the Stoics and the Peripatetics talk as if facts follow from other facts. (The Stoics do not distinguish the relation between antecedent and consequent of a true conditional and the relation between the premises and the conclusion of a valid argument; in both cases they talk of akolouthia.) And it seems that neither the Stoics nor the Peripatetics ever say that an argument is valid because of its logical form, which would be strange if they actually had thought that the validity had to be explained as being due to the form. And even when it is said that a certain form of argument is valid for every matter (i.e., for every suitable substitution of the letters), this does not seem to be the same as saying that the validity is *due* to the form.[3]

So we should consider the possibility that the validity of an argument was thought to be due to a real relation that holds between the facts referred to in the argument, if the premises are true. An argument, on this view, would be valid because, given that what is asserted by the premises is in fact the case, what is asserted by the conclusion cannot but be the case, too; for, in the nature of things, the one follows from the other. If this is the way ancient logicians understood validity, how they explain the validity of arguments will depend upon how they view things following from one another.

Now the Stoics seem to regard consequence and (possibly various kinds of) incompatibility as the relations between states of affairs or facts in terms of which one can explain that something follows from something. If then our hypothesis about validity were correct, it would not be surprising that their syllogisms should take the form of hypothetical syllogisms, and that they should think that every valid argument, if properly reconstructed, turns out to be a hypothetical syllogism. What would be wrong with Aristotelian syllogisms, on this view, is that they do not accurately reflect how, given the truth of the premises, the conclusion really follows. This will become clear only if, for example, appropriate hypothetical premises are added.

Let us consider an example. "All men are mortal; Socrates is a man; therefore Socrates is mortal" will hardly qualify as a syllogism in Aristotle's system in *An. pr.* A 4–6. But later in the *Analytics* (cf. 47^b 15ff.; 70^a 16ff.) Aristotle does not seem to object to singular terms as such in syllogisms, and S.E. (*P.H.* II, 196–97) uses arguments of that form as standard examples for Peripatetic syllogisms. So let us assume that the Stoics, too, would have regarded such an argument as an Aristotelian syllogism. Before we consider why, on the explanation suggested above, they would not regard this as a real syllogism, let us first look at the following argument which would also not qualify as a syllogism: "If something is a man, then he is mortal; Socrates is a man; therefore Socrates is mortal." This, on the present interpretation, would not be a syllogism because what accounts for the fact that Socrates is mortal (or that from which it really follows that Socrates is mortal) is (a) the fact that Socrates' being mortal is a real consequence of Socrates' being a man and (b) the fact that Socrates is a man. To see how, given the premises, it follows that Socrates is mortal, we should therefore add the premises "if Socrates is a man then Socrates is mortal." Now this may be regarded as the real consequence of "if something is a man then he is mortal." If we make this assumption explicit, too, then we shall get the following reasoning: "if (if something is a man then he is mortal) then (if Socrates is a man then Socrates is mortal); if something is a man then he is mortal; therefore if Socrates is a man then Socrates is mortal; if Socrates is a man then Socrates is mortal; Socrates is a man; therefore Socrates is mortal." And this reasoning will by syllogistic because it reflects how the conclusion really follows.

For similar reasons the Peripatetic syllogism mentioned above will not reflect how the conclusion really follows. Either the premise "all men are mortal" would have to be replaced by "if Socrates is a man then Socrates is mortal" or, if we wanted to give a more detailed reason for Socrates' being mortal, we would have to replace "all men are mortal" by "if something is a man then he is mortal" and reconstruct the argument as above.

The Peripatetic position on this question would be: if it follows from something that Socrates is mortal, then this has to be explained as being due to the fact that the two "terms" or entities referred to by "Socrates" and "mortal" are in the nature of things related in a certain way to a third term such that this term, so related, accounts for Socrates' being mortal. And this will be reflected by a categorical syllogism.

An objection to the ontological view of validity which I have been suggesting might be made along the following lines. It might be said that there are cases in which an assumption follows from certain other assumptions (possibly even follows logically from certain other assumptions) and where, given a particular account of real consequence, it is not possible to explain the validity of the corresponding argument as being due to a real relation between the assumed and the inferred facts, because the argument could not be reconstructed in such a way as to exhibit the supposed real relation however liberal one was about reconstruction. In these cases it would be quite clear that what accounts for the validity is not the nature of things but a logical relation between the propositions used. But this objection for the ancient logicians would not have the obvious force it may have for us. For though such a reconstruction of logically valid arguments may be unacceptable for us (and may in many cases not have been very plausible even then), the Stoics at least were able to offer such a recontsruction in each case.

The Peripatetics were not in such a fortunate position. But for various reasons they still could escape noticing the point. Hypothetical syllogisms should have been the stumbling block. But by putting a certain interpretation on the hypothetical premise, the Peripatetics, as we shall see, could always avoid the admission that there are cases in which something follows from certain premises and in which the validity cannot be explained as being due to a certain real relation between the terms which would hold if the premises were true. Moreover, actual Stoic examples of hypothetical syllogisms would be of such a kind as to strengthen the belief that consequence is based on a relation between terms. The Stoic truth-conditions for conditionals and disjunctions are so strong that examples of such propositions always seem to be true owing to certain relation between the terms, e.g., "if something is a man, he is mortal," "if something is walking, then it is in motion." It is therefore not surprising that authors who, at least in logic, follow the Peripatetic tradition treat hypothetical arguments as if they depended on a relation between terms (Ps.-Amm. XI 7ff.; XI, 27ff.; 68, 16–18; 68, 34ff.; Philoponus In an. pr. 244, 31ff.). So Mates (Stoic Logic, p.

70n53) can say of examples these authors give for a hypothetical syllogism: "These are very nearly versions of the syllogism in Barbara." Boethius even talks as if the general form of a simple hypothetical proposition were either "si hoc est, illud non est" or "aut hoc est aut illud est" where "hoc" and "illud," as one can see from the context, do duty for terms (*De syll, hyp*. I, 3, 1f.; cf. I, 4, 2ff.; I, 5, 1).[4]

If we assumed, then, either that the Stoics or that both the Stoics and the Peripatetics tried to give an ontological account for " . . . follows from . . . ," there would have been a dispute about how things really follow from something and for that reason a dispute about what is to count as a syllogism. But the evidence we have seems to be much too weak to show that a disagreement actually arose for that reason. In the following, therefore, I shall completely neglect this approach to our problem.

Similarly, the second requirement as such could not have given rise to a dispute. For, as we shall see, Aristotle, too, seems to have thought that it is characteristic of syllogisms that all the assumptions on which they are based have been made explicit. But there seems to have been a disagreement about what is to be counted as an assumption. If we had to draw the line between what is to be counted as an assumption and what is not, we would presumably say that logically true assumptions are not really assumptions and therefore do not have to be made explicit. They belong to the machinery which we can safely use in arguing from something to something rather than to the assumptions from which we argue. But, however this may be, the Stoics certainly did not draw the line there. Otherwise they would have regarded Aristotelian syllogisms as syllogisms. For an argument of the form "A belongs to very B; B belongs to every C; therefore A belongs to every C" is based on an assumption of the form "if A belongs to every B and B belongs to every C then A belongs to every C" which is logically true and which, if added to the Aristotelian syllogism, would turn it into a Stoic syllogism.

Now the Stoics obviously were interested in arguments whose validity can be explained as due to the way in which elementary propositional connectives like "and," "if . . . , then . . . ," and "or" are used in them. So one may suspect that they accordingly tried to divide propositions by drawing the line between those propositions which are true in virtue of the way these propositional connectives are used in them and those propositions which are true for some other reason. But this, too, does not seem to be the case. For they did not accept the so-called totally hypothetical syllogisms (i.e., arguments of the form "if p then q; if q then r; therefore if p then r") as syllogisms, either[5], though a proposition of the form "if, if p then q and if q then r, then if p then r" is a paradigm of such a truth.

One can, I think, settle the question which propositions according to the Stoics ought not to be counted as assumptions and therefore do not need to be made explicit as premises by looking at Stoic syllogistic. The Stoics define arguments of five classes as indemonstrable. These seem to be thought of as the axioms of the system. And then there are themata by means of which every complex syllogism can be reduced to these axioms. Now the assumptions that need not be made explicit should be exactly those which are embodied in these axioms and rules. And, to judge from Stoic practice, that is actually so (with the exception of the assumptions of commutativity for "and" and "or" which were presupposed).

Now all these assumptions are logically true and therefore all syllogisms will be logically valid; but they will be only a small subset of formally valid arguments. The question, then, is· why are the Stoics so restrictive about the propositions that can be taken for granted and why do they not admit as syllogisms all arguments which are based on logically true assumptions whichever these may be?

The main reason, I think, is that Greek logicans barely had a notion of logically or formally true propositions and certainly did not attempt systematically to develop criteria by means of which they would be able to decide whether a proposition is true in virtue of its form or not. There are several passages which show that they were at least aware of the fact that some propositions are formally true and moreover taught this; but the examples given in this context never go beyond trivial forms like "if p then p" and "p or not p" (S.F. A.M. VIII, 281–282; 466–467; Cicero Acad. pr. 97; 98; N.D. I, 70). There is a curious title in the catalog of Chrysippus' writings (D.L. VII, 194): "Logika synhēmmena pros Timokratēn kai Philomathē: eis ta peri logōn kai tropōn." This may suggest that Chrysippus also used the general criterion for the validity of arguments the other way round as a principle of conditionalization to get logically true conditionals from syllogisms. Since he has criteria for what is to count as a syllogism which arc independent of the general criteria of validity, there would be no objection to such a use of the criterion as a principle of conditionalization. But, first, this would give Chrysippus only a very limited set of logically true propositions; and, second, there is no evidence whatever to suggest that he was interested in these conditionals qua logical truths. In view of this lack of criteria for logical truth, it is suggested, the Stoics restricted the assumptions they were willing to take for granted to the bare minimum which one could hardly challenge without taking this very minimum for granted.

If this is correct then a main deficiency of Aristotelian syllogisms would be that they presuppose more than this bare minimum. Peripatetics, of course, could argue that it was hardly less safe to assume the validity of a syllogism in Barbara, or the truth of the corresponding conditional, than the truth of a proposition of the form "if if p then q and p, then q." But to this the Stoics could object that, although this may be so, for that matter it was also safe to assume that if a equals b and b equals c then a equals c, or if a is bigger than b and b is etc.

So, if one accepted that argument, then, as far as that argument goes, many arguments could claim to qualify as candidates for the title of 'syllogism.' It would be up to the Peripatetics to show that assumptions about "belonging to" are in a logically privileged position whereas assumptions about "being equal to" or "being bigger than" or "being a relative of" are not in that position. But it is difficult to think of any satisfactory argument which would have shown that "belonging to" is in a privileged position and at the same time would not have indicated that other expressions are in the same privileged position and which therefore would have forced the Peripatetics to admit arguments as syllogisms which they did not want to count as such.

The Stoics, then, require of a syllogism that all the assumptions it is based on be made explicit, whether they are logically true or not, with the exception of a few logical assumptions, or rather a few sets of logically true assumptions, which are embodied in the axioms and the rules of the system. And on this basis they reject Aristotelian syllogisms not as valid arguments but as syllogisms.

The third requirement, i.e., that of canonical formulation, is due to the Stoics' formalism. They deliberately seem to have defined all the terms which are used to define the classes of axiomatically valid inferences in such a way that one could see from the wording of an argument whether it was an indemonstrable argument or not. It is for this reason that an argument of the form "q follows from p; but p; therefore q" is not counted as a syllogism, though "q follows from p" and "if p then q" are supposed to be equivalent. Of course, there is no point in making the external form of an expression the criterion for the logical form unless one is also willing to standardize one's language accordingly, i.e., one has to introduce criteria such that one uses a certain form of expression only if, and preferably whenever, one wants to say a certain thing. This, I assume, is the reason why the Stoics not only give formal definitions of the various kinds of simple and molecular propositions but also specify truth-conditions for them. If, then, Chrysippus is reported by Cicero (*De fato* 8, 15ff.) to have told the astrologers that they should used negated conjunctions instead of conditionals, this does not mean that Chrysippus told them that implication and conjunction and negation are interdefinable; nor does it mean that Chrysippus thought that the astrologers did not know ordinary Greek properly. Chrysippus' point rather seems to be that the theorems of astrology, just like the theorems of other empirical sciences, do not meet the criteria he has laid down for the use of conditionals.

This request for canonical formulation of syllogisms gave rise to a controversy with the Peripatetics for which, at least, we have some direct evidence. For the Peripatetics apparently did not appreciate the advantages of a system which tries to make the question of the validity of an argument as independent as possible from the acceptance or nonacceptance of assumptions or interpretations of expressions. One can see how generous Aristotle had been in this respect if one looks, e.g., at *An. pr.* 26ᵃ 23. He tries there to explain that syllogisms of the mood Darii are valid, in fact perfect, given the initial definition of "to be predicated of every . . . " But then instead of using the formulation "Let A be predicated of every B and B of some C," he cheerfully says "Let A belong to very B and B to some C. If, then, to be predicated of every is what was said in the beginning it is necessary that A belong to some C." Alexander (*In an. pr.* 84, 15ff.; 373 29ff.; cf. Galen *I.L.* 9.11; 11, 5ff.) talks about the Stoics as if they maintained that the validity of an argument depended on the expressions used, whereas he thinks that the wording is quite irrelevant because the validity depends on what is signified by the expressions used. But it is clear that the Stoics would deny that they think the validity depends on the expressions used. Not only the fact that hyposyllogistical arguments are treated as one class of valid arguments but also the general criterion for the validity of arguments shows the contrary. What Alexander seems to fail to see is that it is advantageous to distinguish the criteria by means of which we decide whether something is a valid argument of a certain kind, i.e., a syllogism, and the reason why it is a syllogism. It is, of course, this disregard for the actual formulation of arguments which allows the Peripatetics to classify all sorts of arguments as categorical syllogisms which, in our view, have very little resemblance to an Aristotelian syllogism, e.g.: "whomever somebody has as his father he is his son; Lamprocles has Socrates as his father; therefore Lamprocles is Socrates' son" (Galen *I.L.* 41, 11–13). It is possible that this was pointed out by the Stoics. For even Galen, who in logic usually sides with the Peripatetics against the Stoics, says with reference to certain arguments that the Peripatetics "do violence" to them to have them classified as categorical syllogisms (*I.L.* 38, 14; 41, 9).

Another disadvantage of the Peripatetic disregard for the actual formulation of arguments is that they easily lose control over the logical form of propositions. So Galen (*I.L.* 9.8–16) argues that only Stoic pedantry can claim that "if it is not day then it is night" is a conditional whereas anybody who pays attention to what is meant will immediately see that this is an exclusive disjunction. Now this proposition not only lacks the external form of a completely disjunctive proposition, it also does not satisfy the truth-conditions for the corresponding exclusive disjunction "it is day or it is night." So Galen, in order to determine the logical form, not only takes into account our use of "if . . . then . . . " and "not" but obviously also the fact that we all know that night and day are of such a kind that if we say "if it is not day then it is night" we may as well say "it is day or it is night." In fact he says (9, 12–13) that attention to the nature of things brings out the fact that the proposition is an exclusive disjunction. And if Alexander (*In an. pr.* 264, 15–17) wonders whether the third Stoic indemonstrable is not really identical with their first indemonstrable, he must be willing to say that, in arguments of that form, propositions with the external form "not both p and q" are really conditionals of the form "if p then not q." There is, of course, nothing wrong with saying that the external form of expressions in ordinary language is no safe guide to their logical form. But when Galen and Alexander accuse the Stoics of foolishly sticking to the external form of expressions, they do not seem to realize that the Stoics have introduced conventions for the use of expressions which allow them to take the external form as representative of the logical form and that they had good reasons to do so.

The request for canonical formulation may have influenced the Stoic attitude toward Aristotelian syllogisms in yet a different way. There is some slight evidence (S.E. *A.M.* XI, 11; cf. XI, 9; 10; *A.M.* I, 86; Epict. II, 20, 2–3) that the Stoics avoided the use of universal propositions in favor of conditionals and, perhaps, negated conjunctions. If that is so, they may have regarded the use of universal propositions in arguments as unmethodical. As a result they may have refused to call Aristotelian syllogisms "syllogisms" for the additional reason that universal propositions are used in them.

B. The Peripatetic Position

(a) Aristotle's definition of syllogism

To understand the Peripatetic position on this issue one obviously has to start with a consideration of Aristotle's definition of the syllogism, which seems to have been accepted by the Peripatetic school throughout its history. This definition, as given in the *Prior Analytics*, 24^b 18–20, may be rendered thus: "a syllogism is a *logos* in which certain things being laid down something which differs from the things laid down follows of necessity in virtue of the fact that these are the case."

With reference to the interpretation of this definition, I want to make two assumptions. First, this definition can be looked at from two different angles. It was originally formulated with reference to a certain dialectical practice. And so its details can be explained with reference to this practice. But later Peripatetic authors, and even Aristotle himself in the *Analytics,* no longer thought of the definition as dependent on this dialectical context. And for this reason, to deal with our problem, we should interpret the definition independently of the context in which it arose.

Second, it is assumed that by *"logos,"* and therefore by "syllogism," Aristotle here does not mean a proposition, let alone a propositional schema with variables, but an inference or an argument. But, as this is a matter of dispute and as the whole discussion depends on the assumption that both Stoics and Peripatetics take syllogisms to be arguments, some justification has to be given for this assumption. There can be little doubt that the Peripatetics thought that Aristotle had arguments in mind when he talked about syllogisms. For otherwise they would not claim, as we have seen, that Stoic syllogisms are merely valid arguments, just as the Stoics would not claim that Aristotelian syllogisms are arguments, which, though valid, are not syllogisms, unless they thought that syllogisms are arguments. Moreover, the ancient commentators in their remarks on Aristotle's definition always presuppose that Aristotle is trying to define a class of arguments. And there seems to be good evidence that they did understand Aristotle correctly.

In other writings Aristotle uses "syllogism" to refer to an argument or an inference (*Top.* 130^a 7; 139^b 30; 156^a 8ff.; 157^a 18; 157^b 38; 158^a 8ff.; *Rhet.* 1356^b 17; 1357^a 10ff.; 1358^a 19; 1368^{b}2; *Met.* 1014^b 2; 1078^b 24). In the *Analytics* themselves there are many passages from which it seems clear that for Aristotle a syllogism is an argument (cf. *An. pr.* 42^a 1ff.; 42^a 31; 42^a 35ff.; 43^a 16; 43^b 34; 44^a 8; 45^a 26; 46^a 9; 46^a 33; 57^b 33; *An. post.* 73^a 24; 74^b 15; 75^b 22; 76^b 25; 78^b 23; 79^a 22). The definitions which Aristotle gives of the syllogism in other texts together with the context in which they occur indicate that he defines a class of arguments (Top. 100^a 25-27; *S.E.* 164^b 27ff.; Rhet. 1356^b 16-17). Since these definitions are almost identical with our definition in the *Analytics,* it would be surprising if Aristotle were not thinking of an argument here. That he has something different in mind in the *Analytics* seems to be excluded by the fact that in 25^b 30 he says that a proof is a syllogism of a certain kind. But clearly proofs are not propositions, and certainly not logical theses, but arguments of a certain kind. The way he talks about syllogistical premises in the introduction (24^a 28ff.) indicates that he is not merely referring to the antecedents of conditionals. The mere fact that he talks of premises and conclusions throughout the treaties would suggest that he is talking about arguments. That in connection with syllogisms he talks about prosyllogisms (42^b 5; 44^a 22) seems to make sense only if syllogisms are arguments. The way Aristotle refers back to the *Prior Analytics* in *An. post.* 73^a 12-16 seems to presuppose that he thinks he has been dealing with arguments in the *Prior Analytics.*

There is no reason to think that syllogistic cannot be both (a) a theory about arguments which tells us which arguments are syllogisms and why they are syllogisms and (b) a theory which still can be called a logical theory. It is such a theory, I think, that Aristotle expounds in *An. Pr.* A, 4–6. But in putting forth this theory, Aristotle uses formulas like (I) "If A is said of every B and B is said of every C, then necessarily A is said of every C." With reference to these formulas it has been maintained that: (a) these formulas are the genuine Aristotelian syllogisms, (b) these formulas are logical theses, which are the axioms of Aristotelian syllogistic or its theorems which Aristotle tries to prove by reducing them to the axioms, and therefore (c) Aristotelian syllogisms are logical theses.[6]

It is this position we have to argue against in order to justify our second assumption that Aristotle has arguments in mind when he talks about syllogisms. Perhaps we can attack this position in the following way. There seems to be little evidence for (a). But there is evidence against it. In two cases, for Baroco II (27^b 1) and Felapton (28^a 26), Aristotle, instead of using a formula like (I), uses a formula like (II): "if M belongs to every N, but not to every X, then there will be a syllogism to the effect that N does not belong to every X." In two cases for Celarent (25^b 40) and for Darapti (28^a 18), we get an elliptical formula like (II'): "If A is said of no B and B of every C, then that A will belong to no C." It is clear from the modal future tense in 26^a 2 and 28^a 19 (hyparxei), and the "necessarily" in 28^a 19, that what is to be understood with "that" in "then that A will belong to no C" is not "it is necessary" but again "there will be a syllogism to the effect . . . ," as in the case of Baroco II and Felapton. So of the fifteen cases (two for Baroco) in which Aristotle uses these letter-formulas in A, 4–6, four seem to be of type (II). Now all these formulas – of whatever type – are used in exactly the same context and seem to have exactly the same function. Therefore, if formulas of type (I) are syllogisms, formulas of type (II) should be syllogisms too. But the occurrence of the term "syllogism" in a formula like (II) makes it clear that Aristotle does not regard these formulae as syllogisms. Therefore, he cannot have regarded any of these formulas as syllogisms.

Similarly, there is evidence against (b). If Aristotle really regarded these formulas as the theses of his syllogistic, which he either assumes as axiomatic or which he tries to prove, it seems impossible to account for the fact that in the case of Darii (26^a 23) and Cesare (27^a 5) he uses formulas like (III): "Let A belong to every B and B to some C. If, then, to be said of everything is what has been said in the beginning, it is necessary that A belong to some C." Whatever the status of the formulas may be, it is clear that a formula of type (III) is not a logical thesis (nor does it look like a logical rule). Therefore one should not assume that any of the formulas are supposed to be logical theses. But, even if one thought that formulas of type (I) as opposed to formulas of type (III) could be logical theses, it cannot be the case that Aristotle tries to prove, or assumes as axiomatic, logical theses as presented by a formula of type (I). For then he would also have to use such a formula in the case of Darii and Cesare, which he does not. Moreover, formulas of type (II) do not look at all like logical theses of the kind Lukasiewicz had in mind. Therefore, even if one thought that formulas of different types may have different status, the fact that in six out of fifteen cases we do not get the formula we would expect should make one hesitant about the other nine cases. Finally, the way Aristotle introduces these formulas makes it implausible to assume that it is his aim in A, 5–6 to prove formulas of that sort. Throughout A, 4–6, Aristotle starts his paragraphs with general claims to the effect that if there are premises of such and such a kind there will be a syllogism. These claims usually cover two, in one case three, syllogistic moods. They are followed each time by as many letter-formulas as there are moods corresponding to the claim, i.e., usually two (in some cases, e.g., in 25^b 35–37, the claim and the formulas are separated by terminological remarks which come, so to speak, in brackets). The first formula in each set is introduced by "gar," the following by "homoiōs de kai," "kai," or "palin." This indicates that the formulae are introduced by Aristotle to specify and justify the initial statement that, given premises of such and such a kind, there will be a syllogism. So what Aristotle seems to be primarily concerned with in these chapters is the justification and, in the case of the second and the third figure, the proof of these general statements as specified by the formulas.

In this connection it may be noticed that, once we realize that it is not the letter-formulas, but the general statements that Aristotle tries to justify or prove, a new interpretation of the letters suggests itself. Those who assume that the letter-formulas have the status of logical theses naturally treat the letters as variables. One of the considerable disadvantages of such an interpretation is that it presupposes that Aristotle introduced variables into logic without even mentioning them. But the most natural interpretation of the fact that he does not care to explain his use of letters is that he thinks that there is no need for such an explanation, since everybody is already familiar with such a use of letters. This assumption he could have made, if he thought that his use of letters in syllogistic did not really differ from the way in which letters were and are used in geometry. In geometry we first state the proposition to be proved, e.g., one about isosceles triangles. We then proceed by saying, "let ABC be such a triangle," prove for ABC what was to be proved for isosceles triangles, and take this, by generalization, to be a proof for the proposition about isosceles triangles in general. Aristotle's procedure in syllogistic is rather similar. To take a derived mood, consider the way he deals with Cesare (27ª 3ff.). First the general proposition to be proved is stated. Aristotle then proceeds to say: "For let M be predicated of no N, but of every X." He then goes on to show that in this case N will belong to no X. And in this way the general proposition is taken to be established. But, if this account is correct, Aristotle argues by instantiation, and hence the letters should not be treated as variables, but as constants.

But, however this may be, if we reject (a) and (b), there is no good reason to assume (c). So we may proceed on the assumption that both Aristotle and the Peripatetics have arguments in mind when they talk about syllogisms. These, then, are the two assumptions I wanted to make with reference to the interpretation of Aristotle's definition of the syllogism.

Now sometimes it is claimed that, as far as this definition is concerned, any valid inference[7] or at least any valid inference with no fewer than two premises[8] will have to count as a syllogism. And in particular it is pointed out that conversions and propositional arguments (like hypothetical syllogisms) fit the definition but do not fit what Aristotle has to say about syllogisms later in the treatise. For there he talks as if only the traditional categorical syllogisms were syllogistical. On the basis of this apparent discrepancy it may be tempting to assume that Aristotle thought that all deductive inference takes the form of a categorical syllogism. But, if one has a closer look at the definition, it turns out that it is by no means as generous as it is supposed to be, though it may still be wide enough to cover inferences Aristotle does not want to regard as syllogisms.

The definition can be split up into two parts:

(a) syllogismos esti logos en hōi tethentōn heteron ti tōn keimenōn ex anankēs symbainei;

(b) (symbainei) tōi tauta einai.

For Aristotle in *An. pr.* A 32, 47ᵃ 22ff. explicitly distinguishes syllogisms from arguments in which something necessarily follows from the premises, i.e., arguments which satisfy only the first part of the definition. So the first part of the definition should define a class, or the class, of valid inferences, and the second part of the definition, we may assume, serves to single out those valid inferences which are syllogisms.

If we look at the first part of the definition it seems to exclude conversion and, in general, logically valid inference from one premise. It does this presumably on two counts. The Greek commentators all agree that the plural of "certain things being laid down" has to be taken seriously as referring to a plurality of premises (Alexander *In. an. pr.* 18, 1–2; Philoponus *In. an. pr.* 33, 10; Ammonius *In an. pr.* 27, 14). The reason seems to be that they think of syllogisms as arguments, and everybody in antiquity (except for Antipater, cf. Sextus Empiricus *P.H.* II, 167) agreed that arguments have to have at least two premises. Moreover, the mere expression "syllogism" suggested that such an inference was a matter of "putting things together." Alexander explicitly refers to the etymology of "syllogism" (*In an. pr.* 17, 12–18). Aristotle himself may have had yet another reason. For in *An. pr.* 58ᵃ 27–29 he says that the premises "B e A" and "A e B" are identical. Of course, he should not really want to say this. For on this assumption all moods which depend only on conversio simplex will collapse into the moods they are reduced to. And Aristotle himself, shortly afterward, in 59ᵃ 10–12, actually denies that "C i B" and "B i C" are identical (cf. also 27ᵃ 16–18). But, as Boethus did later (cf. Themistius *In Maximum,* p. 171, in: Badawi, *Transmission de la philosophie grecque au monde arabe,* Paris 1968), Aristotle still might want to say that they are identical in meaning or equivalent and that the requirement of the definition that the conclusion of a syllogism be different from any of the premises will be met only by a conclusion which is not just a different proposition but also different in meaning or even nonequivalent. So if conversion is regarded as a way of restating what has been said (in the case of conversio simplex) or a way of restating part of what has been said (in the case of conversio per accidens), then conversion will be excluded by the definition on two grounds. From what has been said it is clear that not just all formally valid one-premises inferences, such as conversion, but all sound inferences from one premise (like "he is breathing; therefore he is alive") are excluded. Also excluded are all inferences that use a premise which is identical with the conclusion, e.g., inferences of the form: "if p then p; but p; therefore p."

Alexander reports (*In an. pr.* 17 5–10) that some commentators assumed that the choice of "tethentōn" instead of "lēphthentōn" indicated that only inferences with categorical premises would count as syllogisms. (The assumption presumably can be explained with refernce (a) to the fact that "lemma" is a term that covers both hypothetical and categorical premises and (b) to the fact that the very term "hypothetical" suggests that hypothetical propositions in some sense are not theses.) This interpretation is in fact favored by Philoponus (*In an. pr.* 33, 6–10). And, if we adopted it, we would have a good chance to explain why Aristotle could think that the definition of the syllogism covers only categorical syllogisms. But this, of course, would just shift our problem. If the definition itself, as Ammonius (*In an. pr.* 27, 6–10) assumes, is wide enough to cover Stoic syllogisms, which have hypothetical premises, we have to look for an additional assumption which could explain why Aristotle actually seems to accept only categorical syllogisms as such, and why Alexander wants to say that hypothetical syllogisms are not really syllogisms. If, on the other hand, Stoic syllogisms are already excluded by the definition itself, we have to ask why the definition is formulated in such a way as to exclude inferences from hypothetical premises. So, for our purposes, we may leave it open whether it is the "tethenton" in the definition that restricts syllogisms to arguments with categorical premises, or whether it is the definition in conjunction with a further assumption that excludes Stoic syllogisms.

In any case it should be clear already from the first part of the definition that Aristotle is not trying to define valid inference in general but a kind of valid inference which can be used to argue for something. In fact, the first part of the definition can be regarded as a definition of valid arguments as opposed to valid inferences.

The second part of the definition then would stipulate that in syllogisms as opposed to other valid inferences, or arguments, the conclusion comes about of necessity just in virtue of the given premises.

Part of what is meant by this is brought out by the explanation Aristotle gives for this part of the definition (24^b 20–22). If, in a syllogism, something follows of necessity that is not due to the fact that the inference is based on some further assumption which has not been made explicit. The syllogism does not need an additional term, i.e., an additional premise involving at least one new term for the necessary to come about. This distinguishes syllogisms from the other valid arguments Aristotle refers to in *An. pr.* A 32. Although, in their case the conclusion comes about of necessity too, it does not come about just in virtue of the given premises, but we would have to add further premises to turn them into syllogisms (47^a 17; 19; 22; 28). So syllogisms are characterized by the fact that all the assumptions on which the inference is based have been made explicit.

But *An. pr.* A 32 also suggests that this is only part of what is meant by "tōi tauta einai." For there Aristotle discusses not only valid arguments which lack premises that in a syllogism would have to be explicit. He also refers to arguments with redundant or irrelevant premises which would have to be dropped if one wanted to turn them into syllogisms. Now Aristotle in the *Topics*, 161[b] 29-30, refers to such a case by saying: "eniote gar pleiō lambanousi tōn anankaiōn, hōste ou tōi taut' einai ginetai ho syllogismos." This seems to justify the assumption that Aristotle by "tōi tauta einai" does not just mean "in virtue of only these" but rather "in virtue of exactly these, i.e., the given premises."

How does Aristotle know that in a given case we have made all the necessary assumptions explicit? To judge from 24[b] 21-22 he seems to think that this is the case if no further assumption is necessary for the conclusion to come about of necessity. By this he cannot just mean that we have got all the assumption we need if, when the premises are true, the conclusion necessarily obtains. For, according to A 32, that is the case even when we have a valid argument which is not yet a syllogism because it still lacks a premise. So the necessity Aristotle has in mind in 24[b] 22 must be something like logical necessity. Hence the criterion Aristotle seems to have in mind is this: all assumptions have been made explicit if the conclusion follows logically from the assumptions.

A syllogism, then, according to Aristotle's definition would be a valid argument in which all the assumptions which are necessary for the conclusion to follow logically are made explicit and no redundant assumptions are made.

(b) the Peripatetic notion of a syllogism

Before we go on to consider how Aristotle and Peripatetics like Alexander could interpret this definition in such a way that it either directly, or in connection with some other assumption, excluded hypothetical syllogisms and in general all arguments which are not categorical syllogisms, let us notice the considerable agreement between the Stoic and the Aristotelian notion of a syllogism as we have outlined it so far.

Both Aristotle and the Stoics seem to agree that syllogisms are a subclass of valid arguments. Both think that syllogisms have to have at least two premises. Both think that syllogisms are characterized by the fact that in them all the assumptions have been made explicit. And whereas the Stoics think that any argument with redundant premises is invalid (S.E. *P.H.* II, 147), Aristotle at least seems to agree that syllogisms should not have redundant premises.

If we look for the discrepancies and leave aside the Stoic requirement for canonical formulation, there seems to be only one disagreement. Whereas Aristotle requires that the conclusion be different from any of the premises, the Stoics reject this restriction. For them even inferences of the form "if p, then p; but p; therefore p" or "if p, then if q, then p; but p; and q; therefore p" will count as syllogisms. This difference, which the commentators do not fail to point out

(Alex. *In an. pr.* 18, 13ff.; Philop. *In an. pr.* 33, 23ff.; Ammon. *In an. pr.* 27, 35ff.), may easily be misinterpreted. For we have tried to explain Aristotle's restriction by saying that he obviously is not interested in valid inference as such but in valid arguments. Now we might suspect that the difference between Stoic and Aristotelian syllogistic is due to the fact that the Stoics are just interested in logically valid inferences, whatever their use may be, whereas Aristotle is only interested in those correct forms of inference that can be used in argument.

Actually there are good reasons to suppose that both systems are set up to serve the needs of a proof-theory and both systems reflect that end. For Aristotle and the Aristotelian tradition this seems to be clear, if we keep in mind that the *Prior* and *Posterior Analytics* form one treatise whose object, as the first sentence of the *Prior Analytics* states, is scientific proof and science. Aristotle himself in 25^b 26–31 explains that he first will deal with syllogisms in general because all proofs are syllogisms. The *Prior Analytics* may be regarded as setting forth the formal conditions an Aristotelian proof has to satisfy, whereas the *Posterior Analytics* will specify the material conditions, e.g., that the premises in proofs have to be true and necessary. As to the Stoics, a remark by Sextus (P.H. II, 247) seems to indicate a similar position. According to Sextus the dialecticians claim that they are not really interested in the validity of arguments as such but in the question of how one can know something to be true or false (cf. Ammon. *In an. pr.* 9, 26–27; S.E. *P.H.* II, 229; Cic. *Ac. pr.* 28, 91; *De or,* II, 38, 157; Diogenes Laertius IV, 45).

But there are two differences, the first of which deserves to be worked out in more detail. To begin with, the notion of what a proof should be like is different. For there is a disagreement about the kinds of propositions that can be proved and about the kind of proposition that can serve as a starting point for a proof. Aristotle thinks these have to be categorical universal propositions. When he sets up the principle of the pons asinorum in chapters 27ff. of the *Prior Analytics,* he even talks as if only syllogisms with universal premises were syllogisms (cf. 43^b 11–14), though he is quite willing to use Darii in 45^a 29–31 and therefore obviously is familiar with other syllogistic forms. The Stoics, on the other hand, think that the truth of singular propositions is a proper object of knowledge and that therefore proofs may have singular conclusions and premises. Moreover, for reasons we have touched on in the beginning, they think that proofs should be based on hypothetical propositions.

The second difference we have to notice here is that the Stoics, once the syllogistical system is set up in the way it is, consider as irrelevant the objection, constantly brought forward by the Peripatetics, that some forms of inference yielded by the system are utterly useless (cf. e.g., Alexander *In an. pr.* 18, 13ff.). So for the Stoics it is not essential that a syllogism can actually be used as an argument or that an argument of its form could be used as a proof. For the Peripatetics, however, this seems to be built into the notion of a syllogism.

It is obvious that this position is a rather dangerous one. For the concept of an argument invites loading, and the more it is loaded the more one gets distracted from that part of the definition of the syllogism which requires that a syllogism be a logically valid inference. And this is bound to happen all the more if one does not have much of an interest in logically valid inferences as such to start with.

That this actually did happen one can see in Alexander. He assumes that a syllogism has to show or establish something. (The Greek words used are "deiknynai" and "deixis" cf. *In an. pr.* 18, 20, 22 263, 9–11; 265, 6–9; 14–16; 19–23.) This, in turn, is taken to entail two things. In the first place, to show or to establish something is to show that something is the case; and that something is the case is expressed by a categorical proposition, whereas a hypothetical proposition serves a different function. Therefore Alexander argues that, strictly speaking, arguments with hypothetical conclusions, and especially the so-called totally hypothetical syllogisms, are not really syllogisms at all (*In an. pr.* 265, 13-17). The second assumption about showing seems to be this: one cannot show that something is the case if one has to presuppose in one's argument that that which is to be shown is a fact. This assumption is used in at least two ways to disqualify inferences as syllogisms. First of all it is, of course, used to exclude Stoic syllogisms in which the conclusion occurs as a premises (cf., e.g., Alex. *In an. pr.* 18, 16ff.). Second, it apparently is used to exclude inferences in which acceptance or knowledge of one of the premises already presupposes acceptance or knowledge of the conclusion. It seems to be for this reason that Galen (*I.L.* p. 32, 17–21; 34, 9–10) rejects Chrysippus' third indemonstrable, i.e., arguments of the form "not both p and q; but p; therefore not q." For in order to know "not both p and q" (if "not . . . and . . . " is defined truthfunctionally and "not both p and q" happens to satisfy just this and not a stronger criterion) one already has to know whether "p" and "q" are true or not. So Galen replaces this form of argument by one which uses the same wording but requires that "p" "q" should be incompatible. Since Alexander, too, has qualms about the third indemonstrable and wonders whether it is not identical with the first one (*In an. pr.* 264, 15-17), we may assume that he, also, objects at least to the Stoic interpretation of the third indemonstrable.

All this makes one wonder whether it could not be an assumption of this kind which, in conjunction with the definition of the syllogism, prompted Peripatetics like Alexander to claim that Stoic syllogisms are not really syllogisms. As a matter of fact, Alexander does say that hypothetical syllogisms, taken by themselves, do not show anything (*in an. pr.* 265, 22-23). And he contrasts them with categorical syllogisms, which can be called syllogisms without qualification, because they can, by themselves, show or establish something (*In an. pr.* 265, 21-22; 265, 12). Philoponus takes this up; and, in an obvious allusion to Aristotle's explanation of his definition of the syllogism, he says that Aristotle is mainly concerned with the categorical syllogism because categorical syllogisms are complete and do not need anything in addition ("toutōn men teleiōn ontōn kai mēdenos exōthen deomenōn"; *In an. pr.* 242, 15–17).

Now why would Alexander and Philoponus think that an inference of the form "if p, then q; but p; therefore q" by itself does not show or establish anything? Alexander seems to argue this way. Assume that both premises, i.e., "if p, then q" and "p" are accepted or known; then there will be no syllogism at all (*In an. pr.* 263, 7–9; 265, 3–7). The reason he gives for this is: in such a case everything will already be known and there will be no use for a syllogism; for a syllogism has to show something which would not be known without this syllogism (263, 9–11; 265, 7–8).

The assumption about 'showing' involved here seems to be different from the two encountered so far. Apparently, Alexander assumes that one cannot show a conclusion C by means of premises P1, P2 . . . Pn if, accepting or knowing premises P1 . . . Pn, one cannot fail to accept or know C. Now in a sense it seems to be perfectly true that in accepting the premises of a hypothetical syllogism one cannot fail to accept the conclusion. But in this sense the same holds true for a categorical syllogism. So this cannot be what Alexander has in mind. Now Aristotle in one passage (*An. Pr.* B 21, 67ᵃ 33–37) suggests that somebody may know two premises but fail to put them together and make the correct inference and instead hold a belief contrary to that conclusion he fails to draw. So Alexander may think that with a categorical syllogism one may know the premises but fail to make the inference, whereas with a hypothetical syllogism one cannot fail to make the inference and know the conclusion once one knows the premises. There is one detail in Alexander's account which suggests that he made such an assumption. For in 262, 32–35 he talks as if, given the assumption that if p then q, we already have established q if we manage to establish p (cf. *In top.* 165, 13–18). And again in 265, 12–13 he talks as if by establishing p we at the same time establish q ("synkataskeuazetai toutōi kai to hepomenon"). So he seems to think that if there is a categorical syllogism "p; q; therefore r" and we already have established "p" and "q" it still takes a syllogism to get "r" because one may accept or know "p" and "q" but fail to accept "r." But if we have a hypothetical syllogism "if p, then q; but p; therefore q" and accept the two premises, it does not take another syllogism to show "q" on the basis of these two premises because that inference will already have been made, so that by establishing "p" we already have established "q."

What could make Alexander think that categorical and hypothetical syllogisms differ in this curious way? The reason seems to be that for Alexander categorical and hypothetical premises do not just differ as propositions but also as premises. When it is convenient for him, he treats hypothetical propositions like "if p then q" not as if they stated a connection between "p" and "q" but as if they either stated "q" with the proviso that p, or stated one's willingness to accept a proof for "p" as a proof for "q." On this interpretation hypothetical premises do not really make explicit an assumption from which one argues, but rather a part of the machinery by means of which one argues.

So there will be a difference between categorical and hypothetical syllogisms in that in categorical syllogisms we have two explicit premises and a nonexplicit logical rule which allows us to draw the conclusion. In hypothetical syllogisms, on the other hand, we have one explicit assumption and one explicit, usually nonlogical, rule which allows us to state the conclusion if the assumption is granted. And Alexander, wrongly, seems to think that because in one case the rule is explicit, and in the other case it is not, in the first case one cannot fail to apply it whereas in the other case one can.

Assuming that hypothetical syllogisms do not show anything if both premises are known, Alexander goes on to consider the case where just one premise is known or accepted. In this case, he tries to argue, it will be the categorical minor which stands in need of proof. For it is characteristic, he says, of hypothetical syllogisms that the hypothetical major is regarded as granted and evident (*In an. pr.* 263, 11–13; 265, 3–5; cf. Ps. Ammonius, *In an. pr.* 65, 39; 67, 13). If one tried to prove the hypothetical major too, the syllogism would cease to be hypothetical (264, 33–265, 3). It is not quite clear what he means by this. And the situation is further complicated by the fact that in one place (263, 22) Alexander admits tentatively, and then (264, 8ff.) without reservation, that the hypothetical premise may stand in need of proof, too. Now we know from Philoponus (*In an. pr.* 252, 2–8) that there was a dispute over the question whether both premises may stand in need of proof or whether just the minor may have to be proved. And Philoponus remarks that Alexander quite rightly adopted the second position (the first position was taken, e.g., by Ammonius, *In de int.* 3, 20ff., and Boethius, *De syll. hyp.* I, 2, 4; II, 1, 2–3; *In Cic. top.* 1132 C). But the reason Philoponus gives for adopting the second position is not very illuminating; he says that if the hypothetical major were not granted, the argument would not get off the ground.

The explanation for the dispute and the reason for Alexander's wavering may be this: if both premises are treated as ordinary premises, as they should be, then there is no reason why both should not stand in need of proof. But if hypothetical premises are supposed to have the strange status I tried to indicate earlier, then by their very nature they do not require a proof. For they represent an agreement as opposed to something that has been proved, and this agreement is not an agreement about facts but about moves to be allowed in the argument. It is such an agreement which makes a hypothetical syllogism hypothetical. If we now assume that Alexander does not distinguish sufficiently between an agreement that a move from "p" to "q' shall be allowed and an agreement that "q" follows from "p," then we may assume that he thinks that, if what was agreed to is proved, the syllogism no longer is hypothetical.

But, whatever the precise reason may be, Alexander in his argument against hypothetical syllogisms only considers the possibility that the minor stands in need of proof. And, in this case, he argues, if the minor is just assumed without proof, nothing will be shown at all and therefore there will be no syllogism (265, 8–10). So, if anything is shown at all, it will be due to the fact that the minor has been proved. And this, being a categorical proposition, will be proved by a categorical syllogism. Therefore, if anything is shown at all, it will be due to this categorical syllogism. And hence the only thing that is syllogistic about a hypothetical syllogism is the categorical syllogism establishing its minor (265, 9–10; 265, 17–19). This argument seems to beg the question by assuming that the minor can be established only by a syllogism that is categorical. But Alexander presumably would argue that if it could be established by a hypothetical syllogism it would have to be one whose minor stands in need of proof. For, if it did not, then the minor of the hypothetical syllogism in question would not require a proof. But if the minor of the second hypothetical syllogism stands in need of proof, either this proof itself, or some proof, will have to be categorical to stop a regress. And it will be in virtue of that categorical syllogism that anything will have been shown at all.

So at least Alexander's attitude toward noncategorical inferences, and especially Stoic syllogisms, seems to be determined by two assumptions:

(1) only inferences of a form such that an inference of that form can show or establish something can be called syllogisms. To show or establish something is supposed to entail:

    (a) what is supposed to be shown is not used as a premise;

    (b) what is supposed to be shown is not presupposed by any of the premises in such a way that one has to accept or know the conclusion in order to accept or know the premise.

    (c) one can fail to know what is supposed to be shown even if one knows the premises.

(2) hypothetical premises, at least in hypothetical syllogisms, are not treated as assumptions about facts but as assumptions about the way one can argue which are to be exploited in the course of the argument in which they are made explicit.

It is on the basis of these assumptions that Alexander may think that only Aristotelian categorical syllogisms are really syllogisms, though he is quite willing to admit that there are many other forms of valid, and even logically valid, inference.

Since Alexander is interpreting Aristotle, we should not be surprised to find at least some evidence in Aristotle to suggest that Aristotle himself had taken a similar position. Aristotle in several places (*An. pr.* 40^b 27; 41^a 21; 41^a 35; 45^a 24) refers to categorical syllogisms as "deiktikoi." Alexander (*In an. pr.*

256, 12–14; cf. 262, 32 and 263, 15) seems to think that by "deiktikos" Aristotle means "categorical" (cf. Philop. *In an. pr.* 248, 2). For Alexander explains that in those days "kategorikos" meant "affirmative" so that Aristotle could not use that expression. This explanation is not very fortunate. For Aristotle also uses "deiktikos" in the sense of "affirmative" (*An. post.* 86^a 32). It seems more natural to assume that by "deiktikos" Aristotle means "capable of showing something" because he, too, thinks that, in some sense, only categorical syllogisms do show something. For in 50^a 16ff. he says with reference to syllogisms from a hypothesis that their conclusion has not been shown but is only granted in virtue of that hypothesis; and again in 50^a 24ff. he says with reference to a particular argument from hypothesis that its conclusion has not been shown though one has to grant it; but one has to grant it not in virtue of a syllogism, but in virtue of a hypothesis. The reason why he, too, thinks that only categorical syllogisms show something unqualifiedly, whereas arguments from a hypothesis may at best be said to show something on the basis of a hypothesis (cf. 40^b 23–25), comes out when he refers to the hypothetical premise not just as a "hypothesis" but also as a "homologia" (41^a 40; cf. 50^a 18; 50^a 25) and a "syntheke" (50^a 18). So hypothetical propositions, understood in this way, can be neither proper conclusions of a syllogism (they are not the kind of thing one can infer) nor are they premises, properly speaking.

On the basis of such an interpretation of hypothetical premises and on the assumption that syllogisms, being defined as arguments, have to show that something is the case, Aristotle may well have thought that his definition of the syllogism fitted exactly what he was going to treat as syllogisms in the *Analytics*.

III. The Dispute over Priority

As we have seen, it is sometimes claimed that the dispute between Peripatetics and Stoics was mainly a dispute over the priority of their respective syllogistics. From what we have said so far, this does not seem to be very plausible. For asking which kind of syllogism is prior to the other seems to presuppose that one accepts both kinds of syllogisms, which neither the Stoics nor the orthodox Peripatetics were prepared to do. So we should expect that this question would be asked by Stoics who have come to accept Aristotelian syllogisms as such, or by Peripatetics who rejected the Aristotelian interpretation of hypothetical propositions and therefore were prepared to accept Stoic syllogisms.

If we look at the evidence for a dispute over priority, it certainly does not confirm the view that it was a debate between Stoic and Peripatetic logicians. In fact there are only two pieces of evidence, both of which had already been adduced by Lukasiewicz (p. 121) as testimony that the Stoics were aware of the logical relation between Aristotelian and Stoic syllogistic. In his commentary on the *Topics* (218, 4–5), Alexander quotes the following question as an example of what he calls a syncritical problem: "Which syllogism is first, the categorical or the hypothetical?" Alexander gives no further details and so all this passage shows is that this was a question which was discussed. The second piece of evidence comes from Galen's *Institutio logica* (17, 4–7): "kai mentoi kai tōn ek tou Peripatou tines hōsper kai Boēthos ou monon anapodeiktous onomazousi tous ek tōn hēgemonikōn lēmmatōn syllogismous, alla kai prōtous, hosoi de ek katē-gorikōn protaseōn eisin anapodeiktoi syllogismoi, toutous ouk eti protous onomazein synchorousi." All we can infer from this passage is that some Peripatetics, like Boethus, were willing to accept hypothetical syllogisms and that they even went so far as to claim priority for them. There is no evidence, then, for the assumption that the two schools engaged in a dispute over the priority of the two systems. Still less can these passages be used as proof that the Stoics had what is supposed to be a proper understanding of the relation between the two systems.

But, it may be argued, we know how much Boethus was influenced by the Stoics, not only in logic; the very fact that he accepts Stoic syllogisms as such and is even willing to grant priority to them confirms this; possibly, therefore, his position and his reasons for granting priority to hyothetical syllogisms reflect Stoic doctrine. Let us ask, then, how Boethus might have come to the conclusion that hypothetical syllogisms are prior. W. Kneale (p. 175) suggests that it was pointed out to the Peripatetics that in the reduction of syllogisms they made un-acknowledged use of principles of Stoic syllogistic. As a matter of fact, some ancient philosophers (cf. Apuleius, *De int.* 191, 5ff.) thought that reductio proofs for the validity of syllogisms are based on the first thema of Stoic syllogistic (an argument-conversion rule). But even if this were true, it would only justify the assumption that, in some sense, Baroco and Bocardo are posterior to the elementary hypothetical syllogisms. And, in general, all interpretations which refer to the reduction of syllogisms will only explain why some categorical syllogisms could have been thought to be posterior. What we need instead is some reason why all categorical syllogisms, including Barbara and Celarent, might be thought of as posterior to the hypothetical syllogisms.

And quite apart from this, Boethus at least cannot have based his claim on the fact that the reduction of syllogisms requires certain principles of Stoic syllogistic. For he seems to have denied that syllogisms in the second and the third figure are less perfect than those in the first figure and therefore have to be reduced to make their validity obvious (Ammon. *In an. pr.* 31, 12ff.; Themistius *In Maximum* pp. 170ff.). So Boethus must have believed—as in fact Galen seems to say—that even Barbara and Celarent are posterior to the Stoic indemonstrables. Hence he perhaps thought that the Stoics were right when they claimed that their syllogisms—as opposed to the Peripatetic syllogisms including Barbara and Celarent—only presuppose the most elementary logical assumptions that could not be avoided anyway.

It is not clear, either, how those Peripatetic and eclectic logicians argued who accepted both kinds of syllogisms but still wanted to maintain that categorical syllogisms are prior. Galen, who does not try to hide his lack of interest in this debate (*I.L.* 17, 14–15), just says that, in a sense, categorical syllogisms are prior because hypothetical premises presuppose the categorical premises they are made up of (17, 9–14).

One of the causes of the controversy may have been that those engaged in the discussion did not have a clear notion of the kind of priority they wanted to argue for. After all, there are various kinds of priority which could be thought to hold between categorical and hypothetical syllogisms. It seems to be a consideration of this kind which Patzig (*Aristotle's Theory of the Syllogism*, p. 184n 7 — *Die aristotelische Syllogistik*, 1969[3], p. 139 nl) has in mind when he says that Aristotle could argue that his syllogistic is elementary and when he remarks that one should not call propositional logic more elementary than Aristotelian syllogistic without qualification.

8

The Original Notion of Cause

However muddled our notion of a cause may be it is clear that we would have difficulties in using the term 'cause' for the kinds of things Aristotle calls 'causes'.[1] We might even find it misleading to talk of Aristotelian causes and wonder whether in translating the relevant passages in Aristotle we should not avoid the term 'cause' altogether. For an end, a form, or matter do not seem to be the right kinds of items to cause anything, let alone to be causes. It is much less clear what our difficulties are due to. We might think that causes are events. Sometimes this is regarded as almost a truism. And, indeed, philosophers since Hume, who still—at least in his language—is wavering on the matter, have tended to think of causes as events. But I doubt that our difficulty with Aristotelian causes is due to the fact that ends, forms, and matter clearly are not events or anything like events. For apart from the fact that one may have doubts about the general thesis that causes are events, we do not have any difficulty in understanding Kant, e.g., when he talks as if a substance, an object, could be the cause of something in another object (*Critique of Pure Reason* B III), as if the sun could be said to be the cause of the warming up of the stone or the melting of the butter. And the reason why we do not have any difficulty in understanding this kind of language seems to me to be the following: a physical object like the sun or a billiard-ball can interact with other things, it can affect them and act on them so as to produce an effect in them. Quite generally our use of causal terms seems to be strongly coloured by the notion that in causation there is something which in some sense does something or other so as to produce or bring about an effect. Even if we do think of causes as events the paradigms we tend to think of, and certainly the paradigms Hume and Kant thought of, are events in which something does something or other; and we feel that we have to explain that it is only in a very metaphorical sense that an event could be said to produce an effect. Thus, though we may want to get away from such a notion, there is a strong tendency to conceive of causes as somehow active. And it seems that our difficulty with the Aristotelian causes is due to the fact that they cannot even be conceived of in this way. A good part of the unfortunate history of the notion of a final cause has its origin in the assumption that the final cause, as a cause, must act and in the vain attempt to explain how it could be so. It is only with Aristotle's moving cause that we think that we readily understand why it should be called a cause. But it would be a mistake to think that Aristotle with his notion of a moving cause tried to capture our notion of cause or at least a notion we would readily recognize as a notion of cause, though it is significant that people have tended to think that among the Aristotelian causes it is only the moving cause which is a cause really. For Aristotle in more theoretical contexts will tell that it is not the sculptor working on his sculpture who is the moving cause, but the art of sculpture. And with the art of sculpture we have the same problems as with ends, forms, and matter.

Aristotle's notion of cause, then, is quite different from ours. But it is by no means peculiar to Aristotle. The same difficulties we have with Aristotle and the Peripatetics we also have with Plato or Epicurus. Ideas do not seem to be the kind of thing that could cause anything, nor does the void (cf. Epicurus in DL X 44). But how did it come about that people got to think that a cause has to be the kind of item which can do something or other so as to bring about an effect?

From a remark in Sextus Empiricus it is clear that it was already in later antiquity that the notion of a cause had been narrowed down to fit the notion of an active cause. For in his discussion of causality Sextus tells us (*PH* III 14) that despite all the differences among philosophers concerning causality we still might assume that they all agree on the following general characterization of a cause: the cause is that because of which in virtue of its being active the effect comes about.[2] Sextus, then, claims that it is generally agreed that causes are items which somehow are active and through their activity bring about an effect. This claim would be puzzling, indeed, given what we have said earlier about Plato, Aristotle, and Epicurus, unless it reflected a general shift in the notion of cause. But we have good reason to accept Sextus' claim. First of all, Sextus shows himself to be quite aware of the fact that even non-active items get called 'causes'. For in the preceding paragraph he tells us that he now wants to turn to a consideration of the active cause in general (*to energetikon aition*). There would be no point in adding the adjective 'active' if Sextus were not aware that non-active items, too, are called causes. So Sextus must assume that though philosophers go on to call such items as Platonic ideas or Aristotelian causes 'causes', they nevertheless are agreed that, strictly speaking, only active items are causes. Second, there is independent evidence that Sextus had good reason to think so. Clement, e.g., tell us (*Strom.* I 17, 82, 3) 'we say . . . that the cause is conceived of as producing, as active, and as doing something'[3] (cf. also *Strom.* VIII 9, 25, 5). As we learn from Simplicius' commentary on the *Catego-*

ries (327, 6ff.), Iamblichus explained a passage in Plato's *Philebus* telling us that it is that which is producing something (*to poioun*) which is, strictly speaking, the cause, whereas matter and form are not causes at all, but auxiliaries (*sunaitia*), and the paradigm and the end only qualifiedly are causes. We find similar remarks throughout the Neoplatonic tradition. Damascius, e.g., tells us that every cause is doing something (*drastērion, in Phileb.* 114, 6 W.). The Peripatetic distinction of kinds of causes is adapted to the shift by claiming that it is the moving cause which is most strictly speaking the cause (*aition to kuriōtaton legomenon*), as we can see from a passage in Simplicius (*in Phys.* 326, 15ff.). The shift in terminology from 'causa movens' to 'causa efficiens' may be another reflection of the change in notion (cf., e.g., Simpl. *in Phys.* 326, 25). Evidence of this kind is easily multiplied, and thus we have good reason to believe that the notion of a cause by Sextus' time had changed in such a way as to be restricted to items which can do something or other and thus cause something. It also seems to be fairly clear how this change in the notion of a cause did come about. Seneca (*Ep.* LXV 11; cf. 2ff.) still criticizes Plato for assuming the five kinds of causes we just saw Iamblichus talking about on the grounds that there is just one kind of cause, that which acts so as to produce the effect: "The Stoics take the view that there is just one cause, that which does something (*facit*)" (LXV 4). In general it is the Stoics who insist that causes are active, and so it seems to be their influence which has brought about the change in question.

But Stoic influence on thought about causes is not restricted to this point. When we look, e.g., at Sextus' discussion of causes in the *Outlines of Pyrrhonism* it turns out that the distinctions of kinds of causes Sextus makes are all of Stoic origin. And hence it might be worthwhile to review our evidence concerning the Stoic doctrine of causes, not just to find out why the Stoics would insist that causes have to be active, but in the hope of getting somewhat clearer on the history of the notion of a cause in general.

Before we go into the details, though, it should be pointed out that the Stoics seem to distinguish at least three uses of 'cause' of increasing narrowness. There is, first of all, a very general use of 'cause'. It seems to be this use we have to think of when Stobaeus (*Ecl.* I, p. 138, 23) says "Chrysippus says that a cause is a because of which (*di' ho*)." Just like the English preposition 'because of' and the German '*wegen*' the Greek '*dia*' with the accusative can cover such a variety of explanatory relations that it would rather comfortably accommodate anything that had been called a cause, in ordinary discourse or by philosophers, including the Aristotelian causes (cf. *Phys.* 198^b 5ff.).

One may, of course, doubt whether Chrysippus' characterization of a cause is supposed to be so generous as to allow us to call all the things causes which actually are called causes. In this case one would have to assume that '*dia*' here is used in a narrower technical sense. But there is evidence that the Stoics were willing to allow for such a generous use of 'cause', though, at the same time, they also insisted on a narrower use. When, then, Clement (VIII 9, 20, 3) says: "It is the same thing, then, which is a cause and which is productive; and if something is a cause and productive it invariably also is a because of which; but if something is a because of which it is not invariably also a cause" and then goes on to give antecedent causes as examples of things which are because of which, but not causes in this sense, it is natural to assume that he is relying on a contrast between a more general notion of a cause according to which any because of which counts as a cause, and a narrower notion which he wants to adopt, according to which a cause not only has to be a because of which, but also productive. Hence it seems that when Chrysippus characterizes the cause as the because of which he allows for a very general notion of a cause.

Then there is the narrower notion of a cause, which Clement in the passage quoted refers to, according to which causes are restricted to those things which actually do something or other to bring about an effect. It is this notion of an active cause of which Sextus claims that it is one all philosophers recognize and accept. It is not just the because of which, but the because of which through whose activity the effect comes about, to use Sextus' characterization. But even this narrower notion of an active cause covers different kinds of causal relations which the Stoics will distinguish by distinguishing various kinds of causes. And among these kinds they will single out that which is the cause, strictly speaking, namely the perfect (*autoteles*) or containing (*sunektikon*) cause. Since the most general notion of a cause is not specifically Stoic, I shall in the following discuss first the general Stoic notion of an active cause and then the various kinds of causes distinguished, in particular causes in the narrowest and strictest sense.

The General Notion of an Active Cause

We said that one had to explain in what sense Aristotelian causes could be called causes. Ends or forms do not seem to be the right kinds of items to be causes. And, as we have seen, one reason for this may be that they are entities, whereas causes, one might think, are events, facts, things one does, in short, items of the kind I shall call propositional items (I take all these items to be propositional items in some very narrow sense, but for our purposes here it will do to take the term in a very generous sense).

Now it is true that at least from the fifth century B.C. onward such propositional items, too, come to be called causes, *aitia*. But throughout antiquity, as far as I can see, it is non-propositional items like Aristotle's causes which are referred to when causes are discussed systematically. This is not to deny that philosophers when they state the cause of something sometimes refer to propositional items ('The cause of this is that . . . '). In this they just follow the shift in ordinary language mentioned above. Aristotle sometimes even refers to propositional items when he gives examples of his kinds of causes. But in other passages it is clear that when he distinguishes kinds of causes he has entities, non-propositional items in mind. And the later tradition quite definitely treats Aristotelian causes as non-propositional. Similarly, Epicurus treats causes as non-propositional when he regards the atoms and the void as the ultimate causes of everything (DL X 44). The same is true of the five causes of the Middle Platonists (Sen. *Ep.* LXV 7–8) and of the six causes of the Neoplatonists (cf. Simp. *in Phys.* II. 2–3; Olymp. *in Phaed.* 207, 27ff.; Philop. *De aet. mundi* 159, 5ff.). And it is certainly true of the Stoics who require a cause to be a being, an entity, a status they deny to propositional items.

The facts of the matter become clearer if we take into account a terminological distinction which Stobaeus attributes to Chrysippus (*Ecl.* I, 139 3f. W.). This distinction has a basis in the original use of the word 'cause' which distinguished between an *aition* and an *aitia*. But this distinction is not preserved by Aristotle; and as a result it is much less clear than it would otherwise have been whether we are considering propositional or non-propositional items when we talk about causes. Chrysippus' distinction is the following. Having explained that an *aition*, a cause, according to Chrysippus is an entity, Stobaeus goes on to say, "But an *aitia*, he says, is an account of the *aition*, or the account about the *aition* as *aition*"[4]). We might have doubts as to the precise meaning of this short characterization of an *aitia*, if we did not have a fragment of Diocles of Carystus (frag. 112 Wellmann) preserved by Galen. Diocles discusses etiology, explanation, in medicine, and in this discussion he uses 'the account about the *aition*' interchangeably with 'the *aitia*' in the sense of 'the reason' or 'the explanation'. Obviously the idea is that the *aitia*, the reason or explanation, is a *logos*, a propositional item of a certain kind, namely a statement or a truth about the *aiton*, the cause, or rather the relevant truth about the cause, the truth in virtue of which it is the cause. And this seems to be exactly the characterization of an *aitia* Stobaeus is attributing to Chrysippus.

By Chrysippus' time ordinary usage of '*aition*' and '*aitia*' no longer followed that distinction. But there was some basis for the terminological distinction in the original use of these words. '*Aiton*' is just the neuter of the adjective '*aitios*' which originally meant 'culpable, responsible, bearing the blame', whereas the '*aitia*' is the accusation, what somebody is charged with having done such that he is responsible for what happened as a result. And if we look at Plato's remarks on explanation in the *Phaedo* we see that such a distinction in use between '*aiton*' and '*aitia*' is still preserved. In spite of its ample use of both the adjective and the noun, the passage reserves the adjective for entities like Anaxagoras' Nous and Socrates' bones and sinews, whereas an *aitia* throughout seems to be a propositional item, the reason or explanation why something is the way it is. It is true that Aristotle does not preserve the terminological distinction. And Galen in one place tells us explicitly that he uses '*aition*' and '*aitia*' interchangeably (IX 458, 7 K). But even if the terminological distinction was not generally accepted, the distinction itself between causes, on the one hand, and reasons and explanations, the truths about causes in virtue of which they are causes, on the other, was generally accepted. In fact, for the very reasons the Stoics rejected, e.g., Aristotelian final causes as causes, properly speaking, they also had to reject propositional items as causes. Since, on the Stoic view, propositional items are not entities, but only *lekta*, somethings, they are not items of the right kind to cause anything. How would an event go about causing something?

So there would be general agreement that causes are non-propositional items. And there would be general agreement that the notion of a cause is closely tied to the notion of an explanation. For an item is a cause only insofar as something is true of it in virtue of which it is the cause. If Brutus is a cause of Caesar's death he is a cause insofar, e.g., as it is true of him that he stabbed Caesar. And it is exactly these truths about the causes of something which will be regarded as affording an explanation of what the causes are causes of.

It is at this point, though, that the disagreement among ancient philosophers will start. For reasons which will become apparent, the question will arise to which of the two notions, cause or explanation, should we give priority. It seems fairly clear that the opponents of the Stoics give priority to the notion of explanation. They are looking for an account of something and they will just call causes those items which have to be referred to in the account. If it is the presence of the idea of justice which accounts for the fact that something is just, then the idea of justice will be a cause. It is clear that on this view the notion of a cause completely loses its connotation of responsibility. The Stoics, on the other hand, are not so much interested in explanation as they are in responsibility.

Though this is a matter which would need a good deal of elaboration, the following statement by Strabo about Posidonius does seem to me to reflect the Stoic attitude in general well enough: "With him [sc. Posidonius] we find a lot of etiology and a lot of Aristotelizing which the members of our school shy away from because of the obscurity of the causes" (II 3, 8). According to Strabo, then, the Stoics in general are hesitant to engage in etiology because the real causes are so hidden and obscure; Posidonius is an exception, and in this respect he is rather more like a Peripatetic. There is abundant evidence to support Strabo's testimony. Later Stoic physics, presumably under the influence of Posidonius, recognizes etiology as a separate part of physics (DL VII 132). It in turn is divided into two parts, one whose subject matter the philosopher shares with the physician, namely physiology and psychology, and another part whose subject matter the philosopher shares with the mathematical sciences, namely natural, in particular meteorological, phenomena. As to the second part of etiology, we not only know how much of an effort Posidonius made to find explanations for particular phenomena like the tides. The relevant part in Diogenes' exposition of Stoic physics (VII 151, 3–156, I), e.g., refers again and again to Posidonius. In fact the only other authority that is mentioned in the whole section is Zeno.

But we also know from a passage in Seneca (*Ep.* LXXXVIII 26–27) and a precious excerpt from Geminus' Epitome of Posidonius'*Meteorologica* (preserved through Alexander's commentary on the *Physics* by Simplicius, *in Phys.* 291, 21ff.) that Posidonius held views concerning causation and explanation which would deserve separate treatment. He took, e.g., the view that only the natural philosopher can have knowledge of the true account of the cause of a phenomenon, whereas the mathematical scientist can only provide us with the hypotheses or possible explanations, as Heraclides Ponticus provided us with a possible explanation of the apparent motion of the sun by assuming a somehow stationary sun and a somehow revolving earth (ibid. 292, 20–23). The other part of etiology which concerns itself with psychology and physiology among other things deals with the passions of the soul (cf. DL VII 158). Of Posidonius' views on this particular topic we are well informed by Galen. Galen in his *De placitis Hippocratis et Platonis* goes to considerable lengths to criticize Chrysippus' views on the matter, and in doing so he relies heavily on Posidonius' criticism of Chrysippus which he also sets out in some detail. It is characteristic that it is a recurring complaint that Chrysippus fails to state the cause or claims that the true explanation is uncertain or too difficult to figure out (cf. 348, 16ff. Mueller; 395, 12ff., 400, 2ff; 401, 9ff.; 439, 4ff., to just mention the Posidonian passages). It is evidence of this kind which supports Strabo's testimony that Posidonius is an exception and that Stoics in general were hesitant to concern themselves with etiology, with the explanation of particular phenomena.

Hence it would seem that the Stoic interest in causes does not arise from an interest in actual explanation. The evidence, rather, suggests that the Stoic interest in causes arises from their interest in responsibility. For when we look at the actual use to which the Stoics put their theory of causes it always seem to be a matter of allotting and distributing responsibility. For example, whatever things do is determined by fate, but fate is a mere helping cause (*sunergon*). The real cause, the things which really are responsible, are the things themselves; they do what they do out of their own nature or character. Or, the wise man may say what is false. But if, as a result, somebody believes it, it is not the wise man who is the cause, but the person who believes it has only himself to blame. Only dumb and wicked people believe falsehoods. It is in contexts of this sort that the Stoics introduce their doctrine of causes. Moreover, as we shall see later, the Stoic distinction of various kinds of causes is a refinement on an ordinary intuitive distinction of various kinds of responsibility.

So for the Stoics the notion of a cause still has a connotation, however tenuous, of responsibility. But for the notion of responsibility to have any content at all that which is responsible must in some sense or other have done something and thus become responsible. It is ultimately for this reason, I take it, that the Stoics insist that causes are active, that they must be the kinds of items that can cause something. But in restricting causes to active items the Stoics seem to loosen the tie between causes and explanation. For to state the causes of something will no longer be a matter of stating all the relevant truths about all the relevant factors which have to enter into a complete explanation, but a matter of referring to just those factors which actively contribute to the effect. And the relevant truths about these will not amount to a complete explanation, or so it would seem. We shall see later, though, that the Stoics conceive of the cause in their narrowest sense in such a way that it recaptures the explanatory force causes seem to lose owing to their restriction to active causes. Nevertheless, it is important to realize that the shift in the notion of a cause threatens the simple and straightforward conceptual link between cause and explanation.

But why should somebody who did not share the Stoics' view that what mattered first of all was the question of responsibility accept the claim that causes, properly speaking, have to be active? The Stoics might argue in the following way: when the question 'What is the *aition*?' was a question of legal, moral, or political responsibility it may have been difficult to come up with the answer in particular cases, but it would have been clear that the person responsible would be a person who had done something or other which he should not have done such that as a result of his doing it something has gone wrong for which he is responsible. (The question of responsibility originally is restricted to cases of blame. It is then extended to all noteworthy cases, including cases in which praise is to be bestowed. It is only then that the question of responsibility gets extended beyond the sphere of human or personal action, which is, of course, facilitated by an unwillingness to determine the limits of personal agency in a narrow way so as to exclude all but human actions. Who knows about the winds and the sea?) When then the use of '*aition*' was extended such that we could ask of anything 'What is its *aition*?' this extension of the use of '*aition*' must have taken place on the assumption that for everything to be explained there is something which plays with reference to it a role analogous to that which the person responsible plays with reference to what has gone wrong; i.e., the extension of the use of '*aition*' across the board is only intelligible on the assumption that with reference to everything there is something which by doing something or other is responsible for it.

This would seem to be a rather questionable assumption. Even in the case of real responsibility we have to construe the notion of doing something quite generously such that forgetting to do something and in general failing to do something which one can be expected to do count as doing something. But if we extend the notion of responsibility across the board, we no longer have a set of expectations such that any violation of these expectations counts as a doing. As a result there are considerable difficulties in determining exactly what is to count as doing something and as being active. If columns support a roof, this, presumably, counts as a case of doing something, but why? Nevertheless, we do have intuitions in this matter which go far beyond, and to some extent correct, the grammatical active-passive distinction. We have a similar difficulty in determining what is to count as the analogue of the thing responsible in a case of real responsibility. In this respect there had been considerable difficulties even when we just had to deal with cases of real responsibility. We had, e.g., to decide that the thing which is responsible has to be a person, rather than an object or an animal. But if the notion of responsibility is to be extended across the board, it seems that we need a new set of instructions as to how one finds what is responsible in this extended sense. To the extent, though, that the Stoics will claim that the common notion of a cause does provide us with such instruction and that they will provide us with further instruction, their point may have some weight, after all.

We find another argument to the effect that causes should be conceived of as active in Seneca, *Ep.* LXV. It seems that, with the exception of the Epicureans, in the case of the swerve all philosophers would have agreed that for any particular thing a complete explanation of that particular thing will involve reference to something which did something or other, i.e., reference to a moving cause in the vulgar sense of 'moving cause'. But once it is agreed that in every case a moving cause is involved, why should we extend the notion of cause to also cover whatever other items do enter into our explanation? Why should we not use Plato's distinction in the *Phaedo* between causes and necessary conditions (or, rather, necessary items, remembering that '*hou*' in the phrase '*aneu hou*' at *Phd.* 99^b does not range over propositional items) and count the other items, e.g. matter, among the necessary conditions? That the presence of something is a necessary condition does not yet mean that it is a cause. This seems to be the line Seneca takes in *Ep.* LXV. He claims that there is just one kind of cause, the active cause, and that if the opponents assume more kinds of causes it is because they think that the effect would not obtain if it were not for the presence of certain other kinds of items in addition to an active cause. In LXV 4–6, e.g. when he lists and explains Aristotle's four causes, in each of the first three cases he explains why the presence of each of them is a necessary condition for obtaining the result. And having explained the fourth cause he adds the rhetorical question 'or don't you think that we have to count among the causes of any work brought about anything such that if that thing had been removed the work would not have been brought about?' (LXV 6). And again in LXV 11 he suggests that the reason why Aristotle and Plato posit a whole bunch of causes ('turba causarum') is that they think that the presence of items of these various kinds is required for a result to come about. But if this is the reason why all these things deserve to be called causes, Seneca argues, the four or five kinds of causes of the Peripatetics and the Platonists do not suffice in the least.

Now, apart from the threat of a proliferation of causes, this argument will only have force if it is already granted that the moving cause does have a privileged status and is not just another necessary condition. Hence, it does presup-

pose some other argument like the one from the basic meaning of 'aition'
presented above. Another argument to fill the gap left by Seneca's argument
could have been the following. We have to remember that the various causes
supposedly involved in a particular case are not necessary conditions the conjunction of which is sufficient. They, rather, are items the necessary conditions
are truths about. What is it, then, that has to be true of the various causes for
the result to come about? In some sense they will all have to be present. But this
will not be sufficient to account for the result. For in the case of the moving
cause it will not just be its presence which is required. It will also be necessary
that it does or has done something or other. And this does seem to set it off from
the other causes for which we only require their mere presence.

That active causes come to be accorded privileged status may also be a matter
of change of perspective. It may or may not be the case that Plato and Aristotle
had committed themselves to a position from which it followed that everything
is determined by antecedent causes. Even if Aristotle was concerned about determinism, his reflections on the matter seem to have been of little influence on his
doctrine in general. Certainly the question had not been a preoccupation of
theirs. But with the Stoics' insistence that everything that happens, including our
actions, is antecedently determined, this problem starts to occupy center-stage.
And the whole technical machinery of explanation gets applied to cases for
which it was not really designed, namely to particular events, to find out whether
they admitted of an explanation which was compatible with the assumption that
not everything is antecedently determined. The problem of determinism makes
one look at particular events as the concrete events they are, happening at the
particular time they do, rather than just as instances of some general pattern of
behavior. As such they could be accounted for in terms of the nature or form
of the thing involved. But if we have to ask why this particular thing behaved
in this particular way at this particular time, it seems clear that a reference to
the general nature of the thing, or its end, or its matter, or its paradigm will not
do. In fact, it seems that these, with whatever their presence entails, only form
the more or less stable background on which we have to explain the particular
event by referring to some particular antecedent change, which, given a stable
background, makes the relevant difference. And hence the item involved in that
change does seem to be in a privileged position, and, if anything, it seems to
be it which deserves to be called the cause.

Once it is admitted that causes have to be active, have to do something or
other in order to bring about the effect, it follows easily for the Stoics that causes
have to be bodies. For only bodies can do something and can be affected, only
bodies can interact. At this point it is important to remember, though, that for
the Stoics not just physical objects, but also stuffs and qualities and mixtures
thereof are bodies. So a quality could qualify as a cause.

Causes, properly speaking, then, for the Stoics are bodies which do something or other such that the fact that they do what they do is at least an important ingredient in the explanation of whatever it is that the causes are causes of.

But what is it that the causes are supposed to be causes of? We so far have been talking as if it were generally agreed that it is propositional items, facts, events, and the like, that are caused or explained. And this seems to fit the common use of *'aitia'* and *'aition'*. It is true that in common use *'aition'* or *'aitios'*, e.g., can be used with a noun in the genitive as in 'the *aitioi* of the murder', i.e. 'those responsible for the murder' (Hdt. IV 200, I). But it is clear that in such cases the noun is the nominalization of an underlying sentence. It is also true that Aristotle often talks as if causes were causes of entities like a statue, a man, or health. But again, we might be inclined to say that this is just a way of speaking; causes of a statue are cause for their being a statue or for something's being a statue.

Nevertheless, there does seem to have been some disagreement. For Clement (*Strom.* VIII 9, 26, 1 = *SVF* II 345) reports that some philosophers assume that causes are causes of bodies. From Sextus (*M* IX 212) we learn more specifically that according to Epicurus the atoms are the causes of their compounds, whereas their incorporeal properties (*sumbebekota*) are the causes of the incorporeal properties of the corresponding compounds. It is not clear, though, whether we should assume that this reflects a serious disagreement about the notion of a cause, or whether we owe this bit of doxography to somebody who was looking very hard to find somebody on whom he could pin the view that causes can be causes of corporeal items as well as of incorporeal items. After all, even if Epicurus had said what is attributed to him, this way of speaking admits of so many constructions that little can be made of these words, unless one assumes that Epicurus chose this manner of speaking because he had taken a position on the issue. But this is hardly plausible, for it would seem that this is exactly the kind of question which Epicurus would regard as sophistical.

We could leave the matter at that, if we did not have additional evidence which suggests that there actually was a dispute over the question what causes are the causes of. This is a disagreement both Clement and Sextus report on. Sextus (*PH* III 14) distinguishes between what we know to be the Stoic view, namely the view that causes are causes of a predicate's being true of something, and the view that causes are causes of appellations (*prosēgoriai*). Clement (*Strom.* VIII 9, 26, 4) attributes the latter view to Aristotle. Unfortunately, it is far from clear what the contrast between the two views is supposed to be, and Sextus' examples does not make the matter any clearer. On the first view, according to Sextus, the sun's heat is the cause of the wax's being melted (*tou cheisthai*), whereas on the second view it is the cause of the melting of the wax (*tēs chuseōs*).

It is fairly clear that the contrast is supposed to be indicated by the use of a verb in the first case and a corresponding noun in the second. This would also fit the examples given by Clement who says "But Aristotle thinks that causes are causes of appellations, i.e. of items of the following sort: a house, a ship, a burning (*kausis*), a cut (*tomē*)," whereas examples of what is caused on the other view seem to be something's being cut (*temnesthai*) or something's coming to be a ship (*gignesthai naun*). Also it would fit the fact that nouns in Greek grammar are called 'appellations' or 'appellatives'; the appellatives in Greek grammar are a word-class which comprises both our nouns and our adjectives. Finally, it is presumably relevant that the term we have rendered by 'predicate', namely '*kategorēma*', sometimes is restricted to what is signified by verbs or even is used synonymously with 'verb' (*rhēma*).

Now it is hardly plausible that according to the view in question causes are causes of expressions of whatever kind. To make reasonable sense of the position we have to assume either that what is meant is that causes are causes of something's being properly called something or other or that 'appellation' here does not refer to a certain kind of expression, but to what is signified by an appellative. There is a passage in Stobaeus (*Ecl.* I, p. 137, 5 W) in which 'appellation' is used in the second way, but this may be due to a confusion on Stobeaus' part. Hence it would be preferable if we got by on the assumption that 'appellation' here has its usual meaning as a grammatical term. But what would be the point of saying that a cause is a cause of something's being properly called (an) *X* where '*X*' is a noun or an adjective? Given the lack of evidence the answer has to be quite speculative. It might, e.g., be the case that verbs are associated with processes or coming-into-beings as opposed to the being of something; hence, perhaps, the contrast in Clement between a ship or the being of a ship or something's being a ship and the coming-into-being of a ship or something's coming to be a ship. But if this is the intended contrast, we have to assume that the nouns corresponding to the verbs are taken not to signify the process signified by the verbs. Given the standard ordinary use of these nouns, this does not seem to be a plausible assumption. But if we look at Simplicius' commentary on the *Categories,* we find that under the category of doing he systematically distinguishes between something's doing something (*poiein*) and a doing (*poiesis*) (301, 29ff.). And we may assume that Simplicius thinks that a corresponding distinction has to be made for all the verbs associated with the category. Similarly, Clement in his discussion of causality refers to a view according to which a cut (*tomē*) has to be distinguished both from something's cutting and somthing's being cut (*Strom.* VIII 9, 26, I; '*temnein*' and '*temnesthai*'). The basis for the distinction in Simplicius is that 'a doing' may refer either to an activity or to its effect (301, 33–35). And this suggests that our appellatives in Sextus and Clement are to be taken in the latter way to refer to the effects. There is an obvious difficulty as to what these effects as distinct from the processes and activities are supposed to be. Presumably a (finished) cut is distinct from the thing cut, the process of its being cut and the activity of cutting it, but not from its being (finally) cut. Are we then supposed to say that a house-building (*oikodomēsis*) is distinct from the thing built? Presumably not, for otherwise the activity of building a house will have two effects, a house and a house-building. It is a house, rather than a house-building, which Clement gives as an example parallel to a cut and a burning, and it is a ship, rather than a ship-building, which he contrasts with the coming-into-being of a ship. But this lack of parallel can be explained as being due to the fact that houses and ships, as opposed to cuts and burnings, are substances. Hence a house-building is distinct from the house's being in the process of being built and the activity of building it, but it is not distinct from the house's being (finally) built and hence not distinct from the being of the house. Thus the text can be read as distinguishing coming-into-beings or processes and beings, between the being of a cut or something's being (finally) cut and the cutting of it or its being cut, between the being of a ship or its being (finally) built and the building of it or its being built. But what would be the point of such a distinction? The idea might be that causes are causes of entities, of the being of things, rather than their coming-into-being, and that their coming-into-being has to be understood in terms of their being rather than the other way around. That Peripatetics should conceive of causes as causes of entities is not so surprising given the Aristotelian program of determining the principles and causes of what there is, where 'what there is' naturally is understood not as referring to all the facts there are, but rather as referring to all the particular entities there are. Really to know all these is to know all that there is to be known (cf. Arist. *Metaph.* M 10 1087^a 15ff).

If, on the other hand, one does not focus one's thought about causes on entities and their being, but on particular events because they are what one is mainly concerned with when one is worried about determinism, it seems natural to make causes causes of propositional items, especially since that corresponds to the ordinary use and the original notion of '*aition*'. It also seems natural to make some room for propositional items in one's ontology. This is exactly what the Stoics do when they admit *lekta*, if not as beings (*onta*), at least as somethings (*tina*). In fact, it is not clear to me that the notion of a *lekton* was introduced by the Stoics in the context of their philosophy of language rather than their ontology. For the first Stoic who we know used the term '*lekton*' is Cleanthes, and he used it precisely to say that causes are causes of *lekta* (Clem. *Strom.* VIII 9, 26).

It seems, though, that the Stoics thought that the canonical representation of the causal relation was not a two-place relation between a body and a propositional item, but as a three-place relation between a body and another body and a predicate true of that body. Thus a knife is the cause for flesh of being cut, fire is the cause for wood of burning. It is in this sense that the Stoics often are reported as claiming that a cause is a cause of a predicate (*katēgorēma*, cf. Clem *Strom.* VIII 9, 26, 4). Now it is true that in Greek there is a widespread use of the construction 'a cause of something for something' where the dative represents the person or the object affected and the genitive represents what, as a result, is true of the object affected. And presumably it is also true that we could rewrite all Greek causal statements so as to satisfy this normal form. But of what importance is this for the notion of cause?

Presumably, this is supposed to be of relevance in at least three respects. It brings out the fact that for there to be a cause there has to be something which is affected, and since only bodies can be affected this has to be a body. Second, whether something does or does not produce a certain effect in something does depend on the nature and state of the thing affected. It has to be the right kind of body. And third, we have to remember that though we want to see how one explains particular facts, we also want to have general explanations which tell us what in general causes a certain predicate to be true of something.

The general notion of a cause, properly speaking, according to the Stoics, then, seems to be the following: a cause is a body which does something or other and by doing so brings it about that another body is affected in such a way that something comes to be true of it. It may very well be the case that the Stoics think that this is just a characterization of the common notion of a cause.

Kinds of Causes and the Cause in the Strict Sense

The Stoics reject the swarm of causes ('turba causarum', Sen. *Ep.* LXV 11) of their opponents and allow only for an active cause. But within the notion of such an active cause as we have outlined it so far they, too, allow for different kinds of relation between cause and effect and hence for different causes. As Alexander puts it, they have a whole swarm of causes (*smēnos aitiōn, Fat.* 192, 18 = *SVF* II, p. 273, 18).

Unfortunately, our sources concerning these various kinds of causes are rather unclear. Hence it may be best to start with what seems to be a quotation from Chrysippus in Cicero's *De fato* 41, in which Chrysippus distinguishes two kinds of causes. Cicero says about Chrysippus: For of causes, he says, some are perfect and principal ("perfectae et principales"), other auxiliary and proximate ("adiuvantes et proximae"). Hence, when we say that everything happens by fate through antecedent causes, we do not want this to be understood as saying "through perfect and principal causes," but in the sense of "through auxiliary and proximate causes."

The point of the distinction, if one looks at the context, would seem to be the following. Chrysippus wants to maintain that everything that happens is fated, is determined by antecedent causes. On the other hand, he also wants to maintain that this does not rule out human responsibility, because, though human actions are determined by antecedent causes, it is nevertheless the human beings themselves, rather than the antecedent causes, who are responsible for these actions.

Quite generally, though what a thing does is determined by an antecedent cause, it is not the antecedent cause but rather the thing itself or something about that thing which is responsible for what it does, though, of course, not necessarily morally responsible; for only with beings of a certain sort and under certain further conditions is responsibility moral responsibility.

We are given two kinds of examples to illustrate the point, one from human behavior and one from the behavior of inanimate objects. Suppose we perceive something and get some impression (e.g., the impression that there is a piece of cake over there or the impression that it would be nice to have that piece of cake now). Now it will depend on us whether we accept or give assent to this impression. If we do, we will think that there is a piece of cake over there or that it would be nice to have that piece of cake now and will feel and act accordingly. And if we do think so and feel and act accordingly, it will have been the impression which brought this about and hence was the antecedent cause of our action. But the impression by itself does not necessitate that we should think, feel, and act that way. Other people or we ourselves at other times would not accept or give assent to the same impressions; it is not the impression, but something about the person which makes the person accept the impression, though the person would not accept the impression and act accordingly if he did not have that impression, and though there is a sense in which the impression does bring about or cause whatever action the person takes as a result.

Chrysippus' point about causes, then, as illustrated by this example is this: everything does have an antecedent cause; our actions, e.g., have as their antecedent cause an impression. But these antecedent causes are not the kind of causes that necessitate the result, they are only 'causae adiuvantes et proximae'. The 'causa perfecta et principalis' which necessitates the result lies in ourselves, it is that about us which makes us accept the impression and act accordingly.

The examples from the behavior of inanimate objects are motions of a cylinder and a cone or spin-top. 'They could not start to move unless they received a push. But once that has happened, he thinks that, for the rest, it is by their own nature that the cylinder rolls and the spin-top turns' (42 fin.). The idea here seems to be that the person who gave the cylinder or the column a push is the antecedent cause. Without the push the cylinder would not roll, but the fact that the person gave it a push does not yet account for the fact that it is rolling. What makes it roll is something about the cylinder itself. And it is that which is the perfect and principal cause of its rolling.

It is important that the examples should not be misinterpreted in the following way: we might think that Chrysippus only wants to point out that if one gives an object a push it will depend very much on the kind of object it is how it will be affected, a cylinder will roll one way, a cone another, and a cube will not roll at all. But Cicero does not just say in 42 that the cylinder rolls in virtue of its own peculiar nature ('suapte natura'), he also tells us in 43 that both in the case of human behavior and the case of the cylinder, once the thing has received an impulse, it will move for the rest 'suapte vi et natura', 'by its own force and nature'. This implies that there are two forces, two *vires* involved: not just the external *vis* of the antecedent cause, the person who gives a push (cf. 'nulla vi extrinsecus excitata' in 42), but also a *vis* on the inside, and it seem to be that *vis* on the inside which keeps the cylinder rolling once it has gotten its initial impulse. This suggests that there also is something active, something which exerts a force, on the inside of the cylinder when the cylinder is rolling. And given what we said about the general notion of a cause this is not surprising. If causes are active and if in the case of the cylinder two causes are supposed to be involved, there should be two things involved, both of which do something or other to bring about the result that the cylinder is rolling.

The picture which we thus get so far is the following: whenever something does something or other there are at least two kinds of active causes involved, an antecedent cause which is classified as an auxiliary and proximate cause and an internal cause which is classified as a 'causa perfecta et principalis'. Though both of them can be said to bring it about that the thing does whatever it does, it really is the internal cause which by its activity is responsible for what is done.

This is not to say that whenever something happens to something, say *A*, there will be two causes involved, one antecedent and one internal to *A*. A mere passive affection of *A* does not require the activity of an internal cause. It is clear from the way Cicero sets out his examples that the antecedent causes do have an effect on the object which is not produced by an internal cause. The person who gives the cylinder a push does give the cylinder a beginning of motion, and the external sight or object does produce an impression in us (43) which is not due to an internal cause. It seems that the need for a second cause only comes in when we want to explain what the thing does, how the thing reacts as a result of being affected this way. This in turn suggests that the 'causa perfecta et principalis' is not essentially an internal cause, as we may have thought. For the 'causa perfecta et principalis' of a mere passive affection of an object will lie outside that object in the object which affects it. And this also seems to be required by what we know about 'causae perfectae' from other sources.

There seems to be no doubt that 'causa perfecta' is just Cicero's rendering of 'aition autoteles'. We do not have a text which claims to give us the Stoic definition of this kind of cause. But we have various texts which distinguish between (i) an *autoteles aition,* (ii) a *sunaition,* and (iii) a *sunergon* ([Gal.] *Def. med.* XIX, 393 K.; Clem. *Strom.* VIII 9, 33 = *SVF* II, p. 121, 25ff.). And since we are told in various places that *'autoteles aition'* and *'sunektikon aition'* are used interchangeably (Clem. *Strom.* VIII 9, 33, 2 = *SVF* II, p. 121, 27; VIII 9, 25, 3 = *SVF* II, p. 120, 2ff.) we may also draw on texts like [Gal.] *Def. med.,* pp. 392–93) K.; S.E. *PH* III 15 and Gal. *Hist. phil.* 19 which distinguish (i) a *sunektikon aition,* (ii) a *sunaition,* and (iii) a *sunergon.* Since Sextus tells us that most philosophers agree on this distinction, we can be reasonably certain that a consideration of these texts will get us near enough to the Stoic notions of these kinds of causes. In fact, it is almost certain that this is a basically Stoic distinction of Stoic origin. And it is also obviously the right distinction to look at in our context, since the 'causa adiuvans' with which the 'causa perfecta' is contrasted in Cicero clearly is a *sunaition* or a *sunergon*.

What, then, is the distinction? The intuitive idea behind it is fairly simple. It always must have been clear that often the question 'Who or what is responsible for this?' does not admit of a simple straighforward answer, because there is no single person or thing to be made responsible, but several things have to be referred to, and among them one would often want to divide the responsibility and distinguish among various degrees of it. Hence in ordinary language, but also in more technical discourse, we soon get such terms as *sunaitios, metaitios, sunergos*. If we went by ordinary usage we would guess that the Stoic distinction amounted to the following: whenever there is exactly one thing which is responsible for what happens this is the *autoteles aition*. If there are two or more things which not individually but collectively have brought about the effect, they are *sunaitia*. If something just in some way contributes to an effect, which is brought about, though, by something else, it is a *sunergon*.

The difficulties arise when it comes to the technical definitions of these kinds. For we are told of all three kinds of causes that they bring about the effect (cf. [Gal.] *Def. med.*). We are also told that the perfect cause *does* bring about the effect by itself ([Gal.] *Def. med.* XIX, 393 K;[5] cf. 'suapte vi et natura' in Cic. *Fat.* 43.) In fact it seems to be this feature of the perfect cause to which it owes its name: '*autoteles*'. As Clement (*Strom.* VIII 9, 33, 2 = *SVF* II, p. 121, 27ff.) tells us: they also call it '*autoteles*', since it produces the effect by itself relying on nothing else. Finally, we know from various souces (e.g., Clem. *Strom.* VIII 9, 33 = SVF II, p. 121, 35ff.) that *sunerga* can appear in conjunction with the perfect cause to help to produce the effect. But in this case, it seems, the perfect cause does not bring about the effect by itself; there is also a *sunergon* which can be said to bring about the effect, too. After all, this is why it, too, is called a cause of this effect.

Ultimately, the only way out of the difficulty I can see is the following: we distinguish between a strict sense of producing or bringing about an effect and a weaker sense. It is true of all three kinds of causes that they somehow bring about the effect. If there were no sense in which the impression could be said to bring about our assent and our action, and if there were no sense in which the person who pushed the cylinder could be said to have brought about the cylinder's rolling, these items could not be said to be causes of their respective effects in the first place. But then our consideration of the cylinder case also has shown that there is a stricter, narrower sense of 'bringing about' in which it is not the person who gives the push, but the perfect cause which brings about the rolling motion of the cylinder 'suapte vi et natura'. Once we make this distinction it is easy to see how we get the threefold classification. Of those things which can be said to bring about an effect in the weaker sense some also can be said to bring about an effect in the narrower sense, namely the perfect causes and the *sunaitia,* whereas in that narrow sense the *sunerga* can only be said to help to bring about the effect. But among those things which bring about an effect in the strict sense, some do bring it about by themselves, namely the perfect causes, whereas others only bring it about in conjunction and cooperation with other causes; these are the *sunaitia.*

What makes a perfect cause perfect or complete, then, is that it does not depend for its causal efficacy on the agency of some other cause outside its control. A potential *sunaition* needs another *sunaition,* a potential *sunergon* needs a perfect cause or *sunaitia* which may or may not be available. This is why the antecedent cause and hence fate by themselves do not necessitate the effect. For whether the antecedent cause does bring about the effect depends on the activity of the perfect cause, and whether the perfect cause does act is outside of the control of the antecedent cause, though it is determined.

So much for the distinction between *autotelē, sunaitia,* and *sunerga.* It rests on an intuitive distinction which divides responsibility. When Chrysippus says that antecedent causes are not *autotelē,* but only *sunerga,* he relies on the fact that intuitively we will understand this as meaning that it is not the antecedent cause which bears the full responsibility. At worst it is something like an accomplice. Given the technical understanding of the distinction Chrysippus' claim amounts to saying that, strictly speaking, it is not the antecedent cause at all which brings about the effect. It is something within the thing itself which produces the effect all by itself.

Given this it is easy to understand why the 'causa perfecta' would be called 'causa perfecta et principalis'. We may assume that the Greek underlying Cicero's 'For of causes some are perfect and principal . . . ' is something like this: ' . . . of causes some are *autotelē* and *kuria* (or *kuriōtata)'.* It is the perfect cause which is the cause, strictly speaking or in the strictest sense. This also seems to be brought out by the Greek names of these three kinds of causes: *'autoteles aition', 'sunaition',* and *'sunergon'.* We never get the phrase *'sunergon aition'* (which also might reflect the fact that *sunerga,* as opposed to *aitia* and *sunaitia,* do not bring about the effect, strictly speaking).

Now, before we have a closer look at the nature of this perfect cause, let us briefly turn to the second kind of cause distinguished by Chrysippus according to Cicero: the auxiliary and proximate causes ('causae adiuvantes et proximae'). So far I have been assuming that these are the *sunerga.* But from what has been said it is clear that 'auxiliary cause' could be a translation either of *'sunergon'* or of *'sunaition'.* This ambiguity is apparent in Cicero's classification of causes in the *Topics* (58ff.), where Cicero refers to the *sunaitia* as those 'which stand in need of help' and to the *sunerga* as 'helping' ('adiuvantia'). Nevertheless, it is clear that here we are talking about *sunerga*. For among the causes of something we can either have *sunaitia* or a perfect cause, but not both. Moreover, we know independently that it was a point of Stoic doctrine that fate, the chain of antecedent causes, only provides a *sunergon* for what things do (cf. Cic. *Top.* 58ff.). And this seems to be exactly what Chrysippus is claiming in our passage when he says that the antecedent causes which somehow constitute fate are not 'causae principlaes', but 'causae adiuvantes'.

But this raises the question how an antecedent cause can be conceived of as a *sunergon,* if a *sunergon* is the kind of item which helps to bring about the effect by making it easier for the effect to be brought about. The examples Sextus and Clement, e.g., give of a *sunergon* are of little help. If somebody lifts a heavy weight and somebody else comes along and gives a helping hand, then the second person is a *sunergon* in so far as he just helps to bring about the effect by making it easier. But the antecedent cause is precisely not the kind of thing which comes in when something is already happening anyway. It is not the case that the cylinder was rolling anyway and that the push just made the rolling easier.

Presumably the idea, rather, is that the ease with which the cylinder rolls depends on the kind of push it got. The push has to be of a sufficient size for it to be easy enough for the cylinder to roll at all, and any increment in size of the push will make the rolling easier. The difficulty about this is that, to apply generally, this presupposes some general physical theory according to which the antecedent cause contributes something to the force with which the effect is brought about by somehow intensifying that force. But that some such theory of forces and their intensification actually is presupposed seems to be clear enough from our testimonies. Cicero, as we have seen, talks about the external and the internal *vis,* ps.-Galen and Sextus characterize *sunaitia* as each exerting an equal force to bring about the result, whereas the *sunergon* is said only to contribute to a minor force. Sextus (*PH* III, 15) talks of the intensification and remission of the perfect cause and a corresponding intensity of the effect. Clement tells us that the *sunergon* helps to intensify the effect (VIII 9, 33, 7; 33, 9). In any case, we know independently that fate, i.e. the antecedent cause, is supposed to help in the production of the effect even if it is not the perfect cause (cf. Josephus *BJ* II 163[6]).

Now, the second kind of cause to be distinguished is not just characterized as a helping cause, but also as a proximate cause. 'Causa proxima' could be a rendering of *'aition proseches'*, *'aition proēgoumenon'*, or *'aition prokatarktikon'*. I assume that it renders *'aition prokatarktikon'* and that the *causae antecedentes* are the *aitia proēgoumena*.

If we take the testimony of Sextus, Clement, and others seriously the class of *sunerga* and the class of *aitia prokatarktika* will not coincide, since not all *sunerga* are antecedent causes. But there is also no evidence that the class of *aitia prokatarktika* was arrived at by further subdivision of the class of *sunerga*. This strongly suggests that the distinction of *aitia prokatarktika* is part of a division of causes quite independent of that into *autotelē, sunaitia,* and *sunerga.* And this seems to be confirmed by the fact that the *prokatarktika* are usually contrasted with the so-called *sunektika,* a kind of cause to which Cicero in §44 of the *De fato* refers as the 'causae continentes', and of which we know from Galen that it along with its name was introduced by the Stoics (*De causis cont.* p. 6, 2; IX 458, 11ff. K.). In fact, ps.-Galen in *Definitiones medicinales* (XIX 392) says that cause is threefold, one is the *prokatarktikon,* the other the *proēgoumenon,* and the third the *sunektikon.* And it is only after definitions of these three kinds that he turns to the distinction into *autotelē, sunaitia,* and *sunerga.* Possibly this threefold distinction is of Stoic origin. For Galen in *De causis continentibus* (p. 8, 8ff.) tells that Athenaeus, the founder of the pneumatic school of medicine, made this distinction and that in this he was influenced by Posidonius (8, 3ff.). He does not say, though, that Athenaeus got this distinction from Posidonius, and it is clear from our passage in Cicero that the distinction does not go back to Chrysippus, quite apart from the fact that Galen tells us elsewhere that the physicians did not get the notion of *sunektikon* straight (*Adv. Jul.,* XVIII A, 279 f. = *SVF* II, p. 122, 22ff.; *Synops. de puls.* IX 458 = *SVF* II, p. 122, 38).

If I understand the medical distinction correctly, the *prokatarktikon* is the external antecedent cause, the *proēgoumenon* is an internal disposition brought about by the *prokatarktikon* which in turn activates the *sunektikon* which is something like the perfect cause internal to the object in our Cicero passage (Galen, *De causis puls.* IX 2, 11ff.). But it is exactly this precise distinction between the last external antecedent cause and the first internal antecedent cause which is neglected in our text. For the impression, an internal antecedent cause, is put on a par with the person who gives a push, an external antecedent cause, and this in spite of the fact that the person who gives a push is also compared to the object which brings about the impression. So in Chrysippus we obviously only have the distinction between the *sunektikon* and the *prokatarktikon.* But it is also clear that given the importance of the external-internal distinction for Chrysippus' causal theory the trichotomy easily comes to mind.

Roughly, it seems to me, the two divisions of kinds of causes are related in this way: perfect causes and synhectic causes coincide; *sunerga* may or may not be antecedent causes, but antecedent causes are *sunerga.* Given that antecedent causes and *sunerga* do not coincide, whereas perfect and synhectic causes do, it is not surprising that we sometimes find a list of four kinds of causes: perfect or synhectic causes, *sunaitia, sunerga,* and antecedent causes (cf. Clem. *Strom.* VIII 9, 31, 7; ps.-Galen, *Hist. phil.* 19, p. 611, 9ff. Diels). Sextus indicates one specific way in which we may arrive at such a list, namely when we distinguish between kinds of causes which are or can be simultaneous with their effects from those which are not or cannot be simultaneous (*PH* III 15–16). But this raises another set of problems which I shall not go into here.

Let us, then, consider in detail the distinction between *sunektika* and *prokatarktika*. Though a distinction under these terms was very widespread, though we have many testimonies for it, and though we still have at least translations of monographs by Galen on each of the two kinds of causes, the Stoic doctrine on the matter is far from clear. There are even doubts as to the explanation of the terms '*prokatarktikon*'[7] and '*sunektikon*'.

As to the term '*sunektikon*' Galen tells us in various places that it was the Stoics who introduced the notion and the name '*sunektikon aition*' (*Synops. de puls.* IX 458, 11ff. K. = *SVF* II, p. 122, 38ff.; *De causis cont.* p. 6, 2ff.; *Adv. Jul.* 6 XVIII A, 279, 13ff. K. = *SVF* II, p. 122, 21ff.). And he also repeatedly tells us that this notion is misunderstood and misused by physicians (cf. the passages mentioned above). What they fail to take note of is that for the Stoics a *sunektikon* is not just a cause of an activity like walking, but the cause of the being of something. And from Galen's *De causis continentibus* and other sources we learn how this is supposed to be so. There is some fine active substance, a mixture of fire and air, the so-called pneuma which pervades every object, holds its parts together, and thus provides it with unity and form and becomes the cause of the being of the thing. In fact it is the Stoic analogue of an Aristotelian form; in animals it is the soul, in human beings it is an intellectual soul. Since it is a primary function of the *sunektikon* to hold together the thing it is the form of, it seems safe to assume that it is this function to which the *sunektikon* originally owes its name. But it also seems to be this very same *sunektikon* which is not just the cause of the being of something, but also of its behavior.

To explain this in a sense should be no more difficult than to explain how a form, e.g. a soul, accounts both for the being of something and for its behavior. The explanation would proceed along the same lines. If anything, it should be easier to explain how the pneuma satisfies both functions, since in this case it is a body which makes a body exhibit a certain behavior. Presumably the pneuma admits of being put into different states and with increasing complexity there will be an increasing number of ranges of such states. Some of these states will be 'active states' such that being in those states the pneuma will act in a certain way. Whether a state is active and how precisely the pneuma will act in such a state will depend on the precise nature of the pneuma, the modifications it has undergone, the dispositions it has acquired, and the other states it is in.

We could, e.g., try to imagine that the pneuma is characterized by a complex set of interdependent tensions in some more or less comfortable equilibrium such that, if certain of these tensions are intensified to a certain degree, we have an active state of the pneuma and a certain kind of action results. Moreover, we might imagine that, if an object is affected, one or more of these tensions are affected and hence, as a result, the whole system of tensions is affected. So we might imagine that if an animal receives a certain impression at least one of these tensions gets intensified. If the whole system of tensions is such that as a result an action producing tension gets sufficiently intensified, this action would be due to the whole system of tensions, but it still might be thought to be literally true that the impression, or more generally the antecedent cause, had contributed some of the force with which the action was executed, insofar as the increased force of the intensified action producing tension in part was the force of the tension intensified by the impression.

But whatever the mechanics of the *aition sunektikon* may have been supposed to be it is clear that most people would not have subscribed to the physical theory underlying it. They might, e.g., deny that the primary active cause for a thing's behavior was to be found in the thing itself. Even if they accepted the view that the pneuma played an important role in the explanation of the behavior of things, they might not, as e.g. Galen did not, accept the view that such a pneuma was needed to account for the existence of objects as that which holds them together (cf. *De causis cont.* VI and VII). Nevertheless, they might want to have some kind of cause which on their physical theory in some way or other plays a role analogous to that of the *sunektikon aition* and which they hence would call by the same name. And in this case it would be clear that the name could no longer be interpreted as referring to the fact that this kind of cause is that which holds the object affected together.

And, as a matter of fact, we do find all sorts of non-Stoic uses of '*sunektikon aition*'. One of them, in Cicero's *De fato* 44, seems to have puzzled editors and commentators no end. Von Arnim, e.g., prints a text (*SVF* II, p. 283, 34ff.) which makes Chrysippus concede that the antecedent cause is the *sunektikon*, i.e. the perfect cause. Cicero refers to a doctrine according to which the proximate and containing cause ('proxima illa et continens causa') would be the impression, if somebody gave assent to it. It is clear that here the *causa continens* is the *aition sunektikon*. But it is equally clear that this term now is not used in the Stoic sense. For the Stoics specifically deny that the antecedent cause is the containing cause. Moreover, the position Cicero describes envisages the possibility that the impression, though it is the containing cause of the assent, also might not have brought about the assent (I take it that the subjunctive of 'moveat' is not just the subjunctive of indirect speech). This again, as we shall see shortly, seems to be incompatible with the Stoic notion of a containing cause. Hence it is not surprising that Cicero should go on to say: "Chrysippus will not admit that the proximate and containing cause of the assent lies in the impression and hence he will also not admit that this cause, i.e. the impression, necessitates the assent."

Cicero's remarks in *De fato* 44 very much suggest that Chrysippus thought that if something were the containing cause of something it would necessitate its effect. And this I actually take to be Chrysippus' view. But in what sense could the containing cause be thought to necessitate its effect? In this connection it is presumably relevant to refer to Stobaeus' characterization of Zeno's notion of a cause (*Ecl.* I, p. 138, 14ff. W). According to Zeno a cause is such that its presence necessitates the effect. And this principle is illustrated by the following examples: it is wisdom which brings about being wise, the soul which brings about living. This reminds one not just of the unreformed giants of Plato's *Sophist* (247^{b}ff.), with whom the Stoics were very much in sympathy (cf. *SVF* II, p. 123, 16ff. = *Soph.* 246^{a}ff.), but also of Socrates' safe causal accounts in the *Phaedo* and Aristotle's formal causes.

The connection between wisdom and being wise and soul and being alive might seem to be trivially necessary insofar as it just is with reference to somebody's wisdom that we call him wise. But this cannot be what Zeno has in mind, for he seems to think of somebody's being wise as an effect produced by wisdom, as if one's wisdom invariably and necessarily brought it about that one is wise. Perhaps the idea is the following. It is true that our common notion of wisdom does not tell us how it is that wisdom makes somebody wise. But if we had a complete technical understanding of what wisdom really is, then we would also understand that wisdom by its very nature brings it about that those who possess it invariably are wise. Looked at in this way the necessity involved still can be regarded as some kind of conceptual necessity. (This is not to attribute to the Stoics a distinction between logical or conceptual and physical or empirical necessity.) Given the correct complete technical notion of wisdom which reflects its nature in all detail, one sees how wisdom cannot fail to produce its characteristic effect. It may be along these lines that the Stoics think that the containing cause necessitates its effects. If one understands the nature of a soul as characterized by wisdom, one sees that it cannot fail to produce the effect that somebody is wise. In this case the necessity involved would just be the necessity which characterizes a Chrysippean conditional whose consequent is the statement that the person is wise and whose antecedent is the relevant truth about his soul.

This brings us back to explanation. To simplify matters let us concentrate on cases in which something does something or other, exhibits a certain piece of behavior. The Stoics assume and argue that nothing happens without a cause. More specifically, they assume that nothing happens without an antecedent cause and argue, e.g., that if things happened without antecedent causes the continuity of the universe would be interrupted. But they also assume that a reference to the antecedent cause is not going to explain why something does something or other. To explain this we have to refer to the *sunektikon,* and we do not have to refer to anything else. For a truth about the *sunektikon* will entail the truth about the object to be explained, whereas no truth about the antecedent cause by itself will be the antecedent of a true Chrysippean conditional with the fact to be explained as the consequent.

These conditionals will be instantiations of universal conditionals of the form 'if the *sunektikon* of x is such-and-such then x is (or does) so-and-so'. We may assume that it is sets of such conditionals which specify the nature of each kind of *sunektikon*, and hence it would be natural to arrange these conditionals according to the kinds of *sunektika*. Since these conditionals are universal and since they can be of any degree of generality, we can also draw on them for general explanations.

Now these conditionals will cover what happens within the thing, so to speak. They tell us how a thing, given its kind of nature, the modification of its nature and the states it is in, will behave. But, though this in some sense gives us a complete explanation of what the thing does – for otherwise the corresponding conditional would not be true – we shall think that we are missing something if we do not get the antecedent cause into the picture. After all, the thing would not have done what we are trying to explain if there had not been an antecedent cause which in some sense had brought it about that the thing would behave in a certain way. In fact, we are very much tempted to think that the real explanation of what the thing did would be in terms of what the antecedent cause did and some general law which connects what the antecedent cause does with what the object does. And it seems clear that our conditionals do not provide us with such laws. According to Cicero's *De fato* it seems that Chrysippus claims that there can be no true conditionals which connect truths about antecedent causes with facts they are the antecedent causes of. Nevertheless, it seems that for the purpose of explanation we shall not need general laws in addition to the conditionals which we already have.

It is true that for other purposes, e.g. divination and prediction, we might want to formulate such general laws. Given his views on cosmic sympathy Chrysippus is not going to deny that events do not occur in isolation of each other, in fact he is going to stress that there is a connection between any two things that happen. He also is not going to deny that by observation we could detect regularities, constant conjunctions, and that it would be worthwhile to formulate and collect corresponding rules or laws for prediction. But he does deny that such rules as 'if somebody is born at the rise of the Dog-star he will die at sea' offer any explanation for somebody's death at sea even if the person was born at the rise of the Dog-star and there in fact is a constant conjunction. For in spite of the fact that he believes in divination in general and does not object to astrological rules as such, he rejects their formulation as conditionals (cf. Cic. *Fat.* 15). And the reason for this would seem to be that the antecedents of such rules established by observation do not amount to a sufficient reason for their consequents, that they do not necessitate the consequent in the way in which the principal, but not the antecedent, cause necessitates its effect, even though it invariably may be accompanied by its consequent, and that the antecedents thus do not provide us with an explanation of the consequent. The question, then, is how we can restrict ourselves to Chrysippean conditionals and nevertheless do justice to the role of antecedent causes.

To see how this perhaps could be done we have to take into account that though the antecedent cause is only the antecedent cause of what the object does, it at the same time is the perfect cause of the state of the *sunektikon* which thus affected makes the object do what it does. Though this will hardly do as it stands, we now can look for an explanation along the following lines: we assume that all antecedent causes are antecedent causes of something *p* by being *sunektika* for a *sunektikon s* of a passive affection *q* such that a *sunektikon s* in state *q* is a perfect cause of *p*. In this case it would turn out that the relation between the antecedent cause and the effect can be analyzed into at least two relations, each of them between a perfect cause and its effect and hence each of them covered by the laws for containing causes.

So it does seem that the theory of causes, in spite of their restriction to active cause, is after all constructed in such a way that we can fully account for any particular fact in terms of these causes. The fact to be explained can be seen and understood as following with necessity from some truth about the cause once we understand the nature of the *sunektikon* involved in its relevant detail. This nature will be spelled out by universal conditionals which are, so to speak, the laws of their particular nature.

That in this way we account for everything in terms of the nature of the thing involved does not as such seem objectionable. For we ourselves might think that ultimately everything has to be accounted for in terms of its nature. We might, e.g., think that there is just one nature, that of an extended body, say, and that the laws of nature amounted just to the specification of that one nature such that if one really knew what an extended body is one would know and understand that to be an extended body was precisely to satisfy these laws. That according to the Stoics we do have a plurality of natures is an inconvenience with which we may have to live anyway. That the Stoics also assume individual natures, though, will create serious problems. That they themselves do not seem to do anything which could count at least as a start of an attempt to specify these hidden causes, in fact rather shy away from it, does raise further questions.

Nevertheless, the Stoic theory of causes may have had a considerable positive effect on actual physical explanation, after all. For, worked out in detail, it presupposes that if an object acts on another object so as to make it react in some way it does so by imparting a force or power to it; there is a transfer of force, an influence into the object affected. For the theory of motion in particular it suggests, as we saw in the case of the rolling cylinder, that we have to work with the notion of an internal force which keeps the body moving and the notion of a force imparted to a body which gets the body moving or increases its motion. It is difficult not to suspect that this may be the ultimate source of Philoponus' theory of imparted forces. It is well known that Philoponus in his discussion of the Aristotelian theory of motion took the position that the motion of a body is caused by an internal force which may be imparted and that it is such an imparted force, rather than the medium, e.g., which accounts for the motion of projectiles. Thus Philoponus has gained a place of honor in the history of science. But in spite of the useful suggestions by Pines, Wolff and G.E.R. Lloyd,[8] we know little about the historical antecedents of Philoponus' theory of motion. And what tends to be overlooked in this connection is the considerable influence Stoicism had on Philoponus' physics. Hence it does not seem farfetched at all to suggest that Philoponus' theory of motion has its ultimate origin in the Stoic theory we have been considering. In this case the Stoic theory of causes would not just have had a deep and lasting influence on the history of the notion of cause, it also would have made considerable contribution to science.

9

Stoics and Skeptics on Clear and Distinct Impressions

The history of Hellenistic philosophy is dominated by the rivalry between Stoics and skeptics, first Academic skeptics and later Pyrrhonian skeptics who tried to revive a more radical form of skepticism when in the second and first centuries B.C. Academic skeptics seemed to have softened their stand to a degree that made it difficult to distinguish them from their Stoic rivals. The debate between Stoics and skeptics primarily concerned the nature and possibility of knowledge. If the skeptics also tried to attack the Stoic position on all other questions, the point of this, at least originally, was in good part to show that the Stoics themselves had failed to attain the knowledge they claimed to be attainable.

Both Stoics and skeptics saw themselves as followers of Socrates, but they took a different view as to the moral to be drawn from Socrates' experience. Socrates by his dialectical practice had shown that, in spite of claims to the contrary, nobody actually possessses the kind of knowledge which would guarantee a rational and happy life, and that, if he himself had any claim to wisdom, it rested only on his ready recognition that he was no less ignorant than anybody else. But Socrates had not resigned himself to his ignorance. And the Stoics seem to have assumed that the reason for this was that Socrates thought that the special kind of knowledge which he had shown people to lack is in fact attainable. They assumed that nature must have constructed human beings in such a way as to make it possible for them to lead a rational and good life. And if this, as Socrates was thought to have shown, is a matter of being wise, nature must also have provided us with the means to gain the kind of knowledge which constitutes wisdom. The skeptics, on the other hand, thought that it remained an open question whether such knowledge could be attained and that hence all one could do meanwhile was go on looking for the truth and subject all claims to the kind of dialectical scrutiny Socrates had subjected them to. Since the Stoa was rapidly developing into the most influential school, it was only natural that the skeptics would turn their dialectical skill in particular against the Stoics who claimed to be on the way to the kind of knowledge Socrates had searched for in vain.

Now when the Stoics claimed that such knowledge is attainable, they also thought that they had to construct an epistemology in terms of which they could show that and how such knowledge is to be gained. On this account nature has provided us with a firm basis for knowledge by providing us with clear and distinct impressions, the so-called kataleptic or cognitive impressions, which by their very nature cannot be false and hence constitute an unfailing guide to the truths one has to know in order to have the wisdom that guarantees the good life. Thus the Stoic theory of knowledge is based on a doctrine of clear and distinct impressions. Given that the skeptics not only were not persuaded that such knowledge had been attained, but even questioned whether such knowledge was attainable, they naturally focused their attack on the Stoic theory of knowledge and in particular on the Stoic doctrine of clear and distinct impressions by means of which we are supposed to be able to acquire the knowledge in question. As a result a lively debate ensued which lasted for more than two centuries and which attracted the best philosophers of the time.

Tradition, though, has developed a view of the Stoic position which makes it so vulnerable to skeptical attacks that it becomes very difficult to understand how the Stoics, through centuries, were able to sustain the criticism without having to concede defeat. If the Stoics had defended the position that tends to be ascribed to them, their school should have been deserted in no time. That instead it was defended by men of the ingenuity of a Chrysippus should encourage us to take a fresh look at the Stoic position to see whether it might not be more attractive or at least easier to defend than tradition would make us believe.

The Stoic Position

Impressions

Animals and human beings are constructed in such a way that their survival and well-being depends essentially on the adequacy of their cognitions. They have to be able to recognize and to shun what is bad for them, and they have to be in a position to realize and seek out what is conducive to their preservation and well-being. For this purpose they are equipped with a sensory apparatus and a soul which, via the senses, receives impressions of the outside world, and thus provides them with some kind of awareness of the world around them. There is a crucial difference, though, between the impressions of rational beings and the impressions of animals. The impressions of rational beings are called "rational impressions" (D.L. VII 51). Rational impressions have a propositional content, they are impressions to the effect that something is the case very much in the sense in which we might say ordinarily, "the impression which one gets, if one looks at the evidence, is that. . . . " Thus rational impressions are thoughts

(D.L. VII 51; Ps.-Gal. *Def. med.* XIX 381 K.) which present themselves to the mind and which the mind either accepts or refuses to accept. To accept or give assent to a thought or impression is to have the belief that the proposition which forms the content of the impression is true, to refuse to accept a thought is to suspend judgment. Thoughts may present themselves to the mind in all sorts of ways. They may come to mind when one considers the evidence concerning a question in doubt. But many of them are brought about by the causal agency of an external object which, through the sense organs, gives rise to an impression in us. Thus to see something, on this view, is to have a certain kind of thought generated in a certain way. But thoughts may also be generated in all sorts of other ways.

Now the Stoics follow Socrates, Plato, and Aristotle in the view that it is a mark of moral knowledge that one never has a mistaken view in moral matters. The Stoics even take the stronger view that the wise man will never have any false beliefs at all (Stob. *Ecl.* II 111, 18 W.), because, for reasons we shall see later, any false belief might stand in the way of one's acquiring the kind of knowledge we are after. One way in which nature could construct a mind which has the ability to avoid any false beliefs whatsoever would be to endow the mind with the ability unfailingly to sort the true impressions from the false ones. But such a mind would be superhuman; nothing like the human physiology would be able to support such a powerful mind. Instead nature provided human beings with the ability unfailingly to distinguish true impressions of a certain kind— namely, clear and distinct impressions—from all other impressions whether they are true or not. In this way human beings are not in a position to know all truths but only those whose truth is guaranteed by clear and distinct impressions. But then we do not need to know all truths to lead a good life, and the clear and distinct impressions we receive in the ordinary course of events provide an ample basis for what we need to know. If our ability to know is restricted this way, our ability to avoid false belief is unlimited: all we need to do is not to accept as true any impression that is not guaranteed to be true by clear and distinct impressions. Thus there will be many true impressions which we nevertheless will not give assent to, but there will be no false impressions which we accept as true.

All this presupposes that there is a class of impressions which by their very nature cannot be false and that the mind can discriminate between these and other impressions. Our main task in the following will be to explain how the Stoics could make these assumptions. To understand this, we first have to have a closer look at the Stoic doctrine of rational impressions quite generally.

On the one hand, rational impressions are not mere sensory affections. This distinguishes them from the impressions of irrational animals. There are several passages according to which the Stoics distinguish rational impressions from mere sense-impressions (cf. Cic. *Acad.* II 21; SE *M* VII 345). Even the most primitive rational impression, like the impression that this is white, already involves the representation of the object by means of a concept, in this case the concept "white." It is in this way that they require a rational mind and manage to be thoughts and to have a definite propositional content. Sometimes commentators talk as if we applied concepts to objects on the basis of impressions which in themselves are preconceptual. But this cannot be the way the Stoics think of rational impressions. For given an impression which does not yet involve the conceptualization of the object, we could have any number of beliefs about the objects on the basis of such an impression. Hence there would not be any one definite proposition that forms the content of the impression, and assent to the impression would not constitute a definite belief. It may be objected that impressions are supposed to be passive affections of the mind, whereas the mind's conceptualization of an object would be an active contribution of the mind to the impression. But it has to be kept in mind that the Stoics characterize an impression as a passive affection of the mind to contrast it with the act of assent and not to deny that the mind has any part in the formation of a thought. As we shall see, the Stoics think that the kind of impression which we have very much depends on whether our mind is in normal working order; and part of what an object does, when it gives rise to an impression in a rational mind that is in working order, is that it makes the mind conceptualize the object in a certain way. In this sense the rational impression is a passive affection of the mind, though it does involve the operation of the mind. It will also be objected that impressions only give rise to concepts and hence cannot themselves already presuppose concepts. This objection overlooks the developmental character of the Stoic account. Human beings, according to the Stoics, start out as irrational animals. As such they have the kind of sense-impressions which animals have. But in the case of human beings these impressions give rise to concepts of very simple perceptual features like colors, shapes, tastes, and the like, and thus reason slowly starts to grow. Once we have these simple concepts, we can have corresponding rational impressions and, what is more important, corresponding cognitive impressions. These will naturally give rise to more complex concepts, like that of a man or a tree, which in turn will enable us to have more complex rational and in particular cognitive impressions (cf. Cic. *Acad.* II 21). Thus these common notions that arise in us naturally on the basis of more primitive impressions turn out to be truly anticipations (Cic. *nd* I 44; *prolēpseis*); for they are needed to form the impressions that afford us a grasp on things (*katalēpsis*); it is in terms of them that the mind has a grasp on things. Thus rational impressions and in particular cognitive impressions do presuppose concepts, but these arise from more primitive impressions that do not presuppose these concepts, and ultimately from sense-impressions that do not presuppose any concepts whatsoever but that are not rational either. Given this developmental account, it is easy to see how the Stoics can claim that concepts only arise from the appropriate impressions and nevertheless maintain that a rational impression involves the conceptualization of the object.

On the other hand, there is more to a rational impression than just the propositional content. We cannot identify an impression by just specifying the proposition it is a thought of. To have a rational impression is to think a certain proposition in a certain way. The kind of impression we have depends not only on the propositional content, but also on the way in which this content is thought. For the same proposition may be thought in any number of ways, and depending on the way it is thought we get different kinds of impressions. One way they differ is the way in which the subject of the proposition—that is, the object of the thought—is represented in the impression. The thought that this (a book in front of me) is green which I have when I look at the book differs considerably from the thought that this (the very same book) is green which I have when I close my eyes and touch the book, though the propositional content, at least in Stoic logic, is exactly the same. The thought that John's cat is gray is quite different depending on whether I see the cat or whether I am just told that John bought a gray cat, though, again, the propositional content may be exactly the same. But thoughts may also differ in the way in which the feature that is attributed to the object is represented. I may be in the habit of thinking of death as something bad and dreadful, in which case it would be a pain for me to accept the thought that I am dying. If, on the other hand, death is matter of indifference to me, the thought that I am dying would be a rather different kind of thought, whose acceptance would not be a pain. In fact, the Stoics seem to think that all emotions and passions are a matter of accepting thoughts thought in a certain way, and that the way these thoughts are thought is entirely a matter of certain further beliefs we have—in particular, beliefs about what is good and what is bad—which we draw on to represent the object of the impression and the feature attributed to it in the thought. Thus all contents of the mind turn out to be thoughts. And it becomes even more apparent why the Stoics should be so concerned with our ability to distinguish between true and false impressions; for on this view even our feelings and desires turn out to be nothing but a matter of accepting true or false thoughts of a certain kind.

For our purposes one difference in the way objects may be represented in our thoughts deserves special emphasis. If one perceives an object, it tends, at least under normal conditions, to be represented in one's thought in such a way that just on the basis of this very representation one could go on to say lots of things about the object in addition to what one thinks about it, and these things that one could say about it may or may not be things one antecedently believed to be true of the object. In cases in which one neither is perceiving the object nor even has perceived it, the object will be represented in one's thought entirely in terms of what one antecedently believed to be true of it. And thus it will be represented in terms of general concepts each of which might equally apply to other objects. But if I see the object and think that it is green, the object may not be represented by general concepts at all, except for the concept "green," though it will be represented in such a way that, just on the basis of the impression, we could go on to represent it in terms of a host of concepts.

From what has been said it should be clear that there is some sense in which impressions have parts corresponding to the various features that are represented in the impression—more particularly, a part or parts corresponding to the features in terms of which the object of the thought or the subject of the proposition is represented, and a part or parts corresponding to the feature or features the object is represented as having—that is, a part or parts that correspond to the predicate of the proposition the impression is a thought of. The Stoics seem to be willing to call such parts of impressions "impressions," too. For they call general notions "impressions" (SE *M* VII 246; Plut. *Comm. not.* 1084F; cf. Cic. *Acad.* II 21). But this seems to be misleading, since parts of impressions are not true or false in the way impressions properly speaking are. Hence it might be better to call such parts of impressions "ideas" and to distinguish the way ideas have a propositional content and are true or false from the way impressions properly speaking are propositional and true or false. The Stoics also seem to distinguish between generic, or abstract, and specific, or concrete, ideas (cf. SE *M* VII 246). The idea of man in general, for example, is abstract, whereas the idea of Socrates and the idea of his complection may be specific, or concrete. The fact that we represent an object in an impression by means of a general concept is reflected by the fact that the corresponding part of the impression is an abstract idea. Moreover, we have to assume that the parts of rational impressions are ordered so that their combination in the appropriate order amounts to the thought of a proposition, whereas their combination in a different order might amount to the thought of a different proposition or to no thought at all.

To sum up: impressions are impressions of an object; in the case of rational impressions this impression consists in a thought concerning the object; such a thought involves the conceptualization of the object, but it need not be, and in the case of perception is not, entirely conceptual; nevertheless, the thought is the thought of a proposition; but it is characterized not only by the proposition it is a thought of, but also by the way this proposition is thought; the way a proposition is thought depends on the way the constituents of the proposition are represented in the thought; this representation does not have to be entirely conceptual—that is, it does not have to consist entirely of abstract ideas—in order to represent a constituent of a proposition and in order to be constitutive of a thought; in the case of perception the thought is partly nonconceptual; it nevertheless is a thought, because it does involve the conceptualization of the object, and in particular because it minimally involves the kind of conceptualization of its object which gives it a propositional content that is true or false, as a result of which the thought itself can be said to be true or false.

Cognitive Impressions

How could there be impressions that cannot fail to be true, not for the trivial reason that they are true or correspond to the facts, but because of some other feature that is logically independent of their truth? It seems that there could be such a feature, namely the property of having a certain kind of causal history, and that the Stoics are relying on this feature.

Impressions have a certain causal history. In the course of this history all sorts of things can go wrong. The mind, for example, may be defective and hence produce the wrong impression. In the case of vision the light may be wrong, the distance too big or too small, the sensory apparatus malfunctioning, and as a result we may get a false impression. On the other hand, it stands to reason that nature has constructed things in such a way that under normal conditions the impression we receive is true. If under normal conditions something appears to be red or appears to be a human being, then it is red or is a human being. Thus impressions with the right kind of history cannot fail to be true, though the fact that they have this kind of history is logically independent of their truth. Let us call such impressions "normal."

There are different kinds of normal impressions. In particular it seems useful to distinguish two kinds. If, for example, I have the impression that $2 + 2 = 4$ because I have a proof for the proposition that $2 + 2 = 4$, my impression will have the right kind of causal history that will guarantee its truth. But it is not a causal history that links the object of the impression, say the number 4, with my impression; the impression, though produced in an appropriate, normal way, is not produced or caused by the object of the impression itself. It is, at least according to the Stoics, only in cases of perception that the normal impression is caused by the object itself. Hence it will be useful to treat normal impressions of this particular kind as a separate class and to call them "perceptual impressions."

That the Stoics think of cognitive impressions as normal is suggested by the following. Sextus Empiricus (*M* VII 247) characterized noncognitive impressions quite generally as those one comes to have because of some abnormal condition (*pathos*). "Abnormal condition" here can hardly refer just to abnormal states of mind; for even in a normal state of mind one will have noncognitive impressions—for example, if one is seeing something from too far away. Hence "abnormal conditions" here has to be understood as referring to a whole set of normal conditions. And in SE *M* VII 424 we are in fact given such a set of conditions for the case of vision. Five conditions have to be met for a visual impression to be cognitive: conditions on the sense organ, on the object of vision, on how the object is placed, on how the impression comes about, and on the state of mind. And though this is not said explicitly, it is strongly suggested that if these conditions are met, the impression will be cognitive. Similarly Cicero (*Acad.* II 19) refers to such a set of sufficient and necessary conditions for cognitive impressions.

Moreover, though this is a matter of considerable controversy, it also seems that the Stoics think of cognitive impressions as perceptual. Aetius (*Plac.* IV 8.1) explicitly says that cognitive impressions come about through a sense organ. Cicero talks of cognitive impressions as if they originated in the senses (*Acad.* II 83). And the way the Stoics define cognitive impressions (they are supposed to arise from an object) and what they have to say about the clearness and distinctness of impressions make straightforward sense only for perceptual impressions.

What seems to stand in the way of this assumption is the following. The Stoics clearly assume that there are nonperceptual cognitions, namely, in those cases where we have a proof of a theorem (DL VII 52). But it is also the case that according to the Stoics even nonperceptual cognitions involve impressions. (SE *M* VII 370). Hence, it seems natural to assume that the impressions involved in cognitions, whether they are perceptual or not, are cognitive. Moreover, there are texts which claim that a cognition consists in the assent to a cognitive impression (SE *M* VII 151; VIII 397). Hence, if there are nonperceptual cognitions, there should be nonperceptual cognitive impressions. Finally, cognitive impressions are supposed to be the criterion of truth. Whatever else this may mean, it must mean that the truth of cognitive impressions is the guarantee of the truth of whatever impressions the wise man accepts as true. But if we restrict cognitive impressions to perceptual impressions, it is difficult to see how their truth would suffice as a basis to guarantee the truth of all other impressions the wise man will accept as true.

To deal with the last point first, we have to take into account that the Stoics seem to think that all features of objects—that is, of sensible bodies—are perceptible. Thus they think that we can even learn to see that something or somebody is beautiful, good, or virtuous (Plut. *Comm. not.* 1062C; *Stoic. rep.* 1042E-F; Cic. *ND* II 145), just as we have to learn to see that something is a man or a horse (Cic. *Acad.* II 21). If this at first sight seems strange, we have to remember that according to the Stoics, qualities of bodily objects like virtue are bodies themselves that form a mixture with the bodies they are the qualities of and hence cannot fail to affect our perception of the objects, given that our perception, at least if trained, is extremely discriminatory; a virtuous body must look quite different from a vicious body to a trained eye. Thus perception, as the Stoics understand it, provides a much broader basis than we would assume. And it will also turn out, when we consider the doctrine of the criterion, that the Stoics do in fact think that all other impressions can be accepted as true to the extent that their truth is guaranteed by the truth of perceptual impressions. Thus Cicero (*Acad.* II 21–22) points out that at some time in our development we come to have the (nonperceptual) cognition that if something is a man, it is a mortal rational animal. But when he explains why this cannot but be true, he does not say that the corresponding impression is cognitive; instead he says that it cannot be false because it is due to impressions that cannot be false, namely, cognitive impressions that are perceptual.

Once we realize that all truths available to us are supposed to be certified by the truth of perceptual impressions, it seems fairly clear that our problem about the scope of cognitive impressions is not so much a problem concerning Stoic doctrine but rather a problem concerning terminology. In fact, it is rather similar, and materially related, to the problem which we have about the scope of "clear" or "evident" and which it seems best to solve by distinguishing between self-evident impressions and impressions whose evidence depends on the evidence of other impressions. Similarly, it seems that the Stoics take the view that only perceptual impressions are cognitive in their own right. Thus other impressions can be called cognitive only to the extent that they have a cognitive content which depends on the cognitive content of impressions which are cognitive in their own right. Thus we may distinguish between self-evident impressions which are cognitive in a narrow sense, and evident impressions which are cognitive in a wider sense. And if we do so, we can say with Sextus Empiricus that a cognition consists in the assent to a cognitive impression, and we can also say that any cognition, whether perceptual or not, involves a cognitive impression, and nevertheless assume that cognitive impressions, strictly speaking, are perceptual.

Perceptual impressions, in addition to being normal and hence true, have certain other features that are of interest for our purposes. In the case of perceptual impressions, the impression represents the object the way it does because the object is this way—that is, all representational features of the impression are due to the object and not to some abnormal condition that would cause the mind to produce an impression different from the one it would produce normally. Thus a perceptual impression in no way misrepresents its object. But considering the purpose for which we have been endowed with cognition, it also stands to reason that nature has constructed things in such a way that under normal conditions we not only have an impression which does not misrepresent things but have one which represents them clearly, that is, affords us a clear answer as to what kinds of objects we are facing. And under normal conditions we do in fact have a clear view of an object we are confronted with, and we can tell without difficulty what its visual features are. Let us call such an impression "clear" or "evident."

The term "evident" has been used, misused, and misunderstood in many ways. To guard against such misunderstanding of the Stoic position some remarks may be in order. The adjective "evident" (*enargēs*) can be used in ordinary Greek to qualify a term "A" to refer to something as being obviously an

A; thus an evident robber is somebody who quite obviously is a robber (Soph. *O.T.* 535). But even in ordinary Greek the term can be used in cases in which appearances are deceptive; the evident ox may not be an ox at all, but Zeus in disguise (cf. Soph. *Tr.* 11). Things also can be said to evidently appear to be a certain way. And hence it is easy for philosophers to move on to talk of evident appearances or evident impressions, though by this they obviously do not mean to suggest that some of our impressions are such that it is evident they are impressions. This move must have been facilitated by the fact that even in ordinary Greek, dream images can be said to be evident (Aesch. *Pers.* 179). Given the ordinary use of the term, evidence suggests but does not guarantee truth. Thus Platonists (cf. SE *M* VII 143) and, of course, Academics (cf. Cic. *Acad.* II 34) do not take evidence to be a criterion of truth. Theophrastus, on the other hand, seems to have been the first philosopher to assume that it does guarantee truth (cf. SE *M* VII 218), and in this he was followed by the Epicureans and the Stoics. Since they cannot rely on ordinary usage for this assumption, we have to look for some argument that would justify this restricted use of the term "evident" or the assumption that even given the ordinary use it turns out that only true impressions are evident. The Stoics may have argued along the following lines: we can learn to see whether something is an ox or a robber; and under normal conditions, if nothing impedes our seeing things clearly, we do see whether something is an ox or only an ox in disguise; for the only things that can really look and move like oxen are oxen; thus something cannot be an evident ox without being a real ox. For it could appear to be an ox without being one only if we had not yet learned to see oxen properly or if our view was somehow impeded because one of the normal conditions was not met; but in this case the ox would not be evident. Evidence is an objective feature of impressions which is not to be confused with a subjective feeling of conviction or certainty, however strong that feeling may be, just as having a clear view of something is a matter of objective fact and not of subjective feeling. How we know that an impression is evident is a different matter, to which we will turn later; for this, our "feeling" may very well be relevant, but it seems, even in optimal circumstances, to be no more than a symptom of the evidence of an impression.

To get clearer about the notion of evidence which is in question here, it may be useful to consider the connection between truth and evidence. Impressions are true, because their propositional content is true, and not because of the way this propositional content is thought, that is, represented in the impression. The same propositional content, as we have seen, can be thought in all sorts of different ways, and correspondingly we get different kinds of impressions; but this difference between the impressions is of no relevance of their truth, which entirely depends on the truth of the proposition. Evidence, on the other hand, is primarily a feature of impressions which does depend on the way a proposition is represented by thought. Thus the same proposition that this is octagonal can be thought by an evident thought when I see an octagonal tower under normal conditions, and by a nonevident thought, if I just know from a book that the tower is octagonal. Propositions only secondarily may be called evident, if there should be any propositions that cannot be thought at all except by evident thoughts. What makes a thought or an impression evident is that it is already part of the representation of the subject of the proposition that the predicate should be true of it and that the representation of the subject is entirely due to the subject itself. Thus evidence is not what makes an impression or a proposition true, but an evident impression cannot but have a true proposition for its content and hence be true itself.

So far it would seem that for the impression that S is P to be evident, the representation of S already has to represent S as being P. But it seems that under normal conditions, when we have a clear view of an object, more than one of its features is clearly represented. And, in fact, Sextus (*M* VII 248, 250, 251) talks as if a cognitive impression captured all the characteristics of the object in precise manner. Cicero, on the other hand, explains that a cognitive impression does not pick up all the features of an object, but only all those features which are appropriate for its kind, visual features in the case of vision, auditory features in the case of hearing, etc. (*Acad.* I 42). Since even the weaker claim is extraordinarily strong, it will be safer to follow Cicero. In this case a cognitive impression will be evident in that it involves a representation of the object which clearly represents all the features of the object that are appropriate for the kind of impression it is; and since it represents all the features of the object in question, it will also represent the particular feature which it represents it as having, that is, the feature attributed to it in the proposition.

Cognitive impressions are not only clear, as opposed to obscure (*amudros;* cf. Alex. Aphrod. *De an.* 71.5ff.), they also are distinct (*ektupos;* cf. DL VII 46), as opposed to confused (*sugkechumenos;* cf. SE *M* VII 171). To see what their distinctness is supposed to consist in, it will be useful to refer to a doctrine which is never explicitly attributed to the Stoics but which we do find in Hellenistic dogmatic medicine and of which we have some reason to believe that it is in part of Stoic origin. According to this doctrine, the discriminatory power of the senses far outruns the ability of the mind to conceptualize the object. Thus, if under normal conditions we see an object clearly, its features are represented in the impression in such detail that our concepts do not capture them in all their detail. Hence, though a normal impression, as a rational impression, has a propositional content, the way it represents the subject of the proposition cannot be exhausted by any number of propositions (cf. Gal. *De loc. aff.* VIII 86.12ff., 87.4, 117.6 339.13, 355; *De praesag. ex puls.* IX 366.10K; *De sanit. tuenda,* CMG V 4.1, p. 185, 16). Now the Stoics assume that the properties of bodies themselves are particular (Cic. *Acad.* II 56). Hence they are called "*idiōmata,*" that is, properties (SE *M* VII 248). And they seem to be particular not in the sense that Socrates' wisdom is Socrates' wisdom rather than Plato's wisdom, but in the sense that they are qualitatively different individuals. After all, on the Stoic theory, Plato's wisdom and Socrates' wisdom quite literally are two particular bodies, which, by the law of the identity of indistinguishables which the Stoics adhere to, should be internally distinct and not just differ in their relational properties. A property, given its intimate connection and interdependence with the whole body it is the property of, cannot but take a certain form reflecting the idiosyncrasy of the object and hence be peculiar to it. Moreover, both Sextus and Cicero emphasize the artistic precision with which the features of the object are represented in a cognitive impression down to their last detail (SE *M* VII 248, 250–251; cf. *"subtiliter impressa"* in Cic. *Acad.* II 34). Hence a cognitive impression of an object will involve a representation of this object which is so articulate that the only object which will fit this representation is the very object the impression has its origin in (cf. SE *M* VII 252). This feature of cognitive impressions, that they represent their objects in such detail as to fit only them, is their distinctness. Since the Stoics assume that clear impressions represent all the relevant features of an object, cognitive impressions will be highly distinct.

Now normal impressions in general and perceptual impressions in particular have been characterized in such a way that their normality or perceptuality is a relational feature of these impressions, a feature which these impressions do not have by themselves, but only in virtue of the fact that they stand in a certain relation to the world. Hence it would seem that to determine whether an impression is cognitive or perceptual it will not suffice just to consider the impression by itself; we also have to consider its relation to the world.

But the Stoics also seem to assume that cognitive impressions by themselves differ from all other impressions, that there is some internal characteristic that serves to mark them off from other kinds of impressions and allows the mind to discriminate between cognitive and noncognitive impressions without having to consider their relation to the world (Cic. *Acad.* I 41). Cognitive impressions are supposed to differ from noncognitive impressions in the way in which horned serpents differ from all other kinds of snakes, that is, by some internal differentiating mark (SE *M* VII 252). The reason the Stoics postulate such a mark is easy to see. All the mind has to go by is its thoughts or impressions. If there is not a privileged set of impressions which we can rely on to be true, we shall be reduced to considerations of plausibility and coherence, to inferences to the best available explanation for our impressions, to decide which of them to accept as true and which to reject as false or to suspend judgment on. But even in the best of all circumstances such considerations could not fail to occasionally produce wrong conclusions, and there is nothing to guard us against the possibility that they generate conclusions which are so much off the mark that they would disrupt our life radically. But the Stoics want to argue that we are entirely responsible for our life and for that reason nature has put us into the position to avoid any false beliefs at all. And the only way to do this, it seems, is to provide us with impressions which cannot but be true and which we can discriminate.

Most of us will be thoroughly disinclined to believe that there is such a qualitative difference between our impressions. But one has to keep in mind that its postulation fits in with Stoic physics without any difficulty. Given that according to Stoic physics all states of the world and all parts of a state of the world are closely interdependent, any variation of the conditions under which an impression arises should affect the impression itself. Thus the assumption that normal impressions have a distinctive character seems not to be ad hoc but to be required by Stoic physics anyway. Even if this were not so, it would not be much of a problem for an omniscient nature to ensure that only impressions which have a normal history have a certain distinctive character which is the effect of the kind of history they have. Moreover, we have to take into account that it is part of the Stoic position that we are so corrupted that we tend to give assent to and to act on cognitive and noncognitive impressions rather indiscriminately. Hence our awareness of their difference is not just seriously retarded but also very distorted. And in any case it does not follow from the fact that we have such difficulties in telling whether an impression is cognitive or not, that there is no clear difference between them. Finally it has to be kept in mind that Plato and Aristotle had already made very strong claims regarding the power of the knowledge they attributed to the wise man; the man of practical wisdom is always right in practical matters. The Stoics explicitly refer to this Aristotelian doctrine (Pap. Herc. 1020, col. 1 n., *SVF* II, p. 41, 25), and they just seem to try to provide a theory that would explain how the wise man might manage to invariably get things right. If one gives up this conception of the wise man, one will, of course, not have the motivation the Stoics had to resort to such a strong assumption. But this conception of wisdom was too firmly embedded to be given up lightly in the face of epistemological difficulties.

Stoic Definitions of Cognitive Impressions

On the basis of what has been said, it should be relatively easy to understand the force of the Stoic definitions of cognitive impressions. These come in basically two versions. In a shorter version, which we find in DL VII 46 and SE *M* XI 183, cognitive impressions are defined by two clauses, whereas on the other, more common, version a further clause is added to the two clauses of the shorter version. There may be some truth in Cicero's claim (*Acad.* II 77) that the shorter definition is the one Zeno originally gave, before he went on to add a third clause to avoid an Academic objection, especially since this notice gets some support from Sextus's remark (*M* VII 252) that the Stoics added the third clause only to block an Academic objection based on an assumption which the Stoics did not share.

Let us, then, first consider the definition in its shorter version. To follow the formulation in DL VII 46, an impression is cognitive exactly if (i) it comes about from what is (*apo huparchontos*) and (ii) it is imprinted and impressed in exact accordance with what is. Though this is by no means obvious from the formulation of the second clause by itself, Sextus's comments on this clause in *M* VII 250–251 show that it is supposed to amount to the requirement that the impression be clear and distinct. And this interpretation is borne out by the characterization of noncognitive impressions which in DL follows immediately on the definition of cognitive impressions. According to this definition an impression is noncognitive if "it either is not from what is or, though it is from what is, is not in exact accordance with what is; one which is not clear nor distinct." Here the phrase "one which is not clear nor distinct" looks like a gloss on "is not in exact accordance with what is," that is, the negative counterpart to the second clause in the definition of cognitive impressions. And if this is correct, the second clause of the definition of a cognitive impression should amount to the requirement that cognitive impressions be clear and distinct.

It is tempting to think that the first clause amounts to the requirement that a cognitive impression have its origin in a real object rather than some disturbance or affection of the mind, that the object the impression presents itself as an impression of be a real object rather than a mere figment of the mind. And this seems to be the way Sextus interprets the clause, as one can see from his comments on the first part of the second clause in *M* VII 249. Nevertheless the interpretation of the first clause has been the subject of considerable controversy, which mainly turns around the force of the term "what is" (*huparchon*). It has been pointed out that Cicero in this context again and again renders "*huparchon*" by "what is true," that is, understands "what is" in the sense of "what is the case" (cf. *Acad.* II 42, 112), and that the Stoics do use "*to huparchon*" for a true proposition. Against this it has to be remembered that there is a great number of examples in which Sextus talks of impressions that have their origin in something or other, and that in his examples the something or other in question never is a proposition but always a real or a fictional object.

Nevertheless, there is some reason to think that Cicero's rendering is not a mere mistranslation or due to misinterpretation, but rests on the correct assumption that the first clause was not meant to amount to the requirement that the impression should have its origin in a real object, but to the stronger requirement that it be altogether true. That this assumption may be correct is suggested by *M* VII 402ff. There Sextus, following Carneades, argues that there are impressions which have their origin in what is not, but which present themselves as impressions which have their origin in what is just as much as purportedly cognitive impressions do. And as an example of such an impression Sextus adduces the case of Heracles who in his madness took his own children to be those of Eurystheus. Heracles here is explicitly said to have an impression that has its origin in his own children who are standing in front of him, that is, in a real external object. And nevertheless this impression, too, is supposed to be an example of an impression that has its origin in what is not. The reason for this must be that the impression is false in that it represents Heracles' children as being Eurystheus's children. In what sense could such an impression be said to have its origin in what is not? The answer seems to be that the impression does not as a whole have its origin in what is; part of it—namely, the part that represents Heracles' children as being Eurystheus's children—is made up by the mind and is not due to the object. We saw earlier that it is characteristic of perceptual impressions that all their representational features are due to the object. In this sense, only true impressions, and more particularly impressions that are true not by accident, have their origin in what is. If we interpret the first clause in this way, not only do we not have to assume that Cicero has misunderstood the Stoic definition, it will also be easy to explain why the third clause of the longer version of the definition—which runs, "it is such that it could not come about from what is not"—is standardly interpreted as meaning that a cognitive impression has to be such that it could not be false (cf. SE *M* VII 152, 252; Cic. *Acad.* II 42, 112). But even a confused and obscure impression may be entirely true and true not by accident but because all of its representational features are due to the object that has given rise to it. Hence, to single out cognitive impressions, the second clause is added. So much about the shorter version of the Stoic definition of cognitive impressions.

Standardly, though, the Stoics define cognitive impressions by adding a third clause. A cognitive impression is supposed to satisfy the further requirement that it be "such that an impression of this character could not come about from what is not" (SE *M* VII 248, 252; DL VII 50). This, as we noted above, is taken to imply that an impression of this character could not be false (cf. SE *M* VII 152, 252). Given the strong reading of "has its origin in what is," it is easy to see how the clause would have this implication. The main question concerning the third clause is the identity of the character referred to. Is this a further characteristic of cognitive impressions which is postulated, but not specified by the definition, or is it the property of satisfying the first two conditions, or is it perhaps just the property of being clear and distinct? The phrase "of this character" (*hoia*) is ambiguous in this respect.

Given what we said earlier about cognitive impressions, it seems most plausible to take this to refer to the distinctive inherent feature that cognitive impressions are supposd to have. And this seems to be confirmed by remarks in Sextus (*M* VII 252) and in Cicero (*Acad.* II 77) which suggest that the Stoics think that any impression which satisfies the first two conditions will in fact also satisfy the third condition, but that they add the third clause because this implication is denied by the Academics, though both agree that cognitive impressions, in order to play the role assigned to them by the Stoics, would have to satisfy the third condition, too. And this dispute about the third clause turns out to be a dispute about whether cognitive impressions have an internal differentiating feature (cf. SE *M* VII 252). Hence, it would seem that the third clause refers to this distinctive feature of cognitive impressions, which is postulated, but not specified.

The Criterion

To get a clearer notion of this feature and of the role it is supposed to play in cognition, it will be useful to briefly consider in which way cognitive impressions are supposed to constitute the criterion or canon of truth. We have already seen that they are not a criterion of truth in the sense that they put us in a position to determine the truth of any proposition whatsoever. There are lots of propositions that cannot be certified by them. Nor are they the criterion of truth in the sense that whenever the truth of a proposition is in question, we at least consider the corresponding impression and try to determine by introspection whether it has the distinctive mark of a cognitive impression. There are several reasons why this can hardly be the Stoic view of the matter.

First of all, cognitive impressions will directly guarantee only the truth of their own propositional content. And if it is true that cognitive impressions are perceptual, the only propositions whose truth they can guarantee directly are propositions that attribute a perceptual feature to a particular object. If they nevertheless are called *the* criterion of truth, it is because in an indirect way they also guarantee the truth of all other propositions that are known to be true by human beings. And they do this in the following way. They give rise to general ideas, the so-called common notions which the mind forms naturally on the basis of cognitive impressions and which in turn allow us to have further cognitive impressions. And since cognitive impressions do represent things as they are, the common notions based on them will represent things as they are. Thus if the common notion of a man represents a man as a biped rational animal, the proposition that man is a biped rational animal will be certified not by an impression that man is a biped rational animal, which is cognitive in its own right, but by the common notion, and this in turn will be certified by the cognitive impressions which give rise to it and which it gives rise to, and these will be cognitive in their own right (cf. Cic. *Acad.* II 22). And the truth of propositions certified by cognitive impressions and of propositions certified by common notions in turn will guarantee the truth of further propositions derived by deductive inference from the former propositions. It is for this reason that Chrysippus sometimes can say that perceptions and common notions constitute the criterion (DL VII 54). Cognitive impressions, then, are the criterion of truth in the sense that their truth guarantees the truth of whatever can be known by human beings. It is only through them that we have any knowledge of what is true and what is not true.

Second, we have to remember that there is no such thing as the impression that corresponds to a given proposition, and, therefore, when the truth of a proposition is in question, we may have to go through a number of impressions all of which have the proposition in question as their propositional content till we hit upon a cognitive impression. Thus we may not be certain of the color of an object we see in the distance. As we move nearer we have a series of different impressions which all may be impressions that the object is blue. Similarly in the case of a theoretical problem our impression of the proposition in question will change as we consider the matter. The impression we have when we have a proof for a proposition is quite different from the impression that we had to start with. Thus cognitive impressions cannot be the criterion in the sense that we just have to look at our impressions to determine whether a proposition is true. It is, rather, by considering the proposition that we may get a clearer and clearer impression.

Most important, though, we have to avoid thinking of Stoic impressions as pictures or images of the world which can be looked at introspectively, with the mind's eye, as it were, to see whether they have this feature that guarantees their truth. What we see and grasp, according to the Stoics, are objects in the world, and not pictures or images of them, though grasping objects does involve the awareness of their representations in the mind, just as it involves an awareness of the mind itself. For we have to take into account that impressions for the Stoics are mental states that are identified as highly complex physical states, as we can see from the fact that originally they were conceived of quite literally as imprints. When Chrysippus objected to this, it was because he thought that they were much more complex than the term "imprint" suggested; in calling them "alterations" or "modifications" (cf. SE *M* VII 229–230; VIII 400; *PH* II 70; DL VII 50) of the mind instead, he deliberately, it seems, left open what their precise nature consists in. There is no suggestion that we could observe them to find out exactly what they are like. It is, of course, true that the Stoics think that impressions reveal themselves along with the object they are impressions of (Aetius, *Plac.* IV 12.2). But all that this means is we can tell what our impressions are; after all, they are our thoughts. But we do not know our thoughts by introspection, nor is there any reason to believe that the Stoics think so. Moreover, if the Stoics thought that we could see by introspection whether an impression has the distinctive feature of a cognitive impression, we would expect them to say, at least on occasion, that the criterion of truth is this feature. But they never say anything of this sort. Also, if they had taken this view, they would have opened themselves to the charge of an infinite regress. For we would have to ask what is supposed to guarantee the truth of the impression that a given impression has this distinctive feature. Quite generally, the criterion will fulfill its role only if it does not require the judgment that an impression is of a certain kind. For this will always raise the question how this judgment is to be certified.

The Stoic theory, I want to suggest, escapes this difficulty because it assumes that the distinctive feature of cognitive impressions is a causal feature of impressions such that cognitive impressions play their criterial role not through our awareness of their distinctive feature, but through the causal effects they have on our minds in virtue of this feature. The word "to discriminate" is ambiguous. It is used in cases in which one recognizes things to be of different kind and, in virtue of this awareness of the difference, treats them differently. But there are also cases in which somebody reacts differently to things of a different kind not in virtue of an awareness of their difference and perhaps even without knowing that there is such a kind of thing which he systematically reacts to in a distinctive manner; there is a causal link between a feature of the object and the behavior of the person, but the awareness of the feature on the part of the person is not an essential part of the causal chain; and nevertheless such a person can be said to discriminate or to discern the feature. Many forms of discrimination in the pejorative sense are of this kind. The suggestion, then, is that the distinctive mark of cognitive impressions is a causal feature in that it makes the mind react in a distinctive way and that it is in this sense that the mind can discriminate cognitive and noncognitive impressions. It can also learn to tell whether an impression is cognitive or not, but that is a different ability not at issue at this point in our argument.

What reason do we have to think that this is the Stoic position? The Stoics assume that cognitive impressions give rise to common notions. Common notions have their privileged status exactly because the mind forms them naturally on the basis of cognitive impressions. Nobody, so at least the Stoics think, can help but end up with the notion of a tree and the notion of a human being and the notion of the color green if he grows up normally in a normal environment. This formation of common notions is not something we engage in deliberately according to certain rules and precepts; if we did, we could make mistakes and end up with the wrong notions. The Stoics clearly assume that the mind sorts out cognitive impressions to form concepts on the basis of them without our being aware of this at all; we just find ourselves having certain concepts that we did not have to start with. Thus the Stoics also must assume that the mind can discriminate cognitive impressions without our being aware of it.

We also have to find some explanation of the fact that the mind gives assent to some impressions but not to others. As soon as the mind has acquired all sorts of beliefs, it is easy to see how it would accept or reject impressions against the background of the beliefs it already has. But in the beginning, it would seem, the mind has no more reason to accept than not to accept any given impression. This problem would be solved if we assume that cognitive impressions cause the mind to accept them. And there is some evidence, though by no means decisive, that this is in fact the Stoic position (cf. SE *M* VII 405, 407; Cic. *Acad.* II 38; Plut. *Adv. Colot.* 1121E, 1122C). This is perfectly compatible with the further Stoic claim that we are responsible for our acts of assent, for it is explicitly not part of the Stoic doctrine of responsibility that we are responsible only for those things which we could have done otherwise. But it clearly cannot be the Stoic view that we acquire our first beliefs by scanning our impressions and by being caused to assent to those which we detect to have the distinctive remark of cognitive impressions. It, rather, must be the case that the Stoics assume that the mind does this without our being aware of it.

Moreover, the Stoics point out (SE *M* VII 258; Cic. *Acad.* II 19) that if we do not have a clear impression we take the appropriate steps to receive an evident impression, in case the subject is of any importance to us; that is, not having a clear impression naturally makes us consider the matter further till we have a clear impression. The suggestion does not seem to be that we recognize that our impression is confused and obscure and hence decide to get a clearer one, but, rather, that there is a causal mechanism that sets us going and would naturally make us stop once we had a clear impression. For these reasons, then, it seems that the differentiating mark of cognitive impressions is a causal feature rather than a phenomenological character to be detected by introspection.

But this is not to say that we cannot be aware of the fact that an impression is cognitive or noncognitive, that we cannot learn to tell whether an impression is clear and distinct or obscure and confused. In fact, the Stoic view seems to be that this is a matter of practice and that in principle one can get so good at it that one will never take a noncognitive impression to be cognitive. But to learn this is not to acquire a mysterious sixth sense which, unlike the other senses, is not subject to the possibility of abnormal conditions and hence unfailingly gives us notice of an equally mysterious feature of cognitive impressions. Judgments regarding the evidence of an impression are notoriously as fallible as any other judgments, and there is no reason to saddle the Stoics with the assumption that this is not so. But we can get better and better at seeing how variations in the conditions under which our impressions arise, especially variations in our mental state and the beliefs we have, do affect our impression.

Cognition, Knowledge, and the Wise Man

Whereas their predecessors had distinguished only between knowledge and mere opinion, the Stoics distinguish between knowledge, cognition, and mere belief (SE *M* VII 151ff.). Cognition consists in the assent to, or acceptance of, the appropriate kind of impression, that is, an impression that is at least cognitive in the wider sense. A mere opinion, on the other hand, even if it is true, may or may not involve the appropriate kind of impression; if it does, it is also a cognition; but whether it does or not is not what one focuses on when one calls it an opinion. Knowledge differs from cognition in that it involves not only the appropriate kind of impression but also the appropriate kind of assent—namely, the kind of firm assent that one cannot be persuaded to withdraw by any argument to the contrary. This presumably is one reason why we have to try to avoid having any false beliefs whatsoever. For if we do accept a false premise we might be led by a chain of reasoning to accept the contradictory of what we had already believed to be true, even if we had accepted it on the basis of a cognitive impression. And as long as one is susceptible to this, one's assent will not be firm. On the other hand, once one has learned to accept true impressions only, no amount of dialectical skill will suffice to make one withdraw one's assent from impressions that are cognitive in the wider sense; and then one's assent will be stable and firm or certain; in this sense of "certain" one will have certain knowledge.

All cases of cognition are cases either of knowledge or of opinion. For though they all involve the appropriate kind of impression, they will be a matter either of opinion or of knowledge depending on whether or not they also involve the appropriate kind of assent. Nevertheless, there is a point to the distinction. It emphasizes the fact that the conditions on knowledge are so strong that only the wise man will have knowledge (SE *M* VII 152, 432). In fact, his wisdom will consist in this kind of knowledge. The ordinary person will have nothing but mere beliefs, for he is not yet able to avoid any false belief and hence his assent is not yet firm. But it is important that many of his beliefs are at least cognitive. For they will afford him a basis to acquire the knowledge that constitutes wisdom.

This view has one consequence that hardly seems to have been noticed, but which is highly relevant to our topic. For the Stoics also assume that there are no wise men or at least that not even the members of their own school have attained the blissful state of wisdom (SE *M* VII 432–33). It immediately follows that there is no knowledge or at least that the Stoics do not have any knowledge. And once we realize this, all sorts of Stoic texts with a strong skeptical flavor come to mind. Thus Seneca (*De ben.* IV 33.2) says: "We never expect completely certain cognition of things, since the exploration of truth is extremely difficult; we follow where likelihood guides us." The Stoic claim is not that they have attained the knowledge Socrates tried to find, but rather that the knowledge Socrates was after is attainable by human beings.

The Skeptical Attack

It should be clear, then, that skepticism did not arise as a reaction to overly confident claims to knowledge on the part of the Stoics. The Stoics were in no mood to make such claims. But the Stoics did claim some expertise, and on the authority of this expertise tried to put forth views on the nature and the material content of the knowledge Socrates had been looking for in vain. Hence the central role of the notion of a dogma and the charges of dogmatism in skeptical attacks on Stoicism. Moreover, the view the Stoics did adopt turned out to be extremely revisionist and literally paradoxical. Thus it would easily occur to one to subject the Stoic claims to exactly the kind of dialectic that Socrates had used to test and expose unfounded claims to expertise. And this is precisely what the skeptics did.

Now there are some crucial features of Socratic dialectic which it is worthwhile to recall if we want to understand the skeptical position. The Socratic method allows one to test expertise in a subject without being oneself an expert in this subject—in fact, without committing oneself to or even having any views on the subject. All one has to do is to show that the person who claims expertise or makes statements with the air of authority involves himself in contradictions concerning the very subject he claims to be an expert in or that he is unable to discard a thesis which is the contradictory of a thesis he has put forth with the air of expertise. For if he were an expert, he should be able to defend his position against theses to the contrary, and he certainly should not involve himself in contradictions. Hence such dialectical arguments are not meant to establish the truth or falsehood of some thesis. All they are meant to show is that the opponent is no authority on the matters in question.

It is important to keep this in mind, because otherwise one might be misled into thinking that the skeptics themselves accept either the premises or the conclusions of their arguments. Thus one might think that the ancient Academic skeptic fits the prevailing modern notion of what a skeptic is, in that he believes that all that is given to us are our impressions and that he tries to convince us that since this is so, there is no way in which we ever can have certain knowledge of what the world that gives rise to these impressions really is like. The skeptic may argue this way, but if he does so, it is just another *ad hominem* argument against those who believe that all that is given to us immediately are our impressions. There is no reason why the skeptic himself should feel committed to this very dogmatic, speculative, unskeptical assumption and the dualism between the mental and the physical, the subject and the object which tends to go with it. Thus it is not surprising that in other contexts the skeptic is quite willing to challenge the dogma of the impression as a given (Gal. *De diff. puls.* VIII 710, 18ff. K.; *De praenot.* XIV 628, 14ff.). He is quite willing to say that some things evidently appear to be the case, as we ordinarily do, but he does not think that this commits him to the view that there are such entities as impressions, assents, and evidence. Nor are the skeptics committed to the conclusions of their arguments—for example, the conclusion that there is no knowledge or the conclusion that nothing can be known, or the conclusion that the wise man will suspend judgment on all questions. He is not even committed to the view that the conclusions of his arguments follow from their premises. For, as he will emphasize, he does not subscribe to the canons of logic worked out by his opponents, either (cf. Cic. *Acad.* II 91ff.). He is just prepared, for the sake of argument, to meet whatever standards of logic are met or required by his opponents. For otherwise his arguments will not have the desired effect on them.

What is the envisaged effect of such arguments? Reporting his experience the skeptic might say that they tend to leave one with the impression that the Stoics have not successfully argued their case concerning the nature and the attainability of knowledge. They may also tend to leave one with the impression that it is doubtful whether such a case can be made at all. More generally, it will appear doubtful whether the case for any revisionist conception of knowledge can be made; we might just have to accept the fact that all that is available to us is the kind of everyday knowledge the vulgar have. Even more generally, it may appear doubtful whether the case for any position can be made. On the other hand, it would not be desirable, from the skeptic's point of view, if one was left with the impression that the positions attacked by him are false, or that, even if they are true, there is no way to definitively establish them as true. This would lead to a dogmatic pseudoskepticism quite alien to true Academic or Pyrrhonean skepticism (cf. SE *PH* I 200, 226, 236; Gal. *De subf. emp.* 84, 22 D.).

Given the central position of the doctrine of cognitive impressions in Stoic epistemology, it is not surprising that the skeptics focused their attack on this doctrine. And here the main point at issue was whether cognitive impressions differ qualitatively from all other impressions. This, as we saw, is an assumption so central to the Stoic position that Zeno already added it to his definition of cognitive impressions. The skeptics were quite willing, at least for the sake of argument, to accept the first part of the definition and to grant that there may be impressions that have their origin in what is and that represent their object faithfully and clearly (SE *M* VII 402). But they took issue with the added assumption that such an impression, just given its internal characteristics, could have no other origin than the object it faithfully represented, that there could not be an impression exactly like it which was nevertheless false. Already Arcesilaus attacked the further assumption (Cic. *Acad.* II 77; SE *M* VII 154), Carneades pursued the same line of attack (SE *M* VII 164, 402ff.), and it was to remain the main point of contention throughout the debate (Cic. *Acad.* II 33, 78; SE *M* VII 252).

We have only a rather general idea of the form this debate took, since its details have not been studied with the care they deserve. Apparently, the skeptics adopted the strategy of arguing for the more general thesis that for any true impression there could be another impression exactly like it which is false (Cic. *Acad.* II 40, 41, 42; 44, 84, 90; SE *M* VII 154, 164, 252, 402, 415, 428), or at least one which differs so minimally from the true one that we cannot distinguish between it and the true one and which, nevertheless, is false (Cic. *Acad.* II 40, 85). More particularly, they seem to have argued the matter for the various kinds of true impressions, kind by kind (Cic. *Acad.* II 42). In the case of cognitive impressions, they did so in at least two ways. To start with, they tried to show that there are impressions which, as far as their representational features are concerned, differ in no way, or at least in no discriminable way, from cognitive impressions, though they themselves are not true. But then they also tried to show that there are impressions which have all the supposed characteristics of cognitive impressions—which, for example, are vivid or striking, or which at least could not be distinguished from a cognitive impression by the person who has the impression at the time he has them, and which nevertheless are false (SE *M* VII 408).

Let us first turn to the impressions that are supposed to be exactly like, or at least indistinguishable from, cognitive impressions in the way in which they represent their object (cf. Cic. *Acad.* II 84ff.; SE *M* VII 408ff.). Suppose that Socrates is standing in full view in front of one; in this case one may have the cognitive impression that this is pale or that this is a man or even that this is Socrates, if one has learned to grasp his Socraticity and has a corresponding idea of Socrates. Now also suppose that Socrates has a twin brother, whom we do not know anything about, but who is exactly like Socrates, or who at least looks exactly like Socrates. In this case, the skeptic rightly claims, the impression one would have of Socrates' twin brother under identical normal conditions would be exactly like the cognitive impression one has of Socrates. Hence, he goes on to argue, it is not the case, as the Stoics claim, that an impression which has all the characteristics of a cognitive impression can have its origin only in the object which gives rise to it and that there could not be another impression exactly like it which does not have its origin in this object. Moreover, suppose (i) that we first see Socrates and have the cognitive impression that this is Socrates and (ii) that then Socrates disappears and his twin brother takes his place. We would have an impression exactly like our first impression and on the basis of it judge again that this is Socrates. But this impression and the corresponding judgment would be false.

The Stoic answer to this relies on the assumption that no two objects are exactly alike (cf. Cic. *Acad.* II 85). Thus Socrates and his twin brother will differ from each other at least minimally. Hence, a cognitive impression of Socrates, being by definition distinct, could not be exactly like an impression that had its origin in his twin brother. If the impression one received of Socrates were exactly like the one which one received of his twin brother, both impressions would be confused and hence not cognitive. But the impressions we receive of Socrates and his twin brother do not need to be indistinguishable and hence confused. For, the Stoics assume, the two brothers do differ from each other at least minimally, and by sufficient training we can learn to distinguish perceptually any two perceptible objects (cf. Cic. *Acad.* II 20; 56; 57; 86). Thus we can learn to distinguish Socrates and his twin brother however much they may look alike, and only if we have learned this can we have the cognitive impression that this is Socrates. Hence, it cannot happen that we first have a cognitive impression of Socrates and then a false impression exactly like it that this (Socrates' twin brother) is Socrates.

The crucial issue here is the metaphysical principle of the internal distinctness of different objects or the identity of indistinguishables. Since this principle is firmly embedded in Stoic metaphysics, their reliance on it here cannot be discounted as an *ad hoc* move. And once this principle is granted, the claim that for any object there could be another object so much like it that we could not possibly discriminate the two is considerably weakened. For though the skeptics can point to many cases in which we could find it exceedingly difficult, if not impossible, to distinguish different objects from each other because of their similarity, the Stoics point out, not without plausibility, that if we just put our mind to it we would also learn to tell these objects apart (Cic. *Acad.* II 56, 57). It also may be mentioned that according to Stoic logic the two impressions one receives when one sees Socrates and his twin brother would differ in one crucial respect even if the two brothers were exactly alike: if they are impressions that this is Socrates, they would differ in propositional content since the demonstrative has a different reference.

Now one may think that the skeptic's case gets a good deal of its force from the fact that it seems to show that even under normal conditions we do not know whether our impression is cognitive, since we do not know whether it is an impression of the object it presents itself as an impression of, or whether it is in fact an impression of an object very much like it which we have not yet learned to distinguish from it. But we have to keep in mind that the Stoics do not deny that we can make the mistake of thinking that an impression is cognitive when it is not. They are committed only to the view that under normal conditions we shall have a cognitive impression of the object in view, that the mind can discriminate the impression as cognitive, and that we could not have the cognitive impression that this is Socrates without being able to distinguish Socrates from all other objects. But this does not mean that we cannot have all sorts of other cognitive impressions of Socrates without being able to distinguish him from all other objects. Similarly, we shall have a cognitive impression of Socrates' twin brother if we see him under normal conditions, even if we do not know him at all, let alone are able to distinguish him from all other objects. But this impression, whichever it is, will be quite different from the cognitive impression that this is Socrates. There is also nothing to prevent us from having the impression, concerning Socrates' twin brother, with him in full view, that this is Socrates. But this impression will not be any of the *cognitive* impressions we have when we have the brother in full view, though we may make the mistake of thinking that it is.

The other line of attack the skeptics choose seems more promising. They point out that even the patently false impressions of dreamers, madmen, and drunkards all seem to have the features supposed to be characteristic of cognitive impressions, or that they at least seem to be indistinguishable from them for the person who has them.

The first thing to notice is that these impressions are due to nonnormal or abnormal states of mind; and it does seem far from obvious that such states of mind do not have an effect on the internal character of the impressions they produce; in fact, often it seems obvious enough that an abnormal state of mind systematically changes the character of our impressions. And, for reasons indicated above, Stoic physics would seem to require that the internal character of impressions implies a certain state of mind. Second, it needs to be noticed that even if it were the case that in certain abnormal states a person is not in a position to tell whether his impressions are cognitive or not, because the noncognitive ones seem to him to have all the features of cognitive ones, this would not show that he does not have cognitive and noncognitive impressions which differ from each other qualitatively and which his mind discriminates accordingly. And correspondingly we do not find the Stoics arguing that even dreamers and madmen can tell that their dreams and hallucinations are noncognitive, but that even dreamers and madmen react differently to cognitive and noncognitive impressions (cf. SE *M* VII 247). And this seems true enough, if we consider the matter in general. The Stoics are, of course, committed to the view that the mind in each case manages to discriminate between cognitive and noncognitive impressions, but their theory also seems to allow them to explain apparent counterexamples. It is exactly a sign of a severely abnormal state of mind, if the mind treats cognitive and noncognitive impressions almost indiscriminately so that in particular cases there may seem to be no difference in observable behavior.

Thus, it seems that the skeptics fail to show that cognitive and noncognitive impressions do not differ from each other qualitatively and that, hence, the mind cannot discriminate between them on the basis of their inherent difference. They even fail to show that it is impossible to tell absolutely reliably whether one's impression is cognitive or not. What they perhaps do show is that we, in our present state, cannot invariably tell whether an impression is cognitive or not. But then the Stoics would be the last to deny that.

Conclusion

Academic skepticism is not characterized by a certain philosophical position, by a set of philosophical views Academics are expected to subscribe to, but by a certain dialectical practice and the impression the pursuit of this dialectical practice left on them. Now it seems that earlier Academic skeptics like Arcesilaus and Carneades were left with the impression that they had no reason to accept philosophical beliefs. Whatever reasons they may have had when they started out had been neutralized by arguments to the contrary. Later Academic skeptics, though, starting with Metrodorus and Philo, seem to have had the impression that however much one argued on both sides of any philosophical or theoretical question, one still may find in the end that, as a matter of fact, one is still inclined toward one side of the matter, that there is no reason to think that this is just due to the fact that one is lacking in dialectical skill or has not considered the matter carefully enough, and that there is no reason not to report which view one feels inclined to, at least as long as one is among one's peers and there is no danger that one's report is mistaken for an authoritative statement, as it might be, for example, by young students. As a result many Academic skeptics came to articulate quite elaborate philosophical beliefs. And given the dominance of Stoicism and the syncretism of the time, these often hardly differed from the views of their Stoic rivals. And since the Stoics did not claim knowledge for their views either, the two positions became more and more difficult to distinguish, as soon as one left the field of epistemology. But given that both sides now tended to have more or less the same beliefs on the basis of the same considerations anyway, the epistemological debate must have started to look somewhat academic and futile, especially since it seemed to have ended in a deadlock. Galen (*De dogm. Plat: et Hipp.* 796, 8ff. M) could even claim the following: the younger Academics say that everything should be judged by means of plausible, tested, incontrovertible impressions (the Carneadean "criterion"), Chrysippus maintains that matters should be judged by cognitive impressions, and common sense tells us that it is all a matter of perception and evident thought; but their disagreement is only verbal: if one considers the matter more closely, Galen says, one will see that they all advocate the same epistemic practice.

Thus it is not surprising that some skeptics thought that the Academy had become unfaithful to its skeptical tradition and that they tried to revive the radical skepticism of the early Academics, but now under the name of "Pyrrhonism" to distinguish themselves from their Academic contemporaries. But by this time, it seems, the Stoics were no longer inclined to engage in a real debate on the matter and to refine their position accordingly. And thus orthodox Stoicism itself was soon a matter of the past, whose views only lived on in the more or less distorted form in which they were assimilated into other systems. And in this distorted form the Stoics' views on cognitive impressions and their clarity and distinctness, in fact the whole Stoic epistemology, have exercised, through surviving Greek and Latin authors like Cicero and Sextus Empiricus, an enormous influence well into modern times.

Skeptics

10

The Skeptic's Beliefs

There are no views or beliefs that define Pyrrhonean Skepticism. Nor are there any specific doctrines or dogmas which a skeptic, rather than a member of one of the 'dogmatic' schools, would have. Even the phrase, "nothing is to be known," is not accepted by the skeptical philosopher as expressing a skeptical doctrine (Sext. Emp. *P.H.* I 200). According to Photius (Bibl. cod. 212, 169[b] 40ff.), Aenesidemus argued that the Academic skeptics really were dogmatists, since some of them did, in fact, claim that nothing is knowable (cf. S.E. *P.H.* I 2–3). There are no specifically Pyrrhonean doctrines, no views which any Pyrrhonist, just by being a Pyrrhonist, would have to accept. Still less is Pyrrhonean skepticism characterized by specifically skeptical views that rely on 'deeper' insights into the true nature of things. It is the dogmatists, not the skeptics, who claim to have such insights (S.E. *P.H.* I 2–3).

The usual interpretation of Pyrrhonean skepticism, of course, ascribes a far more radical stance to these skeptics. According to this interpretation, the skeptic not only claims to have no deeper insight into things, he also claims not to know anything at all; not only does he maintain no specifically skeptical doctrines, he also has no views or beliefs about anything. Such a characterization of Pyrrhonism typically relies on the following: as far as knowledge is concerned, the Pyrrhonist, as a full-blooded skeptic, can hardly assume that he knows anything without undermining his skepticism; and, as for beliefs, the ancient skeptics assure us that they are withholding judgment on whatever issue is under consideration. The skeptic refuses to assent to any proposition.

Any interpretation along these lines, however, seems fundamentally mistaken to me. No matter how ingenious he may be, the skeptic cannot avoid knowing many things. It might even turn out that, with great effort, imagination, and cleverness, he could bring about that he knows less and less. There is, however, no reason to suppose that the skeptic is pursuing such a strategy. If he, then, simply cannot avoid knowing many things, he will also often be aware of knowing, and not merely supposing, certain things. And if we turn from our own conception of skepticism to the words of Sextus Empiricus, we can see clearly that the skeptic, in many instances, does think of himself as knowing something. I can, in fact, see no reason why he should not think this; it is perfectly compatible with his skepticism. Yet, whatever the case may be with regard to knowledge, it seems clear to me both that there are many things the skeptic thinks or believes are the case and that it is perfectly compatible with his skepticism for him to have all sorts of views and beliefs. And it is just this last point which shall be our concern here—can the skeptic have beliefs?

Given how much speaks in its favor, it is hardly surprising that the received interpretation has won almost universal acceptance; indeed so much speaks in its favor that its defenders have not even been deterred by the fact that, on this interpretation, the skeptical position turns out to be inconsistent. For it is generally assumed that ordinary, everyday life is simply not possible without any beliefs or views; and so it is generally assumed that the skeptic refutes himself, when he insists on total suspension of judgment while, at the same time, constantly relying on all sorts of judgments in his actual life. Hume's version of this objection is perhaps the most familiar; without a doubt, it has contributed substantially to the standard picture of the skeptic as a person who, if only he took his own views seriously, would be completely helpless in ordinary life.

Of course, the ancient skeptics, starting with Arcesilaus at the latest, were quite familiar with this objection. Clearly, they felt it did not really tell against their position. Since the issue was raised again and again over the course of centuries, it seems reasonable to suppose that the skeptics had, in fact, considered the matter quite carefully, when they claimed that this objection did not tell against them. That in turn should lead us to suspect that the skeptics' position is more complicated than the objection would have it, that the objection somehow overlooks some crucial aspect of their position. Still, it is hardly a coincidence that, all their protests to the contrary notwithstanding, the skeptics find themselves faced with basically the same objection time and again. The skeptical position must be one that positively provokes such an objection. Yet it seems to me that one violates the canons of interpretation if one does not take the skeptics' constant protests—that this objection does not really tell against their position—at least as seriously as the fact that they were constantly confronted by it.

If we, then, take seriously the skeptics' protestations and try to understand how they could think that this objection somehow misses the mark, there seem to be basically two lines along which the skeptics could argue, in defending themselves against this objection. The objectors claim that the skeptics, in theory, suspend judgment on all matters, but that, in practice, they simply cannot avoid making all kinds of judgments. Thus, one could argue against the objection by (i) trying to show that the skeptics denied that one could not avoid making judgments in practice, in everyday life—judgments like 'it is very hot today' or 'this car is about to run me over'. The skeptics could grant that it is extraordinarily difficult to bring oneself into such a state that one no longer even feels any temptation to have any view but insist that it is, in principle, possible and, indeed, is compatible with living a life worth living. Or, (ii) one could argue that the skeptics thought that even if one suspended judgment on all matters, at least suspended judgment in the sense in which they recommend that one suspend judgment, one would still have many beliefs and views, quite enough, at any rate, to lead a worthwhile life.

For various reasons—which I shall come to—it seems as if the skeptics opted for the second line. Since, however, there are some indications that they pursued the first line, to meet the standard objection, I want to consider this interpretation of their position at least briefly. There are basically three points that make this interpretation seem attractive: (i) As I have already indicated, there are a large number of passages that seem to show that the skeptic suspends judgment about everything and hence has no views or beliefs. Precisely because this part of their position is so well attested, one might suppose that the only way out was for the skeptic to hold that one could go through life without any views or beliefs; (ii) there are at least some reasons for thinking that Pyrrho himself attempted to lead a life entirely without beliefs or views—and Pyrrho is generally thought to have been the source for Pyrrhonean skepticism; (iii) quite a number of skeptical arguments survive that seem to set out to show that human action and human life is possible even without beliefs, that acting does not presuppose that one believes this or that is the case. And this third point seems to fit in very well with the first two.

For the time being, I want to pass over (i) and note that it will turn out that it is only true in a restricted sense that the skeptics suspend judgment on all matters and that everything depends on how one construes this restriction. As for (ii) it may well be that Antigonus of Carystus, virtually a contemporary of Pyrrho's, thought that Pyrrho undertook leading a life without beliefs. Diogenes Laertius, whose report ultimately derives from Antigonus' biography, writes: "In his life he followed [his skepticism]; he avoided nothing, took no precautions, but faced all risks, carts, precipices, dogs or whatever else it happened to be; he left nothing to the guidance of the senses; but he was . . . saved from harm by his friends who always accompanied him" (D.L. IX 61). We cannot rule out that Antigonus' remarks, on which this report depends, were intended as a sort of critical caricature of skeptical philosophers. In that case we would have here yet another instance of the standard objection that skepticism and normal life are incompatible. Still, it is clear that Diogenes Laertius himself does not take his source in this way, and so we must, with all due caveats, perhaps suppose that Antigonus did see Pyrrho's life as an attempt at leading a life without beliefs. This interpretation is compatible with his regarding that attempt as a failure; for the comment about Pyrrho's friends suggests that Pyrrho leads his life under false pretenses, that the appearance of living like a serious skeptic is achieved only by relying on the judgments of his friends. Whatever Antigonus' view may have been, it is this passage of Diogenes Laertius' that one will turn to, if one wants to claim that Pyrrho did attempt to live his life without any beliefs, even without beliefs of the sort we rely on in our ordinary, everyday life. However straightforward and simple, nontheoretical and nonphilosophical these beliefs may be, the serious followers of Pyrrho, on this view of skepticism, will seek to manage without them. He will not even think things like, e.g., that he has forgotten his watch or that he must do some shopping.

If our main interest, however, is in the position that later goes under the name of Pyrrhonean skepticism, we need not be especially interested in what Pyrrho actually thought about this matter; and that for at least two reasons:

(A) It is striking that Pyrrho is the only ancient skeptic to whom the doxographers ascribe a life that can easily be regarded as at least an attempt at a life without beliefs. All the other skeptics seem to have led conventional lives; Sextus Empiricus even emphasizes that the skeptical life is, and should be expected to be, a conventional one. It seems clear that the later skeptics all sought a life which—on any ordinary criterion—would count as a satisfactory life. Their lives cannot readily be construed as lives without beliefs or even as attempts at lives without beliefs, rather they seem like lives guided by beliefs, whatever the skeptics may say. It is revealing that Aenesidemus, the philosopher presumably most responsible for Pyrrhonism, seems to have objected to those features of Pyrrho's life we found described by Antigonus of Carystus. According to Aenesidemus, Pyrrho did not act as foolishly as Antigonus had said he did (D.L. IX 62). An indication of how Pyrrhonists after Aenesidemus viewed Pyrrho's life is provided by Galen (*De subfiguratione empirica* XI, p. 82, 23ff. Deichgräber): Here Pyrrho is described in the way the Pyrrhonists see themselves—in practical life, the Pyrrhonist follows what seems evident to him. That, precisely, is what the Pyrrho of Antigonus' biography had not done; otherwise, he would not have needed his friends to save him from harm. Thus, when later skeptics, both Pyrrhonists and Academics, do recommend a life without beliefs, this surely is not the sort of life that the historical Pyrrho had recommended, but a life that at any rate superficially looked like a life led by someone who was guided by ordinary, everyday beliefs.

(B) I also think that it might very well be the case that Pyrrho's influence on Pyrrhonean skepticism is far less than generally assumed. The ancient doxographers already failed in their attempts to construct a continuous tradition linking Aenesidemus and Sextus with Pyrrho (D.L. IX 115ff.). Menodotus, a prominent Pyrrhonist himself, pointed out that the tradition was broken after Pyrrho. Since Pyrrho left no writings, later authors had to rely on the testimony of Timon, Pyrrho's student, a testimony of dubious value, as I have tried to show elsewhere (*J. Phil.* 70, 1973; p. 806). How badly matters stood when it came to reconstructing Pyrrho's views is shown by these lines of Diogenes', which are clearly meant to give the sources for reports about Pyrrho: "Pyrrho himself left no writings, but those who knew him, Timon, Aenesidemus, Numenius, Nausiphanes and others like them, did" (D.L. IX 102). Aenesidemus here seems in all likelihood to be the familiar Pyrrhonist; and if that is so, we cannot conclude, from the "those who knew him," that Numenius is not the well-known Platonist. If that is correct, it is clear just how bad the situation with respect to sources on Pyrrho really is.

Not surprisingly, then, it seems as if later Pyrronists were unclear about how their position was related to that of the historical Pyrrho. When Sextus (*P.H.* I 7) tells us that skepticism is sometimes called 'Pyrrhonean' because Pyrrho seems to have turned to skepticism "more than his predecessors," it is difficult to avoid the impression that Sextus has certain doubts about the position of the historical Pyrrho. When we hear of Theodosius' suggestion (D.L. IX 70) that the label 'Pyrrhonists' be dropped, since one cannot know what another person is thinking and hence cannot know what Pyrrho had actually intended, we ought not to see this primarily as raising an epistemological worry about other minds; rather, Theodosius seems to want to distance himself from the position of the historical Pyrrho or at least to leave open the question, to what extent was Pyrrho already a Pyrrhonist.

Thus, for these two reasons, it seems of relatively little significance for our question, what Pyrrho himself thought. Even if Pyrrho had really thought that a proper skeptic has no beliefs, this would have few implications for Pyrrhonean skepticism.

Finally (iii), there are whole series of skeptical arguments that purport to show that human action is possible without beliefs, that suspension of judgment does not lead to complete inactivity. Arcesilaus, for example, argued that human action requires nothing more than that things appear to us in a certain way and that we be so constructed that when things do appear to us in a certain way, a drive or instinct leading to action is triggered and that this does not require our also assenting to the appearances (see Plutarch *Adv. Colot.* 1122 B-D; *De Stoic. rep.* 1057 A-B). Put more simply, if not as precisely, the point is just this: suppose someone is, say, hungry and is given his favorite food; why should he need—in addition to his hunger and the impression that he is being given his favorite food—the judgment that, in fact, he is being given his favorite food, to lead him to actually eat?

Given such arguments, one might think that we now have the solution to our problem: the skeptics *do* have an argument which—though we may not accept it—allows us to see why they thought that it is possible to manage without judgments or beliefs even in everyday life. Such a diagnosis of the situation, however, involves overlooking that the skeptic, in this case, would be doing precisely what he usually criticizes the dogmatist for doing: he would be trying to deny what quite obviously is the case, viz., that actions presuppose beliefs, by relying on a theoretical, dogmatic argument which purports to show that action is possible even without assent to appearances, even without judgments. The claim that actions do not presuppose beliefs, especially if based on an argument like the one outlined above, is no less dogmatic than the dogmatic claim that actions do presuppose beliefs. As soon as one sees this, it also becomes clear that the skeptics do not offer these arguments to try to show that we could not act without beliefs. That would be pure dogmatism. These arguments are rather offered to counterbalance the weight of the dogmatic arguments which tend to make us believe that it is not possible to act without beliefs (cf. Cicero *Acad. pr.* 34, 108). We cannot, then, assume, on the basis of such arguments, that the skeptics really did think that life is possible without beliefs, and thus they cannot escape the charge of self-refutation in this way. Indeed, it seems as if in this case, too, the skeptics are simply following their usual strategy of providing equipollent arguments on both sides of every issue.

Closer examination, thus, shows that the considerations which might have led us to defend the skeptic on these grounds—that he supposes, perhaps correctly, that it is possible to manage without beliefs even in everyday life—are, in light of the historical facts, unconvincing. But a skeptical position grounded in this way would itself also be scarcely plausible. Roughly speaking, the claim that it is possible to live without beliefs involves both a theoretical and a practical problem. If we suppose, as it seems we must, that all humans, in the course of their normal development, come to have a large number of beliefs, the practical question is whether or not it is possible, in practice, for a person both to rid himself of these beliefs as well as to prevent himself from acquiring any new ones, and this in such a way that he does not so diminish his capacity for acting that it no longer seems appropriate to speak of human action and a human life. Even if this practical question could be answered affirmatively, it is difficult to see what, besides sheer dogmatism, would lead someone to make use of this possibility. The dogmatist, who has certain views about what real knowledge is and who rejects everything else as mere belief, who believes that everything depends on his beliefs not being merely beliefs and who, like the Stoics, thinks mere beliefs are sinful—such a dogmatist will also believe that he must somehow resist the ordinary way of doing things, of thinking about things, and that he must get rid of his beliefs, once he has been shown that even what he had previously taken for certain knowledge has turned out to be, by his own dogmatic criteria, merely belief. The dilemma—either one must have certain knowledge or one must manage in life without beliefs—is not a dilemma with which the skeptic is confronted; on the contrary, he confronts the dogmatist with it, the dogmatist who rejects our ordinary beliefs and even our ordinary knowledge as 'unscientific' or 'unphilosophical', hence as irresponsible.

It will be objected that it is not dogmatism but experience that leads the skpetic to resist the ordinary way of thinking about things, in particular, the surprising experience that suspending judgment is accompanied by what he had hoped for from right reason, from judging correctly, namely, peace of mind.

Against this, we can say that it is only suspension of judgment understood in a special, qualified sense, alluded to above, that leads the skeptic to his goal. I shall have more to say about this sense later. However, by looking at *P.H.* I 12 and I 29, we can already see that the skeptic's experience, his discovery, is not that it is entirely possible to live without beliefs but that, if one considers things only on the basis of theory and reflection, one finds that, for every proposition, as much speaks in its favor as against it; thus, one cannot but suspend judgment, because the arguments always end up balancing each other, and, surprisingly, it turns out that it does not matter that one cannot form any judgments in *this* way; one even finds oneself in a wonderful state of calm. It seems to me that we can imagine ourselves in the situation of someone who thinks he has made such a discovery, but it also seems to me that this situation is not at all like that of someone who thinks he has discovered that a life without beliefs is accompanied by peace of mind.

Furthermore, the objection, that it is not dogmatism but his discovery (that a life without beliefs brings peace of mind) that leads the skeptic to give up all of his beliefs, does not solve our problem. For while this objection could perhaps explain why the skeptic leads a life without beliefs, once he has discovered that a life without beliefs is a tranquil one, our problem was seeing what would lead the skeptic to discover this in the first place. For the skeptic to make this discovery, however, he must either bring it about that he is in a state in which he has no beliefs or somehow be put into such a state. What, though, could bring him into such a state, on what grounds could he bring himself into such a state; they could only be dogmatic ones. It is relatively easy, though, to see how someone could find himself more and more able at contriving arguments for and against any position and thus also find it ever harder to reach a decision or make a judgment, and we can see how someone might end up in the skeptic's position without particularly trying to end up in such a position.

Perhaps, someone could, in practice, come to live without beliefs by acting *as if* he had a belief that something was the case in every situation in which he previously would have believed that something was the case? What, though, is he now supposed to do in those cases where, previously, he only would have acted as if he believed that something was the case? Is not the very distinction, between acting as if one believed something was the case and acting because one believes something to be the case, a dogmatic one, with no content, no implications for practice? For reasons of this sort, a skeptical position relying on the claim that it is possible, in practice, to live without beliefs, seems quite unsatisfactory to me; and a skeptical position relying on a *theory* of action which implied that human action does not presuppose beliefs would, of course, be still more unsatisfactory. Thus, for philosophical as well as historical reasons this sort of defense for the skeptic seems unattractive to me.

Fortunately, the problem is solved for us by Sextus Empiricus' own words. In *P.H.* I 13ff., Sextus explains in what sense the skeptic is not dogmatic. What is not in question, at least if we follow Sextus, is whether the skeptic has no dogmas, no beliefs at all but whether he has no beliefs of a certain sort. Sextus distinguishes between a wider (koinoteron) and a narrower sense of 'belief'; and only beliefs in the narrower sense count as dogmatic. Hence, there can be no doubt whatsoever that, according to Sextus, a serious Pyrrhonean skeptic can have beliefs.

What needs to be asked is what sorts of beliefs these are, and how is the fact that the skeptic does have beliefs compatible with the claim that the skeptic suspends judgment about every issue. Those who incline toward an interpretation according to which the skeptic has no beliefs even in everyday life have the following answer. They will say that it is necessary to distinguish between how things are and how they appear. The skeptic will suspend judgment on how things are, and, if he wants to be consistent, he will also have no beliefs on how things are. This, however, by no means rules out that he should have beliefs about how things appear to him.

As a matter of fact, various passages seem to support this view. We find Sextus, for example, saying, "no one, presumably, disputes that the underlying thing appears to be such or such; what is in question is whether the thing is as it appears to be" (*P.H.* I 22). This second question, whether the thing is as it appears to be, is the one the dogmatists think they have the answer to, while the skeptic suspends judgment. So it seems as if the skeptic has no beliefs about how things are and thus not really any beliefs at all. Of course, one can, if one wants to, say that the skeptic has beliefs about how things appear to him; and it is with reference to these beliefs that Sextus (in *P.H.* I, 13ff.) speaks as if there were nondogmatic beliefs.

Against this interpretation, I want to maintain that, although there is a sense in which the skeptic has no beliefs about how things are—namely, he has no beliefs about how things *really* are—there is a perfectly good sense in which he does have beliefs about how things are—namely, to the extent that it seems to be the case that things are so or so. Obviously, this distinction needs textual support as well as some clarification. Sextus repeatedly points out that when the skeptic uses expressions of the form ' . . . is . . . ', these are to be construed as ' . . . appears . . . ' (phainetai—cf. *P.H.* II 135; 198; 200; *Adv. math.* XI 19); but ' . . . is . . . ' is also used in the sense of ' . . . is in reality (or, in the nature of things) . . . ' (physei, pros ten physin, kata ten physin—cf. *P.H.* I 27, 78, 140). This second use of ' . . . is . . . ', Sextus in one passage at least, seems to gloss as follows: "but if [honey] also *is* sweet, to the extent that this is a question for reason, we [i.e., the skeptics] call into question" (*P.H.* I 20).

The explanation for this distinction depends, above all, on the following: it is characteristic of the dogmatists that they believe it is possible to go behind the surface phenomena to the essence of things, to the nature of things, to true reality. We believe that the objects around us are colored; in reality, however, they only reflect light of certin wave-lengths that makes them appear colored. The dogmatists further believe that it is reason—if only we would follow it—that can lead us beyond the world of appearances to the world of real being; and thus for them it is a matter of reason, what is to count as real and as true, and what is to count as appearance. It is in the sense of *this* distinction that the skeptic suspends judgment on how things really are. He has discovered by experience that he can reach no decision, if he leaves a question to reason. When all that is at issue, however, is whether something seems to him to be the case, the skeptic too will not deny that something seems to him to be the case. It may well seem to him that something is red, or sweet. What he does suspend judgment on is whether it really, in the nature of things, is red, or sweet. And so, the skeptic will also have beliefs about how things are, not only about how they appear to him. Against this, it will be urged that the skeptic uses "seem" or "appears" (phainesthai) in a nonepistemic sense; when he says, "it seems to me that p," this does not mean that he thinks or believes that p is the case, only that things appear as if p were the case. If, for example, we see a partially submerged oar, while it may appear as if the oar were bent, we do not believe that it is. According to this objection, it is just in this nonepistemic sense of appears that many things appear to be the case for the skeptic; for he suspends judgment on how things are.

Three things, it seems to me, tell against this objection: (i) the assumption that the skeptics use "appears" only in this nonepistemic sense is based on the false presupposition that it is true, without qualification, that the skeptic suspends judgment about how things are; (ii) the objection relies on an inadequate understanding of the contrast between appearance and reality, between how things seem and how they are; (iii) it ultimately leads to what I take to be a disastrous misunderstanding of the epistemological problem, the misunderstanding that certain mental contents (ideas or representations) are directly accessible and that the problem is only how to get from these representations to knowledge of the things that the representations represent. This division into the inner world of the I with its immediately accessible contents and a problematic outer world which needs to be reconstructed, strikes me as dogmatic and philosophically problematic; certainly this division is not just a matter of common sense; it would require some argument to see things in this way.

(i) It is true only with qualifications that the skeptic suspends judgment on how things are. At *P.H.* I 215, Sextus distinguishes between the stance of the

Pyrrhonists and that of the Cyrenaics with these words, "as for the objects in the external world, we suspend judgment insofar as it is a matter of reason" (epechomen hoson epi to logo). Sextus does indeed say that the skeptic suspends judgment on how things are. Yet, it is important to note how he qualifies this claim — insofar as it is a matter of reason. The qualification or restriction is not that the skeptic suspends judgment about how things are but not about how they appear; the restriction, rather, is that the skeptic suspends judgment about how things are in a certain respect. That, however, implies that there is another respect in which the skeptic does not suspend judgment about how things are. Once we have noticed this curious restriction here, we can see that such restrictions, "hoson epi + dative" occur again and again in the Outlines of Pyrrhonism (e.g., III 65, hoson epi to philosopho logo, cf. also II 26; 104; III 6; 13; 29; 65; 81; 135; 167). This construction also occurs in the gloss on the one sense of ' . . . is . . . ' which we considered above. There we had, "if [honey] also is sweet, to the extent that this is a matter of reason, we call into question" (P.H. I 20). We may, thus, assume that the import of this restriction is that the skeptic suspends judgment on how things really are; but that is not the same as claiming that the skeptic suspends judgment on how things are without any restriction.

Sextus' discussion of the sign, at P.H. II 97ff. and Adv. math., 141ff., illustrates this nicely. Suppose that the question arises, are there signs, i.e., can anything count as the sign of another thing? The dogmatists, of course, believe that there are signs; they have a theory of signs, and they construct arguments which supposedly show that there are signs. The skeptic will, as usual, produce a whole series of arguments, which purports to show that there are no signs, in order to neutralize the persuasive force of the dogmatists' arguments. With plausible arguments on both sides of the question, an equilibrium is reached; one no longer knows which argument to trust. Sextus proceeds in exactly this way. Yet, despite all of his arguments against the existence of signs, it is clear that Sextus himself thinks that there are signs, namely, the so-called commemorative ones (P.H. II 104; Adv. math. VIII 151–58). Sextus does not say that it only seems as if there were signs, that the skeptic only has the idea of signs but does not think that there actually are any; his point, rather, is that even the skeptic takes certain things as signs of other things, e.g., smoke as a sign of fire. Sextus' discussion of signs, thus, is a good example of how, in a certain sense, the skeptic does suspend judgment about how things are — namely, to the extent that one considers this matter for arguments, for reason — but also of how, despite his suspension of judgment, the skeptic does think that, given how things are, there are signs.

When the skeptic reports that he regards the existence of signs as a phenomenon, that it seems to him that there are signs, this report does not merely indicate that it appears to him that there are signs, though he does not believe there actually are any; rather, this report indicates that it appears to him that there are signs in the sense that he thinks there are signs. How this is supposed to be compatible with the claim that the skeptic does not believe that there are really, in the nature of things (physei, ontōs, alethōs), may be a difficult question. But it would be naive to suppose that one cannot make out a meaningful contrast between how things are and how things really are and thus think that someone who has no view about how things really are can only have a view about how things seem (nonepistemically) to him.

(ii) It is necessary, then, to get a clearer understanding of the contrast between appearance and reality, at least sufficiently clear to see how it is possible that someone can really believe something to be the case without believing this is how things are in reality.

If something seems to us to be the case, we can, at least in some cases, come to regard the matter differently, if we are, say, given an explanation of why the thing only appears that way. It is necessary to distinguish between two quite different sorts of cases: (a) it can happen that something no longer seems to be the case. If, for example, it is pointed out that we have not properly seen the thing, that we falsely presupposed this or that, that we inferred something incorrectly etc., we shall no longer think that what seemed to be the case is so. In certain especially interesting cases, an impression that things are thus or thus persistently recurs, despite the fact that we know quite well that things are not as they appear; the illusions of the senses are a good example of this type of case.

For example, I might, when I see an oar partially submerged in water, say that 'it appears bent to me,' where 'appears to me' has the sense that I believe that the oar is bent; if, however, someone explains to me why it only appears bent to me, I shall no longer think that the oar is bent. Nonetheless, the oar still *looks* bent. And thus I can still say that the oar appears to be bent, but now I shall be using 'appears' nonepistemically. (b) It can, however, also happen that, even after we have been given an explanation of why something only appears a certain way and even after we have accepted this explanation, we still think the thing is as it appears to be. Suppose, for example, that a particular wine seems quite sweet to me. Someone might explain, it only seems sweet, because I had eaten something sour just before tasting the wine. If I accept this explanation, I shall no longer think that the wine is sweet; at most, I shall think the wine only seems to be sweet. Yet, someone might also try to provide a quite different explanation. He might say that there is, in reality, no such thing as sweetness, no such thing as sweetness in wine; the wine, rather, has certain chemical properties which, in normal circumstances, make it taste such that we call it sweet. It may even be that I am convinced by an explanation of this sort and come to view how things taste in an entirely new light. Nonetheless, such an explanation might seem rather puzzling, because it is not entirely clear how it is supposed to bear on my claim that the wine is quite sweet. Even if I accept this explanation, the wine will still seem sweet, and I shall still think that it is. Thus, in a sense, it will still be true that it does not merely seem as if the wine is sweet, even if I believe that, in reality, there is no such thing as sweetness.

Cases of the second sort, it seems to me, show that the contrast between how things really are and how they appear nonepistemically is insufficient. If one does not think that something is so and so in the true nature of things, this does not yet mean it only seems as if the thing were so and so. Thus, if the skeptic suspends judgment on how things are in reality, this does not mean that he only has impressions, but no beliefs, about things.

That, in fact, something like this more complex contrast is what is involved here seems clear to me not only from the problem itself but also from the situation of the skeptic. Ancient skepticism is essentially a reaction to dogmatism, to the attempt to get behind the phenomena, with the aid of reason, to true reality and, thus, to dissolve the real or apparent contradictions among the phenomena, the contradictions in the world as it appears to us (cf. *P.H.* I 12). However, it is characteristic of dogmatism that this attempt, to move beyond the phenomena, calls into question the status of the phenomena themselves. Parmenides and Plato are particularly clear examples of this, but, in the last analysis, the same is true of all the other dogmatic philosophers. But in calling into question the status of the phenomena, they also call into question the status of our ordinary beliefs and claims, as these are beliefs and claims that reflect how things appear to us. Since, however, the dogmatists, generally speaking, do not deny that the phenomena have at least some objective status, it does not follow that if someone suspends judgment about how things really are, he only has impressions about how things are, and, no beliefs. Plato, for example, ascribes a precarious intermediate status to the objects of belief or *doxa* in the *Republic;* they come between what really is, the objects of reason and knowledge, and what does not exist at all. He does not say that what we ordinarily call 'reality' is nothing but appearance, that our ordinary beliefs and impressions are no better than hallucinations. Though they fail to capture true being and, thus, are not really true, this does not mean that they are simply false in the way that it is simply false that Socrates died in 398. Another example is the role the assumption that, in the case of an ordinary object, for any predicate F, it is never really F, plays in so many interpretations of Plato. Obviously, the import of this assumption is not that for some reason or other water, say, is never heated long enough to be really hot. To put the point rather simply, what is at issue is not whether or not Socrates died in 399, but whether it is appropriate, given the true nature of things, whether it correctly mirrors reality, to speak of Socrates' having died in 399. This question is not at all settled by the fact that it is clear that we ordinarily do say Socartes died in 399. For it might be that, given the true nature of things, it is inappropriate to speak of persons and times. Yet, even if someone believed this, that would not mean that he could not continue to think and say that Socrates died in 399; and there is no reason to suppose that his belief would differ from anyone else's who believes that Socrates died in 399. Thus, there is a perfectly good sense in which someone who suspends judgment about how things really are can have beliefs about how things are.

What is to stop the skeptic from having such beliefs? It is the dogmatists who talk endlessly about the need to go beyond the phenomena, who insist on the need to rely on reason and reason alone, which is also why, at least in medicine, they are called logikoi, i.e., rationalists (cf. *Adv. math.* VIII 156). For they think that reason and reason alone has access to how things really are. It is the dogmatists who believe that it is necessary for us to revise our beliefs, or at least all the important and central ones, in the light of reason. The Stoics even think we ought to give up all beliefs that do not meet the strict criteria of reason and thus are not validated by reason. They, thus, expect us to rid ouselves of all the beliefs we have acquired in ordinary ways, if these should fail to meet the rigorous criteria of reason. Beliefs that do meet these criteria are beliefs about how things are, to the extent that this is a matter of reason, i.e., beliefs about how things really are. The skeptic indeed has no such beliefs; and if he followed the dogmatists' strictures—to accept only those beliefs validated by reason—he would, in fact, have no beliefs about how things are.

Yet why should he accept their strictures? What could lead him to follow only reason? It has been his experience that whenever he tries to rely only on reason, he fails to reach a decision; this past experience could hardly motivate him to follow only reason. We can imagine someone being faced with the following conflict: he has certain beliefs, acquired in some ordinary way which not only cannot be validated by reason but which turn out to conflict with certain insights of reason. If we believe the Eleatics, or the Atomists, or Plato, or Aristotle, or the Stoics, we should expect to be faced with conflicts of this sort rather often. In such a case, we would need to choose whether to follow reason or our ordinary beliefs. The skeptic, however, is not in this situation. Whenever he follows reason seriously and fully, he can form no judgment, hence also no judgment that conflicts with his ordinary beliefs. Thus, he is not even faced with the choice, should he follow only reason (against his ordinary beliefs), at least not in this way.

Since he has not been dissuaded from doing so, the skeptic will continue to rely on how things appear to him, on what seems to him to be the case. He will not think that it only seems as if things were so and so; for that thought presupposes that he believes what the dogmatists believe, namely, that, in reality, things are quite different from the way they seem to be. For him, of course, nothing rules out the possibility that, in reality, things should be exactly as they appear to be. Since he suspends judgment on how things are in reality, he will not think that it merely seems to him that things are thus or thus. If it had been his discovery that, in every instance, it only seems to him that this or that is the case, he would indeed have no beliefs on how things are. When the skeptic, however, speaks of what seems to him to be the case, and when he says that he is only reporting how it appears to him, he cannot be speaking of something which he thinks *only seems* to be the case; and that for the reasons indicated.

Thus, it seems to me that if we properly construe the contrast between how things really are and how they seem to us, it does not follow that the skeptic has no beliefs about how things are just in virtue of his suspending judgment about how they are in reality.

(iii) As a matter of fact, Sextus often does speak as if ideas or impressions (phantasiai) were directly accessible and the problem was to determine whether or not to assent to these impressions, that is, whether or not one should think that things are the way our impressions represent them as being. The conventional interpretation holds that the skeptic does indeed have such impressions but that he consistently refuses to assent to them and, hence, has no beliefs about how things are.

The question, though, is does Sextus Empiricus speak this way because this is how *he* sees the problem of knowledge or because he needs to tailor his argument to his dogmatic opponents' way of regarding matters. After all, his goal is to get the dogmatist to suspend judgment on the basis of his own principles and theories. This much at least is clear: it is the dogmatists, especially the Stoics, who assume that certain impressions arise in us, impressions which we voluntarily either do or do not assent to, which we—if we proceed responsibly—need to judge by a criterion of truth, before we assent to them and form a judgment. Such a view seems wholly dogmatic, because it presupposes a theory about what beliefs actually are, how they arise and how they *ought* to arise. I very much doubt that Sextus shares the view that our beliefs are formed thus: certain impressions arise in us, and, by some means or other, we decide whether or not to assent to them. At any rate, it is conspicuous that Sextus himself, whenever he speaks of the circumstances in which the skeptic, too, will give his assent, avoids speaking as if the skeptic were assenting to an impression. The explanation for this does not seem to be Arcesilaus' criticism of this way of talking (cf. Sext. Emp. *Adv. math.* VII 154) but, rather, something deeper. Moreover, the skeptic has no criterion, on the basis of which he could decide whether or not to assent to an impression. In fact, certain things just seem to him to be the case; the skeptic has no theory on how or why this is so. If, however, someone insists on using dogmatic terminology, he can say that things affect the skeptic in such a way that he comes to assent to something (cf. *P.H.* I 19; 113, 193). Yet, it is hardly plausible that Sextus, when he speaks this way, means to commit himself to the view that there are mental acts of assenting which, together with the appropriate impressions, constitute having beliefs and forming judgments. For these reasons, I am inclined to believe that the skeptic has beliefs not only about how things seem to him but also about how they are, and to believe that things appear to him to be the case, in the sense that he believes they are the case without, of course, believing this is the way they are in reality, this is the way they are insofar as it is a matter for reason to determine what is true and what is real.

If Sextus believes that a skeptic can have beliefs about how things are, we would expect to be able to see this in the passage already mentioned, where Sextus explains in what sense the skeptic can have beliefs (*dogmata*). Conversely, if it really were true that the skeptic can only have beliefs about how things seem to him, this too we should be able to see from this passage. At any rate, it strikes me as methodologically sound to base one's interpretation of an author's views primarily on those passages where he explicitly sets them out and not rest content with indirect indications of what they might be. Since Sextus Empiricus explicitly considers our question in *P.H.* I 13, let us turn to this passage: "We say that the skeptic does not dogmatize, not in the sense of 'belief' (dogma) in which some say, speaking quite generally, a belief consists in consenting to a thing (eudokein tini pragmati); for the skeptic does assent to such affections which necessarily result when things appear to him in certain ways; he would not, for example, when he is hot or cold, say, 'I believe I am not hot (cold)'; We rather say, he does not dogmatize, in the sense of 'belief', in which some say a belief consists in assenting to one of the nonevident things which the sciences have as their objects of inquiry; for the Pyrrhonean assents to nothing nonevident."

The expression on which a lot depends here is, "consenting to something." "Eudokein," to judge form its frequent occurence in papyri, is quite a common word, especially in legal contexts. It also occurs frequently in Hellenistic literature, e.g., in Polybius. On the other hand, it hardly appears at all in philosophical texts; as a philosophical term, it occurs nowhere else. Thus, it has no philosophical or technical meaning, no philosophical associations and is connected with no special philosophical claims; presumably, it is exactly this fact that leads Sextus to choose the word. Eudokein and eudokeisthai are used in the sense of 'be content with', 'assent to', 'agree', 'consent to', 'recognize', 'accept', or 'suppose'. The *Suida* has, s.v. eudokein, the following entry: "synkatatitesthai. ho de ephe eudokein tois legomenois, ei labe pisteis. anti tou areskesthai." First we are given a synonym, then a quote from Polybius, finally a gloss on his use of the term. In the *Etymologicum Magnum* (ed. Gaisford), there is an entry for eudokein, which is of no interest for us here, but also a gloss on eudokoumenos, which we encounter again in the Lexeis rhetorikai (Anecdota Graeca Bekkeri, v. I, p. 260); it runs as follows: "ho synkatatithemenos kai me antilegon." This gloss seems to fit in very well with our Sextus passage, because its two parts seem to correspond to the two parts of Sextus' explanation of how the skeptic consents to something: (a) the skeptic assents to something (synkatatithetai), (b) he does not oppose it and does not protest.

Precisely which meaning of eudokein, however, should we ascribe to Sextus here? The following sentence from Polybius (I, 8, 4) provides a good example of the ordinary use of eudokein: hoste . . . pantas . . . eudokesai strategon hauton hyparchein Hierona. Out of context, this sentence could mean any number of things—they decided, voted, decreed, agreed, that Hiero was to be their *strategos,* they all thought it would be a good thing, would be proper, if Hiero would be their *strategos.* In fact, the sentence means that they accepted the fact that Hiero was to be their *strategos,* they recognized (in the legal sense) that Hiero was their *strategos.*

Obviously, in our passage, beliefs, not decisions, are being discussed. Therefore, our task is to find an interpretation on which eudokein has its usual meaning even though it is beliefs which are being talked about.

It seems as if the following interpretation would satisfy this condition: what the skeptic literally accepts, what he is content with, what he has no objection to is whatever seems to him to be the case, whatever seems evident to him. He accepts the judgment of phantasia; at least he raises no objection against its verdict; if it says things are thus or thus, he does not challenge this. The gloss and Sextus' explanation (hoion oun an . . .) do indeed suggest that the principle, that one consents if one does not object, is at work here. Such an interpretation fits in well with our observations on the question whether Sextus accepts the dogmatists views about the origin of beliefs. The dogmatists see assent as a voluntary act, a judgment about the impressions which presents itself to us; it is only this judgment that leads to a belief. Sextus, to judge by the passage at hand, sees things differently: something which can count as a belief, a judgment, arises in us when we do not object and consequently consent. In the case of those illusions of the senses familiar to us, we do object; otherwise we would falsely believe that the oar was bent. That what the skeptic does not object to is what seems evident to him, what seems to him to be the case, is clear from the next bit of our passage; for there Sextus says that the skeptic refuses to assent to anything nonevident. If he does not refuse to assent to something, it will be a phenomenon, something evident, something that seems to him to be the case.

Why is the skeptic content with what seems to him to be the case; why does he raise no objection? If he were a dogmatist, he certainly would not be content; the dogmatist is so concerned that things might, in reality, be quite different, that he does not accept the verdict of *phantasia;* instead, he relies on reason in order to find out how things really are (cf. *P.H.* I 12). He is also not disturbed by the fact that his reason, in its reckless haste, contradicts the phenomena (cf. *P.H.* I 20). The skeptic, on the other hand, has learned from experience, that reason, if he tries to follow it seriously and fully, gets him no further and, thus that, he must rest content with how things appear (cf. *P.H.* I 12). It may be objected that skeptics will also argue against what seems evident to them, since they argue against everything; but Sextus himself explains that the skeptic only argues against phenomena for dialectical reasons (*P.H.* I 20).

In the second part of our passage, Sextus tells us the sense in which the skeptic has no beliefs. The relevant sense of 'belief' seems surprisingly narrow at first, especially if one assumes that the skeptic has no beliefs about how things are. Only those beliefs will count as dogmatic which involve an assumption or claim about one of the nonevident objects of scientific inquiry. Sextus clearly has the theorems of philosophers and scientists in mind, theorems which they attempt to establish in their efforts to go beyond the phenomena and what is evident in order to get a grip on true reality. These are the doctrines which serve to characterize the various dogmatic schools and allow us to distinguish among them. Menodotus apparently has the same sense of belief in mind when he says that all of Asclepiades' beliefs are false (omnia eius dogmata esse false — Galen De subf. emp. 84, 21-22 D). If Sextus had only such typical school doctrines in mind here, it would be clear that the skeptic could have all sorts of beliefs about how things are. For our ordinary, everyday beliefs are, in general, not theoretical doctrines, not assumptions that are part of any science. The skeptic would thus be free to have such 'unscientific' beliefs. Actually, however, matters are presumably more complicated. Since the skeptic suspends judgment — either in a restricted or in an unrestricted sense — on every matter, even those things that are evident to him must, in a certain respect, be nonevident. Presumably, we need to understand this as follows: everything, if considered only as an object for reason, can be called into question; every question can be regarded as a question to be answered by reason, a question requiring a theoretical answer derived from first principles which are immediately evident to reason. Nothing, looked at in this way, will be evident to the skeptic, not even the most lowly, ordinary belief. Any belief, whatever its content may be, can be a dogmatic belief; conversely, every belief can be an undogmatic one. Thus, it is not the content of theoretical views (though, as we shall see, content is not entirely irrelevant) that makes them dogmatic views; it is, rather, the attitude of the dogmatist who believes his rationalist science actually answers questions, actually gives him good reasons for believing his theoretical doctrines. Sextus probably does have primarily the doctrines of the dogmatic schools in mind here, but it would presumably be a mistake to construe the notion of dogmatic belief so narrowly that it could not, in principle, apply to any belief, regardless of content.

What then, does this passage tell us about our question? It seems to me that the text does not even so much as suggest that the skeptic can have beliefs but only ones about how things seem to him not ones about how things are. As far as the second part of our passage is concerned, it says only that the skeptic may not have beliefs of a certain kind, viz., philosophical or scientific ones which depend on reasoned grounds (here, of course, he is presupposing a dogmatic notion of knowledge and science; if there can be such a thing as skeptical science remains to be seen). Whichever way we choose to interpret the text, there will be a large number of beliefs about things which are not dogmatic beliefs. As far as the first part of our passage is concerned, here too the claim is not that the beliefs which the skeptic may have are only ones about his own impressions. On the contrary, the text says, at least on the interpretation suggested, that the skeptic will be content with what seems to him to be the case; surely, that will include a large number of observations about the world around him.

Whoever wants to find the claim, that the skeptic only accepts such beliefs as are about his own impressions, in this passage, will refer to two details: (a) Sextus says that the skeptic assents to certain affections (pathe); (b) the example he provides seems – if translated in the usual way – to show that the skeptic will not deny that he feels so or so, if that is how he does feel. As for (a), we need to get clearer about what Sextus means by affections, when he says the skeptic assents to them. There are two main possibilities (though it is not clear that, from a skeptical perspective, they do not collapse into one): (1) Referring to, say, *P.H.* I 22, we could say Sextus means to talk of impressions (phantasiai) when he speaks of affections here. In that case, Sextus would be using only a slight variant of the dogmatists' way of speaking; the dogmatists talk as if (and Arcesilaus criticizes them for this – cf. *Adv. math.* VII 154) what we assent to is an impression, a way of talking which, as we have noted, Sextus seems to take pains to avoid. These impressions, however, are impressions of things which appear thus or thus to us; and assenting to them is assuming that things are the way they appear to be. (2) Sextus might, when talking of affections, be referring to the disposition to be affected by things in a certain way, whether one wants to be so affected or not. And assenting to these affections would consist in acquiescing: that it is *this* that seems to be the case, this and nothing else, and *that* it seems to be the case. Neither (1) nor (2), however, give us any reason to think that the belief will only be about the skeptic's own impressions. In any event, "assenting to such impressions" cannot mean "assenting to the claim that one is affected in this way, that one has such impressions." Yet, such a meaning is required, if the first detail is to bear on the issue at hand.

So, only the example remains. A precise analysis of the example is difficult for both linguistic and intrinsic reasons. For example, how exactly is "I am hot" to be understood; how is "thermainesthai" to be translated – 'to be heated' or perhaps 'to feel hot'? Fabricius, in his revision of Henricus Stephanus' translation, opts for the first, literal meaning; Bury and Hossenfelder opt for the second one. It is by no means clear if the word can even have this second meaning. It can mean 'having a fever'; and the dictionary (LSJ) refers to at least one passage (Plato. *Theaet.* 186 D) where it unquestionably means 'feel heat' or 'sense heat', a meaning we perhaps also find in one place in Sextus (*P.H.* II 56). If we followed ordinary usage, we would be inclined to think that here as well "thermainesthai" is to be translated by 'be heated', especially since this seems to conform to Sextus' usual usage. The context certainly provides no reason not to translate it so; one will, thus, translate it differently only under the influence of a preconceived notion of what Sextus' position is.

Nevertheless, let us suppose that "thermainesthai" does refer here to the sub-jective feeling, to sensation. In that case, the expression "dokō mē ther-mainesthai" ('I do not think I am feeling any warmth') creates difficulties. Now the translation presumably must read, when the skeptic feels warmth he will not say, 'I do not think I am feeling any warmth'. Presumably now the "ther-mainomenos," in the previous line, refers to the affection of the skeptic, the affection which he does not refuse to assent to by objecting to it. If the skeptic, however, feels or notices warmth, the objection should not be, "I do not think I am feeling warmth," but it should rather be, "I do not think that there is any warmth," or, "it seems to me that it is not warm." For, as we have just seen, assenting to an affection does not consist in assuming that it exists. What the skeptic does not deny, when he senses warmth, is that something is warm. Per-haps, however, we should still assume that thermainomai can mean 'I am hot' or 'I feel hot'. One passage in Sextus (*Adv. math.* I 147) shows that the transition to this meaning would be easy. In that case, we could say that the affection con-sists in the impression that one is feeling hot; and the skeptic will not go against this impression by saying, 'I do not think that I am feeling hot'. Perhaps nothing rules out this interpretation. Yet, it is worth considering that (1) it assumes a very strange meaning for thermainesthai, (2) the text does not suggest this mean-ing, and (3) even if translated this way, the passage still will not yield the in-tended interpretation. Sextus is interested in providing an especially clear exam-ple of something that is evident even to the skeptic. If Sextus chooses the example of feeling hot, this by no means implies that only his own impressions will be evident to the skeptic; rather, it is just an exceptionally clear example of the sort of thing that could be evident to someone.

In summary, we can say that the passage, in which Sextus explicitly discusses what sorts of beliefs the skeptic can have without being dogmatic, not only does not come out and say, but does not even suggest, that the skeptic can have beliefs only about his own impressions, only about how things seem to him.

It might be objected that what, on our interpretation, Sextus is prepared to call 'dogmata' are not even beliefs. We might, for example, think that the mere feeling that something is the case is not to be regarded as a belief just because we do not object to this feeling or impression. It may very well be the case that the skeptic's beliefs do not satisfy some specific, dogmatic definition of 'belief.' If, however, we stay with the ordinary use of verbs like 'believe', 'think', or 'sup-pose' (or the ordinary use of "dokein"), it is clear that the conditions for employ-ing these verbs are so weak that the skeptic's beliefs will satisfy them without any difficulty. If someone steps into the house, and we ask him if it is still raining outside, and he, without hesitating, answers that it is, we would regard this as an expression of his belief that it is still raining. One would need to have a dogmatic view about what is to count as a belief to be prepared to deny this. There is no reason to suppose that the skeptic, if asked such a question, would not answer either yes or no; and there is no reason to suppose that the skeptic would mean anything different by his answer than anyone else (cf. also Cicero *Acad. pr.* 104).

It is true that the skeptic does not believe that it is *really* still raining. His answer is not grounded in some insight into the true nature of things, an insight such that reason could not but give the answer it does. For reason throws up an unlimited number of possibilities about how it might, after all, be the case that it is no longer raining, without itself being able, as the skeptic has discovered all too often, to eliminate these possibilities. His answer, rather, tells us only what seems to him to be the case; if we ask *him,* that is how it strikes him. In this respect, however, his answer does not differ from that of the man on the street. He, too, only reports his impressions and does not also think that things *really* are the way he takes them to be, the way they appear to him.

How then does the skeptic differ from the man on the street? He differs, it seems to me, in two respects: (i) presumably the average person is quite dogmatic about some of his views, especially moral or ethical ones. As far as scientific speculation is concerned, he may be quite content to leave that to others, but when moral or political questions are at stake, he will tend to claim that he does have some deeper insight, even if his experience seems to tell against it, he has views about what is really good or really bad (cf. *P.H.* I 27; 30). (ii) In contrast to the man on the street, the skeptic is acutely aware of the fact that in all sorts of ways things might, in reality, be quite different from how they appear to be. He takes the phenomena as they come, but he knows better than anyone else that nothing rules out the possibility that things could really be radically different.

Does the skeptic differ from other people in regard to what he believes or thinks? We might think that the skeptic only believes what is evident to him, what is a phenomenon, and that only those things are evident to him which are accessible through observation and experience; and so we might go on to think that the skeptic will refuse to believe anything that is not accessible through observation. Any interpretation along these lines, however, seems false to me. I shall leave aside the fact that experience is extraordinarily complicated and that perception and observation, in the ordinary sense, play a comparatively subordinate role in experience. The skeptic simply has no general answer to the question, 'What is evident?'. There are things that are evident to him, and he could list any number of them. There is no reason, however, why the same things should be evident to other people, or to most people, much less to all people; there is also no reason to suppose that only things which can be perceived or observed should be evident to the skeptic. The text of Sextus Empiricus shows that he believes many things are the case which cannot be observed. Even if it should turn out that all the things that seem evident to a skeptic are also things that can be observed, this could not be because the skeptic only considers things that can be observed as true. For if he thought that, he would be, just like the dogmatists, using a criterion to distinguish between true and false impressions. But the skeptic does not rely on any criterion for his beliefs.

This, of course, does not mean that his skepticism will have no influence on the content of his beliefs. There are, for example, large numbers of views which one in all likelihood would not have unless one relied on reason dogmatically, unless one thought one had arguments which justified these views. It is not very likely that someone would think that there is no motion or no change without also thinking he had some special insight and some good reason for thinking this. Not very likely, but not impossible. For we can imagine someone who has been raised by Stoics and who thus has the Stoic concept of God. As a skeptic, he no longer believes that the Stoic proofs of God's existence entail their conclusion; since, however, his belief was not induced by these arguments, nothing about his belief need change even when the arguments no longer carry conviction. On the whole, though, the skeptic will mostly believe what experience suggests to him.

What fundamentally distinguishes the skeptic from other people are not the beliefs he has but his attitude toward them. He no longer has the more or less naive and partially dogmatic attitude of the 'ordinary' man; his relation to his beliefs is permeated by the awareness that things are quite possibly different in reality, but this possibility no longer worries him. This distinguishes him from the dogmatist who is so worried by the question, how are things in reality, that he succumbs to the illusion that reason could guarantee the truth of his beliefs, could give him the knowledge which would be secure because of his awareness that things could not, in reality, be different from the way reason says they are. This dogmatic craving for the security of true belief as a necessary, perhaps even a sufficient condition for the tranquility and healing of the soul strikes the skeptic as, at best, futile, perhaps even pathological and harmful. As the passage quoted at the end of this paper shows, the skeptics were not alone in this view; but it was a view that quickly lost ground during the second and third centuries. We know of only one successor of Sextus in the third century, Saturninus (D.L. IX 116). The temptation had become too great: if mere reason could not lead us to the truth we need for our salvation and beatitude, it would require cleansed, purified, and illuminated reason, perhaps even reason in the light of some revelation; but whatever it takes, we must have the real truth if our lives are not to fail.

These are the introductory sentences to Heron's treatise on artillery: "The largest and most important part of philosophical activity is that which is devoted to peace of mind. Those who want to attain wisdom have carried out and, indeed, carry out to this very day a large number of investigations concerned with peace of mind. In fact, I believe that theoretical inquiry about this will never end. In the meantime, however, mechanics has progressed beyond the theoretical study of peace of mind, and it has taught all men, how, with the help of part of it—a very small part indeed—to live with peace of mind, I mean the part concerned with artillery." (Hero's *Belopoiika* ed. by H. Diels and E. Schramm; Abh. Preuss. Akad. d. Wiss., Berlin, 1918, p. 5.). The skeptic saw his task as, on the one hand, not giving in to the temptation to expect more from reason and philosophical thinking than these can provide without, on the other hand, coming to hold reason in contempt.[1]

11

The Skeptic's Two Kinds of Assent and the Question of the Possibility of Knowledge

Traditionally one associates skepticism with the position that nothing is, or can be, known for certain. Hence it was only natural that for a long time one should have approached the ancient skeptics with the assumption that they were the first to try to establish or to defend the view that nothing is, or can be, known for certain, especially since there is abundant evidence which would have seemed to bear out the correctness of this approach. After all, extensive arguments to the effect that there is no certain knowledge or that things are unknowable play a central role in our ancient sources on skepticism. And thus Hegel, Brandis, Zeller, and their successors were naturally led to take these arguments at face value and to assume that the skeptics were trying to show that nothing can be known. Closer consideration of the matter, though, shows that it cannot have been the position of the major exponents of ancient skepticism, whether Academic or Pyrrhonean, that nothing is, or can be, known. And this for the simple reason that the major ancient skeptics were not concerned to establish or to defend any position, let alone the position that nothing is, or can be, known. In fact, they went out of their way to point out that, though they produced arguments for it, they did not actually take the position that nothing can be known (cf. S.E., *PH* I., 200–1).[1] And they went on to criticize those who did claim that nothing can be known as being as dogmatic as those philosophers who claimed that something can be known, as being pseudo-skeptics (cf. S.E., *PH* I., 3, 226; Photius, *Bibl.* 212, 169^b).[2] Hence, in the following I shall call the position they criticize 'dogmatic skepticism', to distinguish it from the skepticism I want to attribute to the major ancient skeptics and which I shall call 'classical skepticism'. I do not want to suggest by this that there are no important differences between Arcesilaus, Carneades, and the Pyrrhoneans. It just seems to me that these differences are minor compared to the difference between classical and dogmatic skepticism.

If there should be a substantial difference between classical skepticism and dogmatic skepticism, the questions arise (I) how did it come about that skepticism turned dogmatic, (2) how did it come about that skepticism was identified with dogmatic skepticism, so much so that even classical skeptics came to be interpreted as dogmatic skeptics, and (3) was something philosophically important lost because one was not aware of classical skepticism as an alternative to dogmatic skepticism? It is these questions I am primarily interested in, but since they only arise if there actually is a substantial difference between classical and dogmatic skepticism, I shall first turn to the question whether it can be made out that there is a significant difference.

Traditionally philosophers and historians of philosophy have not seen a substantial difference. For they have treated Arcesilaus, Carneades, and the Pyrrhoneans as if they, just like the dogmatic skeptics, had taken, defended, and argued for the position that nothing can be known. Now this only seems possible if one does not take seriously the classical skeptic's remark that he, unlike the dogmatic skeptic, does not take the position that nothing can be known. And the only reason I can see for not taking this remark seriously is the following: one has reason to believe that the classical skeptic, like the dogmatic skeptic, does have the view that nothing can be known; and thus one thinks that the classical skeptic only says that he does not take this position because he not only cannot consistently claim to know that nothing can be known, but cannot even take the position that nothing can be known, if he wants to preserve consistency with a main tenet of skepticism, namely the principle that one should not commit oneself to any position, that one should suspend judgment, withhold assent on any matter whatsoever. Hence, since I do want to take the classical skeptic's remark seriously, I have to argue either that the classical skeptic does in fact not have the view that nothing can be known or that there is a substantial difference between having a view, on the one hand, and taking a position or making a claim, on the other. Since I believe that there is some sense in which even the classical skeptic might have the view that nothing is, or can be, known, I shall try to argue the latter by distinguishing, following the classical skeptic, two kinds of assent such that having a view involves one kind of assent, whereas taking a position, or making a claim, involves a different kind of assent, namely the kind of assent a skeptic will withhold.

But before we turn to this distinction of two kinds of assent, it will be of use to consider the view that one should withhold assent. For it is this view which, supposedly, the classical skeptic tries to preserve consistency with, in denying that he takes the position that nothing can be known.

What, then, is the status of this view that it is wise to withhold assent? To start with, it is the conclusion of an argument the skeptic produces which is supposed to show that the wise man will always withhold assent. But it clearly is not the case that the skeptic, in arguing this way, thinks that he commits himself to the position that it is wise always to withhold assent. For to commit oneself to this position would be to give assent. In this particular case it is easy to see why the skeptic is not committed to the conclusion of his argument. It is an argument drawn from premises which only his opponent, by granting them, is committed to: an argument designed to show his opponent that he is in a dilemma, that he is committed to conflicting claims and hence had better consider the matter further until he is in a position to decide between them. For it is central to the position of his opponent that the wise man often does have the kind of justification for his views which will allow him to give assent. To be shown then that he also is committed to the view that the wise man will never give assent puts him into a fundamental dilemma.

What is clear in the case of this argument, namely that the skeptic is not committed to its conclusion because he is just trying to show his opponent that he is committed to a claim which conflicts with his original claim, seems to me to be true of all skeptical arguments. The skeptic never tries to argue for a position, he never argues against a claim in the sense that he tries to establish a conflicting claim and thereby tries to show the falsehood of the original claim. He rather thinks of himself as following Socrates, submitting the claims of others to the kind of test Socrates had subjected them to. Socrates saw himself in the unfortunate position of lacking the knowledge and expertise in ethical matters which others claimed to have. He was more than eager to learn from those who were qualified to speak on these matters. But how, given his own ignorance, would he be able to tell whether somebody really had some special qualification to speak on these matters? The method he used was the following: he would ask the person whose qualification he wanted to test a question to which the person would have to know the answer if he were knowledgeable and expert, qualified to speak on the given subject-matter. He would then try to show by an argument drawn for assumptions accepted by his opponent that his opponent also was committed to a belief which was incompatible with his answer to the original question. In case Socrates succeeded, this would have the effect that the opponent would have to admit that by his own standards of rationality he did not have the required qualification, the expertise, or knowledge Socrates was looking for. For if he did have the knowledge he would have sufficient reason to reject one of the two conflicting claims. As it is, he, by his own standards does not even have any reason to maintain one rather than the other of the two claims. For he must have had some reason for his original claim. But this reason is now balanced by another reason which he is shown to have in support of the conflicting claim. And it is because he is not in a position to adjudicate between the two that he ends in an aporia, that he is in a dilemma, that he does not know what to do about the conflict.

For our purposes one crucial feature of this kind of Socratic argument is that all its premises are supplied by the opponent. Socrates does not have to know their truth, he does not even have to have any view as to their truth, nor does he have to know the truth or have a view as to the truth of the conclusion of his argument, to achieve his aim of finding out whether his opponent can be trusted to know the truth on the matters in question. Another crucial feature is that it not only reveals that the opponent by his own standards lacks the knowledge in question, but that it also shows to the opponent that he would have to give the matter further consideration because, as it is, he does not seem to be even in a position to just make the claim.

What I want to suggest is that Arcesilaus and his followers thought of themselves as just following Socratic practice, and that they understood their arguments in the indicated way. In fact, I believe that they went one step further: they not only did not want to be committed themselves to the truth of the premises and the conclusion of their arguments, they also did not want to be committed to the validity of their arguments. More generally, they thought that their opponents had committed themselves to a certain view as to what counts as knowledge, good reason, sufficient reason, justification, and that their opponents had developed something called 'logic' to formulate canons and standards for argument and justification, canons whose strict application would guarantee the truth of the conclusions arrived at in this way. Since the skeptic wants to see whether his opponent at least by his own standards or canons has knowledge, he in his own arguments adheres to these standards. But this does not mean that he himself is committed to them. He is aware of the fact, e.g., that ordinarily we do not operate by these standards and that it is because his opponents want more than we ordinarily have that they try to subject themselves to these stricter canons; they want 'real' knowledge, certain knowledge.

For these reasons, then, the skeptics also would see no reason why their arguments that it is wise to always withhold assent would commit them to the position that one should always withhold assent. Their arguments just show that this is a conclusion their opponents are committed to. But the skeptics not only produce arguments to the effect that one should withhold assent, they also, as we can see from Sextus Empiricus, are in the habit of saying, at the conclusion of their various arguments against the various claims they address themselves to, that one ought to suspend judgment, to withhold assent on the matter. Since these remarks are not part of the skeptical arguments themselves, one might think that at least now the skeptics are committing themselves to a position in saying that one should withhold assent on this or that matter. And since the skeptics seem to be willing to make this kind of remark on any subject-matter whatsoever, one might even think that this reflects the general position that one should always withhold assent. But, of course, there is another interpretation of these remarks. Their aim might just be to point out to the opponent that by his own standards it would seem that he ought to withhold assent. But since the skeptic has not committed himself to these standards there is also no reason to think, just on the basis of these remarks, that he is committed to the claim that one ought to withhold assent on a particular subject, let alone to the generalization that one ought always to withhold assent.

What reason, then, do we have at all to assume that the skeptic thinks that one ought to withhold assent? I think that what may allow us to assume after all that the skeptic has the view that one ought to withhold assent is the fact that his opponents try to refute the skeptic by challenging this view and that the skeptic accepts that challenge. But one has to keep in mind that the fact that the skeptic accepts the challenge also admits of a different interpretation. The opponent, in challenging the view that it is wise to withhold assent, may be trying to re-move one horn of the dilemma into which he has been put by the skeptical argu-ment that the wise man will not give assent, and the skeptic may be taking up the challenge to show that his opponent is not in a position to rule out this possi-bility and thus to remove the conflict of his beliefs. In fact, I think that in classi-cal skepticism this is one function of, e.g., the accounts of the so-called practical criterion, i.e., I think that it should not be taken for granted that the skeptical accounts of the practical criterion are just straightforward accounts of how a skeptic may proceed in real life. They, first of all, serve the purpose to show that the possibility that the wise man will not give assent cannot be ruled out just because it would be impossible to lead a life, let alone a wise life, without assent. The accounts of the practical criterion are supposed to show that even on the Stoics' own assumptions it might be possible to live without assent. Still, it also seems clear from the way the skeptic's opponents attack the skeptic on this point that they do not regard the skeptic's remarks as just a move in the dialectical game, but think that the skeptic does have the view that one ought to withhold assent. But in what sense could the skeptic have the view that one ought always to withhold assent without involving himself in immediate contradiction? If to have a view is to give assent a skeptic cannot heed his own precept without vio-lating it. Thus we must assume that there is a kind of assent, namely the kind of assent the skeptic will withhold, such that having a view in itself does not in-volve that kind of assent, if we also want to assume that the skeptic does think that one ought to withhold assent and that he does not thereby involve himself in contradiction.

In what sense, then, could the skeptic have the view that one always ought to withhold assent? The only possibility I see is this: it turns out in his ex-perience, having considered claim after claim, that given certain standards or canons it seems that one ought to withhold assent. And this might suggest to him, leave him with the impression that, given these standards, one ought to withhold assent. But this does not mean that he is ready to make the claim that one ought to withhold assent. For he knows too well that his claim would invite a skeptical counterargument. It would be pointed out to him that his experience was quite limited, that it was possibly quite idiosyncratic, that the future might be radically different, etc. Knowing all this he does not feel in a position to make the claim that one ought to withhold assent, but he also still might have the impression that, given certain canons, one ought to withhold assent, just as he might still have the impression that there is motion, and yet not be ready to make that claim because he acknowledges that there are impressive arguments, like Zeno's paradoxes, on both sides of the question and that he is in no position to adjudicate between them. More generally, the reason why he does not feel like making a claim, let alone a claim to knowledge, is that he thinks that there is a philosophical practice of making claims, and in particular a practice of making claims to knowledge, and that to engage in this practice is to subject oneself to certain canons, and that he has the impression that, given these canons, one ought to withhold assent. To be more precise, according to these canons, one has to have some special reason to make a claim, and given what counts as a reason according to these canons, he does not see himself in a position to make a claim, and thus thinks he ought to withhold assent.

I want to emphasize that this view not only has a rather complicated, tenuous status, it also has this further complexity which tends to be overlooked. It is a view relative to the canons and standards of rationality espoused by dogmatic philosophy, which the dogmatic philosopher insists on applying to any claim whatsoever, whether it be in mathematics or in ordinary life. It is only given these standards that it seems that one should withhold assent. But they are not the skeptic's standards, though he does not reject them, either. And thus Sextus often qualifies his remark that we have to withhold assent by saying that we have to withhold assent as far as this is a matter of reason or philosophical reason (*hoson epi tō philosophō logō; PH* III, 65; 1, 215; II, 26, 104; III, 6, 13, 29, 81, 135, 167). Thus there is room for another kind of assent, though one which will be threatened by the possibility that one ought to conform to the standards postulated by dogmatic philosophy if it should turn out that there is a choice in the matter.

On the basis of this one might try to make a distinction between just having a view and making a claim, taking a position. To just have a view is to find oneself being left with an impression, to find oneself having an impression after having considered the matter, maybe even for a long time, carefully, diligently, the way one considers matters depending on the importance one attaches to them. But however carefully one has considered a matter it does not follow that the impression one is left with is true, nor that one thinks that it is true, let alone that one thinks that it meets the standards which the dogmatic philosophers claim it has to meet if one is to think of it as true. To make a claim, on the other hand, is to subject oneself to certain canons. It does, e.g., require that one should think that one's impression is true and that one has the appropriate kind of reason for thinking it to be true. To be left with the impression or thought that p, on the other hand, does not involve the further thought that it is true that p, let alone the yet further thought that one has reason to think that p, that it is reasonable that p. Even on the principles of Stoic logic the propositions (i) that p, (ii) that it is true that p, and (iii) that it is reasonable that p, are different propositions, and hence the corresponding thoughts or impressions are different thoughts. And though the propositions that p and that it is true that p may be necessarily equivalent, it does not follow from this that the impression that p involves, or is identical with, the impression that it is true that p.

Now it seems to me that there is such a distinction between having a view and taking a position, but that it is quite difficult to articulate it. And one reason for this seems to be that there is a whole spectrum of distinctions with a very weak notion of having a view at one extreme and a strong notion of taking a position at the other extreme. The problem is to draw the distinction in such a way that it does correspond to the distinction the skeptics actually made.

One way the skeptics draw the distinction is in terms of two kinds of assent, and since I think that it is a difficulty about the way in which the distinction is to be drawn in terms of two kinds of assent which historically give rise to dogmatic skepticism, I focus on the distinction thus drawn. But it is important to realize from the outset that this is just one way in which the skeptics draw the distinction, and that they draw the distinction in this way because their opponents speak about assent in such a way that they are in no position to assail the skeptical distinction.

A clue to how we might distinguish two kinds of assent for the classical skeptic, we get from Sextus. For Sextus, too, distinguishes two kinds of assent. Though at times he says that the skeptic invariably withholds assent, he also says that the skeptic does give assent to those impressions which are forced upon him (I. 13), or that the skeptic does not want to overturn those views which lead us, having been impressed by things in a certain way, toward assent without our will. The addition 'without our will' is crucial. For it guards this kind of assent against the threat that we might find out we ought to conform to the canons of rationality postulated by dogmatism. This kind of assent is not a matter of choice, unlike the assent of the Stoic wise man. In the first of these passages Sextus also uses the verb *eudokein* as a variant for the verb normally used in this context, *synkatatithesthai*. And indeed, the Suida, the Etymologicum Magnum, and the Lexeis Rhetorikai (*Anecdota Graeca*, I, p. 260[3] treat *synkatatithesthai* as a synonym of *eudokein*. And if we consider the ordinary use of this verb, it turns out that it might refer to an explicit act of acknowledgment, approval, consent, acceptance, the kind of thing one does for a reason. Or it might refer to a passive acquiescence or acceptance of something, in the way in which a people might accept a ruler, not by some act of approval or acknowledgment, but by acquiescence in his rule, by failing to resist, to effectively reject his rule. Correspondingly there are two ways or senses in which one might accept or approve of an impression. When the Stoics speak of 'assent', they talk of an act of approval, the kind of thing one should do for an appropriate reason;

they think that to assent to an impression is to take it to be true, and that one should have good reason for taking something to be true. But there is also the other sense of 'assent'. One might, having considered matters, just acquiesce in the impression one is left with, resign oneself to it, accept the fact that this is the impression one is left with, without though taking the step to accept the impression positively by thinking the further thought that the impression is true. One might also not acquiesce in the impression one is left with and think that the matter needs further consideration. But whether one does or does not acquiesce in it is not by itself dependent on whether one takes the impression to be true. Assent may be a purely passive matter. It may be the case that human beings work in such a way that impressions are more or less evident to us. Evidence is a purely internal feature of our impressions. Now we also attribute different importance to different questions. We might be constructed in such a way that if we have an impression on a matter whose degree of evidence does not correspond to the degree of importance we attach to the matter, we naturally, unless we are prevented, e.g., by lack of time or energy or have decided to take a risk, go on to consider the matter further till we get an impression which has a sufficient degree of evidence. It would not even have to be the case that at a certain point we decide that we now have a clear enough impression and stop to consider the matter further. It may just be the case that as soon as we have a clear enough impression we, without any further thought, act on it. And this may be all acquiescence and assent consist in.

One might object that both cases of assent constitute some kind of acceptance, and that to accept an impression surely is to accept it as true. After all, how could somebody be said to have the view that p without thinking that it is the case that p or that it is true that p?

Here is at least one way in which this might be possible. It might be the case that action does not require that one take the impression one is acting on to be true. It might be the case that action does not, in addition to the impression that p, require a positive act of assent or the further thought that it is true that p. All that may be needed is one's acquiescence in the impression, and all this may amount to is that in the series of impressions one has reached an impression which produces an action rather than the kind of disquiet which would make one go on to consider the matter further till one reached an impression which one no longer resists and which produces an action. Indeed, one may have the view that p without even entertaining the thought that p, let alone the further thought that p is true. Things may have left us with the impression that p, and we may act on that view, without being aware of it. We may leave aside here cases in which something prevents us from realizing that this is the view we have (e.g., cases of suppression or self-deception). For even if we know that we have a certain view and on some occasion act on it, it is not necessary that in order to act on it we on that occasion have to entertain explicitly the corresponding thought and to assent positively to it. An expert craftsman is still acting on his expert beliefs, even though he is not actually thinking of what he is doing when he is acting on them. Indeed thinking of them might interfere with his activity. But having finished his work he might well explain to us which views guided his activity. And for some of these views it might be true that this would be the first time he ever formulated them, either to himself or to somebody else. Nevertheless he could properly claim to have acted on them.

The skeptic might think that his opponents will have to grant that there are these kinds of cases and that they can be characterized in terms of assent to an impression. For even the Stoics assume that the wise man will often act, not on the basis of certain knowledge, but of wise conjecture. He is not omniscient, and his rationality and wisdom are characterized exactly by his ability to be rational or reasonable in his assumptions and actions even when he lacks knowledge, as he inevitably will, in the complex situations of everyday life. Nevertheless, he will do what is fitting or appropriate because he will be able, as the Stoics themselves say, to give a reasonable (*eulogon*) account of what he has done. I want to suggest that the past tense of 'what he has done' is to be taken seriously. The view is rather like Aristotle's; the person who has chosen to act in a certain way does not actually have to have gone through some moral reasoning and to have actually decided to act accordingly; what makes the action voluntary, rather, is that one correctly explain the action after the fact as being done for reasons of a certain kind. Similarly, the Stoic wise man, in order to do what is fitting, does not necessarily actually have to go through some reasoning, overtly accept or assent to the conclusion, and act on the basis of this. It, rather, is that his action in hindsight can be explained in terms of such reasoning. Thus even on the Stoics' theory there will be cases where the wise man, in fact, just acts on an impression of an appropriate kind and where, if we want to talk about assent, the assent consists in nothing but the fact that the wise man does not resist the impression he is acting on, but, in acting on it, implicitly accepts it. This, then, would seem to be a kind of case where acceptance of, or assent to, an impression does not involve taking it to be true. And if this is so, and if withholding assent is counted as an action, one might, e.g., say that the skeptic has the view that one ought to withhold assent in the sense that he might explain his withholding assent in terms of his acquiescence in this impression, pointing out that he is not resisting or fighting against this impression, but implicitly accepts it by acting on it.

Thus the skeptic may have views which account for his behavior. He behaves exactly in the way in which somebody who believed these views to be true would behave. But he insists that there is no need to assume that action, in addition to the appropriate kind of impression, requires the additional belief that the impression is true.

Now one might also ask the skeptic about his view on this or that matter. And he might be ready to try to articulate his view. And in this case it might be objected that he now is taking a position about what he takes to be the truth of the matter. But, as we can see from Sextus, it is open to him to reply that he is merely trying to articulate the views which guide his behavior, he is merely, as it were, giving an autobiographical report, without taking a stand on the truth of his views.

At this point it is also worth taking note of another crucial fact. It is assumed by Greek philosophers that knowledge and truth are correlatives. For them those things count as truths which on the true account of things would come out as truths. But given that dogmatic philosophy has raised the conditions for what is to count as knowledge, it thereby has raised the requirements for what is to count as true. Now things which we ordinarily would count as true no longer necessarily qualify as such. We might think that it is true that this book is brown. But it might turn out that on the true theory of things this is a mere appearance, that, in fact, there only is a certain configuration of atoms which may, or may not, produce this appearance. And similarly for all other ordinary truths. It is in this way that dogmatic philosophy creates a global contrast between apppearance and truth or reality. For dogmatic philosophy insists on calling into question all the truths we ordinarily go by.

And given this contrast, the skeptic, of course, does not take his impressions to be true, i.e., he does not think that his impressions are such that they will come out true on the true theory of things. For what reason would he have to think this? And he can point to the fact that not even the Stoic wise man takes all his impressions to be true in this way. The very point of the doctrine of the reasonable is that it allows the wise man to accept impressions and thus not to be reduced to inaction, without thereby taking them to be true. It is in this way that the Stoic wise man avoids having false beliefs, even though some of his impressions, however reasonable, may be false. For though he goes by the impression that *p,* he does not accept it as true, but only as reasonable.

Thus one may argue that the Stoics, given their own theory, can hardly reject the suggestion that there is a difference between having a view and taking a position, between just going by an impression and going by an impression because one takes it to be true, between two kinds of assent, merely passive acceptance and active acceptance as true.

There is one important difference between having a view and taking a position which was emphasized by the skeptics and which is still reflected by our ordinary notion of dogmatism. The skeptic has no stake in the truth of the impression he is left with. He is ever ready to consider the matter further, to change his mind. He has no attachment to the impressions he is left with. He is not responsible for having them, he did not seek them out. He is not out to prove anything, and hence feels no need to defend anything. For the dogmatic, on the other hand, something is at stake. It does make a great difference to him whether his impressions really are true and whether he has made a mistake in taking them to be true. For in actively giving assent to them he has become responsible for them, and hence feels a need to defend them and to prove them to be true. The dogmatic, in taking a position, has made a deliberate choice, a hairesis, for which he is accountable. But because so much is at stake for him, he no longer is in a position openly to consider alternatives, to realize and accept the weight of objections; he has become dogmatic in his attitude.

If we now apply this distinction of two kinds of assent and correspondingly the distinction between having a view and taking a position to the question of knowledge, we might say that the classical skeptic perhaps comes to be left with the impression that nothing is, or even can be, known, whereas the dogmatic skeptic takes the position that nothing can be known. How could the classical skeptic come to have this impression? In his experience it turns out that claim after claim does not pass his scrutiny which, at least given the standards his opponents themselves are committed to, these claims should pass if they were made from knowledge. Thus he naturally is left with the impression that, given these standards, nothing will pass the test and hence that nothing is, or even can be, known. And in the course of time he might even acquiesce in this impression. He might stop to think that this cannot be right and that just some further consideration will change his impression. And yet he might not feel the slightest inclination to claim that nothing can be known. He knows the objections too well: limited experience, experience with the wrong claims, experience with the wrong opponents, one day we shall know, etc. And there is, of course, the troublesome tag 'given these standards'. He is not committed to these standards, but he does see their attraction. He himself originally had hoped that by following these standards he would arrive at certain knowledge and thus could adjudicate all the conflicts which were troubling him. But he also knows of powerful arguments against these standards, like the paradox of the liar. He cannot rule out the possibility that other standards would fare better. He is aware of the fact that in ordinary life and in ordinary language we do not subject ourselves to these standards. We do not ordinarily require of somebody who claims to know that he should have the kind of reason and justification for his belief which allows him to rule out all incompatible beliefs, that knowledge has to be firm or certain exactly in the sense that somebody who really knows cannot be argued out of his belief on the basis of assumptions incompatible with it. It seems that ordinarily we only expect satisfaction of these standards to an extent and degree which is proportional to the importance we attribute to the matter in question. And thus, following common usage, a skeptic might well be moved to say, in perfect consistency with his skepticism, that he knows this or that. There is no reason why the skeptic should not follow the common custom to mark the fact that he is saying what he is saying having given the matter appropriate consideration in the way one ordinarily goes about doing this, by using the verb 'to know'. This, in fact, is what we find Sextus doing occasionally (cf. *Adversus Mathematicos* VIII. 157). Aenesidemus obviously was prepared to go so far as to say that a wise man knows that he does not know anything for certain and that if he does know something he is still going to withhold assent (Photius, *Bibl.* 212, 169[b] 28ff.). A skeptic might take the view that all one could sensibly do was to follow this very complicated common practice. But if he would follow this practice it would be with the thought that what one said one knew could be radically otherwise, and that the whole practice of using the verb 'to know' the way we ordinarily do could be radically mistaken. For we cannot, e.g., rule out the possibility that we should subject ourselves to the rigorous standards and canons philosophers have been trying to impose, but which their own claims do not meet. There is the possibility that one day they will be able to formulate a set of canons which will find general acceptance. There is the possibility that one day they will make claims which meet these standards and which will pass the test.

It seems to me that this rather differentiated view is quite different from the dogmatic position that nothing can be known. It is a view the classical skeptic finds himself stranded with, not a position he is out to demonstrate, to establish, to defend, not a position he thinks he has reason to adopt and adopts for that reason. He is not out to show that some particular person, or some group of people, or people in general do not have knowledge, he is not out to show anything. He is willing to find out. But so far, all his search has left him with is the impression that nothing is known. If this is correct, then there is a substantial difference between classical skepticism and dogmatic skepticism, and the ancient representatives of classical skepticism were not just deluding themselves when they saw a difference between their own view and that of dogmatic skeptics. But if this is so, then the question does arise how this complex attitude of the classical skeptic collapsed into the dogmatic position that nothing can be known.

It seems that the major step in the direction of a dogmatic skepticism was already taken in antiquity. For, as we saw, in antiquity some skeptics accused other skeptics of being dogmatic in their assertion that nothing can be known. This is the charge Aenesidemus levels against the late Academics (cf. Photius, *Bibl.* 212, 169[b]), and a charge, Sextus thinks, which might be leveled against the Academics in general (*PH* I, 226). We find evidence that some late Academics did, in fact, espouse such a dogmatic skepticism. At the end of Cicero's *Academica priora* (148), Catulus is made to say:

> I return to the position of my father, which he said to be that of Carneades; I believe that nothing can be known, but I also believe that the wise man will give assent, i.e. will have opinions, but this in such a way that he is aware that he is only opining and that he knows that there is nothing which can be comprehended and known; hence I approve of this kind of with-

holding assent in all matters, but I vehemently assent to this other view that there is nothing which can be known.

These remarks reveal their dogmatism in the vehemence with which Catulus assents to the impression that nothing can be known, in the strong attachment which he has to this view, attachment of a kind which is quite alien to the classical skeptic and which is explicitly criticized by Sextus Empiricus (*PH* I, 230). Moreover, it reveals its dogmatism in that it allows the skeptic to have opinions, i.e., beliefs on how things are. This passage and its context also supply us with some crucial information about the source of this dogmatism. To start with, it is clear from Cicero's following remarks that he does not think that the view Catulus expresses is the general view of the Academy; Cicero himself thinks that this was not Carneades' view. Second, as we can see from Catulus' own remarks, this view is presented as an interpretation of Carneades, but as one which is controversial.

Now we know from the earlier parts of the *Academica* of at least one respect in which this interpretation of Carneades was controversial among Carneades' pupils. We are told that there was disagreement between Clitomachus, on the one hand, and Metrodorus and Philo, on the other, on whether, in reality and according to Carneades, the wise man will give assent and hence have opinions. The question is whether we can reconstruct enough of this controversy to see how it might have led to the kind of dogmatic skepticism which we find in the later Academy and which is represented by Catulus' remarks. In this case we also would have some explanation why later authors, like Sextus, entertain the possibility, or even assume as a fact, that Academic skeptics in general were dogmatic. For the view presents itself as an interpretation of Carneades and as the position of the Academy in general.

What, then, could have given rise to the view that according to Carneades the wise man will assent to what is not known, i.e., will have opinions, and how could this lead to the kind of dogmatic skepticism we are considering? The following seems to me to be a possibility. The notion of the probable (*pithanon*) plays a central role in Carneades. Among other things it is a matter of probability for Carneades that nothing can be known (Cic., *Ac. pr.* 110). Now there are two different interpretations of, and attitudes toward, the probable. These seem to correspond to two different interpretations of Carneades' so-called practical criterion. Asked how the skeptic will know what to do if he universally withholds assent, Carneades points out that he will just follow the probable, what seems to be the case, and that depending on the importance of the matter he will go through certain procedures to make sure that his impression is relatively reliable. It is clear that Carneades' account, first of all, is a dialectical move against a dogmatic objection and thus does not commit him to any view at all. But I also think that is does reflect Carneades' view of how people actually go about gaining an impression they are willing to rely on. And taken this way, it admits of two interpretations. It may be taken in just the sense that this is how human beings in general seem to proceed, or it may be taken in the sense that this is how one ought to proceed if one wants to get a reliable impression, one which if not true, at least has a good chance to be true. Whereas on the first interpretation it is just noted that human beings, as a matter of fact, go about considering matters in a certain way when in doubt, on the second interpretation proper consideration is regarded as conferring some epistemological status on the impression thus arrived at: it at least has a good chance to be true. And thus, though it is agreed on all sides that the probable is that which seems to be the case, this is interpreted in two different ways. On one interpretation what on due consideration appears to be the case offers us some guidance about what is actually true. Though we are in no position to say that it is true, we may expect it to have a good chance of being true, to be like the truth (*verisimilis*), or else to be the truth itself (Cic., *Ac. pr.* 7; 32; 66; 99; 107). On the other interpretation, the fact that something appears to be the case goes no way to show that it is true; however much it appears to be the case, this does not it itself make it any more likely to be true. The probable is just the plausible, and there is no reason to assume that plausibility and truth, or even evidence and truth, go hand in hand.

Another piece of relevant information seems to be the following: Carneades subscribed to the skeptic tenet that one should always withhold assent. But it also seems to have been agreed that Carneades did say that it is sometimes wise to give assent (*Ac. pr.* 67). Obviously, this needed interpretation, because it had to be made compatible with the general skeptical tenet to withhold assent, but presumably also because Arcesilaus had said nothing of the sort and hence Carneades' remark might be taken to indicate a significant departure from the position of Arcesilaus. Thus we find Clitomachus making a distinction of two kinds of assent, obviously trying to give an interpretation of the distinction which will not commit Carneades to the view that it is wise to have mere opinions (Cic., *Ac. pr.* 104). And it seems clear from Catulus' remarks that the opposing party similarly made a distinction of two kinds of assent, but exactly in such a way that Carneades would be committed to the view that the wise man will have opinions. For Catulus distinguishes between the universal withholding of assent and the vehement assent he gives to the view that nothing can be known and remarks that the wise man will give some kind of assent, i.e., will have opinions.

Now there is an obvious connection between the two interpretations of the probable and the two interpretations of the two kinds of assent Carneades must already have distinguished. To see this we have to notice that the skeptics sometimes speak of two kinds of assent; at other times they reserve the term 'assent' to the mental act, to something one does for a reason, to the positive acceptance of an impression because one thinks one has reason to take it to be true; and then they refer to the other kind of assent by talking of just following or approving or accepting an impression. At this point they rely on an etymological and conceptual connection between *pithanon* (probable) and *peithestai* (to follow; cf. *PH* I, 230). It is this connection which Cicero tries to preserve when he renders *pithanon* by *probabile* to make it correspond to the verb for 'approve' or 'accept' which he likes to use, namely *probare* (Cic., *Ac. pr.* 99; 139). So the probable quite literally is that which invites approval or assent in the sense in which the skeptic is free to give assent. But now there is a disagreement about this sense, and hence about the way the probable is to be understood, and hence a disagreement about whether Carneades allows for mere opinion. This dogmatic skeptic seems to take the view that the only kind of assent which is illegitimate is assent of the kind where one takes something to be true, i.e., commits oneself to a belief about what will come out as true on the true theory of things, about what would turn out to be true if one really knew what things are like. And since it is one thing to take something to be true and quite another to take it to be probable, he thinks it is quite legitimate to give the kind of assent to an impression which would consist in taking it to be probable. And though we may not be able to ascertain what is to count as true, we can consider the matter with appropriate care and thus arrive at an impression which is probable and then assent to it as probable. But to take something to be probable is, on this interpretation of the probable, to take it to be either true or at least sufficiently like what is true. Thus somebody who does give assent in this sense does have beliefs about how things are, i.e., mere opinions.

Clitomachus' interpretation of the two kinds of assent, on the other hand, is very much along the lines of the distinction I earlier on attributed to Sextus, as we can see from Cicero (*Ac. pr.* 104), who spells out Clitomachus' view in some detail. On this interpretation, a view one acts on and a view one is willing to communicate do not presuppose either that one takes them to be true or that at least one takes them to be likely to be true, because one has considered the matter carefully. It is rather that, as a matter of fact, we sometimes only act on an impression, if we have considered the matter further, but not because we now think it more likely to be true. It surely is relevant to keep in mind in this connection, though this is not pointed out in our ancient texts, that sometimes we, quite reasonably, act on views which we ourselves find less likely to be true than their alternatives.

Now to take something to be true or at least likely to be true is not the same thing as to take it to be true. And thus even the kind of dogmatic Academic skeptic we are considering can insist that he, too, distinguishes between having a view and taking a position if to take a position is to take one's impression to be true, and that he does not take a position in saying that nothing can be known. This is what allows him to think that he is still a skeptic and not dogmatic. But since having a view for him might be a matter of actively adopting a view because he thinks that it is true or at least likely to be true, it is only a thin line which distinguishes him from the dogmatic who adopts a view because he takes it to be true. Both have views on how things are, both may be equally firmly convinced that they are true (remember Catulus' vehement assent), but one believes that the kind of justification or knowledge which would establish the truth of a view is available, whereas the other believes that it is not available. But as for the particular question we are concerned with, namely the possibility of knowledge, one cannot be more dogmatic than our dogmatic skeptic already is. For one cannot consistently claim that on the true account of things, i.e., if we really know how things are, it will turn out that nothing can be known. Thus, though there is a fine distinction between the dogmatism of the dogmatists and the dogmatism of late Academic skeptics, this fine distinction collapses when it comes to the view that nothing can be known. To preserve whatever distinction there is, one might distinguish between adopting a view and taking a position and contrast both with having a view. But I shall in the following use 'taking a position' in a wide sense to cover both, to emphasize the similarity which—in the eyes of the classical skeptic—dogmatic skepticism has with ordinary dogmatism.

If this should be correct, we can see what gives rise to dogmatic skepticism. Having considered a matter carefully, one finds oneself with a view which one finds persuasive. But this is now taken to mean that because one has considered the matter carefully the view has some likelihood of being true, though, of course, there is no guarantee or certainty that it is true. Thus Cicero can talk of the probable as the canon of truth and falsehood (*Ac. pr.* 32), and can talk of the Academic method of arguing pro and con, of considering a matter from all sides, as a method he pursues in the hope of finding what is true or at least very much like the truth (*Ac. pr.* 7). Thus the probability of the impression that nothing can be known, too, is interpreted as the likelihood, though not certainty, that nothing can be known, a likelihood one may be so convinced of that one vehemently assents. By contrast, the classical skeptic just finds himself with the view that nothing can be known and may finally acquiesce in it.

Thus a certain interpretation of the Carneadean criterion, and hence the probable, and along with it a certain interpretation of the distinction of two kinds of assent, is the first step on the road to dogmatic skepticism. It allows the skeptic to have opinions about how things are, as long as he is aware that his opinions are not a matter of certain knowledge. And it allows him to take the position that nothing can be known, if only it, too, is qualified by the proviso that it itself is not a matter of certain knowledge. For given his experience with skeptical arguments, it seems at least probable that nothing can be known.

Now the view that, in spite of all the skeptical arguments one has been producing and the effect they have had, one might still be left with an impression of how things are and that, on the basis of this impression, one may take a position, has an effect on the way skeptical arguments in general and the arguments concerning the possibility of knowledge in particular are viewed. On the old view, the skeptical method to argue against any claim and—by implication—for any claim, since one would argue against the contradictory of a claim as much as against the claim itself, was seen as a purely negative, critical method. It might have been granted that the considerations pro and con might still leave one with an impression, that however much one argued for and against the existence of motion one might still be left with the impression that things move. But it was not assumed that this impression gained any epistemological status in virtue of the fact that one was still left with it after having gone through all the arguments pro and con. Now it comes to be assumed that the skeptical method of arguing pro and con is also a method of truth, a method which allows one to approximate the truth, though it does not guarantee the truth of the resulting impression (cf. Cic., *Ac. pr.* 7). And hence the dogmatic skeptic might well take the view that having carefully considered the Stoic arguments for the possibility of knowledge and the skeptical arguments against it, and finding, on balance, the skeptical arguments to be weightier, he is in a position to claim that nothing can be known.

Moreover, once the skeptic takes the liberty to take positions, his positions, given the eclecticism of the time, tend to become more or less identical to those of the Stoics, except on the question of knowledge itself. Thus he does come to believe in mental items like impressions and mental acts like assents. And he comes to believe in the premises of the arguments the classical skeptics had formulated to show that the Stoics themselves were committed to the view that nothing is, or can be, known. And now these arguments will have a pull on him, which is reflected by the quite unskeptical vehemence with which Catulus assents to the view that nothing can be known. Now skeptical arguments to the effect that nothing can be known can come to be interpreted as arguments which go some way, though not all the way, to establish the truth of the claim that nothing can be known. This, then, is the second major step on the road to dogmatic skepticism. The skeptic now, though qualifiedly, himself espouses the dogmatic framework of concepts and assumptions which seem to make knowledge impossible.

It should be noticed that at this point the classical and the dogmatic skeptic no longer differ only in the kind of assent they might feel free to give, but also in the impressions they give assent to. The difference between classical and dogmatic skeptics does not just consist in the different qualifiers attached to their views. For given his, albeit qualified, trust in the ability of philosophical arguments to get one somewhere, the dogmatic skeptic will have views induced by nothing but such arguments, whereas it would seem that in the case of the classical skeptic such arguments only threaten to undermine even those views which had been induced quite independently of philosophical argument.

Finally, the second step, the acceptance of the dogmatic framework, seems to involve a third step. The classical skeptic had started out being attracted by certain knowledge. He certainly had not committed himself to the view that knowledge is certain knowledge. But the dogmatic skeptic now seems to accept the Stoic view that knowledge has to be certain. In fact, I am inclined to think that Philo provoked such an outcry among dogmatic skeptics because he maintained that though the kind of certain knowledge the Stoics were after was impossible this did not mean that knowledge as such was impossible, that this had never been the position of the Academy, and that hence the supposed break of the New Academy with the Old was an illusion.

In this way, then, we arrive by Cicero's time at the dogmatic skeptical position that since all we ever have are impressions of how things are and since there is nothing to ever guarantee the truth of an impression, nothing about how things are can be known for certain.

The next question I raised was how it happened that skepticism came to be identified with dogmatic skepticism, so much so that even classical skepticism was identified as dogmatic skepticism and that to the present day we associate skepticism with the dogmatic skeptical position. To understand this we have to see that skepticism of any form in antiquity soon came to be a dead issue. Dogmatic skepticism did not have a future in later ancient thought. Rather, it provoked a revival of classical skepticism. For it seems that Pyrrhonism is not so much a revival of Pyrrho's philosophy, but a revival of classical Academic skepticism under the name of Pyrronism, to distinguish it from the dogmatism which Aenesidemus and Sextus Empiricus associated with the later skeptical Academy. But neither form of skepticism suited the temper of late antiquity; later antiquity found some form of Platonism or other, in Christian or pagan garb, more congenial, and thus skepticism, with some odd exceptions like Uranius in the sixth century (cf. Agathias, *Historiarum libri quinque* II, 29, 7),[4] came to be a historical position to be vehemently rejected, rather than to be carefully understood. Thus it was largely a matter of ignorance that in late antiquity skepticism came to be identified with dogmatic skepticism. In the Latin West this was, no doubt, in good part due to Cicero's influence, who himself was a dogmatic skeptic and who, moreover, would be the only substantial source concerning skepticism available to those who did not read Greek. And Cicero's influence was magnified by St. Augustine's authority, who for his attack on skepticism in his *Contra Academicos* primarily, if not exclusively, relied on Cicero, but unlike Cicero, gave no indication of the possibility of a nondogmatic skepticism and treated Carneades as taking the kind of position espoused by Cicero. And given Augustine's standing far into early modern times, it is not surprising that the Western view of skepticism should have been determined by him throughout the Middle Ages, especially since for a long time his *Contra Academicos* would have been the only readily available source which discussed skepticism in any detail. And the impression gained from Augustine would be confirmed by the odd remark in the Latin Fathers, Arnobius (*Adv. Nationes* II, 9–10[5] or Lactantius (*Div. Inst.* III. 6),[6] for example. It may also be of relevance in this context that the question of knowledge became a live issue again in the late Middle Ages owing in part to Ockham's doctrine of intuitive cognitions. Ockham took the view that cognitions are entities. He also took the view that God, by his absolute power, can destroy any one of two separate entities, while preserving the other. Thus God could preserve a cognition we have while destroying the object of the cognition. Yet Ockham wanted to maintain that there are cognitions, namely intuitive cognitions, which warrant an evident judgment. Naturally his view raised questions. And at least one author, Nicolaus of Autrecourt, in his letters to Bernhard of Arezzo, took the view that, given the doctrine of cognitions or impressions and the doctrine of divine omnipotence he had to infer 'that every awareness which we have of the existence of objects outside our minds, can be false', and moreover that 'by natural cognitive means we cannot be certain when our awareness of the existence of external objects is true or false' (First Letter, p. 5 11).[7] Thus the question of the possibility of knowledge came to be a live issue again more or less exactly in those terms in which dogmatic skepticism had formulated it. In fact it may well have been this debate kindled by Ockham which created an interest in Cicero's *Academica* and Sextus Empiricus. A fourteenth-century manuscript of a Latin translation of Sextus' *Outlines* and a fifteenth-century manuscript of the same translation in any case show a revival of interest in ancient skepticism which must have been generated by developments in medieval philosophy itself.

Thus the West came to think of skepticism as dogmatic and even thought of classical skeptics as dogmatic skeptics. And the influence of the East during the Renaissance did not change this view. For the Greek East, too, already in antiquity, had settled for a dogmatic interpretation of skepticism. This is true for secular authors as much as ecclesiastical authors. To take the latter first, nobody would be able to gather from Clement's discussion (*Stromateis* VIII, V, 15.2ff.)[8] that not all skeptics asserted it as true that nothing can be known. Similarly, Eusebius (*Praeparatio Evangelica* XIV, 17, 10)[9] talks as if the skeptics took the position that nothing can be known. A particularly striking example of how even classical skeptics are interpreted as dogmatic skeptics is offered by Photius in his report on Aenesidemus' *Pyrrhonean Arguments* (Bibl. cod. 212, 1169[b]). Aenesidemus, in reaction to the dogmatism of the later Academy, had tried to revive classical skepticism under the name of Pyrrhonism. But though Photius tells us in the course of his report that Aenesidemus thought that the Academics had become dogmatic in claiming that nothing can be known, he starts out by telling us that Aenesidemus wrote his book to establish the thesis that nothing is known for certain. As for secular Greek writers one may compare the *Anonymous Prolegomena* (p. 21, 1ff.)[10] and Olympiodorus' *Prolegomena* (3, 32ff.).

Thus it was part of the medieval heritage that skepticism should be thought of as dogmatic skepticism and that even classical skeptics should be considered as dogmatic skeptics. But we have to ask why in early modern times, when most of the evidence concerning classical skepticism was available again, and when Cicero and Sextus Empiricus were reread with a new frame of mind, skepticism continued to be regarded as a dogmatical position, either as the extreme skepticism of the Pyrrhoneans or as the mitigated skepticism of the Academics.

I am not in a position to answer this question, but I do have some suggestions about how it might be answered. There is, first, mere inertia; this notion of skepticism, after all, was the notion inherited from the Middle Ages. Second, the early modern debate concerning the possibility of knowledge must have been a continuation of the medieval debate we referred to earlier. It surely is not accidental that the skeptical arguments against causality found, e.g., in Hume are very much like the arguments to be found in Nicolaus of Autrecourt or in Ghazali and Avervoes' refutation of Ghazali. But at issue in this debate was a version of dogmatic skepticism. Third, early modern philosophy, in part in following the tradition of late medieval epistemology, in part in reaction to Aristotelianism and Scholasticism, came largely to adopt the framework of dogmatic Hellenistic epistemology and thereby invited dogmatic skepticism. The very term 'impressions', for example, may be due to Cicero's influence (*Ac. pr.* 58). Fourth, dogmatic skepticism satisfied various ideological needs of the time. It could be used to reject Aristotelian science, a curious preoccupation of that period. It could be used to point out the need for faith and revelation. Fifth, the attitude toward historical philosophical texts was very different from ours. Philosophers of the past were studied as paradigmatic philosophers, as authorities, as exponents of a philosophical position worth considering, i.e., they were approached with a preconception of what one expected from them which was determined by one's own needs. Obviously this attitude is not conducive to an understanding of the history of philosophy. One way in which this may be relevant for our question is this: at least on the face of it, classical skeptics seem to differ from dogmatic skeptics primarily in that the latter allowed the skeptic to have beliefs about how things are, whereas the former seem to require a life without beliefs. But this seemed so obviously to be such an untenable position that, until very recently, not even historians of philosophy gave it serious consideration. As a result one focused on the part of classical skepticism which was concerned with the possibility of knowledge, as if that part could be understood in isolation from the classical skeptic's attitude toward belief. But as we have seen, the difference between classical and dogmatic skepticism lies exactly in a different attitude toward belief or assent. Thus we can do justice to the classical skeptic's attitude toward knowledge only if we take his remarks concerning belief seriously. Sixth, when the texts were read again, it must have seemed that there were basically two forms of skepticism in antiquity, Pyrrhonean skepticism, going back to Pyrrho, and Academic skepticism going back to Arcesilaus.

Pyrrhonean skepticism seemed hopeless as a philosophical position because one misunderstood the Pyrrhonean attitude toward beliefs and thought that a Pyrrhonean was supposed to live without beliefs. Hence the mitigated skepticism of the late Academy seemed to be the only skeptical position of promise. But remarks in Sextus suggested that the dogmatic skepticism of the late Academy was the position of the Academy in general. For Sextus in part relied on Antiochus for his view of the Academic position, and Antiochus saw Carneades, perhaps Arcesilaus and Carneades, as dogmatic skeptics. Moreover, Sextus himself had a vested interest in seeing the Academy in general as dogmatic. After all, the supposed dogmatism of the Academy is the main rationale for Pyrrhonism. Thus, if one concentrates on Academic skepticism as the viable skeptical position, and under the influence of Augustine and Sextus interprets Academic skepticism quite generally as dogmatic, one naturally arrives at a dogmatic conception of skepticism. But a more scholarly reading of Sextus or Cicero would have shown that this was never the position of the Academy.

To turn finally to our last question, it seems to me that early modern philosophy might have profited from a better historical understanding of ancient skepticism and the realization that dogmatic skepticism is only a degenerate form of skepticism. For it was because of this distorted notion of skepticism that the question at issue was understood as the question how we ever could be justified, on the basis of the impressions or ideas which are immediately given to us, to have any views about how things are, let alone to be certain about how things are. Descartes answered this question very much along the lines the Stoics had answered it, but Hume, in spite of an obvious tendency to go in this direction, was prevented from answering it in the way in which classical skepticism had answered it, since he to a good extent, too, accepted the dogmatic framework in which the question was posed by ancient dogmatic skepticism. But once we see that this framework in which the question is posed is the framework of dogmatic Hellenistic epistemology, and only thus comes to be the framework of ancient dogmatic skepticism, it is easy to realize that the classical skeptic will have no part of it. For all he knows it might be a mistake to distinguish quite generally and globally between how things appear and how they really are. There are some cases where it seems to be useful to make such a distinction, e.g., in the case of illusions, or in the case of deception. But for these cases we have ways to ascertain what really is the case which allow us in the first place to draw, for these cases, a reasonably clear distinction between how things appear and how they really are. But how are we supposed to know what is asked for when we are asked what things are really like in cases where we have not yet found that out? In short, I see no reason why a classical skeptic should accept the global contrast between appearance and reality. I also see no reason why a classical skeptic would believe in such mental entities as impressions or ideas. It is not that he is not willing to accept that people have impressions in the sense that one may have the impression that all this is not very clear, or that people have a mind. He explicitly says that he accepts this. But it is one thing to accept this and quite another to believe in mental entities like impressions. There is no reason to think that he believes in mental acts like assents. It is true that he talks as if he accepted impressions and assents. But this is because his opponents believe in these things. And when, for a change, he does use this language to talk about his own attitude, he is careful not to commit himself to the dogmatic assumptions associated with this language. Thus the assent the skeptic is free to give becomes a matter, for example, of his being ready to say 'yes' or 'no' if asked (Cic., *Ac. pr.* II, 104). Moreover, he has no reason to think that impressions are immediately given and unquestionable. Anybody who has written a paper knows how difficult it is to be clear about one's impressions of the subject which one tries to articulate. Similarly, it is by no means easy to tell in detail what the impressions one is acting on actually are like. Again, it is true that the skeptic talks as if there were no question about what our impressions are when he addresses his opponents. Sextus explicitly says that how something appears to one is not an issue. But by good luck we know from two passages in Galen that a radical Pyrrhonean will also challenge reports of impressions if the question should arise (*De diff puls.* VIII, 708ff.; cf. XIV, 628).[11] Moreover, there is no reason why the skeptic should accept what we do not accept in ordinary life, namely that there is a single answer to the question 'what is to count as knowledge?' What we expect from somebody who knows varies enormously from context to context. What counts as knowledge in an ordinary context may not count as such in the context of a scholarly or scientific discussion where we have higher demands. It also varies with the importance we attach to a matter.

So what in good part has happened is that, because one has failed to understand the classical skeptic's attitude toward belief, one also has failed to understand the peculiar nature and status of the arguments of classical skepticism, one has read and keeps reading them as if they represented the skeptical view of the problem of the possibility of knowledge. In fact, their primary function is to present the dogmatic with the difficulties which arise from the framework of notions and assumptions within which the dogmatic moves. And we should expect a proper skeptic to question not only the assumptions arrived at within this framework, but the very framework itself. This is what, from the point of view of classical skepticism, the later skeptical tradition failed to do. A better knowledge of the history of philosophy would have made this failure apparent.[12]

Medicine

12

Philosophy and Medicine in Antiquity

Throughout antiquity the relation between philosophy and medicine was very close. The author of "Decorum," a treatise in the Hippocratic corpus, advised that philosophy be carried into medicine and medicine into philosophy (chap. 5). Obviously the advice was heeded by many doctors and philosophers. Burnet (*Early Greek Philosophy*, p. 201 n. 4) went so far as to claim that from the times of Empedocles onward "it is impossible to understand the history of philosophy . . . without keeping the history of medicine constantly in view." And as far as medicine is concerned, it is generally agreed, and indeed obvious, that ancient medical authors, from the times of the Hippocratic writers onward, relied heavily on philosophers, not just for their views on physiology, but also for their conception of their art and their moral precepts for the doctor. Often they also formed fairly detailed philosophical views of their own. In fact, there is a whole tradition of philosophical thought in ancient medicine, particularly concerning the nature of medical knowledge, which is fairly independent of the thought of the philosophers, and which was substantial enough at times even to influence the views of the philosophers.

Ancient philosophers reveal a suprising amount of interest in medical questions. Part of this, no doubt, is due to the fact that ever since medicine became an intellectually respectable discipline in the fifth century B.C., educated men quite generally took an interest in it. To a large extent this interest was practical. The health-system required it. Often, especially in small communities, no doctors were available, and one had to care for oneself as well as one could. Access to the medical profession was completely unregulated; since doctors tended to be itinerant, it was practically impossible to hold them responsible. Hence there were many quacks and incompetent doctors; one had to try to make some informed judgment about whether one should trust the competence of the doctor who offered his help. The relationship between the doctor and the patient was different then from what it is today. Much of the responsibility for treatment was carried by the patient. Epid. I, 11 tells us that it is the patient who must combat the disease with the help of the doctor. Especially if the patient was educated, hence, as a rule, socially superior to the doctor who, again as a rule, was regarded as a simple artisan, the doctor merely offered explanation, advice, and help. The choice of treatment, hence the primary responsibility, was the patient's. Therefore, the patient tried to be as informed as possible. The author of "Regimen for Health" (chap. 9) advises the wise man to learn to take care of his ills by his own judgment. At least as early as the fourth century, and possibly even earlier, there were people who had a complete knowledge of the medicine of the times (Ar. Pol. 1282^{a}4; Plato, Pol. 259A), though they were not practicing doctors, at least not professionally, presumably in part because their social status would make it very difficult and, in any case, unnecessary for them to join the medical profession. How knowledgeable a layman in antiquity could be we can see in the case of Celsus, the author of a large handbook on medicine in the reign of Tiberius which is still extant. Historians of medicine have had great difficulty determining whether Celsus was a doctor. His vast knowledge of medicine seemed to suggest that he was. But we also know that Celsus, like Varro before him, was an encyclopedic author who had covered various arts and who wrote for an audience that regarded medicine as one of the liberal arts, a good knowledge of which was fitting for, if not to be expected from, any educated free man. Gellius tells us a revealing story about how he once was visited by Calvisius Taurus, the leading Platonist of his day, and a group of his followers, when he was being attended upon by his doctor since he lay ill with a fever (XVIII, 10). The doctor claimed that Gellius was getting better and that Taurus could see this for himself by feeling his vein. Taurus' following was consternated by so much ignorance, for the doctor meant the artery. Gellius decided that it was shameful "not just for the doctor, but for all free men with a liberal education, to be ignorant of even those things which are relevant for a knowledge of our body and which are not too deep and too hidden." And he started to read up on the medical literature.

But the philosopher's interest in medical questions was not the more or less passive interest he, as an uncommonly educated man, was supposed to take in medicine anyway. Philosophers from very early on showed an active concern for medicine, in particular medical theory, which we may find surprising. But we have to keep in mind that the first philosophers were trying to give a general, unified account of nature in terms of which one could explain the most conspicuous, interesting, important, curious natural phenomena. The persuasiveness of such general accounts was in good part measured by their ability to explain particular phenomena. Thus it was natural that philosophers should try to show the strength of their account by trying to explain the most complicated phenomenon of nature: the constitution of humans, the way they function and behave, or fail to function. And their interest in a physiological explanation of human beings got stronger in the course of the fifth century when humans and human behavior became more and more the center of attention of philosophers, so much so that it took philosophers like Plato and Aristotle to ensure the continued study of natural philosophy in general. Thus the physiological study of human beings was an important part of the very enterprise of natural philosophers almost from the beginning. And in pursuing these studies the philosophers did not feel that they were intruding on someone else's territory. For when they started to concern themselves with medical questions, medicine itself was still traditional and doctors did not yet rely on any medical theories, or at least not on anything the philosophers would have regarded as such. There was, of course, the magical view that illness is a matter of the intrusion of a foreign entity, spiritual or grossly bodily, into the body; and there were more specific views that correlated different diseases with different spirits, demons, or gods (cf. *Sacred Disease* 1ff.; *Airs, Waters, Places* 3; *Celsus Prooem.* 4). But for the most part, medical practice relied on the tradition of an accumulated experience with wounds, fractures, dislocations, and some vaguely diagnosed internal diseases. Thus it was the philosophers who started medical theory, and at least in principle they never gave up their claim to the subject. As late a survey of natural philosophy as the post-Posidonian account of the Stoic philosophy of nature in Diogenes Laertius tells us that of the three subdivisions of natural philosophy one, namely etiology, has two parts of which one is the common concern of both the physician and the philosopher (VII, 132).

Now one could have imagined some division of labor, e.g., one according to which the philosopher deals with the soul and the doctor takes care of the body. There is, after all, from the fifth century onward, a widespread tradition of regarding philosophy as some kind of therapy of the soul. But this division presupposes a conception of the dualism between body and soul which was not widely shared. Both philosophers and physicians tended to assume that an interest in the soul was an interest in the various life-functions, like procreation, growth and nutrition, respiration, perception, thought—and both had an interest in all these functions. Thus it was not uncommon for doctors to write treatises on the soul. Asclepiades of Bithynia wrote one, and so did Soranus and Sextus Empiricus. Moreover, doctors tended to concern themselves with all kinds of disturbances as long as they clearly also involved bodily disturbances, whether it be insanity (mania), effeminacy, lethargy, morbid hunger, or melancholy. Caelius Aurelianus devotes a chapter to the rejection of the claim that hydrophobia is a disease of the soul and not the body (*Acut.* III, 13), and hence, it seems to be suggested, not of concern to the doctor. To dismiss the suggestion, he points to the bodily symptoms, the physical cause, and the sympathetic accord of body and soul. Doctors attended not just to the bodily effects of mental disturbances, but also to the mental effects of what they regarded as bodily disturbances. Thus Soranus in the case of insanity (Caelius Aurelianus, *Chron.* I, 166-

67), in addition to complex dietary measures, prescribes attendance of philosophical discussions for those who are willing: "for by their words they (i.e., the philosophers) diminish fear, sadness, and anger, and no small amount of good arises from them for the body." Thus, given that most philosophers and doctors did not accept a simple, sharp dualism between body and soul, a division of labor along these lines was not possible, even if it had been desired.

It is for the reasons given, then, that philosophers took a very active interest in medical theory and continued to do so even after the rise of a science of medicine in medical schools. Aristotle claimed: "It is also the task of the natural philosopher to have a view of the first principles of health and disease. Hence most natural philosophers . . . finish discussing the matters which fall under medicine (*De sensu* 436^a 17–22), and again "the most refined philosophers of nature end up by discussing the principles of medicine" (*De resp.* 480^b 28–30). These Aristotelian testimonies are fully born out by the evidence we still have. The first Presocratic who we are explicitly told took an interest in medicine is Pythagoras (D.L. VIII, 12). It is difficult for us to determine the core of truth in the legend which grew up around him and which the Pythagoreans themselves seem to have fostered. Given what else we know about Pythagoras, it seems reasonable to believe that, as Diogenes Laertius (VIII, 33, 35) claims, health for Pythagoras consisted in the harmony of the bodily constituents and, correspondingly, disease in upset of this harmony. He seems to have thought that this harmony or balance is upset primarily by a lack of proportion between bodily exertion, intake of nourishment, and rest (Iamblichus, V.P. 163; cf. 244), that diseases arise from excess in any of these respects (Iambl. V.P. 218; Diod. Sic. X, 7), that such excess leads to indigestion, which in turn is the cause of most diseases (Diod. Sic. X, 7). These views are extremely general, but they did provide an extremely useful framework for thought about internal diseases and suggested a way of dealing with them, namely by regimen. Internal diseases caused the greatest difficulties for traditional medicine. Here was a promising approach to them. It was taken up by Iccus of Tarentum and Herodicus of Selymbria, a gymnastic trainer a generation before Hippocrates, whom tradition made one of Hippocrates' teachers, presumably because the Hippocratic Corpus in so many of its parts already reflects the dietary approach, which changed medical thought and medical practice thoroughly. The author of "On Ancient Medicine," e.g., in his account of the rise of medicine talks as if medicine were a matter of regimen and does not even mention surgery and pharmacology, though it had been surgery and drugs which traditional doctors had relied on. As we can see from Celsus' Prooemium (9) already in antiquity the rise of scientific medicine was associated with the rise of dietetics, as opposed to surgery and pharmacology. Dietetics seemed to presuppose some kind of theory about the constitution of the human body and its exchange with the environment. And it was this kind of theory which the physicians of the fifth and fourth centuries tried to provide. In Alcmaeon of Croton at the beginning of the fifth century we find a philosopher whose primary concern seems to have been medical theory. Diogenes Laertius tells us that Alcmaeon wrote mainly on medicine (VIII, 83); and most of what we know about him does, in fact, concern medical theory. Hence, historians have often talked of Alcmaeon as a philosopher and a doctor, but it should be clear from what has been said here that there is no reason to think that he was a doctor just because he took such an interest in medicine. Like the Pythagoreans, Alcmaeon starts out from a very general schematic view about the constitution of the human body and the nature of health and disease. The body is constituted by a large number of pairs of opposites, the moist and the dry, the hot and the cold, the bitter and the sweet, etc. Health obtains if we have a harmonious blending (krasis) of these constituents, if each of them does not play a larger role than is appropriate for it (if there is isonomia); disease is produced by an undue preponderance, by a domination (monarchia) of one of the constituents which is destructive of its opposite and hence prevents it from playing its role (*Aet. Plac.* V, 30, 1).

But Alcmaeon also clearly tries to construct this schema in such a way that it fits experience and can be increasingly adapted to it. For Aristotle explicitly points out (*Met.* 986^a 22ff.) that Alcmaeon, unlike the Pythagoreans, assumed concrete opposites which could actually be observed, and that he did not settle for a definite list of them. Moreover, Alcmaeon seems to have been intent to fill out this schema with as much concrete detail as possible. Thus, he tried to locate the origin of disease in particular parts of the body, the blood, the marrow, or the brain (*Aet.* V, 30, 1). He seems to have been the first to recognize the central importance of the brain, in part as a result of anatomical studies which revealed the connection between the sense-organs, in particular the eyes, and the brain (Theophrastus, *De Sensu* 26). There is no reason to suppose that he was the first to do dissections, but his work will have made it very clear that substantial progress could be made by a closer and systematic study of anatomy.

Empedocles, it seems, played a bigger role in the history of ancient medicine than any other philosopher. Among his students were doctors, e.g., Pausanias and Acron of Acragas, whom later tradition sometimes took to be the first Empiricist doctor (cf. Galen, *De. subf. emp.* p. 43, 1 D). Empedocles tries to give an account of how living beings, including humans, came into existence, and of how they are constituted by the four elements blended according to different ratios which accounts for the different kinds of constituents of the body. This approach also allows him to account for the difference between human beings. For the mixture in different humans may vary to some extent. Thus, he can assume individual natures (B 110, 5), a notion of great importance for Hippocratic medicine because it helps to justify the view that treatment has to be individualized to the individual patient. He apparently attempts to develop a physiological doctrine of all the major vital functions, reproduction and the growth of the embryo, presumably growth and nutrition quite generally, respiration, sleep and death, perception and thought. However inadequate Empedocles' physiology seems, and must have seemed then, it served the important function of persuading people that it was important and possible to arrive at an adequate and comprehensive physiological account of human beings.

And thus from Empedocles onward all major Presocratics, in particular Anaxagoras, Diogenes of Apollonia, and Democritus, tried to develop a more or less detailed physiology. Diogenes even wrote a treatise on the nature of humans. Democritus wrote various medical treatises, among them one on the nature of humans and one on the causes of disease (D.L. ix, 46).

Thus, the philosophers in the course of the fifth century developed more and more elaborate medical theories. When we come to the fourth century, the situation has hardly changed, as we can see from the detail with which Plato in the *Timaeus* discusses the constitution of the human body, health and disease, and from Aristotle's remarks referred to earlier. The situation did change significantly in Hellenistic times. Philosophers now were primarily concerned with ethics, the best of them exercising their ingenuity on the theory of knowledge. The school which we might expect to contribute most to medical theory, namely the Stoic, scrupled by profound skepticism, was very hesitant to engage in detailed etiological research. Ironically enough, the defenders of the theoretical possibility of certain knowledge took a rather dim view of our ability in practice to gain a scientific understanding of the concrete phenomena of nature. It also must have made a difference that by now physicians had developed quite intricate medical theories and clearly had taken the lead in a subject which one could no longer master without specializing in it. Nevertheless, as we see from the passage in Diogenes Laertius referred to earlier, philosophers did not give up their interest in medical theory. It surely is no accident that Posidonius, who—unlike his fellow Stoics—did pursue etiological research in great detail (Strabo II, 3, 8), also studied medicine in Alexandria under Zopyrus (Apollonius Citiensis, De articulis p. 12, 5).

It would also be a mistake to assume that the interest of the philosophers in medical theory was marginal to their philosophical interests. Work on the physiology of the senses had a considerable influence on the theory of perception. The theory of growth and nutrition has considerable metaphysical ramifications, as we can see from Aristotle's *De generatione et corruptione* and the history of the Growing Argument from Epicharmus onward; it raises questions concerning matter and the continued identity of objects. The question of the central organ, heart or brain, was closely connected with the much discussed question of the seat of the ruling part of the soul, the distinction of nerves and that of different kinds of nerves was of obvious relevance for the explanation of motion and action. Moreover, speculation concerning human physiology had an effect on general physical theory. The theory of pores, e.g., seems to have its origin in the physiology of Alcmaeon and Empedocles, but it was used by Empedocles and later authors to account for mixtures of substances, magnetism, and other natural phenomena outside the human body.

The interest of the philosophers in medicine was not restricted to the theoretical level, though. We shall hardly give much credence to Celsus' claim (prooem 6–7): "At first the science of healing was supposed to be part of philosophy such that both the cure of disease and the contemplation of the nature of things originated with the same authorities, i.e., with those who most needed the cure, since they had weakened the strength of their body by restless thinking and nocturnal vigil. Thus we find that many teachers of philosophy were experts in medicine, the most famous among them being Pythagoras, Empedocles, and Democritus." But it does seem that in the fifth century philosophers became more and more convinced that the new knowledge should be put to practical purpose to improve the lot of the human kind. Thus, Empedocles is said to have brought to an end a plague at Selinus caused by water pollution by diverting two rivers into the river which ran through Selinus to clear its water (Diogenes Laertius VIII, 70). Empedocles himself promises to impart knowledge of all drugs against illness and old age (B 111, 1) and boasts that people come to him to hear the word of healing for all sorts of diseases (B 112, 9–10). Similarly, Democritus must have taken a practical interest in medicine, if indeed he is the author of a treatise on regimen (Diog. Laert. IX, 46). But the interest of philosophers in the practice of medicine presumably also was due to a moral concern for a rational healthy life. This seems fairly clear in the case of Pythagoras and the Pythagoreans who laid so much emphasis on a proper regimen (Diod. Sic. X, 7; Iambl. V.P. 97; 163ff.; Porph. V.P. 34; Diog. Laert. VIII, 19; cf. Plato *Rep.* 600A).

Such, then, was the concern of philosophers for medical questions. But to get a complete picture of the role medical questions and the art of medicine played in philosophy one would also have to talk about the influence that particular medical views and more general philosophical views developed by doctors had on philosophers, and about the role medicine played in philosophy as an example of an art. It is fairly clear, e.g., that Aristotle's views in ethics about the difficulty of finding the mean appropriate to one have their paradigm in the difficulty of the doctor to find the balanced regimen appropriate for the individual patient, an analogy which extends far into the details. But more about the influence the views of doctors had on philosophers will be said later.

To understand the attitude of doctors toward philosophy, we have to distinguish two kinds of doctors. There were the traditional healers who had learned their craft, case by case, as assistants of a doctor. Their status was low, their education negligible, they were just following their craft uncritically, as it had been handed down to them, with no understanding of what they were doing. But, at least from the fifth century onward, there were also carefully trained, sometimes highly educated doctors, who took a critical attitude toward tradition, tried to gain some theoretical understanding and to find new ways of healing, and who, because of their competence and their learning, might enjoy a considerable reputation and command respect (cf. Plato, *Leg.* 720A-C; 857C-D; Arist. *Pol.* 1282ᵃ 3-4). This distinction is a rather crude simplification. For there will have been physicians with very little learning who relied largely on traditional practice, and there will have been traditional practitioners to whom some of the learning and the practice of physicians will, in one way or another, have filtered down. Still, the distinction is clear and marked enough. And what we in the following will be concerned with are the physicians.

Their interest in philosophy was very much part of the very origin of the art of the physician, or scientific medicine. Traditional medicine had suffered from severe limitations. Doctors knew how to handle fractures and dislocations, they also could help with wounds, but they were largely powerless in the case of internal diseases. We rightly admire the 42 case histories of the Epidemics, but the fact is that 26 of them ended with the death of the patient.

Yet these limitations on the doctor's art for a long time were accepted by the public. There were a large number of defenses, which made the limitations seem natural, a given nothing could be done about; e.g., the defense that once the illness has gained mastery over the body, there is nothing anybody can do; there is nothing one can do against the will of the gods; many diseases are hidden from the understanding of human beings; patients are unreliable and weak, do not follow the perhaps arduous and painful treatment prescribed, etc. In the course of the fifth century, however, the educated part of the public became less and less willing to accept these defenses. It now was so obvious that the limitations on the art of the doctor were not just due to the nature of things, but also to a large extent to the fact that doctors did not know things which could be known, that doctors had not made sufficient efforts to overcome the extrinsic limitations of their art. Some people went so far as to argue that there is no such thing as the art of medicine, that the doctor can do no more than what an educated, thoughtful layman could do, and that the rest is mere chance (Art 1ff.; Reg. in morb. acut. 8; vet. med. 4 et passim). In this situation, at least educated doctors naturally felt very threatened. Doctors were regarded with a good deal of distrust and suspicion anyway. Even a good doctor had to make an enormous effort to win the confidence and trust of a clientele, often to no avail. For if his patients died, the public might hold it against him, even if no blame fell on him. Thus, ancient doctors were very hesitant in the first place to take on obviously dangerous cases. This, of course, all the more raised the question of what one needed doctors for. For the harmless cases, one could take care of oneself, or perhaps, rather, they took care of themselves. Nevertheless, the good doctor still had been able to live with the thought that at least *he* knew that he had mastered a complicated and important art, though the public might find it difficult to recognize this and to distinguish him from the incompetent doctor and the quack. But now his very art came under criticism, and it was called into question whether he really had any special expertise. His art had lost the intellectual respect of those by whom the educated doctors wanted most dearly to be respected, and on whom he depended for the kind of living he was accustomed to, the educated elite. For the educated doctor must have been upwardly mobile in social background. Otherwise, he would not have had an education, and certainly would not have been able to pay the fees that the schools of medicine which arose toward the middle of the fifth century were asking. On the other hand, he cannot by background have been part of the upper class. For in this case he would not have practiced medicine, certainly not for a living. Thus, it was exactly the educated doctors who must have felt particularly threatened, whereas the ordinary, traditional healers could continue to rely on an unbroken consensus with the vast uneducated majority of the population, especially in backward areas. This threat provided the motivation for the attempt to reform medicine systematically.

What made it easier for the educated doctor to acknowledge the fact that his art was severely limited and stood in need of reform was a view characteristic of the enlightenment of the later fifth century. On this view, the various arts and crafts had evolved in the course of the history of humankind to enable human beings who originally had been exposed rather helplessly to a hostile environment to gain a secure life, and if one just systematically turned one's reason to it, instead of mindlessly following traditional belief and practice, ever further areas of life would be brought under rational control, and human beings would flourish. Socratic ethics is perhaps the most splendid and extreme reflection of this attitude. Thus, medicine was naturally conceived of as an art that had arisen rather late, but that could be set on the road of firm progress, if one merely put one's mind to it instead of following the traditional practices and beliefs as the ordinary doctors did.

Given the conflicting practices and views of doctors, which now, with increased travel and with the rise of a medical literature, became all the more apparent, it was clear that what was needed was reliable knowledge rather than mere opinion. And given the limitations of the art, owing to ignorance, it was also clear that this knowledge had to be extended systematically, so that in the end it would form an organized body of knowledge which would put one in a position to deal with all disease to the extent that this is humanly possible. The need for such a systematic body of knowledge must have become particularly apparent when, in the new schools of medicine, doctors started to give systematic lectures instead of just teaching their students case by case in the way traditional healers did.

The question, then, was "what is to count as knowledge, and by which method does one manage to systematically arrive at medical knowledge?" Thus a concern for epistemological and methodological questions stood at the very beginning of the new art of the physician. And this all the more so since his art had been called into question to the extent that it had been asked whether there was, or even whether there could be, an art or an expertise to be mastered by the doctor. This concern continued to characterize physicians throughout antiquity. For answers to these questions the physicians naturally turned to the philosophers who themselves in the course of the fifth century had become more and more concerned with epistemological questions and who by the fourth century had developed rather elaborate views of what an organized body of knowledge had to look like and how it would be arrived at.

But from the very beginning there were also physicians who objected to the way in which their fellow-physicians tended to follow the philosophers' methods. Thus, the author of "On Ancient Medicine" criticizes physicians who proceed by the hypothetical method, i.e., postulate certain basic constituents of the body and try to derive the appropriate treatment from the assumption, e.g., of an imbalance between the postulated basic constituents. Against such physicians he claims that medicine has long found its own method, the method of trial and error, that many discoveries have been made by this method, and that on the basis of these discoveries medical knowledge will grow further, if one just follows the method by which medicine has progressed thus far. The new philosophical methods, on the other hand, he claims, do not lead anywhere (chap. 2). Thus, there developed in medicine from the start a tradition of independent thought concerning the origin, nature, and scope of medical knowledge and of knowledge in general. Part of the reason for this was the special situation of medicine. It conceived of itself as a growing subject. For this was the only way in which one could acknowledge the inability of the art in its present state to deal with a large variety of cases, and yet maintain that it was a true and worthy art. Hence, physicians, much more than philosophers, took an interest in methods of discovery. Moreover, whereas the philosophers were mainly concerned with theoretical knowledge, the physicians' concern was eminently practical knowledge, on whose reliability much depended in a very obvious and concrete way. Much more than the philosophers they were concerned with the application of general knowledge to particular cases, especially since most of them took the view that the individuality of each case and of each patient had to be taken into consideration. They reflected on the inherent limits of practical arts; no matter how knowledgeable and skillful a doctor is, he may not achieve his aim for reasons which do not reflect badly on his competence or the state of the art. For the most part, though, they were concerned with the nature of the general practical knowledge which the doctor applies to the particular case. And on the nature of this knowledge they disagreed radically.

Most physicians down to Herophilus and Erasistratus, especially those who followed the philosophers, tended to adopt a Rationalist position, i.e., they thought that reason allowed us to determine the nature of a disease, to find out its cause, and, on the basis of this, to find the kind of treatment which would remove the cause of the disease. Thus, they thought that the practical knowledge the doctor relied on was based on some theoretical knowledge which would enable the doctor to account for his practice. In the extreme case, they looked for a theory from first principles from which these results could be obtained. But many Rationalists, as they came to be called, it seems, took a more cautious position. Diocles, perhaps the most distinguished physician of the fourth century, warned against the temptation to look for this kind of theoretical causal account for everything (Gal. VI, 455; Wellmann frg. 112). For, he said, such knowledge is rarely of practical use; moreover, many facts of nature are primitive, hence have to be accepted as such, and do not allow for derivation from a theory; also, such theories often depend on questionable assumptions. One should, rather, trust what one has learned from experience. Similarly, Herophilus, the first of the great Alexandrian physicians, pointed out that in medicine one often has to take as a given or a principle what in the true nature of things is not a principle (Anon. Lond. xxi, 21; Galen De meth. med. x, 107, 15). Galen even chides Herophilus for refusing to pronounce on the nature of the primary bodies (Gal. De meth. med. X, 461, 17). That Herophilus developed a list of arguments against causality which closely resemble those Diogenes Laertius attributes to the Pyrrhonean skeptics suggests, too, that he had strong doubts about theories of the extreme Rationalist type (Galen, De causis procatarcticis 197ff.). Perhaps the kinds of doubts we find in Diocles and in Herophilus were what had already moved the author of "Nature of Man" (chap. 1) to say that though we need some account of human physiology, we do not in medicine need the kind of questionable account from ultimate principles which the philosophers give.

Nevertheless, all the Rationalists agreed that the mere experience of the practitioners did not suffice to provide the doctor with the practical knowledge he needed. Herophilus and Erasistratus must have argued the point explicitly (Galen De sect. ingr. 9, 14; De meth. med. X, 184; Pliny H.N. xxix, 5, 6). This does not necessarily mean that this view had been explicitly defended by any physicians. Some Sophists and rhetoricians had taken the view that rhetoric is a matter of mere experience (e.g., Polus in Plato's Gorgias). There was, early in the third century B.C., the view that political expertise may be a matter of experience and practice (Philod. Rhet. B, I, 27–28). Plato had characterized the lowly practitioner of medicine as someone who relied only on experience (Leg. 720A–C; 857C–D). And both Plato and Aristotle has argued quite generally that knowledge, properly speaking, i.e., scientific knowledge, had to go beyond mere experience and to advance, by means of reason, to a theoretical understanding of the phenomena.

But the fourth century saw a bewildering proliferation of such medical theories. What was worse, they all seemed to be in conflict with one another, yet there seemed to be no way to decide between them. All had arguments in favor of them, and all had their drawbacks. Moreover, Rationalist medicine had a tendency to become academic and scholastic, a term actually used by Galen to refer to the Alexandrian physicians who no longer cared to look at patients (In Hipp. *De. nat. hom.*, CMG V, 9, 1, p. 88, 1ff.). As we know from another passage in Galen (*De dogm. Hipp. et Platon.* p. 598 M.), Erasistratus had stopped practicing medicine altogether. Presumably he and Herophilus devoted all their efforts to the development of their physiological and anatomical theories and thus turned medicine into an academic subject of great subtlety and complexity (cf. Plin. *H.N.* XI, 219; XXVI, 11). Pliny (*H.N.* XXVI, 11) puts the matter this way: "This celebrated rational discipline, though actual practice is the most efficent teacher of all things, but in particular of medicine, little by little degenerated into mere words and garrulity. For it was more pleasant to sit in school and devote one's time to lectures than to walk in the wild to look for the different herbs at the different times of the year."

It was in reaction to this proliferation of competing theories and the neglect of practice and the experience that accrues from practice that in the first part of the third century a new school of thought arose, the Empiricists, as they called themselves. The Empiricists[1] took the position that all knowledge, and in particular all medical knowledge, is a matter of mere experience which one only acquires in actual practice; experience in the sense that through long observation we come to know what is harmful and what is beneficial. Thus, the Empiricists got themselves into the position where they had to show (a) how experience, as a matter of fact, would account for all medical knowledge, (b) that the Rationalist arguments to the contrary were inconclusive, and (c) that Rationalism did not provide an alternative way to gain medical knowledge.

According to the Empiricist, all the doctor has to know is what is beneficial and what is harmful to a patient. For his aim is to heal, and not to understand. Hence, he does not need a theory that allows him to gain a theoretical understanding of his practice. But what is harmful or beneficial can be known by mere observation of what turns out to harm or benefit people. What is more, the Empiricist, relying on skeptical arguments, denies that the hidden natures and hidden causes, that anything hidden to normal observation, can be known. Hence, he rejects all medical theory, not just the physiologies of the Rationalists, but also the anatomy of Herophilus and Erasistratus. For though the facts of descriptive anatomy in some sense are open to observation, the observation is not normal in that it presupposes an artifical interference with the object to be observed, namely the cutting up of the body which may affect it in a way we have no control over (cf. Celsus, *Prooem.* 40ff.).

Whereas the Rationalists, before the rise of Empiricism, had not seen themselves as a group, and, in fact, continued to disagree among themselves, they were united by being attacked by the Empiricists and by having to rebut the Empiricist arguments against them. Thus, one came to talk of a Rationalist and of an Empiricist school of medicine.

An interesting feature of the debate between the two schools was that it turned out to be rather academic. The Empiricists, apparently more ready to rely on traditional forms of treatment, made more use of drugs, whereas Rationalists tended more to a dietary treatment, but there was no real basic disagreement about the actual practice of medicine (Galen, *De sect. ingr.* 1, 12ff.; 7, 16ff.; 12, 12ff.). The Empiricists did not deny that good Rationalist doctors were good doctors, and they were ready to adopt whatever practice showed promise.

The situation changed when late in the first century B.C. a new school arose, that of the Methodists.[2] The Methodists challenged the practice of Rationalists and Empiricists, claiming that neither had understood by which method one comes to know the right form of treatment. They claimed that all internal diseases were forms of constriction or dilation or both, and hence required the corresponding forms of dilation or constriction or both. To know that constriction requires dilation is obvious to reason and is not something which we just know by experience. But nor is it a matter of theoretical knowledge. With some training, we can learn to directly recognize states of dilation or constriction. They are not theoretical states whose existence we have to infer from the observable symptoms. They themselves are observable. In this way the Methodists tried to find a position of their own between Rationalism and Empiricism. The practical knowledge the doctor relies on is a matter of reason, rather than experience; but it is not a matter of reason in the sense that it is based on some theoretical knowledge which we have a priori or which we acquire by inference from the observable to the unobservable.

Rationalism, Empiricism, and Methodism were the major positions adopted by Hellenistic doctors. Yet Galen, in the second half of the second century A.D., found none of them acceptable. He took the position that experience did suffice to gain knowledge which would make one a competent doctor. But he also thought that if the practical knowledge of the doctor was to be complete, if he was to know all that was practically relevant, he also had to master the theory of medicine (Gal. *De meth. med.* X, 29; 31; 122; 159; 272). For all his stress on, and love for, medical theory, Galen also seems to have lost the often naive trust in theory construction which characterized the Rationalists. He suggests that one should clearly separate the body of knowledge one has acquired by theory-construction from the body of knowledge acquired by experience, because in this way theory can be confirmed by experience (*De meth. med.* X, 31; 127; 159; 246).

Thus physicians developed elaborate accounts of the nature of medical knowledge. But Rationalists, Empiricists, and Methodists also thought that their accounts, mutatis mutandis, applied to human knowledge quite generally. And thus philosophers had to take notice of the epistemological views of the physicians. The first reflection of this are Plato's famous remarks in the *Phaedrus* (270C) about Hippocrates' method. Later it was primarily the Empiricists whom the philosophers took an interest in. The Stoic view of the nature of an art like divination, as it is represented in Cicero's *De divinatione,* seems to be Empiricist. Demetrius Laco (fr. 12 De Falco), Philodemus (*De signis* xxxviii, 25), Cicero (*Ac. pr.* 122), and Sextus Empiricus, of course, (*P.H.* I, 236ff.; *A.M.* VIII, 327) refer to the Empiricists. And the version of Pyrrhonean skepticism that we find in Sextus in some respects, e.g., in the use of the notion of historia, i.e., reports of one's own experience, clearly is influenced by Empiricism.

The first physicians, then, by the very nature of their enterprise started a rich tradition of epistemological thought within the schools of medicine. But because most of them saw the solution to their problem in the development of a medical theory, of a science of medicine, they also got engaged in the philosophy of nature. And again, naturally enough, they turned to the philosophers for an appropriate physical and physiological theory. It has been pointed out often enough and in sufficient detail how much physicians throughout antiquity depended on philosophers for the elements of their physical theory. Some of the authors of the Hippocratic Corpus clearly are influenced by Heraclitus, others by Diogenes of Apollonia. There may be an influence of the Pythagoreans and Democritus. The author of "On Ancient Medicine" (20) himself points to the influence of Empedocles. Those medical theories based on the assumption of four elements clearly are Empedoclean in inspiration; but so, presumably, also doctrines based on the assumption of four basic powers and the doctrine of four humors. Diocles and Erasistratus are influenced by the Peripatus, other Rationalists are indebted to Stoicism, Asclepiades relies on Atomism, the Pneumatists are influenced by the Stoics and in particular Posidonius. But, again, there was, almost immediately, a reaction against the uncritical acceptance of philosophical views. The author of "On Ancient Medicine" went so far as to say that one had to be a doctor to be able to develop an adequate physiology (20). And the author of "Nature of Man" takes the view that medicine cannot rely on the philosophers' physiology, but has to develop its own. It is obvious how much physicians contributed to physiology and anatomy. But it may well be the case that even in the theory of nature in general they had something to contribute and exercised an influence on the history of philosophy. Thus, Asclepiades of Bithynia may well be the first to use the notion of a law of nature (Anon. Lond. 36, 47ff; 39, 5), which is not the law of the nature of a particular kind of thing, but a law that guarantees the uniformity of nature and hence allows us to make inferences from what has been observed to what has not been observed, from what can be observed to what cannot on principle be observed. If it is true, as I think it is, that a passage in Cicero's *De oratore* (I, 62) forces us to assume that his floruit is well into the second century B.C., his great reputation in Rome may well be responsible for the widespread acceptance of Epicureanism in Rome in the first century B.C. It may also be the case that some physicians not only wrote their own physiologies in which they developed their own notions concerning the theory of nature in general, but that they felt confident enough to write their own physical treatises. Thus, Galen refers to a treatise "Physica" in several books by Praxagoras (XVII, 838).

For our purposes, though, it may be more interesting to briefly consider the role of these theories than to look at their details. On the Rationalist view, these theories provided the foundation for the practical knowledge the doctor relied on. But the role medical theories actually played is much more complicated. Given that ancient natural theory was by no means sufficiently developed to allow for the construction of a medical theory which came near to fulfilling the role it was supposed to play, we have to suspect that the great interest in medical theory can hardly have been due only to the expectation that it would greatly improve medical practice. There clearly was a social motivation. As we saw earlier, traditional medicine was no longer intellectually acceptable. And this threatened the position of the educated doctor. Had he been looked at basically just as an artisan, even his artisanship was now called into question. Thus, educated doctors had a strong social motiviation to turn medicine into a scientific subject. It helped them to regain intellectual and thus social respectability. At the same time, this learning helped them to set themselves off from the ordinary, lowly practitioner. And it helped them to distinguish themselves from the class of artisans quite generally. In fact, as we have seen, some of the Alexandrian physicians removed themselves from practice altogether. Moreover, theory played a role in the practice of medicine which was quite independent of the role ascribed to it by Rationalism. The doctor was supposed to give the patient an account of the illness and the proposed treatment. In this way, he tried to convince the patient that he was a competent doctor who knew what he was doing. But just as he tried to give an accurate prognosis, mainly to win the confidence of a clientele and not necessarily for any practical medical purpose, so too he was under considerable pressure to produce a theoretical account, whether or not his treatment actually was based on this account. Already the author of "On Ancient Medicine" (chap. 5) suspected that there was no actual connection between the account the doctor gave and what he then did; if he was a good doctor, he would do what good doctors would do in a similar case, except that he vacuously added a story. The Empiricists similarly claimed that medical theories had been constructed in hindsight after the cures had already been found by experience (Celsus *Prooem.* 36), and that it was this experience which good doctors, even if they were Rationalists, were actually relying on. Similarly, Methodists like Soranus (*Gyn.* p. 4, 7; 6, 6ff.) maintained that one had to know medical theory, not because it provided a reliable basis for sound treatment, but because otherwise patients might think that one was incompetent and because it was a matter of good education. Thus, theory did play, and was recognized to play, a social role. If one reads Galen, especially his criticism of the Methodists, the social function of the physician's learning becomes very apparent. Galen, like many Rationalists, does not think that the doctor should know only the intricacies of medical theory and philosophy, he also thinks that the doctor, for medical purposes, should have some knowledge of the liberal arts, geometry, and astronomy, e.g., which are supposed to have some application in medicine. He is quite aware that the kind of training and education which he received and which he demands from the best doctors is available only to the few who can afford it. It is very clear from his discussion of the Methodists that he deeply resents the fact that they promise to provide an adequate medical training in a short time which does not require any great learning (*De sect. ingr.* 15, 6; 24, 22; *De meth. med.* 10, 5, 2) and thus opens up the profession to what Galen regards as the rabble (*De meth. med.* 10, 4, 17ff.; 5, 9ff.). Again and again he refers to the humble social background of Thessalus, who is the main proponent of Methodism, as if this disqualified Thessalus from taking a critical attitude toward established medicine (*De meth. med.* 10, 8, 17ff.; 10, 5ff.; 11, 7). Soranus, on the other hand, a man, perhaps, of no less education and learning than Galen, is treated by him with respect, though he is a Methodist, too. One can see here very clearly how education is used to draw social boundaries and to protect social status.

In any case, the physicians, for the reasons given, took a great professional interest in epistemology and methodology, or logic as it was then called, and in physics. But they were also concerned with ethics. The distrust of doctors was not just because so many of them were incompetent quacks; doctors also had to fight against a good amount of suspicion against them as human beings. Part of this may have been the primitive fear of the powers of the medicine man. But part of it was no doubt owing to the callous way in which some doctors misused the trust placed in them. There will be good reason why the Hippocratic Oath asks the doctor to promise: "I will use treatment which will benefit the sick to the best of my ability and knowledge, and refrain form injury and injustice. . . . Into whichever house I go, I will enter for the benefit of the sick; I will abstain from any willing injustice or harm, in all other respects and in particular in sexual matters, in the case of female and male bodies, whether they be slaves or free." The doctors defended themselves against such suspicion by adopting a manner and bearing which would instill trust and respect. But they also strove to be rigorously reliable in their moral behavior, or at least to give the public this impression. In this effort they tended to adopt rather conservative ethical views. Thus, the Oath enjoins the doctor not to perform any abortions, though this was standard practice throughout antiquity, accepted even by philosophers like Plato (*Rep.* 460E–461C) and Aristotle (*Pol.* 1335[b] 22ff.), though Aristotle in this context also discusses the question up to which point of the development of the fetus should abortion be legal. Doctors were suspected of greed, and the Corpus Hippocraticum contains a good deal of advice for the doctor about how to deal with the problem of fees. Galen found it very upsetting that the Empiricist Menodotus had claimed that doctors were practicing for reputation and money (*De dogm. Plat. et Hipp.* 764 M.). Doctors liked to see themselves as motivated by philanthropy (*Precepts* 6; *On the Physician* 1; Galen, *De dogm. Plat. et Hipp.* 765 M.)

Given their somewhat insecure status, it was natural that doctors would try to convince the public of the elated worth and dignity of their subject. Thus, the author of *Lex* (1; cf. *Vet. med.* 14) claims that medicine is the most important art. Similarly, the Methodist Thessalus proclaimed the superiority of medicine over all other disciplines (Galen, *De meth. med.* 10, 11, 8). What made this possible was the great value antiquity placed on health. Sextus Empiricus can attribute even to Herophilus the view that health is the highest good; for without health all the other goods are of no avail (*A.M.* XI, 49–50). It may well have been the case that Herodicus of Selymbria not only saw in his dietetics a way to maintain and regain health, but the way to lead a good life. Otherwise, it is difficult to understand why Plato in the *Republic* would criticize Herodicus so sharply. Hence, it may very well be true that some physicians and some philosophers saw medicine and philosophical ethics as rival arts of life. In any case, both their subject and their social situation forced educated doctors to develop moral views concerning their role and practice.

Given all this, it is not surprising that Galen was able to write a whole treatise to show that the best physician will be a philosopher. Already the author of "Decorum" had written (5) that a doctor who is also a philosopher will be godlike. And he had gone on to explain how medicine has all the marks of wisdom. Galen himself, in fact, in his own work did go much beyond a discussion of those topics philosophically minded physicians traditionally had concerned themselves with. He obviously had the ambition to be recognized as a philospher as well. And this recognition he was almost immediately granted, though perhaps somewhat grudgingly. His contemporary, Alexander of Aphrodisias, the greatest of the Aristotelian commentators, devoted monographs to the criticism of some of Galen's philosophical views. Similarly, the later commentators refer to Galen's views on a variety of topics. Galen was not the only physician who managed to acquire a reputation as a general philosopher. Sextus Empiricus, too, was a doctor and a medical author, but is best known for his two extant philosophical works, the "Outlines of Pyrrhonism" and "Adversus Mathematicos," our main sources for Pyrrhonean skepticism. In fact, unlike Galen, Sextus Empiricus does not seem to have made any significant contribution to medicine properly speaking. His distinction as an Empiricist doctor relied entirely on his elaboration of Empiricist doctrine (Ps.-Galen, *Med.* 14, 683, 11ff.). It is clear from his remarks in "Outlines of Pyrrhonism" (1, 236ff.) that he was dissatisfied with the dogmatism of the traditional Empiricist doctrine of the nature of medical knowledge. But the evidence also clearly indicates that he never gave up Empiricism. Thus, the contribution to Empiricism Ps. Galen refers to must have consisted in his attempt to bring Empiricism further into line with Pyrrhonism. In Sextus Empiricus, then, we have a doctor whose reputation rests entirely on his philosophical work which secures him a place in the history of philosophy, whereas he is little more than a name in the history of medicine.

Philosophy and medicine in antiquity were so intertwined that we find philosophers like Alcamaeon of Croton whose fame rests entirely on his contributions to medical theory and doctors like Sextus who were primarily philosophers. As a result of the close connection between the two subjects, there evolved in medicine a rather independent tradition of philosophical thought, mainly concerning the nature of medical knowledge. Unfortunately, this tradition has not received the attention it deserves. Historians of medicine tend to leave it to historians of philosophy. But historians of philosophy tend to overlook it, because it is not part of the history of the philosophy of the philosophers. This is most unfortunate. For in this way a large amount of material which is both of intrinsic interest and of considerable use to historians of philosophy and historians of medicine lies waste.

13

The Ancient Empiricists

It is well known that throughout antiquity the connection between philosophy and medicine was very close. Burnet (*E. G. Ph.*, p. 201n 4) went so far as to claim that from the times of Empedocles onward "it is impossible to understand the history of philosophy . . . without keeping the history of medicine constantly in view." If this sounds like an exaggeration to us, this is partly because that given our very different conception of philosophy and our very different philosophical concerns we do not pay much attention to the surprisingly active interest ancient philosophers did take in physiology, anatomy, and even pathology.

Aristotle claimed: "It is also the task of the natural philosopher to have a view of the first principles of health and disease. Hence most natural philosophers . . . finish by discussing the matters which fall under medicine" (*De Sensu* 436^a 17–21), and again "the most refined philosophers of nature end up by discussing the principles of medicine" (*De resp.* 480^b 28–30). Even much later, in the Post-Posidonian account of Stoic physics in Diogenes Laertius, we are told that of the three subdivisions of the philosophy of nature, namely cosmology, the theory of elements, and etiology (VII, 132), etiology has two parts of which one is the common concern of both the physician and the philosopher. There is no reason to doubt the testimony of Aristotle and the Stoic account of physics. For there is an abundant amount of evidence that ancient philosophers, from the Presocratics onward, did in fact actively concern themselves with medical questions.

It would not do justice to the facts, either, to think that these medical questions were of just peripheral importance to philosophy. A satisfactory account of growth and nutrition, e.g., was thought to involve fairly central metaphysical questions concerning identity, the subject of change, and matter.

Nevertheless, it seems fair to grant that the role of medicine in philosophy, and hence the influence of medicine on philosophy, was rather modest. The role of philosophy in medicine, and hence the influence of philosophy on medicine, on the other hand, can hardly be exaggerated. The debt to philosophy was already acknowledged by ancient historians of medicine, e.g., when they attributed the origin of medicine as a proper discipline to the Presocratics. Thus Celsus tells us (prooem. 6–7): "At first the science of healing was supposed to be part of philosophy such that the cure of diseases and the contemplation of the nature of things was originated by the same authorities, i.e., by those who most needed the cure, since they had weakened the strength of their body by restless thinking and nocturnal vigil. Thus we find that many teachers of philosophy were experts in medicine, the most famous among them being Pythagoras, Empedocles, and Democritus." But though medicine in the fifth century managed to establish itself as an independent discipline, a feat later associated with the name of Hippocrates (cf. Celsus prooem. 8), throughout antiquity it very much remained under the influence of philosophy.

There were in particular two areas in which physicians tended to rely heavily on philosophers for their views, namely physiology and methodology or epistemology. It is true that from an early point onward there were physicians who had misgivings about the way in which physicians relied on philosophy. Thus when the author of "On Ancient Medicine" tells us (cap. II) that medicine long ago found its method through which, over the course of time, many great discoveries were made, and then goes on to say that those who instead proceed by a new method and claim to make discoveries by this new method suffer from delusion, he clearly is referring to physicians who try to turn the traditional art of healing with its own inherent laws of growth and development into a scientific discipline modeled on philosophical conceptions of scientific knowledge. And when the same author objects to physicians who start out by postulating the hot or the cold, the moist or the dry, it is clear that he is criticizing physicians who just adopt a philosophical theory of elements and try to build a physiology on this philosophical theory. For it is apparent from his later remarks that he does not object to physiological theory as such. Thus we see that medicine, as early as the Hippocratic Corpus, tries to establish and maintain its independence from philosophy. But it does not do so by becoming unphilosophical; rather, it insists on its right to have its own philosophical views on physiology and the epistemological character of the art of medicine.

Nevertheless, in physiology physicians always remained very much dependent on philosophers for their basic assumptions. But perhaps even here physicians contributed to the philosophy of nature beyond the narrow confines of human physiology and anatomy. Thus, I wonder whether Asclepiades of Bithynia, a physician of the second part of the second century B.C., may not have been the first to conceive of laws of nature which things, irrespective of their kind, observe (cf. Anonymus Londinensis, col. 39, 5ff.; 36, 48ff., ed. W.H.S. Jones, Cambridge 1947).

There can be no doubt, though, that the physicians had a lot to say about the epistemological nature of the art of medicine and about human knowledge in general, that they had views on this subject which went much beyond anything philosophers had to say on the topic. In fact, the matter assumed such importance in the thought of physicians that in Hellenistic times the schools of medicine divided themselves along epistemological lines into Rationalists, Empiricists, and Methodists. And the thought of physicians seems to have had some influence both on how philosophers conceived of human knowledge and on how the students of other disciplines thought of their subject. Both Epicureans like Demetrius Laco and Philodemus and Academics like Cicero refer to the thought of the Empiricist doctors; it seems fairly clear that Empiricist medicine contributed to the revival of Pyrrhonism in the first century B.C., and the form Pyrrhonean skepticism takes in Sextus Empiricus clearly is influenced by Empiricist medicine; moreover, I suspect that the way Academics and later Stoics conceived of arts and crafts was very much influenced by Empiricism. Dionysius Thrax's famous definition of grammar at the outset of his treatise reflects an Empiricist point of view, as does Varro's introductory remark on the method of agriculture (I, 18, 7). Thus, we find in Greek medicine from the time of the writings of the Hippocratic Corpus down to Galen, and beyond, a rich tradition of philosophical controversy concerning the nature of medical knowledge, which — though very much influenced by the discussions in the schools of the philosophers — nevertheless maintained a high degree of independence and originality and even had some influence on the thought of philosophers and the representatives of other arts and sciences.

Unfortunately, this is a tradition which has not received much attention. As a result, it does not yet seem possible to give an account of it even in rough outline. But I hope it will be possible to gain at least some impression of this tradition by considering in some detail a particularly important part of it: the doctrine of the so-called Empirical school of medicine. The following account of this doctrine is based primarily on a short treatise by Galen ("Subfiguratio empirica," or "An Outline of Empiricism," published by K. Deichgräber in his "Die griechische Empirikerschule." [Berlin, 1965]).

The Empirical school of medicine arose in the first half of the third century B.C. as a reaction against what the Empiricists regarded as the Rationalism of the successors of Hippocrates. These Rationalist physicians thought that medical knowledge, to deserve that name, had to be based on a theory concerning the constitution of the human body, its normal and abnormal states, and the causes of its abnormal states. As a result they produced an ever-increasing number of conflicting theories. Facing the proliferation of such theories and finding no way to decide between them, especially since none of them seemed to recommend itself over the others by its practical consequences, the Empiricists decided to take the position that it was a mistake to assume that medical knowledge had to have its foundation in a medical theory and that one should assume instead that medical knowledge is just a matter of experience.

Now the notion that medical knowledge might be just a matter of experience was not entirely new. Some rhetoricians, like Gorgias's pupil Polus, had taken the position—and presumably had even elaborated on it in some detail—that the art of rhetoric is merely a matter of experience. And Plato in the Laws (cf. 720A–C; 857C–D) had distinguished two kinds of doctors: the physicians who had received a systematical theoretical training and hence would treat patients on the basis of their theoretical knowledge, and doctors who had learned from experience, perhaps by watching real physicians, how to take care of a good variety of medical tasks and cases, without, though, having any theoretical understanding of what they were doing. Thus, already in Plato's time there must have been a distinction somewhat analogous to the distinction in early modern times between physicians and empirics. Now there is no reason to suppose that Plato's empirics tried to develop a conception of medicine according to which medicine is just a matter of experience. But their mere existence and the fact that others, like the rhetoricians noted above, took the view that a discipline might be a matter of mere experience, would be enough to explain why the physicians would develop the negative conception that medicine is not a matter of mere experience. In this they were encouraged by philosophers like Plato and Aristotle and their students, who stressed in no uncertain evaluative terms that a respectable discipline had to have a theoretical understanding of its doctrine and practice. For this reason, it already was an essential part of the position of the Rationalists in reaction against whom Empiricism arose that medicine cannot be just a matter of mere experience and, because of this, has to go beyond experience by means of reason to construct a medical theory which allows us to identify and to explain whatever phenomena of disease we may encounter. And they followed the philosophers in believing that reason allows us to construct such a theory, because reason allows us to make inferences from the observable to the nonobservable and thus to advance beyond the observable world of experience to the underlying nonobservable reality of things.

Thus, the task of the very first Empiricists was twofold: (1) they had to show positively that the art of medicine in fact could just be a matter of experience, and they had to show this in such a way that all the objections, on the basis of which their predecessors thought they had to go beyond experience, were taken care of; (ii) they had to show negatively that the Rationalist attempt to base medical knowledge on theory was a failure, hence that Rationalist medicine was no alternative to Empirical medicine.

The strategy that the Empiricists adopted seems to have been strikingly similar to, though not entirely like that of, the author of "On Ancient Medicine." Very much in the tradition of the cultural anthropology of the fifth and sixth centuries and like the author of "On Ancient Medicine," they constructed a story of the origin of medicine. In fact, they seem to have referred to Herodotus' account of how the sick are treated in Babylon for their reconstruction of the state that would naturally lead to the origin of the art of healing (I, 197; Severus I, 7). This story was supposed to show how human beings naturally were led to make certain observations about what is conducive or detrimental to health, how they would try again and again what had shown itself to be conducive to health, and how from a careful observation of all this there would grow an accumulated experience of sufficient richness and complexity to require people who would pay special attention to these matters, and how the experience of these people would grow, until it would fully account for the competence of the most successful doctors. Like the author of "On Ancient Medicine," they thought that such a story showed that medicine arose and grew, as it were naturally, according to a certain pattern or method, namely by observation of what was tried and by trial of what had been observed, and they concluded that this was the time-proven method to follow in medicine by which it ultimately would be completed, but which arbitrarily had been abandoned by the Rationalists. By carefully analyzing the steps by which experience gets started and grows, they thought they could show that the accumulated experience over a sufficiently long stretch of time would by itself get organized in such a rich and complex way that the claim that the art of medicine is just a matter of experience would no longer be open to at least those Rationalist objections that called in doubt whether experience was sufficient for practical purposes, i.e., for successful healing. Thus the Rationalists had claimed that, given the infinite manifold of experience, we would not without the guidance of reason know what to observe, which features of a situation to focus on. The Empiricist answer now would be that experience itself will tell us over the course of time which features seem to be relevant and which irrelevant, and so experience itself will guide our observation. Objections, on the other hand, which did not question the practical efficacy of experience, did not impress the Empiricists. Thus, they were quite willing to grant that experience does not give us any understanding of why the remedies suggested by experience are effective. But then, they argued, their aim was healing and not understanding. And as long as it could not be shown that this lack of understanding interfered with their effectiveness as practitioners, there was no reason for them to be concerned with it.

Negatively, the Empiricists argued against the Rationalists, again rather like the author of "On Ancient Medicine," that the theories the Rationalists want to base medicine on are entirely speculative, that their truth is hidden and in doubt. But they went further than the author of "On Ancient Medicine" seems to go, when they claimed that all theory has to be rejected since theory by its very nature makes reference to entities and states which cannot be observed, and since we cannot have any knowledge of such nonobservable entities and states. Thus, they rejected any kind of physiology. But somewhat to our surprise, they also rejected anatomy, which had made such enormous progress under their immediate predecessors Herophilus and Erasistratus and which we might conceive of as an empirical enterprise. But the Empiricists argued that we cannot observe from a dead body the facts about a living body and that the very dissection of a living body would interfere so much with its state that one could not observe from it the facts about an ordinary living body, let alone a normally functioning living body.

It is clear that in rejecting assumptions about what cannot be directly observed the Empiricists were relying on some kind of skepticism. Traditionally, it has been assumed that they were relying on Pyrrhonean skepticism. For later Empiricists quite explicitly based their position on Pyrrhonism. Since it makes a considerable difference to the way we reconstruct their positive doctrine of experience whether in fact they subscribed to what came to be known as Pyrrhonean skepticism, it is important to briefly consider this question. It seems to me that the early Empiricists clearly were not Pyrrhonists, if by Pyrrhonism we mean the kind of position espoused by Aenesidemus in the first century B.C. and later authors like Sextus Empiricus. For the early Empiricists seem to simply espouse a dogmatic extreme skepticism concerning reason. Whereas the Pyrrhonists insist that it is an open question whether what is not observable can be known by reason, the early Empiricists flatly deny the ability of reason or anything else to grasp what is not observable. But their position is even more extreme. Whereas the Pyrrhonists insist that human beings are rational, that there is a natural, proper use of reason as much as there is a natural use of the senses, the early Empiricists seem to go out of their way to avoid having to acknowledge any legitimate use of reason in the acquisition of medical knowledge, even if this involves them in utter implausibility. Thus Galen in *De methodo medendi* (K. 10, 164) reports how the Empiricists maintain that some composite drugs were found by accident, perhaps because someone accidentally poured the ingredients together and then the mixture got administered, when in fact it is so obvious that the composite owes its origin to the fact that someone figured out that, as the ingredients all individually have the same effect – though some are much more effective on some persons and others more effective on others – their composition in one drug would greatly increase the chance of effectiveness. Thus, the early Empiricists do not just deny that reason puts us in a position to know what is not observable, they deny that reason puts us in a position to know anything, whether observable or nonobservable; they deny that reason plays any substantive role in the acquisition of knowledge. It seems to me that this point deserves emphasis. For, since later Empiricists will acknowledge a use of reason in the acquisition of knowledge (cf. Galen, *Subfiguratio emp.* 87, 23ff.; 50, 3, ed. Deichgräber) and Rationalists increasingly recognize the importance of experience, it becomes more and more difficult to draw the contrast between Empiricism and Rationalism. At this early point, owing to the extreme position the early Empiricists take, the contrast is very clear and simple. Finally, unlike the Pyrrhonists, the early Empiricists do not show a trace of skeptical reservation concerning the faculties by means of which we do, according to them, attain knowledge, namely the senses and memory. This lack of reservation concerning the knowability of the observable, of course, is just the counterpart of their dogmatism concerning the unknowability of the unobservable. Thus, I conclude that the early Empiricists were not Pyrrhonean skeptics. They used a battery of skeptical arguments against reason to come to the unskeptical conclusion not only that theory-building is an empty and vain enterprise, but also that any use of reason is to be avoided. The conclusion that the early Empiricists were not Pyrrhoneans, though they relied on some form of skepticism concerning the unobservable, is not that surprising, since it is just a welcome confirmation of the suspicion one may have anyway, namely the suspicion that what is called Pyrrhonean skepticism is not what it pretends to be and what it is usually taken to be, namely a revival of Pyrrho's skepticism, but, rather, a fabrication of the first century B.C. The early Empiricists cannot have been Pyrrhonean skeptics, since at their time Pyrrhonean skepticism did not yet exist.

If we assume that the early Empiricists rejected any claim that reason plays a role in the acquisition of knowledge, we may also have to conclude that the positive account of medical knowledge which is standardly attributed to the Empiricists in general only characterizes the school at a later stage. According to this account, medical experience has three components or sources: (i) autopsy (i.e., one's own observations and the experience that has arisen from them); (ii) history (i.e., the reports others have given of their observations and experience); (iii) the transition from the similar to the similar. Intuitively the idea behind this scheme is simple: a competent doctor by and large will know from his own experience what to do in a case of disease. But there will be diseases that he himself does not have any experience with. In this case he will resort to history, i.e., to the observations and experience of others, as we find them recorded in the medical literature.

It may be remarked here, incidentally, that the Empiricists later developed a complex doctrine concerning the reliability of the reports of others, that they found Hippocrates to be singularly reliable, that they were among the first to write commentaries on Hippocrates and thus greatly contributed to the establishment of Hippocrates not just as a medical authority but also as an object of philological scholarship. And it should also be noted in passing that the fact that the Empiricist is supposed to take into account the observations and experience of others does affect his position in the following way: whatever successful remedies the Rationalists may have managed to think up will become integrated into the experience of the Empiricist so that *his* medical knowledge of the remedy would be a matter of experience, even if it were true that it had been discovered by reason. Thus, the question how remedies actually were first found took on some importance. But on this question the Empiricist was in a relatively secure position. The actual historical facts about the discovery of a remedy would be difficult to ascertain. Moreoever, even the early Empiricist could easily grant that some discoveries were made by the use of reason, as long as it was understood that it is just by accident that reason sometimes hits upon a remedy, just as, according to the Empiricist, it happens that people quite literally dream up remedies which prove to be successful. But just as nobody would suggest that we should rely on dreams in medicine just because occasionally we dream of a remedy that proves successful, we should not assume either that we can rely on reason just because reason occasionally makes a correct suggestion. Even when reason is useful, it is not the use of reason, but experience, which turns the suggestions of reason into reliable knowledge. What the Rationalists would have to show is that such discoveries by reason are not accidental, that there is a use of reason which by its very nature guarantees the reliability or even truth of the conclusions we come to.

As we have seen, then, the Empiricist doctor relies on his autopsy; and for cases in which he has no experience, on history, the experience of others. But what happens if the doctor comes across a case for which there is no experience? Neither observation nor the experience based on it, either one's own or somebody else's, will give one any clue about how to deal with such cases. Now the doctrine that later Empiricists clearly come to adopt at this point is the view that the Empiricist will use the "transition from the similar to the similar": for the new disease he will appropriately adapt the treatment for that disease in his experience which comes closest, is most similar, to the new disease. The question is whether this procedure is legitimized by the position of the early Empiricists. And it seems clear that it is not legitimized by that position. For no amount of observation of cases of disease by itself will suggest this procedure. It is true that experience may justify the procedure in the sense that we might learn from experience that it is a good thing to proceed by transition from the similar to the similar, and this clearly is the position that the later Empiricists take. But this experience no longer is an experience based on observation of cases of disease, but, rather, an experience based on observation of how one proceeds in unfamiliar cases. And the early Empiricists do not only not seem to have made any provisions for how this kind of experience would get started, they also do not seem to have the appropriate notion of observation. For when they talk about observation, they obviously are thinking of perception, whereas the observation of how one proceeds in unfamiliar cases seems to be a much more complex matter. And it seems fairly clear that this kind of observation and the experience based on it could arise only from some rational reflection. One might either reflect on one's experience and notice that similar diseases are cured by similar treatments and hence test this assumption in unfamiliar cases and thus start to acquire the experience that would justify the procedure. Or, upon facing an entirely new case, one might by reflection arrive at the conclusion that the way to proceed may be by choosing the treatment for a similar disease or an appropriate modification of it. But, as we have seen, the early Empiricists do not allow for such rational reflection in their reconstruction of medical knowledge.

Now it is surely no accident that later Empiricists raised the question whether Serapion, who seems to have been the first Empiricist to write about Empiricism, did regard the transition to the similar along with autopsy and history as a constitutive source of medical knowledge (on this and the following, compare Galen, *Subfiguratio emp.* 49, 23ff. ed. Deichgräber). Menodotus answered the question in the negative. And Cassius is supposed to have written a whole book to show that Serapion not only did not appeal to the transition to the similar as a constitutive principle of Empiricist medicine, but did not even make use of it. Since we may assume that Serapion's writings were still available to later Empiricists, we have to assume that the transition to the similar did not occur in Serapion's account of the constitution of medical knowledge. Hence, we may conclude that the doctrine of the transition to the similar was a later addition to Empiricist doctrine.

We can, incidentally, infer from a passage in Philodemus' *Rhetoric* (BI, 27–28; cf. Usener, *Epicurea*, fr. 47) that at the beginning of the third century B.C. one finds the conception that rhetoric and politics are a matter of experience which comes about from personal experience (tribe) and history. If it is true, as I suggested above, that the rhetoricians' conception of rhetoric served as a model for the Empiricist conception of medicine, it would fit this picture if the Empiricists started out by assuming, like the rhetoricians, two sources of medical knowledge, experience and history.

We can still see why the early Empiricists may have thought that autopsy and history sufficed to account for the medical knowledge of a competent doctor. In Hellenistic times, the question whether there are any new diseases received wide attention; it even became a topic of one of Plutarch's Table-Talks (VIII, 9). The early Empiricists may have gone on the assumption that given just enough time all diseases and remedies against them would be covered by history.

Now modern accounts of Empiricism might give one the impression that with some minor variations there was basically one doctrine to which all Empiricists adhered. We have already seen that this impression would be quite mistaken. Empiricism seems to have undergone considerable changes between the time of its origin in the third century B.C. and its abandonment in the third century A.D. I am not in a position to trace this evolution of Empiricist doctrine, but I am now convinced that Empiricism became radically transformed under the growing influence of Pyrrhonism in the Empirical school of medicine. It is difficult to state when this transformation started. If it is true, as is usually assumed, that the famous Empiricist physician Heraclides of Tarentum is identical with the teacher of the philosopher Aenesidemus, who gave Pyrrhonean skepticism its detailed form, the process may have started as early as 100 B.C. with Heraclides of Tarentum. It certainly was in full progress in the second century A.D., when the main representatives of the Empirical school of medicine, Menodotus, Theodas, and Sextus Empiricus, at the same time were the main representatives of Pyrrhonean skepticism. It is this transformation of traditional Empiricism in the light of Pyrrhonean skepticism which I take the author of Ps.-Galen's *Isagage* (K. 14, 683, 11ff.) to refer to when he concludes his very brief account of the history of the Empirical school by saying that Menodotus and Sextus greatly strengthened it.

Thus one can draw on Sextus's surviving philosophical works to reconstruct the position of this later Pyrrhonean Empiricism. Before we can do so, though, we have to face an objection. Sextus Empiricus in the Outlines of Pyrrhonism claims that it is a mistake to identify the position of the Pyrrhonists with the position of the Empiricists, and he even goes so far as to claim that the doctrine of the Methodical school of medicine is more in line with skepticism than that of the Empirical school. This passage has always puzzled commentators enormously. It has been suggested that Sextus was not an Empiricist, or that he turned Methodist. The explanation seems to me to be simple. Sextus was highly critical of the traditional position of the Empirical school of medicine and did think that it needed thorough revision. We know from Sextus's own testimony (*A.M.* I, 61) that he did write a work on Empirical medicine in which he discussed epistemological questions. And tradition from an early point onward recognized his contribution to the development of Empiricist doctrine. Hence, the name "Empiricus" already in Diogenes Laertius, his mention in Ps.-Galen's *Isagage* in the first part of the third century A.D. as a prominent exponent of Empiricism, his almost invariable appearance on short lists of important empiricists in various medical treatises, and his mention in Agathias (II, 29, 7) as an exponent of skeptical empiricism, as if this were a particular brand of empiricism.

Now, if we follow Sextus, it seems that the narrow notions of observation as perception and experience as based on perception that we find in the early Empiricists get embedded in a wider notion of experience. In Sextus the notion of an ordinary life and of what is conducive to an ordinary life plays a considerable role; and so does the notion of a general experience of what is conducive and what is detrimental to this life. And this notion of life-experience in turn is embedded in a much more sophisiticated version of skepticism than we find in the early Empiricists. To put the matter in a nutshell: the Pyrrhonean follows what appears to him to be the case without committing himself to the view that what appears to him to be the case actually is the case. What appears to him to be the case, among other things, depends on what his life-experience suggests. Life-experience suggests to him that one should do medicine very much in the way the early Empiricists suggest. But there is a difference in detail, and there is a difference in the account of the detail. It is these differences that largely account for the change from early Empiricism to later Pyrrhonean Empiricism.

Perhaps the best way to approach Pyrrhonean Empiricism is to ask how a Pyrrhonean skeptic can have an epistemology in the first place. Skeptics, after all, are supposed to think that we do not know anything; worse still, Pyrrhoneans are supposed to be extreme skeptics who not only reject claims to knowledge, but even think that any belief is unworthy of a proper skeptic; a Pyrrhonean is supposed to suspend judgment on any question whatsoever. Hence, it will seem that it is difficult enough to see how a Pyrrhonean could maintain his skepticism in ordinary life if he invariably has to suspend judgment; to maintain that a Pyrrhonean consistently could entertain scientific, e.g., medical, beliefs, is to stretch credulity to the extreme. To assume, then, that according to the Pyrrhonean there is such a thing as knowledge, and in particular such a thing as medical knowledge, to assume, moreover, that it is possible for a Pyrrhonean to have a detailed view of what medical knowledge may consist would seem to commit one to an indefensible position.

It seems to me, though, that the assumption that any form of an Empiricist account of knowledge is incompatible with Pyrrhonean skepticism rests on a misunderstanding of Pyrrhonism and of ancient skepticism in general. There is no reason why Pyrrhoneans should not formulate a view of how, as a matter of their experience, people in ordinary life or in some field of special expertise come to have such beliefs that they can be said to know, in the ordinary sense of the word.

The Pyrrhonean position is the following: it seems that we just cannot help the fact that certain things appear to us to be the case and that we thus, with more or less confidence, take them to be the case. This just seems to be a fact of human life. Similarly, it just seems to be a fact that often the question arises whether what appears to be the case actually is the case and that hence we give the matter further consideration. It may, e.g., be of considerable importance to us whether our impression is correct, and yet our confidence in our impression may be very low. In such a situation, we may well be driven to give the matter further consideration. Now there are two ways in which we might give the matter further consideration. We might treat the question whether what appears to be the case actually is the case as an ordinary question to be settled by ordinary means, i.e., by the procedures we use in ordinary life to settle such questions, e.g., by having another look, by reading up on it, by asking other people, by consulting experts, etc. There is a whole array of such procedures which, as a matter of fact, people ordinarly follow. And ordinarily they follow such procedures until they feel sufficiently confident that their impression is correct. And what degree of confidence they are satisfied by depends, among other things, on the importance they attach to the matter. Thus, as a matter of fact, there seems to be a whole pattern of cognitive behavior that people ordinarily follow and that we could study by merely observing what people do. Experience suggests that following these procedures is conducive to life; hence, following them is a matter of life-experience. And this, presumably, is why people ordinarily follow these procedures.

But then there are also some people, namely philosophers, who at least some of the time are unwilling to follow the ordinary pattern of cognitive behavior. They have a curious attachment to truth which makes them place such importance on whether their impressions are correct that they go on to consider a matter long after everybody else has stopped and acquiesced in whatever view he may have arrived at. Now some of these philosophers realize that however far one goes in following these ordinary cognitive procedures and however diligently one follows them they do not guarantee the truth of the view one arrives at. If one is just willing to push far enough, there is always another way to look at the matter; however much consideration one may have given to it, there always seem to be further questions one could raise, the answer to which could change one's mind.

This may be just how things, as a matter of fact, are. But the philosophers, given their curious attachment to truth, find it difficult to acquiesce in such a view. It crosses their mind that the reason why we think about the world the way we ordinarily do may just be because we follow these ordinary cognitive procedures, and that the world in reality may be quite different. And it now seems to them not only that our ordinary cognitive practice does not really settle a question like whether Socrates is standing still or is in motion, but that to answer such a question we first of all have to ask ourselves whether there are such things as motion and rest, whether there are objects like Socrates.

This extra-push for truth has the curious effect that truth now seems to be further removed than ever. The new questions raised cannot be effectively answered by using our ordinary cognitive procedures. For they were raised to explore the possibility that our ordinary cognitive practice may be radically misleading. The philosophers who raise them know that the answer to the question whether there is motion is "yes," if we follow our ordinary practice. For we have ordinary ways to find out whether something is in motion; and given these ways, we know that there is motion. Similarly, our philosophers will not be impressed by the suggestion that we have ordinary procedures to find out whether the thing in front of us is our right hand and that, given these procedures, we know that there are external objects. For these philosophers raise these questions because they have come to wonder not just whether our ordinary procedures ever guarantee the truth of their results, but whether they are not radically and systematically misleading.

For this reason they are naturally led to look for a new procedure to settle such questions. And some of them, namely the dogmatic philosophers, actually think they have found such a method; though different philosophers take different views on what this method, this new philosophical procedure to settle questions, may be, they all agree that it involves a certain use of reason. Hence, this method is called the rational method. And on the basis of this rational method they develop theories of how things really are, which puts them into a position to criticize our ordinary views which are the result of our ordinary cognitive procedures. And since the new method provides us with a true standard on how things really are, these philosophers reserve the term "knowledge" for those beliefs that are certified by the new method.

Some philosophers, though, namely the skeptics, question whether such a rational method has been found. They recognize the possibility that in any particular case the conclusion our ordinary cognitive practice leads us to may be false. They also recognize the possibility that the world may be quite different from what, given our ordinary cognitive practice, it appears to be. They also recognize the possibility that there may be a method that allows us to determine how things really are. What they do not accept is the claim that such a method has been found.

Hence, the skeptic does not see any acceptable alternative to our ordinary cognitive practices. Thus, he acquiesces in following them and in accepting the views they lead him to, though he is quite aware of the fact that they may not just be plainly and straightforwardly false, but that they might be radically misguided because in reality things might be entirely different from what we ordinarily conceive them to be. His life-experience makes him follow these procedures in spite of his skepticism about their outcome, because there is no alternative way to follow.

Now it is part of our practice to mark the fact that a view has been arrived at by following certain cognitive procedures in a certain way by speaking of knowledge. Experience suggests that this practice is conducive to life. And the skeptic sees no reason not to follow this practice, as long as it is understood that in marking certain beliefs as being a matter of knowledge he is not excluding the possibility that they are false or even radically false.

In this sense, the Pyrrhonean, in perfect consistency with his skepticism, can study, analyze, and describe the ways by means of which we attain knowledge, and he can study by observation the particular way in which one in fact does acquire some body of technical knowledge or expertise, e.g., medical knowledge. He can even think of new ways to attain knowledge, if experience can show that they are conducive to life. Given the dogmatism of early Empiricism and the a priori character of certain modern Empiricist doctrines, it might deserve emphasis that the Pyrrhonean Empiricist's conception of knowledge and of how we attain knowledge is itself supposed to be merely a matter of experience. We observe how people have come and still do come to attain knowledge, and under which conditions it is thought that knowledge has been attained. The difficulty which the Empiricist runs into, though, is that in medicine, as in many other disciplines, there is no agreement about what constitutes technical knowledge and by which procedures one attains it. And the reason for this is that most of the major physicians have espoused the rational method. Relying on some version or other of this method, they have constructed medical theories that are supposed to show what the true reality underlying the phenomena of disease is, and they claim to derive their knowledge of how to treat patients from these theories. Now it is exactly because they profess to derive their theoretical claims by the philosophical method that the skeptic can subject these claims to theoretical knowledge to skeptical criticism; and since they do not stand up to this criticism, he does not have to consider them in his account of how one arrives at medical knowledge. What is then left to account for is the concrete knowledge how to treat patients, the knowledge that gets directly applied to particular cases. Those who engage in medical theory claim to derive this knowledge from their theories. Or rather, given their view of medical knowledge, this concrete knowledge that they apply in practice should be derived from their theories.

But closer consideration shows that this knowledge which they actually make use of in treating patients is exactly the same knowledge which the Empiricists rely on and which the Empiricists claim to derive from experience. Moreover, it turns out that this knowledge can be accounted for by our ordinary cognitive behavior very much along the lines suggested by the Empiricists. Hence, the natural conclusion is that we do not need these theories to arrive at medical knowledge, and that what makes this medical knowledge knowledge is not that it is derived from theory, but rather that it is covered in the appropriate way by our ordinary cognitive behavior. In fact, one has to have the suspicion that the Rationalists did not arrive at the medical views they apply in practice by deriving them from their theory, but that they, in fact, acquire these views by experience and only afterward make up the theories.

Given all this, it is fairly clear which direction a Pyrrhonean revision of Empiricism will take. First, the Pyrrhoneans do agree that medical knowledge is a matter of experience. But they will analyze the ways in which we come to have the experience which constitutes our medical knowledge in terms of their analysis of our ordinary cognitive behavior. Or, more generally, of cognitive behavior proven by experience. And since they assume that the use of reason does play an important role in our ordinary cognitive behavior, they will also make room for the use of reason in their account of medical experience. They do agree with the earlier Empiricists that the use of reason by itself does not give us medical knowledge, but they insist that experience shows that a proper use of reason does allows us, e.g., to find new remedies, not by supplying us with the knowledge that a certain treatment will help, but supplying us with a reasonably reliable conjecture which then needs to be confirmed by the outcome of the treatment. Second, the Pyrrhonean will take a skeptical attitude toward this empiricist knowledge which seems to be quite lacking in early Empiricists. Third, the Pyrrhonean Empiricist will have a different attitude toward medical theory. The attitude of the early Empiricist toward theory seems to be entirely negative. They reject the use of reason, and they dogmatically claim that theoretical truths cannot be known. The Pyrrhonean Empiricist, on the other hand, does allow for the use of reason, he does not reject the possibility that reason may advance beyond appearances and that we may come to find a rational method that allows us to know theoretical truths. It is just that he thinks that such a method has not been found and that the theoretical claims advanced in philosophy or in medicine are not known to be true either by the standards of the purported new method or by our ordinary standards of knowledge. Thus, Pyrrhonean Empiricists, unlike the early Empiricists, allow for the possibility that there may be a true theory of how things really are which one day we may discover.

At first sight, it might seem that this admission of the possibility of theory is a purely abstract move designed to guard the Pyrrhonean against the charge of dogmatism. And it has always been assumed that the Pyrrhoneans in practice are as anti-theoretical as the early Empiricists. This may be true. But there is one fact that makes one wonder. It is generally agreed that the Pyrrhonism of later antiquity was a position first formulated in detail by Aenesidemus in the first century B.C. Now there are a good number of passages in which Sextus attributes highly theoretical positive philosophical views to Aenesidemus. In contexts like this, Sextus tends to talk of Aenesidemus as "Aenesidemus in accordance with Heraclitus." Apparently, Aenesidemus had developed some curious form of Heracliteanism, and when Sextus wants to talk about these views of Aenesidemus rather than about his skepticism, he refers to "Aenesidemus in accordance with Heraclitus." Commentators have had great difficulties fitting Aenesidemus' Heracliteanism into a plausible picture of Aenesidemus' philosophical development. They invariably assume that Aenesidemus cannot have been a Pyrrhonean and at the same time held some Heraclitean view. This now seems to me to be a mistake. The Pyrrhonean is committed to the view that we have no way to settle such theoretical questions. Unlike the later Academics, against whom he is reacting in this respect, he is also committed to the position that there is no way in which we could be justified in thinking that such a theoretical view was at least likely to be true or sufficiently like the truth. Recognizing all this, a Pyrrhonean may, nevertheless, feel inclined, as a matter of sheer speculation, toward one theoretical view rather than another. We have to take into account that the attitude of the Pyrrhonean Empiricist toward medical theory was not an abstract, dogmatic negative one that dismissed all theory without consideration. To start with, the Pyrrhonean, given his attitude toward history, had to carefully read all the medical literature anyway. Moreover, he had to take the theories proposed in it seriously, at least to the extent which would put him into the position to show in the case of each single theory that it was not known to be true. Further still, he was committed to an open-minded consideration of each new theory; for all he knew, the next theory he encountered might be true and might turn out to be known to be true. Thus a Pyrrhonean, because of his skepticism toward medical theory, would be as thoroughly familiar with medical theory as any Rationalist physician could be. And there seems to be nothing to exclude the possibility that a Pyrrhonean, thoroughly familiar with medical theories, might find himself attracted by some particular theory.

At this point, the parallel to Methodist medicine may be instructive. The Methodists, like the Empiricists, reject medical theory. Medical treatment, they argue, should be safe and hence based on knowledge and not on speculation. They then use skeptical arguments to show that medical theory is a matter of speculation and not of firm knowledge. To our surprise, though, we find that one of the most distinguished Methodists, Soranus, does write treatises on physiology and even on the soul. Scholars assume that by the time of Soranus skepticism must have lost its grip on Methodism. Closer consideration, though, shows that Methodists all along had no qualms about entertaining elaborate physiological theories. Obviously the position of the school all along was that it was perfectly all right to engage in medical theory as long as one realized that this was sheer speculation and did not base one's practice on it.

Thus, we could imagine that Pyrrhonean Empiricists similarly entertained medical theories and engaged in medical theorizing. Unfortunately, there is not much evidence to justify such a conclusion. There is, though, the curious fact that Sextus, like the Methodists Antipater and Soranus, wrote a treatise on the soul (*A.M.* VI, 55, X, 284). Though this may have been purely critical of the assumption of the existence of souls and of particular theories of the soul and the vital functions, there is no parallel to such a treatise in the Empirical or the Skeptical tradition. Hence, it might very well be inspired by similar Methodist treatises, which after a skeptical consideration of the topic seem to have gone on to develop a speculative positive view of the matter. And it is also clear that Heraclides, who acknowledged a use of reason, did have elaborate theoretical views (cf. Cael. Aur. Ac. I, 166; 181; II, 53; III, 45; 169).

But even if further study did show that Pyrrhonean Empiricists took a positive interest in medical theory, which led them to formulate medical theories, it is not clear whether they would have been willing and able to find an adequate account for such theories in their account of knowledge. This is a problem which not just the Empiricists faced. For it seems that the Empiricists were so effective in their criticism of medical theory that the physicians' confidence in theory was seriously undermined. But the effect of this was not that medical theory was given up altogether. It, rather, was that physicians were looking for a new account of the role of theory. We have already seen that the Methodists were unwilling to base medical practice on medical theory, and yet did go on to entertain theoretical views in medicine, without being able, though, to give a satisfactory account of the role of these theories. Soranus, e.g., claimed that one had to know medical theory as a matter of education and because otherwise people would doubt one's competence as a physician. Celsus thought that medical theory is not part of the art of medicine, because medical practice should not be based on something as uncertain as medical theory; but he also thought that a good physician should know medical theory because it stimulates his mind (prooem. 47). Even Galen's trust in theory was undermined at least to the extent that he thought that wherever possible the findings of theory should be confirmed by experience.

Now the reason for this state of affairs seems to be that the body of knowledge physicians actually relied on in their practice, on the one hand, and medical theory, on the other, never linked up in an appropriate way. The body of empirical knowledge doctors actually relied on was so rich that a theory to account for the facts, or the assumptions actually relied on, would have had to be extremely rich. But antiquity was not in a position to construct a rich enough theory. Instead, we get theories which are sufficiently vague, abstract, and general to avoid conflict with the known or assumed facts, but which for that reason also have very little impact on the growth of medical knowledge and hence little to recommend themselves over any number of rival theories of equal vagueness and generality. It is this poverty of available medical theory compared to the wealth of empirical knowledge which explains why physicians had such difficulty in conceiving a proper role for theory, once their confidence in Rationalistic science had been undermined.

A passage in Sextus Empiricus gives us a clear indication of how theory could have been given a positive role even in Pyrrhonean Empiricism. Sextus, when he turns to the criticism of astronomy (*A.M.* V, 1–2), tells us that he is not objecting to "the ability to predict which one finds in the followers of Eudoxus and Hipparchus and their likes, which some also call astronomy. For it, like agriculture and navigation, is constituted by observation of the phenomena, which allows one to predict droughts and rainstorms, plagues and quakes, and other changes of this kind in the environment." It is of little importance for our purposes that Sextus seems to have a rather curious notion of the predictive power of Eudoxus' or Hipparchus' astronomy; presumably, his remarks are rather inspired by the last part of Aratus' Phainomena. What is of interest, rather, is that Sextus does allow for some kind of theory if it puts us in a position to make predictions.

One feature that Pyrrhonean Empiricists stress in their discussion of experience, history, and the transition to the similar is that these factors have an effect on our expectation that a certain treatment will be beneficial. They do not just raise or lower it, they also make it more reliable, i.e., their combination allows us to make the most reliable predictions about whether a certain treatment will have the desired effect. And it is because experience shows that this is so that the Pyrrhonean Empiricist bases his treatment on his own experience, history, and the transition to the similar. If, then, experience showed that there was a use of reason, namely theoreticizing, which improved the reliability of our expectations and thus was conducive to life, it would be just a matter of following life-experience to start to engage in theoreticizing. And if experience showed that such theories had to take a certain form to increase the realiability of our expectations, the Pyrrhonean Empiricist would start to construct theories of this kind. And this would be perfectly compatible with his thorough-going skepticism concerning reason, just as it is perfectly compatible with his thorough-going skepticism concerning the senses that he patiently observes medical cases. Thus, there would seem to be a place for theory in Pyrrhonean skepticism. The question is whether the Pyrrhoneans saw it this way. So far we have not been able to find the answer. But one may hope that by following the time-proven method of just going on looking, consulting the observations and experience of others, and by considering similar cases like that of the Methodists we still may come up with a positive answer.

14

The Method of the So-Called
Methodical School of Medicine

I. Introduction

Later antiquity, as a rule, distinguishes three schools of medicine, the Rationalists, the Empiricists, and the Methodists (cf. Galen, *De sect. ingr.*, chs 1 and 6; ps.-Galen, *De optima secta,* I, 118ff. Kühn; but also cf. ps.-Galen, *Def. med.* 14–17, XIX 353 K).[1] What is at issue between these schools is the nature, origin, and scope of medical knowledge. Usually their views on this matter are based on views about human knowledge in general; Rationalists, Empiricists, and Methodists in medicine tend to be Rationalists, Empiricists, or Methodists concerning human knowledge and science quite generally (for the Methodists cf. Galen, *De sect. ingr.* 14, I Marquardt). But it is only medicine they are immediately concerned with, and hence they argue their case only for medical knowledge.

In medicine the issue came to take the form of the question 'How does the doctor, in a particular case, know how the patient is to be treated?' And one particular way this question was formulated was the following: 'Which is the correct method of treatment?' (cf. Galen's *De methodo medendi*). Obviously 'method of treatment' here does not mean the way one treats a patient, but rather the way in which one arrives at a certain treatment, i.e., the way one come to think, or arrives at the conclusion, that a certain treatment is the right treatment. This is the sense in which what was at issue was the method. And accordingly one talked of a rational method and an empirical method. For the Empiricists claimed that it is all a matter of experience, that it is by experience that we have the general knowledge we have, and that it is from experience that we know what to do in a particular case. The Rationalists, on the other hand, claimed that it is, at least in part, by reason that we have the general knowledge we have and hence know what to do in a particular case (Gal. *De sect. ingr.* I, 12ff. M). In part they thought so because they assumed that professional medical practice had to be based on scientific theory and that a scientific theory had to account for the phenomena in terms of the underlying reality and that this reality included hidden natures, causes, and actions, not open to observation, but only accessible to reason, e.g., atoms, invisible pores, functions of organs, or essences. Thus the rational method involves the knowledge of truths about nonobservable items which can be obtained only by reason (Gal. *De. sect. ingr.* 4, 18ff. M).

Methodism arises in the first century A.D. in reaction to both Empiricism and Rationalism. It is a movement of radical reform. The dispute between Rationalists and Empiricists, at least by this time, is somewhat academic; Galen sometimes even tells us (*De sect. ingr.* I, 12; 7, 16; 12, 12) that they agree on the treatment, though they disagree on the method which leads to this treatment. We shall hesitate to accept Galen's claim that they agree on the treatment. For we know from Galen's own writings that there were significant differences in their approach to therapy. But presumably in the *De sectis* Galen tries to minimize the practical differences between the established schools of the Rationalists and the Empiricists to be in a position to characterize the innovations of the Methodists as wanton, unasked for, irresponsible departure from the established, respectable practice of traditional medicine. In any case, in the *De sectis* he goes on to claim that the Methodists, on the other hand, do not just disagree on the method, but also object to the actual medical practice of Rationalists and Empiricists (*De sect. ingr.* 12, 13ff.; 15, 25ff.). And they object to their practice precisely because, in their view, it is fundamentally misguided by a wrong method, basically flawed by the lack of the true method (Gal. ibid. 12, 9ff.). They conceive of themselves as finally putting medical practice on a firm, solid, reliable basis by providing medicine with a safe, simple, scientific method. They just call it 'the method' (Celsus, *prooem.* 57), and themselves 'the methodical ones' (Gal. *De sect. ingr.* 12, 9; *De meth. med.* X 76, 2; 380, 5 K). The following is an attempt to characterize the new method advocated by the methodical school at least in rough outline.

Medicine, as conceived of by the Methodists, is supposed to be very simple. Life is long, and the art is short, a matter of about six months, they like to say, and thus with a few words manage to outrage the representatives of traditional medicine in more than one way (Gal. *De. sect. ingr.* 15, 6; 24, 22; *De meth. med.* X 5, 2 K). Their definition of methodical medicine bears the same character of provocative simplicity in expression and content. Medicine, according to the Methodists, amounts to no more than a "knowledge of manifest generalities" (*gnōsis phainomenōn koinoteton*), i.e., of certain general, recurrent features whose presence or absence can be determined by inspection (Gal. *De sect. ingr.* 13, 24; 23, 1; *De meth. med.* X 206, 11 K; ps.-Galen, *De opt. secta* I 175, 18; 182, 2 K). This characterization obviously is meant to emphasize the simplicity and clarity of medicine, once we have grasped the true method, and though at first it seems unduly simple, it turns out, on closer inspection, to amount to an admirably clear, concise, and economical summary of the Methodist position.

It is true that some Methodist characterizations of methodical medicine are slightly more complex. But this is owing to the fact that this very general characterization is supposed to apply not just to medicine, but to any art whatsoever (Gal. *De sect. ingr.* 14, 1). It thus reflects the Methodist, as opposed to the Empiricist or Rationalist, conception of the art of medicine as a true art. When the Methodists want to distinguish medicine from other arts, they go on to specify the generalities which are the particular concern of medicine. Thus, standardly, they say that medicine is knowledge of manifest generalities which are relevant to the aim of medicine (Gal. *De sect. ingr.* 14, 1–7); some of them, among them Thessalus, a main exponent of the school, more restrictively say that medicine is the knowledge of manifest generalities which are proximate to and necessary for health (ibid. 14. 7ff.; ps.-Gal. *De opt. secta* I 172, 7K; *Def. med.* XIX 353, 13 K). "More restrictively," because it seems that Thessalus wants to insist that although there also may be all sorts of general features which are of more or less remote relevance to the presence or absence of health, the methodical doctor should not, and does not have to, occupy himself with these, for he knows the crucial features which are imediately relevant to the health of patient. But since we are concerned with the method, the Methodist conception of medicine as a methodical art, we shall concentrate on this very general characterization of methodical medicine. In fact, the following will be no more than a first attempt to elucidate the terms of this characterization in some detail.

II. Indication

Before we start to consider the details of this general characterization, though, we have to ask ourselves how this possibly could amount to a characterization of methodical medicine, of the true method. For, as we saw above, the method is what is supposed to enable us to find the right treatment for a patient. But this general characterization does not seem to tell us anything at all about the way in which we find out how to treat a patient. The matter is even more puzzling if we take into account that the manifest generalities the Methodists are thinking of when they give the very general characterization, seem to be the various affections and diseases themselves (Gal. *De sect. ingr.* 23, 2–12). But it is difficult to see, unless one is a philosopher, how the mere knowledge of a disease by itself could provide one with a knowledge of its treatment. And yet this is what the Methodists do want to maintain. The very brevity and apparent deficiency of their characterization just serves to draw our attention to the point that all the doctor really has to know are the affections and diseases themselves; knowing them he will also know their treatment; and to know their treatment he does not have to know anything but the affections and diseases themselves.

But how is knowledge of the disease by itself supposed to provide one with a knowledge of its treatment? The Methodists claim that the disease in itself is indicative of its own treatment (Gal. *De sect. ingr.* 12, 14ff.; 13, 13; 17, 5ff.; *De meth. med.* X 351, 7 K; *Med.* XIV 677, 12 K; ps.-Galen, *De opt. secta* I 125, 2ff.; 164, 1ff. K). To see what is meant by this we have to consider the Methodist conception of indication (*endeixis*). The notion of indication is not of Methodist origin. It comes into use in later Hellenistic epistemology, most commonly to distinguish kinds of signs and, correspondingly, kinds of conditionals. Roughly speaking, something A is a suggestive or commemorative sign of something B, if we know from experience that B obtains if A obtains. Thus, to use a traditional example, the presence of smoke is a suggestive sign of the presence of fire. Something A, on the other hand, is not a suggestive, but an indicative sign of something B, if we know, not by experience, but by reason that B obtains if A obtains. An Atomist, for example, might regard the presence of motion as an indicative sign of the presence of void. The application of these notions to conditionals should be obvious (cf. Sextus Emp. *PH* II 100ff.).

If, then, the Methodists claim that the disease itself is indicative of its treatment, they obviously mean to say that it is not by experience, as the Empiricists claim, that we know that a certain disease needs a certain treatment (cf. Gal. *De sect. ingr.* 14, 10–12). But it also turns out not to be a matter of reason in the way the Rationalists assume, either (cf. ibid. 13, 19ff.). In fact, this, in a nut-shell, is the ultimate source of the difference between the three schools. To see this more clearly, we have to take a closer look at the Methodist use of the notion of indication.

Sextus Empiricus (*PH* I 240) tells us: "The Methodist in an undogmatic manner also makes use of the term 'indication' to refer to the guidance which both natural and unnatural affections provide towards what seems to be (the) fitting (treatment) for them as I pointed out in the case of thirst, hunger, and the rest." He is referring back here to what he had said a few sentences earlier in *PH* I 238: "As . . . the sceptic is guided by thirst towards drink, by hunger towards food, and thus with the rest, in a similar fashion the methodical doctor is guided by the affections towards what is fitting for them, by constriction to dilation, just as somebody tries to escape from condensation due to intensified cold by getting to a warm spot." A few lines further down Sextus goes on to refer to the example of a dog which, pricked by a thorn, moves to do what is indicated and removes the thorn which is alien to its body.

On Sextus' account, then, a disease is supposed to be indicative of its treatment in the way in which hunger is indicative of the need for food. If there is a relevant difference between affections like thirst and hunger, on the one hand, and disease, on the other, it just seems to lie in the fact that it takes a doctor to know the diseases in the way in which we all know thirst and hunger. There is no suggestion that there is a relevant difference in the way in which affections and diseases are indicative of what needs to be done to remove them. The peculiarly Methodist notion seems to be that once one has recognized the affection or disease for what it is, it is immediately obvious what needs to be done; "immediately obvious" in the sense that it is neither a matter of observation, nor a matter of inference, if we know what needs to be done once we have recognized the disorder (cf. ps-Galen, *De optima secta* I 131, 6ff. K). The Rationalists think that the manifest state of the body does not make it immediately obvious what needs to be done. For them the manifest state is indicative of a hidden state which causes the affection or the disease. And it is only if we know this hidden state that we know how to treat the patient. Thus, for the Rationalist, knowledge of the appropriate treatment on the basis of the manifest condition is a matter of inference, and indication is a relation between a manifest and a non-manifest state. More specifically, there is, on the one hand, the relation between the manifest state of the body and the underlying, hidden abnormal state, and, on the other hand, the relation between this hidden state and the treatment indicated by it (and not directly by the manifest state). It is the distinctively Rationalist position that reason can grasp such relations (cf. Gal. *De sect. ingr.* 2, 3; 5, 17; 10, 22ff.). Like the Empiricists the Methodists reject such inferences to and from hidden states; according to the Methodists there is no need for such a detour via the non-manifest (Gal. *De sect. ingr.* 14, 9–11). The manifest affection makes it immediately evident what needs to be done; "immediately evident" in the sense that we do not require the mediation of assumptions about hidden states, but presumably also in the sense that it does not take any chain of reasons to see that constriction requires dilation and that dilation requires constriction. The point of Sextus' examples seems to be that the connection between a state and what is indicated by it is so immediately obvious that even a dog "knows" immediately what is indicated; there is no inference involved.

But the Methodists, in claiming that the affection by itself is indicative of its treatment, also deny the Empiricist claim that the connection between disease and appropriate treatment is just a matter of experience (cf. Gal. *De sect. ingr.* 14, 11–12). It does not take experience to know that a state of constriction requires dilation, that depletion asks for replenishment. These, if properly interpreted, are truths of reason. But we have to be careful not to rush to unwarranted conclusions about the sense in which they are supposed to be truths of reason. There is no reason, for example, to think that the Methodists take them to be conceptually or analytically true. For all we know, the Methodists may just insist that, whatever the explanation for it may be, it is immediately obvious to common reason that somebody who is suffering from constriction will find relief in dilation, that we do not feel any need to justify such a claim by reference to past experience, that we not only do not expect any counter-example, but in fact do not see how there could be counter-examples (cf. Cels. *prooem.* 62–63; Gal. *De meth. med.* X 208, 10ff. .K).

Since knowledge of what is indicated is not a matter of observation, nor a matter of experience, the Methodists are willing to say that it is a matter of reason. Thus, on this point the Methodists do side with the Rationalists against the Empiricists and grant that reason does play a constitutive role in medical knowledge (cf. Celsus, *prooem.* 62). But at the same time they do not accept the dogmatic Rationalist conception of the role reason plays in the acquisition of medical knowledge. They do not accept the Rationalist claims that reason can, and has to, grasp hidden entities to acquire the necessary medical knowledge. They refuse to attribute to reason any obscure powers which we would not have dreamed of in ordinary life. They are just noting, in this and in other contexts, what seems to be an obvious fact, but which the Empiricists in their dogmatism do not want to recognize, that there are certain things which are obvious to rational creatures, though it does not seem to be by observation or experience that they are obvious. To admit, though, against the Empiricists, that certain things are obvious to reason, is not to admit that they are obvious to reason on the basis of some scientific theory constructed in accordance with the canons of the rational method or logic. The Methodists insist that it is obvious to reason that somebody who is hungry needs some food prior to, and quite independently of, any theory which would prove that and explain why this is so. In particular, the Methodist does not see how only a theory which operates in terms of hidden, theoretical entities can make it really obvious, or evident, that someone who is thirsty needs to drink. The Methodist is content to stay with what is obviously obvious rather than really obvious.

Thus, in taking the view on indication he does, the Methodist merely tries to stay with the phenomena. He does accept truths of reason, but he does not accept the Rationalist canons for truths of reason, which would commit him to the assumption of hidden, theoretical entities. This, according to our ancient commentators, is the fundamental source of the differences between the Methodists, on the one hand, and the Empiricists and the Rationalists, on the other (Gal. *De sect. ingr.* 13, 19ff. and 14, 10ff.; Celsus, *prooem.* 57; ps.-Gal. *De. opt. secta* I 119 K).

According to the Methodists, then, the disease itself is indicative of its treatment in the sense that once we are aware of the disease in the appropriate way it will also be obvious to us how it is to be treated. It is for this reason that the Methodists can characterize methodical medicine simply as knowledge of certain manifest generalities. With this in mind, let us turn to the characterization itself.

III. Generalities

From what has been said, it is clear that we have to pay particular attention to two features of this characterization: (i) It seems to be important for an understanding of the method that diseases are conceived of as generalities and that they are conceived of as manifest; (ii) Obviously it is not any kind of awareness of a disease which gives us the knowledge of its treatment; it must be the kind of awareness the Methodist doctor has; hence we have to find out what kind of knowledge the Methodists are referring to. Let us then first consider why the Methodists insist that medical knowledge is knowledge of generalities. 'Generality' (*koinotēs*) is a term of dogmatic metaphysics. It refers to a common, general, recurrent feature. As Sextus (*PH* I 240) tells us, the Methodists adopt this term, but use it, like all other terms, in an undogmatic manner; i.e., they are willing to talk of generalities, but they do not mean by this to commit themselves to the assumptions involved in the dogmatic use of this term. They do not commit themselves to any particular metaphysical view concerning the nature of generalities, nor do they even commit themselves to the metaphysical assumption that there are such common properties or qualities. This is important, because it means that the Methodists in talking of diseases as generalities do not really commit themselves to the existence of diseases as separate entities. The sense in which they are willing to talk of diseases as generalities is a perfectly simple and straightforward one: we ordinarily say that two persons who suffer from pneumonia have the same disease, and in saying "the same disease" we do not commit ourselves, let alone mean to commit ourselves, to the existence of a universal called "pneumonia," all we commit ourselves to is that the two persons in question in certain respects are very much alike, so much alike that in this respect we do not care to distinguish between them. Thus, Methodist talk about generalities is entirely based on ordinary talk about similarlity and likeness between objects (cf. ps.-Galen, *De opt. secta* I 191, 4ff. K, where the point is explicitly made). On the other hand, the Method ist also would not want to commit himself to the view that such common entities do not really exist; i.e., when he explains his use of "generality" in terms of the way we ordinarily talk about the similarity or likeness between objects, he does not mean to commit himself to some form of nominalism. It is in this noncommittal sense, then, that the Methodists talk of "generalities." With this in mind, let us return to our question: of what importance is it that diseases should be conceived of as generalities in this sense?

This question has to be seen on the background of a long tradition in Greek medicine according to which treatment has to be individualized to do justice to the individuality of the particular cases to be treated, none of which is exactly like any other (cf. Hipp. *Epid.* I 23; *De vet. med.* 20). There are a large number of factors which are supposed to make a relevant difference to the particular case, and which hence have to be taken into account when one tries to decide on the right treatment for the particular case. Rationalists, especially those under Stoic influence, tend to assume that individuals have an individual nature or essence which has an effect on the form and the course a disease takes (cf. Galen,

De. sect. ingr. 5, 200ff.; *De. meth. med.* X 209, 4ff. K). In addition, there are differentiating and particularizing factors like age, sex, constitution, and habits of the patient, the part of the body affected, antecedent causes, the place and its climate, the season of the year, and whatever else may be relevant (cf., e.g., Galen *De sect. ingr.* ch. 3). This view tended to be combined with the view that knowledge, at least scientific knowledge, is of the universal, whereas the individual and its condition are ineffable, i.e., cannot be captured by general notions, however scientific they may be (cf. Galen, *De meth. med.* X 209, 7 K; *De loc. aff.* VIII 117, 6ff.; 339, 13ff. K), and hence cannot be known scientifically. As a result, it tended to be assumed that diagnosis and treatment, though based on a scientific theory, cannot be more than a matter of artful conjecture (cf. Gal. *De. plenit.* VII 581, 1ff. K; *De. sanit, tuenda* VII 129, 4ff. K; *De rat. cur.* XI 285, 10ff. K; *De meth. med.* X 181, 17ff.; 206, 5ff. K). Hence, the classification of medicine as a conjectural art.

The Methodists claim that medicine as a whole is a matter of firm knowledge (ps.-Gal. *Med.* XIV 684 K) and thus deny that treatment cannot but be conjectural. If medicine is to be safe and reliable, treatment should be a matter of firm and certain knowledge. And that it can be a matter of knowledge we see, once we have grasped the true method. For the fact that traditional medicine does indeed proceed by mere conjecture and that its representatives think that it cannot but be conjectural, is due to a mistaken conception of the method. According to the Methodists all these differentiating and individualizing features are of no relevance in determining the appropriate treatment. There is no need to take into account mere symptoms (ps.-Gal. *De opt. secta* I 162, 9ff.; 163, 12ff.; 164 2ff.; 170, 18ff. K), sex is irrelevant (Soran. *Gyn.* p. 95, 4), so are causes (Celsus, *prooem,* 54; ps.-Galen, *Med.* XIV 683, 2 K; Gal. *Ad pis.* XIV 278, 11; 279, 4 K; Cael. Aur. *Ac.* III 45; 190), whether hidden (Gal. *De sect. ingr.* 17, 3ff.; Cael. Aurel. *Chron.* 14, 83) or antecedent (Gal. *De sect. ingr.* 16, 12ff.; Cael. Aur. *Ac.* II 187); there is no need to know the part of the body affected (Cael. Aur. *Ac.* I 53; II 148) or to take note of the age, constitution, habits of the patient, the season, the location, and its climate (Gal. *De sect. ingr.* 6, 10ff.; 12, 14ff.; 17, 7ff.; 19, 20ff.; *De meth. med.* X 629, 14ff.; *On med. exp.* P. 87ff.; Cael. Aur. *Ac.* I 157; Celsus, *prooem.* 65). As Galen puts it (*De meth. med.* X 206, 12 K), the Methodists talk as if their patient was not an individual, but the universal man. The Methodists take the position that thirst is the same, whatever the nature, age, sex, constitution, and habits of the patient, the clime of the place, the time of the year, and there is one and the same treatment which is asked for, namely the administration of drink. And since this affection is a generality, which asks for one and the same treatment whenever it occurs, we do not even have to worry about the problem whether individuals can be known scientifically or not and how we can apply our general knowledge to the particular case; we do not have to worry that our theorems only hold for the most part, because some idiosyncratic feature of a particular case may cause an exception to the general rule. The rules hold without exception, exactly because no account needs to be taken of the various differentiating and individualizing features. Thus, they are truly scientific, firm, and stable (Gal. *De meth. med.* X 206, 10; 208, 10 K; *De cris.* IX 657, 18K; Celsus, *prooem.* 62). Rationalists and Empiricists just confuse matters by dragging in all these irrelevant facts. Hence, it is not surprising that their theorems should be hopelessly unreliable. At the same time it is not surprising that their doctrine should be excessively and needlessly complicated and difficult to master, whereas the true method shows medical knowledge to be a rather clear and straightforward matter.

It has to be added, though, that—as Galen points out (*De meth. med.* X 630 K)—the Methodists do take into account differentiating features, after all, when it comes to administering the indicated treatment; the differentiating features may, e.g., offer counterindications to certain ways the treatment might be administered (cf. Gal. *De sect. ingr.* 20, 3ff.; 20, 16ff.). In fact, to be precise, in order to determine the appropriate timing and dosage of the indicated treatment, the Methodist doctor in addition to the generality is also supposed to know the stage of the disease and its intensity (Gal. *De sect. ingr.* 13, 12ff.; 26, 21ff.; ps-Galen, *De opt. secta* I 162; 194; 211 K; Celsus, *prooem.* 55-6).

IV. The Manifest

Some generalities, e.g., colors, clearly are manifest, i.e., open to inspection. There also may be hidden generalities, not open to inspection, but accessible only to reason. And some of them may be relevant to medicine in the sense that truths about them may entail truths about diseases and their treatment. This is why Thessalus, unlike most Methodists, does not characterize the generalities medicine is concerned with as those which are relevant to the aim of medicine, but as those which are proximate and necessary. The ones which one has to know in medical practice, the ones which immediately determine the treatment, are manifest generalities. Though, then, the Methodist grants that there may be hidden generalities relevant to the aim of medicine, he will only rely on assumptions about obvious or manifest entities, and more particularly only on those assumptions about manifest entities which themselves are obvious. But what does count as obvious or manifest? We might think that those things are obvious or manifest which one can perceive or perceive to be the case. And in the *De sectis* Galen talks as if this was the Methodist view (24, 12ff.; 24, 19ff.). But we have already seen that the Methodists also take truths of reason to be obvious. And it seems that there is some unclarity in Galen's mind about whether they think that generalities can be perceived (*De meth. med.* X 36, 5ff.; 38, 5K). The author of *De optima secta* is quite unequivocal about this. He tells us (I 175, 18ff. K) that by "manifest" the Methodists here do not mean "grasped by perception." But what, then, distinguishes the Methodist's generalities from the Rationalist's hidden entities? The claim seems to be that everybody can be taught to recognize these generalities by careful observation; one learns to "see" them, develops an eye for them, whereas no amount of training will teach one to recognize an atom or a complex of atoms as such.

But why does the Methodist insist that the doctor should restrict himself to the manifest? Rationalist physicians have postulated the existence of all sorts of hidden entities. In each case it has turned out that there is some reasonable doubt about their existence, and there does not seem to be any clear way to settle these doubts, once and for all (Cael. Aur. Ac. II 8). Moreover, even given their existence, assumptions about them seem to be a matter of endless speculation and controversy. The Methodist does not deny that such entities may exist and that one can have knowledge about them (Gal. De sect. ingr. 14, 14; Cael. Aur. Ac. I 9). But since he is determined to provide safe medical treatment, he refuses to rely on such controversial and speculative assumptions. And since medical theories are characterized by such assumptions, he also quite generally refuses to rely on such theories for his practice. Whereas the Rationalists think that it is only in virtue of these theories that medical practice can have a sound, scientific basis, the methodists argue that these theories fail to provide a reliable basis, because they themselves are controversial.

Fortunately, according to the Methodists, there is no need to rely on such assumptions and theories. For our knowledge of what is manifest is entirely sufficient to determine the correct treatment for a disease. Thus, even if these assumptions and theories were not controversial, but well established, knowledge of them would be redundant and superfluous, as far as the aim of medicine is concerned (Gal. De sect. ingr. 16, 11ff.; 18, 20ff.; De meth. med. X 268, 17 K; ps.-Galen, De opt. secta 122, 6ff. K). Hence, the Methodists refuse to accept physiology or anatomy as part of the art of medicine (Gal. De meth. med. X 9, 10; 107, 11ff.; 319, 17; 349, 16A; 928, 5ff. K; Soran. Gyn. 6, 6ff.). They claim that others, in pursuing these subjects, go beyond the boundaries of the art (Gal. De meth. med. X 106, 2 K; cf. Celsus, prooem. 64).

In this refusal to rely on anything but the obvious and manifest, the Methodists are taking the side of the Empiricists against the Rationalists. But the Methodists' position on the hidden and the obvious is not quite the same as that of the Empiricists. To start with, as we have seen, the obvious for the Methodists includes truths of reason. In addition, the Methodists accuse the Empiricists of dogmatism because of their attitude toward hidden entities. The Empiricists tend to claim that such entities do not exist and that, even if they do exist, nothing can be known about them. The Methodist will not commit himself on these questions; he just observes that in fact nothing seems to be known about such entities.

In keeping with this, the Methodist does not claim that there are no true theories, or that, even if there were, they could not be known. In fact, it seems that the Methodist takes a much more positive attitude toward theories. It is true that he refuses to rely on theories for his practice, but this does not mean that his interest in medical theory is entirely negative or critical.

If we look at Caelius Aurelianus we see a Methodist author who not infrequently gives causal accounts of diseases (cf. *Ac.* I 33; *Chron.* II 125; V 109) and even refers to hidden entities like hidden dissolutions (cf. *Ac.* II 172, *adēlos diaphorēsis;* 217, *occulta diaphorēsis;* cf. also *Chron.* III 19). Given that he himself refers to them in this way, we have to assume that he thinks that it is in perfect agreement with his Methodism to consider such theoretical assumptions with approval of some kind. That this is not an aberration on Caelius' part we can see from the fact that even Soranus wrote treatises on etiology and physiology. And from various passages in Caelius Aurelianus (cf. *Ac.* II 28, 147–48; *Chron.* IV 1, 5) it is clear that Soranus thought that there is nothing wrong with having theoretical views, as long as one keeps in mind that they are purely speculative, and as long as one does not base one's treatment on these views.

Soranus himself tells us (*Gyn.* 6, 6ff. I 1b.) that though anatomy is useless, it is good to know it; for otherwise people might think that one is rejecting it out of ignorance. He also acknowledges that there is real anatomical knowledge; after all, anatomy in good part is a matter of experience (*Gyn.* 6, 8; 10, 12; 12, 3). We may also assume that the Methodists think that it would be dogmatic to reject theories out of hand without having carefully considered them; after all, one of them may turn out to be obviously true. Soranus also tells us of both anatomy and physiology that, though they are useless, one should take account of them '*pros chrēstomatheian*' (*Gyn.* 4, 6ff.; 6, 6ff. 1 1b.). This suggests that knowledge of these theories satisfies learned curiosity, is, as it were, an amenity of life, a decorative ornament of the educated person.

Somehow, though, I am inclined to think that there must be, according to the Methodists, a more positive connection between medical theory and the art practiced by the doctor. Celsus obviously does assume that there is such a positive connection, and though he does not attribute this view to the Methodists, there is at least some faint reason to suppose that it does reflect the Methodist position. He says (*prooem.* 74): "Though I think that medicine should be rational, I also think that one should take one's instructions from manifest causes, all hidden matters being rejected, not from the thought of the practitioner, but from the art itself." The point of these lines seems to be this: though the doctor in his practice should only be guided by what is evident, he also in his thinking, as opposed to his practice, should engage in medical theory. Celsus clearly thinks that such theoretical activity is of more than ornamental value; for otherwise he would not say that in his view medicine has to be rational. But what reason is there to suppose that these remarks reflect Methodical thought? It seems to me that the contrast between the art itself and the thought of the practitioner, the restriction of the art, but not of the thought of the practitioner, to what is evident, and the insistence that treatment should be guided by the evident cannot but remind one of the Methodist position. Moreover, it also seems that there are certain features of Methodism which are most easily understood, if we assume that the Methodists allowed theoretical speculation to have a positive influence on the art itself.

For, if one thinks of the noncommittal attitude of the Methodists toward theories, it does strike one that they would hardly have arrived at their central doctrine that all diseases are forms of one of three basic generalities (constriction, dilation, and the combination of both) if they had not been thoroughly influenced by Asclepiades' rather speculative physiology. Asclepiades' physiology was based on the assumption that the body is constituted by atoms and invisible pores. He explained many illnesses as owing to the constriction of these invisible pores, some as owing to an excessive flow through them (cf. Gal. *De tremore* VII 615, 3ff. K; Cael. Aur. *Ac.* I 6ff.; 106ff.), i.e., as owing to dilation. The Methodist position obviously is reached by two moves: (i) They generalize the Asclepiadean position by assuming that all illnesses are a matter of constriction, dilation, or a combination of both; (ii) But constriction and dilation in Asclepiades' account are hidden states postulated by the theory; after all, invisible pores and atoms are paradigms of hidden entities to be grasped only by reason; thus, the Methodists have to leave it an open question whether underlying the phenomena there are hidden states of constriction and dilation of the kind postulated by Asclepiades; instead, they assume that there are manifest states of constriction and dilation, whether or not underlying these there are also corresponding hidden states of constriction and dilation of the kind assumed by Asclepiades which are the cause of the manifest dilation or constriction. Thus, sometimes the Methodists criticize Asclepiades for basing his account of a disease on these hidden states (Cael. Aur. *Ac.* I 9). But there is also some evidence that in some sense Methodists did accept Asclepiades' view of the reality behind the manifest states of dilation and constriction (Cael. Aur. *Ac.* II 52; III 189ff.; Gal. *De temp. et virtut. simpl. med.* XI 783, 5ff. K). If such a speculative view were ascribed only to Themison, we might think that this was just further evidence that Themison had not yet managed to free himself entirely from his Asclepiadean views and to take a consistently Methodist position (cf. Cael. Aur. *Chron.* I 50; IV 6). But the fact that Galen (*l.c.*) seems to attribute such views to Thessalus also makes this explanation far less plausible. It, rather, seems that at least some Methodists saw the relation between Asclepiades' theory concerning the hidden states and their own view concerning the corresponding manifest states in the following way: If one was to speculate about such matters, they were willing to accept Asclepiades' account; this account seemed so much more plausible than any other account, though this did not change the crucial fact that it still was only a matter of speculation; in fact, quite literally a matter of speculation, for the hidden entities involved in this account were called *logotheorēta* (i.e., to be seen by reason; cf. Cael. Aur. *Ac.* I 105; 106; *Chron.* V 105), and *'theōria'*, *'theōrētikos'* etc., not only came to be rendered *'speculatio'*, *'speculativus'*, etc., but also to take on the sense of 'speculation', 'speculative' (cf. Gal. *De dogm. Plat. et. Hipp.* p. 815 M). But though it is just speculation, it does have two positive effects: First of all Asclepiades' theoretical speculation suggested something which was borne out by careful attention to the phenomena; if it had not been for Asclepiades' theory, we might never have become aware of the manifest generalities. After all, it is extremely unlikely that by merely looking at the phenomena without the guidance of some theory we would ever have realized that all diseases are forms of the three generalities. Nevertheless, it was not speculation but observation which provided us with the knowledge of these generalities. But speculation did help us to focus our attention in the right direction. This is one way in which medical theory, though not part of the art of medicine itself, may be more than a mere ornament of the educated doctor. Second, the theory, though not itself part of medical knowledge and irrelevant for treatment, does provide some understanding and makes sense of our medical knowledge.

The reason why the Methodist for his treatment will rely only on what is obvious is that it is only in this way that safe and reliable treatment can be guaranteed; for only what is manifest can be known reliably. But it is really the case that the generalities the Methodist claims to take his indications from are manifest? Galen repeatedly points out (cf., e.g., *adv. Iul.* 50, 2ff. Wenkebach) that the Methodists themselves disagree in their definitions or characterizations of even the most basic generalities. If they were manifest, Galen claims, there should be universal agreement on their definition.

At this point it may be useful to consider briefly the Methodists' attitude toward definitions. The evidence on the matter is somewhat confused. In Ps.-Soranus, *Quaestiones medicinales* §46, for example, we are told that whereas the Rationalists rely on definitions and the Empiricists on descriptions, the Methodists use both. The distinction between definitions and descriptions, *horoi* and *hupotupōseis* or *hupographai,* is part of dogmatic dialectic (cf. DL VII 60). A definition specifies the essence of something in terms of the true theory, a description captures the notion of something in pretheoretical terms accessible to everybody, e.g., by capturing the common notion or the ordinary meaning of a term. Now sometimes we are told about the Methodists, in particular about Soranus, that they refuse to give definitions (cf. Cael. Aur. *Ac.* II 142; 163). And given what we have said, this is easily understood. Definitions in the technical sense involve a commitment to a theory and to theoretical entities, a commitment Methodists reject. Caelius Aurelianus, for example, repeatedly rejects definitions of diseases because they make reference to hidden entities (*Ac.* I 9; II 8). Nevertheless, they often do give us definitions and talk of them as definitions. But this apparent inconsistency is easily explained by their general policy to use dogmatic terms like 'definition', without feeling committed to the dogmatic theories and distinctions associated with these terms. Thus, in this case they feel free to talk of definitions, when in fact, from a dogmatic point of view, they should be talking of descriptions. So the Methodists refuse to give definitions in the technical sense, but they do not refuse to give definitions in the sense of descriptions. But the fact that they call these both 'definitions' and 'descriptions' has given rise to the confusion we find in ps.-Soranus.

If the Methodists had meant to give definitions in the technical sense, the fact that different Methodists give different definitions of the various generalities would have raised a serious problem. For in the technical sense each kind of thing can only have one definition. But once we see that, from a dogmatic point of view, the Methodists are only giving descriptions even if they themselves may call them 'definitions', it no longer seems problematic that they should offer different characterizations of one and the same generality. For, obviously, one thing may be characterized in different ways. And even the fact that they disagree about the most suitable and appropriate characterization no longer seems problematic. For suppose that we all manage to focus our awareness on a certain phenomenon and that this phenomenon does stand out in our mind with all desirable clarity; we still might disagree about how we should characterize it in such a way that others who are not familiar with it know what to pay attention to and thus may come to see it too. Methodist definition, and Methodist language quite generally, does not pretend to be more than a pragmatic attempt to draw our attention to the phenomena, to help us to become aware of them in our own experience. This familiarity with the phenomena is what counts; it can never be replaced by the mere possession of a phrase; however appropriate and precise the phrase may be, it will never quite capture the phenomenon.

One might object that if the generalities really were manifest, they should be constituted by a set of phenomenal features. And hence, if one had a clear awareness of a generality, it should be possible to give a list of its constitutive features, and hence a definition all Methodists should be able to agree upon. But this presupposes that there is a set of basic, simple phenomenal features such that all complex phenomena can be resolved into these simple features, and though this is an assumption which philosophers throughout the ages have been very tempted to accept, it is entirely speculative and dogmatic; the phenomena themselves do not justify it. It is only when we try to develop certain kinds of epistemologies that this assumption seems to be attractive.

Thus the fact that the Methodists themselves disagree about how the generalities should be characterized does not show that the generalities are not manifest. What it does show is that something can be manifest without being immediately manifest to everybody. It does take some training till the medical generalities become manifest to one with sufficient clarity. Otherwise we would not need any doctors. This brings us to the third and last part of the general characterization of methodical medicine, the doctor's knowledge.

V. The Doctor's Knowledge

As we have seen, the Methodist position is very much influenced by the consideration that medical treatment should not, and need not, be a matter of speculation and conjecture, as in fact it is in the hands of Rationalist and Empiricist doctors. If we restrict ourselves to manifest generalities our treatment will be a matter of firm and certain knowledge, based on our knowledge of these manifest generalities and thereby of what they indicate. What, then, is it to know these generalities and how do we come to know them?

It seems to be a safe assumption that the kind of knowledge of generalities in question is supposed to involve the ability to recognize a generality when one comes across it. Moreover, it would seem to be an ability to recognize a generality, rather than an instance of it. For what we are supposed to be aware of are the generalities themselves, and not instances of them. This, in turn, suggests that the generalities themselves, rather than instances of them, are the kind of thing we can be familiar or acquainted with, and that we can know them in the way in which we can know other things we are familiar with, like people, trees, colors, or pain. Presumably it is significant that the term the Methodists use in this connection is 'gnōsis', a term which suggests direct acquaintance. Mere familiarity in this sense, though, does not suffice for the doctor. He has to acquire a sufficiently articulate and clear notion of the disease to have a clear indication of its treatment. This he achieves by carefully observing the various diseases, by comparing them with each other, noting their similarities and their dissimilarities (cf. ps.-Gal. *Med.* XIV 680, 3 K; also consider Caelius' differential diagnoses). In this way he learns to distinguish between the disease itself and symptoms which tend to accompany it (Cael. Aur. *Ac.* II 30), and slowly he comes to see that the diseases themselves are just different forms of the three basic generalities. At this point everything falls into place, he can now clearly see the various diseases for what they are and knows their indicated treatment.

The Methodist in acquiring knowledge of the generalities and their treatment does acquire some general knowledge. But, unlike the Rationalist's or the Empiricist's purported general knowledge, the Methodist's knowledge is firm and certain, not subject to revision by future experience (Gal. *De cris.* IX 657, 18 K; *De meth. med.* X 206, 8–10; 208, 10–11 K; Celsus, prooem. 62; cf. 63). Now, one might think that it is by applying this general knowledge to the particular case that the Methodist is supposed to know with certainty how to treat the particular case. But it should be clear from what has been said that this would be an unmethodical way of looking at the matter. The Methodist does not deal with a particular case, except incidentally; he deals with a disease, a generality, and not with an instance of it. Moreover, once we know the disease, and hence have the general knowledge how to treat it, the awareness of the disease will produce the thought how it is to be treated not by inference, but immediately. This is part of what is meant by 'indication'. Thus the question of the application of our general knowledge to the particular case and the question of the validity of logical inference does not even arise. This last point is not without relevance, since, as we may have suspected, the Methodists also refuse to rely on logic and its various subdisciplines (Gal. *De meth. med.* X 5, 4–7; 30, 1ff.). They have no need for a theory of proof and inference and conspicuously refrain from presenting canonical proofs for their theses (Gal. *De meth. med.* X 30, 1ff.; 109, 4ff. K; *In Hipp. de vict. acut. CMG* V 9, I, 286, 27ff.). Since, as we already have seen, they reject definitions in the strict sense, they also have no use for a logical theory of definitions. Nor are they interested in the method of resolution (cf. Galen, *De meth. med.* X 30, 2 K). Obviously, the Methodist rejection of logic also involves a rejection of the Rationalist conception of the role reason plays in medical knowledge, since for the Rationalist logic defines the way in which we come to have knowledge by reason. In this respect, again, the Methodists side with the Empiricists.

It is in this sense, then, that the art of medicine, according to the Methodist, does not involve more than the knowledge of certain manifest generalities.

VI. Skepticism

Given their emphasis on the necessity of safe and certain knowledge and their claim to actually possess this knowledge, it comes as a considerable surprise when we are told by Sextus Empiricus (*PH* I 236ff.) that of all the medical sects the Methodical school is the one which is most attractive for a skeptic. Sextus does not say that the Methodists are skeptics. But he does say that Methodism is more in line with skepticism than Empiricism. And since Empiricism and Pyrrhonean skepticism were closely associated with each other, so much so that Sextus finds it necessary to explicitly reject their identification (*PH* I 236ff.), the relation between Methodism and skepticism, at least in Sextus' mind, must be very close. Unfortunately, we have no further evidence which explicitly links Methodism with skepticism. There is a notice in Eusebius (*PE* XIV 5, 6) which shows that somebody called 'Mnaseas' took the kind of interest in the history of skepticism which would suggest that he himself was a skeptic; and it so happens that there also is a leading, widely known Methodist of the same name; hence it is generally assumed that the skeptical author mentioned by Eusebius is identical with the Methodist, though the basis for this identification is rather tenuous, especially in light of the fact that the name 'Mnaseas' is not that uncommon. Given that there is no other evidence which directly links Methodism with skepticism, one might be inclined to think that such skeptical leanings may have been peculiar to Mnaseas and his followers, especially since we know that Mnaseas had distinctive views of his own on other matters, too (cf. Cael. Aur. *Chron* II 97).

But if one looks at the reasons Sextus gives for his association of Methodism with skepticism, all of them turn out to rely on features which are characteristic of Methodism in general: their undogmatic use of terms, the undogmatic attitude toward hidden entities, their letting themselves be guided by manifest affections. And this suggests that Sextus is not thinking of some particular group of Methodists, or mistakenly identifying the position of a particular group of Methodists with that of the school as a whole, but, rather, of the school in general, when he links Methodism with skepticism.

Thus, we have to see whether we can find a way in which the general Methodist position, as we have outlined it above, might be thought to be compatible with some form of skepticism. The resolution of the puzzle seems to me to lie in the following: when the Methodists talk about certain knowledge, they again do so in an undogmatic manner. We do say in ordinary life that we know this or that for certain. It is in this trivial, ordinary sense that the Methodists talk of 'certain knowledge'. By doing so, they do not have the slightest intention of taking a position on the question whether there really is such a thing as certain knowledge, let alone whether there could be such a thing as certain knowledge in the sense in which dogmatic philosophers claim certainty. Their point rather seems to be that their Rationalist opponents in their attempt to gain certain knowledge in the philosopher's sense not only seem to fail in that endeavor, but also fail to acquire knowledge in the uncontroversial ordinary sense. It is because the Methodists content themselves with vulgar knowledge that they have been able to gain at least that much. This position is perfectly compatible with an unrestricted skepticism about how things really are. For vulgar knowledge is knowledge of the phenomena, of how things appear to us. And the Methodists do not lay claim to more. It is hardly an accident that Sextus, in his characterization of the Methodist use of indication (*PH* I 240), says that the affection guides us toward what 'appears' to be the fitting treatment. Thus even our firm and certain knowledge of the indicated treatment is a matter of appearance. The Methodist, like the skeptic, just follows the phenomena.

One might object that a proper ancient skeptic will not just refuse to rely on anything which is not a phenomenon, but that he will also not have as much as a mere opinion on matters hidden, whereas the Methodist, as we have seen, does engage in theoretical speculation and mentions theoretical views with approval, though he refuses to base his practice on them. But it is not true that ancient skeptics quite generally reject any kind of theoretical belief. There is a whole tradition of Academic skepticism, of which Metrodorus, Philo, Cicero, Favorinus, and Plutarch are a part, which allows for the possibility of theoretical or philosophical beliefs. And this suggests that if we are to associate Methodism with a particular kind of skepticism, it may be with a brand of late Academic skepticism, rather than with Pyrrhonean skepticism, as Edelstein has suggested ("The Methodists," *Ancient Medicine* (Baltimore, 167), 187). But however this may be, there does not seem to me to be any difficulty in understanding how the Methodist claim to certain knowledge could be compatible with a thorough-going skepticism. In fact, it is worth noting that Sextus, though he carefully refrains from fully endorsing Methodism as a skeptical position, does not give a single reason for this hesitation. This is all the more remarkable, since in the preceding discussion (*PH* I 210ff.) Sextus had gone out of his way to show in which respects the various positions which might be thought to be skeptical fall short of true skepticism.

VII. Conclusion

Galen (*De sect. ingr.* 12, 12ff.; 15, 17ff.) gives us the impression that if the Methodists were right, there would have to be a radical change of medical practice. And this is an impression which, it seems, the Methodists themselves meant to create. Hence, at first sight, we would seem to have a case in which a philosophical view has an enormous impact on the actual practice of an art. And it would be extremely useful to investigate in detail which effect these philosophical views had on the actual practice of medicine. But such an investigation, I suspect, would show that once we come to Methodist authors like Soranus, the actual change in practice stood in no proportion to the revolutionary zeal with which Thessalus offended the medical profession when he set out to propagate the new method. Thessalus had his tomb inscribed '*iatronikēs*' (Plin. *NH* 29, 9). But it was largely traditional medical practice which happily survived, even under the guise of Methodism.

15

On Galen's Epistemology

There is a question about whether Galen should be regarded as a philosopher or merely as a learned physician with philosophical ambitions. And there seems to be a tendency to answer this question negatively.[1] It is not that anyone would doubt that Galen has rather detailed views on a vast number of philosophical subjects covering all traditional parts of philosophy: logic, physics, and ethics. For his medical writings abound in philosophical remarks, and Galen even wrote a great number of monographs on philosophical topics. But it is suggested that Galen's philosophical knowledge is derivative, second-hand, that he does not have any philosophical views of his own, that he is just a very well-educated physician who has acquired, and likes to display, an admittedly quite extensive knowledge of philosophy. It is also pointed out that Galen thinks that the perfect doctor needs a certain amount of philosophical knowledge (cf. *Quod optimus medicus philosophus*); and since, as we shall see, Galen systematically avoids certain basic philosophical questions which have no bearing on medicine, one might be tempted to think that Galen's extensive philosophical knowledge primarily reflects his good education and his belief that the ideal physician has to be philosophically educated and hence goes no way to show that Galen should be considered as a philosopher in his own right.

The question is complicated by the fact that we have to distinguish two traditions. There is the general philosophical tradition carried by the schools of philosophy; but then there is also a long tradition of physician-philosophers, of physicians who thought of themselves as dealing as physicians with certain questions which standardly were also treated by philosophers, questions of natural philosophy, the nature and constitution of the human body, the soul, or epistemological questions like the nature and the methods of an art like medicine. This tradition is not as continuous as the general philosophical tradition, and very often it is very much dependent on the development of the general philosophical tradition. Nevertheless, it seems continuous, independent, and weighty enough to be considered a separate tradition. It seems clear, e.g., that the discussion Asclepiades of Bithynia, Soranus, Menodotus, and Theodas participated in was not part of mainstream philosophy, that it did form a sufficiently independent tradition with a considerable amount of philosophical substance of its own so as to deserve to be treated in its own right. There can be no doubt that Galen took a very decisive part in the shaping of this second tradition, so much so that we speak of the Galenism of his successors.

It seems, though, that Galen should not only be accorded his clearly deserved place in the tradition of the physician-philosophers, but that he also deserves to be taken into account as part of the general philosophical tradition. It is not just that Galen himself seems to think that he has something to contribute to the general philosophical tradition. For in his philosophical writings he goes far beyond the list of topics which have some relevance, however generously construed, for medicine. It seems to be a position accorded to him by the professional philosophers of his time and of later antiquity. It is true that their esteem for Galen as a philosopher is not particularly high, but Alexander of Aphrodisias (*In top.* 549, 24; *In soph. el.* 22, 7; 142, 19), Themistius (*In phys.* 114 9ff.; 144, 29; 149, 4), Simplicius (*In phys.* 325, 24; 573, 19; 708, 28; 718, 14ff.; 1039, 13), and Philoponus (*In phys.* 576, 13ff.; *De aet. mundi* 319, 7; 599, 23ff.; *In de an.* 155, 33) all find it at least worthwhile to mention Galen repeatedly. Philoponus in *De aeternitate mundi* (599, 23ff.) even comments rather favorably on Galen's competence as a philosopher. Now one might think that this is just due to Galen's reputation for extraordinary learning in later antiquity. But this can hardly account for the fact that already Galen's younger contemporary, Alexander of Aphrodisias, one of the most important philosophers of antiquity, found it worthwhile to write essays against Galen's doctrine of the possible and Galen's criticism of Aristotle's doctrine of motion.[2] Alexander must have thought of Galen as a contributor to the general philosophical discussion who very much deserved to be taken note of. This, or course, does not settle the question whether Galen did in fact have a significant influence on the general history of philosophy of his time, or whether his writings just passively reflect the general philosophical thought of his period.

The way to settle this question is to look in detail at Galen's philosophical position and to compare it to that of his predecessors and his contemporaries. Unfortunately, this is not an easy task. For very little work has been done on Galen's philosophy.[3] One of the reasons for this obviously is that the amount of material which would have to be studied if one wanted to give a precise and detailed reconstruction of his philosophical views is truly forbidding. But we also know very little about Galen's philosophical contemporaries and predecessors. Hence, given the present state of knowledge of the relevant period of the history of philosophy, i.e., the period from roughly 100 B.C. to 200 A.D., it is almost impossible to form a reliable view of Galen's place in the history of philosophy. It deserves to be noted, though, that since Galen is an extremely rich source for this period there is no way in which we can avoid the detailed study of Galen's work if we ever want to arrive at an adequate account of the philosophical thought of the period, even if we should come to think that Galen's own contribution is rather modest.

It is, of course, this view, or rather, given our state of knowledge, this prejudice that Galen did not have anything to contribute to the philosophical thought of his time, which has further deterred historians of philosophy from studying Galen's philosophy in sufficient detail. And hence some remarks on what seems to be the most important source of this prejudice are in place.

If historians of philosophy tend to take such a low view of Galen's philosophical achievements as to question whether he deserves to be considered as a philosopher in his own right, this in good part is due to the fact that one tends to think of Galen as an eclectic. And eclectic Galen, in some sense, no doubt, is; in fact, this is how he sees himself (*De libr. propr.* 1; XIX 13 [SM II 95]; *De dign. aff.* 8: V 41ff. [CMG V 4, 1, 1, 28ff.]). But if we are to avoid the wrong inferences from this epithet, we have to understand the sense in which it applies to Galen; it applies to Galen's philosophical position very much as it applies to Galen's position in medicine; and nobody would infer from his medical eclecticism that Galen's role in the history of medicine is negligible.

To understand the epithet properly one has to see that it applies to Galen's philosophy in two different, though closely related, ways, namely in a more general and in a more precise sense. First of all, Galen is an eclectic in the more general sense in which most philosophers of the period are eclectic. Eclecticism in this sense is an important and rather complex phenomenon of the period which deserves systematic study in its own right. The following factors seem to contribute to it and at the same time to shed some light on Galen's position: (1) presumably the most important factor is the rapid disintegration of the authority of the great schools of Athens in the second part of the second century B.C. and the apparent disintegration of the schools themselves in the first part of the first century B.C. They had defined some kind of orthodoxy. They had attracted the most promising and talented philosophers from all over the Hellenistic world and dominated the philosophical thought of their time. But as the Athenian schools disintegrate, we find the major representatives of the schools no longer in Athens, but setting up schools all over the eastern Mediterranean and developing their own version of the school doctrine. Yet none of these "provincial" schools, at least during the period in question, ever gained the status to be recognized as authoritative for the school of thought as a whole; Posidonius' position, e.g., never came to be recognized as the Stoic position. Hence, the boundaries between the schools became less well-defined. Moreover, major cities, at least in Imperial times, seem to have tried systematically to attract representatives of each of the four major schools. This in itself already reflects an eclectic attitude, and it certainly invites eclecticism. For students will try out the various schools and not necessarily settle for one, especially since the schools differ in their interests and strengths and in the subjects they cover. Even someone who saw himself as basically a Platonist at this time would be inclined to study Peripatetic or Stoic logic or Peripatetic physics.

In fact, it is exactly in this way that Galen came to be exposed to the philosophy of his day. In his native Pergamum his father deliberately had him attend lectures by representatives of all four schools (*De dign. aff.* 8: V 41 [CMG V 4, 1, 1, 28]), apparently rather mediocre figures; for Galen does not even find it worthwhile to give us their names, though for three of them he gives us the names of their teachers which include the famous Platonist Gaius and the equally distinguished Peripatetic Aspasius. Given his intelligence and his education it would have been surprising if Galen had identified himself with the doctrine of any of his Pergamene teachers (cf. the rather disparaging remarks about his teachers in philosophy in *De libr. prop.* 11: XIX 40 [SM II 116]).

(2) Another important factor in the rise of eclecticism was Academic skepticism. Skeptics take a pride in their learning; they study the doctrines of all the other schools. At least from the generation after Carneades onward there is an interpretation of skepticism according to which it is perfectly acceptable for a skeptic to have philosophical beliefs of his own as long as he is undogmatic about these views. Skeptics came to think that the careful consideration of opposite views on a question does not necessarily result in a state of mind in which we are no more inclined toward one view than to its opposite. Thus, even after the most careful consideration of the conflicting views of the different philosophical schools, a skeptic may find himself adopting the view of one of the schools on a particular question. Now it is extremely unlikely that the skeptic would find himself siding invariably with one and the same school; for this would suggest that there was a school of philosophy which had arrived at a true view of the world, after all. Thus, there is a kind of skepticism in the Academy which leads naturally and directly to eclecticism, the kind of eclecticism we find, e.g., in Cicero.

As we can see from his remarks in *De libris prop.* 11: XIX 40 (SM II 116) and his *De optima doctrina,* Galen, though tempted by skepticism, rejected both Pyrrhonism and Academic skepticism. But it is worth noting that if we did not have his explicit remarks to the contrary, and if Galen did not explicitly claim not to adhere to any school, he might well be thought to be an Academic of the kind represented by Philo of Larissa, Cicero, or Plutarch. His sympathies clearly are on the side of Plato's school. He shares the eclecticism of these men. As we shall see, he refuses to to have any views on a large number of central philosophical questions. His writings are full of remarks against dogmatism which remind one of the antidogmatic tradition of the Academy, and which, in fact, have close parallels in the antidogmatic statements in Cicero's *Academica* e.g., in the remarks about men who enslave themselves to the dogma of a school or the authority of a person and hence can no longer consider the evidence on a matter with detachment and decide freely, just in the light of the evidence, which view they should adopt.[4] And though Galen believes that there is certain knowledge, this does not serve to distinguish his position from the very weak skepticism of Academics like Philo and Cicero who readily grant that there is some sense in which we have certain knowledge. What they primarily are concerned to deny is that there is the kind of self-certifyingly evident knowledge the Stoics claim to have. But then Galen himself does not seem to accept the Stoic notion of certain knowledge. For otherwise he would not claim that we have to try to confirm by experience what we think we know by reason. Thus, though Galen claims to reject skepticism, his own position is remarkably similar to that of Academic skeptics like Philo and Cicero. Presumably, Galen shares the view of those like Antiochus and Aenesidemus who think that Academics like Philo really have abandoned skepticism. What he means to reject, when he rejects skepticism, is Pyrrhonean skepticism and the earlier, more radical version of Academic skepticism represented by Arcesilaus and Carneades.

(3) Yet another factor which contributes to the rise of eclecticism in general, but which is also highly relevant in Galen's case, is what one might call the neoclassicism of the period. In philosophy it is reflected by the distinction between the "ancient philosophers," which include the Old Academy, the Old Peripatus, and sometimes the Old Stoa, and the "younger philosophers:" The ancient philosophers, first among them Plato, but then also Aristotle, are regarded as somehow paradigmatic. Their authority is such that the differences between them somehow seem less significant than the differences between them and the younger philosophers of any school. Already Panaetius and then Posidonius are occasionally willing to side with Plato rather than Stoic orthodoxy; Posidonius also is regarded as having strong Aristotelian leanings (Strabo II, 3, 8). Thus, the Academic Antiochus finds the ground prepared for his influential interpretation of the history of philosophy according to which originally the differences between Platonists, Aristotelians, and Stoics were minimal. Given this view of the history of philosophy and the high regard for the classical philosophers, it is not surprising that philosophy should come to be regarded mainly as a matter of reconstructing the original common doctrine on the basis of the classical texts. Galen does not share Antiochus' view of the history of philosophy, nor are Plato or Aristotle beyond criticism for him. But the ancient philosophers do have a special status for him, he studies their texts carefully, and in fact repeatedly chides the Platonists and Peripatetics of his time for not knowing the classical texts of their schools properly. Obviously, this would make him even less inclined to identify himself with any of the contemporary schools of philosophy.

(4) Finally there is one further crucial feature of eclecticism in this sense which needs to be mentioned. Given the way we use the term "eclectic," and

given some of the things that have been said, one might imagine that eclecticism gave rise to a vast number of philosophical systems freely constructed out of the elements of the doctrines of the existing schools according to the predilections of each author. In reality the eclecticism of the time followed highly selective patterns. And Galen is no exception to this: he is just following what seems to be the most common of these patterns:

(i) Like most of his contemporaries he has no sympathy whatsoever for Epicureanism;

(ii) Among all the classical philosophers Plato for him stands out in the way in which Hippocrates stands out among physicians;

(iii) Nevertheless, and in spite of his critical attitude toward the younger philosophers in general and the Stoics in every part of philosophy in particular, he is, like all of his contemporaries, deeply influenced by Stoicism;

(iv) Like most, but not all, philosophers of the period who are heavily dependent on Plato and the Stoics, he also draws freely on Aristotle and the early Peripatus.

In all this he does not differ from the vast majority of Platonists of the period, and hence scholars have been tempted to classify him as just another eclectic Middle Platonist. And indeed, if one wanted to work out his position in detail, one would have to compare his views in particular to those of the Middle Platonists.

In classifying Galen as an eclectic Middle Platonist, though, one does not do justice to his own refusal to identify himself with any of the schools, or to the particular form his eclecticism takes. Whereas almost all philosophers of the period see themselves as Platonists, Peripatetics, Stoics, Epicureans, or Skeptics, Galen refuses to accept even such a general classification. He is not the first to do so. According to Diogenes Laertius (I, 21), Potamo of Alexandria at the end of the first century B.C. started a so-called Eclectic School. Unfortuantely, we do not know anything about the philosophical motivations of Potamo. But if Potamo set out to establish a new school of philosophy defined by its own, albeit eclectic, dogma, we may be certain that Galen would not have approved of this, either. We have to realize that Galen's is a very specific form of eclecticism which has at least two distinctive features which set it off from the general eclecticism of the time:

(i) It is, rather like the eclecticism of the skeptical Academy, characterized by strong antidogmatism, which not only makes him reject an identification with any of the existing schools, but which seems to make him disapprove of the very idea of an identification with one school of thought; it is one's own careful consideration of a matter, rather than the doctrine of a school or an authority which should determine one's views. Given Galen's position in this matter, the status Galenism achieved in history is highly ironic;

(ii) Given this kind of antidogmatism Galen sees himself unable to take a position on a large number of central philosophical questions, because he does not see how in the light of one's own reason and knowledge one could decide questions, e.g., concerning the nature of the soul; but since it is these very questions to which a philosopher of the time was supposed to have an answer, and since it was the answers to these questions which tended to define the borderlines between the different schools, Galen cannot possibly identify himself with any of these schools.

Thus, it turns out that a close consideration of the claim that Galen is an eclectic shows that Galen is not just another eclectic in the sense in which most of his contemporaries were eclectics; and hence the claim, though true, does not justify the conclusion that Galen's philosophical position is of no particular interest to the historian of philosophy. The opposite seems to be the case. Galen's very eclecticism turns out to be of such a distinctive kind as to set him apart from his philosophical contemporaries.

Now, obviously, this distinctive kind of eclecticism rests on certain epistemological views. And these epistemological views, I suggest, Galen acquired in good part by reflecting on the history of medicine and the nature, scope, and origin of medical knowledge. Hence, I want to consider in some detail his epistemological views on the nature of medical knowledge, before I return toward the end to the question how these views may help to explain the two distinctive characters of his eclecticism and thus, perhaps, to set him apart as a philosopher of some originality and distinction.

Questions concerning the nature, scope, and origin of medical knowledge are at least as old as the earliest parts of the *Corpus Hippocraticum*. In ways and for reasons which still have to be clarified, these questions received a sharper focus in the third century when they started to divide physicians into two groups, the so-called rationalists ("logikoi," which sometimes in this context, misleadingly, is rendered as "logicians") or dogmatists and the so-called empiricists. It seems that in the following centuries discussion of these questions was dominated by the controversy between the two "schools" of medicine. Though one would imagine that the philosophers would take a strong interest in the debate, especially since it was extended to disciplines other than medicine, explicit references to it in the philosophical literature are extremely rare (cf., e.g., Cicero, *Academica priora* II, 122). But we have to remind ourselves that of the four major Hellenistic schools of philosophy three, namely Stoics, Peripatetics, and Epicureans, all were dogmatic or rationalist and thus presumably did not regard the question as an issue still to be settled. As to the

fourth major school, the Academic Skeptics were mainly concerned to undermine the dogmatism of the rationalists. And for the same reason for which
Sextus Empiricus (*P.H.* I, 236ff.) will later take exception to the epistemology
of the empiricists, the Academics would reject the empiricist account of knowledge if it claimed for itself the status of a competing theory of knowledge. It
is only with the rise of Pyrrhonism in the first century B.C. that we find a group
of philosophers who take a marked interest in the empiricism of the empirical
school. But the connections between Pyrrhonean skepticism and empiricism so
far remain rather obscure. For all we know it may, rather, have been the empiricists who started to have an interest in the Pyrrhonean tradition and helped
to revive Pyrrhonean skepticism, though this seems less likely. For reasons of
this sort, then, the debate between rationalism and empiricism was a debate
which took place mainly between the schools of medicine.

Galen's own views on the nature of medical knowledge are very much determined by this controversy in the schools of medicine, and hence it seems appropriate to discuss them within the framework of this debate. It is well known
that Galen refuses to identify himself with any of the schools of medicine (*De
lib. prop.* 1: XIX 13, [SM II 95]). He reject the school-doctrines of the various
rational schools as much as those of the empiricists and the methodists. Part of
this refusal clearly is due to the fact that Galen is unwilling to subscribe to the
characteristic medical doctrine of any of the schools. It may not seem so clear
whether he is also rejecting the epistemological positions of all of these schools,
in particular whether he is rejecting the rationalism of the rationalists. There is
no doubt that Galen sees no merit in the epistemological position of the methodical school. He does show a considerable amount of sympathy for empiricism,
not just in his medical writings, but also in two monographs on empiricism,
namely in *On Medical Experience* and in *Subfiguratio empirica*. Both treatises
on balance turn out to be defenses of empiricism against certain standard rationalist criticisms of empiricism. But even these two treatises at least indicate that
Galen is unwilling to accept empiricism, either. The crucial point, as Galen
notes in the opening paragraph of *On Medical Experience,* is that the empiricists
reject the so-called rational or logical method (*methodos logike*). Now this
method, which we shall have to consider later in some detail, is characteristic
of the rational school. Thus, in rejecting empiricism for this reason and adopting
the rational method, Galen seems to put himself squarely into the camp of the
rationalists.

But Galen does not adopt rationalism without qualification. It is clear that
there is some sense in which Galen is a rationalist. Thus, various students of
Galen, among them Ilberg and Helmreich, have thought it obvious that Galen
shares the epistemological position of the rationalists. Already in antiquity Galen
seems to have been classified as a rationalist.[5] Galen himself sometimes, (e.g.,
in *De differentiis febrium* I.3: VII 282) characterizes the rationalist position in

such a way that there can be no doubt that he regards himself as a rationalist in the sense of this characterization. Again, sometimes he rejects empiricism quite emphatically to leave no room for doubt about whether he is a rationalist (e.g., *De dign. puls.* II.2: VIII 856). Nevertheless, I want to argue that Galen does not accept the epistemological position of the rationalist school, either, but, rather, as Walzer (*Gnomon* 8, 1932, p. 442) and others have suggested, tries to take a position mediating between the two schools. To be more precise: Galen is a rationalist, he regards himself as a rationalist, but he rejects the particular kind of rationalism adopted by the rationalists.

To get a clearer perspective on this question it might be best to first briefly consider the problem to which rationalism and empiricism were supposed to be an answer, then to look for Galen's answer to this problem, and finally to compare Galen's position to that of the rationalists.

All sides to the dispute will agree that a competent doctor, a doctor who has mastered the art, in a sufficiently large and varied number of particular cases, even in cases of a kind he has not come across so far either in theory or in practice, will be able to find out what is conducive to health in the case in question, in particular which therapy will turn out to be helpful to the patient. Moreover, all sides will agree that part of this competence is due to the fact that the doctor has acquired a certain body of general medical knowledge. In one sense of the term "art," it is this body of general medical knowledge that the doctor has acquired which constitutes the art of medicine.

There is, of course, more to the competence of the able doctor than his possession of a body of general medical knowledge. And this to some extent is captured by a narrower, more concrete use of the term "art," as when we say that somebody who has just acquired a certain amount of general medical knowledge has not yet thereby mastered the art of medicine. The art in the more concrete sense does, e.g., involve the ability to identify particular cases as being of a certain kind, though cases of this kind may vary enormously in appearance, and yet one also has to have a sense for their relevant particularities; it obviously involves a certain amount of practical skill; one has to be able to extrapolate from familiar to unfamiliar cases. Thus, the connection between the art in the more abstract and the art in the more concrete sense raises many interesting epistemological problems. And Galen has quite a bit to say on them. He does, e.g., have views about the effect the exercise of the art in the narrow sense has on one's general, abstract knowledge (*De comp. med. per gen.* VI.7: XIII 887), or about armchair medicine (*De ven. sect. adv. Eras.* 4: XI 159); and he frequently comments on the stochastic, as he calls it, nature of the art in the more concrete sense, both in diagnosis and in treatment.[6]

But the main point at issue between the rationalists and the empiricists seems to be the nature and origin of the general knowledge, of the art of medicine in the more abstract sense. And hence I restrict myself to this point. The empiricists claim that the general knowledge of the doctor, as for that matter all of his knowledge, is acquired by experience alone, whereas the rationalists claim that the acquisition of this knowledge also involves reason. To quote Galen (*De sect.* 1: I 65 [SM III 1], "But whence the knowledge of these things is arrived at, is no longer a matter of general agreement. For some (i.e., the empiricists) say that experience alone suffices for the art, whereas others (i.e., the rationalists) claim that reason, too, to no small degree contributes to it."

One striking feature of this characterization of the dispute is its emphasis on the way of inquiry, on how we come to find out about things. And, indeed, "*zetesis,*" "*methodos,*" and "*heuresis*" are crucial terms in the debate. This feature needs to be noted, for it seems to be indicative of a general shift of focus. If we consider, e.g., Aristotle's theory of science in the *Posterior Analytics,* and more generally views on knowledge in classical Greek philosophy, knowledge is not primarily a matter of finding out new things, but first of all a matter of gaining a theoretical understanding of what one, in a way, had known all along. Hence, in classical Greek philosophy there is comparatively little concern for the question how we actually go about finding out new things, and how we might do this in a systematic and methodical way.

This shift in focus reflects at least two things. On the part of the empiricists it reflects the position not only that medical knowledge is empirical, but that the very question of the nature of medical knowledge is empirical, but that the very question of the nature of medical knowledge is an empirical question; if there is an issue about whether it is by reason or by experience that we know, one safe way to settle this question would seem to be to go and see how we actually came to have the knowledge as all agree we as a matter of fact do have. On the part of the rationalists it reflects an interest in a method of discovery, an *ars inveniendi.* It is difficult to trace back the history of this interest. It is there in Cicero (cf. *Topica,* 6; *De orat.* II, 157–59; *De fin.* IV 10). And there is a whole tradition based on Cicero which runs through Quintilian and Boethius (*In Cic. top.* 1045 A), and which plays a considerable role in the Renaissance. Cicero himself ascribes an interest in a method of invention to the Peripatetics. And we do find traces of a strong interest in this, e.g., in the account of Aristotle's doctrine in Diogenes Laertius (V. 28–29) or in Alexander's commentary on Aristotle's *Prior Analytics* (p. 1, 7ff.). In fact, the passages referred to suggest a view of logic or dialectic as having essentially two parts, one concerned with invention and the other concerned with the positive determination of the truth of what has been "invented." A particularly clear case of this contrast is supposed to be the contrast between mathematical analysis, the finding of a solution of a mathematical problem by analysis, i.e., by reduction to a problem already solved, and the positive proof or the truth of the solution by deduction or, more generally, by synthesis.

This contrast appears in Galen in the following way. Galen distinguishes between instruments (*organa*) or means of invention and instruments or means of judging or deciding the truth (*krisis*) or of confirming it (*pistis*). Galen assumes that both reason and experience serve to find the truth (*De meth. mned.* V.1: X 306; *De cur. rat. per ven. sect.* 3: XI 255; *De elem. ex Hipp.* I.2: I 422; *In Hipp. aphor. I.1: XVIIB 346); and he assumes that both reason and experience serve to judge and confirm the truth; in particular, experience is needed to confirm truths found by reason (De probis pravisque sucis 14: VI 814 (CMG V 4, 2, 429); In Hipp. epid. I comm. I.praef.: XVII A 13; De comp. med. sec. gen. VI.7: XIII 887).* In the case of invention, Galen instead of "reason" also talks of "indication" (e.g., *De meth. med.* V.10: X 347) or, quite generally, of "the rational methods" (*De meth. med.* I.3: X 29). What he has in mind when he talks of the rational method in this context seems to be what other authors call the analytical method (cf., e.g., Albinus, *Isag.* 5, p. 156 H.; Plotinus I 3, 4, 12ff.; Proclus, *In Tim.* I, 276, 10ff.). Galen himself occasionally talks of analysis (*Ars medica.* pr.: I 305; *De pecc. dign.* 5: V 80 (CMG V 4, 1, 1, 54); V 84 (CMG V 4, 1, 1, 57); *De meth. med.* I.3: X 30) and synthesis and the synthetical method (*Ars,* prooem.: I 305ff.; *De diff. puls.* II.6: VIII 601; II.7: VIII 608ff.; *De dogm. Plat. et Hipp.* IX.5: V 753 [CMG V 4, 1, 2, 566]). And there is good reason to believe that his remarks on analysis and synthesis in the introduction to the *Ars medica* which were extensively commented on, directly or indirectly, had an influence on the formation of methods of analysis and synthesis, resolution and composition which were to play such an important role in early modern science and philosophy.[7] In any case, Galen shares with the rationalists the view that there is a systematic, logical method of discovery (cf. *De meth. med.* I.3: X 29).

To properly identify Galen's position in this dispute concerning the origin of medical knowledge, it is useful to make two distinctions: (i) We should distinguish the question how we come to know a particular bit of medical knowledge from the question how we come to know the whole body of medical knowledge which is the art of medicine in this abstract sense. Obviously, knowing the art of medicine even just in this sense involves much more than just knowing the particular bits of general medical knowledge. It does, e.g., involve some notion of how the various truths one knows fit together to form some kind of unity, amount to knowledge of one subject matter, hang together to cover that subject coherently and the like. It is natural to think that even if reason is not involved in the acquisition of particular bits of truth, nevertheless acquisition of the art as a whole involves reason. (ii) We also have to distinguish between a body of medical knowledge which is adequate enough to be called an art of medicine, because it allows the person who has acquired it to treat the ordinary range of patients by and large artfully, and a body of knowledge which is complete or perfect in the sense either that it is not only adequate but it includes all the medical knowledge which is available at the time or that is the art of medicine in the very abstract sense that it includes all the truths of medicine whether these have been discovered or not. Obviously, it might turn out to be the case that the acquisition of the perfect art would involve reason, whereas the merely adequate art only presupposes experience.

As to particular bits of general medical knowledge, Galen's position is that some are known by reason alone, some by a combination of reason and experience, some by both reason and by experience, and some by experience only.[8] From this one has to infer that for Galen the perfect art as a whole has two sources of knowledge, reason and experience. But it would be a mistake to infer that for Galen the art has to be based on both reason and experience. And in fact, Galen insists repeatedly that there is an absolute body of knowledge which deserves the name of the art, but which rests entirely on experience, namely empirical medicine.[9] Indeed, Galen claims that it was the very purpose of his *Subfiguratio empirica* to establish this point: "And now I have written this book to show how it is possible that somebody should acquire the art of medicine by experience without the use of reason being involved, if only he gives up to find the whole matter (i.e., to acquire the whole of the art of medicine)."[10] The qualification at the end, no doubt, is crucial, but it is equally crucial to take note of the fact that there is a sense in which Galen admits that experience suffices for the art of medicine. It is difficult to determine whether Galen ever withdrew this concession to empiricism. At least he never, even in his later writings, says that even the merely adequate art presupposes reason.

On the other hand, we have also seen that Galen thinks that there are medical theorems which are known by reason or not without reason, and hence his position must be that perfect medicine relies on both reason and experience. In fact, Galen does tell us again and again that, as with all other arts, there are two sources of knowledge in medicine, reason and experience.[11] It should also be noted that Galen thinks that besides reason and experience there are no other sources of knowledge, either in medicine or elsewhere (*De meth. med.* IV.4: X 272).

Now, there are many philosophers who have claimed that reason and experience are the two sources of all of our knowledge. Hence, in a detailed treatment of Galen's epistemology one would have to clarify his position to the degree that it became apparent in precisely which way he differed from other philosophers who made the same claim. I shall restrict myself to three remarks: (i) Galen's claim is not that the two sources of knowledge are reason and perception. Experience may be based on perception, and the experience Galen has in mind in medicine is based on perception, but perception by itself does not amount to experience in the relevant sense; one cannot, e.g., say that one knows something from experience just because one has seen it. (ii) Galen's claim is not that there would be no knowledge without experience, though perhaps all knowledge is knowledge by reason. One may think, as Aristotle seems to have thought, that for human beings knowledge causally is not possible without experience, because, e.g., it is only through experience that we come to have the concepts we have, and nevertheless one may think that one's knowledge is not justified by this experience it causally rests on, but by an insight of reason into the nature and principles of things by means of the concepts we have acquired. Galen's own view is that some of our knowledge is of this latter, a priori kind, and that in that sense reason is one of the sources of knowledge. But he does not restrict the term "knowledge," as Aristotle had done, to knowledge of this kind. He also accepts genuinely empirical knowledge, i.e., knowledge which is based purely on experience, as knowledge, and in this sense experience is a second, independent source of knowledge for him. (iii) The claim that reason is a source of knowledge is not the trivial claim that some of the things we know we know by having thought about the matter, by having exercised our natural ability to reason. To understand rationalism and the dispute between the rationalists and the empiricists one has to understand that the sense of "reason" involved is a technical one. It is very difficult to grasp the relevant sense of "reason," and it is presumably in part this difficulty which accounts for the problems the use of the labels "rationalist" and "empiricist" raise when they are applied to early modern philosophy.

Given the importance of this point for our topic, I shall at least try to clarify the matter somewhat. Let us start by considering truths of reason quite generally, i.e., things we come to know by the use of reason. Among these truths we have, according to Galen, to distinguish between those which are known by inference, and thus by reason, and those which are known non-inferentially. Now there are lots of things in everyday life which we know by inference, and so, thus far, there is nothing mysterious or controversial about the claim that certain things are known by reason and not by experience or observation. Even the empiricists grant that in that sense there are things known by reason. They do not deny the obvious, namely that people do think and reason, and that in this way they do find out things which they otherwise would not know. The empiricists do not even deny that it takes some thought to arrive at medical knowledge or, quite generally, at some expert, technical kind of knowledge. What they do deny is that it takes some special kind of thought or reasoning to arrive at such knowledge. And to mark the difference they call ordinary thought "*epilogismos*" and any supposedly special, technical kind of reasoning "*analogismos*" (*De sect.* 5:I 78 (SM III.11)). The rationalists, on the other hand, take the view that the kind of reasoning which we use in everyday life does not lead to technical or scientific knowledge; and hence they claim that to arrive at true knowledge we have to use reasoning of a special kind, namely scientific, methodical reasoning. Thus, the question at issue is not whether it takes thought to acquire the art of medicine, but, rather, whether it takes a special, technical kind of reasoning. And since there is a discipline whose main aim it is to develop a theory of scientific reasoning, namely logic, the method of reasoning by means of which we arrive at scientific or technical knowledge is also called the logical or rational method (*methodos logike*). Different rationalists take different views on what the rational method consists in, and correspondingly their rationalism expresses itself in different ways.

Unfortunately, we know very little about the kind of logic Galen has in mind when he talks of the rational method. His little treatise *Institutio logica* deals only with various kinds of deductive inference and thus shows us only a fragment of the rational method. Given his basically Middle Platonic background one might assume that this conception of the method is not significantly different from that of Albinus, especially since Galen had also been a student of Albinus in Smyrna, and since the conception of the rational method which we find in Albinus comes to be the dominant one from the third century onward. On this conception the four dialectical methods are the methods of division, definition, induction, and proof (Albinus, *Isag.* III, p. 153 H.; cf. Sextus Empiricus *P.H.* II, 213), or the methods of division, definition, inference, and analysis (Albinus *Isag.* V, p. 156 H.; *Didasc.* 23–25 Louis). Similarly, Galen does not only talk of the rational method, but also of the rational methods (*De meth. med.* I.3: X 28ff.; II.5: X 115); and though he never gives us a complete list of what he takes to be the rational methods, the ones he refers to are the ones which we find in Albinus.

His insistence on thorough familiarity with the canons of scientific proof is well known and hardly needs an explanation. He himself devoted a compendious treatise to the topic, and he tells us (*De ord. lib.* 1:XIX 53 [SM II 82]) that a student of medicine would do well to study this subject first. There are also numerous passages from which it is clear what importance Galen attributes to the method of division.[12] Similarly, there are a number of passages in which Galen talks about definition, though this topic is markedly less prominent in his writings (cf. *De diff. puls.* IV.7: VIII 736).

From what has been said it should be clear that the rational method for Galen involves much more than the ability to argue correctly or even the ability to produce formally, logically correct deductive inferences. It involves the supposed ability of reason to determine the kinds of things there are in the nature of things and their distinguishing marks by the method of division, the ability to recognize similarities between things in a methodical way which will allow one to determine the genera of things and the most general truths about the various kinds of things, and the ability to define things, not just names, but things as they essentially are in the nature of things. These abilities are not the abilities of ordinary reason which we all are familiar with from everyday life and which we all have come to trust. They are special abilities which the rationalist ascribes to a philosophically and scientifically trained reason, and it is the postulation of and trust in these special abilities which characterizes the rationalist.

There is one feature of the rational method as defended by Galen and the rationalists which requires some comment. Reason is supposed to be in a position to recognize consequences and incompatibilities. It is not just claimed that we can find out by experience that certain states of affairs regularly precede, accompany, or follow certain other states of affairs and that certain states of affairs never occur in conjunction with certain other states of affairs. We are also supposed to be able to see by reason that this must be so by the nature of things, that it is in virtue of the very nature of things that certain states of affairs exclude each other, whereas others are natural consequences of each other. This relation of consequence is also called "indication" (*endeixis;* cf. *In Hipp. Progn.* III.44: XVIIIB 307 [CMG V 9, 2, 373]), and it plays such an important role in rationalism that Galen sometimes characterizes the rational method as being based on indication as opposed to experience.[13] More particularly, the rationalists believe that there are indicative signs by means of which one can make inferences from observable states of affairs to unobservable, hidden states and entities, which are implied by them. Thus, we shall be able to proceed deductively from what can be observed to what cannot be observed, from the existence of objects of experience to the existence of theoretical entities. There are then two ways in which reason can advance beyond phenomena, by direct insight into the nature of things and by inference from what can be observed. Thus, the theory of the rational method is supposed to provide a justification for the old assumption that medical knowledge should be based on a theory of the underlying hidden nature of things.

Galen, then, thinks that nature has provided us with the ability to discern matters which lie beyond our experience. And he also thinks that nature has provided us with trust (*pistis*) in our natural powers of discernment. But the rational method is a very difficult, technical method, which requires considerable intellectual gifts and an extensive training in logic which very few people have, and which even the professed adherents of the method, the rationalists, almost invariably lack.[14] Hence the trust which the rationalists put in their conclusions is mostly unjustified. For they do not actually follow the rational method (*De meth. med.* I.4: X 32). To begin with, they would have to start from proper first principles, which they would have to establish on the basis of truths obvious to everybody in such a way that they could be seen to be true even by those who have no expertise of the subject (*De rat. cur. per ven. sect.* 3: XI 255ff.; *De meth. med.* I.4: X 32). But in fact there is complete disagreement among them concerning first principles (*De meth med.* ibid.). What is worse, most so-called rationalists accept principles on authority, different rationalists following different authorities (*In Hipp. epid.* VI *comm.* II.28: XVIIA 952). Of course, it is often difficult to judge whether something is true by mere reason. One might, e.g., think that "everything that comes into being passes away" and hence "man is mortal" are truths of reason, and yet at least the former is not (*De marc.*

2: VII 671). But it is not just that the rationalists start from arbitrary principles, they also have not learned how to construct scientific proofs (*De simpl. med.* II.2: XI 462), and content themselves with probability arguments, legislating truths rather than proving them (*De meth. med.* I.4: X 32). How difficult the method is we can also see from the fact that many rationalists do not even try to keep up the pretence of following it throughout; they actually are only half-rationalists (*De meth. med.* I.5: X 108; *In Hipp. de nat. hom.* Praef.: XV 8 [CMG V 9, 1, 7]).

The rational method is not just very difficult; in the hand of dilettantes it can be positively dangerous (*De purg. facult.* 5: XI 342). Since we have a natural trust in the method and since it is a feature of it that it leads to conclusions which the ordinary man finds incredible or of which at least he doubts whether such things can be known, there is a tendency to put trust into the findings of reason even in those cases where, because of a failure of reason, they conflict with what we perceive or know from experience (*De rat. cur. per ven. sect.* 3: XI 256; *De simpl. med.* I.13: XI 403). Thus we get dogmas and dogmatists in the pejorative sense of the word (*De plenit.* 2: VII 521; *De simpl. med.* III.6: XI 549; I.28: XI 430; *De meth. med.* II.6: X 122), men who are blinded against the phenomena (*De comp. med. sec. loc.* VIII.1: XIII 117) and who will not even refrain from lying and cheating to preserve their dogma (*In Hipp. de artic.* IV.40: XVIIIA 735). What is worse, they will give up and unlearn what they already come to know from experience or deny what they could know from experience (*De marc.* 2: VII 671; *De simpl. med. temp.* II.5: XI 477; I.36: XI 444; II.1: XI 459). They will start to argue against the use of experience or even the reliability of the senses.[15]

Nevertheless, in spite of all the difficulties and dangers of the rational method, Galen insists that reason does contribute to medical knowledge, that the rational method is a more powerful method than the method of experience (*De comp. med. per gen.* III.2: XIII 582; *De meth. med.* III.3: X 183).

But besides reason and the rational method, Galen also recognizes experience as a source of technical knowledge. We have already commented on his qualified acceptance of empirical medicine as an art. But empirical knowledge, according to Galen, has severe limitations. Though technical, it is not scientific because it does not provide us with any understanding of why the things we know from experience are the way they are; experience can just give us the facts, but not their explanation (*De simpl. med.* II.5: XI 476; *De caus. puls.* III.1: IX 106). Thus, Galen thinks that the physician should pursue both methods, the rational and the experiential method, and that only by their combination shall we arrive at a body of medical knowledge which is perfect and complete and which we can confidently trust to be true (*De comp. med. sec. locos.* VIII.1: XIII 117).

The rational method needs to be supplemented by experience for the following reasons. To start with, we have seen that Galen thinks that the starting points of science are truths of reason. Thus, Galen rejects the notion that the first principles of a science are hypotheses whose acceptance completely depends on the degree of confirmation they receive from their observable consequences. Reason for Galen has the power not just to draw inferences, but to grasp first principles. At the same time, Galen seems to take a rather dim view of our ability to tell confidently in a given case whether we really have a grasp on the first principles of the discipline. Unlike the Stoics or some other rationalists Galen does not believe that our insights into first principles are self-certifying. In sharp contrast with this somewhat diffident trust in reason is Galen's confidence in the reliability of perception and experience. Thus, he tells us that he wished that everything could be perceived; in that case there soon would be no more disagreement and nothing would be left in doubt, and there would be no need to resort to reason (*De simpl. med.* II 2: XI 462). He insists that experience by itself is the most reliable criterion (*De simpl. med.* I.40: XI 456), he repeatedly gives the advice that one should restrict oneself to what can be known by experience unless one has had a thorough training in the rational method.[16] He is unwilling to consider the possibility that right reason and experience could ever clash. But if there is an apparent clash between reason and experience, he takes it for granted that something must have gone wrong on the side of reason; if a theory does not accord with the phenomena, it is not the phenomena, but the theory which has to be rejected.[17] Thus experience is the ultimate judge. Because of this he thinks that the conclusions of reason stand in need of confirmation by experience.[18] Hence, one should try to ascertain as much as possible by both reason and experience. Moreover, one should distinguish between those things which have been found by experience and those things which have been found by the rational method so that the latter can be checked against the former as an independent source of knowledge (*De meth. med.* I.4: X 31; II.7: X 127; III.1: X 159; IV.3: X 246). Thus, the rational method needs the check of experience. There are certain truths which are only found by experience (*De meth. med.* IV.3: X 245; *De antidotis* I.2: XIV, 12; *In Hipp. de acut. morb. victu.* IV.85: XV 871 [CMG V 9, 1, 34]).

But similarly the experiental method stands to gain greatly if it is combined with the rational method. Only the rational method provides a scientific understanding. Moreover certain theorems are arrived at only by reason (*De meth. med.* IX.16: X 655; XIV.5: X 962; *De comp. med. per. gen.* VI.7: XIII 887). Proposed theorems arrived at by experience tend to lack the proper qualifications (*De comp. med. sec. loc.* VIII.2: XIII 128). Though experience puts one into a position to deal with familiar situations, it is not as resourceful as the rational method when it comes to dealing with qualitatively new cases (*De meth. med.* III.6: X 204; II.8: X 211). Hence, the ideal physician will rely not just on the rational method, or just on experience, but on both.

On the basis of the preceding it should be clear that Galen rejects the rationalism of the rationalists in two respects; though he does accept the rational method, he neither fully accepts the rationalists' positive account of the power of reason and the rational method, nor does he fully accept their criticism of experience and empiricism. The rationalists claim that the one way to acquire medical knowledge is by the rational method.[19] Now we have to assume that apart from some radical rationalists, most rationalists would agree that there was some sense in which one could also come to know medical truths by experience. If they insisted that the one way to acquire medical knowledge is by the rational method, their point must have been that knowledge by experience does not amount to true scientific knowledge based on an insight and understanding of why things could not be otherwise. Nothing short of this is to count as real knowledge. And knowledge arrived at by the rational method not only satisfies this requirement, but also any demands one could reasonably have of knowledge.

Against this Galen seems to take the view that knowledge arrived at by the rational method is not perfect. For, as we have seen, he thinks that it stands in need of confirmation wherever possible. Moreover, he seems to think that experience does affect the content of one's general knowledge by making it clearer and more precise.[20] (*De usu part.* XII.8: IV 30; *De fac. nat.* II.8: II 109 [SM III 180]). Finally, there is medical knowledge which we cannot arrive at by the rational method. Thus, to restrict oneself to the rational method is to deny oneself useful and reliable knowledge. To try to derive all medical knowledge by the rational method is to overstep the limits of the method. (*De simpl. med.* II.3: XI 466). And to claim, as Asclepiades did, that experience does not give us any knowledge in any sense of the word is just so wrong that it suggests sophistry. Thus Galen seems to think that the rationalists fail to see the limits of the rational method in at least two respects: it does not provide us with all the knowledge we need, and it does not provide all the knowledge it does provide with the firmness, certainty, and clarity which can be achieved if we also rely on experience.

Neither does Galen fully accept the rationalists' criticism of empiricism. In *De sectis* 5, 1, he distinguishes three groups of rationalist critics of empiricism. From this chapter and chapter 8,3 of *On Medical Experience* we can see that these three groups correspond to three standard lines of attack against empiricism: (i) There is no such thing as empirical knowledge; (ii) Empirical medical knowledge is so limited in scope as to be insufficient to constitute an art; (iii) Empirical knowledge is unmethodical, unwieldy, unmanageable; it lacks the precision, clarity, systematic character of an art. Galen recognizes some truth in the second and the third of these criticisms, but *On Medical Experience* also shows that he knows how these criticisms can be answered on behalf of the empiricists.

This, then, is a brief account of Galen's epistemological position. And if this account is correct at least in its basic outline, it would seem that Galen does have a philosophical position of his own which is by no means negligible. But instead of pursuing the merits of this position, I want to return to the distinctive kind of eclecticism which characterizes Galen's thought and which can now be seen to be firmly grounded in his general epistemological position.

One feature which characterized Galen's distinctive kind of eclecticism was his strikingly skeptical attitude toward a good number of central philosophical questions. He refuses to have a view on questions concerning the essence of God and the substance of the soul, its embodiment, transmigration, and immortality, the eternity of the world, whether there is one world or more than one or even an infinite number of them, whether it is finite or infinite, whether it is surrounded by the void, questions the answers to which mark the divisions between the schools.[21] In part his refusal is due to the view that an answer to these questions is not necessary, since nothing of practical use depends on them. But the main point seems to be that he thinks that there is no way to decide these questions undogmatically by looking at the evidence in a detached and critical way; there just is no clear evidence on the basis of which one could come to a judgment (*In Hipp. de acut. morbl. victu* I.12: XV 434 [CMG V 9, 1, 125]). In *De dogm. Plac. et Hipp. et Plat.* IX.6, 19[22] he even talks as if the reason why such questions could not be decided is that there was no experience to judge them by. And when a few pages later[23] he tells us that such questions belong to the theoretical rather than practical philosophy, one very much suspects that "*theoretike*" here already has some of the pejorative connotation its translation "*speculativa*" was to gain. In any case, one gets the impression that Galen's position, though not antitheoretical, definitely is antispeculative. It is difficult not to regard this antispeculative attitude as a result of his views on medical knowledge and the role of experience in the acquisition of this knowledge.

Second, there was Galen's refusal to identify himself with any of the philosophical schools. Philosophy is supposed to proceed by the rational method. And we have seen how difficult Galen thinks the pursuit of the rational method is in medicine. In philosophy it seems to be even more difficult, so difficult indeed, that many of the issues which divide the schools do not get settled by it. Hence, Galen can hardly be expected to subscribe to the doctrine of any one school. Moreover all his criticisms of reliance on authority, sectarianism, and dogmatism in medicine too obviously apply in philosophy at least as well. And given his historical knowledge, it would have been strange if Galen had not drawn the same consequences in philosophy which he had drawn in medicine: to trust nothing but reason and experience, the two criteria nature has given us, but most of all experience.

For all his eclecticism Galen was perhaps a philosopher of some distinction after all. He certainly stands out from most of his contemporaries with a position of his own and hence deserves the careful attention of the historian of philosophy.

Grammar

16

Principles of Stoic Grammar

I

H. von Arnim did not make a systematic effort to include testimonies on matters of grammatical doctrine in his *Stoicorum Veterum Fragmenta*.[1] So, for this part of Stoic doctrine one still has to rely on R. Schmidt's *Stoicorum Grammatica* which appeared in 1839. In this monograph Schmidt quotes and discusses many of the important texts. Since then, however, our general knowledge of ancient grammatical thought has grown considerably, and much has also been written on the Stoic contributions to the subject; one may mention here the work of Lersch, Steinthal, Pohlenz, Dahlmann, and, in particular, that of Barwick. Also most of the relevant texts are now available in critical editions.

After all this work we should now be in a position to write a monograph on Stoic grammar which would be much more complete and, in points of detail more adequate and accurate than Schmidt's opusculum. It seems, however, that certain general questions have not been clarified sufficiently, and that this neglect has often vitiated the treatment of matters of detail. We still, for example, do not really know whether the Stoics had the notion of a discipline that somehow corresponds to something we could call grammar or why they had such an interest in grammatical questions or on what principles and with what methods they tried to resolve grammatical questions. It is to these general problems rather than to the details of Stoic grammatical doctrine that I would like to turn. In particular I want to discuss the question of whether there is such a subject as Stoic grammar for us to be concerned with. (For these purposes I shall use "grammar" in a very generous and vague sense for any discipline that tries to set forth rules for a language as a whole such that purported sentences that satisfy these rules qualify as sentences of the language.)

The reader of the following pages may wonder why one should insist on a rather tedious treatment of this question. Historians of grammar have usually proceeded as if their subject had a continuous history starting in the fifth century B.C., with the Sophists. But even if one is willing to credit Sophists like Protagoras and Prodicus, and later philosophers like Plato and Aristotle, with a theory of language, it is obvious that their theories were not grammatical theories: they were not interested in finding out how a particular language, Greek, actually works in such detail as to be in a position even to attempt to start formulating the canons for correct Greek. Hence, to treat them as part of one continuous tradition along with the later grammarians is to invite neglect of important questions. We may, for example, assume that those who actually started grammar had certain notions concerning the nature of language, and that these and other philosophical views influenced the way they set up their subject and thus also its later development. We may also assume that they had certain reasons for starting this enterprise and that these reasons influenced the way they went about it and hence, indirectly, the outlines of later grammar. For reasons of this sort it is important that we should have a better notion of the actual origins of the grammatical tradition.

Now our question concerning the Stoics is important, since it has been claimed that it was the Stoics themselves who first formulated traditional grammar. To substantiate this claim it will not be sufficient to show that traditional grammar is influenced in many respects by Stoic notions. For such a state of affairs would be completely compatible with the assumption that the Stoics still formed part of the earlier philosophical tradition, though they contributed more to this tradition than their predecessors, but that grammar itself only began among the classical scholars of Alexandria, who exploited the available philosophical tradition and the Stoic contributions to it. To substantiate the claim that grammar originated with the philosophers we have to show that it formed a definite part of Stoic philosophy (the evidence seems to rule out the other schools of philosophy as plausible candidates). But the origin of traditional grammar is not the concern of this paper. Even if grammar originated with the Alexandrians, it would be important to know whether in matters of language the Stoics still formed part of the earlier philosophical tradition or whether they were already engaged in doing grammar. For the evidence on the Stoic theory of language is so fragmentary that the context of the fragments and testimonies makes an enormous difference to their interpretation and evaluation.

II

The answer to the question whether there is such a subject as Stoic grammar is far from obvious for the following reasons. At least since the first century B.C. we find, besides rhetoric and dialectic, grammar as a third discipline supposed to deal with speech; hence, later the "trivium" of the "artes sermocinales." But the Stoics in their division of philosophy seem to recognize only two disciplines dealing with speech (*legein*): they distinguish rhetoric and dialectic as the two parts of logic. And though these two parts are further divided, none of the subdivisions corresponds to grammar. Later Stoics, of course, could not fail to realize that there were grammarians pursuing a particular discipline. And since there is no doubt that some Stoics had considerable interest in grammatical questions, one might think that they simply joined the grammarians in their own pursuits, either for ulterior philosophical reasons or merely out of interest in the subject itself. So we would have Stoic grammar in the sense that there were Stoics who also happened to be engaged in grammatical studies.

This is, in fact, a view one might obtain from a superficial reading of Seneca's letters. In *Epistle 88* Seneca considers the liberal studies or arts, among which he includes grammar (88.3). But he wonders whether they are genuinely liberal, that is, whether they really help make us virtuous and hence truly free, as philosophy supposedly does (88.2). And hence, later in the letter (88.42), he criticizes philosophers for losing themselves in such petty matters as the distinction of syllables and the properties of conjunctions and prepositions, matters that have no proper place in philosophy; philosophers, Seneca says, should not try to compete with the grammarians. Yet though Seneca here takes the view that such grammatical studies are external to philosophy, his language both here and elsewhere (e.g., *Ep.* 48.11) shows that the philosophers criticized think that it is very much their business as philosophers to discuss such questions. And there is ample evidence that in this they just followed a well-established tradition. In the case of the Stoics we have only to look at the catalog of Chrysippus's writings (D.L. 7.189–202) or at the two surveys of Stoic logic given in Diogenes Laertius (7.41–48 and 7.49–83). There we see how Chrysippus and his students dealt under the heading of "dialectic" with almost all the important topics that we find covered in treatises of grammar some centuries later. So it is clear, at least for the orthodox Stoic philosophers, that engaging in grammatical studies is an integral part of philosophy. And, hence, we may assert that to talk of Stoic grammar is more than to talk of grammatical studies that just happen to catch the interest of particular Stoic philosophers.

But this still leaves open the question whether the Stoics regarded all these grammatical studies as being part of one project covered by the notion of a discipline which more or less corresponds to the traditional notion of grammar. And it seems as if the answer to this question would have to be negative. The Stoics distinguished two parts of dialectic, one dealing with what is (or could be) said or meant or signified (the so-called *lekton*), the other with the way the human voice is articulated to say, express, mean, signify things (cf., e.g., D.L. 7.43; 62). Now many of the distinctions we would regard as grammatical are made in the part of dialectic concerning things said (*lekta*) rather than, as we would expect, in the part concerning expressions, whereas other grammatical points are made in fact where we would expect them, in the section dealing with expressions. Our knowledge of the Stoic doctrine of the *genera verbi,* for example, is largely derived from Diogenes Laertius 7.64. There Diogenes discusses various kinds of predicates, that is, incomplete *lekta* of a kind, which correspond to verbs, but which are explicitly distinguished from verbs as the corresponding *lekta* (D.L. 7.58). We can see that this distinction between *lekta* and the corresponding expressions is to be taken seriously, and that one has to keep in mind that many of the apparently grammatical distinctions are introduced as they apply to *lekta* rather than to expressions, from the fact that as an example of what would correspond to active verbs we are given *"dialegesthai"* (D.L. 7.58). The same point has to be kept in mind, though it has tended to be overlooked by historians of grammar, in connection with the two pieces of Stoic doctrine which are generally regarded as their main contribution to grammar: their doctrine of the cases of the noun and their verbal tense system.

As opposed to Aristotle's cases of the noun, which are noun-forms in the oblique cases, inflected from the form in the nominative (cf. *De. int.,* 16ª 32ff.), there is in Stoicism no immediate connection between cases and inflection. For inflection characterizes words, whereas Stoic cases are not words or features thereof; rather they seem to be what corresponds to the different forms of a noun on the level of what is signified or meant. This is strongly suggested by the fact that in the account of Stoic dialectic in Diogenes Laertius cases are introduced in the section concerning *lekta* and their parts (7.64–65; 70), and, moreover, by the positions of the treatise "On the five cases, in one book" in Chrysippus's list of writings (D.L. 7.192). This in turn suggests that for the Stoics cases are the qualities that are said by Diogenes Laertius (7.58) to be signified by proper names and common, or rather appellative, nouns. (That qualities of material objects are held to be corporeal by the Stoics is perfectly compatible with their belonging to the level of what is signified and their being parts of *lekta;* there is no reason why material objects or corporeal entities should not be constituents of incorporeal *lekta,* e.g., states-of-affairs. Clement of Alexandria (*Strom.* 8, 9 p. 97, 6–7) operates on the assumption that a case is incorporeal, but this is due to the fact that he is not a Stoic and hence naturally thinks of properties as something incorporeal.) The qualities signified by nouns, including proper names, have to be distinguished from the external objects that have the qualities signified and which hence are called *tynchanonta.*[2]

Correspondingly the cases, being the qualities characterizing the external objects, are also called *teukta* (Simpl., *In cat.,* 209 13). They are called "cases" because they fall (cadere, *piptein*) under a concept (Stob., *Ecl.* I, p. 137, 1 W.). It is not the concepts themselves which are constituents of the *lekta* signified by sentences but only their cases. For according to the Stoics, concepts or ideas are figments without real substance,[3] they are at best quasi-subsistent.[4] *Lekta,* on the other hand, and hence their constituents, are something quite real in the way, for example, facts are. Though the Stoics refuse to call them "beings," since they are incorporeal, they grant *lekta* the status of "somethings," whereas concepts or ideas are denied even that status. Hence, cases rather than the corresponding concepts are constituents of *lekta*. Now cases enter the constitution of *lekta* in various ways, depending on how they are related to, or constructed with, the other constituents of the *lekton*. Corresponding to these ways we get the analogue of the distinction between the traditional cases of the noun. But to understand the Stoic doctrine of cases, it is important not to overlook the fact that the Stoic distinction of cases does not primarily apply to nouns, but to their counterparts, to the constituents of what is signified, rather than to the constituents of what has signification. If one overlooks this crucial difference one will not, for example, be able to understand how the Stoics could insist that a nominative case is a case strictly speaking, and as much so as any other case (cf. e.g., Ammon., *In de int.* 42, 30ff.). But what is of importance for our argument in this paper is that a Stoic doctrine which historians of grammar regard as an important part of Stoic grammar is not dealt with in the part of dialectic concerned with expressions, where we would expect to find it, and where in fact other matters of grammar like the parts of speech are treated.

The same, it seems, may be said with reference to the other piece of Stoic doctrine to which historians of grammar attach particular importance, the Stoic verbal tense system. The Stoics, like Aristotle before and the grammarians afterward, distinguish between past, present, and future. But whereas the grammarians tend to neglect aspect and to regard imperfect, perfect, aorist, and pluperfect as primarily differing in their temporal distance from the present (the aorist leaving it open whether something is near or far away in the past), the Stoics emphasize the importance of aspect in the tense-system, in particular whether an action is complete or incomplete (hence the terms "perfect" and "imperfect"). And so they call the present "present imperfect," the perfect "present perfect," the imperfect "past imperfect," and the pluperfect "past perfect" (cf., e.g., *Schol. in Dion. Th.* 250, 26ff.). In this connection Pohlenz and others have suggested that Zeno and Chrysippus, because of their Phoenician background, would be particularly sensitive to the difference in aspect of the various tenses. And in general it seems to be assumed that the Stoics came to make this classification according to aspect because of careful observation of the use of differently tensed verbs.

Another explanation, though, seems to be much more plausible. Aristotle had tried to distinguish two kinds of activities (in a suitably wide sense of the word); those which have their end in themselves, which are complete or perfect at any time at which they can be said to take place, and those which are incomplete. As one test for this distinction he used the following: to see something is complete because at any time at which one can be said to see something one can also be said to have seen it; on the other hand, to build something is incomplete because at no time at which one can be said to be building a house can one be said to have built the house; to build something is not to have built it, but rather to have not built it. It would be clear from this test that there is no essential connection between the Greek perfect tense as such and the past; hence the test would draw attention to the importance of aspect in the tense-system. Since the test occurs in various crucial contexts in Aristotle, the Stoics cannot but have been familiar with it and have recognized its significance.

More to the point, however, is the distinction between perfect and imperfect propositions in an argument reported by Sextus Empiricus (*Adv. Math.* 10.85ff.). Diodorus Cronus maintains that there is no motion; it is never true to say of something that it moves or that it is moving or that it is in motion; all one can say of something is that it did move or that it has moved. Against this the critics (who use Stoic terminology) argue that such a claim wrongly presupposes that perfect propositions could be true without the corresponding so-called "imperfect" propositions being true also: that is, "A has moved" cannot be true unless "A moves" or "A is moving" is true also (*Adv. Math.* 10.92). It seems clear that the argument is not stated precisely. For it cannot be claimed that for "A has moved" to be true now it must be true now that A moves or is moving. The claim rather must be that for "A has moved" to be true it must be true at some time that A moves or is moving, and hence, that there is motion. Diodorus tries to counter this argument in various ways which, in turn, are answered by his opponents. For example, he points out that it may be true that Helena had or had had three husbands without its ever being true that she has three husbands. But we are only concerned with this argument to the extent that it sheds light on the distinction between perfect and imperfect propositions. Translators and commentators tend to suggest that the distinction is one made in terms of the tense of the verb. But though the "imperfect" propositions are all specified by means of present-tensed verbs, in the case of the "perfect" propositions both the perfect (10.92, 101) and the aorist (10.92, 97, 98, 101, 102) are used indiscriminately. Moreover, though the Aristotelian test may not suffice to make the distinction Aristotle wants to make, it does show that it would be a mistake to assume that the present tense necessarily marks imperfection. Hence, the distinction does not seem to be in terms of tense, but rather between propositions whose truth presupposes that the activity referred to is complete or completed, and propositions whose truth does not require such completion.

So what we have is a logical rather than a grammatical distinction in Diodorus and also, as it seems from the terminology, in the Stoics, to discuss a philosophical problem. Now the terms used in this discussion to distinguish the two kinds of propositions are basically the terms used by the Stoics to characterize the aspects. *Paratatikon* is the term used by the Stoics both in this discussion and later to mark imperfectness. The agreement is all the more remarkable since the use of the term in non-Stoic grammarians will be restricted to verbs in the imperfect tense, whereas in this discussion it is used for propositions expressed by means of verbs in the present tense, just as the Stoics used it for both present tensed and imperfect tensed verbs. The term for perfect propositions in this discussion is *syntelestikon,* an expression not extant in this sense in any other source and put to quite different purposes by Epicurus, whereas the Stoics use the term *syntelikon.* But the correspondence is close enough, in fact so close as to suggest that the distinction of aspects which is characteristic of the Stoic verbal tense system is derived from, and secondary to, a corresponding distinction of propositions, which for the Stoics will be a distinction of *lekta* rather than of expressions.

That the Stoics were in fact interested in such a distinction can be seen from two titles in the section of Chrysippus's catalog which concerns *lekta:* "On things said according to tenses, in two books" and "On perfect propositions, in two books" (D.L. 7.190), and, moreover, from the fact that Chrysippus in his *Logical Investigations* (SVF 2.96ff.), repeatedly speaks of present, past, and future predicates, which he regards as incomplete *lekta* and not as expressions. So there seems to be an analogue of the whole verbal tense system on the level of the *lekton.* And of this analogue there is, as we have seen, good reason to believe that, with regard to the distinction of aspect, it was prior to the verbal tense system. In fact, whereas we have at least some evidence of the analogue for the time of Chrysippus and Diogenes of Babylon, it is quite unclear when the verbal tense system itself was introduced. Hence, for the Old Stoa the situation in the case of the tense system is rather similar to what we found with regard to the cases of the noun: there is evidence for a piece of doctrine of obvious grammatical relevance, which is therefore often treated by historians of grammar as a piece of grammatical doctrine. Insufficient attention is paid to the fact that it is a fragment of a theory concerned with *lekta* and their parts, rather than with sentences and their constituents.

So the position seems to be as follows: the evidence for many of the grammatical distinctions attributed to the Stoics comes from the part of dialectic concerned with *lekta.* If we proceeded as if the distinctions on the level of *lekta* were grammatical distinctions, it would be clear that there is no such subject as Stoic grammar in any interesting sense; for its reconstruction would be patched up from pieces taken out of context from the two quite different parts of Stoic dialectic. So if there is to be Stoic grammar in a sufficiently strong sense, it has to have its systematic place in one of the two parts of dialectic. It lies in the nature of the subject that this can hardly be the part concerned with *lekta* and their parts. And even if it were, we should expect to find within that part of dialectic some division between grammatical and other questions, for example, logical questions. But there is no trace of such a division in this part of dialectic, and a glance at the way these quasi-grammatical categories come to be introduced in this part of dialectic shows why it would be misguided to expect these apparently grammatical notions to form part of a subtheory of their own. What the

Stoics in this part of dialectic are concerned with is an investigation of the kinds of things that could be said (and hence thought). This investigation is to supply us with criteria by means of which we can decide what we should say and what we should avoid saying: in the simplest case, that of propositions, criteria for truth to help us avoid saying what is false. Such an investigation of course, involves the classification, characterization, and analysis of *lekta*. And for this we need a fairly complex conceptual framework. It appears that the seemingly grammatical categories that we find in this part of dialectic come in naturally as part of this conceptual framework. We shall, for example, pay special attention to tensed propositions and their relations to one another in order to be able to deal with Diodorus's Master Argument or The Sea-Battle Tomorrow; hence, the distinction of tenses will come in. We have seen above how an analogue to the distinction of aspects would be introduced. Similarly for logical reasons, we will be interested in various kinds of negations and, hence, will distinguish between various kinds of negatives (cf. D.L. 7.69, 70, 190). Both the distinction of various kinds of simple propositions and that of various kinds of predicates seems for the Stoics to involve the notion of case and the distinction between oblique and direct cases (D.L. 7.64–65, 70). The distinction between kinds of atomic propositions involves in addition the notions of a demonstrative and an indefinite particle (D.L. 7.70). The *genera verbi,* or rather their analogues, are introduced to distinguish kinds of predicates (D.L. 7.64). The notion of a conjunction and its various kinds is needed to characterize molecular propositions and their kinds (D.L. 7.71–73). One could extend this list, but the examples given should suffice to show that these quasi-grammatical distinctions in this part of dialectic form an integral part of the machinery by means of which the Stoics try to do logic.

So Stoic grammar would seem to have to be part of the theory of expressions. But if we take this position and try to reconstruct a Stoic system of grammar just from evidence concerning the Stoic theory of expressions, our subject again seems to be in danger of disappearing for lack of substance: for to get a sufficiently substantial system of grammar we have to have many distinctions of the kind for which we only can get evidence from the Stoic theory of *lekta*. And this lack of evidence from the theory of expressions casts doubt on the very existence of the subject as a part of the theory of expressions. We could try to evade this difficulty by assuming that the Stoic theory of expressions will have counterparts for those parts of the theory of *lekta* which are of obvious grammatical relevance. But that would be to beg the question. For we are only justified in postulating such counterparts if we are justified in believing that a system of grammar formed part of the Stoic theory of expressions. But this is exactly what is in question.

What reason, then, do we have for attributing to the Stoics a system of grammar as part of the theory of expressions? Very little, it would seem. For if we look at the relevant part of Diocles Magnes' account of Stoic dialectic in Diogenes Laertius (7.55ff.), the most comprehensive ancient report of the matter, it is apparent that grammar cannot be identified with the whole part of dialectic which deals with expressions. After all, it is supposed to deal also with such matters as definition, concepts, genera, species, and divisions of various kinds (D.L. 7.60–62). It could be argued on the basis of Diogenes Laertius 7.44 that these topics do not really belong to the theory of expressions, but found a place there because they had to go somewhere; but then there are still such topics as poetics (D.L. 7.60) and ambiguity (ibid., 62), or even meter and music (ibid., 44) which have to be dealt with under this head. So it seems that we cannot identify grammar with this whole part of dialectic. But neither is grammar set off in any way as a separate part within this part of dialectic. It is true that the first paragraphs of Diocles' account (D.L. 7.55–59) cover grammatical topics, but it is difficult to see how the treatment of these topics would amount to a grammar. And, what is more, the paragraph on the virtues and vices of speech (D.L. 7.59), which follows sections on, roughly, phonology and the parts of speech, seems to presuppose a point of view according to which the grammaticality of an expression (its Hellenism, as it is called) is just one, though perhaps the most important, of the features that are constitutive of good style. Thus the comparatively detailed account of Diocles in Diogenes Laertius gives us very much the impression that grammar is not a special part of the theory of expressions or, for that matter, of Stoic logic. And the short survey of Stoic logic at Diogenes Laertius 7.44 reinforces this impression: if grammar had been regarded as a separate subject, it would have been natural to refer to it as one of the items dealt with under the appropriate heading.

Hence, it seems to be a problem whether there is such a subject as Stoic grammar in the sense of a separate discipline pursued systematically, as opposed to a collection of grammatical remarks made in the pursuit of various other enterprises. In spite of these difficulties I shall, in what follows, try to argue that there is such a Stoic discipline as grammar or, at least, that what the Stoics are doing in the first part of the theory of expressions comes sufficiently close to such a separate discipline.

III

To start with, it seems that there is evidence that the Stoics had the notion of such a discipline before grammar had become an established subject of its own. We have already had occasion to refer to a section in Diocles' account of Stoic dialectic on the virtues and vices of speech (D.L. 7.59). This doctrine of virtues and vices of speech goes back at least to the third book of the *Rhetoric,* in which Aristotle deals with diction or good style. He recognizes (1404b 1–2) one virtue of diction or speech (*lexis*): clarity (*saphē einai*). Theophrastus apparently tried to elaborate this and distinguished four virtues of diction. Good speech for him is (I) pure, proper Greek, (II) clear, (III) fitting, and (IV) ornate (cf. Cicero, *Orator* 79). The Stoics, in turn, adopted the doctrine from Theophrastus and incorporated it into their dialectic. For the virtues of speech attributed to them in Diogenes Laertius (7.59) turn out to be those of Theophrastus in exactly that order, except that between the second and the third virtue the Stoics added another, conciseness, a virtue they cherished so much that Cicero could say of Cleanthes' and Chrysippus's treatises on rhetoric that they provided ideal instruction for one desiring to fall silent (*De fin.* 4.3.7).

Of these virtues obviously the most important is the first, Hellenism. Aristotle already had said (*Rhet.* 3, 5 [1407[a] 19–20]) that Hellenism is the principle of diction. What one says may not be concise, need not be particularly elegant, could be less than crystal clear, and might not be completely appropriate, but it at least has to be proper Greek. The relative importance of this virtue was generally stressed. Dionysius of Halicarnassus, for example, says that the other virtues are of no use if they are not accompanied by this primary virtue (*Ad Pompeium* 3). In our text the prominence of this virtue is indicated not only by its first place on the list of virtues but also by the fact that the only vices of speech explicitly mentioned in Diogenes Laertius (7.59) are those associated with the virtue of Hellenism: barbarism and solecism.

According to the account in Diogenes (7.59) Hellenism or pure Greek is defined as a way of speaking which is in accordance with the technical, and not some (random or) arbitrary usage. It is not very clear what this definition amounts to, but it does not seem to be the following: "Not any usage which is in accordance with the usage of some Greek-speaking community is acceptable; it has to be the technical usage." It, rather, seems that "arbitrary" here characterizes the kind of usage rejected and that "and not some arbitrary" is supposed to clarify by contrast what is meant by "technical."

What, then, may the Stoics have in mind when they talk of a random or arbitrary usage? Since we are talking about usage, that is, a specifiable way of speaking and hence a way of speaking covered by some set of rules, they cannot have in mind that the rejected usage is random or arbitrary in that it lacks a set of rules or principles which govern it. Its arbitrariness must, rather, consist in some arbitrariness of its rules. By contrast the technical usage must be characterized by the fact that its rules are subject to certain constraints or principles; because of these constraints they are nonarbitrary. If one looks around for the kind of principle the Stoics may have in mind, one comes across a whole number of passages in which it is said that pure Greek (or Latin) is constituted or determined or defined by factors like etymology, reason, analogy, age, usage, nature. Quintilian, for example, says of good Latin that it is determined by reason, age, authority, and usage (*Inst.* 1.6.1). Leaving aside the details, it seems to be fairly clear how these princples are supposed to be used. If we employ a word or a phrase or a construction that is not immediately recognizable as part of common or educated Roman usage, we may appeal to reason, age, or authority for support; we may, for example, point out that it is already to be found in Ennius or that it is accepted by Cicero. But if our usage cannot be justified by reference to one of these principles and if we still insist on speaking in this way, our usage will be arbitrary even if a whole group adopts it. That the ancient grammarians in general have in mind principles of this kind when they try to distinguish the pure language from some other (arbitrary) form of the language (say the Greek used by the Egyptians) seems to be clear form the way Sextus Empiricus criticizes them. In *Adversus Mathematicos* (11.176–247) he considers the question whether, as the grammarians maintain, there is an art of Hellenism, that is, whether there is a theory that supplies us with canons for the distinction. And he apparently believes he has shown that there is no such discipline by showing that the two principles of analogy and etymology cannot be accepted as criteria for Hellenism. Hence it is plausible to assume that when the Stoics talk of a technical usage, as opposed to some arbitrary one, they have in mind a way of speaking which is governed by a set of principles of the kind we have mentioned, as opposed to a way of speaking which cannot be justified with references to such principles.

If this is what the Stoics have in mind when they speak of the technical usage, we may still wonder why they use the term "technical" rather than some adjective like "proper," "correct," "natural," "rational," or "common," all of which would have been appropriate and in accord with their doctrine. It may be the case that "technical" is used here to indicate that the proper usage is not acquired, as Sextus tries to argue, merely by experience and observation (*empeiria, paratērē-sis, Adv. Math.* 1.177); and it is not a matter of scientific knowledge either. That such epistemological questions concerning the status of grammatical knowledge were widely treated in Hellenistic times one can see, for example, from the discussion in Sextus (*Adv. Math.* 1.60–89) and from the Scholia on Dionysius Thrax (cf. p. 6, 31ff; 118, 19ff.). Sometimes, in fact, scholars tried to divide philology (of which philologists then took grammar to be a part) according to the supposed epistemological status of its divisions. Of this kind is the division suggested by Tauriscus, a pupil of the Stoic Crates, into a rational (*logikon*), an empirical (*tribikon*), and a "historical" (*historikon*) part (Sext. Emp., *Adv. Math.* 1.248). It would take some effort to specify exactly what Tauriscus meant by these terms, but if one looks at the terminology used to describe empirical medicine, or at the language of Sextus Empiricus, it is obvious that the terms used by Tauriscus are taken from epistemology. The same is true, just to mention one other example, of the division of "grammatica" into "methodice" and "historice" to be found in Quintilian (1.9.1). The Stoics can hardly have failed to take a position on this matter. Hence, it is natural to assume that, in the definition of Hellenism, "technical" is chosen to mark the Stoic attitude.

But if the Stoics thought of proper useage as being technical in this way, it is difficult to believe that they did not entertain the notion of a *technē*, a discipline or art, which would set for the principles and canons by means of which we could judge whether some usage is proper; and this all the more so since the educated general public of the time regarded a pure Greek language, to be shared by all who wanted to use Greek, as highly desirable. In fact, in view of such a desire,it is difficult to believe that no effort was made by the Stoics to work out such a discipline. That some scholars engaged in such an enterprise can be seen from the way Sextus deals with the question "Whether there is an art of Hellensim?" (*Adv. Math.* 1.176ff.) and from what remains of such treatises as Varro's *De Lingua Latina*.

That this enterprise, which ultimately led to the art of grammar, was originally regarded as an extension of the theory of the virtues of speech in a doctrine of style or diction, is suggested by the following: one can still see from the third book of Cicero's *De Oratore* (10. 28, 13, 48ff.) that a division of labor was envisaged according to which it fell to the grammarian to teach pure and clear Latin (or Greek), whereas the teacher of style or rhetoric would concern himself with the other, higher virtues of speech. Quintilian, too, presupposes such a division of tasks between the grammarian and the rhetorician. He distinguishes (*Inst.* 1.5.1) three virtues of speech, of which the first, correctness, corresponds to Hellenism (or Latinity). And this virtue—as opposed to the others—is dealt with by the first part of grammar. Now, by "the first part of grammar" he means, as the context shows (cf. 1. 4. 2 and I.9. 11), what we would call "grammar," as opposed to philology (or the rest of philology), which makes up Quintilian's second part of grammar. Since it would be understood that it is not philology that deals with the other virtues of speech, it would be clear that these were to be handled by the rhetoricians. Of relevance here may also be the corresponding distinction between *loqui* and *dicere* as falling within the province of the dialectician and the rhetorician respectively (cf. Cic., *Orat.* 32.113).

Once we are willing to entertain the assumption that the Stoics had the notion of a discipline at least in its aims sufficiently like grammar, a notion, moreover, which led to the development of grammar, we may also be willing to reconsider the question whether Diocles' account of Stoic dialectic does not after all provide evidence for the existence of such a Stoic discipline. It seems clear that if the subject is to be found anywhere, it has to be found in the part of dialectic concerned with expressions. Now the main reasons that seemed to tell against this possibility were two: (1) though the topics discussed in Diogenes Laertius 7.55–58 could be dealt with in a treatise of grammar, it is difficult to see how a treatment on just these topics could amount to a grammar; and (2) wherever we might consider drawing the line in Diogenes' account between a survey of grammar and a survey of something else, there seems to be no natural point of division; certainly no such point is indicated explicitly—which is strange if grammar was regarded as a distinct part of dialectic.

Perhaps these difficulties can be overcome. As to the first, we are, fortunately, able to point out that this is a problem that arises for the historian of ancient grammar in any case. For the contents of the majority of ancient grammatical treatises correspond very closely to the topics dealt with in Diogenes Laertius 7.55–59: they contain some general introductory remarks and basic definitions along the lines of 7.55–56, have a section on phonology corresponding to chapters 56–57, then mainly deal with the parts of speech, and, finally, may have a section on the virtues and vices of speech. Sometimes treatises on grammar would deal only with the parts of speech. Hence, the first difficulty does not arise just for those who want to attribute a system of grammar to the Stoics. Hence, the apparent incompleteness of Diogenes Laertius 7.55ff. as a survey of grammar should not be counted as evidence against assuming a Stoic discipline of grammar. Although it calls for an explanation, such an explanation is also called for by other texts.

Nevertheless, to disperse possible doubts on this score, we may proceed further. As a first step we distinguish between the elements of grammar and scholarly grammar. The topics discussed in Diogenes Laertius 7.55ff., in the ancient grammatical treatises of the type referred to above, and in such surveys of grammar as we find in Sextus and Quintilian's first book, correspond to the elements of grammar rather than to a full fledged scholarly grammar. Such a distinction is suggested, for example, by Quintilian (*Inst.* I.4–7). Quintilian there goes through the topics in grammar which a boy should have covered before he can profitably proceed to the study of rhetoric. That the topics mentioned are not supposed to exhaust the subject of grammar is clear from the fact that Quintilian insists that boys should also learn to inflect nouns and verbs before they pass on to more advanced grammatical subjects. There is a suggestion that some schoolmasters pass over the matter (I.4.22). In general we have to keep in mind that the introductory grammatical treatises cover the material to be taught to children at about the age of twelve. So what is in question is certainly not the scope of *scholarly* grammar, but the elements of grammar with which the young student would be confronted upon entering secondary school. If this distinction is granted we may say that, once grammar was an established subject represented in the curriculum, the topics discussed in Diogenes Laertius 7.55ff. might be referred to as the elements of grammar. When, for example, Seneca complains (*Ep.* 48.11) that the philosophers, having promised heaven, descend to the elements of the grammarians, we may safely assume that it is the part of dialectic corresponding to Diogenes 7.55ff. which he is thinking of.[5] Now clearly the Stoics were not interested in outlining an elementary grammar course for children. But if we could explain that the account in Diogenes Laertius was supposed to represent no more than the elements of grammar, we would be in a better position to explain the apparent incompleteness of the account as a survey of grammar as a whole.

Our second step is to see how what we have called the elements of grammar could be thought of as elements of grammar, how a treatment of them might serve as an introduction to grammar not just for children but even at a rather advanced level. It is easy enough to see how the material referred to in Diogenes Laertius 7, paragraphs 55, 56, and the first part of 57, could serve as an introduction at any level. This explanation, though, puts the main burden of representing grammar on to the section concerning the parts of speech; too much of a burden, it would seem. But a look at ancient treatises of grammar, such as Priscian's *Institutiones* or the remains of Apollonius's special treatises on the various parts of speech, shows that at least the ancients thought that most of the material covered in grammar *could* be organized around the various parts of speech. Even syntax could be covered this way to a considerable extent, as one can see from the organization of Apollonius's Syntax. In fact, both of Apollonius's treatises on pronouns and adverbs contain sections on the syntax of these parts of speech. We do not at this point have to discuss what the Stoics themselves dealt with under the parts of speech. For our present argument it is sufficient to see that even a treatment of the parts of speech could be, and was, regarded as an introduction to grammar even at a rather advanced level. Thus, the apparent incompleteness of the survey in Diogenes is by itself no evidence that the Stoics did not recognize grammar as a distinct part of dialectic.

Now it might be objected that if Diogenes Laertius 7.55ff. was not supposed to represent Stoic grammar as a whole, but only the elements of grammar, one might expect at least a comment to that effect. This objection brings us to our second difficulty: not only is no part of the account in Diogenes marked off as covering grammar (or, for that matter, the elements of grammar), but one cannot even see where such a cut could be made.

The explanation may be as follows: the items that later were treated as the elements of grammar were originally not introduced as such. They were there, at the position in this part of dialectic which they still occupy in Diocles' account, not as the elements of grammar, but as part of a theory of diction or style (*lexis*). The account in Diogenes might be thought of as representing a stage in which grammar has grown from a negligible part of such a theory of diction to a fullblown and complex discipline, which, however, at least formally, was still regarded as part of the theory of diction. Hence, the treatment of the virtues and vices of speech – and among the virtues of speech the treatment of Hellenism – is not set off from the discussion of the other virtues as the subject matter of a distinct discipline.

What, then, is the evidence for saying that the elements of grammar originally formed part of a theory of diction and that even later the Stoics still considered grammar as embedded in such a theory?

According to Alexander (*In Top.* 1.10ff.), the Stoics regarded dialectic as the discipline that tells us how to speak well (*eu legein*); and to speak well, Alexander says, they make a matter of saying what is true and saying what is fitting. Saying what is true is the concern of that part of Stoic dialectic which deals with what is signified. Hence, it contains an epistemology (D.L. 7.43, 41, 45 [6] a doctrine of truth-conditions for the various kinds of propositions (D.L. 7.73–74), a theory of arguments, in particular syllogisms (D.L. 7.76ff., 45),[7] and a treatment of fallacies (D.L. 7.82, 44). But it would be imprecise to say that this part of dialectic is exclusively concerned with truth. For among things signified or said, the Stoics distinguish not only propositions but also commands, questions, wishes, oaths, and the like (cf. e.g., D.L. 7.6ff.). So it would be more precise to say that this part of dialectic is concerned quite generally with what it is that should be said, though, of course, it would mainly deal with truth and falsehood. This raises the question whether it was this very point that Alexander had in mind when he explained that Stoic dialectic is also concerned with saying what is fitting. But this is very improbable. For by the time of Alexander it seems to have been complete forgotten that Stoic dialectic was conceived by Chrysippus as also dealing wtih such topics as the logic of commands or the logic of questions. What then does Alexander have in mind? The most plausible assumption seems to be that he wants to point out that for the Stoics to speak well amounted to two things: that it is the right or true thing that is said, and that what is said is said the proper way. This, in turn, would suggest that the two main parts of dialectic (cf. D.L. 7.43) corresponded to the double function of dialectic: the theory of what is signified or said tells us what it is that we should or could say; the theory of expressions tells us how it is to be said.

More light may be shed on this by a further passage of Diogenes. Unfortunately, the remarks he makes at 7.83 about the general aims of Stoic dialectic are too short; and in addition the text seems to have suffered considerably. But the passage still shows that the dialectician tries to provide us with criteria for what one should say. From the end of the paragraph we may infer that knowledge of what one should or should not say involves a two-fold competence. For the dialectician will know both what things are and what they should be called. Presumably this can be generalized so that the dialectician's expertise amounts to both knowledge of what it is that should be said and knowledge of how it should be said. If this is regarded as the characteristic competence of the dialectician, then it is natural to regard the two main parts of Stoic dialectic as corresponding to this two-fold competence: the theory of *lekta* tells us what it is that should be said, whereas the theory of expressions will tell us how we should say it.

Traditionally, dialectic had been concerned with truth. But where would one turn if one tried to develop a theory of how one should express oneself as a second part of dialectic? It seems that the theory of diction would be a natural source to draw on. Rhetoric was familiar with the contrast between knowing what to say and knowing how to say it; it was exactly this contrast that Aristotle used to introduce the theory of diction in the third book of the *Rhetoric* (1403^b 14ff.) as being concerned with the way in which we should speak.

The theory of diction seems also to have become a repository for much earlier Greek speculation on language; one associates grammar in the fifth and fourth centuries B.C. very much with philosophical debates concerning the nature and origin of language, in particular the correctness of names. There is no doubt that as a result of these debates there existed in the fourth century a considerable body of linguistic notions and assumptions. What is in doubt is what happened to this body of knowledge when the Early Academy and the Stoa started to divide philosophy into sections and subsections. They attempted to make the division on principles which gave them confidence that somehow all that there is to be known by philosophers could find its place in the schema. There was a natural tendency to make the cuts follow the boundaries of the established disciplines that had to be incorporated. But this meant that for subjects which had not yet been safely established, there was a tendency to pursue them just to the extent to which they fitted into the program of study suggsted by the division of philosophy, and with that program in view. One of the subjects discriminated against in this way would be language in general and the Greek language in particular. For even with an author as late as Aristotle, whose works do contain numerous short remarks on the topic, there is no suggestion that there is a place in philosophy where language would be dealt with systematically and on its own. It is significant that by far the most grammatical text in the Aristotelian corpus is the passage on diction in the *Poetics*. Hence, there is no reason to expect that philosophers like Xenocrates and the first Stoics would try to provide a separate place for the study of Greek in their classification of philosophy. So we should not be surprised to find that the tradition of philosophical speculation about language, when channeled through this classificatory scheme, should come up in a subordinate place like the theory of diction. That this place is not necessarily entirely inappropriate, however, can be seen from the fact that of the five points Aristotle mentions as particularly important for Hellenism (the principle, as he says, of diction) the first concerns conjunctions (*Rhet.* 1407^a 20ff.), the fourth grammatical gender (1407^b 6ff.), and the fifth grammatical number (1407^b 9ff.). How the philosophical tradition is integrated at this point can be seen, for example, from the references to Protagoras in the *Rhetoric* (1407^b 6) and the *Poetics* (19.1456^b 15ff.).

In any case, it is clear that the Stoics turned to the theory of diction. The account in Diogenes (7.55–59) can be read as a report of a theory which culminates in a doctrine of the virtues and vices of speech. It certainly has to be read as a report of a theory in which the virtues and vices of speech play an important role. But, as we have seen, the doctrine of the virtues and vices of speech was regarded as a central part of the theory of diction. What is more, we have already seen that in their doctrine of the virtues and vices of speech the Stoics depend heavily on Theophrastus's theory of diction. So at least for this important part of their theory they must have turned to the theory of diction.

Our survey in Diogenes also shares another important topic with Theophrastus's *On diction;* a large part of Diocles' account is taken up by the section on the parts of speech, and this seems also to have been one of the main topics in Theophrastus's treatise. For it is generally agreed that a list of topics that Simplicius (*In cat.* 10, 23ff.) says are discussed by Theophrastus in *On the elements of speech* represents the contents of one part of Theophrastus's *On diction;* and in this list the parts of speech figure very prominently. At all events it seems clear both that the parts of speech would be discussed in theories of diction and why this was so.

A certain Theodectes is said to have distinguished just three parts of speech: nouns, verbs, and conjunctions (Dion. Hal., *De comp. verb.,* 2.8; Quint. 1.4.18). Whence could this information ultimately be derived if not from Theodectes' remarks on diction in one of his rhetorical writings? Morover, when Diocles reports (D.L. 7.57) that the Stoic Antipater suggested the adverb as a sixth part of speech, he gives as the title of Antipater's treatise *On diction and things said.* It is also fairly clear why the parts of speech would be mentioned in a theory of diction or style. Dionysius of Halicarnassus tells us in the second chapter of his treatise on compositioin that composition is a certain arrangement of the parts of speech, and then goes on to give a short account of how the number of parts of speech was increased after Aristotle. We may also notice that the four parts of speech that, it is generally assumed, were already distinguished by Zeno and Cleanthes, namely noun, verb, conjunction, and article (supposing that Chrysippus introduced the distinction between proper name and common noun as separate parts of speech), are exactly those on which we find remarks in theories of diction in the fourth century B.C.[8] In any case, it is clear at least for Theophrastus that another important topic of the Stoic theory, the parts of speech, had been the topic of systematic discussion within the theory of diction.

Many of our texts, especially the chapters on diction from Aristotle's *Poetics,* also show that *most* of the topics dealt with in this part of dialectic, certainly those covered in Diogenes Laertius 7.55–59, were also regarded as falling within the province of the theory of diction.[9]

So it turns out that the topics of this part of dialectic can be regarded as topics of the theory of diction; and it is also clear that at least for some of them the Stoics turned to the theory of diction. But, on the other hand, it is also clear that their treatment of these topics does not amount to a theory of style of the kind we find in Aristotle, Demetrius, or Dionysius of Halicanrassus. Too many of the standard topics of such a theory are missing. Hence, the claim that this part of Stoic dialectic was conceived of as some kind of theory of diction needs further qualification and explanation.

To start with, it is obvious that in this part of dialectic the Stoics are not interested in a *rhetorical* theory of style. For the theory whose original purpose we are trying to grasp more clearly is pursued as part of dialectic rather than rhetoric. The rhetorical theory of style is concerned with the composition of artful speeches or, when we come to the age of the book, with the kind of "Kunstprosa" we find, for example, in Thucydides. Dialectic, on the other hand, is concerned with language, or at least educated language, in general. (If it was sometimes said that dialectic was concerned with dialectical discussion, this was an anachronistic attempt to preserve the traditional contrast between dialectic and rhetoric; the actual scope of Stoic dialectic gives no indication of such a restriction). So the material covered by the original rhetorical theory of diction will be divided into two parts, one part that deals in a general way with any (educated) use of language, and which will become the part of dialectic with which we are concerned as, so to speak, a general theory of diction; and another part that deals with the specifically rhetorical use of language, and which will remain a part of rhetoric.

This distinction between a general theory of diction and a specifically rhetorical doctrine of style was to have an enormous effect on the general part of the original theory of diction. The primary concern of the original theory was rhetorical or stylistic; hence, linguistic or grammatical matters would come in only incidentally and would not be developed systematically. Once a systematic division was made between a general theory of diction and a specifically rhetorical part, the grammatical questions, which philosophers had in any case taken particular interest in, had to be treated more systematically.

This division of labor also had another advantage. A theory of diction was needed not just for artful prose but also for poetry. Hence, diction was dealt with in two places, in rhetoric and in poetics (cf. Arist., *Poetics* 19, 1456^b 8–18; *Rhet.* 1404^a 28–39). Aristotle tries to justify this by saying that poetical diction and rhetorical diction are two quite different matters (1404^a 24–29); hence, each should be the subject of a different study. But even given two such theories, there would still be the problem of whether the general part of the theory of diction, which is neither tied to rhetoric nor to poetics, should be dealt with not only in rhetoric but also in poetics, as in fact happens in Aristotle (*Poet.* 20–21). For the Stoics this problem does not arise. They have one general theory of diction which is then immediately followed by "poetics" (D.L. 7.60; cf. 44), and which will be presupposed by rhetoric.

The whole matter might be much clearer if we knew more about Theophrastus's theory of diction. For Theophrastus may already have, in practice, made the distinction between a general and a specific theory of diction by treating of language quite generally in the first part of *On diction*. The matter would also be much clearer if we knew more about Xenocrates' treatment of dialectic. Zeno had been a student of Xenocrates (D.L. 7.2; Eus., *P.E.* 13.5, 11), and the Stoics seem to have followed Xenocrates in the relevant part of the division of philosophy. Like him they divided philosophy into logic, physics, and ethics (Sext. Emp., *Adv. Math.* 7.16), and they followed him in the division of logic into rhetoric and dialectic as well as in the definition of rhetoric (*Adv. Math.* 2.6–7). Like the Stoics Xenocrates made one part of dialectic deal with voice (*phōnē,* Porph., *In Harm. Ptol.,* 193 W., frg. 10 Heinze), and like the Stoics he dealt with both prose and verse under this heading (*ibid.*). Now, on the authority of Aristoxenus, Xenocrates is reported to have been rightly criticized for including the discussion of voice in dialectic. This may suggest that Xenocrates' procedure was a novelty. In that case it would be particularly significant that the Stoics followed Xenocrates. And, hence, for our problem it would be important to know what role Xenocrates attributed to the treatment of voice within the system of dialectic. The catalog of Xenocrates' writings lists two *Studies on Diction,* in 15 and 16 books respectively, immediately after a treatise on dialectic in 14 books. But this will hardly suffice as evidence that Xenocrates regarded the part of dialectic in question as a theory of diction.

So there is some reason to believe that the first part of the Stoic doctrine of expression, the part corresponding to D.L. 7.55–59, was originally conceived of as a general theory of diction or style. We have also seen that, given such a division between a general theory, on the one hand, and specific rhetorical and poetical theories on the other, questions concerning language in general could now be dealt with in a more systematic way. But it is still the case that a theory of diction or style, however general, is not a grammar. So some further explanation is still necessary.

It may be relevant that one could take two positions with reference to the theory of diction. One could take the attitude that the grammatical part of it was trivial and negligible, because anybody with a decent upbringing would know Greek anyway. What he might still lack in this regard was much too subtle to be acquired through a "discipline"; for that he had to read good authors and to associate with the right people; experience of the right kind rather than doctrine was needed. Hence, the important, difficult, and really technical part of the theory would be the one concerned with the finer virtues of speech which would give it elegance and effectiveness. Not that excellence in these virtues could be achieved just by reading treatises, but that there is an enormous amount of technical knowledge which can be acquired in this way. This is the attitude that we still find in Cicero's *De oratore* (cf., e.g., 3.37ff., 151). But if one did not follow

Cicero in his praise of rich style and preferred instead a very plain language, as the Stoics did, the treatment of the other virtues of speech would lose much of its urgency.

Moreover, though the higher virtues of speech would be regarded as being relevant to language in general, it would commonly be granted that they were the particular concern of the rhetorician. We saw above how a divison of labor was envisaged according to which it was the grammarian who was responsible for Hellenism, whereas the rhetorician dealt with the higher virtues. Even if he did not agree in theory that the higher virtues quite generally fell into the province of rhetoric (as a Stoic obviously did not), in practice a representative of the general theory of diction will have concentrated on what was indisputably his own area. The general and, in a way, justified concern for Hellenism, a common dialect of pure Greek (*koinē, kathareuein*), would considerably increase the relative importance of the primary virtue of speech. But quite apart from his general interest in Hellenism, it was never called in doubt—rather it was often stressed by authors on style like Dionysius of Halicarnassus—that there is no excellence of style unless the requirements of Hellenism have been met. So if one believed that Hellenism admitted of the kind of systematic treatment on the basis of which canons of correct usage could be established, it was only natural that one would devote most of one's energy to this primary virtue of speech.

The Stoics may also have been impressed by the idea that it was in ordinary rather than in highly refined language in which reason articulated itself, and that, hence, a study of ordinary language was philosophically much more relevant. It should also be kept in mind that the questions concerning language in which philosophers had traditionally taken an interest would now be classified as problems concerning Hellenism. Their systematic treatment seems to have gathered such momentum that it vastly outgrew investigation into the higher virtues of speech. For all these reasons one should not be surprised that a treatment of what was originally conceived of as a general theory of diction would later turn out to be little more than a treatment of Hellenism, that is, a grammar of some sort.

If there is any truth in this account, we have also removed our second difficulty, that grammar in Diocles' account is not marked off as a distinct part of dialectic; indeed that it could not be so marked off because no radical distinction is made among the virtues of speech between grammatical correctness and the higher virtues of diction. The explanation would be that grammar has grown out of a general theory of diction from which the specifically rhetorical elements have been removed and in which so much emphasis is placed on the primary virtue of speech that the remaining general theory of diction amounts basically to the elements of grammar. This is the subject matter of Diogenes Laertius 7.55–59; and to this are appended certain other subjects that, given the division of Stoic philosophy, would naturally go there, as we explained in the case of poetics, or which would not find a suitable place elsewhere, like definition, genus, and species. Grammar originally would not be marked off, because in the time of Chrysippus and Diogenes of Babylon, on whom Diocles seems mainly to draw, grammar had not yet been established as a discipline of its own, let alone as one distinguished from dialectic. Later the Stoics would feel no particular need to mark it off, since it would be clear that it basically corresponds to what is covered in Diogenes 7.55–59. That this, in addition to grammar, also included at least a short treatment of the higher virtues of speech does not seem to have been regarded as a disadvantage. For even much later we find treatises that profess to be treatises on grammar but which still at least touch on the other virtues of speech (or the corresponding vices.)[10] Some treatises, at least in a very rudimentary form, even cover the topics of definition, genus, and species.[11] Charisius's treatise, in fact, also covers such topics as the tropes.

In any case, grammar came to be a subject of its own, independent of dialectic, only by being lifted out of this context and being put into a new one: it was made the first, introductory part of philology, sometimes also called "the technical part" (cf. Sext. Emp., *Adv. Math.* 1.91). And since philology was called "grammar," our subject acquired the labels "grammar" or "art of grammar." It is for this trivial reason that the Stoics at the time of Chrysippus or Diogenes of Babylon were not in a position to say something like "this part of dialectic starts with grammar, and then deals with . . . " Grammar came to have its name only when and because it was put in a different context. Some Stoics who also taught philology as Crates and his followers would, of course, also teach grammar in the new context (cf. Sext. Emp., *Adv. Math.* 1.79 and 248). In fact they may be responsible for the introduction of the technical part of philology as a discipline, and in this way for the establishment of grammar as a discipline distinguished from both dialectic and rhetoric. But there was no need for the Stoics in general to lift grammar out of its original context. For though the Stoics had a great interest in the classical authors, and, hence, in the philology needed to deal with them, philology, after all, was not a part of philosophy. In fact, there would have been systematic reasons for leaving grammar in its place. The notion of Hellenism was normative, and, hence, grammar would naturally go with the doctrine of the other virtues of speech. More important, there was, as we shall see, a systematic connection between grammar and the theory of *lekta* which would be obscured by separating grammar from dialectic. Finally, one might argue that such a radical separation of logic and grammar proves to be disastrous, at least for grammar.

It turns out, then, that the facts which at first sight seemed to tell against the existence of Stoic grammar also fit a plausible picture according to which grammar was already a fairly well defined and rather developed part of Stoic doctrine. So we seem to have reached the following point in our argument: (1) the evidence considered does not rule out the possibility that the Stoics recognized grammar as a philosophical subject; (2) the Stoics seem to have the notion of such a subject as grammar; (3) there is a clearly distinct part of Stoic dialectic, a general theory of diction, which we could identify with their grammar; (4) it is very tempting to identify this part of dialectic with Stoic grammar, since in its contents it seems to correspond to the elements of grammar; and (5), as nobody will deny, the Stoics do deal with a great number of grammatical questions: they contribute to the terminology and conceptual framework of grammar; they have an influence on grammatical doctrine from Dionysius Thrax onward; and they are even in antiquity regarded as being particularly concerned with language.[12]

But all this is still compatible with the assumption that the Stoics failed to pursue grammar systematically as a distinct subject within dialectic. Hence, the existence of Stoic grammar in this sense is still an open question. In what follows I shall try to provide some positive evidence for this assumption by trying to reconstruct the basic structure of Stoic grammar, so that it may become clearer whether their grammatical studies amount to systematic grammar or not.

There is reason to believe that the Stoics divided the subject into two parts, one concerned with individual words taken in isolation, the other with the assembling of words into sentences. This is what one would expect if it were true that grammar developed out of the theory of diction. For the theory of diction has two primary parts, the first concerned with individual words, particularly the choice of words, the second with the assembling of these words (cf., e.g., Cic., *De orat.* 3.149). This seems to be a natural way of bringing order into the material of the grammarian, and it is in fact followed by later grammarians like Priscian, who first deals with the parts of speech and then their organization into sentences. It is referred to as a principle of organization in Quintilian (1.29.2); it is used in treatises that are agreed to be heavily influenced by Stoic doctrine, like Varro's *De lingua latina* and Augustine's *Dialectica*. When Seneca characterizes logic in the Stoic sense, he says "It goes into the properties of words, into their combination, and into arguments to ensure that falsehoods do not creep in in place of truth" (*Ep.* 89.9). A comparison with *Ep.* 88.42 suggests that Seneca, when he talks of the properties of words, is thinking of the characterization of words as the different parts of speech. Thus, he seems to characterize dialectic by referring to what he regards as the main topics of its two parts: the theory of argument representing the parts concerning *lekta,* grammar representing the part concerning expressions; and grammar, it would seem, is referred to under its two main topics, the doctrine of the parts of speech and the theory of their combination. Furthermore, the two vices that are associated with the virtue of Hellenism, barbarism and solecism, come to be distinguished accordingly: mistakes about individual words are barbarisms; violations of the rules of composition are solecisms.

Let us first consider composition. It seems appropriate to start with this for two reasons. First of all, there does not seem to be anything in Diocles' account to correspond to it. And this throws doubt on our suggestion about the basic organization of Stoic grammar. Second, as one can infer from the definition of solecism in Diogenes Laertius (7.59), composition in grammar amounts to syntax. But partly because syntax seems to be missing in Diocles' account, this subject is often thought to be of much later origin.

There are two considerations that may help to explain the apparent lack of a syntax. To start with, we may argue that the omission of syntax in Diocles' account is simply due to the fact that syntax did not belong to the elements of grammar. And there is independent evidence for this; for syntax is covered neither in Sextus's discussion of grammar in *Adversus Mathematicos*, book 1, nor is it dealt with in Quintilian or in many of the Roman introductions to grammar. But then, of course, the question arises why syntax, given its importance, is not counted among the elements of grammar. A number of factors may have come togehter to bring this about. If, for example, it should be the case that the elements of grammar are topics of the theory of diction reconstituted as the elements of grammar, we should not expect syntax to be among them. For syntax, though touched on (cf. Cic., *De orat.* 3.40), does not seem to have been dealt with systematically in the theory of diction. Or, as we have seen earlier, syntax could be dealt with to some extent under the different parts of speech; and this may have been thought to be sufficient for an introduction. There is one further factor, however, which deserves to be treated in more detail.

We noted earlier that in the theory of *lekta* the Stoics were also concerned with the *analysis* of *lekta*. In fact, they seem to have distinguished various kinds of elements of *lekta* and to have investigated how these are put together to form various kinds of complete *lekta* corresponding to complete thoughts and sentences. Cases are one kind of element (D.L. 7.64, 70), predicates of a certain sort another kind (cf., e.g., D.L. 7.58, 64, 70), and there are still others, such as various kinds of particles (D.L. 7.67, 70) and conjunctives (*ibid.* 71ff.). These elements are thought to enter compounds according to certain laws of composition. The term regularly used for their composition is *syntattein*, the verb from which "syntax" is derived as the corresponding noun (cf. D.L. 7.58, 59, 64 four times, 72 twice). This syntax of *lekta* seems to have been the object of systematic study. For among the titles of Chrysippus's writings we find *On the syntax of the things said*, in four books, and *On the syntax and the elements of the things said, to Philippus*, in three books (D.L. 7.193). Since the things said are *lekta* (cf. D.L. 7.57), we have here two treatises on the syntax of *lekta* (and, incidentally, confirmation for the assumption that the Stoics worked with the notion of elements of *lekta*). That there was such a topic as the syntax of *lekta* we can also see from the fact that Plutarch refers to it in these very terms. (*Adv. Colot.*, 1119F).

Now if one has such a syntax of *lekta* and if one thinks that there is a very close correspondence between the parts or elements of speech and the elements of *lekta,* one may think that to construct a syntactically acceptable sentence was basically a matter of putting together elements of speech in such a way that the corresponding elements of *lekta* form a *lekton* which satisfies the laws of the syntax of *lekta.* It seems that the Stoics adopted a version of this view, and that even Apollonius Dyscolus still wrote his *Syntax* on some assumption of this sort (cf. *De synt* I.2. p. 2, 10ff., replacing "intelligibles" by "elements of *lekta*"). We shall deal with the correspondence between the elements of *lekta* and the elements of speech when we come to the latter; for the moment I shall suppose that the Stoics assumed such a correspondence. That they approached syntax in this way is suggested by the following facts: if we inspect the relevant section of the catalog of Chrysippus's writings (D.L. 7.192–193), we notice that the two treatises concerning the syntax of *lekta* mentioned above are preceded and followed by treatises dealing with the parts of speech. This suggests a systematic connection between the syntax of *lekta* and the parts of speech. Moreover, the first in this group of four treatises is not just on the parts of speech, but on the elements of speech and the things said, that is, it seems to compare and correlate the parts of speech and the elements of *lekta.* Similarly, the third treatise is not just on the syntax of *lekta,* but on the syntax and the elements of things said. This suggests a systematic connection between parts of speech, elements of *lekta,* and the syntax of *lekta,* which could be accounted for if we assume that the Stoics took the approach to syntax mentioned above.

Moreover, it should be noticed that the series of four writings just referred to is listed in the catalog under the heading "Logical topics concerning expressions and the corresponding *logos,*" that is, they are not listed in the part of the catalog which covers the theory of *lekta.* There would be a justification for putting treatises dealing with the syntax of *lekta* among treatises dealing with expressions and the sentences they constitiute if the syntax of *lekta* was also supposed indirectly to serve the suggested function of a syntax for sentences. Similarly, it may be pointed out that when Plutarch mentions (*Adv. Colot.* 1119 F) three topics in the theory of language, "syntax of *lekta*" is preceded by "sounds of some kind or other" and followed by "usage of words."

The most important passage however, for our purposes is one from Dionysius's *On composition* (4.32). Dionysius explains that for his treatise on composition he turned to two writings of Chrysippus, both entitled *On the syntax of the parts of speech,* but found them of no use for his purposes. For they dealt with dialectical matters, "the composition of true and false, possible and impossible propositions, propositions which are contingent and change their truth-value, ambiguous ones and others of such a kind." It is clear, both from the title and the reference to ambiguity, that in these treatises Chrysippus was also dealing with sentences and their composition. But though we may suspect that Dionysius selects examples of what was dealt with in these treatises in a rather one-sided way, to make his point that they were useless for composition as he was interested in it, the examples themselves make it clear that Chrysippus here too must have dealt with various kinds of *lekta,* and, what is more, with kinds of *lekta* in which the logician would be interested but which would be of no particular concern to the grammarian. An explanation for this, again, would be that the Stoics do syntax of expressions by recourse to the dialectician's syntax of *lekta* via the parts of speech and the elements of *lekta.* That the syntax of *lekta* would be determined very much by logical interests would help to explain why Dionysius, who is interested in style, would not find Stoic treatises on the composition of expressions particularly useful.

That the Stoics thought that by putting together parts of speech in the appropriate way we construct, as it were, the intended corresponding *lekton,* can also be seen from the characterization of the various kinds of molecular propositions in Diogenes Laertius 7.71ff. These propositions are *lekta* and hence not expressions. Nevertheless, they are characterized in terms of kinds of conjunctions which are supposed to be characteristic for the various kinds of proposition in question. But the text makes it clear that these conjunctions are thought of as expressions and, hence, not as constituents of the propositions to be characterized. If then Chrysippus and Diogenes are said to claim that the implicative proposition is formed by means of the implicative conjunction "if," their assumption must be that it is by putting parts of speech together in an appropriate way that we get the intended *lekton,* formed by parts corresponding to the parts of speech. So, if an account along these lines is acceptable, we have another explanation of why syntax was not counted among the elements of grammar. On the one hand, it relied so much on the syntax of *lekta* that, given the knowledge of this syntax and the correspondence between parts of speech and elements of *lekta,* one was supposed to know the basic facts of the syntax of expressions anyway; on the other hand, the syntax of *lekta* carried one far into the details of Stoic logic in a narrow sense—which would be inappropriate at least for elementary instruction in grammar.

But from what has been said it should also be clear that the Stoics did deal with syntax systematically: they not only had a syntax of *lekta;* they also had a syntax of expressions or parts of speech, that is, a syntax in the strict sense, though it was closely tied to the syntax of *lekta.* Hence, there should be no doubt on this score that the Stoics, even in the days of Chrysippus and Diogenes of Babylon, systematically pursued grammatical studies.

IV

Having dealt briefly with composition or syntax, let us turn to the part of grammar which deals with words taken in isolation. From what has been said, it is fairly clear that an important, if not the most important, topic here is the parts of speech. But if the suggested program of grammar is taken seriously, this part of grammar has to do more than deal with questions that we associate with the doctrine of the parts of speech; it has, after all, to supply us with the criteria for what is to count as a proper Greek word. The Stoics certainly try to provide us with such criteria, for example, when they give us a definition of barbarism (D.L. 7.59).

It is in this context that authors like Sextus and Quintilian discuss such factors as etymology and analogy as criteria for Hellenism. Hence, the question arises how discussion of these questions was related to the discussion of the parts of speech. No light is thrown on this by Diocles' account, and it is unclear how the question is to be answered. Since later the parts of speech and the criteria for Hellenism were discussed separately (cf. Sext. Emp., *Adv. Math.* 1), we shall proceed on the assumption that to qualify as words all expressions have to fall under one of the parts of speech, and, hence, have to meet the conditions for belonging to the part of speech that is relevant to them. But, in addition, they have to satisfy certain further requirements in order not to be disqualified as barbaric. Our difficulty may be connected with the fact that in later antiquity, besides the treatises on the art of grammar, there was a separate class of treatises *On Latinity* (or *On Hellenism*) which are introductions dealing with the nature and origin of language and the criteria for Hellenism (or Latinity), and then proceeding to discuss the choice of words, their inflection, and sometimes also their orthography (cf. Barwick, *Remmius Palaemon* 228ff.).

The doctrine of the parts of speech was regarded by the Stoics as highly important from the start. When Epictetus characterizes the genuine philosopher and asks which theorems he is after, he answers, "Those which Zeno talks of, to know the elements of speech, what each of them is like, and how they fit together, and what is along those lines" (*Disc.* 4.8.12). This passage seems to indicate that Zeno already had an interest in the parts of speech, in fact even at least a rudimentary interest in their syntax. But beyond this, the remark taken in its context suggests a motive for this interest which we have not touched upon so far. For Epictetus begins his characterization by saying that the true philosopher deals with reason and that it is his end to possess right reason. Now the word rendered by "reason" here, and above, in "elements of speech," by "speech," is the very same word, *logos*. And it also seems that Epictetus means to use the same word throughout the characterization of the true philosopher. Hence, some authors have doubted whether Epictetus is talking here of anything as trivial as the parts of speech. But this seems to be guaranteed by the fact that "parts of speech" and "elements of speech" are such firmly established technical terms that it would be highly misleading for Epictetus to use them in any but their usual technical meaning, unless the context fully determined a different sense—which it does not in our case. Hence, we might be inclined to see in this apparent move from one sense of *logos* to another a piece of cheap rhetoric. But that, too, must be ruled out. For we find almost the same characterization, involving the same apparent equivocation, in a papyrus-text (Herc. 1020 = SVF 2.131) attributed to Chrysippus. According to this text "philosophy, whether it is the care for, or the knowledge of, right reason, is the discipline concerned with reason (*logos*). For if we are completely familiar with the parts of speech (*logos*) and their syntax, we will make use of it (i.e., the *logos*) in an expert way. By *logos* I mean the one that by nature belongs to all rational beings."

What is the supposed connection between the rightness of reason and the parts of speech and their syntax which would make such language understandable? There are various possibilities. According to the Stoics, the discipline that is primarily responsible for the correctness of reason is dialectic. But for Zeno the main function of dialectic was avoiding and dissolving fallacies (cf. Plut., *S.R.* 1034E; D.L. 7.25; Stob., *Ecl.* II, 22, 13ff. W.). Now we can see from Aristotle's *Sophistical Refutations,* especially from the section on fallacies in diction, from Galen's treatise on such fallacies (SVF 2.153), and from various fallacies in which the Stoics took a particular interest (cf., e.g., D.L. 82; Simpl., *In cat.* 105, 13ff.) that a distinction of parts of speech and a consideration of their construction was regarded as useful or even necessary for the analysis of fallacies. So Zeno may have seen the relevance of the parts of speech and their composition to the correctness of reason in their relevance to the analysis of fallacies. But the way Epictetus and Chrysippus speak suggest some "deeper" connection.

Reason is articulated in thought. Now the articulation of thought in which we are interested when we are interested in the correctness of reason is the articulation of its content. But thought, in this sense of the content of thought, according to Stoic doctrine, is a *lekton*. Hence we are interested in the articulation of *lekta*. We can see the way in which knowledge of the articulation of *lekta* is essential for the correctness of reason by looking at Diocles' account of Stoic logic. According to his arguments, and in particular syllogisms, are *lekta* (D.L. 7.63, 76). And one can easily see also how in a very literal sense the articulation of the argument is decisive for the question whether we have a valid syllogism or not. What, then, does this have to do with the parts of speech and their syntax? The articulation of thought is described in terms of the elements of *lekta* and their syntax. Given the supposed close correspondence between the elements of *lekta* and their syntax and the parts of speech and their syntax, it is clear how an investigation into the parts of speech and their syntax is relevant to an investigation of the articulation of thought, and, hence, to correct reason; how, in fact, it could be regarded as an investigation of the elements of thought and their syntax. But, though this may be part of what Chrysippus had in mind, we may doubt whether it was a concern of Zeno's. For it is not clear that Zeno was already thinking in terms of *lekta* and their constitutive elements as opposed to sentences and their constituents, the parts of speech. Furthermore, Zeno does not seem to have been concerned with the elaboration of a positive theory of inference as an aid to correct reason.

There is yet another possibility, though admittedly a rather speculative and obscure one, by which we may explain the relevance of the doctrine of the parts of speech and their syntax to the correctness of reason. It may have been assumed that ordinary language, at least in its basic structure, is a reflection of the rationality and common sense of human beings. And it may have been assumed that this rationality is reflected in particular by the kinds of units from which speech is composed and by the laws of its composition. Hence, one might hope that an investigation of the parts of speech and their syntax would reveal aspects of rationality to the extent that a linguistic community had achieved it. In any case, the two passages referred to can be taken as evidence that right from the start the Stoics had a strong interest in the parts of speech, because of their relevance to the correctness of reason.

This interpretation again suggests that the Stoics, at least from Chrysippus on, relied on a very strong correspondence between the elements of *lekta* and the parts of speech. We should now examine this assumption more closely. In the *Quaestiones Platonicae* Plutarch devotes an entire essay to the question whether there are only two parts of speech, nouns and verbs, as a passage in Plato's *Sophist* (262 C) might suggest, or whether there are, in addition, all sorts of other parts of speech, as the Stoics claimed. Plutarch himself concludes that there are only two parts or elements of speech (1011E), and he refers to others who take the same view (1010B). Later this position will be shared by authors like Ammonius (*In de int.* 12, 20ff.; cf. 11 1ff.), who goes so far as to attribute to Aristotle himself the view that conjunctions, articles, prepositions, and the like are not properly speaking parts of speech, (ibid. 12, 24; 14, 19ff.).[13] Ammonius suggests that we should distinguish between parts of speech and parts of diction (*lexeos*, cf. 12.30ff.) and regard the other so-called parts of speech as parts of diction. By chance we know that this distinction had already been made by Theophrastus, and that already in his day it had been a matter of some discussion (Simpl., *In cat.* 10.24ff.). It may be for this reason that some authors preferred the expression "elements of diction," instead of "elements" or "parts of speech" (cf. Dion. Hal., *De comp. verb.* 2.7–8). If, then, the Stoics insist on calling all parts "parts of speech," we may suspect that they are trying to make a point, especially since Theophrastus is supposed to have made this distinction in his treatise on diction—which we have seen that the Stoics followed in other respects.

Unfortunately, our rather late sources are not very clear about the grounds on which the distinction had been suggested; they also do not seem to have a clear notion of how the various parts of speech had been treated in Theophrastus' day. Simplicius (*In cat.,* 10.25ff.), presumably following Porphyry, talks as if Theophrastus had dealt with the question "whether noun and verb are parts of speech or whether there are also articles and conjunctions and other kinds." Here the "and other kinds" is not to be taken as evidence that Theophrastus recognized other parts of speech or diction than the four explicitly mentioned. It seems certain that Theophrastus did not distinguish more than these four parts, and Simplicius did not find more than these specified in his source; but he still would want to add the phrase "and other kinds," since to him the list of four parts of speech would look curiously incomplete. Similarly, we find Plutarch and Ammonius trying to explain why adverbs and participles are not properly speaking parts of speech. But their discussion, as a report of the views of the ancients, is highly misleading, since in Theophrastus' day participles and adverbs were still classified as nouns or verbs, and so for "the ancients" would be parts of speech in the strict sense.

Hence, the question really is why Theophrastus and others wanted to maintain that conjunctions and articles (in the larger old sense of the terms) are just parts of diction, whereas the Stoics insisted that they, too, like nouns and verbs, are parts of speech. Given this clarification, it is tempting to assume that the distinction has something to do with the Peripatetic tenet that only nouns and verbs have signification, that is, are the kinds of expressions that have corresponding items in ontology, and that the notion of these items is evoked by the particular term (cf. Aristotle, *De int.* 16^a 3ff.; 16^b 20–21). (It may be noted that on this count adverbs and participles would not be just parts of diction.) Now it is still Plutarch's first move to argue that, as opposed to nouns and verbs, the other parts of speech do not signify (1009D). Ammonius similarly says of these parts of speech that they do not signify (*In de int.* 12, 13–15). But of what relevance is this for the distinction between parts of speech and parts of diction? The idea may have been that in the case of a statement, for example, we have to distinguish between what is claimed, that is, what would make the statement a true statement, and the way we happen to make this claim, that is, how we express it (cf. Ammon., *In de int.* 13, 9ff.). Now for the Peripatetics truths would be configurations of the ontological items signified by what they call nouns and verbs. These truths would be represented canonically in the language for which syllogistic is developed in the *Analytics* or in the simpler language of the *Categories*. This very simple language contains only nouns, verbs, and a negation-sign; in the more complex form it may contain, in addition, quantifiers. But, as one can see from the *De interpretatione,* it does not contain sentence-connectives, the paradigms of conjunctions. The *De interpretatione,* of course, does refer to conjunctions (cf. 17^a 9; 17^a 16; cf. also 18^a 18ff.), but only, it seems, to point out that propositions formed by means of them are not strictly speaking one or simple. It then neglects them completely for the rest of the treatise. This might lead to the idea that conjunctions and articles owe their existence just to our way of speaking about things and dealing with facts; there is nothing in the basic facts themselves which corresponds to them. Hence, they are just parts of diction, whereas nouns and verbs are also parts of speech.

If this was Theophrastus' point, we can easily see why the Stoics would disagree. As far as conjunctions are concerned, the Stoics maintained that there are real connections between states of affairs in the nature of things, implication, disjunction, incompatibility, which are reflected in language by the different conjunctions, especially those crucial in logic. When Apollonius Dyscolus (*De coni.* 247, 22ff.) reports that most authors agree that expletive conjunctions do not have signification, we may assume that the minority includes Stoics, who even in the case of expletive conjunctions want to maintain that there is signification. Apollonius does, in fact, tell us in another passage (*De coni.* 214, 4–6) that Posidonius in his treatise on conjunctions argued against those who maintain that conjunctions do not signify but only tie expressions together.

As far as articles are concerned, let us consider "This (pointing to Socrates) runs," to use a simple example (at this time the class of articles would include pronouns). According to our interpretation, for Theophrastus and his party the state of affairs relevant to this statement would be that Socrates runs; its canonical expression would be "Socrates runs." It is for reasons of style, convenience, ignorance of Socrates, his kind, or his name, and the like, that instead we might say "this runs." The *logos,* what is claimed, is the same; just the expressions differ. Again the Stoics would disagree. For them there are many important logical differences between "This runs" and "Socrates runs"; hence, they assume that there are two different *lekta* corresponding to the two sentences (cf. Sext. Emp., *Adv. Math.* 8.97–98). So for the Stoics both conjunctions and articles will be parts of speech, since they have their counterpart in what would make the statement come out true and do not owe their existence merely to our way of speaking about the world.

If this is why the Stoics insisted that all words can be classified as parts of speech, then the very term "part of speech," as opposed to "part of diction," is meant to suggest that there is a correspondence between the parts of speech and the elements constitutive of *lekta.* It is because of this supposed correspondence that even conjunctions and articles can claim to be parts of speech. It is tempting to think that the Stoics not only assumed that something on the level of the *lekta* corresponded to the parts of speech but that the different parts of speech corresponded to the different elements of *lekta* kind by kind. Even Apollonius Dyscolus in one passage (*De pron.* 67.5–7) claims that the parts of speech should be distinguished according to what they signify, implying not only that all parts of speech have signification but also that each of them has a kind of signification peculiar to itself. The most important text in this connection is the part of Diocles' account in which we are given the definitions of the various parts of speech (D.L. 7.58). There the first three parts of speech are indeed distinguished by the different kinds of elements of *lekta* they signify; an appellative noun signifies a common quality, a proper name an individuating quality, a verb a certain kind of predicate.

So far, then, the assumption seems to be confirmed. It derives further confirmation from the fact that the Stoics, following Chrysippus, distinguished between appellative and proper names as two parts of speech, a distinction not accepted by Aristarchus, by Dionysius Thrax in the *Technē* (cf. though *Schol. in D. Th.* p. 160, 26–28 H.), and by later traditional grammar. For though differences in the inflectional pattern were claimed as evidence for the distinction, the main reason for it was clearly the difference between common and proper qualities.

Difficulties with the assumption that the parts of speech can be distinguished with reference to the kind of element of *lekta* to which they correspond arise with the fourth part of speech, the conjunction; it is defined syntactically and by its morphology. This complication seems to be due to the following: the class of conjunctions is supposed to include both the conjunctions proper and the prepositions (cf. Apoll. Dysc., *De coni.* 214, 7–8). And it is difficult to see how one could specify one kind of signification for both conjunctions and prepositions. It is, of course, possible that in the representation of the form of *lekta* both conjunctions and prepositions could be represented by the same operator with a characteristic function in the syntax of *lekta*. And, hence, it would still be true that even to conjunctions in the broad Stoic sense there corresponds one kind of element of *lekta*. But unity of this kind would be due to the function of elements of this kind in the syntax, not to a common denominator in the signification of conjunctions. Since the Stoic Chaeremon was willing to speak of conjunctions in the case of expletive conjunctions, though they could not be regarded as sentence-connectives (cf. Apoll. Dysc., *De coni.* 248.1ff.), it may also be the case that some Stoics were willing to admit that at least some conjunctions do not have signification. Hence, such conjunctions would not be covered by a definition of a supposed characteristic signification of conjunctions. But they would be covered by a definition of the kind given in Diocles' account.

Much more difficult to deal with are the so-called articles that include both our articles and pronouns (cf. Apoll. Dysc., *De pron.* 5.13). Part of the difficulty is that so far we do not have a clear view of how the Stoics treated articles, except that we know that they tried to construe the definite article as an indefinite pronoun. For reasons analogous to those in the case of conjunctions, we can understand why this class of articles cannot be characterized by what they signify in the way proper names, for example, can. But in their case it is even difficult to see how one could give plausibility to the claim that on the level of *lekta* there is one kind of element which corresponds to all articles. Hence, it does not seem plausible to assume that the Stoics maintained a strict kind by kind correspondence between parts of speech and elements of *lekta*. But in this case the question arises how the parts of speech were identified, if not with reference to the kind of things they signfy. There cannot have been a clear answer to this question, for the parts of speech tended to proliferate, a proliferation associated with the Stoics in particular (cf. Quint., 1.4.19; Dion. Hal.,

2.8-9; D.L 7.57). As late as the second century A.D. Apollonius Dyscolus devoted a monograph to the problem of the division of the parts of speech, which, unfortunately, is not extant.[14] As it is we have very little evidence concerning the principles used by the Stoics to determine what is to count as a part of speech.[15]

In any case, it is clear that the Stoics had a strong interest in the parts of speech. They wrote special treatises on the subject long before the grammarians, and they even devoted monographs to individual parts of speech, as we can see from Posidonius' *On conjunctions* (Apoll. Dysc., *De coni.* 214.4). The next question, then, is what they dealt with under the parts of speech. Since this was a matter of debate, we may assume that they would discuss the division of the parts of speech. Under each part they would presumably discuss the appropriate definition of this part of speech. Given that they insisted that all the parts of speech have signification, they would have to discuss the signification characteristics of the part of speech in question. In the case of conjunctions and articles, this would immediately lead to a distinction of various kinds of conjunctions and articles. We can see in Dionysius Thrax how the conjunctions proper are classified, obviously under Stoic influence, according to their signification (p. 87, 1ff.); the Stoic influence is apparent from the logical terminology.

Another topic that would be raised under the relevant parts of speech are the so-called accidents or secondary grammatical categories like gender, number, case, tense. Barwick (*Remmius Palaemon* 97ff., 107ff.) has argued that the very term "accident" in this use is of Stoic origin. This may very well be so, but the explanation given for the use of the term seems to be doubtful: supposedly the accidents are accidental in the Aristotelian sense; it is not essential for a word to appear with particular accidents; a noun remains the same noun whether it appears in the singular or the plural, the dative or the nominative.[16] The fact that Greek grammarians standardly use the term "consequents" (*parepomena*) instead of "accidents" suggests that, to use Aristotelian terminology again, these accidents in one respect are thought of as being rather like per se accidents in the way oddness and evenness are per se accidents of number; just as natural numbers come as odd or even, so a noun necessarily comes in one of the cases, in one of the *numeri,* in one of the genders, and so forth. The word (the *genikon onoma*), to occur in a concrete context, has to take on a determination in each of the relevant secondary categories; a noun, for example, would have to take on determinations with reference to number, case, gender, and whatever other accidents of nouns one may want to distinguish. Which particular accidents the Stoics distinguished under the various parts of speech is so far unclear. Similarly one would wish to know whether and to what extent the Stoics discussed syntax under the parts of speech, or inflection.

But in any case it seems to be fairly clear that, even given the doctrine of the parts of speech, more needed to be said about the grammatically adequate choice of words. To avoid barbarisms, that is, mistakes about individual words rather than their composition, more had to be taken into account than what had been laid down in the doctrine of the parts of speech. There is no guarantee that a word that satisfies the conditions specified under the relevant part of speech is not, nevertheless, a barbarism as defined in D.L. 7.59. A barbarism is the use of an expression "against the useage of those Greeks who have a good reputation." This definition seems to suggest that "Hellenism," beyond the doctrine of the parts of speech and syntax, is not a technical matter, to be covered by rules and theorems, but rather a matter of long familiarity with good authors. From this, one gets some kind of feeling for the proper choice of words and phrases.

On the other hand, there is evidence that the Stoics were more ambitious than this and had some sympathy for those grammarians who thought that even this aspect of the choice of words could be captured by rules of art. It is well known that the Stoics were the main proponents of the study of etymology. We also know that etymology was regarded as one of the most promising tools to test the "Hellenicity" of an expression (cf. Sext. Emp., *Adv. Math.* 1.241.ff.). To understand how the Stoics could use etymology as a criterion for the "Hellenicity" of a word, one has to know something about the Stoic doctrine of the origin of language, another dark matter, complicated by the fact that important testimonies concerning the subject (like Ptolemacus' *De criterio,* p. 7, 18ff. Lammert) present positions whose origin is not easily identified.

In the old controversy whether names are significant by nature or by convention, the Stoics took the view that the relation between names and what they signify is natural (cf. Origen, *Contra Celsum* 1.24. p. 74.13K). That immediately raised the objection that, if this were so, we should expect all human beings to use basically the same language. But the Stoics clarified their thesis by saying, it seems, that names are not formed by nature; they are not, for example, fully determined by the nature of human beings and the nature of things; rather, they are formed by human imposition, which may differ from group to group, and, hence, would produce different languages. Nevertheless, names are natural because they have been imposed in such a way that they naturally reflect the nature of things by somehow imitating them.[17] To bring such an imposition about it took wise men who had grasped the nature of things and who knew how best to impose names (cf. Philo, *De opif. mundi* 148; *Quaest. in Genes.* 1.20). And being wise, they would arrange this imposition in the most reasonable way possible. If the same things in different cases, for example, Socrates in the dative and Socrates in the accusative, had different names, say "Sophroniscus" and "Philoxenus," or if related things like Athens and the Athenians, justice and the just, running and the runner, did not have systematically related names, we would not be able to remember the correct names of things and, hence, would never learn the language (Varro, *De lin. lat.* 8.5). Varro mentions Cosconius who had said that if there were one thousand primitive words, there could be five hundred thousand words or word-forms by derivation (*De ling. lat.* 6.36; cf. 37); and he goes on to explain that one could easily have as many as five million different forms if one took prefixes into account (6.38). Hence, the wise man puts down a certain number of basic, primitive names, and then has everything systematically related to what is named by the primitive words named by systematically related names. The original imposition of names is at first accepted by the whole community. For at this early, incorrupt stage of society its members are at least reasonable enough to recognize the superiority of the wise who, for this reason, will also be kings.[18] This would seem to answer the Epicurean objection about how the mysterious name-giver could be supposed to make his fellow human beings adopt his names.[19]

Given such a picture of the origin of our languages, it is apparent how one could try to establish the Hellenicity of a word: it is necessary to show that it is one of the original impositions of the wise responsible for the origin of Greek, or that it is systematically derived from one of the original impositions. And in this way etymology, which is the doctrine of the original impositions and the derivatives from them, could be thought to serve as a criterion for the Hellenicity of a word. A word derived from a Latin or Persian primitive will be disqualified unless some special justification is given why it should be accepted after all. Now the fact that a word somehow can be traced to a Greek primitive word shows only that it is somehow Greek rather than barbarian. But the mere existence of some historical causal link between a word and a Greek primitive surely does not qualify an expression as a proper Greek word. The derivation of nonprimitives from primitives has to follow certain rules.

We noted above that the name-givers proceeded economically: they envisaged two kinds of derivation, inflection (*klisis*) and derivation in a narrow sense (*paragōgē*). Inflection we have, for example, in the case of declension or conjugation; derivation we have in cases like "Romulus"-"Rome," "Rome"-"Roman," or "justice"-"just." It would be difficult, though very important, to make the distinction precise; important, for example, because the question what is to count as one word will depend on where we draw the line between inflection and derivation. In addition to these two kinds of derivation, we shall also have to have assumptions about the phonetic changes words may undergo in their history, if we are to have any chance of retracing the derivation of a word to its origin (cf. Varro, *De lin lat.* 5.6; Aug., *Princ. dial.* c. 1321A).

Derivation in the narrow sense seems to have been guided by two sets of principles, one covering the relation in meaning between terms in the derivational chain, the other covering the phonetic relations. The first set of principles seems to conform to Stoic notions about the associations of ideas and the formation of concepts. It is assumed that, if a word A is used for x, then it is natural and reasonable that a derivative of A should be used for something similar to x or something in the vicinity of x or something contrary to x. How exactly derivatives of patronyms and the like were fitted into this scheme is unclear. The principles governing the phonetic changes in the chain similarly seem to have been rather loose and mechanical. The changes allowed include the dropping of letters, the acquisition of letters, and the change of letters (Varro, *De lin. lat.*, 6.2).

If the principles of word-derivation in the narrow sense are so loose as to lead to absurd derivations and to expose Stoic etymology to ridicule, inflection was so obviously guided by more stringent principles that any work on inflection could not fail to be more successful than Stoic etymology. The declension of nouns, for example, shows a striking amount of regularity. This basic regularity was generally accepted, but its precise nature, status, and explanation were a matter of some dispute. The participants in this dispute are called "analogists" and "anomalists" depending on whether they stress the regularity, or even demand the elimination of anomalies, or whether they stress the anomalies and resist their elimination in texts and in speech.

Presumably the most important testimony concerning this debate comes from Varro's *De lingua latina* (9.1). According to Varro, the Stoic Crates takes the position of an anomalist and, relying for this on Chrysippus, argues against Aristarchus who had defended analogy. But, Varro says, Crates seems to have misunderstood both Chrysippus and Aristarchus: Chrysippus and Aristarchus are talking about different things when they discuss anomaly and analogy and, hence, arc not really in disagreement. Aristarchus maintains that similar words should have a similar declension to the extent that usage permits this (Varro, *De lin. lat.* 9.1). And he tries to single out the relevant features with reference to which one could decide whether two nouns have the kind of similarity that would make us expect that they have the same declension. The features he suggests as relevant are six: gender, case, word-ending, number of syllables, accent, and figure (i.e., whether a word is simple or composite) (Charis. p. 149, 26ff. Barwick). Obviously, this set of features will not be sufficient if one tries to formulate a set of rules in terms of such features which will completely cover Greek declension; in fact, no such nontrivial set will do. But later grammarians introduced more and more features to capture the analogy in declension. The point that needs to be emphasized in connection with Aristarchus is that he did not maintain that there could be a complete set of rules or canons in terms of such features. His claim that declension is governed by analogy is severely restricted by the qualification "to the extent that usage permits this." But this qualification tended to be overlooked later. In Gellius' report of the controversy, for example, Aristarchus' position is described as if the Alexandrian had defended the unqualified thesis. And it is clear from the extensive criticism by Sextus (*Adv. Math.* 1.176ff.; cf. 1.97–99) that there was a faction among the grammarians who were tempted to "reform" ordinary language by regularizing its patterns of inflection against established usage.

Chrysippus, on the other hand, says Varro, maintained that language is anomalous because similar things are referred to by dissimilar names and similar names refer to things quite unlike each other. The anomaly Chrysippus had in mind seems to be of the following kind: "immortal" is formed by means of a privative prefix as if immortality were a privation (Simpl., *In cat.* 396, 5ff., esp. 396, 12ff.), Athens has a name in the plural though it is just one place (Sext. Emp., *Adv. Math.* 1.154), words do not have their natural gender, and so on. Chrysippus devoted a special treatise to such anomalies (D.L. 7.192). This insistence by Chrysippus on anomaly has tended to be misunderstood, as if Chrysippus thought that language is utterly irregular and irrational.

Varro suggests (*De lin. lat.* 91) that the positions of Chrysippus and Aristarchus are perfectly compatible, and that, hence, Crates misunderstood them; and this is certainly true if we just go by Varro's characterization of their positions. But we may wonder whether Crates could have been so entirely wrong on the matter. As the later history of the work on declension shows, Aristarchus was not just overoptimistic when he thought that six features would be sufficient to formulate canons of declension, and that the odd exception could be written off as being due to usage. Chrysippus seems to have taken a much dimmer view of the possibility of bringing order into the system of declensions. For according to Varro (*De lin. lat.* 10.59) he said that only sometimes it is possible to reconstruct the nominative from an oblique case or an oblique case from the nominative. This difference in attitude could make a great difference in the establishment of texts, where one constantly has to decide whether one is facing another anomaly or a corruption.

Moreover, the reason why the positions of Chrysippus and Aristarchus appear to be quite compatible is that Chrysippus is concerned with the anomaly between meaning and word-form, whereas Aristarchus is concerned with the analogy between word-forms in inflection. But the very fact that Aristophanes of Byzantium and Aristarchus try to establish classes of nouns with analogous declension, without reference to the meaning of the nouns, may invite criticism by the Stoics. The Stoics may have argued that in a rationally constructed language the different declensions should have a semantic function; that, hence, the classes of analogous nouns should be set up with a view to some such function; and that, if this did not turn out to be feasible, this just showed the amount of anomaly pervading the declension system, anomaly exactly of the kind Chrysippus had talked about when he pointed out that the correspondence between inflection or word-form and meaning often breaks down. That the Stoics may have argued in this way can be seen from the fact that they tried to show that proper names and common nouns differ in declension; that is, the difference between individuating and common qualities is supposed to be reflected by the declension of the names that stand for these qualities (*Schol. in D. Th.* 214.19ff., 356.27ff.; Charis., 80.1ff. Barwick). In fact, Varro himself tells us (*De lin. lat.* 10.68) that Aristophanes had written on analogy in declension exactly in the sense in which Chrysippus stressed anomaly. And Aristarchus, too, on the basis of analogy in this sense, argued for the accent *pterýgos* rather than *ptérygos* in Homer B 316 and Ψ 875. Hence, Crates may have had good reason, after all, to see a conflict between the Alexandrian and Stoic positions on this matter. But even if he was mistaken, it does not seem to make much sense to deny that he managed to start a lively controversy. For otherwise it is difficult to understand why the relative claims of analogy and usage should be given such attention in Sextus, Quintilian, and Varro.

That Stoic etymology did not find general acceptance, and that the debate concerning analogy and anomaly did not come to a decisive conclusion meant, of course, that attempts along these lines to establish criteria for the "Hellenicity" of words did not result in a generally recognized *technē*. Given the lack of satis-factory criteria, the Stoics seem to have taken a conservative attitude toward or-dinary language, which would be reinforced by their notion of style. Hence, the notion underlying their definition of barbarism in Diocles (D.L. 7.59) may be more representative of their position than it first seemed: in the choice of words and their forms we have to follow the usage of good authors.

V

We are left with the doctrine of the parts of speech and a syntax as the two parts of Stoic grammar sufficiently elaborated and established. These two more or less amount to a grammar. They correspond to what was done later in antiquity un-der the title of "grammar," which, in turn, corresponds to traditional grammar. There is good reason to believe that the Stoics had a notion of grammar and that they came to pursue the study of the parts of speech and syntax as parts of this discipline. Hence, there seems to be a fairly straightforward and strong sense in which we may speak of Stoic grammar. It is a discipline pursued by the Stoics as part of their philosophy; partly for historical, but also for systematic reasons, it is so much embedded in their dialectic that we had considerable difficulties finding it and isolating it from its context. In its details it is very much influenced by philosophical views concerning meaning, reference, the origin and rationality of language, metaphysical views concerning facts, states of affairs, qualities, and individuals, and finally by Stoic logic in a narrow sense. Hence, there is such a subject as Stoic grammar, and it would deserve a treatment that incorporates the material uncovered since Schmidt's monograph appeared almost 140 years ago. But such a treatment should not approach the topic as if it were from the outside; it should reconstruct a Stoic notion of grammar as a part of Stoic philos-ophy and follow its natural articulation; and it should do more justice to the con-nections between Stoic grammar and other parts of their philosophy. The effort is worthwhile, especially since there is reason to believe that traditional gram-mar has its origin in Stoic grammar. Many of the real or apparent incongruities of traditional grammar should appear in a different light once we have a better understanding of the philosophical background.

17

The Origins of Traditional Grammar

By 'traditional grammar' I mean the kind of grammatical system set out in and presupposed by standard modern grammars of Greek and Latin like Kühner-Gerth or Kühner-Stegmann.[1] Since grammars of this kind traditionally have been followed quite closely by grammarians of other languages, one may speak of traditional grammar quite generally. Grammars of this type consist of three parts: a phonology, dealing among other things with the sounds of the language, a morphology, dealing with word-formation and -inflection, and finally a syntax in which we are told which combinations of words constitute a phrase or a sentence. Moreover, such grammars are characterized by a certain set of concepts, especially the so-called grammatical categories, that is, notions of various parts of speech like that of a noun or a verb, and notions of various features of these parts of speech which traditionally are called 'accidents' or 'secondary categories'. Examples of such accidents are gender, number, case, mood, tense.

The only ancient text which more or less fits this characterization is Priscian's Institutiones, written in the early 6th century A.D. But we do know that earlier ancient grammarians like Apollonius Dyscolus in the second century A.D. covered in their writings the whole of traditional grammar, and we can see from his extant writings on various parts of speech and on syntax that by his time the concepts of traditional grammar were already fairly well established. Hence, we have to look for the origins of traditional grammar in antiquity.

Some of the concepts of traditional grammar can, in fact, be traced back to the fifth century B.C. Protagoras distinguished the three genders (Aristotle *Rhet.* 1407[b] 6; cf. *Soph. El.* 173[b] 17), and during the following centuries the familiar concepts seem to make their appearance one after the other. Hence, historians of ancient grammar like Steinthal tend to treat their subject as if it had a more or less continuous history. If one treats of the subject in this way, though, one runs the risk of overlooking the motives and guiding principles followed by those who first tried to write something like a systematical grammar as opposed

338

to those who just occasionally would care to note a point of grammar. Hence, when I talk of 'the origins of traditional grammar,' I am trying to talk about the first attempts to write something like a traditional grammar.

Unfortunately, the origins of traditional grammar in this sense are very obscure, mainly because all the texts of the formative period, with one exception, have been lost. The exception is Dionysius Thrax' Technē grammatikē, and this text poses such problems that even its authenticity has been doubted (cf. Di Benedetto, Dionisio Trace e la Techne a lui attribuita, *Annali, Scuola Norm. Sup.*, Pisa, v. 27, 1958, pp. 169ff.), though nowadays the text is generally accepted as genuine. But the origins of grammar are also very much obscured by an ambiguity in the ancient terms for grammar or the grammarian. Grammar may just be the modest art of reading and writing, sometimes also called 'small' or 'lower grammar' (Scholia Vaticana in Dionysium Th. 114, 23ff. Hilgard; cf. atelestera Philo De congr. erud. causa § 148 or 'grammatistikē', Sextus Emp., *A.M.* I, 44; Philo ibid.). In Hellenistic and later times 'grammarian' primarily refers to those Alexandrian scholars and their followers, including the schoolmasters, who are concerned with the restitution, the proper reading, the explanation and interpretation of the classical texts, and their literary criticism. This art was also called 'great' or 'higher grammar' (Schol. Vat. 114, 27ff.), 'perfect' or 'complete grammar' (e.g. entelēs S.E. *A.M.* I, 44; teleios I, 46; teleia I, 76; teleiotera Philo l.c.). High grammar is basicaly what we call 'philology'. And it was, in fact, one of these Alexandrian scholars, Eratosthenes, who first wanted to be referred to as a 'philologos' (Sueton. *De gramm.* 10, 4). Finally, incorporated as a part of this grammar, we find a discipline called 'the technical part of grammar' (S.E. *A.M.* I, 91; 96) or 'methodical grammar' (Quintilian I, 9, 1). It is this technical grammar which corresponds to our traditional grammar; and, hence, what we are concerned with are the origins of this technical grammar.

Since the earliest grammar of this type we know of is the one I referred to above, written toward the end of the second century B.C. by the Alexandrian scholar Dionysius Thrax and often thought to be the first grammar ever to be written in our tradition (cf. Susemihl, *Geschichte der griechischen Literatur in der Alexandrinerzeit,* II, p. 170, and more recently R. H. Robins, *Dionysius Thrax and the Western Grammatical Tradition,* Transactions of the Philological Society, 1957, p. 67) and since technical grammar subsequently seems to fall within the domain of scholars and grammar-school masters, it is natural to assume that grammar had its origins in the tradition of Alexandrian scholarship (cf. Robins, "The development of the word-class system of the European grammatical tradition," *Foundations of Language* 2, 1966, p. 6). But, though it seem safe to assume that grammar owes its independence, as a subject on a par with rhetoric and dialectic, to this tradition as it was received in the schools, a look at the facts makes it difficult to believe that it owes its origin to Alexandrian philology.

Dionysius Thrax' *Techne* starts out with a definition of grammar: "Grammar is knowledge by experience of what is said for the most part by poets and prose-writers." He goes on to specify six parts of grammar: (1) the skillful reading of texts, (2) the explanation of poetical tropes, (3) the explanation of peculiar words and realia, (4) etymology, (5) analogy, i.e., the explanation of declined and, perhaps, conjugated word-forms, (6) literary criticism, the finest part of grammar, as Dionysius adds. It may be easier to understand this list if we assume that it is a development of an earlier list of four parts referred to by the scholiasts (e.g., p. 12, 3ff.) and Varro (ap. Diomedem, Grammatici Latini I, 426 Keil), though they do not agree on the order: (1) the correction of the text, (2) its reading, (3) its explanation, and (4) its criticism, i.e., its evaluation. It is obvious that these four parts correspond to the topics somebody in philology would go through in lecturing and commenting on literary texts. Hence, Dionysius in the introduction seems to think of Alexandrian philology when he promises us a treatise on grammar. For the next four paragraphs our expectations are fulfilled, for he talks of reading, accents, and punctuation (and has three lines on rhapsody). But then, without any warning or explanation, he starts with a treatise on technical grammar covering letters, the corresponding sounds, syllables, and then the parts of speech. Not the slightest explanation is given of how this technical grammar fits the notion of grammar as it is defined in the first sentence or how it is related to the six parts of grammar referred to. The best explanation for this abrupt juxtaposition seems to be the following: at the time Dionysius wrote his *Techne* there was no established systematic connection between philology and technical grammar such that a few sentences, to keep in style with the rest of the text, would have sufficed to explain what role grammar plays in philology.

It is, of course, possible that philology and technical grammar had been pursued in the Alexandrian school alongside each other for some time and that only now Dionysius tried to incorporate the study of technical grammar into some philological curriculum. After all, given the nature of the philological enterprise, one hardly gets along without the use of grammatical notions. But if we look at the testimonies concerning the work of Dionysius' Alexandrian predecessors, there is no hint that any of them wrote on technical grammar. It is only for Dionysius' successors that treatises on technical grammar are attested, e.g., one on the parts of speech for his student Tyrannio (Suida s.v.). Claims as to the achievements of Dionysius' Alexandrian predecessors in this area are usually supported by reference to the following facts:

(1) Aristarchus, Dionysius' teacher, is said to have distinguished the canonical eight parts of speech (Quint. I, 4, 20);

(2) Aristarchus and his predecessor, Aristophanes of Byzantium, tried to set up rules of declension (Charisius, p. 149, 26ff. Barwick).

And it is, in fact, in this connection that Pfeiffer (*History of Classical Scholarship*, p. 203) says: "The term 'grammar', so far consciously avoided, can now indeed be used; we can see that as part of scholarship in general a separate discipline was being built up which reached its height in the second generation after Aristophanes, in the Technē grammatikē of Dionysius Thrax, the pupil of Aristarchus." In support of this Pfeiffer refers to Sextus Empiricus who says (*A.M.* I, 44) that 'grammar' more specifically is called that perfect discipline worked out by the followers of Crates Mallotes, Aristophanes, and Aristarchus. But it should be clear from what was said in the beginning about the ambiguity of the term 'grammar' that this statement may refer to philology quite generally; and that it actually does so is brought out by the etymology of 'grammar' offered by Sextus a few paragraphs later (I, 47ff.).

This, then, leaves us with the two facts referred to as the main evidence for Alexandrian contributions to technical grammar before Dionysius. So let us consider these in turn. According to Quintilian (I, 4, 20), Aristarchus assumed eight parts of speech. As we can see from the context, Quintilian refers to the eight parts we also find in Dionysius Thrax and which then came to be commonly accepted for Greek grammar (for Latin interjections were added as a separate class, but the number 8 was preserved, since Latin does not have the definite article; cf., e.g., Quint. I, 4, 19). It is very difficult to evaluate this testimony. Since Aristarchus does not seem to have written on the parts of speech, the testimony may rest on no more than the observation that Aristarchus in his writings in practice distinguishes eight classes of words which exactly correspond to the eight parts of speech. But from this it would by no means follow that Aristarchus distinguished eight parts of speech. For one might talk of proper names and common nouns, or common nouns and adjectives, and it still might be left open whether one considers these as one or two parts of speech (consider, e.g., the question whether one should say on the basis of *De congr. erud. causa* §149 that Philo distinguished proper name and common noun as two parts of speech). It may also be pointed out that Quintilian does not suggest that it was a major achievement of Aristarchus to establish this canon of eight parts of speech, whereas Aristotle, as Quintilian believes (I, 4, 18), had only recognized three. For he says that the number of parts of speech was slowly raised from Aristotle's times by the philosophers and in particular by the Stoics (I, 4, 19), and Aristarchus is only referred to as an authority among those who accepted the list of eight parts which later was to become canonical. There is no suggestion that the list was accepted because it was thought that Aristarchus had cleared the matter up. Even his best students, Dionysius and Apollodorus, did not agree, at least at times (Apol. Dysc. *De pron.* 5, 18–19; Schol. Vat. in D.Th. 160, 26–28), nor did Didymus (*Prisc. Inst.* XI, 1, 1, p. 548, 7ff.; for the whole matter cf. also, e.g., Schol. in D.Th. 58, 21; Quint. I, 4, 20; Dionys. Halic. *De comp.*

verb. 2; Apol. Dysc. *De coni.* 214, 25–26; Ps. Herodian *De soloescismo,* Nauck Lexicon Vindob. p. 295; Papyrus Yale V c.I lines 3 and 10).

Of more substance is the other testimony. According to Charisius (p. 149, 26ff.). Aristophanes and Aristarchus were concerned with the analogy of declinable words. Similar words should be expected to have a similar declension. The question is just with reference to which features we determine the relevant similarity of words. Aristophanes specifies five such features: gender, case, word-ending, number of syllables, and accent; to which Aristarchus added a sixth: figure, i.e., whether a word is simple or composite. Words being the same with reference to these features should have the same declension. Following this approach later grammarians added further features and tried to formulate rules of declension in terms of these.

So there seems to be a concern with declension, out of which an interest in inflection in general would grow naturally. Later inflection was dealt with in treatises on Hellenismos (or Latinitas), i.e., treatises trying to specify what is to count as proper Greek (or Latin). In these treatiese analogy and etymology were regarded as the major criteria to judge the acceptibility of an expression. Hence, it is tempting to assume that when, as we saw above, Dionysius Thrax in addition to the four regular parts of grammar also lists analogy and etymology, he is taking into account a traditional concern of the Alexandrian school at least for inflection. But it is significant that though Dionysius may refer to such studies in his introductory characterization of grammar, he himself in the treatise does not deal with declension. Hence, it would seem that the evidence usually relied on for the claim that technical grammar is of Alexandrian origin is rather insufficient.

One could, of course, proceed to list as further evidence grammatical concepts or assumptions Aristarchus or his Alexandrian predecessors used. What such a survey would show is that Dionysius' *Techne* cannot be regarded as an elaboration, let alone as a codification of the grammatical system presupped by the Alexandrians.

So, to save the assumption of an Alexandrian origin of this kind of technical grammar, one would have to assume that it was developed by Dionysius Thrax himself. But a look at his treatise shows that this hypothesis is extremely implausible. It has the character of a very elementary handbook in which a fairly rich system for didactic purposes has been reduced to basic definitions, classifications, and examples of the classes referred to. In fact, it has been discussed as a paradigm of such an elementary handbook in antiquity by Fuhrmann in his "Das systematische Lehrbuch." And we may assume that the *Techne* owed its later success to the radical simplification with which it treated its complex material. It is definitely not the kind of text that would be written to introduce a new discipline of such interest and importance.

Now, if one looks for the origin of grammar outside the Alexandrian tradition of philology, one has to turn to the philosophers who ever since the fifth century had taken an interest in language. In fact, there are traces of Peripatetic influence in ancient grammar. But I think that it can be shown that most of these traces either are due to the influence of the Aristotelians on the early Stoics or are of much later origin when some form of Peripatetic logic became part of what was accepted by any educated person (i.e., at least from the late second century onward). One of the reasons, it seems, why the medieval speculative grammarians tried to reconstruct grammar was that traditional grammar did not fit their views on language shaped by Aristotle's *Categories* and *De interpretatione*.

So we have to turn to the Stoics. It has been argued by Pohlenz (cf. his "Die Begründung der abendländischen Sprachlehre durch die Stoa," *Nachr. Ges. d. W. Göttingen* 3, 1938, pp. 151ff.) and in much detail by Barwick that traditional grammar is of Stoic origin. Pohlenz argued in particular that the case-system and the verbal tense-system are basically Stoic. This conclusion seems to be generally accepted, and, hence, all authors admit some Stoic influence. But there seems to be a general feeling of uncertainty concerning the extent of this influence. Some authors tend to minimize it. Robins, e.g., says "there seems to be little to substantiate the alleged Stoic influences" (*Dionysius Thrax*, p. 76n4), in support of which he refers to M. Schmidt's famous paper on Dionysius in *Philologus*, 1853. Other authors show a significant tendency to waver on this point from one page to another. This skepticism and the uncertainty to a good extent seem to be due to the fact that we still know so little about the details of Stoic grammar or even its scope. Hence, the Stoics' contribution to the subject might still seem to be insignificant and incidental.

The difficulties begin with the fact that among the many parts of philosophy recognized by the Stoics there is none which is called 'grammar' nor is there one which could at least be identified as grammar. Those who claim Stoic origin for grammar point to the *Technē peri phōnēs* by Diogenes of Babylon as the probable source for handbooks of grammar like that by Dionysius Thrax. But though this may be right, it would be a mistake to think that Stoic grammar is to be identified with that part of Stoic dialectic which deals with human or Greek utterances or any part thereof.

The Stoics standardly divided philosophy into logic, physics, and ethics. One may say that logic for them is the doctrine of what somebody says who is guided by reason. Traditionally logic was divided into rhetoric and dialectic. But dialectic came to be concerned with rational (Greek) utterances quite generally, at least insofar as their study did not fall into the province of rhetoric. Hence, the general study of language would belong to dialectic. Dialectic, in turn, was divided into two parts, one concerned with the utterances, the other with what was said by uttering these sounds (or writing these letters). To use Stoic language, one part of dialectic is concerned with what is signified or what is said, the other with what is signifying or with voice. It seems to me, then, that it is a mistake to think that Stoic grammar could be identified with that part of dialectic which deals with signs or with a part thereof. For a large number of the traditional notions of grammar like those of a case, casus rectus and obliquus, active and passive, past, present and future, singular and plural, construction or syntax, and many other seem to have been introduced by the Stoics in the part of dialectic concerned with what is signified, and their application to utterances appears to be secondary. Hence, let us start with a consideration of the relevant parts of the Stoic doctrine of what is said or signified.

According to Stoic doctrine if one says something two kinds of items are involved. There is (1) the utterance one produces and (2) that which one is saying is producing this utterance. An item of the first kind is a sound of a certain sort, according to the Stoics air modulated or articulated in a certain way. An item of the second kind, on the other hand, is supposed to be immaterial; it is called a *lekton* by the Stoics, i.e., something which is or can be said. The Stoic doctrine of *lekta* is a notoriously difficult subject-matter. *Lekta* in Stoic philosophy seem to have two functions, of which the first tends to be overlooked, particularly by those who are interested in Stoic logic and their philosophy of language. Since this function is of some importance for one point in our investigation, I shall have to consider it at least briefly.

The first philosopher who is attested to have used the term *lekton* is Cleanthes: according to Clement of Alexandria (Strom. VIII, 9, p. 96, 23ff.) some (i.e., the Stoics) say that causes are causes of predicates or "as some put it, of lekta, for Cleanthes and Archedemus called these predicates lekta." We know from many sources that for the Stoics both causes and what is affected by these causes are bodies, but that which is effected or brought about by these causes is something immaterial. For what is brought about is that something is so-and-so, e.g., cold, but that something is cold is not a body, though it is a body which is cold. This assumption created a certain difficulty for Stoic ontology. For it was claimed by them, strikingly along the lines of the Earth-born giants in Plato's *Sophist,* that everything which is real, including qualities, is corporeal and that it is the test for the reality of something whether it can act upon or be affected by something. But, on the other hand, the Stoics did need in their physics certain incorporeal items anyway, namely place, time, and the void. And, hence, to cover these and the *lekta* brought about by causes, they felt forced to introduce the notion of a something (ti) which may subsist though it does not exist or is not real (S.E. *A.M.* X, 218). Behind this recognition of *lekta* at least under the limited status of a subsistent something lies, I think, a criticism of Aristotle. Aristotle accepts entities like a man or health, also such compound entities as a healthy man. But there seems to be no place in Aristotle's ontology for such items as being healthy or being pink or the fact that Socrates is healthy. It is the color pink which for Aristotle and the Stoics is a quality and not an item such as being pink. Hence, the Stoics think that if Socrates is healthy there are at least three items involved, namely the two recognized by Aristotle, Socrates and the quality health, but then also a third one, being healthy or that x is healthy. It is this kind of item which, we are told, they call a *predicate* or a *lekton*. As opposed to the first two items it is incorporeal.

This notion of a *lekton* and in particular of a *predicate* occurs not infrequently, but primarily in two contexts: in explications of the notion of a cause and in remarks about the proper objects of choice, desire, wishes and the like (cf. Stobaeus *Ecl.* II p. 98, 5W.).

More important, though, seems to be the second function *lekta* serve. *Lekta* are also something like the meanings of sentences in the following sense: as we saw above, the Stoics assumed that when we say something two kinds of items are involved, the utterance and the *lekton*. Since it is also assumed that whenever we say something we either make a claim, ask a question, give an oath, address or invoke somebody, give an order, pray or ask for something or do something else of this kind which involves producing an utterance, the Stoics divided the *lekta* accordingly into claims or propositions, orders, questions, oaths etc. (S.E. *A.M.* VIII 70; D.L. VII, 65–68). There was some interest in non-propositional *lekta*. Chrysippus devoted several writings to questions and one in two books to orders (D.L. VII, 191). There are some interesting remarks concerning the relation between oaths and truth (cf. Simplicius *In cat.* 406, 23; Stob. *Flor.* 28, 14; 28, 15). And the badly damaged papyrus with a book of Chrysippus' *Logical Investigations* shows at least that Chrysippus considered utterances like "walk, since it is day" (col. 11n, *Stoicorum vet. fragm.* II p. 107, 36–37 von Arnim), "walk, or if you don't do that, sit down" (12n), "either walk or sit down" (col. 13n). But most of the attention was given to propositions, and, hence, in the following I shall restrict myself to these and the corresponding sentences, except to note that the traditional terms for two of the moods of the verb, 'optative' and 'imperative', seem to be derived from the names of two kinds of such non-propositional *lekta*, prayers and orders,[2] and similarly the term 'vocative' seems to be derived from the name of another kind, the address.[3] What happens in these cases is something which we shall observe again and again: distinctions are made on the level of the *lekta* which are reflected by certain features on the level of the expressions which features then get named after the corresponding features of the *lekta*. A standard way to pray for something or to express a wish is to use a sentence with the verb in the optative, to give an order one standardly uses the imperative, and if one addresses somebody one uses the vocative. To say this and to assume such a correspondence is not to commit oneself to the view that to use the optative is to express a wish or that the only way to express a wish is to use an optative.

Parts of the Stoic doctrine of propositions are of interest for our purposes because the Stoics treated even simple propositions as in a way complex (cf. e.g., S.E. *A.M.* VIII, 79; 83; 94). Though, as is well known, Stoic logic is basically propositional, the Stoics made considerable efforts to analyze propositions, developed a doctrine of elements of propositions (and *lekta* in general) and something like a syntax to specify which of these elements would go together in which way to form a *lekton*. There is every reason to believe that our use of the term 'syntax' is derived from their use for the syntax of *lekta* (cf. D.L. VII, 192; 193; also compare the corresponding use of *syntattein*, e.g., in D.L. VII, 58; 59; 64 four times; 72 twice). I shall return to this point later.

We have some information concerning the syntax of propositions. These *lekta* are talked of as if they were generated (cf. D.L. VII, 64; Suida s.v. axioma p. 255, 2 Adler) or put together from the elements. Hence, the expressions 'constructio' and 'syntaxis' which literally mean 'putting together'. It seems that this construction was supposed to take place in a certain order. We start with the construction of the predicate we have encountered above. But the predicate is essentially incomplete, in fact, it is called an incomplete *lekton* (D.L. VII, 64). Hence, we proceed to the construction of a simple propositions. From there we may proceed to the construction of various kinds of negative simple propositions (but c.f. D.L. VII, 70) and then to the construction of non-simple propositions by combination of the propositions constructed so far.

Let us start with a consideration of the elements of propositions. There is, first of all, the predicate. Since we have talked above about the construction of predicates, it is clear that either the term 'predicate' does not refer to a kind of element since predicates themselves may be complex or that the term is ambiguous. It seems that Stoic terminology in this respect is not uniform, but there is at least one terminology according to which the term is ambiguous. For in D.L. VII, 64 it is said that those predicates are direct which, combined with an oblique case, will from a predicate (pros katēgorēmatos genesin). The language here strongly suggests that there is a sense in which the predicate taken without the oblique case is not yet a predicate. And so we do have predicates in the sense of parts of propositions which satisfy certain conditions such that from them one may proceed to the construction of a proposition. These predicates may be simple or complex. In the latter case they themselves would have to be constructed before one could proceed to the construction of a proposition. But then there are, second, predicates in the sense of elements of propositions. It is these that we are concerned with right now. Let us call them elementary predicates as opposed to syntactical predicates.

These elementary predicates are what corresponds to the verb in the corresponding sentences. There is a very rich and complex tradition concerning various kinds of elementary predicates. The Stoics distinguished, e.g., between direct predicates, which correspond to active or active transitive verbs, and oblique predicates, which correspond to middle and passive verbs. A distinction between middle and passive then may have been drawn within the class of oblique predicates (cf. D.L. VII, 191; Chrysippus, Q.L., *SVF* II, p. 97, 37-99,

36 von Arnim; D.L. VII, 64). Predicates were also distinguished by number (Chrysippus, Q.L. *SVF* II, p. 99, 39) and tense. The tense distinction stressed aspect which later tended to be neglected by Greek grammarians, partly owing to a change in the language itself.

Another important kind of element of the proposition which like the elementary predicate perhaps is needed for the construction of any proposition (but, again, cf. D.L. VII, 70) is the so-called case (ptōsis). Several kinds of cases are distinguished. A case is supposed to come either as a casus rectus or a casus obliquus (D.L. VII, 64–65), and among the casus obliqui the Stoics distinguished between the genitive, the dative, and the accusative. It is obvious that our case-system and the corresponding terminology are derived from this.

Among the many problems concerning the doctrine of cases, I would like to comment on two closely related ones. The first was already raised in antiquity: why is the nominative a case? The Peripatetics claimed that it was only called a case by courtesy (katachrēstikōs) since it was not itself a case of anything in any sense. And this explanation seems to have remained the standard one. But it is almost certainly wrong. For the Stoics insisted that the nominative is a case straightforwardly (Ammonius *In de int.* 43, 4–5; Stephanus *In de int.* 10, 22–26). Hence, in late antiquity and in Byzantine times there was a considerable amount of speculation about what the nominative might be thought to be the case of. Some of this speculation is quite interesting. It leads, e.g., to the abstraction of a word as opposed to its inflected realization. But as far as our problem is concerned, all this speculation seems to be off the mark.

The correct solution seems to be suggested by a solution of the second problem. This problem arises in the following way: it is clear that one class of cases corresponds to nouns. In the sentence "Socrates is wise" 'is wise' would correspond to a complex syntactical predicate and 'Socrates' to a case in the underlying proposition. Now predicates are incomplete *lekta* and as such incorporeal items. Hence, one should suppose that cases, being elements of *lekta* too, will also be incomplete *lekta* and hence incorporeal. And this is the position usually taken by commentators, with some uneasiness, though, because we are also told that according to the Stoics nouns signify qualities (D.L. VII, 58) but also that qualities, at least those of bodies, are themselves corporeal. So there seems to be an incoherence.

In looking for a solution to this problem, it is useful to notice that in the many lists of kinds of *lekta* the only incomplete *lekta* ever to be mentioned are predicates (cf., e.g., D.L. VII, 43; 63; Plut. *De comm. not.* 1074D), that these are syntactical predicates, and that this is what we should expect if we consider the metaphysical function of *lekta* referred to above. The Stoics want to account for the fact that Socrates is wise (which is considered by them as a complete *lekton*), and they think that to account for this we need more than the two entities Socrates and wisdom. We also need the predicate of being wise. But if we have the predicate of being wise, or that *x* is wise, and if we have Socrates there is no need to postulate an additional item to correspond to Socrates. Socrates and the incomplete *lekton* that he is wise will suffice to make up the complete *lekton* that Socrates is wise. There is also no need to assume that since facts are not bodies no constituent part of a fact can be a body. Hence, so far there is no reason to think that cases are incorporeal. Quite the opposite, on the basis of what has been said, we should expect cases to be corporeal. And that, of course, would fit the testimony perfectly which says that nouns signify qualities, that is, according to the Stoics, corporeal entities.

But I think there is not only good reason to believe that the apparent contradiction can be solved by assuming that cases as opposed to predicates are thought to be corporeal, there is more direct evidence that the Stoics did regard them as corporeal.

To understand this evidence one has to take into account that Platonists (some claim even Plato himself) assumed two kinds of forms, the transcendent forms or ideas (ahyla eidē) and the immanent forms as they are found in concrete objects (enhyla eide). There is the transcendent form wisdom and, in addition, the form wisdom, a realization of the idea, which is to be found in a concrete individual, e.g., Socrates' wisdom. The second kind of form corresponds, it appears, to the Aristotelian forms of the Peripatetics. Both Platonists and Peripatetics agreed that these forms in themselves are incorporeal, though they are embodied, whereas the Stoics believed such qualities or forms to be as corporeal as the bodies they are the qualities of.

Now, the evidence I have referred to seems to be evidence to the effect that cases in the Stoic system correspond to the embodied forms of the Platonists and the Aristotelians. Stobaeus in a notoriously obscure and difficult passage (*Ecl.* I, p. 136, 21ff. W.) says that according to the Stoics "concepts (ennoēmata) are . . . quasi-somethings (hōsanei tina; cf. D.L. VII, 60; Origenes *In Joh.* II, 13, 93). They are called ideas by the ancients. For the ideas are ideas of the things which according to the concepts fall under them. . . . Of these (sc. ideas) the Stoic philosophers say that they do not subsist and that we participate in these concepts, whereas the cases, which they call appellatives, we do possess (tynchanein)." A closely related passage is one in which Simplicius compares Stoic and Platonistic terminology (*In cat.* 209, 12–14): "the concepts they called participibilia (methekta) because they are participated in, and the cases they call possessibles (teukta) because they can be possessed (tynchanein), and the predicates they call accidents." Finally a third passage should be mentioned: Clement, *Strom.* VIII, 9, p. 97, 6–7). Here it is said that the case is something which the concrete object possesses (tynchanei).

It appears from these three passages that there are items, namely the cases, of which both Stoics and non-Stoics say that they are somehow possessed (as opposed to participated in) by objects in this world. In this respect they are contrasted with the ideas which things in this world only participate in (but do not possess). It seems clear, then, that these cases are or correspond to the embodied forms of the Peripatetics and the Platonists, i.e., they are qualities of some sort.

There is some apparent counterevidence which it now should be easier to deal with. There is first of all the famous passage (*A.M.* VIII, 12) in which Sextus Empiricus explains that the Stoics distinguish between the utterance, the *lekton* and the external object the utterance is about and that they make the *lekton* the primary bearer of truth and falsehood. As an example Sextus gives 'Dion'. Hence, interpreters naturally have assumed that the Stoics distinguished between (1) the reference of a term, in our case the person Dio, (2) its meaning or sense, an incorporeal *lekton,* and (3) the word 'Dion'. But, unfortunately, 'Dion' is not an example of something which is true or false, and so it is clear that something has gone wrong with Sextus' report (it is not a simple slip on Sextus' part; for cf. *A.M.* VIII, 75). To judge from parallel passages (e.g., Seneca *Ep.* 117, 13) the claim must have been, rather, that in the case of an utterance like "Dio walks" we have to distinguish between (1) the expression (2) the correspoonding *lekton* that Dion walks (it is this which is true or false), and (3) the external object we are talking about, Dio.

I am all the more inclined to think that we have to treat the passage in Sextus in this way as in one respect his report fits the interpretation we have given so far extremely well. Sextus says that the Stoics call the external object 'to tynchanon' (cf., e.g., Philoponus *In an. pr.* 243, 2 and Plut. *Adv. Colot.* 1119F). Translators and commentators had some difficulty with this expression. The explanation for this use should be clear now. 'Tynchanein' was the expression used in the three passages quoted above to characterize the relation between cases or qualities and the object which possesses the quality or case signified by the noun.

If this is correct, it is clear that the common view according to which the Stoics distinguished between the meaning and the reference of terms and posited *lekta* as the meanings is quite inadequate. The term 'horse' signifies the quality characteristic of horses. If in addition to this there is something faintly like the meaning of the term, it is the concept. But of this the Stoics repeatedly (e.g., in the passage quoted above from Stobaeus) say that it does not exist, that it is not even a something but only an as-if-it-were something. Hence, it cannot be a *lekton* since *lekta* are somethings. Moreover, it seems that the Stoics did not make use of these concepts in their theory of meaning. And, hence, it would seem that they thought that all that was needed for such terms as 'horse' (appellatives and names) was the corresponding corporeal quality. Similarly, for predicate-phrases like 'runs' we do not have two kinds of items corresponding to them but only one, the respective incomplete *lekton.* It is only in the case of utterances about something that we have to distinguish three kinds of items, the utterance, the *lekton,* and the external object.

I think it would be misleading to say here 'the object the statement or utter-

ance is about' or 'the subject' instead of 'the external object'. At least some clarification is needed. For from what has been said, it is clear that in a sentence with
a proper name or a common noun in subject-position the subject-expression does
not signify a subject of which the predicate has to be true if the sentence is to
be true, to use Aristotelian language. There only has to be such an object which
has the quality signified by the name or noun for the statement to be true. Hence,
there would seem to be room for a distinction between that which the statement
is about, i.e., that which is signified by the subject-expression, i.e., the respective quality, and an object thus qualified, of which the predicate has to be true
if the statement is to be true. There might be a parallel here to Aristotle's treatment of unquantified general propositions (the so-called 'indefinite' ones) in the
Categories and *De interpretatione*. According to that account 'anthrōpos trechei'
would have the species or universal 'man' as it subject (hypokeimenon), but it
would be true in virtue of the fact that there is some particular of which the
predicate is true. In any case, later grammarians were puzzled by the Stoic assumption that names and common nouns signify qualities rather than something
qualified in a certain way. And their attempts to modify the Stoic definitions
resulted in a considerable variety of partly rather obscure definitions which gave
rise to further problems. The introduction of the term 'substance' (ousia) into the
definition, e.g., would raise the question whether substantial objects or essences
were referred to, and in either case, but particularly in the latter, a problem
would arise how adjectives would fit the definition (they so far had been treated
as appellative nouns).

So much about what Sextus Empiricus has to say in *A.M.* VIII, 12 and some
of the problems raised by this passage. But there is more evidence against our
suggestion that cases, for the Stoics, are not incorporeal *lekta,* but corporeal
qualities. The counter-evidence consists of two remarks in Clement's *Stromateis,*
separated by only a few lines. Clement says that a case is incorporeal (VIII, 9,
p. 97, 6–7) and that it is agreed to be incorporeal. This testimony surely should
settle the matter against us.

Fortunately, the matter is more complicated. It is not difficult to explain how
Clement's remark, that a case is incorporeal, could be compatible with our view
that cases for the Stoics are corporeal. Starting in the first century B.C. attempts
were made to synthesize the doctrines of the rival schools, and all later Greek
philosophy is heavily influenced by this syncretism. Hence, we should not be
surprised to find the term 'case' used by non-Stoics who would claim, though,
that cases are incorporeal because they do not share the Stoic view that qualities
are bodies. This was still a debated question in Clement's time as we can see
from the fact that Galen (?), his contemporary, wrote a short treatise on the question (ed. Kühn vol. 19). An example of how a non-Stoic use of 'case' may perhaps be found in a fragment of Iamblichus (Simpl. *In cat.* 53, 17; cf. 53, 9ff.).
Now the philosophy of Stromateis VIII is highly syncretistic (as has been pointed

out again recently by S. Lilla in his book on Clement). In the theory of meaning Clement follows the Peripatetics (cf. VIII, 8, p. 94, 5ff.). Hence, we should not be surprised to find that he uses the term 'case' but claims that cases are incorporeal because he thinks that qualities are incorporeal.

Much more difficult to deal with is his other remark, made a few lines earlier (p. 97, 3), that cases are agreed to be incorporeal. Part of the problem is that the text and its argument are so difficult to follow that editors have been tempted to change its reading in several places. But whichever interpretation we adopt, it seems to be clear that the notion of a case with reference to which Clement here says that cases are agreed to be incorporeal cannot be the Stoic one in question. For the remark that cases are agreed to be incorporeal is made with reference to a remark three lines earlier (96, 26), that to be cut is a case, and a remark two lines earlier (97, 1), that for a ship to come into being is a case. These items certainly would be agreed to be incorporeal. But they would not be considered as cases by the Stoics. Hence, Clement's notion of a case which not only covers the case of a house (cf. 97, 7) but also the two examples just mentioned must be different from the Stoic notion. For this reason and because the items with reference to which Clement says that cases are agreed to be incorporeal are in fact agreed to be incorporeal by the Stoics, I do not think that Clement's remark can be used as evidence against the suggestion that Stoic cases are corporeal.

Given this, we may try to solve our first problem: why is the nominative called a case? It should now be clear that the problem arose because two quite different terms were conflated, since the same word 'ptōsis' or 'case' was used for both and since both terms were used to refer to grammatical cases. There was the term of Aristotelian origin (cf. De int. 16ᵃ 32ff.) according to which the word in the nominative is the noun whereas the word with the genitive inflection is not the noun but a case since it is thought of as falling from or being derived or inflected from the word in the nominative. Hence, in this tradition the nominative could be called a case only by courtesy. But the Stoic case is called a case, as we are told in the passage I quoted from Stobaeus, because it falls under a concept or an idea. And since, of course, it falls under this concept quite independently of whether it comes in the nominative or the genitive, the nominative for the Stoics is as much a case as any other (for possible traces of the correct explanation cf. Ammonius In de int. 43, 9-10).

Besides elementary predicates and cases, the Stoics distinguished other kinds of elements of *lekta*. But I shall not go into the matter here. Nor shall I discuss here the reconstruction of the syntax of *lekta*. All I am concerned with now is to point out that the Stoics had something like a syntax of *lekta* and that a good part of the traditional grammatical terminology is derived from the Stoic specification and characterization of the elements of *lekta* whose combination is studied in the syntax of *lekta*.

This raises the question how these terms used or introduced to characterize items on the level of *lekta* came to be applied to items on the level of expressions. The answer, it seems, will have to take into account at least three factors. Apparently, the Stoics believed that the relation between *lekta* and the sentences used to express them is basically simple and rational though disturbed over the ages by careless usage and tendencies toward abbreviation, euphony, and the like. Chrysippus dealt extensively with such anomalies as they occur in the formation of words (cf. D.L. VII, 192). But the mere fact that such anomalies are singled out for special treatment appears to indicate confidence in the basic regularity with which features of the *lekta* and syntactical or morphological features of the expression correspond to each other. A good example of this confidence may be the following: the Stoics distinguished between individualizing qualities, i.e., features which make their owners the particular individuals they are, individual essences so to speak, and common qualities. But they were not content to distinguish correspondingly between proper names and general nouns (appellatives), they tried to confirm this distinction by showing that proper names are inflected differently from general nouns (*Schol. in D.Th.* 214, 19ff.; 356, 27ff.; Charisius p. 80, 1ff. Barwick). In a highly inflected language like Greek, correspondences in gender, case, and number, e.g., would be fairly conspicuous anyway. And, hence, it would be natural for the Stoics to use the same terms to refer to a feature of the *lekton* and the corresponding feature of the expression, as in fact we see they did (cf. 'henikon' and 'plēthyntikon' in D.L. VII, 192 and Chrysipp's *Logical Investigations*). Second, most philosophers and even some Stoics (S.E. *A.M.* VIII, 258) rejected the postulation of *lekta*. Hence, they would be inclined to transfer the use of Stoic terms they found useful, where possible, to expressions. Third, partly as a result of the two factors mentioned, considerable confusion seems to have set in. This may have been aided by the fact that the expression *lekton* itself is ambiguous and was in fact used by the influential grammarian Chaeres for expressions as opposed to what they signify (S.E. *A.M.* I, 76; 77; 78), a use we then also find, e.g., in Apollonius Dyscolus (*De pron.* 59, 5–6; *De adv.* 158, 20; *De coni.* 233, 2ff.). Hence, one finds that the two levels, so carefully distinguished by the Stoics in theory, are constantly confused even in good sources like Plutarch who in *Q.P.* (1009 C) claims that 'case' is the Stoic term for 'noun' and 'predicate' their term for 'verb'. This confusion is so widespread that some modern authors like A.C. Lloyd ("Grammar and Metaphysics in the Stoa", p. 58 in A.A. Long, *Problems in Stoicism*) have been misled into thinking that *lekta* are the expressions insofar as they are meaningful. A good Greek example of the terminological confusion is Ps.-Alexander on *Soph. El.,* p. 20, 27ff., where it is claimed that entities have to be divided into two classes, *lekta* and tynchanonta, i.e., expressions and the things referred to by them. Hence, there will be no shortage of explanations for the transfer of terms from *lekta* to expressions and the resulting confusions.

Let us now turn to the second part of the Stoic dialectic which is concerned

with voice and with expressions. To judge from the short survey given by Diocles Magnes in D.L. VII, 55–62, the Stoics under this heading dealt with a wide
variety of topics, and it is not at all clear how these topics would form a systematic unity. But it is fairly clear that those of relevance for us are the first
three, i.e., the sections on sounds, the parts of speech, and the virtues and vices
of speech.

The idea behind this division seems to be fairly clear. In this part of dialectic
we are concerned with the utterances we make, or expressions we use, when we
claim, order, ask, express a wish, or the like. These utterances may be regarded
under two aspects: they may be regarded just insofar as certain sounds are articulated, or they may be regarded insofar as they are used to do or to express
something. The first of the three parts mentioned clearly corresponds to a study
of utterances under the first aspect. It is obvious why such a study would be of
interest or relevance. To mention a less conspicuous reason one may point out
that some Stoics insisted that one should also judge poetry by its mere sound (cf.
Crates fr. 82 Mette). In the following I shall not go into the details of Stoic phonology. The second part concerning the parts of speech corresponds to the study
of utterances insofar as they are made to say something. This is less than obvious, hence I shall return to this point shortly. The section on the virtues and vices
of speech, finally, is of traditional origin. Theophrastus, e.g., had dealt with the
subject, and the Stoics show themselves to be influenced by him. This third part
is of interest here insofar as it reveals to us a part of the motivation which made
the Stoics go into technical grammar: the Stoic wise man is absolutely infallible,
infallible also in any of the ways one may go wrong in speaking; to make him
immune against such mistakes he has to acquire the relevant knowledge.

Given our initial rough characterization of traditional grammar, one may
wonder what happened to morphology and syntax. A consideration of this question will also help us to come to a better understanding of the second part concerning the parts of speech and the dominating role it plays in ancient grammar.
The doctrine of the parts of speech plays such a dominating role that treatises
on technical grammar very often are nothing more than treatises on the parts of
speech. It is often maintained that syntax was developed long after the Stoics and
Dionysius Thrax (Steinthal, *Geschichte der Sprachwissenschaft, vol. 2, p. 393,
and Robins, Dionysius Thrax.,* p. 102, e.g., claim that it is the work of Apollonius Dyscolus), and it is certainly significant that even in later times not many
treatises on syntax were written: there are, besides Apollonius Dyscolus, the last
two books of Priscian's *Institutiones,* and then the Byzantine tracts by Arcadius,
Michael Syncellus, and Gregory of Corinth, though Priscian's remarks (*Inst.*
XVII, 1) suggest that he had other authors to rely on besides Apollonius Dyscolus. And so we also have to look for an explanation of this phenomenon.

It seems to me that at least part of the explanation may be that the Stoics had
some kind of syntax after all, but pursued it in a peculiar way. They certainly

used the notions of concord, governance, and order (cf., e.g., D.L. VII 59; S.E. *A.M.* VIII, 90; Apulcius *De int.* p. 177, 27 Thomas). Apollonius Dyscolus in the introduction to his syntax (I, 2, p. 2, 10–3, 2; cf. also Priscian XVII. 3) tells us that to each word there corresponds an intelligible item (noēton) such that, in a way, it is these intelligible items which are the elements of the meaningful sentence. It is by combining the words that we combine the intelligible elements in such a way as to get a meaningful sentence. And we get a complete or perfect sentence (autotelēs logos) if the intelligible items fit each other or, as Apollonius puts it, if the intelligibles have the required katallēlotēs. "Katallēlotēs" is the standard Greek term, used by Apollonius and others, for syntactical propriety.

These remarks by Apollonius are easily translated into Stoic language, especially since a good part of the terminology of the passage – including that for syntactical propriety (cf. D.L. VII, 59) – is of Stoic origin anyway. In translation Apollonius would say: corresponding to each word there is an element in the *lekton;* in putting the words together we put the elements of the *lekton* together, i.e., construct a *lekton.* Whether we get a syntactically proper sentence depends on whether the *lekton* we construct satisfies the syntax for *lekta.*

So it may turn out that the reason why we would look in vain for a syntax in the part of dialectic concerned with expressions is that even for Apollonius the syntax of sentences is still basically the syntax of the corresponding *lekta,* except that Apollonius has replaced the Stoic *lekta* and their elements by something like our meanings which he refers to as intelligibles.

But the connection between Stoic syntax and Apollonius' approach to syntax is even closer. So far we have talked as if the Stoics had just been concerned with something like a syntax for *lekta.* But a closer look at the evidence shows that the Stoics also were concerned with the question how we use words such that by combining these words in a certain way we get a *lekton* which satisfies the laws of the syntax of *lekta.* Dionysius of Halicarnassus in his 'Composition of Words', e.g., reports that Chrysippus wrote two treatises on the syntax of all sorts of propositions (p. 22, 14ff. Usener-Radermacher). Among these propositions he lists ambiguous propositions. Now it is sentences, but not propositions which according to the Stoics could be ambiguous. Hence, Chryssipus in these treatises on syntax must also have talked about the composition of sentences to express the various kinds of propositions. How this could be so we can see from many passages; e.g., from the description of molecular propositions in Diogenes Laertius. There (VII, 71–72) we are told that a disjunctive proposition is formed by means of a disjunctive conjunction in such-and-such a way, and similarly for other kinds of molecular propositions.

Passages like this also suggest an answer to the question why we need a fairly elaborate doctrine of the parts of speech. Only such a theory would provide us with the conceptual apparatus needed to describe how we use words to put together sentences to express the kinds of *lekta* distingusihed by the syntax of *lekta*. That this is so is put beyond reasonable doubt by the fact that Dionysius of Halicarnassus gives as the title of the writings of Chrysippus he refers to "On the syntax of the parts of speech." Matters become even clearer if we have a look at the relevant part of the catalog of Chrysippus' writings (D.L. VII, 192–193). There the following four titles are listed in sequence "On the elements of speech and what is said (5 books)," "On the syntax of what is said (4 books)," "On the syntax and the elements of what is said, to Philippus (3 books)," and "On the elements of speech, to Nicias (1 book)." What these titles and their relative position in the catalog reveal, if we keep in mind that the 'what is said' in these titles refers to the *lekta,* is that the parts of speech or elements of speech were talked of and discussed in connection with the elements of *lekta* and their composition. Seneca (*ep.* 89, 9) mentions as one of the most important tasks of Stoic logic an investigation of the 'structura (sc. verborum)', i.e., the composition of words to form sentences. Similarly, Epictetus (*Diss.* IV, 8, 12) attributes to Zeno the view that one of the most important tasks of the philosopher is to determine the elements of speech, to characterize them, and to see how they fit each other (pōs harmottetai; pros allēla). Hence, it seems that the Stoic school right from the start had taken a strong interest in something like the syntax of sentences. And the question is why among the sections of the second part of Stoic dialectic do we not find one on syntax.[4]

The very terminology for parts of speech seems to fit this picture very well. The parts of speech are the parts of a sentence which, in being combined, make up a sentence and in making up sentences make up speech. Chrysippus apparently wanted to stress their character of being elements of sentences and, hence, preferred the expression 'elements of speech' (Galen, *De Plat. et Hipp. dogm.* p. 673, 6 Müller; Theodosius Alex. p. 17 Göttling). Now, if we keep in mind that utterances are regarded under two aspects, as articulated sounds and as sentences, i.e., as utterances insofar as they express a *lekton,* then it becomes clear that the parts or elements of speech owe their very name to the fact that they are the elements which by being combined in a certain way will give us a *lekton* of a certain kind. All this, then, makes one inclined to think that the doctrine of the syntax of *lekta* together with the doctrine of the parts of speech is also supposed to serve the function of a syntax, and that one reason why the doctrine of the parts of speech plays such a prominent role is that it supplies us with the concepts we need to describe how one combines expressions to get a sentence and, hence, a *lekton.* And one reason why so few treatises on syntax were written may be that it was thought that this was basically a matter of the syntax of *lekta* and, hence, belonged to dialectic.

Again I shall not consider the details of the doctrine of the parts of speech. As we should expect, the parts of speech are made to correspond to the elements of *lekta.* Even later Apollonius Dyscolus (*De pron.* 67, 6–7) will claim that the parts of speech are divided according to their meanings. Hence, the so-called notional character of the traditional definitions of the parts of speech. For the Stoics this is clear in the case of proper names, appellatives, and verbs, which are defined by them as corresponding to individualizing qualities, common qualities, and simple predicates, respectively. It is not as clear for the definition of the article which is defined as determining gender and number. And it even seems to be shown wrong by the definition of the conjunction as an undeclinable part of speech binding together the parts of speech (cf. D.L. VII, 58). Yet this exception in an important sense is only apparent. Behind it there seems to be a discussion in the Stoic school concerning the so-called expletive conjunctions, i.e., particles like 'now' in "well, now, let us do so-and-so" which are used in Greek, e.g., to ensure proper sentence-rhythm. The discussion as reported by later authors concerns the question whether conjunctions have a meaning, i.e., whether to the conjunction in the sentence there always corresponds an element in the *lekton*. According to Apollonius Dyscolus (*De coni.* 248 1ff.) the Stoic grammarian Chaeremo denied this with reference to the expletive conjunctions but explained that they, nevertheless, could be called conjunctions because of their morphology which they share with the 'true' conjunctions. This should help to explain the apparently deviant definition of the conjunction.

This dispute concerning conjunctions is of interest in other respects, too. It shows, e.g., that the Stoics were aware of the fact that the structure of the sentence is not determined exclusively by the structure of the underlying *lekton*. It also shows a concern for the morphology characteristic of the various parts of speech. This interest is not surprising. After all, it is not very helpful to be told that one forms a disjunctive proposition by means of a disjunctive conjunction unless one knows what counts as a conjunction and what, in particular, counts as a disjunctive conjunction. Hence, attempts were made to distinguish the parts of speech and their sub-kinds and forms by their morphology and surface syntax. And hence, perhaps, one resorted in those cases where such distinctions could no longer be made, to lists of words, e.g., in the case of the various kinds of conjunctions and prepositions (cf. Dionysius Thrax p. 71, 1ff.).

So much for a very rough sketch of the parts of Stoic dialectic insofar as they are relevant for traditional grammar. I should also have dealt with the question to what extent the Stoics were really interested in an analysis of the Greek language in general (or at least some form of it). This question arises because so many of the grammatical distinctions the Stoics make may seem to be made out of a logical interest. One's suspicions could grow if one sees that Dionysius of Halicarnassus (*De comp. verb.* p. 22) says that when he wanted to treat composition he turned to the Stoics because of their renown in linguistics (lektikos topos), but that he was quite disappointed by Chrysippus' writings on syntax because they, rather, seemed to belong to dialectic. Similarly, one might become suspicious when Apollonius Dycolus in the introduction to "On conjunctions" says that the Stoics have written a lot on the matter but warns against those grammarians who introduce Stoic terms and notions which are alien to or not useful for grammar.

To deal with this question adequately one would have to have a clear notion of the relation between logic and grammar in general and in the Stoics in particular. From what has been said, it is clearly not their ignorance of or lack of interest in grammar which makes them fail to recognize grammar as a discipline separate from dialectic. But all I can do now is to point out that disparaging remarks like the ones referred to can easily be explained and that many of the grammatical distinctions made by the Stoics are not systematically connected with what we regard as the logic of the Stoics and, hence, have to be explained as due to an interest in the language. The remark by Dionysius is easily explained by the fact that he, as he says, is interested in rhetorical composition. And somebody primarily interested in style and rhetoric would regard a treatise on syntax, however grammatical in orientation it was, as dialectical. The grammarians in the Alexandrian tradition would not be too happy with Stoic grammar because they want to understand the language of Homer, the poets, and in general the classical authors, whereas the Stoics, though they are very much interested in Homer, primarily want to construct or reconstruct the language the wise man would use. It later will become a common-place that Chrysippus and the Stoics try to tell even the Athenians how to speak Greek properly (Galen *De diff. puls.* 10, SVF II, 24 von Arnim; cf. S.E. *A.M.* VIII, 125–26; Cicero *De fato* 8, 15). But if the Stoics tried to 'legislate' the use of language, as their opponents put it, they must at least themselves have thought that they knew something about the way language works.

It is time to return to our argument concerning the origins of traditional grammar. We saw that a closer look at the evidence shows that it is very unlikely that traditional grammar started with Dionysius Thrax or his Alexandrian predecessors. But we also felt uncertain whether we should attribute the origins of traditional grammar to the Stoics. And one reason why we felt uncertain about this was that the Stoics may not have done more than to make some, perhaps important, but nevertheless incidental contributions to grammar.

But from what has been said it should be clear that Stoic contributions to grammar were not incidental. They were made as part of a larger theory which also served the purpose of accounting for utterances or sentences of Greek. Moreover, we have seen that some grammatically relevant parts of this larger theory had been worked out by the Stoics in considerable detail, that a very large portion of the notions of traditional grammar were incorporated into or made their first appearance in this theory, and that the work of later ancient grammarians can be regarded as taking up well-defined parts of the Stoic project of a study of the Greek language as outlined above. We have also seen that we may be able to explain the curious prominence of the doctrine of the parts of speech in later grammar if we assume that this grammar developed out of Stoic dialectic. Hence, the claim that traditional grammar is of Stoic origin seems to be quite promising. With this in mind it should be easier to evaluate some further evidence.

There is general agreement that among the Stoics with an interest in grammar Diogenes of Babylon was of particular influence. In the short survey in Diogenes Laertius he is referred to eight times within the five paragraphs we are concerned with (VII, 55–59). Now among the pupils of Diogenes of Babylon there are two of importance for us. One of them is Crates who went to Pergamum to establish a 'school' there which rivaled that of the Alexandrian philologists. Crates spent some time on a mission in Rome where he lectured on grammar. If we follow Suetonius in his *Grammarians and Rhetoricians* (Chap. 2) these lectures by Crates, "the equal of Aristarchus," started grammar in Rome. Of course, "grammar" here has to be understood in the wide sense. But we can be fairly certain that this for Crates included the type of Stoic grammar we have discussed above. For Sextus Empiricus (*A.M.* I, 79) tells us that Crates required of a grammarian (whom Crates called a "critic") that he should be familiar with logic. It seems plausible to assume that Crates had in mind that the grammarians of the Alexandrian kind lacked the knowledge of Stoic logic including the kind of grammar discussed above which is required to do philology properly. And this may get some confirmation from the fact that a later Cratetean, Tauriscus, called the technical part of grammar "the logical part" (S.E. *A.M.* I, 248). In any case, Roman technical grammar was centered around the doctrine of the parts of speech, sometimes preceded by a phonology and sometimes followed by a part on the virtues and vices of speech, i.e., it seems to follow the basic structure of the relevant part of Stoic dialectic. Perhaps most telling is the way the Roman art of grammar preserved in some instances a part of the Stoic techne we have not referred to at all because it does not belong to traditional grammar (cf. K. Barwick's *Remmius Palaemon*). We know that the Stoics in the theory of expressions or utterances at least sometimes also dealt with the notions of the definition, the species, and the genus. Like a fossil we still find these topics dealt with in a few lines by Charisius (p. 192, 20–193, 2 Barwick), with no connection to the preceding or the following. Later Roman grammarians know even less what to do with this fossil, and, hence, Diomedes, Maximus Victorinus, and Audax at least keep a definition of 'definition' in an unobtrusive position. Diomedes even manages to put in definitions of 'genus' and 'species' in some other place (326, 30–35). In many ways, then, the Roman art of grammar suggests that it is of Stoic origin. Priscian, at the end of a long tradition in Latin grammar, tells us in fact that Roman writers on technical grammar tended to follow the Stoics (XI, 1, 1, p. 548, 12ff.).

Another student of Diogenes of Babylon was Apollodorus, who afterward went to Alexandria to work with Aristarchus and who was to become, with Dionysius Thrax, the most important pupil of Aristarch. We may assume that he was quite familiar with Diogenes' grammatical ideas, and the only thing we know about his views on technical grammar makes him side with the Stoics rather than with Dionysius' *Techne* and later Greek grammar: he classified pronouns as demonstrative articles (Ap. Dysc. *De pron.* r, 18–19). Now it is certainly not the case that the Alexandrians had to rely on oral reports to learn about the theories of Diogenes of Babylon. But it is equally difficult to believe that a distinguished scholar like Apollodorus, trained in Stoic logic, should not be of considerable influence on the Alexandrians in this respect. And, hence, it is tempting to see some significance in the fact that in all three cases in which we know that Dionysius at some time defended a point of view different from the one he took in the *Techne* he was siding with the Stoics and that at least on one of the these points he was in company with Apollodorus. Like Apollodorus, at some stage he thought of pronouns as demonstrative articles (Ap. Dysc. *De pron.* 5, 18–19). In addition, like the Stoics, he defined the verb as signifying a predicate (*Schol. in D.Th.* p. 161, 6; Ap. Dysc. *Fragm.*. p. 71, 29ff.), and finally, like the Stoics, he at some point counted proper names and common nouns as two parts of speech (*Schol. in D.Th.* 160, 26–28). If we want to maintain the authenticity of Dionysius' *Techne,* the easiest explanation of the facts may be that Dionysius, perhaps through Apollodorus, got interested in Stoic grammar, but then modified it; modified it under the influence of the enormous experience and feeling for the Greek language the Alexandrians had at least up to the time of Aristarchus. Parts of Dionysius' *Techne* in any case cannot be understood except as modifications of Stoic doctrine. Thus the classification of conjunctions, e.g., in its content and its terminology reflects the Stoic doctrine at a certain, not fully developed stage. The lines on syllogistical conjunctions clearly presuppose Stoic rather than Aristotelian logic, and a Homeric scholar would hardly introduce a class of syllogistic conjunctions in the first place unless he was following a Stoic source fairly closely.

One could proceed to list more details of this sort. One certainly should mention that in 'De congressu eruditionis causa' Philo tries to make us believe that grammar had its origin in philosophy, Stoic philosophy as his terminology shows (sections 146–50). But I think we are now in a position to see that and in what sense Philo may be right. The Stoics certainly did not write grammars like Kühner-Gerth's or Schwyzer-Debrunner's. But, on the other hand, they did something their philological and philosophical predecessors failed to do, however much they may have contributed to grammar. It was the Stoics who first tried to develop a theory on the basis of which one would know what could pass as correct Greek. To the extent that later ancient grammarians took up the subject where it had been left by the Stoics and established the tradition which was to last to these days, we can talk of the Stoic origin of traditional grammar. Why and how grammar was separated from logic or dialectic and came to fall within the province of the grammarian should deserve an account of its own.

Notes

Notes

Introduction. The Study of Ancient Philosophy

1. I would like to thank John Cooper and Raymond Geuss for the generous help they gave me in writing this introduction.

Chapter 2. The Title, Unity, and Authenticity
of the Aristotelian *Categories*

1. Olymp., *Prol.* 22, 38ff.; *Schol.* 33a 28ff.; Brandis.

2. Ammon., *In Cat.* 13, 25.

3. The question of authenticity is either not discussed at all (cf. Ockham, *Expositio aurea*, Bologna 1469, f. gii) or discussed only very superficially and mechanically (cf. De Soto, *Absolutissima commentaria*, Venice 1574, 247ff.; Complutenses, *Disputationes in Arist. dialecticam*, Leiden 1668, 160; Gennadios, *Oeuvres*, VII, 119, 9, Paris 1936).

4. Cf. Peter Abailard, *Logica Ingredientibus*, 116; Conimbricenses, *In universam dialecticam*, Cologne 1607, c. 297.

5. *De causis corrupt.*, art. 99 (according to Fabricius, *Bibl. Gr.*, vol. II, 109).

6. *Discuss. Peripat.*, vol. I, Basle 1581, 20.

7. C. Prantl, *Geschichte der Logik*, I, 90; C. Prantl, in: *Zeitschrift für die Altherthumswissenschaft* IV (1846) 641–652; L. Spengel, in: *Gelehrte Anzeigen* (München), 1845, c. 33–56; V. Rose, *De Aristotelis librorum ord.*, 234ff.; A. Gercke, in: *Arch. f. G. d. Ph.* 4 (1891) 424–441; E. Dupreel, in: *Arch. f. G. d. Ph.* 22 (1909) 230–251.

8. *Über die Kategorien des Aristoteles*, in: *Sitzungsber. Wien* 1853, 593.

9. *La logique de Théophraste*, 32.

10. "La doctrine aristotélicienne de la substance et le Traité des Categories" in: *Proc. 10th Internat. Congr. of Philosophy*, Amsterdam 1949, 1097–1100; cf. also her earlier paper, "La première doctrine de la substance: la substance selon Aristote" in: *Rev. Philos. de Louvain* 44 (1946) 349–360.

11. I. Düring says only that the authenticity of the *Postpraedicamenta* is likely (*Aristoteles*, 55); D. Ross thought that the *Postpraedicamenta* were generally regarded as spurious (*Aristotle*, 24 n. 2).

12. See J. G. Buhle, *Aristotelis Opera*, vol. I, 1791, 436; Ch. A. Brandis in: *Abh. Berlin* 1833, 268ff.; E. Zeller, *Philos. d. Gr.*, II 2⁴, 1921, 67 n. 1; Th. Gomperz, *Greek Thinkers*, IV, 514; Überweg-Praechter, 379; D. Ross, *Aristotle*, 10; L. M. De Rijk, *The Authenticity*, in: *Mnemos.* 4 (1951), 159; I. Düring, *R E Suppl.* XI, s.v. Aristoteles, 205, 61; J. L. Ackrill, 70; V. Sainati,

Storia, 151ff. Some ancient authors took this line (Olymp., *In cat.* 133, 14), especially Andronicus (Simpl., *In cat.* 379, 8ff.).

13. E.g., J. G. Buhle, 436; E. Zeller, II 2^4, 1921, 67; H. Maier, *Die Syllogistik,* II 2, 292 n. We hear of this view being taken by some in antiquity (Ammon., *In cat.* 14, 18ff.; Olymp., *In cat.* 133, 14ff.). Whether Andronicus was among these, as is often claimed, is doubtful; at any rate, we never hear that he argued against the authenticity of the *Postpraedicamenta;* we would assume, if this had been the case, that he would be referred to by name when their authenticity was being discussed.

14. J. G. Buhle, 436.

15. O. Hamelin, Le système d'Aristote, 27 and 131.

16. *GGA* (1880) 465–469; also, E. Zeller, II 2^4, 1921, 69 note; H. Maier, *Die Syllogistik,* II 2, 292 note.

17. In his edition, *Praef.* V n. 1.

18. J. L. Ackrill, 31; I. Düring, *Aristoteles,* 54ff.; *R E Suppl.* XI, s.v. Aristoteles, 205, 59ff.; V. Sainati, *Storia,* 150.

19. Aristotle, *Organon,* 749ff.

20. But cf. the variant reading in 8^b 21.

21. In connection with this, it is relevant that there supposedly were two versions, of equal length and with more or less the same contents, of the *Categories* in Hellenistic times (Ammon., *In cat.* 13, 20ff.; Simpl., *In cat.* 18, 16ff.; Philop., *In cat.* 7, 26ff. and 13, 1; Olymp., *Prol.* 24, 14ff.; Elias, *In cat.* 133, 16; Boethius, *In cat.* 161 E-162 A). The explanation for this may just be that, given the condition of the text, it could only be published with the help of editorial intervention and that, in this case as in others, at least two editions were prepared by Aristotle's students which differed from each other because of different editorial changes in each. Of course, we should recall that according to Olympiodorus (*Prol.* 24, 19ff.), the second version was considered spurious. On the other hand, Adrastus, on whom perhaps all surviving remarks on the second version depend, reports (Simpl., *In cat.* 18, 18) that this version too circulated under Aristotle's name. Also, none of the other authors confirms Olympiodorus' claim, though some express themselves in a way that could easily lead one to conclude that the second version was not thought to be by Aristotle. Olympidorus' remark perhaps ultimately indicates that, in Hellenistic times, our version of the text was preferred and taken to be by Aristotle, while the origin of the second version was left an open question.

22. "Über die Reihenfolge," in: *Abh. Berlin* 1833, 26; *Griech.-röm. Philos.,* II b, 407, cf. I. Düring, *Aristoteles,* 54.

23. H. Maier, *Die Syllogistik,* II 2, 292, note.

24. II 2^4, 1921, 69, note.

25. L. Minio-Paluello, app. crit. 11b 1–8, doubts whether this is even the fragment of an independent chapter; his suggestion to transpose the lines (after 11^a 14), however, makes little sense.

26. Simpl., *In cat.* 379, 9ff.

27. Simpl., *In cat.* 379, 12ff.

28. Simpl., *In cat.* 379, 21.

29. Porph., *In cat.* 56, 8.

30. Simpl., *In cat.* 17, 10–26.

31. *Organon* I, 265

32. Olymp., *Prol.* 24, 9; Elias, *In cat.* 133, 12.

33. Cf., e.g., Porph., *In cat.* 56 14ff.

34. Porph., *In cat.,* 56, 15.

35. Simpl., *In cat.,* 15, 29.

36. Porph., *In cat.,* 56, 19; Simpl., *In cat.,* 15, 29.

37. Porph., *In cat.,* 57, 14.

38. Porph., *In cat.*, 56, 18; Simpl., *In cat.*, 15, 28.

39. Porph., *In cat.*, 56, 18; further references *infra*.

40. Th. Waitz, *Organon,* I, 265; E. Zeller, *Philos. e. Gr.*, II 2^4, 1921, 67 n. 1. Presumably this was already Andronicus' view.

41. J. Bernays, *Die Dialoge des Aristoteles,* 133ff.; E. Heitz, *Die verlorenen Schriften des Aristoteles,* 238ff.; P. Moraux, *Les listes,* 131; 187ff.; 204; I. Düring, *Aristotle in the Biographical Tradition,* 40. Cf. V. Rose, *De Arist. lib. ord.*, 32.

42. Cf. Simpl., *In cat.*, 16, 14ff.

43. Ibid.

44. Simpl., *In cat.*, 379, 8ff.

45. Porph., *In cat.*, 56, 14ff.

46. Ammon., *In cat.*, 14, 18ff.

47. Simpl., *In cat.*, 15, 28ff. and 379, 8ff.

48. Boethius, *In cat.*, 162 C and 263 B, where the text clearly should read *qui hunc libellum Ante Topica <in> scripserit,* cf. J. Shiel, "Boethius and Andronicus of Rhodes" in: *Vig. Christ.* 11 (1957) 179ff. and now P. Moraux, *Der Aristotelismus b.d. Gr.* I, 100.

49. Olymp., *Prol.* 22, 34ff.

50. Elias, *In cat.*, 132, 26 and 241, 30.

51. 32b 36 Brandis.

52. Th. Waitz, *Organon,* I, 81.

53. Simpl., *In cat.*, 16, 1; Elias, *In cat.*, 132, 26–27 (obviously, Adrastus and Archytas are permuted, as has often been pointed out. Cf. H. Schmidt, *De Hermino Peripatetico,* Diss. Marburg 1907, 21 n. 1; P. Moraux, *Listes anciennes,* 63ff.).

54. Simpl., *In cat.*, 16, 1ff. and 18, 16ff

55. Elias, *In cat.*, 241, 30.

56. Cf. Luc., *Vita Demon.* 56.

57. Olymp., *Prol.* 22, 34.

58. Simpl., *In cat.*, 16, 31.

59. P. Moraux, *Les listes* 58ff.; I. Düring, *Aristotle,* 45. But now see P. Moraux, *Der Aristotelismus,* I, 101 n. 14. The indications against this identification are weak: (i) in Alexander's commentary on the *Topics,* we read (5, 27–28) that some people called the first book of the *Topics, Pro tōn topōn;* (ii) Olympiodorus reports (*In cat.*, 134, 1ff.) that some people used this title for the *Postpraedicamenta.* It is obvious that we can draw no conclusions about the title in Hellenistic times from this second passage. The first passage is controversial. M. Wallies deleted the sentence; though, as he himself, to some extent, saw (preface XXVI), for the wrong reasons. For we find the sentence also in the codex Paris. 1832, and, in the *Suida,* it does not occur at the wrong place. Nevertheless, the sentence seems doubtful, since it does not really fit in with the context, and since it looks more like a gloss on 5, 18–19. Still, even if we retain the sentence, we should think of it in connection with the title, *Horoi pro tōn topikōn,* which we find for the first book of the *Topics* in the catalogs (cf. P. Moraux, *Les listes,* 58; I. Düring, *Aristotle,* 44). If this, however, is the origin of the title mentioned by Alexander, there is no reason to suppose that the other title (from the catalogs) also refers to the first book of the *Topics.*

60. E. Heitz, *Die verl. Schr. d. Arist.*, 239 and, apparently, also W. Jaeger, *Stud. z. Entwicklungsgesh. d. Metaph.*, 151.

61. E. Heitz (*Die verl. Schr.*) wanted to bracket *ta*; the title of Theophrastus' work, which is exactly the same (D. L. V 49), seems, though, to confirm this form of the title.

62. D. L. V 49.

63. "Theophrastus," *R E Suppl.* VII (1940) 1381. Cf. also A. Graeser, *Die logischen Fr. d. Theophrast,* 54.

64. "Theophrastus," 1380.

65. Cf. also I. M. Bochenski, *La logique de Théophr.*, 29 and L. Repici, *La logica di Teofr.*, 167ff.

66. Cf. Olymp., *In cat.*, 134, 3ff.

67. Simpl., *In cat.*, 15, 31ff. and 16, 14ff.

68. *Die Kateogrien des Aristoteles*, Diss. Rostock 1903; cf. also his paper in *Arch. f. G. d. Ph.* 17 (1904) 52–59.

69. *Gr.-röm. Philos.* II b, 408.

70. As was already pointed out by Ch. A. Brandis, *Gr.-röm.*, 408.

71. A. Gercke in: *Arch. f. G. d. Phil.* 4 (1891) 438.

72. *Gr.-röm. Philos.*, II b, 408.

73. Philop., *In cat.*, 7, 20–21

74. David, *In Porph. Isag.* 102, 4dd.

75. Ch. A. Brandis in: *Rh. Mus.* 1 (1827) 270ff. and his "Über die Reihenfolge" in' *Abh. Berlin* 1833, 269ff.; H. Usener, *Anecdota Theophr.*, 21; E. Zeller, *Philos. d. Gr.* II, 2, 68 note.; I. M. Bochenski, *Log. Theophr.*, 32; Fr. Wehrli, *Die Schule d. Arist.*, VIII, 79 and further references provided there, IX 28. Cf. A. Gråeser, *Die log. Fr. d. Theophr.*, 58, and L. Repici, *La log. di Teofr.*, 180.

76. Olymp., *Prol.* 13, 24–25; Ps.-Elias *In Porph Isag.* 28, 44 Westerink; *Anon. Coisl.* 160 *In Int.* (on him, cf. CAG IV 5, *Praef.* XIXff.); *Anon. Laur.* 85, 1 f. 17 (in V. Rose, *Arist. Pseudepigr.*, 129).

77. C. Boethius, *De syll. hyp.* I 3.

78. In the *Anon. Laur.* 85, 1 quoted by Rose (see n. 76 supra), we read that Kleinias, Eudemus, and Theophrastus wrote *Categories*. As Rose already noted, we should presumably read Phanias for Kleinias.

79. Alex., *In top.* 131, 15; Fr. Wehrli, *Die Schule des Arist.*, VIII, 79.

80. Ammon., *In Porph. Isag.* 26, 13ff.; Olymp., *Prol.* 24, 12ff. Cf. Elias, *In Porph. Isag.* 36, 35.

81. Besides Philoponus and David: Olymp., *Prol.* 13, 24ff.; Ps.-Elias, *In Porph. Isag.* 28, 44 Westerink; *Anon. Coisl.* 160 *In Int.* (see n. 76 supra); *Anon. Laur.* 85, 1. Al-Qifti according to M. Steinschneider, *Die arab. Übers. aus dem Griech.*, 36 (p. 74); cf. J. G. Wenrich, *De autorum Gr.*, 176 n. 71.

82. Olymp., *Prol* 13, 32ff.

83. Cf. Alex., *In top.* 69, 15, *In Anal. Pr.* 16, 16.

84. Galen, *De libr. propr.* XIX 42K. = 118, 16–17 *Scr. Min.* II Müller.

85. Olymp., *Prol.* 13, 29ff.

86. Ibn al-Nadim, *Fihrist*, p. 13 Müller.

87. p. 22 Müller.

88. Ch. A. Brandis in "Über die Reinhenfolge," 270, has pointed out that the *Anon. Coisl.* 160 claims that such treatises were titled *Peri lexeos;* this was a further reason for Brandis to deny that Theophrastus and Eudemus had written Categories, since this identification could not possibly be correct. Now, it is certain that Theophrastus' as well as Eudemus' *Peri lexeos* treat of things other than categories; on the basis of what we know about these works, however, it is quite possible that they also discussed categories. Both treatises seem, among other things, to treat of the elements of propositions; i.e., the *aneu symplokes legomena;* and it is quite possible that, in connection with this, they also considered categories. Since both works were quite lengthy, it is possible that a book of each was devoted to categories.

89. *Aristoteles*, 45; cf. also G. R. G. Mure, *Aristotle*, 268.

90. "On the Categories of Aristotle" in: *Phil Rev.* 13 (1904) 514–528; "The Authenticity of Aristotle's Categories" in: *J. Philos.* 36 (1939) 427–431.

91. Olymp., *Prol.* 23, 28ff.; *Anon. Urb.* 35, *Schol.* 33b 1, Brandis. Cf. also Dex., *In cat.* 44, 32ff.; Ammon., *In cat.*, 36, 6ff.; Simpl., *In cat.*, 82, 1ff.; Philop., *In cat.*, 50, 23ff.

92. According to Fabricius, *Bibl. Gr.* vol. II, 109, the work in question presumably is *Accorambonis Commentarium obscuriorum locorum,* Rone 1590.

93. "Aristotle et le Traité des Categories" in: *Arch. f. G. d. Ph.* 22 (1909) 230–251.

Chapter 3. Categories in Aristotle

1. Cf. Ammon. *In cat.* 14, 18ff.: Simpl. *In cat.* 379, 8ff.

2. Bonitz's *Index* s.v. ousia 544b 15–17.

3. I would like to thank R. Dancy, A. Code, and J. Fjeld for their helpful written comments on earlier versions of this paper.

Chapter 4. Individuals in Aristotle

1. Cf., however, Thesaurus L.I., sv., and Th. Kobusch, "Individuum, Individualitat," in: *Historisches Wörterbuch der Philosophie,* ed. J. Ritter, Bd. 4, cc. 300–304.

2. With Boethius' translation, compare Porphyrius Introductio vers. lat., p. 27, 3 Busse; with Marius Victorius' translation, Boethius *In Porph.*, ed. prima, p. 44, 12 Brandt.

3. The view of genera and species I want to ascribe to Aristotle in the *Categories* is one that at least since Abelard would be described as a realist view. Realism in this original sense, where the genera and species of objects also are *res* not *nomina,* of course, *res* of a special kind, is a view which, it seems to me, has recently been hardly considered, though it was the dominant view, in one form or another from late antiquity to Abelard's time. What is not at issue is whether there are things like Platonic ideas because these can also be accepted by nominalists, as being ideas in the divine mind. What is, rather, at issue is whether individual men constitute an object, which one could call Man or Mankind, whose parts they then would be. Man or Mankind cannot be related to individual man in the way forms, from Plato's middle dialogues, whether in the divine mind or not, are related to individuals; rather, the relationship is like that between the police and a policeman, between the forest and the trees, or between a language and its phonemes. If one sees a policeman, one also see the police and can say, 'the police is here'. Thus, too, with Man: he is what we see, when we see Socrates; it is also Man who sinned in Adam. He exists in his parts, but as in the case of the forest or the police, the parts can and do change, without the identity of the forest or police changing. An example of such a view can be found in Gregory of Nyssa, Ad Ablabium Quod non sint tres dei, p. 40, 5ff. Mueller; according to him, we can speak only catachrestically of many men.

4. See, G. F. Stout, "The Nature of Universals and Propositions," *Proceedings of the British Academy,* vol. X, 1921–22; G. E. Moore, G. F. Stout, and G. Dawes Hicks, "Are the Characteristics of Particular Things Universal or Particular?" *P.A.S.S.*, vol. III, 1923, pp. 95–128.

5. G. E. L. Owen, "Inherence," *Phronesis* X, 1955, pp. 97–105. Owen's view is, as far as I know, shared only by Montgomery Furth in an unpublished book on Aristotelian essentialism.

6. See, for example, E. D. Sylla, "Medieval Concepts of the Latitude of Forms: The Oxford Calculators," *Arch. Hist. Doctr. Litt. Moyen Age* 48, 1974, pp. 203ff.

Chapter 5. Substance in Aristotle's *Metaphysics*

1. This is a revised version of a paper given in 1972 in which I tried to develop the view presented by R. Albritton, *Journal of Philosophy,* 1957, 699–708, that substantial forms are particular; meanwhile others, e.g., Robert Heinaman and Charlotte Witt, and most recently A. C. Lloyd in his monograph "Form and Universal in Aristotle" have taken up the same position, though from a different point of view.

2. I shall, in the following, talk of properties when I mean qualities, quantities, and the other non-substantial kinds of entities Aristotle assumes.

Chapter 7. Stoic vs. Aristotelian Syllogistic

1. I assume familiarity with Ian Mueller's extremely useful paper "Stoic and Peripatetic Logic" which appeared in *Journal of Philosophy,* vol. 51, 1969. pp. 173–87.

2. Cf. also M. Kneale (*The Development of Logic,* p. 115): "We do not know whether this (sc. Eubulides' attack on Aristotle) was the beginning of the hostility between the Peripatetics and the Megarians; but it is certain that, inherited by the Stoics from the Megarians, the quarrel continued for many centuries and had a bad effect on the development of logic. For, although Aristotelian and Stoic theories are in fact complementary, they were treated as alternatives."

3. There are, of course, passages where the distinction we are looking for seems to be made, and each of which would have to be dealt with individually. E.g., Boethius says about arguments of the form "si non est a, est b; est b; non est igitur a" that the conclusion does not follow "quantum ad complexionem propositionum" but only "quantum ad rerum naturam" (*De syll. hyp.* II, 2, 4–5; cf. II, 3, 6; II, 4, 2). But he goes on to explain that these arguments are valid because premises of the form "si non est a, est b" actually are used in this context in such a way that the inference will be valid. So all he wants to say may be that if we go by the external form of the proposition the argument does not seem to be valid, but that we should notice that arguments of this form actually are used only if a and b are thought to be incompatible and for that reason arguments of this form are valid. Galen (*I.L.* 9, 8–16), using the same examples as Boethius ("if it is not day it is night"), had argued that such a proposition is not really conditional but a disjunctive proposition. For similar reasons Boethius (*In Cic. top.* 1145A) does not mind listing arguments of the form "not both p and q; but not p; therefore q" as a 7th kind of hypothetical syllogism along with six kinds of formally valid arguments. Another example is a remark in Ps.-Ammonius (*In an. pr.* 70, 11–12). Here the mathematicians are told that they should not say "a equals b; b equals c; therefore a equals c." For that inference is correct "ou dia ten ploken, alla dia ten hylen."

4. In *De syll. hyp.* I, 3, 5 Boethius gives as an example of a conditional "cum ignis calidus sit, caelum rotundum est"; but he says this is only a per accidens conditional; genuine conditionals which have "aliquam naturae consequentiam" seem to be of the indicated form.

5. The evidence for this is, admittedly, indirect: (a) the indemonstrable inferences and the themata are, as a matter of fact, not such that they would allow the reduction of the totally hypothetical syllogisms to indemonstrable syllogisms (that the themata are of such a kind I shall try to show in a different place); (b) in late Greek and Byzantine texts one finds a list of forms of indemonstrable arguments in which the totally hypothetical ones are added to the Stoic indemonstrables (e.g., in the Anonymous Heiberg or in Vat. gr. 244, f. 136r); this presupposes the assumption that they cannot be reduced to the indemonstrables; (c) Alexander (*In an. pr.* 390, 17–19) seems to distinguish between the Stoic syllogisms which he refers to as "the hypothetical ones" in 390, 17 and the totally hypothetical syllogism to which he refers as "ho dia triōn" in 390, 19.

6. This is the position taken by the authorities in the subject, Lukasiewicz ("Zur Geschichte der Aussagenlogik," *Erkenntnis,* v. 5, 1935, p. 113; *Aristotle's Syllogistic,* 1957[2], pp. 20ff.) and, with reservations, Patzig (*Aristotle's Theory of the Syllogism,* 1968, pp. 4; 12–13; *Die aristotelische Syllogistik,* 1969[3], pp. 14; 23–24; 48).

7. Cf. Ross, *Aristotle's Prior and Posterior Analytics,* p. 291; Ebbinghaus, *Ein formales Modell der Syllogistik des Aristoteles,* Hypomnemata 9, pp. 29–30; Mignucci, *Aristotele, Gli Analitici Primi,* p. 190; Lejewski, *Edward's Encyclopedia of Philosophy,* s.v. "Logic, History of," p. 516.

8. Cf. Joseph, *An Introduction to Logic,* p. 225.

Chapter 8. The Original Notion of Cause

1. I would like to thank the members of the conference for their useful comments. I am particularly grateful to Robert Bolton, Myles Burnyeat, Dorothea Frede, Thomas Rosenmeyer, and Richard Sorabji, who were kind enough to provide me with written comments which were very helpful in revising this paper.

2. di' ho energoun ginetai to apotelesma.

3. phamen . . . to aition en tō poiein kai energein kai dran noeisthai.

4. aitian d'einai logon aitiou, ē logon ton peri tou aitiou hōs aitiou.

5. The way this is put, though, suggests a false etymology: to auto kath' hauto poioun telos.

6. kai to men prattein ta dikaia kai mē kata to pleiston epi tois anthrōpois keisthai, boēthein d' eis hekaston kai tēn heimarmenēn.

7. A clue to the sense of the term 'prokatarktikon' we get from the use of 'katarchein' in passages like this: tōn hamartēmatōn prohairesis kai hormē katarchei (Clem. *Strom.* I 84, 2), or when Galen says that the hēgemonikon is to katarchon aisthēseōs te kai tēs kath' hormēn kinēseōs (*Plac. Hipp. Plat.*, p. 583, 10–11 M.; cf. also the use of katarchē in a fragment of Chrysippus preserved in *Plac. Hipp.*, p. 216, 13 M). The katarchē of something seems to be that in which it has its origin. By contrast, to say of something that it is the prokatarchon or the prokatarktikon of something would be to deny that the effect has its origin in it and to say that it preceeds that which is the real origin and source of the effect.

8. S. Pines. *Omne quod movetur necesse est ab aliquo moveri:* A Refutation of Galen by Alexander of Aphrodisias and the Theory of Motion, *Isis* 52 (1961), 21–54; M. Wolff, *Fallgesetz and Massebegriff* (Berlin, 1971), Part I; G. E. R. Lloyd, *Greek Science after Aristotle* (London, 1973), 158ff.

Chapter 10. The Skeptic's Beliefs

1. With this paper, compare Myles Burnyeat's "Can the Sceptic Live His Scepticism" in: *Doubt and Dogmatism* ed. M. Burnyeat et al., (Oxford, 1983).

Chapter 11. The Skeptic's Two Kinds of Assent and the Question of the Possibility of Knowledge

1. Sextus Empiricus, *Outlines of Pyrrhonism* (hereinafter *PH*).

2. Photius, *Bibliotheke,* ed. R. Henry (Paris, 1959).

3. Ed. I. Bekker (Berlin, 1814).

4. Ed. R. Keydell (Berlin, 1967).

5. Ed. A. Reifferscheid CSEL IV (Vienna, 1875).

6. Ed. S. Brandt, CSEL XIX (Vienna, 1890).

7. In H. Shapiro, *Medieval Philosophy, Selected Reading* (New York, 1964).

8. Ed. O. Stählin, GCS III (Leipzig, 1909).

9. Ed. K. Mras, GCS VIII. 1 (Berlin, 1954).

10. Ed. L. G. Westerink (Amsterdam, 1962).

11. *Galeni Opera,* ed. C. G. Kühn (Leipzig, 1821-33).

12. In writing this paper I have been greatly helped by discussions with Myles Burnyeat, John Cooper, Richard Jeffrey, Barry Stroud, and many others, but in particular Charlotte Stough, who took the care to write up her extensive comments on it.

Chapter 12. Philosophy and Medicine in Antiquity

1. For an account of Empiricism, the most important sources are: Galen, *De sectis ingredientibus, Subfiguratio empirica, On Medical Experience, De methodo medendi;* ps.-Galen, *De optima secta;* and Celsus, *De medicina, prooemium.*

2. For a convenient summary of the Methodist position, see Galen, *De sectis ingredientibus* p. 12, 9ff.

Chapter 14. The Method of the So-Called Methodical School of Medicine

1. I am grateful for the generous help I received in writing this paper. In particular, I would like to thank Jonathan Barnes, Geoffrey Lloyd, Don Morrison, and Mario Vegetti.

Chapter 15. On Galen's Epistemology

1. Cf. J. Dillon, *The Middle Platonists,* London 1977, pp. 339ff.

2. Cf. A. Dietrich, *Die arabische Version einer unbekannten Schrift des Alexander von Aphrodisias,* (Göttingen 1964, p. 96, 99; S. Pines, "Omne quod movetur necesse est ab aliquo moveri," *Isis* 52, 1961, pp. 21ff.

3. Although some of it is extremely useful; I am, e.g. particularly indebted to De Lacy's "Galen's Platonism," *AJPh.* 1972.

4. *De ord. lib. suor.* 1: XIX 50 (SM II 80); *De meth. med.* IV.4: X 274; II.6: X 122; *De prob. prav. suc.* 1: VI 754 (CMG V 4, 2, 391); *De loc. aff.* III.5: VIII 158; *De simp. med. temp.* ac. fac. I.28: XI 430; III.6: XI 549; *De comp. med. sec. loc.* VIII.1: XIII 117.

5. Cf. O. Temkin, *The Double Face,* p. 195.

6. *De plenit.* 11: VII 581; *De sanit. tuend.* II.7: VI 129 (CMG V 4, 2, 57); *De rat. cur. per venae sect.* 12: XI 285; *In Hipp. de vict. ac. comm.* II.37: XV 585 (CMG V 9, 1, 197); *De meth med.* III.7: X 206.

7. "Galen in the Renaissance," *Galen: Problems and Prospects,* ed. V. Nutton (London, 1981), pp. 238–45.

8. *De meth. med.* V.1: X 306; XIV.5: X 962; *De comp. med. per gen.* VI.7: XIII 887.

9. *Subfig. emp.* 11: Deichgräber, *Empirikerschule,* p. 80; *De meth. med.* II.6: X 122.

10. *Subfig. emp.* 12: Deichgräber, *Empirikerschule,* p. 88.

11. Ibid.; *De meth. med.* I.3: X 29; I.4: X 31; II.6: X 122; II.1: X 159; XIV.17: X 1012; *De comp. med. sec. loc.* VIII.1: XIII 117; *De exper. med.* 1: p. 85 Walzer,; *In Hipp. Epid.* VI comm. I.2: XVIIA 814 (CMG V 10, 2, 2, 14); *De cur. rat. per venae sect.* 3: XI 255; *De elem. sec. Hipp.* I.2: I 422 (p. 7 Helmr.); *In Hipp. Aph. comm.* I.1: XVIIB 346; VI.44: XVIIIA 70.

12. *Plac. Hipp. et Plat.* IX.5ff.: V 753ff. (CMG V 4, 1, 2, 566ff.); *De meth. med.* II.6: X 115; *De diff. puls.* II.6: VIII 601; II.7: VIII 608ff.; IV.7: VIII 736; *De cur. rat. per venae sect.* 3: XI 258; *Quod opt. med.* 3: I 59 (SM II 6); *De diff. resp.* III.3: VII 895.

13. *De sectis* 1:I 65 (SM II 2); *In Hipp. Epid.* VI comm. I.1: XVIIA 814 (CMG V 10, 2, 2, 14).

14. *De alim. fac.* I.1: VI 454 (CMG V 4, 2, 202); *De simp. med. temp. ac fac.* I.13: XI 403; *In Hipp. Aph.* comm. I.1: XVIIB 346.

15. *De exper. med.* 1–2; pp. 85–87 Walzer; *De sectis* 5: I 75 (SM III 9); *De simp. med. temp. ac fac.* I.31: XI 434; II.1: XI 459, 461.

16. *De meth med.* II.6: X 123; XIII.16: X 916, *De temper.* I.5: I 534 (p. 16 Helmr.); *De alim. fac.* I.1: VI 454 (CMG V 4, 2, 202).

17. *De fac. nat.* I.13: II 43 (SM III 132); II.8: II 117 (SM III 186); *De semine* II.4: IV 620–623.

18. *In Hipp. Epid.* I comm. I.pr.: XVIIA 13 (CMG V 10, 1, 10); *De comp. med. per. gen.* I.4: XIII 376.

19. *De sectis* 4: I 74 (SM III 9); *De meth. med.* I.4: X 32.

20. *De usu part.* XII.8: IV 30 (II, p. 203 Helmr.); *De fac. nat.* II.8: II 109 (SM III 180).

21. *Plac. HIpp. et Plat.* IX.6, 19-9, 9: V 765-794 (CMG V 4, 1, 2, 576-600); *In Hipp. de morb. ac.* comm. I.12: XV 434 (CMG V 9, 1, 125); *De subst. nat. fac.: IV* 762 (=*De sent.* 15.1); *Quod animi mor. 3: IV 773 (SM II 36); De sent.* 2 N.

22. *Plac. Hipp. et. Plat.* IX.6, 19,; V 765 (CMG V 4, 1, 2, 576),

23. Ibid. IX.9, 9: V 794 (CMG V 4, 1, 2, 600).

Chapter 16. Principles of Stoic Grammar

1. This paper was dedicated to Jürgen Mau on his sixtieth birthday. The reader may find it useful to consult the excellent survey of ancient Greek grammar by Jan Pinborg in *Current Trends in Linguistics*, vol. 13, *Historiography of Linguistics* (The Hauge, 1975), "Classical Antiquity: Greece," 69-126. Some questions only raised briefly in the present paper are discussed at length in "Some Remarks on the Origins of Traditional Grammar" in R. Butts and J. Hintikka ed., *Logic, Methodology, and Philosophy of Science* (Dordrecht, 1976), 609-637.

2. Cf. Sextus Empiricus, *Adv. math.* 8.12, 13, 75; Plut., *Adv. Col.* 1119ff.; Phil, *Leg. All* 2.15; Philop., *In an. pr.* 243, 2ff.; Ammon., *In an. pr.* 68, 5ff.; Alex., *In soph. el.* 20, 29ff. and Stob., *Ecl.,* 1.137, 6W.; Simpl., *In cat.* 209, 13; Clem., *Strom.,* 8.9 p. 97, 6-7.

3. Stob., *Ecl.* 1. 137, 4W.

4. Stob., *Ecl.* 1. 136, 21ff. W.; cf. D.L. 7.60; Orig., *In Joh.* 2, 13, 93; cf. also Simpl., *In cat.* 105, 8ff.; Syr., *In met.* 106, 7ff.

5. Cf. also the *elementa loquendi* in Cic., *Ac. pr.* 24. 92.

6. Though, for a different arrangement, cf. D.L. 7.41, 49 and 55.

7. On the whole matter cf. Sext. Emp., *P.H.* 2.194, 247; Ammon., *In an. pr.* 9, 27.

8. Cf., e.g., Arist. *Rhet.*, 1404^b 5; 1407^a 20ff.; the whole of *Rhet. ad Alex.* 25; *Poet.* 20; for the *Technē* of Isocrates (?) cf. Syrianus, *In Hermog.* 1, 28, 6ff. Rabe = Radermacher, *Artium Scriptores* B 24, 22.

9. As noted above, the remark in D.L. 7.44 that according to some Stoics definition and division do not belong to this part of dialectic (cf. also D.L. 7.41) would justify the suggestion that the sections in D.L. 7. 60-62 on definition, concepts, genus, species, division, and partition were not regarded as forming part of the core of the theory of expressions. One may have doubts concerning poetry—on which see D.L. 7.44 and 60. These doubts are easily removed since for this section on poetry Diocles refers to a treatise by Posidonius entitled *Introduction to Diction;* but more on this below.

10. Cf. K. Barwick, *Remmius Palaemon* 95ff.

11. Charisius, p. 192, 20-193, 2 Barwick; Diomedes p. 326, 30-35; p. 420, 24ff.

12. Dion. Hal., *De comp. verb.* 4, 31; Apollonius Dyscolus, *De coni.* 213, 8ff.

13. The basis for this in Aristotle is presumably chap. 20 of the *Poetics.* There (1456^b 20ff.) the parts of speech occur in a list of parts of diction, and both conjunctions and articles are said to lack signification (1456^b 38ff.; 1457^a 6ff.).

14. For the testimonies and fragments, cf. *Grammatici Graeci*, vol. 2. 3, ed Schneider-Uhlig.

15. Cf. Schol. in D. Th. 214, 19ff.; 356, 27ff.; Charis, p. 80, 1ff. Barwick; Apoll. Dysc., *De pron.* 5. 20ff.; *De coni.* 214, 17ff.; 248. 1ff.

16. Barwick, *Probleme der stoischen Sprachlehre und Rhetorik* 48; A.C. Lloyd, "Grammar and Metaphysics in the Stoa," 59, in A. A. Long, *Problems in Stoicism.*

17. Orig., *Contra Celsum,* 1.24; Ammon., *In de int.* 35. 1ff.; 30, 23ff.; Aug., *Princ. dial.* c. 1319Aff.; cf. Procl., *In Crat.* 8. 1ff.; 8.7ff.; Dion. Hal., *De comp. verb.* p. 62, 9-12; Varro, *De lin. lat.* 6.3; Philo, *Quaest. in Genes.* 1.20; Diogenes of Oenoanda, fr. 10, c. 3, 9ff. Chilton.

18. Cf. Varro, *De lin. lat.* 5.8, 9; Philo, *De opif. mundi* 148; *Quaest in Genes.* 1.20.

19. Diog. Oen., fr. 10, c. IV f.; if we take this passage, as suggested, to be a criticism of the Stoic view, it seems that in 4. line 11 we should restore *basilees* with Heberdey and Kalinka.

Chapter 17. The Origins of Traditional Grammar

1. I would like to thank Professor Julius Moravcsik for his kind discussion of points raised in this paper and related topics.

2. The standard Greek terms are 'euktike' and 'prostaktike' (cf. D. Th. 47, 3). Of these the second comes straightforwardly from the Stoic 'prostaktikon' (cf. D. L. VII, 67). The first comes from euktikos (sc. logos) a term the Peripatetics preferred to the Stoic 'aratikon' (cf. Ammon. *In de it.* 2, 27), presumably under the influence of Aristotle, De int. 17 a 4, who in turn may have followed Protagoras' 'euchole' (D. L. IX, 53), but avoided the epic form.

3. The standard Greek term is 'kletike' (cf. D. Th. 31, 6). But D. Th. also gives an alternative 'prosagoreutike' (32, 1; cf. Choerob. 11, 3; Prisc. V, 73, p. 186, 1). 'Kletikos' is the Peripatetic equivalent of the Stoic 'prosagoreutikon' (cf. Ammon. *In de int.* 2, 7), which is their standard term to refer to an address (cf. D. L. VII, 67).

4. Syntacticality is, of course, referred to in the part on the virtues and vices of speech in the definition of a solecism (cf. D. L. VII, 59). But to judge from grammar treatises on solecism it seems that it was not under this heading that syntax was developed systematically.

Indexes

Index of Ancient Authors

Index of Subjects

Kategorikos, 122

Language, origin of, 333
Laws of nature, 238, 244
Lekton, 137ff., 323ff., 344, 345, 349, 354
Liberal arts, 303
Logic, 20, 171, 276, 292, 303, 319
Logically true, 107
Logotheoreton, 273

Manifest, 269ff.
Medicine: as art, 226, 241;
    limitations on art, 232;
    medical theory, 239, 270ff.;
    origin of, 229f., 233, 247;
    traditional, 227f.;
    ultimate principles, 235
Mental disorders, 227ff.
Metaphysics: demonstrative, 94ff.;
    metaphysica generalis, 83;
    metaphysica specialis, 83;
    "metaphysics," 81ff.;
    a series of disciplines, 93
Method, 261, 262, 288;
    analytical, synthetical, 289;
    rational, 289, 292, 293, 294;
    of truth, 217
Methodism and skepticism, 276ff.

Name-giver, 334
Necessitation, 146, 147
Nominative case, 347ff.
Normal conditions, 157ff.
Noun, 352

Opinion, 213 (cf. Belief, Dogma)
Optative, 345, 372

Paratatikon, 306
Parts: conceptual, 61;
    subjective, 52
Perception, 3ff., 158
Perfect, 305
Perfect propositions, 306
Philanthropy, 241
"Philologos," 339
Philology, 311, 312, 321, 339
Physicians-healers, 231f., 246
Poetics, 318
Predicate, 137, 346, 348

Prediction, 259
Present, 305
"Probable," 215
Probable, 213ff., 215
Prolepsis, 154 (cf. Common notions)
Proper names, 331, 352, 356
Proshegoria, 135ff. (cf. Appellative)
"Pyrrhonean," 183

"Rationalist," 285
Realism, 367

Sextus's Empiricism, 252
Signification, 333
Signs, 188
Skepticism: and empiricism, 248ff.;
    and theory, 257ff.
Socratic dialectic, 151ff., 203ff.
Solecism, 310
"Speculative," 273
Speech: elements of, 317, 326, 328, 355;
    parts of, 309, 313, 314, 317, 327, 328,
    329, 330, 332, 341, 353, 355;
    virtues of, 309ff., 312, 317, 319, 320,
    321
Stoic "skepticism," 130ff., 170
Style, theory of, 318
"Substance," 70, 73
Substance, 64ff.
Syllogism, 100ff., 110ff.
Syntacticality, 372
Syntax, 323, 324, 327, 346, 353, 354, 372;
    of lekta, 323, 324, 354ff.
Synthetical method, 289
Syntelikon, 307

Tenses, 305
Teukta, 304
Theory, 195, 258ff.;
    and experience, 237 (cf. Diction, Style)
Third indemonstrable, 109ff., 118
Transition to the similar, 251
Transsubstantiation, 57ff.
Trivium, 302
Truths of reason, 294
Tynchanon, 304, 348, 349, 352

Unity, generic, specific, numeric, 52ff.
Universals, 55, 63
Usage, 310, 311, 335, 336, 337, 357

Michael Frede earned his Ph.D. in 1966 at the University of Göttingen, where he taught until 1971; he taught philosophy at the University of California, Berkeley, from 1971–1976, and since 1976 has been professor of philosophy at Princeton University. Frede is the author of *Prädikation und Existenzaussage* and *Die Stoische Logik*, and his essays have appeared in several German- and English-language publications.